1st Workshop on Machine Learning for Ancient Languages (ML4AL 2024)

Bangkok, Thailand
15 August 2024

ISBN: 979-8-3313-0170-5

Printed from e-media with permission by:

Curran Associates, Inc.
57 Morehouse Lane
Red Hook, NY 12571

Some format issues inherent in the e-media version may also appear in this print version.

Printed with permission by Curran Associates, Inc. (2025)

Association for Computational Linguistics
209 N. Eighth Street
Stroudsburg, Pennsylvania 18360

Phone: 1-570-476-8006
Fax: 1-570-476-0860

acl@aclweb.org

Additional copies of this publication are available from:

Curran Associates, Inc.
57 Morehouse Lane
Red Hook, NY 12571 USA
Phone: 845-758-0400
Fax: 845-758-2633
Email: curran@proceedings.com
Web: www.proceedings.com

ML4AL 2024

1st Workshop on Machine Learning for Ancient Languages

Proceedings of the Workshop

August 15, 2024

The ML4AL organizers gratefully acknowledge the support from the following sponsors.

Diamond Tier

Google DeepMind

Silver Tier

Vesuvius Challenge

Supporting Organisations

ARCHIMEDES
Research & Innovation Information Technologies / ATHENA

Association for Computational Linguistics (ACL)
317 Sidney Baker St. S
Suite 400 - 134
Kerrville, TX 78028
USA
Tel: +1-855-225-1962
acl@aclweb.org

Preface by the General Chair

Welcome to the proceedings of the 1st Machine Learning for Ancient Languages (**ML4AL**) Workshop, held as part of the Annual Conference of the Association for Computational Linguistics (ACL) 2024. Taking place on August 15th, 2024, this is a hybrid event with virtual and on-site participation in Thailand.

ML4AL showcases the scientific opportunities at the intersection of the Humanities and ML, representing a unique convergence between the two and spotlighting promising directions for future endeavors within this rising field. By leveraging advances in AI and by focusing on the study and preservation of ancient texts, ML4AL aims to inspire collaboration and support research momentum in the emerging field of ML for the study of ancient languages.

On its 1st year, ML4AL received 50 submissions from a global community of researchers. The submissions concerned multiple languages, including Ancient Greek, Latin, Sumerian and Akkadian, Classical and Old Chinese, ancient Egyptian, Coptic, etc. 18 papers were accepted for oral presentation (36%) and 10 were accepted as posters (20%). The accepted submissions covered diverse topics, such as digitization, restoration, attribution, linguistic analysis, textual criticism, translation, and decipherment of ancient texts. These contributions reflect the depth and breadth of current research and highlight the innovative approaches being developed to tackle the unique challenges posed by ancient languages.

Besides the oral and poster presentations, ML4AL features two distinguished keynote talks to provide valuable perspectives on the integration of machine learning for the study of ancient texts. The talk of Dr Stephen Parsons from Educe Lab, University of Kentucky, USA concerns the virtual unwrapping of the Herculaneum Scrolls. The talk of Professor JinYeong Bak from the Department of Computer Science and Engineering, Sungkyunkwan University, South Korea focuses on monarchical ruling styles when applying ML to historical corpora.

The ML4AL Organising Committee is grateful: to the keynote speakers for their stimulating talks; the authors for their valuable contributions; the members of the Program Committee for their hard work. We would like to particularly thank our emergency reviewers, who provided very valuable expertise in a very limited time window. We would also like to extend our gratitude to the ACL 2024 Workshop Chairs for their kind assistance, and to our sponsors and supporting organization for their generous contributions. Specifically, Google DeepMind was our diamond-tier sponsor, the Vezuvius Challenge was our silver-tier sponsor, and Archimedes/Athena RC was our supporting organization.

Hopefully, the discussions and collaborations initiated at this workshop will lead to significant advancements in the study of ancient languages and foster a deeper understanding of our shared human heritage.

Sincerely,

John Pavlopoulos, General Chair

Organizing Committee

General Chair

John Pavlopoulos, Athens University of Economics and Business, Archimedes/Athena RC, Greece

Co-Chair

Thea Sommerschield, University of Nottingham, UK
Yannis Assael, Google DeepMind, UK
Shai Gordin, Ariel University, Israel

Organizing Committee

Kyunghyun Cho, NYU, CIFAR, Genentech, USA
Marco Passarotti, Università Cattolica del Sacro Cuore, Italy
Rachele Sprugnoli, Università di Parma, Italy
Yudong Liu, Western Washington University, USA
Bin Li, Nanjing Normal University, China
Adam Anderson, UC Berkeley, USA

Program Committee

Program Chairs

Adam G Anderson, University of California, Berkeley
Yannis Assael, Google DeepMind
Kyunghyun Cho, Genentech and New York University
Shai Gordin, Ariel University
Bin Li
Yudong Liu, Western Washington University
Marco Carlo Passarotti, Università Cattolica del Sacro Cuore
John Pavlopoulos, Athens University of Economics and Business
Thea Sommerschield
Rachele Sprugnoli, University of Parma

Reviewers

Masayuki Asahara

John Bodel

Flavio Massimiliano Cecchini, Heo Chul, Claudia Corbetta

Angelo Mario Del Grosso, Mark Depauw

Hanne Martine Eckhoff

Margherita Fantoli, Ethan Fetaya, Theodorus Fransen

Federica Gamba

Petra Heřmánková, Marietta Horster, Renfen Hu

Federica Iurescia

Kyle Johnson

Alek Keersmaekers

Els Lefever, Chaya Liebeskind, Eliese-Sophia Lincke, Chao-Lin Liu, Liu Liu, Jiaming Luo

Massimo Maiocchi, Isabelle Marthot-Santaniello, Barbara McGillivray, M. Willis Monroe, Alex Mullen

Chiara Palladino, Chanjun Park, Matteo Pellegrini, Edoardo Ponti, Mladen Popović, Jonathan R.w. Prag

Avital Romach, Edgar Roman-Rangel, Matteo Romanello

William Seales, Andrew Senior, Si Shen, Gustav Ryberg Smidt, Richard Sproat, Gabriel Stanovsky, Silvia Stopponi, Qi Su, Matthew I. Swindall

Xuri Tang, Charlotte Tupman

Haneul Yoo

Chongsheng Zhang

Table of Contents

Program

Thursday, August 15, 2024

09:15 - 09:30	*Introduction*
09:30 - 10:30	*Session 1*
	Towards Context-aware Normalization of Variant Characters in Classical Chinese Using Parallel Editions and BERT Florian Kessler
	Ancient Wisdom, Modern Tools: Exploring Retrieval-Augmented LLMs for Ancient Indian Philosophy Priyanka Mandikal
	A new machine-actionable corpus for ancient text restoration Will Fitzgerald and Justin Barney
	Lacuna Language Learning: Leveraging RNNs for Ranked Text Completion in Digitized Coptic Manuscripts Lauren Elizabeth Levine, Cindy Tung Li, Lydia BremerMcCollum, Nicholas E. Wagner and Amir Zeldes
	A deep learning pipeline for the palaeographical dating of ancient Greek papyrus fragments Graham West, Matthew I. Swindall, James H. Brusuelas and John Wallin
	Coarse-to-Fine Generative Model for Oracle Bone Inscriptions Inpainting Shibin Wang, Wenjie Guo, Yubo Xu, Dong Liu and Xueshan Li
10:30 - 11:00	*Coffee and Posters I*
	Exploring intertextuality across the Homeric poems through language models Maria Konstantinidou, John Pavlopoulos and Elton Barker
	The Metronome Approach to Sanskrit Meter: Analysis for the Rigveda Yuzuki Tsukagoshi and Ikki Ohmukai
	UD-ETCSUX: Toward a Better Understanding of Sumerian Syntax Kenan Jiang and Adam G Anderson

	Adapting transformer models to morphological tagging of two highly inflectional languages: a case study on Ancient Greek and Latin Alek Keersmaekers and Wouter Mercelis
	Gotta catch 'em all!": Retrieving people in Ancient Greek texts combining transformer models and domain knowledge Marijke Beersmans, Alek Keersmaekers, Evelien de Graaf, Tim Van De Cruys, Mark Depauw and Margherita Fantoli
11:00 - 11:30	*Keynote Talk by Dr Stephen Parsons, University of Kentucky, USA*
11:30 - 12:30	*Session 2*
	Classification of Paleographic Artifacts at Scale: Mitigating Confounds and Distribution Shift in Cuneiform Tablet Dating Danlu Chen, Jiahe Tian, Yufei Weng, Taylor Berg-Kirkpatrick and Jacobo Myerston
	Latin Treebanks in Review: An Evaluation of Morphological Tagging Across Time Marisa Hudspeth, Brendan O'Connor and Laure Thompson
	Leveraging Part-of-Speech Tagging for Enhanced Stylometry of Latin Literature Sarah Li Chen, Patrick J. Burns, Thomas J. Bolt, Pramit Chaudhuri and Joseph P. Dexter
	SumTablets: A Transliteration Dataset of Sumerian Tablets Cole Simmons, Richard Diehl Martinez and Dan Jurafsky
	UFCNet: Unsupervised Network based on Fourier transform and Convolutional attention for Oracle Character Recognition Yanan Zhou, Guoqi Liu, Yiping Yang, Linyuan Ru, Dong Liu and Xueshan Li
	Long Unit Word Tokenization and Bunsetsu Segmentation of Historical Japanese Hiroaki Ozaki, Kanako Komiya, Masayuki Asahara and Toshinobu Ogiso
12:30 - 14:00	*Lunch Break*
14:00 - 14:30	*Keynote Talk by Professor JinYeong Bak, Sungkyunkwan University, South Korea*

Thursday, August 15, 2024 (continued)

14:30 - 15:30 *Session 3*

CuReD: Deep Learning Optical Character Recognition for Cuneiform Text Editions and Legacy Materials
Shai Gordin, Morris Alper, Avital Romach, Luis Daniel Saenz Santos, Naama Yochai and Roey Lalazar

Neural Lemmatization and POS-tagging models for Coptic, Demotic and Earlier Egyptian
Aleksi Sahala and Eliese-Sophia Lincke

Challenging Error Correction in Recognised Byzantine Greek
John Pavlopoulos, Vasiliki Kougia, Esteban Garces Arias, Paraskevi Platanou, Stepan Shabalin, Konstantina Liagkou, Emmanouil Papadatos, Holger Essler, Jean-Baptiste Camps and Franz Fischer

MsBERT: A New Model for the Reconstruction of Lacunae in Hebrew Manuscripts
Avi Shmidman, Ometz Shmidman, Hillel Gershuni and Moshe Koppel

Deep Learning Meets Egyptology: a Hieroglyphic Transformer for Translating Ancient Egyptian
Mattia De Cao, Nicola De Cao, Angelo Colonna and Alessandro Lenci

Classifier identification in Ancient Egyptian as a low-resource sequence-labelling task
Dmitry Nikolaev, Jorke Grotenhuis, Haleli Harel and Orly Goldwasser

15:30 - 16:00 *Coffee and Posters II*

Detecting Narrative Patterns in Biblical Hebrew and Greek
Hope McGovern, Hale Sirin, Tom Lippincott and Andrew Caines

Restoring Mycenaean Linear B 'A&B' series tablets using supervised and transfer learning
Katerina Papavassileiou and Dimitrios Kosmopoulos

Application of Machine Learning to the Critical Edition of Ancient Greek Inscriptions: Ithaca and the Corpus of Oracular Inscriptions of Dodona
Elena Martín González

A Dataset for Metaphor Detection in Early Medieval Hebrew Poetry
Michael Toker, Oren Mishali, Ophir Münz-Manor, Benny Kimelfeld and Yonatan Belinkov

Thursday, August 15, 2024 (continued)

	Predicate Sense Disambiguation for UMR Annotation of Latin: Challenges and Insights Federica Gamba
16:00 - 17:00	*Round Table*
17:00 - 17:30	*Best Paper Award*
17:30 - 17:45	*Closing Remarks*

Challenging Error Correction in Recognised Byzantine Greek

**John Pavlopoulos[1,2], Vasiliki Kougia[3], Esteban Garces Arias[4], Paraskevi Platanou[5]
Stepan Shabalin[6], Konstantina Liagkou[6], Emmanouil Papadatos[6]
Holger Essler[6], Jean-Baptiste Camps[6], Franz Fischer[6]**
[1] Department of Informatics, Athens University of Economics and Business, Greece
[2] Archimedes/Athena RC, Greece (annis@aueb.gr)
[3] Faculty of Computer Science, University of Vienna, Vienna, Austria
[4] Department of Statistics, LMU Munich, Munich Center for Machine Learning, Germany
[5] University of Athens, Greece
[6] Ca'Foscari University of Venice, Italy

Abstract

Automatic correction of errors in Handwritten Text Recognition (HTR) output poses persistent challenges yet to be fully resolved. In this study, we introduce a shared task aimed at addressing this challenge, which attracted 271 submissions, yielding only a handful of promising approaches. This paper presents the datasets, the most effective methods, and an experimental analysis in error-correcting HTRed manuscripts and papyri in Byzantine Greek, the language that followed Classical and preceded Modern Greek. By using recognised and transcribed data from seven centuries, the two best-performing methods are compared, one based on a neural encoder-decoder architecture and the other based on engineered linguistic rules. We show that the recognition error rate can be reduced by both, up to 2.5 points at the level of characters and up to 15 at the level of words, while also elucidating their respective strengths and weaknesses.

1 Introduction

The digitisation of ancient texts plays a crucial role in both analysing ancient corpora and preserving cultural heritage. However, transcribing ancient handwritten text using optical character and text recognition methods remains a challenging task. Handwritten text recognition (HTR) concerns the conversion of scanned images of handwritten text into machine-readable text. In contrast to recently printed materials, the analysis of images containing handwritten documents presents more intricate difficulties, particularly when dealing with historical and premodern manuscripts. These challenges may result in recognised text containing numerous errors or, at times, a complete inability to recognise the text. This is especially true when there is a low availability of suitable training data for specific scripts, such as medieval scripts.

1.1 Motivation

Natural language processing (NLP) can assist with the task of detecting and correcting erroneous text. When errors come from human learners of well-resourced languages, the task is undoubtedly challenging, yet notable advancements have been documented in recent research (Bryant et al., 2017, 2022). In the case of low-resource languages, however, the task can be more difficult and expensive, posing an additional hurdle not only to experts but also to systems. An example is the correction of recognition errors in historical newspapers, where recognition error rates of 10% (Chiron et al., 2017) have been reported. In this study, we escalate the difficulty by concentrating on the task of rectifying recognition errors in handwritten text. These errors tend to pose a greater challenge compared to those in printed text, primarily owing to the diversity in letter shapes and the distinct scripts employed by scribes. Error correction algorithms are applicable to HTRed material, benefiting macro-analytical applications, such as collation (Perdiki, 2022). They also concern transcribed text, e.g. by proposing corrections arising, for instance, due to distraction or fatigue during the annotation process.

1.2 Background

The written language of the Byzantine manuscripts and papyri,[1] such as the ones we shared with the challenge (see Section 3.2.3), reflects the language of the Byzantine times, following classical Greek and preceding the modern Greek language. Within these texts, morphological categories such as the optative, the pluperfect, and the perfect have disappeared, while others, such as the dative case have gradually decreased. Infinitives and participles are still there in the texts, serving as remnants of the

[1] We refer to Byzantine Greek, also known as Medieval or Middle Greek.

Proceedings of the 1st Workshop on Machine Learning for Ancient Languages (ML4AL 2024), pages 1–12
August 15, 2024

classical tradition, prompting one to regard the language as a distinct variant, separate from modern Greek. There are several spelling conventions that deviate from the older orthographic rules while the ancient punctuation signs are still in use, albeit not always with the same function. A more detailed description of this language is available in Papaioannou (2021).

1.3 Contributions

We study the benefits of error-correcting HTRed Byzantine text from the 10th to the 16th cent. CE. To conduct our research, we utilised a collection of transcribed images of Byzantine papyri and manuscripts documented by Platanou et al. (2022). For recognition, we used Transkribus (Kahle et al., 2017) to train an HTR model on seven images, one per century, and we used the trained model to recognise approx. one hundred pages. By using the recognised and transcribed images,[2] we introduced and successfully ran a shared task, challenging systems to correct errors in HTRed material (Fig. 1). Here:

- we present an overview of this challenge, which attracted 271 submissions, discussing the timeline, the evaluation, and the task difficulty that was introduced by a recognition error rate that varied across centuries;
- we introduce and publicly release a machine-actionable dataset for the correction of errors in HTRed Byzantine text.[3] Additionally, we offer three other resources: a synthetic dataset for evaluating error correction algorithms, and two corpora created specifically for this challenge, which we also make publicly available;
- by benchmarking the two best approaches—one based on engineered linguistic rules and the other on deep learning (the developers are co-authors)—we demonstrate that both effectively reduce the recognition-error rate, also outlining and analysing the merits of each approach.

2 Related work

Most studies approach the task of post-correction by focusing on printed text and by employing encoder-decoder architectures (Chiron et al., 2017; Rigaud et al., 2019; Schaefer and Neudecker, 2020; Lyu et al., 2021). The underlying idea is to encode the recognized erroneous text and then decode it into the corrected text, frequently employing methods from machine translation (Nguyen et al., 2020; Amrhein and Clematide, 2018).

2.1 Error correction

Error-correcting recognised text is a common approach when working with printed text (Schulz and Kuhn, 2017), where techniques such as spell checking, edit distance from lexicons, and the output of a statistical machine translation (SMT) model (Koehn et al., 2007) have been employed. A language model (i.e., the SMT decoder) decides the most probable correction, and to prevent the false alteration of a correct word, the authors introduce an additional input feature to the decision module. This feature indicates whether a word was found in a corpus alongside the preceding or following word. More generally, SMT is preferred in error correction while neural machine translation (NMT) has been reported advantageous in error detection (Amrhein and Clematide, 2018). More recently, an encoder-decoder model has been used to correct recognised printed text (on a character level) from historical books in German (Lyu et al., 2021). All the aforementioned studies pertain to printed text, where a recognition error rate of 10% is deemed challenging (Chiron et al., 2017). While we also experiment with statistical and neural error correction methods, our primary focus is on handwritten text, where the error rate is often higher (Figure 4).

2.2 Error detection for error correction

Error detection benefits error correction (Pavlopoulos et al., 2023). In 2017, ICDAR organised a competition focused on post-correcting recognised output (Chiron et al., 2017). The competition used a dataset comprising 12 million characters of printed text in English and French, and consisted of two subtasks. The first concerned error detection, aiming at the accurate identification of the position and the length of the errors. The second concerned error correction, where the errors were already provided to the participants (Chiron et al., 2017; Rigaud et al., 2019). The organisers noted 35 registrations, indicating a substantial interest from the community. However, it was also noted that only half of the submissions were deemed successful, underscoring the challenging nature of the task.

[2]To distinguish between the two, we will refer to 'transcribed' when the text is generated by a human expert and to 'recognised' when it is generated by a system.

[3]`https://github.com/htrec-gr/challenge`.

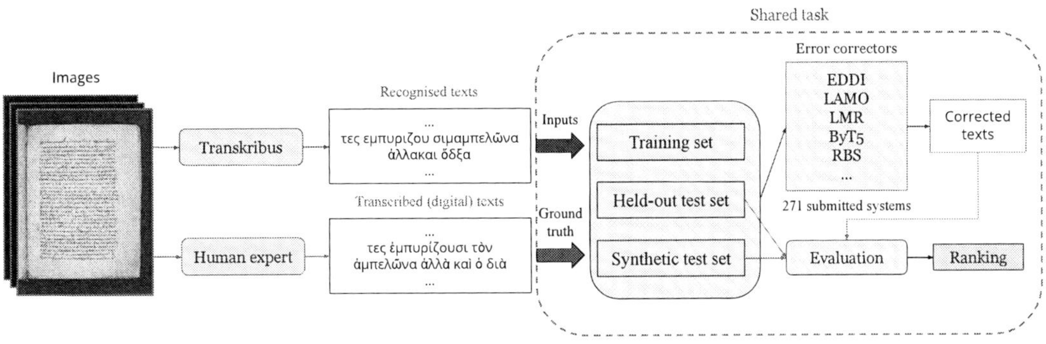

Figure 1: Overview of the organised shared task (details hidden to preserve anonymity)

In 2019, the competition was repeated, and the dataset's size was doubled, with the introduction of ten European languages (Rigaud et al., 2019). The texts used in both competitions were sourced from collections of national libraries or universities and encompassed a variety of formats, such as newspapers, historical books, and shopping receipts. In the 2017 edition, the most effective error correction method consisted of an ensemble combining statistical and neural machine translation models. In contrast, in the 2019 competition a character-level neural encoder-decoder took the top position, based on BiLSTM (Hochreiter and Schmidhuber, 1997) and BERT (Devlin et al., 2018).

BERT, fine-tuned on a named entity recognition task, was also used to perform error detection at the token level (Nguyen et al., 2020). After the subtoken tokenisation, the authors obtained GloVe or fastText word embeddings; combined with segment and positional embeddings, these were given as input to BERT. The hidden states were fed to a dense layer on top that classified each token as erroneous or not. Error correction, then, followed with a character-based NMT model. Error detection has been considered a reasonable first step to avoid the false alteration of already correctly recognised lines (Schaefer and Neudecker, 2020). The authors used a recurrent neural network (RNN) as a first step to detect erroneous characters in the recognised printed text. Then, a neural encoder-decoder translation model was fed only with sentences that comprised (detected) erroneous characters. Their two-step post-correction resulted in an 18.2% relative improvement in the recognition error rate.

3 The Shared Task

We used a dataset (§3.2) to set up a shared task on error-correcting the HTR output of Byzantine papyri and manuscripts. The challenge lasted from May 1st to July 1st, 2022, counting one hundred thirty-six registered participants from around the world,[4] and 271 submissions.

3.1 The language

We used images from Byzantine papyri and manuscripts from seven centuries (10th-16th c. CE). As was discussed already (§1.2), the written text reflects the language of the Byzantine times, a language during an intermediary phase of linguistic evolution between Classical and Modern Greek.

We employed the Handwritten Paleographic Greek Text Recognition (HPGTR) dataset (Platanou et al., 2022), comprising images from the digitised Barocci manuscript collection of the Bodleian Library that display text dating back from 10th to 17th c. CE. The scripts found in the respective manuscripts are the Greek minuscule script and the cursive style of the minuscule script, an example of which is shown in Figure 2(a). As shown in Figure 2(b), characters may join each other, disallowing empty space between words and leading to joined words that often characterise the cursive style. Also, joined characters can form ligatures, as shown in Figure 2(c), while the character position is not strict, as is shown with the character 'α' at the end of the word 'τάλαινα' in Figure 2(d).

Figure 2 also shows that lowercase and uppercase letters appear interchangeably in the text. Scriptura continua exists (not consistently) along

[4] India had the most participants (26), followed by the United States (7), Russia (6), Greece (6), and Japan (3).

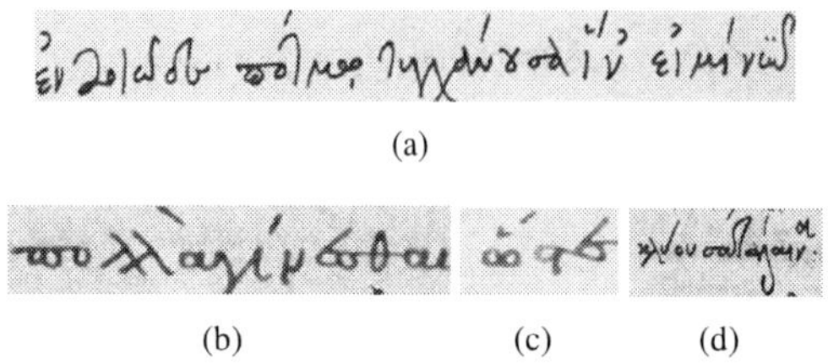

Figure 2: Visual examples of the language in the HPGTR dataset. An example of the cursive style of the minuscule script (a). The words 'πολλά' and 'γίνεσϑαι' are joined, leaving no empty space between them (b). In the word 'ὥστε', the characters 'σ', 'τ' and 'ε' are combined to form the ligature 'στε' (c). The words 'χλύουσα' and 'τάλαινα' are shown in (d), with the final 'α' written above the latter.

with abbreviations. Furthermore, characters of various sizes may appear regardless of their neighbouring ones, such as in Figure 2(d) where the bigger letter 'T' is written between two small letters 'α'.

3.2 The dataset

The dataset of the challenge comprises texts that are recognised (HTRed) and transcribed, with the latter serving as ground truth (hidden during evaluation).

3.2.1 The HTR model

To recognise text from images of handwritten Byzantine papyri and manuscripts, we opted for Transkribus (Kahle et al., 2017).[5] This is an industrial platform that encompasses a wide range of functions (e.g., layout analysis, transcription, HTR training/prediction). To yield a rich material for our task and, hence, a diversity of recognition errors, we trained our model only on seven randomly-selected images (and transcriptions) from the HPGTR dataset, one per century. The centuries from 11th to 13th are better supported when counting words compared to the next three centuries, with the 16th being the least supported.

3.2.2 Training data

We used the lines from ninety-eight HPGTR images. Each was transcribed by both a human expert, yielding the ground truth, and by our HTR network, yielding the input (see Fig. 1). To ensure a balanced representation across centuries, we randomly selected ten images per century (from the 10th to the 16th c. CE). However, the images from the 16th century contained fewer lines compared to other centuries, which we addressed by including additional images from that period. Overall, the training dataset comprises a (parallel) corpus of 1,800 lines (see also Table 5 in Appendix A).

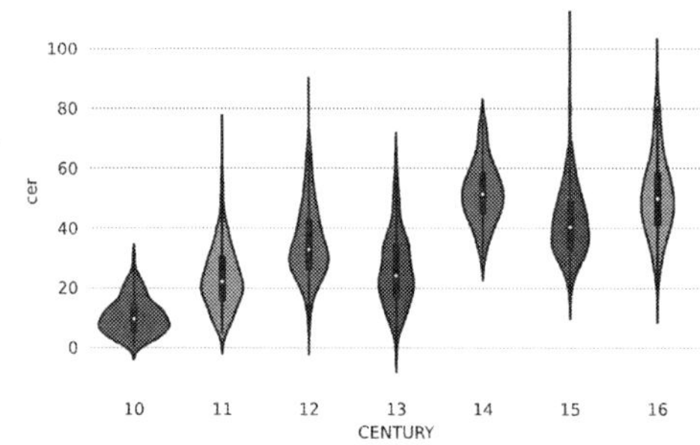

Figure 3: CER of recognised lines per century

CER per century When we group the character error rate (CER) by century, we notice that the rate tends to be higher for lines originating from the three most recent centuries (Fig. 3). This trend is consistent with findings from recognition systems trained on larger datasets (Platanou et al., 2022). Here, however, it is worth noting that lines with low CER present a more manageable correction task, whereas those with high CER pose greater challenges for parsing and correction.

HTR error analysis A common error in lines with a low CER is mistaken word division (i.e., space mistakenly added, e.g., by pushing away the final "s" of a word) and merging. Figure 4 shows that approx. 200 lines have a CER that is lower than 10% (fifty of which have less than 5%), while 500 have less than 20%. Further, approximately 400 lines have a CER of 50% or higher.

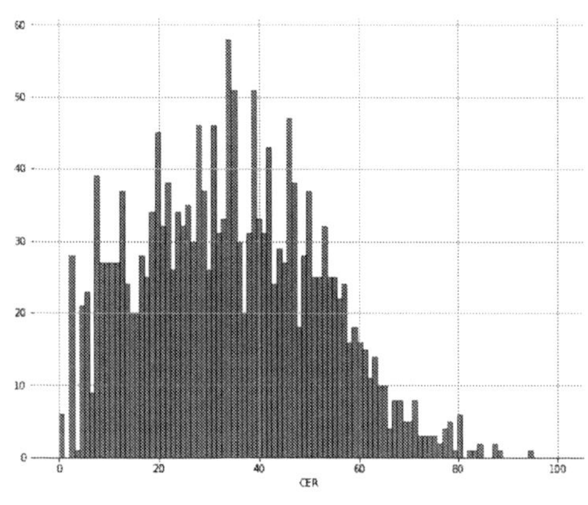

Figure 4: Number of recognised lines per CER

[5] https://readcoop.eu/transkribus, Version 1.15.1.

3.2.3 Evaluation data

For evaluation purposes, a held-out test set was created, comprising 180 recognised lines but excluding their respective 180 transcriptions (hidden ground truth). These lines were taken from seven randomly selected HPGTR images, one per century, different from the ones used for creating the training set.

Synthetic data The test set comprised also synthetic recognised lines, designed by "attacking" human transcriptions of seven randomly selected images (153 lines), one per century (synthetic test set), as outlined in Table 5. Synthetic data had been shared also with the participants to serve validation purposes while avoiding overfitting the evaluation data. Our error-introducing attacks are based on five categories, shown in Table 1. We remove (I) or add (II) words in the text; add (III) or swap (IV) characters, and merge consecutive words (V).[6] Although different in nature when compared to data coming from an HTR system, we opt for this synthetic dataset to unlock a detailed error analysis.

Error type	Example
I. *Remove randomly selected words*	this is a test > this is a __
II. *Add random words at random positions*	this is a test > this is **word** a test
III. *Add random characters at random positions*	this is a test > this is a tes**k**t
IV. *Swap random characters*	this is a test > thiis __s a test
V. *Merge random consecutive words*	this is a test > this is **atest**

Table 1: Types of errors introduced (attacks) to yield the synthetic dataset. Instead of transcriptions, the same example sentence is shown to highlight the error types.

3.3 The evaluation metric

For evaluation we employ relative error reduction (ERr), which is applicable to CER and WER. We consider a (human) transcription t_i^D for line i in document D; the recognised text r_i^D for the same line, and the corrected text $C(r_i^D)$, assuming the application of an error correction system. Then, assuming an error rate method ER (e.g., CER), we define ERr for line i of D as:

$$ERr(i, D) = ER(t_i^D, r_i^D) - ER(t_i^D, C(r_i^D)) \quad (1)$$

[6]The positions of the attacks are selected randomly.

A positive ERr means that the error rate is reduced and that the applied correction (by C) yields a text that is closer to the human transcription. Negative values, on the other hand, mean that errors are introduced, increasing the edits needed to reach the transcribed text.

3.4 Leaderboard

A leaderboard was set up using the character error rate reduction (CERr) as the official evaluation metric but also reporting the word error rate reduction (WERr). The scores of the leaderboard were computed on the whole evaluation set, comprising system and synthetic transcriptions. The official ranking, however, ignores the synthetic transcriptions. We opted for adding instead of hiding data (i.e., using only a small part of the data for the leaderboard), for two reasons. First, synthetic errors provide valuable information regarding the generalisation ability of systems. Second, a small evaluation set is easier to overfit, which could yield a deceiving leaderboard.

4 Methods

For our error correction task, which aims to push the system transcription closer to the respective human transcription, we opted for three baselines (§4.1), which were shared with the participants of the challenge. Upon the evaluation of all the submissions, using the system and the synthetic transcriptions as input, we investigate further the two best-performing submitted approaches: one based on predefined rules and the other utilising a text-to-text Transformer.[7]

4.1 Baselines

We considered three baselines, which were based on edit distance (EDDI), a language model (LAMO), and linguistic rules (LMR).

EDDI replaces unknown words in the text by using the edit distance and a lexicon. Tokens that are not in the lexicon are replaced by the word in the lexicon with the lowest edit distance. As a lexicon, we use all the words of the training set.[8]

LAMO is similar to EDDI in that it uses a lexicon

[7]The developers of these two algorithms are co-authors of this paper. Other submissions were excluded due to their lower performance and a lack of accompanying system descriptions.

[8]The method returns the input text when the count of unknown words is larger than three, and only lexicon entries with low distance (lower than twenty-five) are considered for replacements. Thresholds are based on preliminary experiments.

to recognise unknown words in the text. However, word replacement is performed by a word-based statistical language model. We use a window of three words for the language model.

LMR is the third baseline, which is based on linguistic rules. Specifically, it focuses on the final "s" letter that is frequently the subject of wrong word division. Then, a character-based statistical language model decides whether it would be deleted (i.e., assuming it was mistakenly added) or merged with the previous word (a mistaken word division).

4.2 Deep learning with ByT5

ByT5 (Xue et al., 2022) is a byte-level pre-trained text-to-text Transformer (Raffel et al., 2020; Vaswani et al., 2017) that allows fine-tuning on various downstream tasks. For small model sizes, it outperforms MT5, which is the multilingual version of T5 (Xue et al., 2020) [9]. We fine-tuned the ByT5 "large" model variant by feeding it with recognised and transcribed texts, in order for it to learn to encode the former and decode the latter. We used a gradient accumulation of four steps, a standard cross-entropy loss, and the efficient Adafactor optimiser (Shazeer and Stern, 2018). At inference time, we used greedy decoding as it produced the best results. More details can be found in Appendix B.

4.3 Linguistic engineering with RBS

The rule-based correction system (RBS) is designed by making use of different rules, derived based on a qualitative analysis of what kind of errors typically occur in hand-written text recognition of Greek texts. These rules are described in more detail below (the algorithm is provided in Appendix C).

Word subset (R1): Any token comprising a word in a lexicon (formed by the transcriptions) is divided into two tokens with a white space.[10]

Edit distance (R2): Tokens that had an edit distance of one with (a) any possible valid alternation of the conjunction "και", and (b) a term in the lexicon (R1), are replaced with these two terms. For tokens of eight characters or more, not affected by this rule, we use an edit distance of two.

Word bigrams (R3): Recognition often produces white spaces at the wrong positions (e.g., "δικαι ονπερι" instead of "δικαιον περι"). To address such errors, any bigram in the text is merged (removing the white space) and passed to R1.

Single-character tokens (R4): Single-character tokens that weren't known articles are merged with the end of the previous token, if the merged token exists in the lexicon, and with the start of the next token otherwise.

Duplicate characters (R5): Tokens comprising two (or more) identical consecutive characters, and that are not present in the lexicon, are collapsed to a single character (e.g., "εεστιν" becomes "εστιν").

Misspelled pronouns (R6): Character order issues of pronouns are fixed by specific replacements. For example, "τνω" is replaced by "των".

Joint pronouns (R7): Pronouns merged with the next token (e.g., "τηνκαρδιαν") are searched and replaced by two words (e.g., the previous token would become "την καρδιαν").

Main prepositions (R8): Words beginning with specific prefixes (e.g., "ειντοις", "εντοις", "ηκτοις", "εκτης") can bypass the previous rules. Hence, a mapping is used to address such tokens.

5 Empirical analysis

5.1 Error rate reduction results

In Table 2, we present the ERr for characters (CERr) and words (WERr), achieved by error-correcting the HTR output or synthetic data. EDDI and LAMO display negative scores in both metrics on both input types. This means that such - rather simplistic - baselines introduce new errors instead of addressing existing ones. The third baseline, LMR, reduces slightly the CER and WER of the HTR output. The focus of this baseline is on a single letter (final "s"), which is a common recognition error, though not the only one. The attacks that are used to create the synthetic data, on the other hand, are applied to random text positions (see §4), none of which concerns this letter. Hence, no correction is made and both scores are zero.

BYT5 and RBS achieve a positive reduction in both metrics. RBS scores higher than LMR when the input is the HTR output. Also, it achieves a positive reduction when the input is synthetic (0.10 in CERr and 1.29 in WERr). Obviously, this method handles many error types, covering more than typical HTR mistakes. BYT5 is the best overall when applied to HTR output. It is more than five times better in terms of CER and more than eight times better in terms of WER compared to RBS. When evaluated on synthetic input, however, the error

[9] In preliminary experiments, MT5 performed considerably worse than ByT5.

[10] A more strict version of this rule uses a list of pronouns (e.g., αυτου) and conjunctions (e.g., και), testing if the token concatenates words from the two resources.

	HTR OUTPUT		SYNTHETIC	
	CERr ↑	WERr ↑	CERr ↑	WERr ↑
EDDI	-0.19	-0.29	-0.54	-2.48
LAMO	-5.88	-0.80	-5.95	-3.13
LMR	0.02	0.06	0.00	-0.00
RBS	0.44	1.82	**0.10**	**1.29**
BYT5	**2.53**	**14.97**	-7.72	-23.14

Table 2: CERr and WERr scores of the baselines (top three rows), of the neural encoder-decoder (BYT5), and the rule-based error correction approach (RBS).

rates increase considerably, displaying a lower performance than RBS and all three baselines, most probably because the model is not trained on synthetic data. This is an indication that the synthetic data may not be very natural, and that rule-based systems are less useful in 'real-world' situations.

5.2 Inter-corrector agreement

In order to investigate closer the relationship between BYT5 and RBS, we compute the CER between the two corrected texts, one per system, of each recognised line. Low scores reflect a high agreement between the two approaches while high scores indicate very different outputs. By sorting the lines based on this score, we can assess the two approaches in different agreement zones. Figure 5 presents these results. Overall, BYT5 is more often above zero and bars are also much higher than RBS. When we look at the left of the diagram, there are almost no differences between the two in their performance, which is reasonable given that the two approaches agree (i.e., they will both be correct or they will both be wrong). As we move to the right, however, we can see that BYT5 achieves more and deeper negative bars. On the other hand, RBS follows a low-risk, low-gain strategy.
Manual investigation of the best and worst handled lines per method (Table 3) reveals that in the worst-case scenario per method (line 8 for RBS, hallucination in 15 for BYT5), the corrections of the other method were minimal (lines 7 and 16, resp.).

5.3 Sensitivity analysis on synthetic data

As was shown in Table 2, RBS achieves a positive CERr in the synthetic data while BYT5 underperforms in this setup. To explore the performance of the two methods further, we computed the mean CERr per attack type (Table 4). For all attack types,

Figure 5: CERr (moving average for better readability with a window of size 5) of BYT5 and RBS per line. Lines have been sorted from the least (left) to the highest (right) agreement (CER) between the two.

BYT5 yields a negative average CERr, with its weakest performance observed when characters are added (Type III), and relatively better results when words are merged (Type V). On the other hand, RBS also struggles with two attack types, specifically when words are removed (Type I) and added (Type II). Its performance remains relatively consistent for the remaining three types of attack.

5.4 Enhanced HTR vs. post-correction

Enhancing HTR with more training data can allow a direct comparison between the performance gains from neural error correction and from increasing the HTR training data.

For the purposes of this experiment, we trained a new HTR model. To avoid the financial cost of train multiple instances, we opted for an open-source alternative to Transkribus. For the experiment described in §5.4, our HTR model achieved a similar performance with Transkribus on the same seven training pages. We release this model publicly at: `https://github.com/htrec-gr/htr`. The architecture of this HTR model is a Swin (Liu et al., 2021) encoder with a BERT-based decoder (Devlin et al., 2019). For the experiment we used a single GPU card, i.e., NVIDIA Tesla V100 (16GB), and the model had 142 million parameters. It was trained for 75 epochs (12 hours). We used as seed 42, batch size of 48, AdamW optimizer, and Transformers V4.25.1. For language generation, we used a max-length of 200 characters, early stopping and a greedy decoding strategy.

Figure 6 shows the CERr and WERr as we transition from 7 pages of training data (our baseline) to 70 pages overall. When training with 28 (+21) pages, CERr goes up to 9.73 and WERr to 12.62. This means that the WERr of BYT5 (correcting the errors of a 7-page-trained HTR model) is better by two points (14.97; Table 2). When training with more pages (e.g., 70), however, CERr and WERr reach up to 15.72 and 27.15 respectively, outperforming the gains from error correction. It is worth

		Transcribed, Recognised, or Corrected line	CERr	
	Human:	σωματος κρειττων τοσουτον των χρημασι βοη		
	HTRed:	ωματος κρειτγων τοσουτον των χρημασιβοη		
	BYT5:	εωματος κρειται το σουτον των χρημασι βοη	-4.88	
B	RBS:	σωματος κρειτγων τοσουτον των χρημασι βοη		4.88
	Human:	λεντιον διεζωσεν εαυτον		
	HTRed:	λεντιον διεζωσενεαυτόν		
	BYT5:	λεντιον διεζωσεν εαυτον	0.00	
W	RBS:	λεντιον διεζωσενε αυτόν		-4.37
	Human:	ψεκτως ποιουσιν εαυτους σαρκα		
	HTRed:	ψκε κτῶς ποι ουσιν εαύτοις σάλρ κα		
B	BYT5:	ψκεκτως ποιουσιν εαυτοις σαλοκα	17.24	
	RBS:	ψκε κτῶς ποι ουσιν εαύτοις σάλρ κα		0.00
	Human:	ῶν δὲ συνεπινοουμενην έχων τῆ ὺπαρξει		
	HTRed:	ῶῶν δὲ συνεπινοουμενην δέχων τῆ ὺπαΈρξει		
W	BYT5:	συνεπινοουμενην συνεπινοουμενην συνεπινοουμενη...	-108	
	RBS:	ῶῶν δὲ συνεπινοουμενην δέχων τῆ ὺπαΈρξει		0.00

Table 3: Error analysis by focusing on the best (B) and worst (W) correction per method based on the achieved CERr. The first two rows per quadruplet show the respective transcription and recognition.

	Type of attack	BYT5	RBS
I.	Remove words	-6.36	0.00
II.	Add words	-7.95	-0.06
III.	Add characters	-12.28	0.18
IV.	Swap characters	-8.42	0.21
V.	Merge words	-3.54	0.18

Table 4: Average CERr per attack type.

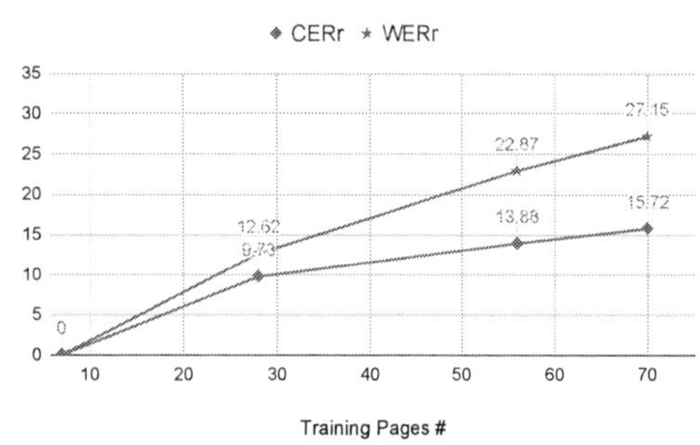

Figure 6: CERr and WERr scores (vertically) when the HTR model is trained on more pages (horizontally).

noting that this improvement requires a substantial increase of HTR training material, which may not be available (e.g., lack of images or transcriptions), making error correction a promising alternative.

6 Discussion

The challenge in error-correcting the HTR output of Byzantine manuscripts and papyri has attracted a significant number of registrations and submissions (§3.2.3), the best of which were discussed in this work. Characteristics of Byzantine Greek and the respective scripts have been discussed in §3.1, in order to highlight the difficulties that recognition and error-correction algorithms need to tackle. The variety of scripts and scribes in this language, along with its evolution, is likely to have caused a varying recognition error rate over time (Figure 3). This error rate variety poses a significant challenge to post-correction methods, which should be able to handle lines that comprise from few to many errors (different types).

When assessing error correction in recognized printed and handwritten material, it's crucial to consider the error rate. As detailed in §2, prior studies have predominantly focused on printed material, characterised by relatively low recognition error rates. However, our findings illustrate a significant variation in the error rate for HTR output, encompassing both accurate recognitions and those with numerous errors (Fig. 4).

We also show that a rule-based approach outperforms the baselines (Table 2), or even a neural encoder-decoder in the case of synthetic data (Table 4). Therefore, error-correcting the HTR output can also be seen as a knowledge-intensive NLP task, for which knowledge-based approaches can be successful (Lewis et al., 2020).

The experimental results presented in Table 2, show that post-correcting the HTR output for Byzantine Greek can reduce the error rate by approximately 2.5 units at the character and 15 units at the word level. This means that error correction can be employed during the recognition of the text in the images of Byzantine manuscripts and papyri, to facilitate human experts with the tedious semi-automated transcription task (i.e., correcting the HTR output). This gain is recorded by post-correcting errors, but the encoding-decoding of BYT5 could possibly be integrated also into the HTR pipeline, incorporated as one of the tasks in a multitask approach (i.e., image to text to text).

7 Conclusions

We presented a challenge of error-correcting HTR output for Byzantine Greek, publicly releasing data with both synthetic and actual HTR errors. A pre-trained BYT5 encoder-decoder model, fine-tuned on recognised (input; encoded) and transcribed (output; decoded) texts, achieves a notably high performance, effectively reducing errors. A comparable reduction of errors could have been achieved if the HTR model had been trained on approximately 30 additional pages. However, generalisation remains a concern, as evidenced by the model's performance on synthetic data, where errors were introduced instead of corrected. A rule-based approach, on the other hand, showed promise by well performing on synthetic data but not on real-world data. Future work will focus on challenging error-correction systems based on HTR models trained on data from specific centuries, aiming to address the diverse range of errors encountered.

Acknowledgements

This work has been partially supported by project MIS 5154714 of the National Recovery and Resilience Plan Greece 2.0 funded by the European Union under the NextGenerationEU Program.

Limitations

- As observed in the results, the performance of the systems varies significantly across centuries, suggesting that century-specific factors need to be considered when designing effective error-correcting systems.

- It's evident that post-correction is often hindered by the low quality of the HTR output. Therefore, there is a need for more advanced approaches that incorporate error detection (Pavlopoulos et al., 2023) and correction before the output is generated, possibly in conjunction with a post-correction module.

- While the results demonstrate the potential of error-correcting systems for some Byzantine Greek corpora, the generalisation potential in the context of low-resource data remains to be explored. This can be achieved by extending this approach to additional corpora and other languages, allowing for a more comprehensive understanding of its effectiveness across different linguistic domains. Still, we hope that this study will be beneficial for the development of new error-correction strategies aimed at improving the quality of recognitions, especially in scenarios with limited data availability.

Ethics Statement

This work involves the use of publicly available datasets and does not involve human subjects or any personally identifiable information. We declare that we have no conflicts of interest that could potentially influence the outcomes, interpretations, or conclusions of this research. All funding sources supporting this study are acknowledged in the acknowledgments section (hidden to preserve anonymity). We have made our best effort to document our methodology, experiments, and results accurately and are committed to sharing our code, data, and other relevant resources to foster reproducibility and further advancements in research.

References

Chantal Amrhein and Simon Clematide. 2018. Supervised ocr error detection and correction using statistical and neural machine translation methods. *Journal for Language Technology and Computational Linguistics (JLCL)*, 33(1):49–76.

Christopher Bryant, Mariano Felice, and Edward Briscoe. 2017. Automatic annotation and evaluation of error types for grammatical error correction. Association for Computational Linguistics.

Christopher Bryant, Zheng Yuan, Muhammad Reza Qorib, Hannan Cao, Hwee Tou Ng, and Ted Briscoe. 2022. Grammatical error correction: A survey of the state of the art. *arXiv preprint arXiv:2211.05166*.

Guillaume Chiron, Antoine Doucet, Mickaël Coustaty, and Jean-Philippe Moreux. 2017. Icdar2017 competition on post-ocr text correction. In *2017 14th IAPR International Conference on Document Analysis and Recognition (ICDAR)*, volume 1, pages 1423–1428, Kyoto, Japan.

Jacob Devlin, Ming-Wei Chang, Kenton Lee, and Kristina Toutanova. 2018. Bert: Pre-training of deep bidirectional transformers for language understanding. *arXiv preprint arXiv:1810.04805*.

Jacob Devlin, Ming-Wei Chang, Kenton Lee, and Kristina Toutanova. 2019. BERT: Pre-training of deep bidirectional transformers for language understanding. In *Proceedings of the 2019 Conference of the North American Chapter of the Association for Computational Linguistics: Human Language Technologies, Volume 1 (Long and Short Papers)*, pages 4171–4186, Minneapolis, Minnesota. Association for Computational Linguistics.

Sepp Hochreiter and Jürgen Schmidhuber. 1997. Long short-term memory. *Neural computation*, 9(8):1735–1780.

Philip Kahle, Sebastian Colutto, Günter Hackl, and Günter Mühlberger. 2017. Transkribus-a service platform for transcription, recognition and retrieval of historical documents. In *2017 14th IAPR International Conference on Document Analysis and Recognition (ICDAR)*, volume 4, pages 19–24. IEEE.

Philipp Koehn, Hieu Hoang, Alexandra Birch, Chris Callison-Burch, Marcello Federico, Nicola Bertoldi, Brooke Cowan, Wade Shen, Christine Moran, Richard Zens, et al. 2007. Moses: Open source toolkit for statistical machine translation. In *Proceedings of the 45th annual meeting of the association for computational linguistics companion volume proceedings of the demo and poster sessions*, pages 177–180, Prague, Czech Republic.

Patrick Lewis, Ethan Perez, Aleksandra Piktus, Fabio Petroni, Vladimir Karpukhin, Naman Goyal, Heinrich Küttler, Mike Lewis, Wen-tau Yih, Tim Rocktäschel, et al. 2020. Retrieval-augmented generation for knowledge-intensive nlp tasks. *Advances in Neural Information Processing Systems*, 33:9459–9474.

Ze Liu, Yutong Lin, Yue Cao, Han Hu, Yixuan Wei, Zheng Zhang, Stephen Lin, and Baining Guo. 2021. Swin transformer: Hierarchical vision transformer using shifted windows. In *Proceedings of the IEEE/CVF International Conference on Computer Vision (ICCV)*.

Lijun Lyu, Maria Koutraki, Martin Krickl, and Besnik Fetahu. 2021. Neural ocr post-hoc correction of historical corpora. *Transactions of the Association for Computational Linguistics*, pages 479–493.

Thi Tuyet Hai Nguyen, Adam Jatowt, Nhu-Van Nguyen, Mickael Coustaty, and Antoine Doucet. 2020. Neural machine translation with bert for post-ocr error detection and correction. In *Proceedings of the ACM/IEEE joint conference on digital libraries in 2020*, pages 333–336.

Stratis Papaioannou. 2021. *The Oxford Handbook of Byzantine Literature*. Oxford University Press.

John Pavlopoulos, Vasiliki Kougia, Paraskevi Platanou, and Holger Essler. 2023. Detecting erroneously recognized handwritten byzantine text. In *Findings of the Association for Computational Linguistics: EMNLP 2023*, pages 7818–7828, Singapore. Association for Computational Linguistics.

Elpida Perdiki. 2022. How to (auto) collate big manuscript data with minimal htr training. *Journal of Data Mining and Digital Humanities*.

Paraskevi Platanou, John Pavlopoulos, and Georgios Papaioannou. 2022. Handwritten paleographic greek text recognition: A century-based approach. In *Proceedings of the Language Resources and Evaluation Conference*, pages 6585–6589, Marseille, France. European Language Resources Association.

Colin Raffel, Noam Shazeer, Adam Roberts, Katherine Lee, Sharan Narang, Michael Matena, Yanqi Zhou, Wei Li, Peter J Liu, et al. 2020. Exploring the limits of transfer learning with a unified text-to-text transformer. *J. Mach. Learn. Res.*, 21(140):1–67.

Christophe Rigaud, Antoine Doucet, Mickaël Coustaty, and Jean-Philippe Moreux. 2019. Icdar 2019 competition on post-ocr text correction. In *2019 international conference on document analysis and recognition (ICDAR)*, pages 1588–1593, Sydney, Australia.

Robin Schaefer and Clemens Neudecker. 2020. A two-step approach for automatic ocr post-correction. In *Proceedings of the The 4th Joint SIGHUM Workshop on Computational Linguistics for Cultural Heritage, Social Sciences, Humanities and Literature*, pages 52–57, held online.

Sarah Schulz and Jonas Kuhn. 2017. Multi-modular domain-tailored ocr post-correction. In *Proceedings of the 2017 Conference on Empirical Methods in Natural Language Processing*, pages 2716–2726, Copenhagen, Denmark.

Noam Shazeer and Mitchell Stern. 2018. Adafactor: Adaptive learning rates with sublinear memory cost. *CoRR*, abs/1804.04235.

Ashish Vaswani, Noam Shazeer, Niki Parmar, Jakob Uszkoreit, Llion Jones, Aidan N Gomez, Łukasz Kaiser, and Illia Polosukhin. 2017. Attention is all you need. *Advances in neural information processing systems*, 30.

Linting Xue, Aditya Barua, Noah Constant, Rami Al-Rfou, Sharan Narang, Mihir Kale, Adam Roberts, and Colin Raffel. 2022. Byt5: Towards a token-free future with pre-trained byte-to-byte models. *Transactions of the Association for Computational Linguistics*, 10:291–306.

Linting Xue, Noah Constant, Adam Roberts, Mihir Kale, Rami Al-Rfou, Aditya Siddhant, Aditya Barua, and Colin Raffel. 2020. mt5: A massively multilingual pre-trained text-to-text transformer. *arXiv preprint arXiv:2010.11934*.

A Dataset configuration

As is shown in Table 5, we compiled a parallel corpus of 1,800 lines for training purposes. Each line comprises a transcription (ground truth) and a recognition, resulted from an under-trained HTR model (trained on the transcriptions of seven held-out pages). Evaluation was performed on synthetic (153 lines) and actual (180 lines) data, resulting to a parallel corpus of 2,133 lines, overall, which we publicly release, along with the HTR model that we used to produce the recognitions.

Purpose	# Pages	# Lines	Dataset
Training	98	1800	HPGTR
Evaluation	8	180	HPGTR
Evaluation	7	153	Synthetic
Total	113	2,133	—

Table 5: Data configuration for the challenge. Each page comprises several lines (texts) and each line has been transcribed and recognised. The transcription of lines used for evaluation was kept hidden from the participants during the testing phase.

B ByT5

We (i.e., a participant at the time of the challenge) opted for a batch size of 1 (i.e., a single line) and a learning rate of 1e-4. Optimum performance was achieved at one and a half epochs. As is shown in Table 6, BYT5 was trained for more epochs but results deteriorated.

Table 6: CERr and WERr of ByT5 when it was trained for more epochs.

	HTR OUTPUT		SYNTHETIC	
EPOCHS	CERr ↑	WERr ↑	CERr ↑	WERr ↑
1.5	2.53	14.97	-7.72	-23.14
3	-2.91	8.62	-15.41	-36.05
12	-8.45	6.08	-18.85	-43.40

C RBS

Algorithm 1 presents the pseudocode for RBS. A rule based system, however, is only as good as the corpus size it has access to. We hypothesize that the system's performance would improve with a bigger corpus. To that end, we provide over 100 books of text in ancient Greek [11] and Byzantine [12], scraped from various online sources. Due to time constraints, these were not utilized by RBS, a task that will be explored in future work. The biggest collection, titled 'Σύνοψις Ιστοριών' from I.Skylitzis totals 5 books, 153,709 words and 885,259 characters [13]. Furthermore, we provide a lexicon [14] of over 42,107 ancient Greek words independent of the collection of books, which was also not utilized by RBS.

[11] http://users.uoa.gr/~nektar/history/tributes/ancient_authors/index.htm

[12] https://byzantium.gr/keimena/keimena.php

[13] https://wordcounter.tools/

[14] https://www.greek-language.gr/digitalResources/ancient_greek/tools/liddel-scott/search.html?start=20&lq=

Algorithm 1 Rule-Based System (RBS)

```
Require: corpus ← list(words) ≥ 0
  for sent ← example_system_transcr do
      sent ← drop_duplicate_char(sent)
      for token ← sent do
          for gold ← corpus_1 do
              if token in gold then
                  gold, subtoken ← split_token(token)
                  sent ← replace_token_in_sentence(token, [gold, subtoken])
              end if
          end for
          list[(gold1, gold2)] ← create_pairs(corpus)
          for pair ← list[(gold1, gold2)] do
              combination ← pair[0] + pair[1]
              if token in combination then
                  gold1, gold2 ← split_combination(token)
                  sent ← replace_token_in_sentence(token, [gold1, gold2])
              end if
          end for
          token ← replace_freq_tokens(token)
          list_and ← ['και', 'καὶ', 'καί']
          for gold ← corpus + list_and do
              if edit_distance(gold, token) == 1 and (token not in list_and) then
                  if gold in list_and) then
                      if gold not in (begin/end_of_the_sentence) then
                          token ← gold
                      end if
                  else if N is odd then
                      token ← gold
                  end if
              end if
              if edit_distance(gold, token) == 2 and length(token) ≥ 8 then
                  token ← gold
              end if
          end for
          list_articles ← ['τὴν', 'κατα', 'τὰ', 'τῶν']
          if token in list_articles then
              if position(token,gold) in begin_or_end_of_token then
                  gold, subtoken ← split_article(token)
                  sent ← replace_token_in_sentence(token, [gold, subtoken])
              end if
          end if
          if length(token)==1 then
              sent ← drop_token(token)
          end if
          for i ← range(0, len(sent_tokens) − 1) do # R3
              w1, w2 ← sent_tokens[i], sent_tokens[i + 1]
              bigram = w1 + w2 # no white space between the consecutive words
              for g ← corpus do # for each gold word in the corpus
                  if edit_distance(g, bigram) == 1 & w1 not in {'ο','η','το','τα'} then
                      token ←g+' '+w2
                  end if
              end for
          end for
      end for
  end for
```

MsBERT: A New Model for the Reconstruction of Lacunae in Hebrew Manuscripts

Avi Shmidman[1,2,†], **Ometz Shmidman**[1,‡], **Hillel Gershuni**[1,2,‡], **Moshe Koppel**[1,2,‡]
[1]DICTA / Jerusalem, Israel [2]Bar Ilan University / Ramat Gan, Israel
[†]avi.shmidman@biu.ac.il
[‡]{ometzshmidman,gershuni,moishk}@gmail.com

Abstract

Hebrew manuscripts provide thousands of textual transmissions of post-Biblical Hebrew texts. In many cases, the text in the manuscripts is not fully decipherable, whether due to deterioration, perforation, burns, or otherwise. Existing BERT models for Hebrew struggle to fill these gaps, due to the many orthographical deviations found in Hebrew manuscripts. We have pretrained a new dedicated BERT model, dubbed MsBERT (short for: Manuscript BERT), designed from the ground up to handle Hebrew manuscript text. MsBERT substantially outperforms all existing Hebrew BERT models regarding the prediction of missing words in fragmentary Hebrew manuscript transcriptions in multiple genres, as well as regarding the task of differentiating between quoted passages and exegetical elaborations. We provide MsBERT for free download and unrestricted use, and we also provide an interactive and user-friendly website to allow manuscript scholars to leverage the power of MsBERT in their scholarly work of reconstructing fragmentary Hebrew manuscripts.[1]

1 Introduction

Hebrew manuscripts preserve thousands of textual transmissions of post-Biblical Hebrew texts from the first millennium (Richler, 2014). In many cases, the text in the manuscripts is not fully decipherable, whether due to deterioration, perforation, burns, or otherwise. Hebrew Studies scholars spend hours upon hours attempting to determine these missing words, in order to reconstruct the original texts.

Prima facie, BERT models are optimally suited for this task, given their Masked Language Modeling objective (Devlin et al., 2019a). Indeed, a variety of high-performing BERT models for Hebrew texts have been released over the last few years, including AlephBERT (Seker et al., 2021), AlephBERTGimmel (Gueta et al., 2023), and BEREL (Shmidman et al., 2022). A recent study even showed that these models can be leveraged to complete Biblical verses (Fono et al., 2024). However, as we will show, these models are not adequately equipped to handle Hebrew manuscript texts. In order to address this need, we have pretrained a new BERT model specifically for Hebrew manuscript transcriptions. Our new model is dubbed MsBERT, short for: Manuscript BERT.

2 Reconstruction of Textual Lacunae via Deep Learning in Other Languages

Over the last few years, deep learning techniques have been utilized for reconstruction of textual lacunae in a number of other languages. For instance, Assael et al. (2019) applied such techniques to Greek epigraphy; Bamman and Burns (2020) did so with Latin; and Fetaya et al. (2020) did so regarding Akkadian texts found in Mesopotamian cuneiform tablets. For a full survey of existing research regarding computational textual restoration, see Sommerschield et al. (2023, Section 4).

3 Challenges of Hebrew Manuscript Texts

Most existing Hebrew BERT models, including AlephBERT and AlephBERTGimmel, were trained on modern Hebrew alone. The historical texts found in Hebrew manuscripts admit to a very different writing style. Differences abound regarding vocabulary, morphology, syntax, semantics, and more. It is therefore not surprising that these models stumble when faced with historical Hebrew texts.

One notable exception is BEREL. This model was specifically trained on a corpus of historical Hebrew texts, and it is thus suited to handle the linguistic norms of such texts. However, although it can handle the *morphology and syntax* of these

[1]Link to model: https://huggingface.co/dicta-il/MsBERT
Link to website: https://mss--dicta-bert-demo.netlify.app/

Proceedings of the 1st Workshop on Machine Learning for Ancient Languages (ML4AL 2024), pages 13–18
August 15, 2024

texts, it falls flat when confronted with the *orthography* of the manuscript transcriptions. Virtually all of BEREL's training data originates from printed editions of historical Hebrew texts. Although these printed editions date as far back as the cradle of printing at the end of the fifteenth century, they still conform to a narrow set of orthographic norms assumed by the Hebrew printing press.

In contrast, the scribes of the Hebrew manuscripts did not adhere to such norms. Examples of where the orthography of the manuscripts deviates from that of the printing press include:

- *Matres lectionis* (consonants representing vowels). Manuscripts use *matres lectionis* in a far more varied set of positions (e.g. מיצטרף rather than מצטרף).
- Acronyms. Manuscripts tend to use multiple apostrophes rather than a single double quote mark (e.g. 'ה'ק'ב'ה rather than הקב"ה).
- Truncated words. The manuscript scribes often transcribed only one or two letters of a given word, relying on the reader to fill in the rest from context. Hebrew manuscripts often contain long sequences of such minimal word subsets (e.g. 'ד' א' כי' ק' ה rather than דבר אחר כי קדוש הוא).[2]
- Treating the preposition של ("of") as a proclitic rather than as an independent word (e.g. שלתרומה vs. של תרומה).

Needless to say, these orthographic discrepancies lead to a situation wherein texts of Hebrew manuscripts are not well supported in the BEREL model. Many of the words in the texts (including words noted above, such as מיצטרף, שלתרומה, and 'ה'ק'ב'ה), end up as sequences of word-pieces that the model was simply not trained for. The orthographic deviations noted above are not occasional but rather rampant throughout these texts, and thus they take their toll on BEREL's ability to handle the text.

Due to all of the foregoing, there is a need for a new specialized model for Hebrew manuscript texts, designed from the ground up - from the tokenization level and through all phases of training - specifically to handle the type of text found in Hebrew manuscripts.[3] The present paper does precisely this.

[2]This particular sequence is attested in a Cairo Genizah fragment of *mekhilta de-rashbi*, a legal midrash; see Kahana (2005), p. 25.

4 Model

4.1 Tokenizer

The first stage of our model design involves the training of a new word-piece tokenizer to build a BERT vocabulary that is optimally suited for Hebrew manuscript texts. For the training corpus for the tokenizer we start with our full set of manuscript transcriptions (section 4.3.1). Additionally, we add in a corpus of standard editions of Hebrew texts from before the printing era (section 4.3.2), to widen the vocabulary with additional words that are likely to be found in Hebrew manuscripts, even if they aren't in our particular corpus of manuscript transcriptions.

We use the Word-Piece tokenization method proposed by Song et al. (2021), with adjustments to handle the apostrophe and double-quote marks, which otherwise would have been tokenized into separate word pieces. Specifically, we avoid breaking on a double-quote between Hebrew letters (e.g., תנ"ך), or on apostrophes which succeed Hebrew letters (e.g., 'א'ע'נ).

Following previous work (Gueta et al., 2023), the tokenizer was trained with a vocabulary size of 128,000 tokens. In addition, in order to properly represent the fragmentary nature of Hebrew manuscripts, we add two special tokens to the vocabulary: `[GAP]` (indicating a large gap, or a gap of an unknown number of words) and `[ONEGAP]` (indicating a single missing word).

4.2 Architecture

The model's architecture is based on the BERT-base architecture (Devlin et al., 2019b), trained

[3]To be sure, to a certain extent, challenges of manuscript orthography can be addressed with existing models if normalization is applied during preprocessing. However, the oddities of manuscript orthography often result in ambiguous forms which must be disambiguated prior to normalization, and aggressively normalizing such forms would likely result in errors early on in the pipeline, adversely impacting the model's capabilities overall. Furthermore, the oddities of manuscript orthography are not entirely predictable, and constructing a completely comprehensive normalization routine would prove difficult. Additionally, for downstream tasks such as handwritten text recognition, it is desirable to have a model which can predict the specific orthographic forms which fits the orthographic norms of the context words; this would not be possible if everything was normalized in advance. For these reasons, we opted to produce the new model presented here, tokenized and pretrained from scratch. Nevertheless, in future work we hope to explore the preprocessing normalization approach as well, and to properly compare the results.

on a DGX-A100 with 4xA100 40GB cards. The training was done with the fused lamb optimizer combined with AMP (Automatic Mixed Precision). A polynomial warmup learning rate scheduler was used to warm up for a portion of the training steps and then decay the learning rate over the total steps.

4.3 Training Data

On the one hand, we wish to train the model specifically for Hebrew manuscript texts; yet our corpus of Hebrew manuscript texts is not sufficiently large to train a BERT model alone, and thus we need to augment it with larger corpora of Hebrew. We first describe the multiple corpora which we used as part of this process, and then describe how we combine them together during the training process.

4.3.1 Hebrew Manuscript Corpus

We collected transcriptions of Hebrew manuscripts from Hebrew Studies scholars who generously agreed to provide their transcriptions for this project. All in all, this corpus consists of over 67 million words, representing texts authored between the 3rd and 13th centuries.

4.3.2 Pre-Print Rabbinic Corpus

The Pre-Print Rabbinic Corpus is a collection of digitized Rabbinic texts authored before the age of printing (that is, before the end of the 15th century). This corpus contains a total of 49 million words.

4.3.3 Comprehensive Rabbinic Corpus

This corpus contains a maximally comprehensive set of digitized Rabbinic Hebrew texts from all available time periods, stretching from the 3rd century until today. It contains over 400 million words, including the full corpus of texts from Sefaria [4], plus many texts which we have scanned and digitized in-house.

4.4 Training Objectives

We train our model on the Masked Language Modeling objective. We implement two restrictions when selecting the random tokens to mask:

1. We don't allow masking of word-piece tokens which are not full words. The task of predicting just one part of a word given the rest of the word is too easy and does not result in significant optimization.

2. We don't allow masking of the `[GAP]` and `[ONEGAP]` tokens, since we wish to train the model to predict actual Hebrew words.

During training we chunk the texts into sequences of up to 256 tokens. To ensure we train on sentences of substance, we remove sentences with fewer than 3 words or where most of the sentence consisted of `[GAP]` tokens.

4.5 Training Phases

In order to leverage the larger Hebrew corpora, while still placing the emphasis specifically on the manuscript transcriptions, we used a three-stage procedure, as follows:

Phase 1: For the first phase of the training - when the model is most malleable - we trained only on the manuscript Corpus (4.3.1) and the Pre-Print Corpus (4.3.2). We trained for one full epoch over these corpora, using a global batch size of 2048 examples per iteration, for a total of 4200 iterations. The learning rate was initialized to 0, and was warmed up to 6e-5 by the end of this phase. Total training time was 7 hours.

Phase 2: For the second phase of the training, we continued training with all three corpora. We trained for a total of 5.5 epochs of the corpora, using a global batch size of 8192 examples, for a total of 15,400 iterations. We continued warming up the learning rate until 6e-3 and then applied a polynomial scheduler with a degree of 0.5. Total training time was 2.1 days.

Phase 3: For the third phase of the training, we confined the training corpus solely to our set of Hebrew manuscript transcriptions. We ran this corpus for 3.5 epochs with a batch size of 1024, for a total of 15,800 iterations. We used a learning rate of 5e-5, with the same scheduler as in phase 2. Total training time was 5.5 hours.

5 Experiments and Results

We evaluate the performance of MsBERT in comparison with the three BERT models discussed above. We evaluate MsBERT both in its final form (*MsBERT-Full*), as well the checkpoint upon completing phase 2 (*MsBERT-Ph2*), before the final training phase on the dedicated manuscript corpus, in order to evaluate the impact of that final training phase.

Our first test evaluates the models' ability to predict a masked word within a Hebrew manuscript transcription. We tested the models on Hebrew manuscript transcriptions from two separate genres: first, manuscripts of a homiletic text from the

[4]sefaria.org.il

5th-6th century (*shir hashirim rabba*),[5] and second, a manuscript of a Hebrew legal text from the fourth quarter of the first millennium dubbed *me'en sh'iltot* (Emanuel, 2019, 82-148). These transcriptions were not part of the training corpus of any of the BERT models.

It should be emphasized that this word prediction task is particularly difficult due to the fragmentary nature of the aforementioned manuscripts. Many words are damaged or indecipherable throughout both manuscripts, and many of the extant words are truncated. It should also be noted that although MsBERT was trained with the special GAP and ONEGAP tokens in order to provide it with optimal knowledge of the type of gaps found in Hebrew manuscript, here we avoided use of those tokens, to allow for a fair comparison with the other models in which those tokens are not available. Instead, we replace any single-word gaps with the universal MASK token, and we treat GAP tokens as paragraph separators, cutting the input samples at that points. We run the word-prediction test on all full words within the text (we don't include truncated words in the test, because they can potentially match multiple forms). In all, we test predictions for 9333 words in the first corpus, and 9475 words in the second corpus.

We report accuracy indicating how often the masked word was correctly predicted within the top 1, top 3, or top 10 (ignoring predictions of truncated words, word pieces, or punctuation). When we test for word equivalence, we ignore medial *vav* and *yod* characters, because words that differ only in their *matres lectionis* are essentially the same word. The results can be seen in Tables 1 and 2. MsBERT outperforms all models on both tests. As expected, BEREL (184M params) performs far better than both AlephBERT (120M params) and AlephBERTGimmel (184M params), due to its exposure to a large Rabbinic Hebrew corpus. Yet, at the same time, the substantial gap between BEREL and MsBERT (also 184M params) demonstrates the critical importance of our new training corpus which reflects the orthographic range of Hebrew manuscripts. Furthermore, the results demonstrate that the final phase of manuscript-only training does in fact provide a boost in the model's ability to handle these fragmentary transcriptions.

Our second test evaluates the models' ability to analyze the content of the texts, by testing whether the models can identify the words that comprise quoted citations. Our evaluation involves two genres: legal midrash and homiletic midrash. Many citations of Biblical verses are interspersed throughout such texts. Unlike modern texts, these texts do not use any form of quotation marks or braces to mark the citations; rather, the reader must figure this out from context. Thus, this test poses an ample challenge for our BERT models, to determine how well they are able to parse the context and to thus determine which words comprise the claims and discussion, and which words are source material interwoven within. The test set includes manuscripts transcriptions of *mekhilta de-rashbi* (a legal midrash),[6] and *shir hashirim rabah* (a homiletic midrash).[7] The training set includes excerpts from standard print editions of *sifre* Deuteronomy (a legal midrash) and *kohelet rabba* (a homiletic midrash). We selected training texts from printed editions in order to increase the challenge: the BERT models must apply the lessons learned from standard Hebrew texts to Hebrew manuscripts with their nonstandardized orthography. This challenge is particularly acute when it comes to identifying citations, because print editions tend to quote sources in full, whereas the manuscript scribes, painstakingly writing by hand, generally sufficed with more subtle references of only two or three words.

All of these texts were annotated by our in-house expert who marked the words that comprise the source citations. We include both full words and truncated words in the experiment. In total, the test set includes 1753 words, 288 of which are citations; the train set includes 3976 words, 1122 of which are citations.

We fine-tune each of the BERT models on the task of classifying words as "Citation" or "Not Citation". We input sequences of 64 tokens (batch size = 2, LR = 5e-5, Epochs = 30). We report the results in Table 3. Although precision is similar across the various models, MsBERT far outperforms all of the other models on the recall.

6 Conclusion

The BERT model we present here is the first of its kind: a model specifically trained to handle

[5] https://schechter.ac.il/midrash/shir-hashirim-raba/; we use the set of 16 Cairo Genizah fragments downloadable there.

[6] We test on fragment 13 from Kahana (2005), p. 161-162.

[7] We test on Cairo Genizah fragments 15 and 16 from https://schechter.ac.il/midrash/shir-hashirim-raba/.

Model	Top	Top 3	Top 10
AlephBERT	22.90	31.95	40.86
AlephBERTGimmel	25.57	34.89	43.96
BEREL	47.33	58.99	67.91
MsBERT-Ph2	56.77	69.50	77.25
MsBERT-Full	**59.99**	**71.99**	**79.10**

Table 1: Word prediction on mss of *shir hashirim rabba*

Model	Top	Top 3	Top 10
AlephBERT	26.37	37.27	46.80
AlephBERTGimmel	31.18	42.91	53.11
BEREL	56.24	68.88	76.89
MsBERT-Ph2	62.43	74.5	82.06
MsBERT-Full	**63.99**	**75.85**	**82.99**

Table 2: Word prediction on the *me'en sh'iltot* manuscript.

the orthographic oddities of Hebrew manuscript transcriptions. As we have shown, our model substantially outperforms all existing Hebrew BERT models on a variety of tests regarding Hebrew manuscript texts. We release the model for unrestricted use and free download.

We expect that this new model will aid Hebrew manuscript scholarship in a number of ways. First and foremost, this model provides a computational foundation to aid scholars in deciphering and reconstructing Hebrew manuscript text. As noted, we have in fact already developed an interactive and user-friendly website to bridge the gap between the scholar and the technology; scholars can input their text as they have deciphered it so far, and then receive predictions from the model which fit the context and any additional extant letters. Moreover, in addition to the basic word-prediction task, we have demonstrated that this model also excels beyond other models in its ability to classify parts of the text. Thus, this model provides a critical foundation for researchers who wish to build deep learning models for automatic analysis of Hebrew manuscripts. Finally, because this model is so keenly aware of the orthographic reality of Hebrew manuscripts, it provides an ideal foundation on which to build Handwritten Text Recognition systems for Hebrew manuscripts.

7 Limitations

When building the training corpus of Hebrew manuscript transcriptions, we endeavored to include as many genres as possible, to ensure maximal applicability of the model. However, we note that there is one specialized genre found in Hebrew manuscripts which is not at all covered in the present model: the genre of Hebrew liturgical poetry. These Hebrew poems draw upon all sorts of unusual and unique words which are not represented in the present model, and which really require a separate specialized model in and of itself. We don't expect this model to perform well on manuscripts containing Hebrew liturgical poetry.

Model	Precision	Recall
AlephBERT	76.99	20.21
AlephBERTGimmel	77.40	47.60
BEREL	78.67	81.94
MsBERT-Ph2	**79.31**	87.85
MsBERT-Full	78.20	**89.93**

Table 3: Evaluation on the citation identification test.

Acknowledgements

This paper has been funded by the Israel Science Foundation (Grant No. 2617/22) and by the European Union (ERC, MiDRASH, Project No. 101071829), for which we are grateful. Views and opinions expressed are, however, those of the authors only and do not necessarily reflect those of the European Union or the European Research Council Executive Agency. Neither the European Union nor the granting authority can be held responsible for them.

We will to express our thanks to Eli Handel for his substantial help in preparing and preprocessing the input corpus.

References

Yannis Assael, Thea Sommerschield, and Jonathan Prag. 2019. Restoring ancient text using deep learning: a case study on Greek epigraphy. In *Proceedings of the 2019 Conference on Empirical Methods in Natural Language Processing and the 9th International Joint Conference on Natural Language Processing (EMNLP-IJCNLP)*, pages 6368–6375, Hong Kong, China. Association for Computational Linguistics.

David Bamman and Patrick J. Burns. 2020. Latin BERT: A contextual language model for classical philology. *CoRR*, abs/2009.10053.

Jacob Devlin, Ming-Wei Chang, Kenton Lee, and Kristina Toutanova. 2019a. Bert: Pre-training of deep bidirectional transformers for language understanding. *Preprint*, arXiv:1810.04805.

Jacob Devlin, Ming-Wei Chang, Kenton Lee, and Kristina Toutanova. 2019b. Bert: Pre-training of deep bidirectional transformers for language understanding. *Preprint*, arXiv:1810.04805.

Simcha Emanuel. 2019. *Hidden Treasures from Europe [Hebrew]*, volume 2. Mekize Nirdamim, Jerusalem.

Ethan Fetaya, Yonatan Lifshitz, Elad Aaron, and Shai Gordin. 2020. Restoration of fragmentary Babylonian texts using recurrent neural networks. *Proceedings of the National Academy of Sciences (PNAS)*, 117 (37):22743—-22751.

Niv Fono, Harel Moshayof, Eldar Karol, Itai Assraf, and Mark Last. 2024. Embible: Reconstruction of Ancient Hebrew and Aramaic texts using transformers. In *Findings of the Association for Computational Linguistics: EACL 2024*, pages 846–852, St. Julian's, Malta. Association for Computational Linguistics.

Eylon Gueta, Avi Shmidman, Shaltiel Shmidman, Cheyn Shmuel Shmidman, Joshua Guedalia, Moshe Koppel, Dan Bareket, Amit Seker, and Reut Tsarfaty. 2023. Large pre-trained models with extra-large vocabularies: A contrastive analysis of hebrew bert models and a new one to outperform them all. *Preprint*, arXiv:2211.15199.

Menachem I. Kahana. 2005. *The Genizah Fragments of the Halakhic Midrashim [Hebrew]*. Magnes Press, Jerusalem.

Benjamin Richler. 2014. *Guide to Hebrew Manuscript Collections*, second, revised edition. The Israel Academy of Sciences and Humanities, Jerusalem.

Amit Seker, Elron Bandel, Dan Bareket, Idan Brusilovsky, Refael Shaked Greenfeld, and Reut Tsarfaty. 2021. Alephbert:a hebrew large pre-trained language model to start-off your hebrew nlp application with. *Preprint*, arXiv:2104.04052.

Avi Shmidman, Joshua Guedalia, Shaltiel Shmidman, Cheyn Shmuel Shmidman, Eli Handel, and Moshe Koppel. 2022. Introducing berel: Bert embeddings for rabbinic-encoded language. *Preprint*, arXiv:2208.01875.

Thea Sommerschield, Yannis Assael, John Pavlopoulos, Vanessa Stefanak, Andrew Senior, Chris Dyer, John Bodel, and Jonathan Prag. 2023. Machine learning for ancient languages: A survey. *Computational Linguistics*, 49(3):703–747.

Xinying Song, Alex Salcianu, Yang Song, Dave Dopson, and Denny Zhou. 2021. Fast wordpiece tokenization. *Preprint*, arXiv:2012.15524.

Predicate Sense Disambiguation for UMR Annotation of Latin: Challenges and Insights

Federica Gamba
Charles University, Faculty of Mathematics and Physics
Institute of Formal and Applied Linguistics
Prague, Czech Republic
gamba@ufal.mff.cuni.cz

Abstract

This paper explores the possibility to exploit different Pretrained Language Models (PLMs) to assist in a manual annotation task consisting in assigning the appropriate sense to verbal predicates in a Latin text. Indeed, this represents a crucial step when annotating data according to the Uniform Meaning Representation (UMR) framework, designed to annotate the semantic content of a text in a cross-linguistic perspective. We approach the study as a Word Sense Disambiguation task, with the primary goal of assessing the feasibility of leveraging available resources for Latin to streamline the labor-intensive annotation process. Our methodology revolves around the exploitation of contextual embeddings to compute token similarity, under the assumption that predicates sharing a similar sense would also share their context of occurrence. We discuss our findings, emphasizing applicability and limitations of this approach in the context of Latin, for which the limited amount of available resources poses additional challenges.

1 Introduction

Word Sense Disambiguation (WSD), i.e. the task of identifying the correct sense of a word in a specific instance or sentence, poses non-trivial challenges especially in the context of languages where resources are relatively scarce. This is the case of Latin, whose few existing resources confront the inherent complexity of the task and often resort to a binary approach revolving around the assumption that the several senses of a word can be reduced to two primary senses. This inevitably leads to resources that are overly coarse-grained. While such simplifications serve as valuable starting points for future experiments, their granularity may not universally cater to the diverse research needs.

The present work originates from the needs of a distinct project, which focuses on the annotation of Latin data according to the Uniform Meaning Representation framework (UMR) (Van Gysel et al., 2021). The text to be annotated is *De Coniuratione Catilinae* 'Conspiracy of Catiline' by Sallust. The UMR framework is designed to annotate the semantic content of a text, and was developed with cross-linguistic scope in mind. It is primarily based on Abstract Meaning Representation (AMR) (Banarescu et al., 2013), and aims at extending it to other languages – in particular to morphologically complex, possibly low-resource languages – in a cross-lingual and typological perspective. In AMR and UMR graphs, nodes represent semantic concepts. If word senses are available, semantic concepts are defined as word senses; participant roles associated to each predicate (e.g., ARG0, ARG1) are included in the graph if realized in the sentence. For instance, the predicate *utimur* in the sentence *Corporis servitio magis utimur* 'Of the body we rather employ the service' corresponds to the semantic concept `utor-03`, i.e. the sense "put into service; make work or employ for a particular purpose or for its inherent or natural purpose" to which ARG0 (first person plural, not overtly realized) and ARG1 (*servitio*) are associated. Within the whole annotation process, manual selection of the correct sense constitutes a time-consuming and demanding sub-task. We thus aim to investigate whether the existing resources allow to develop a strategy to expedite this process, by deriving annotation suggestions for unannotated predicates based on already manually annotated ones.

The paper is structured as follows. Section 2 presents an overview of related work, while Section 3 discusses Latin Vallex as the main linguistic resource that has been exploited, as well as the limitations it presents. Section 4 describes the methodology designed for the task, while its outcomes are evaluated in Section 5. Section 6 highlights some conclusive remarks and possible future research directions.

Proceedings of the 1st Workshop on Machine Learning for Ancient Languages (ML4AL 2024), pages 19–29
August 15, 2024 ©2024 Association for Computational Linguistics

2 Related Work

The exploration of WSD tasks for classical languages, and notably Latin, has recently gained attention, especially from a diachronic perspective with regard to lexical semantic change (Beelen et al., 2021; McGillivray, 2021; McGillivray et al., 2022, 2023a; Marongiu and McGillivray, 2023). However, the granularity of available resources remains a significant obstacle to successful WSD, as discussed by Navigli (2006) and McGillivray et al. (2023b). In the context of introducing the Latin BERT model, Bamman and Burns (2020) discuss a WSD task framed as a binary classification task, where only the first two major senses are selected for each headword and, thus, the sense to be predicted has to be chosen out of two possible candidates only. Building on their work, Lendvai and Wick (2022) create a new dataset based on a subset of sense representations from the *Thesaurus Linguae Latinae*,[1] and use it to fine-tune Latin BERT on a supervised WSD task. Despite achieving more robust performances, the task remains configured as binary classification, retaining only the first two sense groups for each lemma.

Pivoting a low-resource language to a high-resource one via parallel corpora has been observed to be a valid strategy to obtain WSD annotations in the under-resourced language (Pasini et al., 2021). As the issue of data scarcity applies to Latin as well, Ghinassi et al. (2024) extend such approach to historical languages, leveraging parallel corpora to pivot Latin to English. Propagating WSD annotations from English to Latin then helps tackle the challenge represented by the lack of large sense annotated corpora.

The need for automated WSD has been observed, particularly for historical languages, in light of the increasing size of corpora to annotate and of the subjectivity involved in the intuitive judgment required by sense disambiguation, even more so when native speakers cannot be exploited, as noted by Manjavacas Arevalo and Fonteyn (2022). However, efforts to expedite the annotation process do represent a more general need. For instance, in the context of expanding an event-type ontology Straková et al. (2023) try to exploit fine-tuned LLMs to generate annotation suggestions that could expedite the manual annotation process of verbs to be included in the ontology. Despite not working with a historical language – as their focus is on Czech – their remarks about the necessity of manual post-inspection and annotation of suggestions as an indispensable step can be generalized.

Furthermore, Scarlini et al. (2020) experiment with developing a semi-supervised approach[2] to obtain sense embeddings for lexical meanings within a lexical knowledge base like WordNet. Although their approach does not include Latin and thus cannot be leveraged in our work, it interestingly builds upon the semantic information already carried by contextual word embeddings.

In general – as it provides a comprehensive lexical inventory for the identification of the different word senses – WordNet is a crucial resource for WSD. The current Latin WordNet[3] (WN) (Franzini et al. 2019; Mambrini et al. 2021) is the outcome of an ongoing and substantial revision of the original LatinWordNet (Minozzi, 2010) as initiated within the MultiWordNet project (Pianta et al., 2002). In WordNet, diverse senses of a polysemic word are assigned to distinct synsets. Within the LiLa Knowledge Base (Passarotti et al., 2020), these WN synsets are mapped with valency frames of the valency lexicon Latin Vallex[4], thanks to the shared lexical entries between the two resources. As a result, the Latin Vallex contains not only valency frames but also synset definitions associated to them.

3 In between Latin Vallex and WordNet

Let us delve deeper into the examination of the linguistic resources exploited, and notably Latin Vallex.[5] Nonetheless, speaking of Vallex implies speaking of WordNet as well, as the two resources are interlinked in LiLa (Section 2).

For each lemma, Vallex contains information about the synset definition (taken from WordNet) and the valency frame associated to it. A closer look at the entries immediately reveals how some synsets are semantically close. In many cases, their strikingly similar definitions are not justified by diverging valency frames. Among the many examples, two senses of *porto*, both with frame ACT (Actor), PAT (Patient), are defined respectively as

[1] https://tll.degruyter.com/about.

[2] ARES (context-AwaRe Embeddings of Senses).

[3] https://lila-erc.eu/lodview/data/lexicalResources/LatinWordNet/Lexicon.

[4] http://lila-erc.eu/lodview/data/lexicalResources/LatinVallex/Lexicon.

[5] https://github.com/CIRCSE/Latin_Vallex2.0.

definition	synset_id
have on one's person	v#00047745
have with oneself; have on one's person	v#02717102

Three very similar entries are associated to *augeo*, all with the same valency frame ACT, PAT:

definition	synset_id
make strong or stronger	v#00220869
make stronger	v#00222472
make more intense, stronger, or more marked	v#00227165

The examples just mentioned represent instances of extremely high similarity of synset definitions. Although not infrequent, such cases are not the majority. *Metior* can serve as a less extreme example, yet still informative about Vallex/WN granularity; see a list of its 9 synsets, all with frame ACT, PAT:

1. measure (distances) by pacing
2. determine the measurements of something or somebody, take measurements of
3. judge tentatively or form an estimate of (quantities or time)
4. evaluate or estimate the nature, quality, ability, extent, or significance of
5. set, mark, or draw the boundaries of something
6. determine the capacity, volume, or contents of by measurement and calculation
7. travel across or pass over
8. give out as one's portion or share
9. administer or bestow, as in small portions

Although with different nuances, synsets 1-6 all revolve around the concept of *measuring*, being possibly too fine-grained for automatic detection. *Metior* does not represent an isolated occurrence, but a standard entry in Vallex/WN: in light of this consideration, it becomes apparent how Vallex itself poses additional challenges to such task of automatic synset detection.

4 Methodology

In response to the aforementioned need of deriving annotation suggestions for verbal senses, we develop a Predicate Sense Disambiguation (henceforth PSD) workflow leveraging contextual embeddings.[6] As the core of the approach, we try to assess the similarity[7] between the verbal tokens in the target text and those in the reference corpus, with the goal of disambiguating the token sense by virtue of its contextual surroundings. Reference and target corpus[8] are defined based on text paragraphs (reference: par. 1-30 + par. 41-61; target: par. 31-40). The workflow consists of the following steps:

Extracting of verbal tokens. We collect a list of all verbal tokens by extracting them from our source text, i.e., Sallust's *De Coniuratione Catilinae* annotated in the XML-based format Prague Markup Language (PML).[9] The PML files of the treebank are organized by annotation layers and linked to each other through stand-off annotation; we exploit the morphological (lemmatization and morphological tagging) and the tectogrammatical (semantic and pragmatic annotation) layers in combination. We retrieve all verbs by extracting nodes with a valency frame and the required POS.[10]
The extracted verbs are split according to the reference/target corpus partition,[11] and are then manually annotated by a single annotator.

Storing annotated synsets. For each of the extracted tokens in the reference corpus, we store the synset definition that was manually assigned to it. Three cases can occur: i) Most verbs receive a synset from the Latin WN/Vallex, as linked in the LiLa Knowledge Base. For instance, *dominor* in *lubidinem dominandi* 'lust of dominion' is assigned the synset `v#02442106` "be master; reign or rule". ii) When no appropriate synset can be found in the resource, a new one is defined. The definition of the new synset can consist either of an existing WN synset which was not yet assigned to the verb, or of a new definition modeled on a dictionary entry for the verb. E.g., for *vivo* there is no entry in WN; to its occurrence in *alii alio more viventes* 'living with different customs' we assign a new frame with synset `v#02614387` "lead a certain kind

[6]Code is available at `https://github.com/fjambe/PSD-Latin-UMR`.

[7]Measured in terms of cosine similarity.

[8]Since we are not training any model, we decided not to call them training and test.

[9]The text is available at `https://itreebank.marginalia.it/view/download.php` as part of the Latin Dependency Treebank (LDT).

[10]Based on the guidelines of the Prague Dependency Treebank, whose annotation the LDT replicates, valency mainly applies to verbs, yet not exclusively. See `https://ufal.mff.cuni.cz/pdt2.0/doc/manuals/en/t-layer/html/`.

[11]The respective sizes of reference and target corpus are: i) tokens: 13,297 and 1,775 tokens; ii) extracted predicate tokens: 1,787 and 259. The division approximately conforms to a 9:1 ratio, while preserving the paragraph structure of the original work.

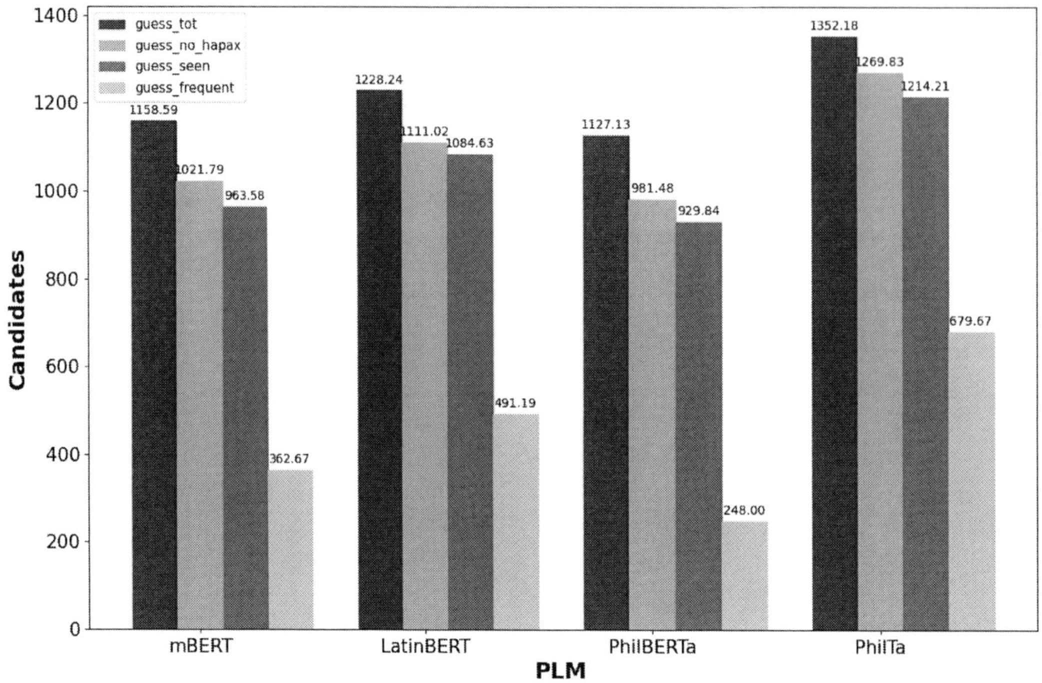

Figure 1: Comparison of different PLMs (mBERT, LatinBERT, PhilBERTa, PhilTa) with lemma constraint. For each of the four defined settings, the number of suggested candidates before retrieving one with same lemma is shown.

of life; live in a certain style". iii) Some tokens lack assigned synsets, as they can be treated as UMR abstract predicates;[12] for instance, the verb *sum* 'to be' can be treated e.g. as *identity-91*, *belong-91*, *have-mod[ification]-91*. We proceed to exclude such tokens from the corpus.

Computing and comparing embeddings. For each verbal token in its respective sentence, both in reference and target corpus, embeddings are computed exploiting the Flair library.[13] We then compute cosine similarity to compare embeddings, and more precisely to quantify the degree of similarity between each target token and each reference token. Similarity scores are then sorted in descending order, so that we can extract the five closest tokens (those with the highest scores — even if the scores are generally low). The synsets of these tokens are then extracted as candidate synsets.

Further constraining candidate tokens. Additionally, we retrieve all the tokens that are extracted as candidates before the first one with the same lemma as the target token[14] is found, i.e. those tokens with higher similarity score than the first one with constrained lemma. As preliminary results did not appear very promising, we decide to apply this additional lemma-based constraint on the candidate extraction. Specifically, we henceforth select as candidates only those tokens which share the lemma with the target token. The same-lemma requirement is merely an artificial constraint intended to facilitate the task, as in a real-case scenario it is possible to derive a correct synset even when the lemma differs. For instance, the synset `v#00406243` "make ready or suitable or equip in advance for a particular purpose or for some use, event, etc." is shared by *pario*, *instituo*, and *facio* among other verbs. In theory, such tokens that share synsets should be retrievable aside from whether they share the same lemma or not. Yet, the necessity of defining a simplified scenario through the imposition of a lemma constraint becomes ap-

[12]UMR features 9 types of abstract predicates, used to represent predication of properties, possession, location. They are identified by special labels serving as artificial lemmas and have their own roleset. For example, *identity-91* has an ARG1 role for the theme, and ARG2 for the equated referent.

[13]`https://flairnlp.github.io/`. We employ Transformer embeddings with default arguments; we only choose a different pooling operation to generate the final token representation from subwords – for which we select `mean`, calculating a `torch.mean` over all subword embeddings.

[14]By target token we mean the token to be annotated.

parent from the initial results of the experiments.

Output. As a result, the output file provides all retrieved information about each token: five annotation suggestions; i.e. the most plausible synsets; the number of incorrect guesses before suggesting a token with the same lemma;[15] the list of lemmas retrieved before a correct one was found.

4.1 Pretrained LMs for Embeddings

The following pretrained language models have been exploited to produce embeddings:

- mBERT (Devlin et al., 2018): multilingual BERT model (base, cased) pre-trained on 104 languages including Latin.
- Latin BERT (Bamman and Burns, 2020): pre-trained on 642.7 million words from a variety of sources spanning the Classical era to the 21st century.
- PhilBERTa (Riemenschneider and Frank, 2023): RoBERTa (Liu et al., 2019) model, pre-trained on Latin, Ancient Greek, and English, and tailored for classical philology (like PhilTa).
- PhilTa (Riemenschneider and Frank, 2023): T5 (Raffel et al., 2020) model, pre-trained on Latin, Ancient Greek, and English.

5 Evaluation

In this section we present and discuss a comparison between outputs yielded by different PLMs (Subsection 4.1), with respect to various criteria. Additionally, we manually evaluate a subset of the target corpus so as to complement the evaluation metrics with a qualitative analysis.

5.1 Quantitative Analysis

OOV. A key observation concerns out-of-vocabulary predicates, i.e. verbs that occur in the target corpus only. The amount of such verbs, for which a candidate with same lemma cannot be retrieved, is considerably high (20%). The percentage of target predicates whose lemma occurs only once in the reference corpus is quite high as well (13.7%). These figures would strongly argue against the constrained-lemma setting, when only candidates with the same lemma as the target token are retrieved. However, as mentioned before, the constraint on the lemma was deemed reasonable since preliminary results did not seem promising.

[15]Of course, the fact that the lemma is shared does not guarantee that the sense is shared as well.

Criteria. We identify four criteria to extract some patterns from the data (see Figure 1). For all four metrics, lower scores are indicative of better performance.

1. `guess_tot`: average number of suggested candidates before retrieving one with the same lemma.
2. `guess_no_hapax`: average number of suggested candidates before retrieving one with same lemma, excluding *hapax legomena*.[16]
3. `guess_seen`: average number of suggested candidates before retrieving one with same lemma, considering only lemma-synset pairs which occur in the reference corpus. In other words, we try to observe what happens when evaluating only cases where there was a chance that the synset could have been guessed correctly. The results of this artificially simplified setup will be analyzed in greater depth also with respect to retrieval of synsets, by exploiting such a controlled setup to lift the lemma constraint and evaluate retrieval of synsets instead of lemmas.
4. `guess_freq`: average number of suggested candidates before retrieving one with same lemma, computed only on the 10 most frequent lemmas[17] of the whole corpus.

In light of the criteria defined, and assuming their representativeness, we observe how PhilBERTa tendentially performs best in all settings, while the worst results are achieved with PhilTa. A pattern emerges when progressively limiting the evaluation scope to 'known', i.e. more frequent, predicates: all four PLMs output slightly improved results, highlighting the effect of frequency on such a task. Specifically, the number of retrieved candidates before finding one with shared lemma is highest in case of overall evaluation, and it gradually decreases first when *hapax* are excluded, then when only lemma-synset pairs occurring in the reference corpus are considered, and finally when the evaluation is limited to the 10 most frequent verbs. In particular, the `guess_frequent` setting seems to impact results to a greater extent, as the number of retrieved candidates is here conspicuously lower.

[16]Lemmas occurring only once, namely only in the target corpus.

[17]*Facio* 'make', *dico* 'say', *video* 'see', *paro* 'prepare', *fio* 'become', *do* 'give', *cognosco* 'know', *coepio* 'begin', *capio* 'take', *valeo* 'be strong'. *Sum* 'be' and *habeo* 'have' have been discarded as they often correspond to UMR abstract concepts.

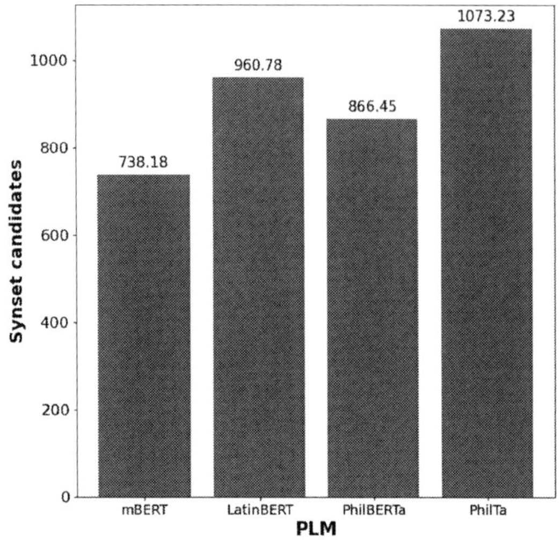

Figure 2: Evaluation of different PLMs (mBERT, LatinBERT, PhilBERTa, PhilTa) in synset retrieval. The *y* axis reports the number of candidates suggested before retrieving the correct synset, without any lemma constraint and by considering only lemma-synset pairs occurring in the reference corpus.

In addition to the evaluation settings based on lemma constraint, we then design an artificially simplified setting to analyze how PLMs behave when retrieving the correct synset without being limited by shared lemma. As mentioned when presenting the `guess_seen` evaluation criterion, in this controlled setup we focus only on lemma-synset pairs which occur in the reference corpus, excluding from the evaluation all those that do not meet this requirement. A similar setup should allow to investigate actual performances without being overly affected by data scarcity. In principle, it should be possible to retrieve tokens sharing the same synset regardless of whether they share the same lemma, as explained through the example of *pario, facio, instituo*, all sharing the synset `v#00406243` (Section 4). However, Figure 2 highlights how the number of attempts before a correct guess is still very high. The pattern is similar to what already observed when constraining on lemma, with PhilTa performing the worst. Yet, here PhilBERTa and multilingual BERT are inverted, with the latter resulting to be the model that on average needs the lowest number of attempts before a correct one.

5.2 Manual Evaluation

To further investigate the performance of the models, we also conduct a manual evaluation of a subset of the results. As a sample, we extract the first 20 predicates that occur in the target text. We first assess how the models perform on this subset within the default lemma-constrained setting (`guess_tot`). We ignore the number of attempts before retrieving the correct lemma, as it is already reflected by evaluation metrics, and focus on the assignments of synsets given a shared lemma. Results are presented in Table 1, to be interpreted in the following way: `1/2` means that two synset candidates are retrieved by the model (given a constrained lemma), and the first out of the two is the correct one based on manual annotation. `1=2/2` implies that two candidates are retrieved, and that they are identical and both correct, while `0/n` means that none of the `n` retrieved candidates is correct. `1=n=5/5` corresponds to a situation where all five retrieved candidates are identical and correct.

The analysis of results shows that the models' performances do not differ substantially one from another in the defined setting. Lemmas for which none of the retrieved candidates are correct (e.g. `0/5` in the table) can be explained by the fact that the sense they have been manually annotated with never occurs in the reference corpus, either at all or in association to that specific lemma. It is e.g. the case of *credo* 'to believe' and *moveo* 'to move', despite both being quite frequent verbs. The same happens with *diffido* 'to distrust'; the sense observed in the target corpus (`v#00687926`, "regard as untrustworthy; regard with suspicion; have no faith or confidence in") never occurs in the reference corpus. In this way, even a classification that should be relatively simple -— like the binary classification of *diffido*, for which only two senses are stored in Latin WordNet – fails. In the case of *permota*, from *permoveo* 'to stir up', we can observe the similarity of definitions that was already discussed in Section 3, as the sense definitions of retrieved candidates are highly similar: "move deeply" and "disturb in mind or make uneasy or cause to be worried or alarmed" (retrieved twice).

The case of *gerere*, from *gero* 'to manage', offers interesting insights as well, since all the five retrieved candidates are assigned the same sense "direct the course of; manage or control". Such cases of candidates leading to the same sense suggestion could probably be grouped, in order to inves-

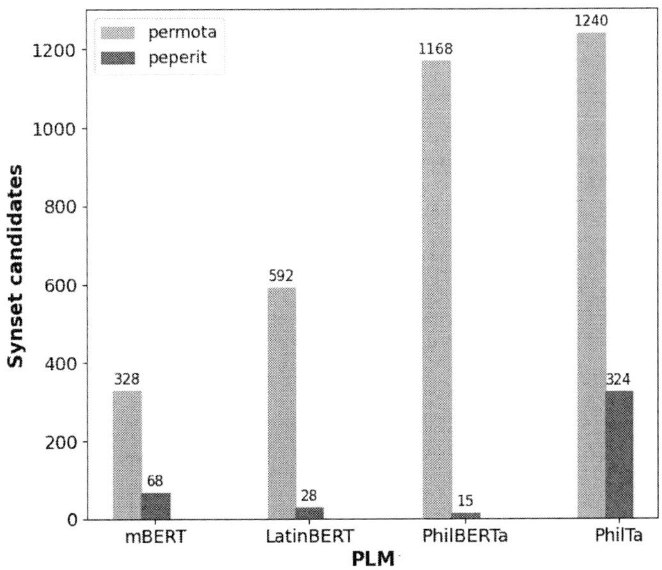

Figure 3: Evaluation of different PLMs in synset retrieval on two examples (*permota*, *peperit*).

token	lemma	hapax	**mBERT**	**Latin BERT**	**PhilBERTa**	**PhilTa**
permota	*permoveo*		1=3/3	2=3/3	2=3/3	2=3/3
pepererat	*pario*		1/2	2/2	2/2	2/2
invasit	*invado*		2/3	3/3	1/3	3/3
festinare	*festino*		1=2/2	1=2/2	1=2/2	1=2/2
trepidare	*trepido*	x				
credere	*credo*		0/5	0/5	0/5	0/5
gerere	*gero*		1=n=5/5	1=n=5/5	1=n=5/5	1=n=5/5
metiri	*metior*	x				
incesserat	*incedo*		1=2/2	1=2/2	1=2/2	1=2/2
adflictare	*afflicto*	x				
tendere	*tendo*		0/1	0/1	0/1	0/1
miserari	*miseror*		0/1	0/1	0/1	0/1
rogitare	*rogito*	x				
pavere	*paveo*	x				
adripere	*arripio*	x				
omissis	*omitto*		2/2	2/2	2/2	2/2
diffidere	*diffido*		0/1	0/1	0/1	0/1
movebat	*moveo*		0/5	0/5	0/5	0/5
parabantur	*paro*		1=3=5/5	1=2=3=5/5	1=2=3=4/5	1=2=3=5/5
interrogatus	*interrogo*		0/2	0/2	0/2	0/2

Table 1: Manual assessment of PLMs' performances (with lemma constraint).

tigate whether additional and different senses are retrieved after the main one; then, retrieved sense suggestions could possibly be weighted by the number of times they are proposed. However, in this specific case in the reference corpus we can find ten occurrences of the verb *gero*, all assigned that same sense. The effect of frequency can be observed with *gero* in the number of total guesses before a token with the same lemma is retrieved: 459 for PhilBERTa and 304 for mBERT, considerably lower than the average number (Figure 1). *Hapax legomena*, marked as such in Table 1, have been set aside also in the manual evaluation, as the lemma-constrained setting inevitably prevents the retrieval of any candidate.
Overall, what emerges from Table 1 is that no PLM consistently outperforms the others, with all models exhibiting similar performance within the defined setting.[18]

Within the proposed manual assessment, we also evaluate the sub-task of synset retrieval. Let us take again the token *permota*[19] as an example. mBERT and PhilBERTa, the two models that have proved to perform better, take respectively 328 and 1168 guesses before retrieving the correct synset. Their performances differ substantially here, with mBERT outperforming PhilBERTa by much. Nonetheless, the synset definitions of the first 5 out of the 328 candidates suggested by mBERT are sufficient to highlight the absence of a clear, reliable rationale in such retrieval, as they appear uncorrelated: "give a certain impression or gave a certain outward aspect", "enter or assume a certain state or condition", "from a critical opinion of", habitually do something (used only in past tense)", "have with oneself; have on one's person".

Moreover, deriving discernible patterns from the outputs of PLMs presents considerable challenges (see Figure 3). In the case of *permota*, beside performances by mBERT and PhilBERTa, we observe the number of guesses by PhilTa and Latin BERT amounting to 592 and 1240 respectively – not totally consistently with the pattern observed e.g. in Figure 1. However, if we take into account the second token of the target corpus, i.e. *peperat* from *pario* with the meaning of "cause to happen, occur or exist", the number of suggestions before retrieving the correct sense does not mirror what has been observed so far (PhilBERTa: 15 suggested candidates; Latin BERT: 28; mBERT: 68; PhilTa: 324). Once again, it is hard to interpret why specific senses associated to candidate suggestions are retrieved. For instance, mBERT retrieves the following: 1) "be willing to concede", 2) "spur on", 3)"impose a penalty on; inflict punishment on", 4) "confess to a punishable or reprehensible deed, usually under pressure", 5) "take or capture by force". PhilBERTa, i.e. the model with lowest retrieval score in this specific case, outputs these candidates: 1) "make a solicitation or entreaty for something; request urgently or persistently", 2) "order, request, or command to come", 3) "get to know or become aware of, usually accidentally", 4) "assign a specified (usually proper name) proper name to", 5) "decide with authority". Not only their similarity to the actually assigned one ("cause to happen, occur or exist") is irrelevant, but the two sets of candidates do not look mutually similar in any way.

6 Conclusions

The complexity of the task has been apparent from the beginning, and is confirmed by observations from related studies. Bamman and Burns (2020) already discuss comparable challenges, emphasizing the inherent difficulty of the WSD task and the lack of suitable resources for Latin – an observation also echoed by Keersmaekers et al. (2023). In light of such complexity, our study was never truly conceived as a solution to a specific task, but rather as a qualitative assessment of the available resources as well as of the results they can lead to. Therefore, our main objective revolved around a thorough examination of the task, its objectives, and challenges, with the intention of critically analyzing and identifying realistic possibilities within the constraints of the available resources. One of the key questions concerned whether we can actually exploit available resources: in particular, can Latin Vallex represent a suitable resource for PSD? At its present stage, its exploitation for PSD does not appear to be feasible; its fine-grained granularity definitely presents challenges for this specific task. Nevertheless, adopting a binary classification approach, as suggested by previous works (Bamman and Burns, 2020; Lendvai and Wick, 2022), may not offer a satisfactory solution either. As an

[18]It is important to note that these results may be influenced by the limited sample size.

[19]Occurring in the sentence *Quibus rebus permota civitas atque inmutata urbis facies erat* (Sall., *De Coniuratione Catiline* XXXI), translated as "By such proceedings as these the citizens were struck with alarm" in Perseus, at `https://www.perseus.tufts.edu/`.

illustrative example, the verb *postulo* demonstrates the need for at least three distinct frames, even under a coarse-grained granularity: i) 'to ask, demand, require' (ACT, ADDR, PAT); ii) 'arraign before a court, to prosecute, accuse' [juridical] (ACT, PAT, REG); iii) 'to contain, measure' [of things] (ACT, PAT). Currently, Latin Vallex/WN provides nine frames for *postulo*. The granularity of Latin Vallex and the simplicity of a binary classification demand a thoughtful exploration of alternative strategies to address such challenges. A possibility could be represented by sense clustering, as described e.g. by Navigli (2006) and Martelli et al. (2022).

Additionally, an important limitation of the study arises from the decision not to fine-tune PLMs, whose performances would most probably be enhanced through fine-tuning. However, fine-tuning requires training data, and the annotated dataset currently at our disposal is of limited size. The quantitative results, as illustrated in Figure 1, clearly highlight the substantial impact of the limited amount of available data on results. Therefore, what can be also inferred from the present study is the need for a larger reference corpus, to be obtained by enlarging the existing dataset with additional data.

An envisioned extension to the presented workflow involves the computation of sentence embeddings for definitions. Without constraining either on same lemma or on same synset, and thus handling even OOV cases, cosine similarity could be leveraged to identify the most probable synset by comparing all the synset definitions associated to the target token against the synset definition of the extracted candidates, to find the most similar one(s). In other words, embeddings for the synset definition of retrieved candidates could be generated, as well as for the list of synset definitions as available in Vallex/WN for the lemma under scrutiny. We could then select candidate synset definitions by computing cosine similarity between all synsets associated in Vallex/WN to the target lemma and synsets of the extracted candidate tokens in the reference corpus, in order to be able to deal not only with synsets shared by verbs with different lemma, but also with synsets that do not occur in the reference corpus. However, we expect the issues encountered so far (to name one, the dataset size) to pose similar challenges even in this further-defined setting.

Acknowledgments

This work has been supported by the Charles University, project GAUK No. 104924. It has also been partially supported by the SVV project number 260 698 and by the grant *Language Understanding: from Syntax to Discourse* (No. 20-16819X) of the Czech Science Foundation.

The project has been using data and tools provided by the *LINDAT/CLARIAH-CZ Research Infrastructure* (https://lindat.cz), supported by the Ministry of Education, Youth and Sports of the Czech Republic (Project No. LM2023062).

References

David Bamman and Patrick J. Burns. 2020. Latin BERT: A contextual language model for classical philology. *CoRR*, abs/2009.10053.

Laura Banarescu, Claire Bonial, Shu Cai, Madalina Georgescu, Kira Griffitt, Ulf Hermjakob, Kevin Knight, Philipp Koehn, Martha Palmer, and Nathan Schneider. 2013. Abstract Meaning Representation for Sembanking. In *Proceedings of the 7th Linguistic Annotation Workshop and Interoperability with Discourse*, pages 178–186, Sofia, Bulgaria. Association for Computational Linguistics.

Kaspar Beelen, Federico Nanni, Mariona Coll Ardanuy, Kasra Hosseini, Giorgia Tolfo, and Barbara McGillivray. 2021. When time makes sense: A historically-aware approach to targeted sense disambiguation. In *Findings of the Association for Computational Linguistics: ACL-IJCNLP 2021*, pages 2751–2761, Online. Association for Computational Linguistics.

Jacob Devlin, Ming-Wei Chang, Kenton Lee, and Kristina Toutanova. 2018. BERT: pre-training of deep bidirectional transformers for language understanding. *CoRR*, abs/1810.04805.

Greta Franzini, Andrea Peverelli, Paolo Ruffolo, Marco Passarotti, Helena Sanna, Edoardo Signoroni, Viviana Ventura, Federica Zampedri, et al. 2019. Nunc Est Aestimandum: Towards an Evaluation of the Latin WordNet. In *Proceedings of the Sixth Italian Conference on Computational Linguistics (CLiC-it 2019)*, Bari, Italy.

Iacopo Ghinassi, Simone Tedeschi, Paola Marongiu, Roberto Navigli, and Barbara McGillivray. 2024. Language pivoting from parallel corpora for word sense disambiguation of historical languages: A case study on Latin. In *Proceedings of the 2024 Joint International Conference on Computational Linguistics, Language Resources and Evaluation (LREC-COLING 2024)*, pages 10073–10084, Torino, Italia. ELRA and ICCL.

Alek Keersmaekers, Wouter Mercelis, and Toon Van Hal. 2023. Word Sense Disambiguation for Ancient Greek: Sourcing a training corpus through translation alignment. In *Proceedings of the Ancient Language Processing Workshop*, pages 148–159.

Piroska Lendvai and Claudia Wick. 2022. Finetuning Latin BERT for Word Sense Disambiguation on the Thesaurus Linguae Latinae. In *Proceedings of the Workshop on Cognitive Aspects of the Lexicon*, pages 37–41, Taipei, Taiwan. Association for Computational Linguistics.

Yinhan Liu, Myle Ott, Naman Goyal, Jingfei Du, Mandar Joshi, Danqi Chen, Omer Levy, Mike Lewis, Luke Zettlemoyer, and Veselin Stoyanov. 2019. RoBERTa: A robustly optimized bert pretraining approach. *Preprint*, arXiv:1907.11692.

Francesco Mambrini, Marco Passarotti, Eleonora Litta, and Giovanni Moretti. 2021. Interlinking valency frames and wordnet synsets in the LiLa knowledge base of linguistic resources for Latin. In *Further with Knowledge Graphs*, pages 16–28. IOS Press.

Enrique Manjavacas Arevalo and Lauren Fonteyn. 2022. Non-parametric word sense disambiguation for historical languages. In *Proceedings of the 2nd International Workshop on Natural Language Processing for Digital Humanities*, pages 123–134, Taipei, Taiwan. Association for Computational Linguistics.

Paola Marongiu and Barbara McGillivray. 2023. Preliminary guidelines for manual annotation of word senses in Latin and ancient Greek corpora.

Federico Martelli, Marco Maru, Cesare Campagnano, Roberto Navigli, Paola Velardi, Rafael-J. Ureña-Ruiz, Francesca Frontini, Valeria Quochi, Jelena Kallas, Kristina Koppel, Margit Langemets, Jesse de Does, Rob Tempelaars, Carole Tiberius, Rute Costa, Ana Salgado, Sanni Nimb, Sussi Olsen, Simon Krek, Jaka Čibej, Kaja Dobrovoljc, Polona Gantar, and Tina Munda. 2022. *D3.8 Lexical-semantic analytics for NLP*. ELEXIS - European Lexicographic Infrastructure.

Barbara McGillivray. 2021. Latin lexical semantic annotation. King's College London. DOI: `10.18742/16974823.v1`.

Barbara McGillivray, Pierluigi Cassotti, Davide Di Pierro, Paola Marongiu, Anas Fahad Khan, Stefano Ferilli, and Pierpaolo Basile. 2023a. Graph databases for diachronic language data modelling. In *Proceedings of the 4th Conference on Language, Data and Knowledge*, pages 86–96, Vienna, Austria. NOVA CLUNL, Portugal.

Barbara McGillivray, Iacopo Ghinassi, and Paola Marongiu. 2023b. The challenges of sense granularity in word sense disambiguation for Latin. In *La memoria digitale: forme del testo e organizzazione della conoscenza. Atti del XII Convegno Annuale AIUCD*, pages 279–283, Siena, Italy. AIUCD.

Barbara McGillivray, Daria Kondakova, Annie Burman, Francesca Dell'Oro, Helena Bermúdez Sabel, Paola Marongiu, and Manuel Márquez Cruz. 2022. A new corpus annotation framework for latin diachronic lexical semantics. *Journal of Latin Linguistics*, 21(1):47–105.

Stefano Minozzi. 2010. The Latin WordNet project. In *Latin Linguistics Today. Akten des 15. Internationalen Kolloquiums zur Lateinischen Linguistik*, pages 707–716, Innsbruck. Institut für Sprachen und Literaturen der Universität Innsbruck.

Roberto Navigli. 2006. Meaningful clustering of senses helps boost word sense disambiguation performance. In *Proceedings of the 21st International Conference on Computational Linguistics and 44th Annual Meeting of the Association for Computational Linguistics*, pages 105–112, Sydney, Australia. Association for Computational Linguistics.

Tommaso Pasini, Alessandro Raganato, and Roberto Navigli. 2021. Xl-wsd: An extra-large and cross-lingual evaluation framework for word sense disambiguation. In *Proceedings of the AAAI Conference on Artificial Intelligence*, volume 35, pages 13648–13656.

Marco Passarotti, Francesco Mambrini, Greta Franzini, Flavio Massimiliano Cecchini, Eleonora Litta, Giovanni Moretti, Paolo Ruffolo, and Rachele Sprugnoli. 2020. Interlinking through lemmas. The lexical collection of the LiLa knowledge base of linguistic resources for Latin. *Studi e Saggi Linguistici*, 58(1):177–212.

Emanuele Pianta, Luisa Bentivogli, and Christian Girardi. 2002. MultiWordNet: developing an aligned multilingual database. In *First international conference on global WordNet*, pages 293–302.

Colin Raffel, Noam Shazeer, Adam Roberts, Katherine Lee, Sharan Narang, Michael Matena, Yanqi Zhou, Wei Li, and Peter J. Liu. 2020. Exploring the limits of transfer learning with a unified text-to-text transformer. *Journal of Machine Learning Research*, 21(140):1–67.

Frederick Riemenschneider and Anette Frank. 2023. Exploring large language models for classical philology. In *Proceedings of the 61st Annual Meeting of the Association for Computational Linguistics (Volume 1: Long Papers)*, pages 15181–15199, Toronto, Canada. Association for Computational Linguistics.

Bianca Scarlini, Tommaso Pasini, and Roberto Navigli. 2020. With more contexts comes better performance: Contextualized sense embeddings for all-round word sense disambiguation. In *Proceedings of the 2020 Conference on Empirical Methods in Natural Language Processing (EMNLP)*, pages 3528–3539, Online. Association for Computational Linguistics.

Jana Straková, Eva Fučíková, Jan Hajič, and Zdeňka Urešová. 2023. Extending an event-type ontology:

Adding verbs and classes using fine-tuned LLMs suggestions. In *Proceedings of the 17th Linguistic Annotation Workshop (LAW-XVII)*, pages 85–95, Toronto, Canada. Association for Computational Linguistics.

Jens EL Van Gysel, Meagan Vigus, Jayeol Chun, Kenneth Lai, Sarah Moeller, Jiarui Yao, Tim O'Gorman, Andrew Cowell, William Croft, Chu-Ren Huang, et al. 2021. Designing a Uniform Meaning Representation for Natural Language Processing. *KI-Künstliche Intelligenz*, 35(3-4):343–360.

Classification of Paleographic Artifacts at Scale: Mitigating Confounds and Distribution Shift in Cuneiform Tablet Dating

Danlu Chen[1], **Jiahe Tian**[2], **Yufei Weng**[1], **Taylor Berg-Kirkpatrick**[1], **Jacobo Myerston**[1]
UC San Diego[1], Fudan University[2]
danlu@ucsd.edu

Abstract

Cuneiform is the oldest writing system used for more than 3,000 years in ancient Mesopotamia. Cuneiform is written on clay tablets, which are hard to date because they often lack explicit references to time periods and their paleographic traits are not always reliable as a dating criterion. In this paper, we systematically analyse cuneiform dating problems using machine learning. We build baseline models for both visual and textual features and identify two major issues: confounds and distribution shift. We apply adversarial regularization and deep domain adaptation to mitigate these issues. On tablets from the same museum collections represented in the training set, we achieve accuracies as high as 84.42%. However, when test tablets are taken from held-out collections, models generalize more poorly. This is only partially mitigated by robust learning techniques, highlighting important challenges for future work.

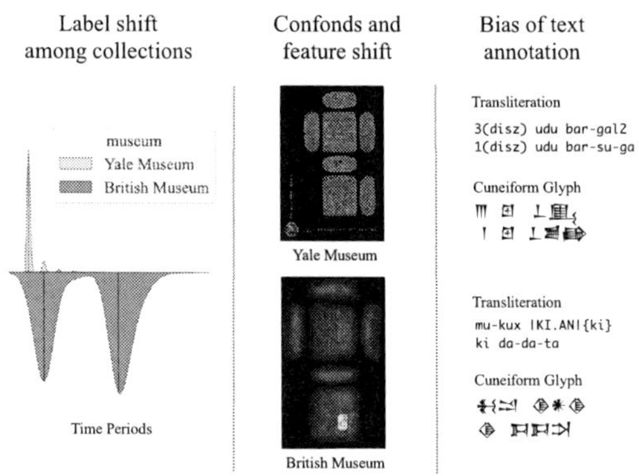

Figure 1: An overview of the cuneiform dating task. Tablets from different collection (museum or private collector) usually in different time period distribution and there is confound (undeier features to machine learning models) from different cameras. The transliteration is usually exhibit bias towards specific time periods.

1 Introduction

Computational paleography (Vidal-Gorène and Decours-Perez, 2021; Srivatsan et al., 2021) is a growing interdisciplinary field that uses computational algorithms to decipher and analyse ancient writing systems. We investigate using machine learning to automate large-scale dating of cuneiform[1], the oldest writing system from around 3,500 BCE. Similar to general chronicle attribution tasks in paleography, cuneiform dating involves classifying cuneiform tablets into specific time periods rather than precise years. For example, Figure 1 shows a tablet comes from Ur III. Different from other historical languages, such as ancient Greek (Assael et al., 2022) or ancient Arabic (Adam et al., 2018), cuneiform tablets are more challenging to convert into a machine readable format because the writing system continually evolved over the 3,000 years it was in use.

For many writing systems, historians and paleographers have been able to identify distinguishing features in textual content and writing style that allow for inferences about date of origin for individual artifacts. For some writing systems, these processes have even been automated with machine learning to some extent. For example, Assael et al. (2022) showed encouraging results using neural networks trained on ancient Greek text to restore and date digitized ancient Greek artifacts.

Can we train similar textual models for cuneiform dating using accompanying manual transcriptions or transliterations? We conduct experiments with a series of light-weight recurrent models that show this is indeed possible. However, relying on manual transcriptions for the purpose of dating is somewhat circular: for Cuneiform, transcription and transliteration is as time-intensive as manually dating tablets. Further, transliterations themselves might exhibit bias—for example, an expert's approach to transliterating a tablet may al-

[1] Code is available at https://github.com/taineleau/CuneiML/tree/main/ml4al_2024_dating.

Proceedings of the 1st Workshop on Machine Learning for Ancient Languages (ML4AL 2024), pages 30–41
August 15, 2024 ©2024 Association for Computational Linguistics

ready be influenced by preconceived notions about its time period—allowing models to overfit to the tendencies of individual transliterators.

Thus, we also study whether *visual representations* of Cuneiform tablets can be used effectively for automatic dating. Visual representations skirt the issues of manually-intensive transcription and confounds due to transliteration style. Further, visual representations may even allow models to automatically extract information about the visual style of writing, which paleographers have found useful for manual dating. In past work, Bogacz and Mara (2020) has shown that relatively accurate dating of cuneiform tablets using 3D scans is possible. However, currently it is not feasible to produce 3D scans of over 100,000 remaining tablets, which are dispersed among museums and private collections around the world.

Therefore, instead we explore the use 2D photographs from CDLI (CDLI contributors, 2024) to address the dating problem—a task that as far as we are aware has not been previously studied. Our experiments using convolutional neural models trained on 2D images demonstrate a new problem however: the different imaging setups used by different collections presents a confound that leads to poor generalization (shown in Figure 3). We find that the gap between performance on tablets from collections that were attested in training data versus those that were not is extremely large. Thus, we also evaluate to what extent robust learning methods that attempt to address out-of-distribution (OOD) generalization can mitigate this issue. We find that while these methods do help, they do not increase generalization to the point where accurate dating of tablets from unseen collections can be performed reliably. Thus, our empirical study highlights this important challenge as an area for future research. We summarize our primary contributions below:

1. We identify and analyze several challenging issues in cuneiform dating related to confounds, distribution shift, and domain generalization. These challenges are likely also present in the classification of other ancient artifacts with text.
2. We study a range of modeling approaches including simple methods like Naive Bayes, as well as neural methods for both images and text features. We demonstrate strong performance when using data splits that reduce distribution shift and OOD effects, but poor performance across museum collections.
3. We applied multiple robust learning techniques to mitigate distribution shift and the effect of confounds. While our results demonstrate improvements from these techniques, overall OOD generalization performance is still prohibitive for broader use.

In the following sections, we first formulate the problem and then describe the data collection splits we created to address our core research questions.

2 Problem Formulation

Technically, the dating task can be formulated as either a classification or a regression problem. However, after careful examination, we concluded that treating inferred dates as continuous variables (using regression) does not make sense in this domain because the annotation standard used for manual dating (the source of supervision for learning and evaluation) includes date categories with overlapping time intervals (see Figure 5). Instead, we represent each time period as a categorical class ID and treat dating as a multi-class classification problem.

Next, we layout the core research questions we attempt to answer in this empirical study. To address each, we will carefully design data splits that contain three separate test sets, each measuring a specific aspect of OOD generalization, along with a train and validation set.

RQ1: What models, configurations, and features—either visual or textual—are most effective for automatically dating cuneiform tablets?

RQ2: How much of a problem do OOD effects pose for generalization in this domain? For example, do models overfit to specific features present in individual museum collections? How well do models generalize to tablets from previously unseen museum collections?

RQ3: How well do existing robust learning techniques address the issue of distribution shift and OOD generalization in the context of cuneiform tablet dating?

In later sections, we will specify the datasets we use, which specific input representations we compare, and which modeling approaches

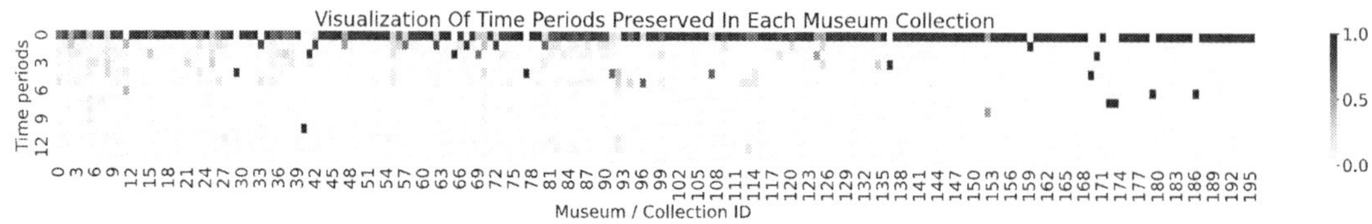

Figure 2: The normalized count density (by collection) of tablets from different time periods across museum collections. Darker colors indicate higher densities, highlighting that tablets from certain collections often belong to the same time period. This supports the hypothesis of distribution shifts between training and testing datasets. For a high-resolution version, see Appendix Figure 8.

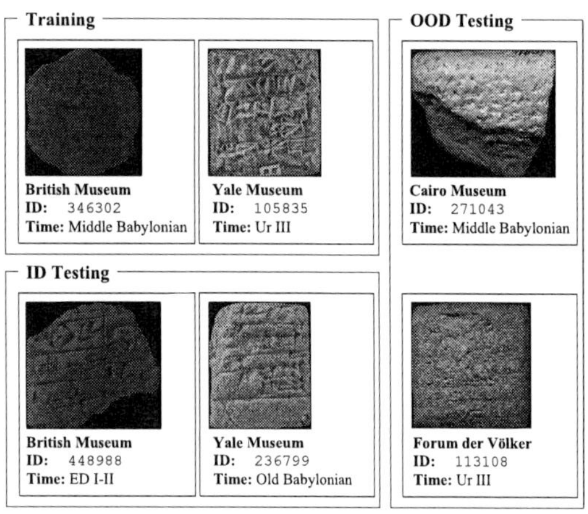

Figure 3: An overview one of the dating tasks using major-face cutouts of photographs to predict time periods. We held out several museums for the out-of-distribution (OOD) setting (e.g., the Cairo Museum), while the ID Testing set contains tablets from the same museums as the training set.

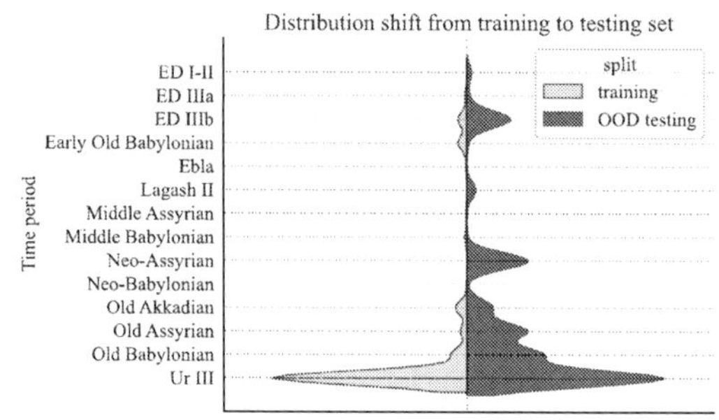

Figure 4: Visualization of *label shift* for the `collection shift` train/test split setting.

we evaluate. We will also carefully design test splits to answer specific questions about OOD generalization. Next, we describe and define some of the potential OOD effects in this domain and distribution shifts we seek to analyze.

Generally speaking, *distribution shift* occurs whenever the underlying distribution that generated the training data diverges from the distribution that will generate future test instances. Distribution shift poses a substantial challenge for learning systems: patterns that hold true on the training data may not generalize to the test set, leading to poor generalization performance. In the domain of cuneiform data the are two important types of distribution shift.

First, cuneiform datasets tend to exhibit substantial *label shift* due to how tablets are distributed across museum collections. We depict the distribution of tablet dates in museum collections in the CuneiML dataset (Chen et al., 2023) (which we use in experiments) in Table 2. Most museums contain tablets from a small range of time periods. Thus, if train and test setups for validating computational approaches are selected based on i.i.d. sampling from this dataset, the test performance may not accurately reflect expected performance on tablets from new, *unseen* museum collections. In Figure 4 we visualize actual label distribution shift in a i.i.d. train/test split.

Second, the input representations from individual museum collections may have properties that make the collection itself identifiable. For instance, as shown in Figures 1 and 3, the scanning methodologies used by separate museums leave artifacts like different amounts of color saturation and blurring. Similarly, it is possible that different transliteration styles may also be identifiable. Because individual collections are biased towards specific date ranges, the confounds mentioned above may cause *covariate shift*—a type of distribution shift where the distribution on the input variables and the relationship between input and output vary between train and test. For example, a model may learn to identify the collection based on properties of the scanning hardware in order to determine date. This may work on training data, but will not generalize

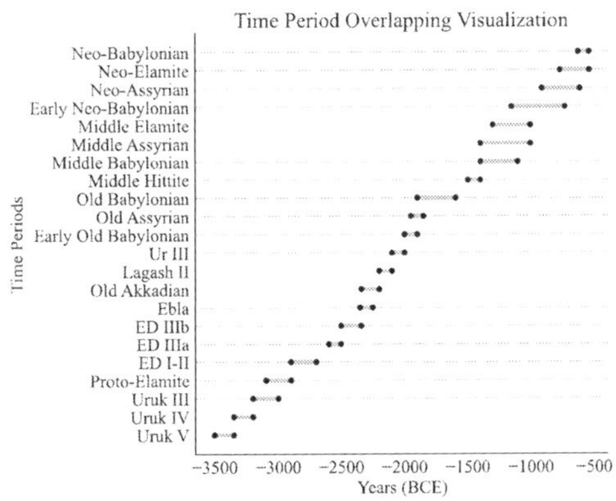

Figure 5: Time period overlapping visualization. The x-axis is years for BCE. Two time period classes can be parallel in time, for example, Middle Babylonian is almost completely overlaps in time with Middle Assyrian.

to new collections. Thus, one of our primary goals is to measure the effects of label and covariate shift for cuneiform dating and to evaluate to what extent robust learning methods may address these issues.

3 Data

We obtain 38,937 tablet images with transliterations from CDLI (CDLI contributors, 2024), using prepossessing from CuneiML (Chen et al., 2023). An example is shown in Figure 6. Besides transliteration and 2D images, we use several other attributes from the metadata entries, including **provenience**, **collection**, and **genre**, which we use in later experiments for both simple baselines and as additional supervision to mitigate distribution shift.

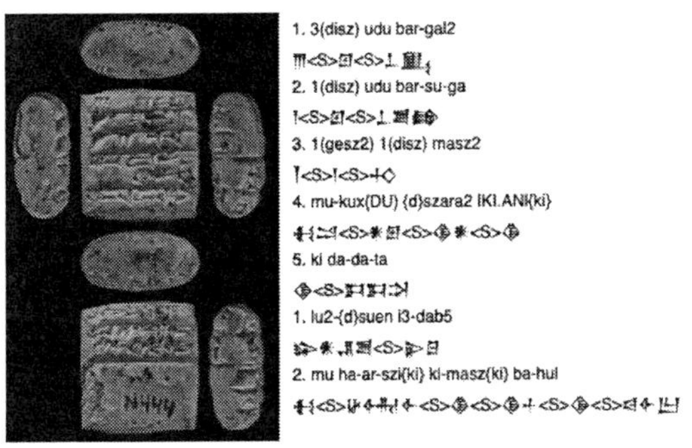

Figure 6: Left: Cuneiform Tablet images with six face photographs. Right: Example of transliteration in ATF format and the tokenization in cuneiform glyph. We use a special token <S> to separate the word in cuneiform.

Split	%	Count	Note
all	100%	38,937	-
train	80%	30,626	-
test 1	5%	2,065	OOD , $p(y)$ shift
valid	5%	2,116	OOD , $p(y)$ shift
test 2	5%	2,065	ID , $p(y)$ shift
test 3	5%	2,065	ID

Table 1: Dataset split statistics. OOD stands for Out-of-distribution compared to training set, and ID stands for in distribution compared to training set.

3.1 Data split

Inspired by Koh et al. (2021), we identify two kinds of distribution shift and would like to create splits that disentangle the issues and better answer the research questions. As we can see in Figure 2, most museum collections only own tablets from one or two time periods and most time periods are collected by a specific museum. To better study the distribution shift across collections, we split the data with regard to the collection id, i.e. tablets from the same collection only present in one split. This split we call OOD test split (test 1). We use $p(y)$ shift to denote a split where the label distribution $p(y)$ is significantly different from that of the training set. We describe briefly how we split the data (Table 1) below.

1. **Step 1: Getting an OOD and $p(y)$ shift set S_1 from the full data.** We sampled about 10% from the full dataset using the following rules: (i) We sample by collections, meaning tablets from an entire collection are either included or excluded. (ii) For a given time period, we do not select collections that constitute more than 30% of the data for that time period, ensuring that we do not remove most of the tablets for certain time periods from the training set. We named the remaining 90% of full data S_2. Figure 4 shows the shift of $p(Y)$.

2. **Step 2: Getting valid and test 1 set.** we evenly split S_1 We obtained from step 1 and we now have **valid** and **test 1** set.

3. **Step 3: Getting test 2.** We sampled 5% of the data from the subset S_2 against the label distribution of **test 1**. Therefore, test 2 has the same sub-population shift from the training set as **test 1**, but consists of in-domain (ID)

data instead of OOD data. We named the remaining 85% of the full data S_3.

4. **Step 4: Getting test 3 and train set.** We randomly sampled 5% of the data from S_3 to constitute **test 3**, and the remaining 80% is the final training set.

Therefore, we have three testing splits setup as shown in Table 1.

4 Methods

We describe the baseline models we used in experiments and also several training strategies, adversarial regularization and , to mitigate the distribution shift issues.

4.1 Baseline models

1. **Naive Bayes.** We use discrete categorical features, including genre, collection, provenance, and size, to predict the time period as a categorical prediction problem. Note that when there is only one feature, the performance indicates a correlation between the feature and the predicted class.

2. **Char-LSTMs.** We use a character-level two-layer bi-directional LSTMs to process cuneiform transliterations and sign tokens for dating ancient texts. The model has a hidden size of 128 and an embedding size of 256. We train for 200 epochs using the ADAMW optimizer with a learning rate of 5e-4 and a weight decay of 1e-3.

3. **ResNet.** Our study utilizes the ResNet (He et al., 2016) architecture, specifically ResNet-50 and ResNet-101. We apply these models to classify images of cuneiform inscriptions, leveraging their powerful feature extraction capabilities. The models are trained using a cross-entropy loss function, with adjustments made to the final layer to suit our specific class labels. The training regimen includes a batch size of 16, 30 epochs, ADAM with a learning rate of 3e-5, and no weight decay.

4.2 Baseline Objective

For all the neural models, we use cross entropy (CE) loss to train the models.

$$L = \text{CE}(y^{(t)}, p^{(t)})$$

4.3 Advanced Algorithms

To address the aforementioned issues, we explore several different robust training algorithms in this paper.

Adversarial Regularization. We use other attributes such as provenience and genre, to optimize a min-max objective. We attach a new branch of MLP to calculate the $p^{(adv)}$.

$L = \text{CE}(y^{(t)}, p^{(t)}) + \text{KLD}(y^{(const)}, p^{(adv)})$

where CE is cross entropy loss and KLD is the KL Divergence loss.

Correlation Alignment for Deep Domain Adaptation (CORAL). CORAL (Sun and Saenko, 2016) measures the divergence of means and covariance between batches of feature representations. The goal of CORAL is to match the feature distributions from different domains.

Invariant risk minimization (IRM). IRM (Arjovsky et al., 2019) penalizes feature distributions that result in different optimal linear classifiers across different domains. where where Φ is the entire invariant predictor, $w = 1.0$ is a fixed classifier, and the gradient norm penalty is the measure of the classifier at each environment.

5 Experiments and Results

5.1 Input Features

We have four different input features for training, describing as below.

1. **Raw image.** The raw images downloaded from CDLI. Each image usually contains photographs of six faces for each tablet.

2. **Major-face image.** The major-face cutout of the raw images, which are usually the front faces of the tablets.

3. **Raw transliteration.** We use the post-processed version from CuneiML, which removes formatting string such as line numbers, broken markers and etc.

4. **Cuneiform sign (glyph) token.** We tokenize cuneiform glyph at a character-level, with a vocabulary size of 764. See Figure 6 for an example. We keep the space between words and line break.

Features	Model	test 1 OOD $p(y)$ shift		test 2 ID $p(y)$ shift		test 3 ID	
		F_1	Acc.	F_1	Acc.	F_1	Acc.
-	random	2.92	7.80	2.91	7.12	2.96	6.30
-	majority	6.56	74.29	6.56	74.29	6.02	72.93
provenience	NBayes	**39.48**	83.63	51.09	79.95	61.15	89.20
genre	NBayes	15.31	72.88	19.77	75.11	22.72	80.63
provenience & genre	NBayes	37.94	83.49	**56.98**	83.24	**62.72**	91.91
museum (collection)	NBayes	6.56	74.29	13.92	75.16	21.78	77.85
transliteration	char-LSTM	16.14	10.72	**26.52**	10.87	**84.42**	95.73
sign token	char-LSTM	**16.59**	11.45	24.25	11.89	78.13	95.39
raw image	ResNet-50	28.46	82.03	64.33	93.51	78.73	94.26
+ OOD mitigate		29.42	83.24	47.46	92.13	48.63	88.17
major cutout	ResNet-50	34.82	87.36	**68.69**	94.74	**80.60**	95.19
+ OOD mitigate		**41.06**	88.37	49.55	91.62	54.78	88.03

Table 2: Main result table for cuneiform dating. Macro F_1 and Accuracy (Acc.) are reported. Macro F_1 denotes the average F_1 score calculated across all classes. Best F_1 scores for each subgroup are in **bold face** and the second best ones are underlined. Colored background highlight the best overall model for each setting.

The bounding boxes for major-face images and the Cuneiform sign (glyph) tokens are obtained from Chen et al. (2023)[2].

5.2 Metrics

As the label distribution $p(y)$ imbalance exists and there is a distribution shift, we primarily use the F_1 score and accuracy to evaluate our methods. Specifically, we use Macro F_1 and accuracy[3] as our major evaluation metrics.

Macro F_1 score computes the F_1 score independently for each class and then takes the average, thus treating all classes equally regardless of their frequency. This dual approach allows us to address both the overall accuracy and the individual class performance, ensuring a thorough evaluation in the face of skewed class distributions and shifts.

5.3 Results and Analysis

The main results for two split settings are shown in Table 2 and several key observation are summarized as follows.

1. **Random and Majority Baseline Models.** These models provide basic benchmarks with the majority model performing based on the most frequent class, note that the majority class contains more than 70% of the models, which accounts for the big discrepency between macro F_1 and accuracy. The low F1 scores, indicating poor performance across all classes evenly.
2. **Neural models perform the best across all settings.** Both visual and textual neural models work fairly good in ID setting (test 3), showing that both textual and visual features provide sufficient information to date tablets.
3. **Raw images contain confounded undesired features: collection.** When using a ResNet-50 model, features extracted from the raw images outperformed those obtained from front face cutouts on ID split (test 3). However, this performance was reversed on an OOD split (test 1). This reversal clearly indicates that raw images include collections as a confounding factor.
4. **Textual features are not effective for dating when label shift exists.** From test 3 to test 2, only the label distribution changes, while the data remains in-domain. However, textual models experience a dramatic drop in performance by 57.9%, revealing that textual features are not robust to label imbalance issues. In contrast, image models are not affected as significantly.
5. **Textual models are not robust to OOD shift; visual models are better but still have room for improvement.** Textual models exhibit nearly a 50% relative decrease in macro F_1 for the OOD setting (test 1) compared to visual models. With the application of OOD

[2]https://github.com/taineleau/CuneiML

[3]For single-label classification, Micro F_1 is equal to accuracy

mitigating algorithms (see section 6.3 for details), visual models improve from 34.82% to 41.06%, achieving the best F_1 score on test 1. This aligns with our earlier concerns that textual features do not capture any writing style of the tablet, making it difficult to determine the time period under OOD shift conditions.

6 Further Analysis

6.1 Zooming in on Textual Models

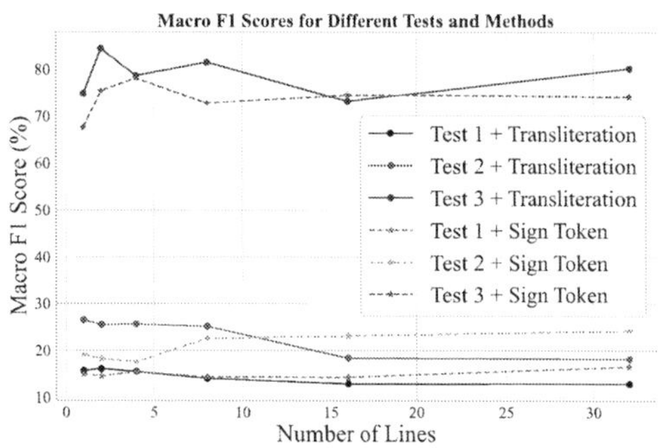

Figure 7: Analysis on best context length for textual features using char-LSTM on three test split.

As shown in Figure 7, we conducted extensive experiments on the number of lines per example fed into the models. As mentioned earlier, we use majority vote by default to ensemble predictions when we divide a full document. The performance of the glyph token features (sign token) increases as the number of lines in an example increases, while the transliteration features typically achieve the best performance with only one or two lines. This observation aligns with our understanding that transliteration already encodes some contextual knowledge, as signs are transliterated into Latin depending on the context. In contrast, for sign token features, the machine learning model requires more lines to discern the underlying information effectively.

6.2 Mitigating Label Imbalance Issues

Table 3 presents the results of label imbalance methods using char-LSTM on transliteration and glyph token features, with loss reweighing (LR) and upsampling (US). While both methods show varied effects on the performance metrics, loss reweighing generally improves F_1 scores and accuracy across the test sets, particularly for transliteration features, achieving a F_1 86.06% on test 3.

Features	test 1		test 2		test 3	
	F_1	Acc.	F_1	Acc.	F_1	Acc.
trans.	15.77	10.53	**26.52**	10.87	74.89	92.62
+ *LR*	**16.54**	11.45	24.98	11.89	**86.06**	85.33
+ *US*	12.63	9.89	25.32	10.63	81.75	94.61
glyph	15.00	8.82	19.14	9.52	67.56	92.08
+ *LR*	**17.63**	12.04	18.63	12.52	**74.08**	94.85
+ *US*	15.57	10.92	**19.17**	12.38	73.22	94.66

Table 3: Result for label Imbalance methods using char-LSTM on transliteraion and glyph token features. LR: loss reweighing, US: up sampling. The models trained with num_of_line=1.

6.3 Distribution shift and Confounds

Adversarial Regularization. Table 4 show results using adversarial regularization. Macro F_1 does not change as much as the accuracy. We also found that adversarial training requires very careful hyper-parameter tuning; otherwise, the model may completely underfit due to the noisy gradients provided by the adversarial branch.

Input	adv. feat	Macro F_1	Acc.
raw	none	25.73	58.34
raw	collection	25.44	62.12
cutout	none	29.09	64.91
cutout	collection	30.39	68.64

Table 4: Adversarial study on image features. ResNet-50 is used for all experiments in this table. We run each experiments five time and report the mean F_1 scores. Note that the result is trained on a slightly different split than the main table.

OOD mitigation. Table 5 shows results using OOD methods. Among the OOD mitigating algorithms, CORAL consistently improves the performance across all test sets for both raw and cutout features. Notably, CORAL achieves the best F_1 scores of 29.42% and 40.46% on test 1 for raw and cutout features, respectively. The other algorithms, IRM and groupDRO, generally show a decline in performance, with groupDRO performing the worst, especially for the cutout features. Overall, the results indicate that while textual models struggle with domain shifts, visual models, particularly those enhanced with cutout features and CORAL, demonstrate a more robust performance, albeit with room for further improvement.

Features	test 1		test 2		test 3	
	F_1	Acc.	F_1	Acc.	F_1	Acc.
raw	28.46	82.03	**64.33**	93.51	**78.73**	94.26
+ *IRM*	26.97	85.28	47.28	90.91	48.63	88.17
+ *CORAL*	**29.42**	83.24	47.46	92.13	46.94	90.08
+ *groupDRO*	24.02	77.97	35.18	87.69	56.54	89.54
cutout	34.82	87.36	**68.69**	94.74	**80.60**	95.19
+ *IRM*	28.31	87.46	43.42	91.11	44.34	88.81
+ *CORAL*	**40.46**	89.39	52.51	93.05	48.61	90.92
+ *groupDRO*	27.94	80.77	50.47	86.82	60.50	86.99

Table 5: OOD setting results trained on images features using ResNet-50.

Num of Examples	ResNet-50		char-LSTM	
	F_1	Acc.	F_1	Acc.
Full	85.34	94.40	53.19	85.89
10,000	67.18	90.86	49.46	84.73
5,000	59.17	89.99	32.93	82.24
1,000	40.89	82.39	17.28	75.09
500	28.03	77.77	7.44	70.62
100	13.21	55.49	5.66	65.67

Table 6: Ablation study on different number of training data, on test 3 using ResNet-50 and BERT. Note that this table is running on a slightly different data split from the main table.

6.4 Cuneiform Dating at Scale

It is not possible to make an apple-to-apple comparison on 2D and 3D scans features because most of the HeiCuBeDa dataset (Bogacz and Mara, 2020) does not accompany with a 2D photo. The paper reported a weighted F_1 of 83% (which is roughly comparable to accuracy in our case). We conduct a set of experiments by varying the number of training examples, as shown in Table 6. Both models show a clear trend of improved performance with increased training data.

7 Related work

7.1 Automated classification for ancient languages

Sommerschield et al. (2023) provides a detailed overview of ancient languages processing using machine learning. Resler et al. (2021) classified artifact images using CNNs and nearest neighbors. Assael et al. (2022) train a BE to restore ancient Greek. There have been work on dating documents in various ancient languages, like Arabic, Korean and Chinese oracles bones among others (Sommerschield et al., 2023)

7.2 Cuneiform studies

There have been important efforts in cuneiform sign recognition, language identification (Bernier-Colborne et al., 2019), and machine translation for Akkadian have been explored (Gutherz et al., 2023). Bogacz and Mara (2020) use high resolution 3D scans to classify time periods, and more recently Yugay et al. (2024) have explored the dating of first millennium Assyrian and Babylonian documents, using stylistic criteria and CNN. As mentioned earlier, it is non-trivial to tokenize the transliteration. Gordin et al. (2020) uses HMM and neural models to automatically transliterate Unicode cuneiform signs. On the contrary, in our paper, we reverse this process by converting the transliteration back to Unicode cuneiform signs to reduce transliteration bias.

7.3 Distribution shift

Historical data always suffers from noise and therefore it is hard to have good generalization on held out data. Specially for cuneiform, the systematic distribution shift is the most salient one. The systematic distribution shift is a special cases in domain adaptation, and therefore can be mitigated by general domain adaptation methods (Koh et al., 2021)). Ahmed et al. (2020) analyses group invariant predictions, where dominant simpler correlations with the target variable. Zare and Nguyen (2022) studied similar scenario in medical diagnosis, which has a shift on several attributes such as sex, age and race. They use invariant risk minimization (IRM) (Arjovsky et al., 2019) to learn invariant features. Another branch of methods is adversarial regularization, which uses adversarial training (Gokhale et al., 2021) to improve the generalization ability. Li et al. (2018) uses Maximum Mean Discrepancy (MMD) to align loss in different class.

8 Conclusion

In this paper, we explore end-to-end cuneiform dating at scale using machine learning. We have identified three major challenges—label imbalance, distribution shift, and circular reasoning—that are prevalent in cuneiform dating. These issues and solutions explored in our paper are broadly applicable to the classification of other ancient artifacts as well. We hope our initial analysis will inspire the community to further adopt machine learning for addressing problems in ancient language processing.

Acknowledgments

All the images and annotations are from CDLI (CDLI contributors, 2024), and our work would not have been possible without the numerous annotations and editorial work provided by their team and collaborators.

References

Kalthoum Adam, Asim Baig, Somaya Al-Maadeed, Ahmed Bouridane, and Sherine El-Menshawy. 2018. Kertas: dataset for automatic dating of ancient arabic manuscripts. *International Journal on Document Analysis and Recognition (IJDAR)*, 21:283–290.

Faruk Ahmed, Yoshua Bengio, Harm Van Seijen, and Aaron Courville. 2020. Systematic generalisation with group invariant predictions. In *International Conference on Learning Representations*.

Martin Arjovsky, Léon Bottou, Ishaan Gulrajani, and David Lopez-Paz. 2019. Invariant risk minimization. *arXiv preprint arXiv:1907.02893*.

Yannis Assael, Thea Sommerschield, Brendan Shillingford, Mahyar Bordbar, John Pavlopoulos, Marita Chatzipanagiotou, Ion Androutsopoulos, Jonathan Prag, and Nando de Freitas. 2022. Restoring and attributing ancient texts using deep neural networks. *Nature*, 603(7900):280–283. Number: 7900 Publisher: Nature Publishing Group.

Gabriel Bernier-Colborne, Cyril Goutte, and Serge Léger. 2019. Improving Cuneiform Language Identification with BERT. In *Proceedings of the Sixth Workshop on NLP for Similar Languages, Varieties and Dialects*, pages 17–25, Ann Arbor, Michigan. Association for Computational Linguistics.

Bartosz Bogacz and Hubert Mara. 2020. Period Classification of 3D Cuneiform Tablets with Geometric Neural Networks. In *2020 17th International Conference on Frontiers in Handwriting Recognition (ICFHR)*, pages 246–251.

CDLI contributors. 2024. Home. https://cdli.mpiwg-berlin.mpg.de/. [Online; accessed 2024-07-04].

Danlu Chen, Aditi Agarwal, Taylor Berg-Kirkpatrick, and Jacobo Myerston. 2023. Cuneiml: A cuneiform dataset for machine learning. *Journal of Open Humanities Data*.

Tejas Gokhale, Rushil Anirudh, Bhavya Kailkhura, Jayaraman J Thiagarajan, Chitta Baral, and Yezhou Yang. 2021. Attribute-guided adversarial training for robustness to natural perturbations. In *Proceedings of the AAAI Conference on Artificial Intelligence*, volume 35, pages 7574–7582.

Shai Gordin, Gai Gutherz, Ariel Elazary, Avital Romach, Enrique Jiménez, Jonathan Berant, and Yoram Cohen. 2020. Reading akkadian cuneiform using natural language processing. *PloS one*, 15(10):e0240511.

Gai Gutherz, Shai Gordin, Luis Sáenz, Omer Levy, and Jonathan Berant. 2023. Translating akkadian to english with neural machine translation. *PNAS nexus*, 2(5):pgad096.

Kaiming He, Xiangyu Zhang, Shaoqing Ren, and Jian Sun. 2016. Deep residual learning for image recognition. In *Proceedings of the IEEE conference on computer vision and pattern recognition*, pages 770–778.

Pang Wei Koh, Shiori Sagawa, Henrik Marklund, Sang Michael Xie, Marvin Zhang, Akshay Balsubramani, Weihua Hu, Michihiro Yasunaga, Richard Lanas Phillips, Irena Gao, Tony Lee, Etienne David, Ian Stavness, Wei Guo, Berton A. Earnshaw, Imran S. Haque, Sara Beery, Jure Leskovec, Anshul Kundaje, Emma Pierson, Sergey Levine, Chelsea Finn, and Percy Liang. 2021. WILDS: A benchmark of in-the-wild distribution shifts. In *International Conference on Machine Learning (ICML)*.

Haoliang Li, Sinno Jialin Pan, Shiqi Wang, and Alex C Kot. 2018. Domain generalization with adversarial feature learning. In *Proceedings of the IEEE conference on computer vision and pattern recognition*, pages 5400–5409.

Abraham Resler, Reuven Yeshurun, Filipe Natalio, and Raja Giryes. 2021. A deep-learning model for predictive archaeology and archaeological community detection. *Humanities and Social Sciences Communications*, 8(1):295.

Thea Sommerschield, Yannis Assael, John Pavlopoulos, Vanessa Stefanak, Andrew Senior, Chris Dyer, John Bodel, Jonathan Prag, Ion Androutsopoulos, and Nando de Freitas. 2023. Machine learning for ancient languages: A survey. *Computational Linguistics*, pages 1–44.

Nikita Srivatsan, Jason Vega, Christina Skelton, and Taylor Berg-Kirkpatrick. 2021. Neural representation learning for scribal hands of linear b. In *Document Analysis and Recognition–ICDAR 2021 Workshops: Lausanne, Switzerland, September 5–10, 2021, Proceedings, Part II 16*, pages 325–338. Springer.

Baochen Sun and Kate Saenko. 2016. Deep coral: Correlation alignment for deep domain adaptation. In *European Conference on Computer Vision (ECCV)*.

Chahan Vidal-Gorène and Aliénor Decours-Perez. 2021. A computational approach of armenian paleography. In *Document Analysis and Recognition – ICDAR 2021 Workshops*, pages 295–305, Cham. Springer International Publishing.

Vasiliy Yugay, Kartik Paliwal, Yunus Cobanoglu, Luis Sáenz, Ekaterine Gogokhia, Shai Gordin, and Enrique Jiménez. 2024. Stylistic classification of cuneiform signs using convolutional neural networks. *it - Information Technology*. Publisher: De Gruyter Oldenbourg.

Samira Zare and Hien Van Nguyen. 2022. Removal of confounders via invariant risk minimization for medical diagnosis. In *Medical Image Computing and Computer Assisted Intervention – MICCAI 2022*, pages 578–587, Cham. Springer Nature Switzerland.

A Appendix

A.1 Tokenization

There are $7,000$ glyphs across different time periods. We use Chen et al. (2023) tokenization of text.

1. **word boundary.** Empty space is manually inserted between word. We by default keep the space by inserting.
2. **Logogram.** A tilde sign before a sign indicate it is a logogram. By default we differentiate whether a sign is syllable or logogram.
3. **Intrusions.** `(...)` indicates unknown number of signs is missing.
4. **Modifier**. In ATF, at-sign precedes a sign or group. For example, `@c` means curved.
5. **Compound.** $|\mathtt{GA}_2 \sim \mathtt{a{\times}EN}|$, means: "the a-allograph of the sign GA_2 containing sign EN".
6. **Breakage.** Hash tag is used to mark breakage.

B Details

B.1 OOD Experiments Details

1. **Raw**
   - (a) **IRM**. We train for 30 epochs with a learning rate of 3e-5, an IRM lambda 1, and seed 2.
   - (b) **CORAL**. We train for 30 epochs with a penalty weight 10 and seed 0.
   - (c) **groupDRO** We train for 30 epochs with a learning rate of 3e-5 and seed 1.
2. **Front**
   - (a) **IRM**. We train for 30 epochs with a learning rate of 3e-5, an IRM lambda 1, and seed 2.
   - (b) **CORAL**. We train for 30 epochs with a penalty weight 10 and seed 2.
   - (c) **groupDRO** We train for 30 epochs with a learning rate of 3e-5 and seed 2.

B.2 Hyperparameters and ablation study

We provide further analysis and conduct a comprehensive ablation study in the following section, exploring the effects of hyperparameters, input feature selection, and the number of training examples on our model's performance.

As shown in Table ??, larger model or larger resolution of input can boost model performance.

C Visualization of tablets counts

A full resolution with number annotated heatmap for the time periods preserved in each museum collection is shown in Figure 8.

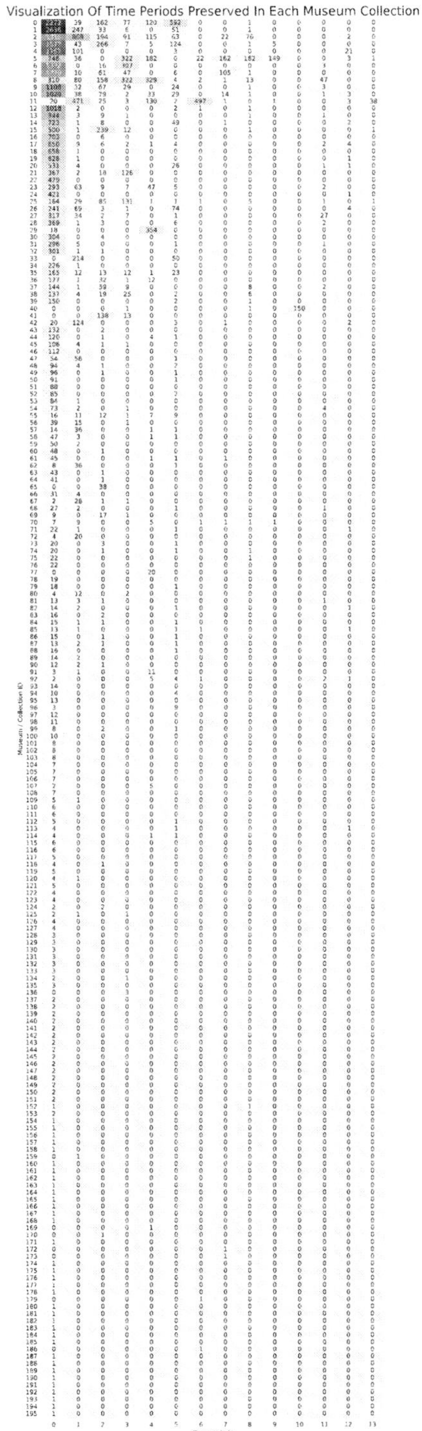

Figure 8: Visualization of the time periods preserved in each museum collection.

Classifier identification in Ancient Egyptian as a low-resource sequence-labelling task

Dmitry Nikolaev[1] **Jorke Grotenhuis**[2] **Haleli Harel**[2] **Orly Goldwasser**[2]
[1]University of Manchester [2]Hebrew University of Jerusalem
dmitry.nikolaev@manchester.ac.uk,
{jorke.grotenhuis,haleli.harel,orly.goldwasser}@mail.huji.ac.il

Abstract

The complex Ancient Egyptian (AE) writing system was characterised by widespread use of graphemic classifiers (determinatives): silent (unpronounced) hieroglyphic signs clarifying the meaning or indicating the pronunciation of the host word. The study of classifiers has intensified in recent years with the launch and quick growth of the iClassifier project, a web-based platform for annotation and analysis of classifiers in ancient and modern languages. Thanks to the data contributed by the project participants, it is now possible to formulate the identification of classifiers in AE texts as an NLP task. In this paper, we make first steps towards solving this task by implementing a series of sequence-labelling neural models, which achieve promising performance despite the modest amount of training data. We discuss tokenisation and operationalisation issues arising from tackling AE texts and contrast our approach with frequency-based baselines.

1 Introduction

The Ancient Egyptian language and writing system, which belong to the earliest stratum of intangible cultural heritage available to researchers, possess a range of interesting features. One of them is widespread use of classificatory signs, called *determinatives* in earlier literature. These classifiers (hereafter CLFs in ambiguous contexts, in order to avoid confusion with classifier models) are hieroglyphic signs attached, singly or in combinations, to words of different parts of speech and used mostly to highlight some aspect of the host word's meaning or pronunciation (Goldwasser, 2023; Goldwasser and Grinevald, 2012). Egyptian graphemic classifiers are usually understood to be a purely written phenomenon, i.e., unlike classifiers in contemporary spoken languages (Grinevald, 2015), they were not pronounced. Classifiers of this type have been most intensively studied in Ancient Egyptian, but they have been also described in Sumerian (Selz et al., 2017) and Luwian (Payne, 2017), and it is argued that the ancient Chinese writing system was built on similar principles (Goldwasser and Handel, 2024).

The computational research on the Ancient Egyptian language is in its infancy. A comprehensive overview of studies of ancient languages utilising machine-learning methods, prepared by Sommerschield et al. (2023), mentions only a couple of works on Egyptian, and all of them deal with technical tasks, such as optical character recognition and spectrography-based dating. Neither do we know of any computational works tackling classifiers/determinatives in other ancient scripts.

At the same time, the field of classifier studies has been progressing rapidly in recent years. To a large extent this is due to the launch of iClassifier (Harel et al., 2024), a dedicated platform for analysis of classifiers in ancient and spoken languages, which ensures comparability between annotated corpora. By providing such a platform, the project aims to facilitate both the study of individual classification traditions and, by means of semantic annotations with CONCEPTICON labels (List et al., 2024), cross-cultural analyses of classification systems.

The particular structure of any given corpus is dependent on its creator, and the project includes resources of two basic types:

1. Full-text corpora, which include annotations for both classified and unclassified wordforms from a particular text or set of texts.

2. Topical corpora, which include data points of a particular type, e.g., lexical borrowings or items from a particular lexical class.

Corpora of the first type are more informative, but in practice they presuppose the existence of already-digitised texts that can be imported in iClassifier wholesale and then annotated. In some cases, the

Proceedings of the 1st Workshop on Machine Learning for Ancient Languages (ML4AL 2024), pages 42–47
August 15, 2024 ©2024 Association for Computational Linguistics

target texts have not yet been digitised, and only words or phrases of particular interest are manually entered.

Work on projects of both types could be facilitated by the existence of a trained classifier model, which would highlight potential CLF tokens in inputs. If such a classifier attains a high degree of accuracy, it will then be possible to conduct fast analyses of large digitised textual corpora, which have been published for, e.g., Ancient Egyptian (Richter and Werning, 2024), Sumerian,[1] Luwian,[2] and ancient Chinese (Xu, 2024). From the research perspective, an accurate discriminative classifier model will serve as a first step towards building a more interpretable generative model for word classification in ancient complex scripts and spoken languages.

In this study, we take first steps towards developing such a classifier on the basis of the Coffin Texts corpus, as of today the largest annotated full-text corpus in the iClassifier system.

2 Data

2.1 The corpus

The main dataset used in this study is a subset of the so-called Coffin Texts (de Buck, 1935–1956), a collection of spells painted on burial coffins of the First Intermediate period (c. 2130–1938 BCE) and the Middle Kingdom (1938 – c. 1630 BCE). A subset of the spells forms one of full-text projects in iClassifier, i.e. it includes both classified and unclassified data points in the proportions reflecting the linguistic usage of the time, which makes it suitable for training a classifier-identification model. The corpus is word based: individual data points are wordforms, which is the standard annotation practice for ancient texts in iClassifier.[3]

This corpus, similarly to other corpora in the project, relies on a broad definition of the term *classifier* that encompasses not only semantic CLFs[4] but also phonograms presenting redundant phonological information, such as phono-repeaters. These sign functions can be tagged in the UI as

U33-Z4:D21-Z1-D21-Z1-D56-D54

Figure 1: A form of the verb *trr* 'to race' represented in hieroglyphs and in the Manuel de Codage transcription. The last two signs are unpronounced semantic classifiers putting 'race' in the [MOVEMENT] category.

'semantic classifiers' and 'phonetic classifiers', respectively. Additional tagged signs pertain to common 'grammatical classifiers', which represent the number or gender of the host word. As a first step we do not distinguish between different CLF types but try and identify all non-autonomous signs (Polis and Rosmorduc, 2015, 157).

The fully-annotated subset of the Coffin Texts corpus contains 74106 data points. However, many wordforms are repeated several times with the same CLFs, which reduces the effective size of the dataset to 8423 types, randomly split into 6739 train, 842 development, and 842 test data points. Table 2 shows the statistics of the number of CLFs per data point.

The setting therefore can be characterised as extremely low resource since not only the dataset itself is small, but there are no language models pre-trained on the target language.[5]

We also use a small (404 data points) corpus of wordforms from Late Egyptian narratives[6] as a separate out-of-domain test set. This smaller corpus represents a different textual genre, a folktale, and was compiled later, in the 13th century BCE, compared to the Coffin Texts, which are dated to 22nd–17th c. BCE.

2.2 The transcription system

The representation format for Ancient Egyptian texts used in iClassifier is the Manuel de Codage (MdC; Buurman et al., 1988) transcription, which, despite some criticism (Nederhof, 2013), remains the standard in Egyptology. Hieroglyphic signs in MdC are represented with their Gardiner numbers (Gardiner, 1957, 438–548),[7] with additional sym-

[1] https://etcsl.orinst.ox.ac.uk/

[2] http://web-corpora.net/LuwianCorpus/search/

[3] Modern languages usually need sentences as data points, while the ancient Chinese corpora, conversely, decompose individual signs into the phonetic and semantic component and treat the latter as a classifier. See Xu (2024) for details.

[4] Including so-called 'repeater CLFs', where an unpronounced pictorial logogram expresses the same meaning as that conveyed by a phonologically-encoded word.

[5] The most closely related language with a sizeable corpus is Coptic, which was written in an alphabetic script and presents a tough low-resource scenario in itself, cf., e.g., Gessler and Zeldes (2022).

[6] https://thesaurus-linguae-aegyptiae.de/text/MTBRL3MIIJDKXAOF2336WRLMZA

[7] https://en.wikipedia.org/wiki/Gardiner%27s_sign_list

bols used for denoting relative positions of signs, damaged signs, ligatures, and other information. An example transcription is shown in Figure 1.

Classifier signs in iClassifier are surrounded with ~'s, so the annotated version of the example from Figure 1 is `U33-Z4-D21-Z1-D21-Z1-~D56~-~D54~`.[8] The simplest operationalisation of the classifier-identification problem is therefore seq2seq transduction with bare transcriptions (in MdC or any other suitable scheme) as inputs and the same encodings with tildes added when necessary as outputs. As we discuss below, however, this operationalisation makes the transduction task unnecessarily hard for the models and considerable gains may be made by means of some straightforward simplifications.

3 Methods

In this section, we describe our approaches to input tokenisation and output formatting (§ 3.1), the baselines (§ 3.2), and the experimental setup (§ 3.3).

3.1 Preprocessing

The aim of the Manuel de Codage transcription system is not only to represent several hundred signs of Egyptian hieroglyphics using numbers and Latin letters but also, as far as possible, to describe their spatial relations in the original inscriptions since the Ancient Egyptian writing was inherently two-dimensional. Additional complexity comes from the ability of the transcription system to handle damaged inscriptionts, empty space, and editorial emendations, among other things. As a result, although it is possible to represent (a somewhat simplified version of) MdC as a context-free grammar,[9] which is used, for example, in the standard MdC-visualisation tool JSesh,[10] this grammar is quite complex and it seems unreasonable to expect seq2seq classifiers to learn it implicitly. Therefore we preprocessed the input by (i) parsing it with a simplistic CFG powerful enough to distinguish between signs, delimiters, and other elements,[11] and (ii) replacing everything except for hieroglyphs and tildes, used to mark CLFs, with spaces.

[8] https://thesaurus-linguae-aegyptiae.de/sentence/IBUBdWH5CJXKnkyQhOCrlBiZSCA

[9] https://mjn.host.cs.st-andrews.ac.uk/egyptian/res/mdc.html

[10] http://jseshdoc.qenherkhopeshef.org/

[11] The parser was implemented using the Python package Lark. The CFG for the grammar is given in the Appendix.

Tokenisation. The output of the previous step is a sequence of hieroglyphs in MdC, with CLFs flanked by tildes, separated by spaces. When fine-tuning a pre-trained model with its own tokeniser, the input must be represented as a string. If we train a model from scratch, however, a trade-off can be made between, on one hand, longer inputs and a very small vocabulary (Latin letters, digits, and the tilde) and, on the other hand, short inputs and a large vocabulary, where each hieroglyph from the dataset gets its own token (784 tokens in total in our data). We call models using the small vocabulary *character based* and models using the large vocabulary *sign based*.

Output formatting. Regardless of the tokenisation approach, reference outputs can be represented in several different ways, for example:

1. In the (simplified) original notation: `U33 Z4 D21 Z1 D21 Z1 D56 D54` → `U33 Z4 D21 Z1 D21 Z1 ~D56~ ~D54~`
2. Without the first tilde, since each classifier in the data is unambiguously identified by a single marker: `U33 Z4 D21 Z1 D21 Z1 D56 D54` → `U33 Z4 D21 Z1 D21 Z1 D56~ D54~`
3. As a sequence of binary labels: `U33 Z4 D21 Z1 D21 Z1 D56 D54` → `0 0 0 0 0 0 1 1`

While the first approach preserves the structure of the data, it forces the models to learn complicated well-formedness constraints. The second approach considerably simplifies them since the models can always first copy the sign and then add a tilde when necessary. However, copying can still be imperfect, especially with character-based models. The third approach completely dispenses with the original data format, but it makes enforcing the structural constraints almost trivial. Preliminary experiments showed that resorting to binary labels gives a strong boost in performance, and we used this approach in all reported experiments.

3.2 Baselines

The existence of frequent classifiers and other imbalances in the sign distribution suggest that we may dispense with using complicated machine-learning methods altogether and predict classifiers using sign statistics. In this study, we use the following approaches as baselines to which we compare our sequence-to-sequence methods:

1. **Top-N**: we mark $N = 5, 10, 20, 30, 50, 100$ signs that are most-frequent classifiers in the

training set as classifiers. N is selected using the validation set.

2. **CLF-only**: we mark signs as classifiers if they only appear as such in the training set.

3. **CLF-majority**: we mark signs as classifiers if they appear more frequently in this function in the training set.

3.3 Experimental setup

Models and training. We contrast the performance of sign-frequency-based baselines with three neural seq2seq models: a character-based 3-layer encoder-decoder LSTM with a hidden dimension of 512, a sign-based 3-layer encoder-decoder LSTM with the same hidden size, and ByT5-small (Xue et al., 2022). We thus cover both RNN-based and Transformer-based models. Given relatively short input lengths, we keep RNNs simple and do not equip them with attention.

Importantly, the small version of ByT5 is still a considerably larger model compared to the seq2seq LSTMs and therefore harder to train on a small dataset. However, there is a possibility that its extensive pre-training on data from other languages gives it enough inductive bias to tackle a novel language, even with a non-orthodox transcription.

The batch size and learning rate for the models reported below were selected using grid search on the development set, and the models were trained until there was no improvement on the development set for 5 epochs.[12]

Evaluation metric. As the evaluation metric, we use the average number of mistakenly classified signs in the test-set data points.

More precisely, we split the output of the decoder on whitespaces, pad the resulting vector of labels with zeros if it is too short, and convert any non-1 elements to zeros as well. This corresponds to a conservative procedure that, given an input sequence of signs, outputs a sequence of signs with marked classifiers and without NAs, which is how the system is arguably supposed to work in practice.

4 Results

The performance of the trained models on the development and test subsets of the Coffin Texts corpus and on the out-of-domain (OOD) data from the Late Egyptian corpus is reported in Table 1. Several observations can be made.

Model	Dev	Test	Narratives
CLF only	1.23	1.23	1.39
Top-50 CLF	0.46	0.47	1.07
CLF majority	0.27	0.28	0.49
LSTM (char)	0.2	0.21	3.07
LSTM (sign)	0.14	0.11	0.38
ByT5 small	0.08	**0.1**	**0.35**

Table 1: Average number of misclassified signs per data point on the Coffin Texts corpus (dev and test) and the Late Egyptian narratives (out-of-domain). **CLF only**: signs only found as CLFs in the training set are marked as CLFs. **Top-50 CLF**: 50 signs that are most frequently found as CLFs marked as CLFs. **CLF majority**: signs that are more frequently found as CLFs than as regular signs marked as CLFs. **LSTM (char)**: character-based 3-layer encoder-decoder model with the hidden dimension of 512. **LSTM (sign)**: sign-based 3-layer encoder-decoder with the hidden dimension of 512.

First, the Coffin Texts are shown to be quite homogeneous: the performance drop between the development and test sets is marginal, with one model (sign-based seq2seq LSTM) even gaining 3 performance percentage points.

Secondly, the character-based LSTM model does not perform well: it barely beats the CLF-majority baseline and suffers performance collapse on the OOD data. The sign-based LSTM, on the other hand, is very competitive, even on the OOD test dataset, where, unlike ByT5, it had to contend with UNK tokens, mapped to SOS tokens.

Thirdly, ByT5, despite not being trained on any directly comparable data and being character based, beats the sign-based seq2seq LSTM model both on the in-domain and on the out-of-domain test sets. This suggests that there may be a decent possibility for knowledge transfer between classifier languages.

Finally, the CLF-majority baseline, despite its conceptual simplicity, demonstrates tolerable performance and with some additional tuning may be used as a lightweight method that can dynamically respond as new data points are added.

It must be pointed out that the array of possible CLFs is very wide, given the existence of phonetic classifiers. Despite the homogeneity of the Coffin Texts data, the test set contains 19 CLFs not found

[12]The code and the dataset used for the analyses are available at `https://git.sr.ht/~macleginn/ml4al-iclassifier-paper-code/tree`

0	1	2	3	4	5	6	7	8
1403	4113	2195	573	112	20	6	0	1

Table 2: Counts of data points with different number of CLFs in the train and dev subsets of the Coffin Texts dataset.

in either test or dev subsets; 17 of them are only used once. Conversely, 156 CLFs were encountered only once in the combined test and dev set. The OOD test set, despite being twice smaller than the in-domain one, also has 13 new CLFs. This does not preclude the possibility of ever identifying such classifiers (human expert annotators can do this by, e.g., analysing the structure of different lexical items across contexts), but this considerably raises the demands on the size of the training set.

5 Conclusion

This study is a first step towards creating a trained system for identification and analysis of classifiers and other sign functions in ancient complex scripts. It demonstrates that it is possible to achieve respectable error rates on this task on in-domain data, with ≈ 0.1 mistakenly identified classifiers per data point. Given a high number of data points with several classifiers (cf. Table 2), this translates to correct analysis of most wordforms. The accuracy falls significantly on out-of-domain data, but it must be noted that our OOD test set is distinguished from the training set not only by a different genre (narratives vs. religious texts) but also by at least 400 years of language evolution.

Future work, in addition to improving model accuracy, could be directed toward providing a more fine-grained classification of sign functions by leveraging the distinction between semantic and grammatical classifiers and phono-repeaters.

Acknowledgments

The research for and preparation of this article were supported by ISF grant number 1704/22, 'Exploring the minds of Ancient Egypt and Ancient China – a comparative network analysis of the classifier systems of the scripts', and ISF grant number 735/17, 'Classifying the other: The classification of Semitic loanwords in the Egyptian script', awarded to ArchaeoMind Lab, The Hebrew University Jerusalem (www.archaeomind.net), PI Orly Goldwasser.

Jorke Grotenhuis' work was supported by the Israel Academy of Sciences and Humanities & Council for Higher Education Excellence Fellowship Program for International Postdoctoral Researchers and the ArchaeoMind Lab.

References

Jan Buurman, Nicolas-Christophe Grimal, Michael Hainsworth, Jochen Hallof, and Dirk van der Plas. 1988. *Inventaire des signes hiéroglyphiques en vue de leur saisie informatique : manuel de codage des textes hiéroglyphiques en vue de leur saisie sur ordinateur = manual for the encoding of hieroglyphic texts for computer-input.* Impr. Lienhart, Paris.

Adriaan de Buck, editor. 1935–1956. *The Egyptian Coffin Texts (vols. I–VII).* University of Chicago Press.

Alan Gardiner. 1957. *Egyptian Grammar, 3rd rev. ed.* Griffith Institute, Oxford.

Luke Gessler and Amir Zeldes. 2022. MicroBERT: Effective training of low-resource monolingual BERTs through parameter reduction and multitask learning. In *Proceedings of the 2nd Workshop on Multi-lingual Representation Learning (MRL)*, pages 86–99, Abu Dhabi, United Arab Emirates (Hybrid). Association for Computational Linguistics.

Orly Goldwasser. 2023. *Guide to the Writing Systems of Ancient Egypt*, chapter From Determinatives to Classifiers: Categorisation in the Ancient Egyptian Writing System. Institut Français d'Archéologie Orientale, Cairo, Egypt.

Orly Goldwasser and Colette Grinevald. 2012. *Lexical semantics in Ancient Egyptian*, chapter What are determinatives good for? Widmaier, Hamburg.

Orly Goldwasser and Zev Handel. 2024. Introduction: Graphemic classifiers in complex script systems. *Journal of Chinese Writing Systems*, 8(1):2–13.

Colette Grinevald. 2015. *International Encyclopedia of the Social & Behavioral Sciences*, 2 edition, volume 3, chapter Classifiers, Linguistics of. Elsevier.

Haleli Harel, Orly Goldwasser, and Dmitry Nikolaev. 2024. iClassifier: A digital research tool for corpus-based classifier networks in complex writing systems. *Journal of Chinese Writing Systems*, 8(1):79–102.

Johann Mattis List, Annika Tjuka, Mathilda van Zantwijk, Frederic Blum, Carlos Barrientos Ugarte, Christoph Rzymski, Simon Greenhill, and Robert Forkel, editors. 2024. *CLLD Concepticon 3.2.0.* Max Planck Institute for Evolutionary Anthropology, Leipzig.

Mark-Jan Nederhof. 2013. *Texts, languages & information: technology in Egyptology*, chapter The 'Manuel de codage' encoding of hieroglyphs impedes development of corpora. Presses universitaires de Liège.

Annick Payne. 2017. Determination in the Anatolian hieroglyphic script. *News from the Lands of the Hittites*, 1:101–112.

Stéphane Polis and Serge Rosmorduc. 2015. *Fuzzy Boundaries: Festschrift für Antonio Loprieno, vol. 1*, chapter The Hieroglyphic Sign Functions: Suggestions for a Revised Taxonomy. Widmaier, Hamburg.

Tonio Sebastian Richter and Daniel A. Werning, editors. 2024. *Thesaurus Linguae Aegyptiae, Corpus issue 18, Web app version 2.1.2, 11/24/2023*.

Gebhard Selz, Colette Grinevald, and Orly Goldwasser. 2017. The question of Sumerian "determinatives". Inventory, classier analysis, and comparison to Egyptian classifiers from the linguistic perspective of noun classification. *Lingua Aegyptia*, 25:281–344.

Thea Sommerschield, Yannis Assael, John Pavlopoulos, Vanessa Stefanak, Andrew Senior, Chris Dyer, John Bodel, Jonathan Prag, Ion Androutsopoulos, and Nando de Freitas. 2023. Machine Learning for Ancient Languages: A Survey. *Computational Linguistics*, 49(3):703–747.

Yanru Xu. 2024. Semantic classifiers in Guodian bamboo manuscripts: Reconstructing categories in the ancient Chinese mind. *Journal of Chinese Writing Systems*, 8(1):14–33.

Linting Xue, Aditya Barua, Noah Constant, Rami Al-Rfou, Sharan Narang, Mihir Kale, Adam Roberts, and Colin Raffel. 2022. ByT5: Towards a Token-Free Future with Pre-trained Byte-to-Byte Models. *Transactions of the Association for Computational Linguistics*, 10:291–306.

Appendix: A CFG for parsing MdC

In Lark notation:

```
token : sequence (delimiters sequence)*

delimiters : delimiter+

sequence : left_paren sequence right_paren
    | tilde sequence tilde
    | sequence delimiters sequence
    | classified_sign

left_paren : "("
right_paren : ")"

classified_sign : code suffix?
    | tilde code tilde suffix?

suffix : ligature_pos
    | damage
    | ligature_pos damage
    | damage ligature_pos

code : /[a-zA-Z]+[0-9]*[a-zA-Z]*/
    | /[0-9]+/
    | "#b-..#e"
    | "#b"
    | "#e"
    | "[&"
    | "&]"
    | "."

damage : /#\d+/

ligature_pos : /\{\{\d+,\d+,\d+\}\}/

delimiter : "-"
    | ":"
    | "\\"
    | "\\\\"
    | "\\\\\\\\"
    | "_GROUPING_"
    | "^"
    | "("
    | ")"
    | "&"
    | "{"
    | "}"
    | ","
    | "*"
    | "_"

tilde : "~"
```

Long Unit Word Tokenization and Bunsetsu Segmentation of Historical Japanese

Hiroaki Ozaki[1] **Komiya Kanako**[1] **Masayuki Asahara**[2] and **Toshinobu Ogiso**[2]
[1]Tokyo University of Agriculture and Technology, Japan
[2]National Institute for Japanese Language and Linguistics, Japan
hiroaki-ozaki@st.go.tuat.ac.jp, kkomiya@go.tuat.ac.jp,
{masayu-a,togiso}@ninjal.ac.jp

Abstract

In Japanese, "bunsetsu" is the natural minimal phrase of a sentence; it serves as a natural boundary of a sentence for native speakers rather than words, and thus grammatical analysis in Japanese linguistics commonly operates on the basis of bunsetsu units. By contrast, because Japanese does not have delimiters between words, there are two major categories of word definitions: Short Unit Words (SUWs) and Long Unit Words (LUWs). SUW dictionaries are available, whereas LUW dictionaries are not. Hence, this study focuses on providing deep learning-based (or LLM-based) bunsetsu and LUWs parser for the Heian period (AD 794-1185) and evaluating its performances. We model the parser as a transformer-based joint sequential labels model that combines the bunsetsu BI tag, LUW BI tag, and LUW Part-of-Speech (POS) tag for each SUW token. We trained our models on the corpora of each period including contemporary and historical Japanese. The results ranged from 0.976 to 0.996 in the f1 value for both bunsetsu and LUW reconstruction indicating that our models achieved comparable performance with models for a contemporary Japanese corpus. Through statistical analysis and a diachronic case study, it was found that the estimation of bunsetsu could be influenced by the grammaticalization of morphemes.

1 Introduction

In Japanese, "bunsetsu" (base-phrase) is the natural minimal phrase of a sentence. It serves as a natural boundary of a sentence for native speakers rather than words; thus grammatical analysis in Japanese linguistics commonly operates on the basis of bunsetsu units. For example, in Universal Dependencies (UD; Nivre et al., 2020), a framework for the consistent annotation of lexical dependency grammar across different human languages, some Japanese corpora have been converted from dependency relations between bunsetsu (Asahara et al., 2018; Omura and Asahara, 2018).

In contrast, because Japanese does not have delimiters between words, there are many definitions of "words" in Japanese. The National Institute for Japanese Language and Linguistics defines two hierarchical word tokenization categories: Short Unit Words (SUWs) and Long Unit Words (LUWs). SUW is a minimal word token in Japanese, and is defined by a bottom-up method that consists of at most two morphological units. In contrast, LUW is defined by a top-down method that divides a bunsetsu into two parts, and it may contain several SUWs. For example, the LUW "北西大西洋 (Northwest Atlantic)" consists of two SUWs "北西 (Northwest)" and "大西洋 (Atlantic)."

Dictionaries of SUWs for historical and contemporary Japanese are already publicly available [1], whereas there is no dictionary for LUWs. Hence, a parser that outputs bunsetsu and LUWs for historical Japanese is necessary to analyze the grammatical changes in Japanese.

For existing historical Japanese literature, a sufficient amount of bunsetsu and LUW annotated text to train the parser is primarily available from the Heian period (AD 794-1185) and later. Therefore, this study mainly focuses on the Heian period, with the subsequent Kamakura (AD 1185-1336) and the Muromachi (AD 1336-1573) periods chosen for comparison.

The existing bunsetsu parser (Kozawa et al., 2014) for these periods is based on Conditional Random Field (CRF), which was used to create the annotated corpus. Thus, this study focuses on providing a deep learning-based (or LLM-based) bunsetsu and Long Unit Words (LUW) parser and evaluating its performances. We model the parser

[1]https://clrd.ninjal.ac.jp/unidic/

Proceedings of the 1st Workshop on Machine Learning for Ancient Languages (ML4AL 2024), pages 48–55
August 15, 2024

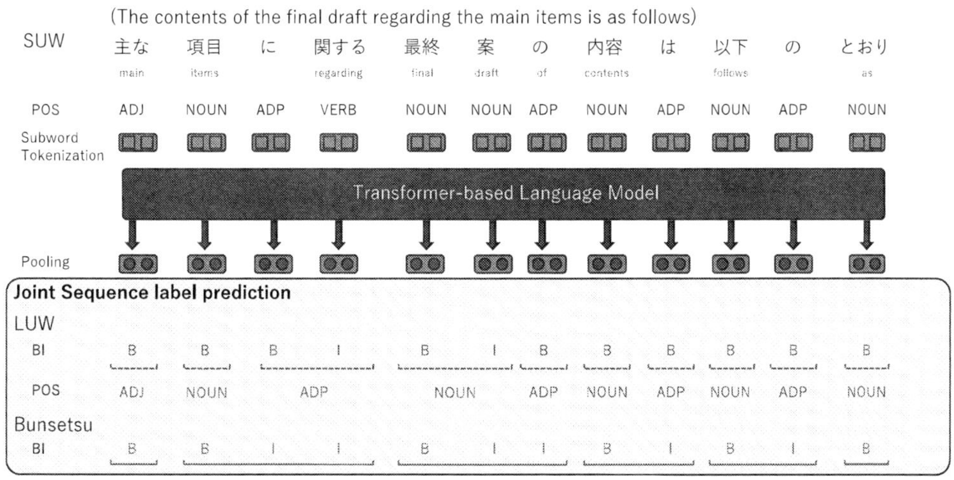

Figure 1: Overview of bunsetsu and Long Unit Words (LUWs) tokenization.

as a joint sequential label that combines the bunsetsu BI tag, LUW BI tag, and LUW Part-of-Speech (POS) tags for each SUW token. We used a Transformer-based Language Model (TLM) to output an SUW token representation by taking the appropriate pooling of subword representations for the last layer of the transformer. We preserved the SUW boundaries when tokenizing a given sentence into subwords. We trained our models on the corpora of each period including contemporary and historical Japanese.

The results indicate that the models trained on historical Japanese achieve comparable performance (0.976-0.996 f1 values) to a model for a contemporary Japanese corpus. To trace grammatical changes in Japanese, we evaluated the zero-shot transfer performance of the Heian, Kamakura, and Muromachi periods for each other. The models trained with a corpus of the Heian and Kamakura periods performed well on each other, whereas the model trained with a corpus of the Muromachi period did not. These results support the consensus among Japanese liguists that the large grammatical changes occurred during the Muromachi period. Furthermore, the analysis focusing on sentence-ending particles revealed that new sentence-ending particle usage has emerged in the Muromachi, and they are difficult to predict by the models of the prior periods.[2]

2 Related Work

Parser for Historical Japanese Comainu, a Japanese bunsetsu and LUW parser, was originally provided for contemporary Japanese (Kozawa et al., 2014), although it can also be applied to historical Japanese. Comainu takes SUW tokens as input, which are tokenized by a CRF-based morphological analyzer MeCab[3], and then outputs the bunsetsu and LUW tokens. As mentioned above, Comainu is a CRF-based parser; thus, we focused on deep-learning-based methods.

Parser for Contemporary Japanese Recent Japanese corpora of UD contain bunsetsu and LUW annotations (Omura et al., 2023); thus, some parsers trained on these corpora support bunsetsu segmentation and LUW tokenization. For example, the spaCy-based [4] Japanese UD parser[5] supports LUW tokenization (Matsuda et al., 2022). The parser was trained with a Transformer-based language model (TLM) through the spaCy pipeline, and it achieved better performance than Comainu by adding some rules. GiNZA (Matsuda, 2020), which is also a spaCy-based parser, supports bunsetsu output.

3 Bunsetsu and Long Unit Word

3.1 Short Unit Word

Short Unit Word (SUW) is a token close to the granularity of typical Japanese word tokens. A

[2]Our code is publicly available at `https://github.com/komiya-lab/monaka`

[3]`https://taku910.github.io/mecab/`

[4]`https://spacy.io/`

[5]`https://github.com/megagonlabs/UD_Japanese-GSD/releases/tag/r2.9-NE/`

	Heian	Kamakura	Muromachi	UD-Japanese-GSD
Number of				
Sentence	196,680	332,575	154,080	8,100
SUW	5,084,245	6,519,090	2,077,960	193,654
LUW	4,576,115	6,003,790	1,923,300	150,244
Bunsetsu	1,986,150	2,700,520	881,015	65,966
Average numbers in a sentence				
Characters	43.029	27.779	21.511	39.371
SUW	25.850	19.602	13.486	23.908
LUW	23.267	18.052	12.482	18.549
Bunsetsu	10.098	8.120	5.718	8.144

Table 1: Statistics of the Corpus of Historical Japanese (CHJ) (Heian, Kamakura, and Muromachi) and UD-Japanese-GSD.

	UD-Japanese-GSD	CHJ
dropout rate	0.5	0.5
dim. POS emb.	256	256
learning rate	2e-05	5e-06
batch size	28	24
num. of epocsh	50	20
gradient clip	5.0	5.0
gradient decay	0.75	0.75
decay step	5000	5000

Table 2: Hyperparamters

dictionary (UniDic) was established for SUWs, enabling high-performance morphological analysis based on UniDic (Den et al., 2008). As shown in the overview Figure 1, bunsetsu and LUWs are also composed of SUWs.

3.2 Bunsetsu (Base-pharase)

A bunsetsu is a (natural) minimal phrase that consists of a Japanese sentence. Generally, a bunsetsu boundary occurs after a particle or a sequence of particles. This is because Japanese functional words typically follow their content words, on which they depend. In Figure 1, all LUW noun (NOUN) and adposition (ADP) pairs are composed into bunsetsu segments.

3.3 Long Unit Word

The Long Unit Word (LUW) is a word unit based on a bunsetsu. Identification of LUW involves identifying bunsetsu and then dividing each bunsetsu into independent and attached LUWs. For example, in Figure 1, bunsetsu "項目に関する" is divided into an independent LUW "項目 (items)" and attached LUW "に関する (regarding)," which is categorized as adposition even if it contains SUW verb "関する."

4 Corpus

We used the Corpus of Historical Japanese (CHJ; NINJAL 2024), which collects documents from the Nara (AD 710-794) to the Meiji (AD 1868-1912). Bunsetsu and LUW annotations were performed on sampled sentences sampled from the CHJ.

We also used UD-Japanese-GSD[6], a contemporary Japanese corpus, for the model comparison and searching for the best model, because there is a deep-learning-based parser that can output bunsetsu and LUW labels (Matsuda et al., 2022).

Table 1 shows the statistics of both the CHJ and UD-Japanese-GSD. There is not a large difference in the number of sentences in each historical period, while that of UD-Japanese-GSD is one-tenth of them. From the Heian to the Muromachi periods, the number of characters, SUWs, LUWs, and bunsetsu per sentence gradually decreases. In UD-Japanese-GSD, the average numbers of characters and SUWs per sentence are almost the same as those of the Heian period, although the average numbers of LUWs and bunsetsu are less than those of the Heian period.

5 Method

5.1 Bunsetsu and LUW Analyzer Model

Figure 1 shows the architecture of our model. We used joint BI (beginning and inside) tagging-based sequential modeling with a Transformer-based language model (TLM). We combined the

[6] https://github.com/UniversalDependencies/UD_Japanese-GSD

sequential labels of LUW BI, LUW POS, and Bunsetsu BI. For example, the target label of the adposition "は" in Figure 1 is "I-B-ADP," where the first "I" represents the target SUW located intermediate of the bunsetsu, and the second "B-ADP" represents the beginning of the LUW and its POS tag. The total number of target labels is 237 for CHJ and 224 for UD-Japanese-GSD.

We first tokenized each SUW token into subwords instead of tokenizing a sentence directly, to avoid breaking the SUW boundary. We then fed each subword token to the TLM. We added a pooling layer to combine each subword representation produced by the TLM into SUW-level representation. We then fed the pooled SUW-level representations into an additional fully connected layer to output the likelihood of the labels with a softmax activation function. The variants of the pooling layers are as follows:

sum Suppose the j-th subword representation $\boldsymbol{v}_{i,j}$ corresponds to the i-th SUW token output from TLM, the sum pooling $\boldsymbol{u}_i$ is calculated as $\boldsymbol{u}_i = \sum_j \boldsymbol{v}_{i,j}$.

max The max pooling layer takes the max function instead of the summation of the sum pooling.

head The head pooling layer outputs the first subword representation ($\boldsymbol{v}_{i,1}$).

We incorporate SUW POS information into the model in a two-pronged way:

Embedding We concatenated POS embedding with the pooled output $\boldsymbol{u}_i$. The POS embedding was determined through the training.

Incontext We appended a text representing the POS information to each word before subword tokenization. For example, when the SUW "項目 (item)" is tokenized into subwords, the input SUW text representation is "項目 NOUN"[7]. This method increases the number of subword tokens fed into the TLM.

5.2 Evaluation Method

Because our model requires SUW tokens as the input, we feed gold SUWs to the model, throughout the entire evaluation process.

We used span-based precision, recall, and f1 values to evaluate the segmentation of both bunsetsu and LUW. We also used labeled span-based precision, recall, and f1 values for the LUW evaluation. The labeled span-based evaluation is based on a triple (b, e, l) reconstruction score, where b, e, and l represent the start, the end, and the POS labels of the span, respectively.

To evaluate UD-Japanese-GSD, we used the original train, dev, and test sets as intended. We also compare the precision, recall, and f1 values of LUW with the existing parse. Because the prior work tokenized the SUW tokens by a morphological analyzer, we also used predicted SUW tokens by MeCab, instead of the gold SUW tokens.

To evaluate the CHJ samples, we calculated these metrics through five times cross-validations and averaged them to obtain the final scores. We randomly sampled 5% of the sentences from the corpus to create the dev and test sets for each CV. In this procedure, we selected each test set not to overlap.

[7]Though example POS tag is written in English, we add POS tag name in Japanese with sub-tags; "名詞-普通名詞-一般".

	Pooling	P	R	F1
Emb.	sum	.98425	.98264	.98344
	max	.98446	.98446	.98446
	head	**.98532**	**.98456**	**.98494**
Incontext	sum	.98433	.96394	.97403

(a) LUW, span-based

	Pooling	P	R	F1
Emb.	sum	**.97487**	**.97330**	**.97408**
	max	.97228	.97228	.97228
	head	.97348	.97279	.97313
Incontext	sum	**.97478**	.95377	.96416

(b) LUW, labeled span-based

	Pooling	P	R	F1
Emb.	sum	**.97524**	.97459	.97492
	max	.97158	.97350	.97254
	head	.97505	**.97591**	**.97548**
Incontext	sum	.97408	.95488	.96434

(c) Bunsetsu

Table 3: Precision, recall and f1 values of LUW and Bunsetsu tokenization on UD-Japanese-GSD.

	P	R	F1
MeCab + Emb. + sum	0.978	0.978	0.978
Matsuda et al. 2022			
Comainu	0.976	0.969	0.973
SudachiPy + spaCy	0.987	0.985	0.986

Table 4: Span-based LUW score comparison with the previous study.

	Heian			Kamakura			Muromachi		
	P	R	F1	P	R	F1	P	R	F1
Trained on Heian									
LUW span	.99647	.99622	.99635	.98184	.97890	.98036	.90478	.91416	.90945
LUW labeled	.99304	.99279	.99291	.95451	.95165	.95308	.76438	.77231	.76832
Bunsetsu	.96445	.97612	.97025	.93377	.94094	.93734	.74055	.80871	.77313
Trained on Kamakura									
LUW span	.99060	.99147	.99103	.99492	.99452	.99472	.91162	.92650	.91900
LUW labeled	.98252	.98338	.98295	.99089	.99049	.99069	.82257	.83600	.82923
Bunsetsu	.94324	.96250	.95278	.97385	.97997	.97690	.79196	.85138	.82059
Trained on Muromachi									
LUW span	.94672	.95750	.95208	.96079	.95897	.95988	.98913	.98996	.98954
LUW labeled	.88427	.89435	.88928	.91468	.91295	.91381	.98039	.98122	.98080
Bunsetsu	.80727	.86853	.83678	.87293	.89999	.88625	.97810	.97927	.97869

Table 5: Span-based precision, recall, and f1 values on CHJ.

5.3 Hyperparameters

Table 2 lists the hyperparameters. We did not perform an intense hyperparameter search, thus there is a possibility for further performance improvements. Since the number of sentences in CHJ corpora is more than ten times compared to that of in UD-Japanese-GSD, we decreased the total number of epochs and the learning rate when we trained on the CHJ. We used "cl-tohoku/bert-base-japanese-whole-word-masking"[8] for the TLM.

6 Results and Discussions

6.1 Contemporary Japanese

We first compared the model variants using UD-Japanese-GSD, as shown in Table 3. The variant with the **Embedding** and **sum** pooling layers generally performed well. The **head** pooling layer performed well for boundary predictions. This suggests that **sum** pooling provides a better representation of the entire SUW content, while **head** pooling adequately preserves the boundary information.

The variant with **incontext** and the sum pooling achieved the highest precision, but a lower recall value. This is because the **incontext** method increases the number of subword tokens and often exceeds the maximum subword token limit (512) to represent an entire sentence. Table 4 presents a span-based LUW score comparison with that in a previous study (Matsuda et al., 2022). Our model and that of Comainu used MeCab(Kudo et al., 2004) for the SUW tokenization using a UniDic dictionary. The spaCy model uses SudachiPy [9] for SUW tokenizer instead of MeCab. Our model showed an improvement compared to Comainu, while spaCy outperformed the other models. This is because of the difference in the SUW tokenizers.

Because SudachiPy only supports contemporary Japanese, we are supposed to use MeCab for the SUW tokenizer and decided to use **Embedding + sum** pooling model for historical Japanese models.

	Heian	Kamakura	Muromachi
LUW span	.74684	.78141	.77547
labeled	.62969	.68091	.66623
Bunsetsu	.62397	.67525	.67230

(a) F1 values of UD-Japanese-Models on samples of each period.

	Heian	Kamakura	Muromachi
LUW span	.84759	.85769	.88904
labeled	.52768	.56726	.57092
Bunsetsu	.57181	.65828	.75237

(b) F1 values of the models of each period on UD-Japanese-GSD.

Table 6: Evaluations of zero-shot transfer between contemporary and historical Japanese.

6.2 Historical Japanese

Table 5 lists the overall results for the CHJ. The results evaluated on samples from the same period as

[8] https://huggingface.co/tohoku-nlp/bert-base-japanese-whole-word-masking

[9] https://github.com/WorksApplications/SudachiPy

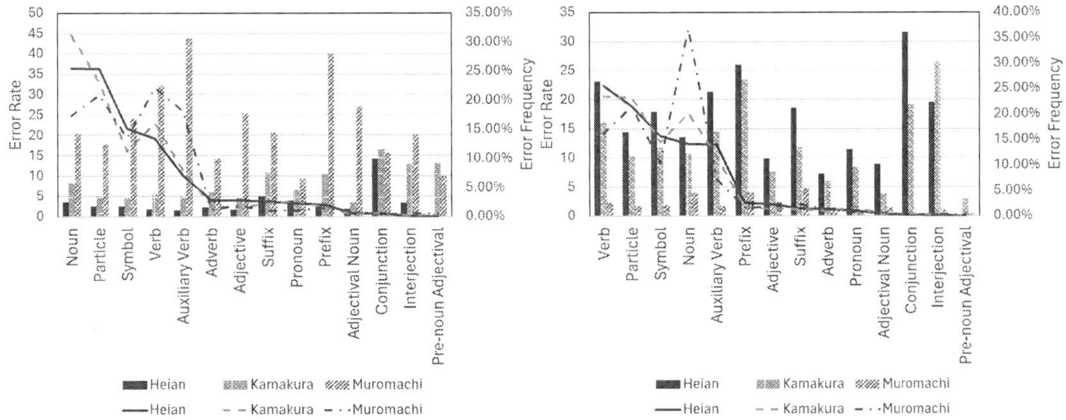

(a) Trained on the Heian period

(b) Trained on the Muromachi period

Figure 2: POS tags contained in bunsetsu versus error rate and normalized frequency.

during training ranged from 0.976 to 0.996. Thus, our historical models have comparable or even superior results to those of contemporary Japanese (UD-Japanese-GSD), as shown in Table 3. This was because the data size of the CHJ was significantly larger than that of UD-Japanese-GSD. The LUW performances degrades with time, while the bunsetsu segmentation performances increase. As time progresses and vocabulary becomes more complex, it is suggested that styles that are more conscious of syntactic structures such as bunsetsu, increase.

Focusing on the transferability between the CHJ corpora, the model trained on samples of newer periods and applied to older periods yielded higher performance than the reverse case. This is because the vocabulary coverage of the newer samples is larger than that of the older samples. The Heian and Kamakura models work well on samples from each other, however, they do not perform well on samples from the Muromachi period, particularly for labeled LUW and bunsetsu evaluations. This implies drastic grammatical changes occured in Japanese during the Muromachi period.

6.3 Transferability between Contemporary and Historical Japanese

Table 6 shows the transferability performances of contemporary and historical Japanese. In this evaluation, the POS embeddings may not work, because there is a large difference in fine-grained POS categories between contemporary and historical Japanese. Thus, we used the highest level of POS tags for the labeled LUW evaluations. The model trained on UD-Japanese-GSD performed similarly in each period (Table 6a). However, the performances of the models on samples from each period increased with time, specifically for the bunsetsu segmentation. This indicates that the syntactic structure of sentences gradually approaches modern syntactic structures over time, while the morphology of LUW is not as high.

6.4 Grammatical Changes during the Muromachi Period

Figure 2 plots the error rates of bunsetsu containing the SUW of a particular POS tag. Figure 2 presents the results of the models trained on samples from the Heian and Muromachi periods. We also plotted the normalized error frequency corresponding to each POS tag for all errors in the same period in Figure 2.

The model trained on Heian period data exhibited a particularly higher error rate when it predicted bunsetsu containing auxiliary verbs or verbs when evaluated on samples from the Muromachi period. This tendency was also observed when samples from the Heian period were evaluated using the Muromachi model. This indicates that there may have been significant changes in sentence endings that usually contained both verbs and auxiliary verbs.

When evaluating samples from the Muromachi period using the Heian model, the error frequency relatively increased in bunsetsu-containing nouns compared with the reverse scenario. This is because the newer model partially contains old vocabularies.

In both cases, the bunsetsu-containing particles resulted in a high error rates and frequencies.

Gold (Heian) and the Kamakura model prediction:													
En	One doesn't do such things, there will surely be regrets												
Ja	| さる	| わざ	| せ	ず	は	、	| 恨むる	| こと	も	| あり	な	む	など |
	such	things	do	not			regrets			there be	surely	will	
LUW	V	N	V	A	P	S	V	N	P	V	A	A	P
The Muromachi model prediction:													
LUW	| C	| V		A	P	S	| V	| N	P	| V	V	A	P |

Table 7: An example of bunsetsu and LUW analysis. V, N, A, P, S, and C stand for verb, noun, auxiliary verb, particle, symbol, and conjunction, respectively. Vertical bars represent bunsetsu boundaries.

Evaluated on	Heian		Muromachi	
	C	R	C	R
Sentence-ending	95	13.67	1835	43.74
Adverbial	1521	15.41	462	27.26
Case-marking	11577	10.46	7395	11.22
Binding	5216	11.55	2026	10.27
Conjunctive	2966	15.99	1615	12.49

Table 8: Error counts (C) and error rate (R) of bunsetsu ending with a particle. We show a result of the Muromachi model evaluated on data in the Heian period, and vice versa.

Case Study: Verbs and Auxiliary Verbs Table 7 presents a sample sentence from the Heian period data and the outputs of our models. The Japanese space-separated tokens in Table 7 are SUW tokens. In this case, the LUWs and SUWs are identical. V, N, A, P, S, and C denote verb, noun, auxiliary verb, particle, symbol, and conjunction, respectively. Vertical bars represent the bunsetsu boundaries.

The Heian and the Kamakura models output perfect LUW and bunsetsu boundaries, respectively. The first word "さる (saru; do such)" is a verb, however, it is often used as an adversative conjunction, and thus the Muromachi model misclassified it as a conjunction. The second verb "せ (se; do)" often composes a LUW with an antecedent noun. The first noun "わざ (waza; thing)" has several senses, such as "ceremony" and "technique"; thus "わざせ" is misunderstood as "doing a ceremony" or "doing the technique" by the Muromachi model. This is because a case marker "を (wo; objective)" is required just after "わざ" to retain the meaning in the Muromachi period.

Both "さる" and "せ" are common words; thus, it is conceivable that the grammaticalization of those words was progressing during the Muromachi period. Since the verbs and auxiliary verbs are often contained in mispredicted bunsetsu in Figure 2, the grammaticalization of those words would be a major part of the grammatical changes.

The auxiliary verb "な (na; complete)" is misclassified as a verb. This may be because the expression "なむ" became less common in the Muromachi period.

Analysis of Particles Table 8 lists the error counts and error rates of bunsetsu prediction when the target bunsetsu ends with a particle for all particle subcategories. During the Heian period, adverbial particles were frequently used. However, during the Muromachi period, they became less common. Conversely, while there were a few examples of sentence-ending particles in the Heian period, they became commonly used in the Muromachi period [10]. The error rates of bunsetsu prediction ending with these particles significantly increased when the Heian model was applied to data from the Muromachi period. This could be because new usages for these particles emerged during the Muromachi period alongside the changes in verb conjugation forms, which often appear with the sentence-ending particles.

7 Conclusion

This study focuses on providing a deep learning-based (or LLM-based) bunsetsu, which is a minimal phrase in Japanese, and Long Unit Words parser for the Heian period (AD 794-1185) to the Muromachi period (AD 1336-1573) and evaluating its performances.

We model the parser as a joint sequential label that combines the bunsetsu BI tag, LUW BI tag, and LUW POS tags for each SUW token. We used the transformer-based language model to output an SUW token representation by taking the appropri-

[10]The samples of the Muromachi period are mainly informal conversations, which used sentence-ending particles frequently. `https://clrd.ninjal.ac.jp/chj/muromachi-en.html`

ately pooling of the subword representations for the last layer of the transformer. We trained our models on the corpora of each period, including contemporary and historical Japanese.

The results ranged from 0.976 to 0.996 in the f1 value for both bunsetsu and LUW reconstructions indicating that our models achieved comparable performance to models trained on a contemporary Japanese corpus.

Through the statistical analysis and case studies comparing each period, the bunsetsu estimation can be influenced by the grammaticalization of morphemes.

In the future, we will expand the applicable periods. We will build a syntactic parser by annotating the dependencies between bunsetsu segments.

Acknowledgments

This research was supported by JSPS KAKENHI grant JP22K12145, as well as the National Institute for Japanese Language and Linguistics Joint Research Projects "Empirical Computational Psycholinguistics Using Annotation Data." and "Extending the Diachronic Corpus through an Open Co-construction Environment."

References

Masayuki Asahara, Hiroshi Kanayama, Takaaki Tanaka, Yusuke Miyao, Sumire Uematsu, Shinsuke Mori, Yuji Matsumoto, Mai Omura, and Yugo Murawaki. 2018. Universal Dependencies version 2 for Japanese. In *Proceedings of the Eleventh International Conference on Language Resources and Evaluation (LREC 2018)*, Miyazaki, Japan. European Language Resources Association (ELRA).

Yasuharu Den, Junpei Nakamura, Toshinobu Ogiso, and Hideki Ogura. 2008. A proper approach to Japanese morphological analysis: Dictionary, model, and evaluation. In *Proceedings of the Sixth International Conference on Language Resources and Evaluation (LREC'08)*, Marrakech, Morocco. European Language Resources Association (ELRA).

Shunsuke Kozawa, Kiyotaka Uchimoto, and Yasuharu Den. 2014. Bccwj ni motozuku cho-tani kaiseki tsuru comainu (in japanese)(long unit word analysis tool comainu based on bccwj). *The Annual Meeting of the Association for Natural Language Processing*.

Taku Kudo, Kaoru Yamamoto, and Yuji Matsumoto. 2004. Applying conditional random fields to Japanese morphological analysis. In *Proceedings of the 2004 Conference on Empirical Methods in Natural Language Processing*, pages 230–237, Barcelona, Spain. Association for Computational Linguistics.

Hiroshi Matsuda. 2020. Ginza - practical japanese nlp based on universal dependencies. *Journal of Natural Language Processing*, 27(3):695–701.

Hiroshi Matsuda, Mai Omura, and Masayuki Asahara. 2022. Ud japanese ni motoduku kokugo-ken chotani kaiseki-kei no kochiku(in japanese) construction of a long unit word analysis system for japanese based on ud japanese. *The Annual Meeting of the Association for Natural Language Processing*.

NINJAL. 2024. Corpus of historical japanese.

Joakim Nivre, Marie-Catherine de Marneffe, Filip Ginter, Jan Hajič, Christopher D. Manning, Sampo Pyysalo, Sebastian Schuster, Francis Tyers, and Daniel Zeman. 2020. Universal Dependencies v2: An evergrowing multilingual treebank collection. In *Proceedings of the Twelfth Language Resources and Evaluation Conference*, pages 4034–4043, Marseille, France. European Language Resources Association.

Mai Omura and Masayuki Asahara. 2018. UD–Japanese BCCWJ: Universal Dependencies annotation for the Balanced Corpus of Contemporary Written Japanese. In *Proceedings of the Second Workshop on Universal Dependencies (UDW 2018)*, pages 117–125, Brussels, Belgium. Association for Computational Linguistics.

Mai Omura, Aya Wakasa, and Masayuki Asahara. 2023. Universal dependencies for japanese based on long-unit words by ninjal. *Journal of Natural Language Processing*, 30(1):4–29.

A new machine-actionable corpus for ancient text restoration

Will Fitzgerald and **Justin Barney**
Western Michigan University
{william.a.fitzgerald, justin.barney}@wmich.edu

Abstract

The Machine-Actionable Ancient Text (MAAT) Corpus is a new resource providing training and evaluation data for restoring lacunae in ancient Greek, Latin, and Coptic texts. Current text restoration systems require large amounts of data for training and task-relevant means for evaluation. The MAAT Corpus addresses this need by converting texts available in EpiDoc XML format into a machine-actionable format that preserves the most textually salient aspects needed for machine learning: the text itself, lacunae, and textual restorations. Structured test cases are generated from the corpus that align with the actual text restoration task performed by papyrologists and epigraphist, enabling more realistic evaluation than the synthetic tasks used previously. The initial 1.0 beta release contains approximately 134,000 text editions, 178,000 text blocks, and 750,000 individual restorations, with Greek and Latin predominating. This corpus aims to facilitate the development of computational methods to assist scholars in accurately restoring ancient texts.

1 Introduction

For the papyrologist and epigraphist, a fundamental task is the creation of an accurate transcription of the text under consideration. Often the physical medium supporting the text has undergone decay, leaving gaps, or "lacunae," in the text. Filling these gaps is a painstaking task. Kleve and Fonnes (1981) first recognized the potential of computer science for assisting with text restorations of this type, specifically by leveraging string-searching algorithms. Advances in computational approaches to text analysis, especially deep learning and large language models, may be able to aid scholars in the task of textual restoration. Developing such systems typically requires large amounts of data, both for training, and ideally for providing task-relevant means for evaluation.

-- -- -- -- -- -- -- -- -- --
[-ca.?-] . [-ca.?-] [-ca.?-]
. . . . [. . . .] ὠνουμένη(*) Ἰσα[ροῦς](*)[ ] ν [. .]ρχοντ[ ]ν[-ca.?- πηχῶν κατ']
ἐμβαδ[ὸ]ν ἑβδομήκοντα [ἢ ὅ]σων ἐὰν ὦσι [-ca.?- καὶ χρηστηρίων καὶ]
ἀνηκόντων πάντων καὶ ε[ἰ]σόδου καὶ ἐξόδου ὧν [ὅλων γείτονες νότου οἰκία Πα-]
θώτου, λιβὸς δημοσία ῥύμη ἐν ᾗ εἴσοδος καὶ ἔξ[οδος τῆς οἰκίας δεῖνος]
Παήσιος βορρᾶ οἱ λοιποὶ τόποι τῆς ὠνουμένης Ἰσαρ[ ] . . . . [ ] [-ca.?-]-
των ὄντων ἐν τοῖς ἀπὸ βορρᾶ πρὸς λίβα μέρ[εσι] τῆς [κ]ώμη[ς -ca.?-]
Πατρὴ κάτωι(*), τ[ὴν] δὲ συνπεφων[ημ]ένην τιμὴν ἀργ[υρίου σεβαστοῦ νομίσμα-]
τος δραχμὰς τρ[ια]κοσίας ἀπεσχηκ[έ]ναι τὸν πωλοῦντ[α -ca.?- παρὰ τῆς ὠνου-]
μένης διὰ χειράς(*) καὶ εἶναι τὴν τοῦ πεπραμένου ψιλοῦ τόπ[ου κυρείαν καὶ κρά-]
[τησι]ν περὶ τ[ὴν] ὠ[νου]μένην [κ]αὶ τοὺ[ς πα]ρ' αὐτῆς χρ[ωμένους -ca.?-]
-- -- -- -- -- -- -- -- -- --

Apparatus

^ 2. or ὠνουμένη
^ 2. or Ἰσά[ριον]
^ 8. l. κάτω
^ 10. l. χειρὸς

Figure 1: Leiden Transcription of P.Flor. 3 324, from Aegyptus.89.240, 2011.

Here we introduce the 1.0 beta version of the Machine-Actionable Ancient Text Corpus (MAAT Corpus), which provides training and evaluation data for the development of machine learning models that aid in the restoration of ancient Greek, Latin, and Coptic texts.

2 Current text restoration corpora

There are several different corpora used in creating systems for text restoration of ancient text. Two existing systems, Pythia (Assael et al., 2019) and its successor Ithaca (Assael et al., 2022) use Greek inscription data from the Packard Humanities Institute (Packard Humanities Institute, 2023) that have been converted to a modified Leiden Convention (Wilcken, 1932) format. Papavassiliou et al. 2020 created a corpus of Mycenaean Linear B texts for the restoration of Linear B tablets. Background large-language models have been trained on corpora as well, such as Latin BERT (Bamman & Burns, 2020) and AristoBERTo (Myerston, 2022), GreBerta (Riemenschneider & Frank, 2023).

Proceedings of the 1st Workshop on Machine Learning for Ancient Languages (ML4AL 2024), pages 56–60
August 15, 2024

```
{
   "corpus_id": "EDH",
   "file_id": "HD056774",
   "block_index": 1,
   "id": "EDH/HD056774/1",
   "title": "Epitaph from Municipium Claudium Virunum, bei - S. Andrä/Lavanttal
(Noricum)",
   "material": "gesteine",
   "language": "la",
   "training_text": " Ursuius vius sibi \nfecit et <gap/>\niurae uxo[ri]",
   "test_cases": [
     {
       "case_index": 1,
       "id": "EDH/HD056774/1/1",
       "test_case": " Ursuius vius sibi \nfecit et <gap />\niurae uxo[..]",
       "alternatives": [
         "ri"
       ]
     }
   ]
}
```

Figure 2: Example JSON representation of a single **ab** block with one test case; \n reflects a **lb** element.

3 Corpora of interest

Papyrologists and epigraphists have generally agreed upon using a specialized schema developed originally for epigraphy, EpiDoc (Elliott et al., 2006), based on the TEI format (*TEI*, 1994). The largest corpus of epigraphy stored in EpiDoc format is maintained by the Epigraphic Database Heidelberg (*Epigraphic Database Heidelberg*, 1993), which focuses primarily on Latin inscriptions from the Roman Empire. The largest corpus of papyrological texts is Papyri.info, a collaboration among several institutions that hosts papyrological data in Greek, Latin, Coptic, and Arabic (*Papyri.Info*, 2007).

The EpiDoc format provides extensive capabilities for describing metadata for inscriptions and papyri. It also has an XML-structured format as an alternative to the Leiden Conventions. Texts are described in **ab** blocks (originally standing for "anonymous block") and provide a richer description language for text editions than the Leiden Conventions. Because the Leiden Conventions format is more compact, we will use this format for examples printed in this paper.

4 Features of MAAT corpus

Unfortunately, for many machine learning and large language models, the structure of the **ab** blocks is too rich, since it provides internal structure for annotations, stylistic information and so on (the Leiden Conventions also communicate some of these features). With respect to building systems for text restoration, a simpler system is required. As Assael et al. 2022 note, these corpora need to be "machine-actionable." For this reason, they ought to be easy to feed into machine learning systems for learning and for evaluation.

Figure 1 shows the text from a typical edition (P.Flor 3 324) from Papyri.info, a contract for the sale of property (*Aegyptus.89.240*, 2011). For this paper, three things should be noted. First, text restorations are provided in square brackets. For example, in line three, the brackets in the phrase [ἢ ὅ]σων̣ indicate that "ἢ ὅ" has been supplied by the papyrologist and that the letter forms are not visible on the papyrus itself. Second, missing text that the editor has not restored is indicated by dots. One dot corresponds to one missing letter; therefore, the number of dots signifies the approximate number of letters known to be missing. The marking "-ca.?" or "- - -" indicates a gap of unknown extent. Third, alternate restorations of the text are sometimes given in the *apparatus criticus*. These alternate readings represent viable textual conjectures, which were not ultimately chosen by the editor as their preferred reading. While digital editions print alternative restorations less commonly than print editions, they are sometimes encoded in the XML

Corpus	Editions	Blocks	Restorations
DCLP (Digital Corpus of Literary Papyri in EpiDoc XML)	1,938	11,581	129,806
DDbDP (Duke Databank of Documentary Papyri)	59,693	85,626	507,985
EDH (Epigraphic Database Heidelberg)	72,353	80,753	113,944
Totals	133,984	177,960	751,735

Table 1: Counts of Editions, Blocks, and Restorations from the corpora represented in the Machine-Actionable Ancient Text Corpus

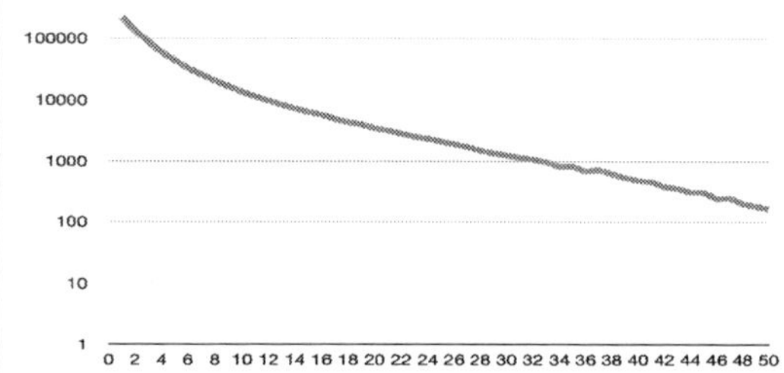

Figure 3: Distribution of gap lengths of text restorations in the MAAT Corpus, logarithmic scale

data. In our sample text from Figure 1, two apparatus notes appear for line two of the transcription.

To make a corpus machine-actionable for learning, especially for large language models, we stripped away all but the most textually salient aspects of the text, using Unicode UTF-8 encoding. Our corpus includes the preserved text, as well as unclear letters and restorations. Although typographical conventions such as casing, interlinear word space, punctuation, accents, breathing marks, and other diacritics are typically not found on the source material, such typography is retained. Line breaks (indicated by the **lb** element in EpiDoc XML) are also preserved. Unclear text, indicated by Leiden Conventions with a sublinear dot, is treated no differently than preserved text; text that has been restored by an editor is bracketed. For example, the text "καὶ ε[ἰ]σ̣ό̣δ̣ο̣υ̣" converted to "καὶ ε[ἰ]σόδου." Occasionally (as in Figure 1) there are alternative readings of a restored text, but since alternative readings are difficult to process, the first primary text restoration is chosen. Abbreviations, especially prevalent in Latin inscriptions, are not expanded.

Gaps in the text that have not been restored by an editor must also be indicated. There are, essentially, three types of gaps: gaps of known length, gaps of approximately known length, and gaps of unknown length. Gaps of known length are converted to a dot for each missing letter. Similarly, gaps of approximate length are treated as if the gap length is known. The EpiDoc XML tag **<gap/>** is used for gaps of unknown length. Gaps are sometimes indicated *within* a restored text, and such gaps are moved outside. For example, the text "τὸν πωλοῦν̣τ̣[α -ca.?- παρὰ]" is converted to "τὸν πωλοῦντ[α]<gap/>[παρὰ]".

In the end, all texts in the MAAT corpus are written in a simplified format for easier use by machine learning models. Texts from the **ab** blocks in EpiDoc XML format are converted to a light, Leiden-like format, but with a bare minimum of annotative markings: text and gaps of known and unknown length, with restored text in brackets. Figure 2 provides our data for a 1st-2nd century CE epitaph from the Roman province Noricum (*EDH HD056774*, 2014).

Typically, in machine learning tasks, a portion of a training corpus is set aside for evaluation. In the most successful system to date for inscription restoration, Ithaca (Assael et al., 2022), one to ten characters are artificially hidden during the testing phase, and the machine (or parallel human evaluator) is tasked with restoring these artificial lacunae. A similar text-masking evaluation method is used in Papavassileiou et al., 2023 for Mycenaean Linear B tablets, although they also ask the model to perform text restoration of some real lacunae.

The large number of restorations created by papyrologists and epigraphists found in the base corpora of Greek, Latin, and Coptic texts provide a rich opportunity to create evaluation data that are aligned with the actual text restoration task. Although it may be useful to train a system using artificial lacunae, it is more valuable to evaluate on the text restorations done by working papyrologists and epigraphists. These practitioners do not work with random lacunae, since lacunae *in situ* are not random: they follow a logarithmic distribution in length (see Figure 3), and tend to occur in certain locations. The immediate textual context of real lacunae also tends to be much deteriorated and uncertain, in comparison to the sites of artificial lacunae.

To that end, we can create test cases by using the actual lacunae and text restorations that are present in papyrological and epigraphic sources and use the (retained) training data with the restored text for evaluation. Because there are possible alternative readings for a restored gap, though, it is better to have a structured test case that retains those readings. This will slightly complicate the evaluation metrics. Rather than using, for example, character error count for a single restoration, we need to use the minimum character error count for a (possibly singleton) set of alternatives. Similarly, calculating the top-*n* rate will need to consider the presence of the proposed restoration in the set of alternatives.

Thus, a single test case needs a little more structure, containing at least the text with a gap to be filled, plus its alternatives. For example, for the text "ὠνουμένη Ἰσα[....]" the two alternative readings "ροῦς" and "ριον" are required. Note that, because letter forms of different types take up different amounts of space on the material substrate (and therefore calculations of the number of missing letters are approximate), alternatives might, in fact, have different character lengths. In these cases, the mask to be restored will comprise the mode of alternative lengths.

5 Format and distribution of data

Data in the MAAT Corpus is structured as a set of JavaScript object notation (JSON) records (Bray, 2014), one record for each **ab** block. Each record contains metadata about the block (an id field, source corpus, source file id, block index within the file, material, and language). It also has the training text, as described above. For each restored text, a test case is created, also containing an id, test case index within the text, the test case itself, and the set of alternatives. For statistical purposes, the number of alternatives, the number, mode, maximum, and minimum lengths of the alternatives are also described.

Currently, there are approximately 134,000 editions processed in the MAAT Corpus, representing approximately 178,000 **ab** blocks and 750,000 individual text restorations.

There is a small representation of Coptic texts in the MAAT Corpus (around 1% of the total, mostly papyri). Latin editions outnumber Greek editions (54% and 45%, respectively). Papyrological texts tend to be longer than inscriptions; papyrological texts tend to be written in Greek and inscriptions in Latin, so the number of Greek blocks is greater than the number of Latin ones (53% and 46%, respectively). The number of text restorations in Greek greatly outnumber Latin ones (83% and 16%, respectively).

The gap lengths of restored text created by papyrologists and epigraphists found in the MAAT Corpus vary widely, and follow an unsurprising logarithmic or Zipfian distribution. Gaps of length 1 (that is, one character) account for 30% of all gaps, and gaps of length 4 or less account for 67%. Gaps of length 10 or less account for 87% of all gaps. Figure 3 shows the distribution.

6 Data availability and next steps

We are now releasing the Machine-Actionable Ancient Text Corpus in a beta state at https://zenodo.org/records/12518435 (Fitzgerald & Barney, 2024). The corpus is not meant to compete with current systems, such as Papyri.info and EDH, whose use cases are different. Instead, we hope that the MAAT Corpus will aid the creation of software systems that can help working papyrologists and epigraphists accurately and efficiently hypothesize text restorations in new editions of current and newly recovered texts and inscriptions. Code for creating the corpus can be found at https://github.com/WMU-Herculaneum-Project/maat.

We welcome the collaboration of other scholars and institutions in the service of adding additional data to the MAAT corpus, including data from other ancient languages. Our specific interest is in text restoration of Greek papyrological texts, but we would like to expand this to Arabic and other non-western texts as well. Given the similarities of the text restoration task and its evaluation methodology among texts of different language traditions, such expansions promise to be fruitful.

In the future, we also intend to create a pathway by which any data made available in DSL-based formats (Del Grosso et al., 2023; Williams et al., 2015) can be converted for inclusion in future versions of the corpus.

7 Conclusion

This paper introduces and announces the publication of the MAAT Corpus, which provides an easily accessible, versioned corpus of machine-actionable ancient texts that can be used in machine learning. It also makes available evaluation data, via its test cases, that closely track the task of text restoration as done by working papyrologists and epigraphists. The MAAT Corpus currently includes approximately 60 Mb of ancient text, making it the largest corpus available for evaluating text restoration tasks. It is also the only dataset that uses actual lacunae and text restorations as test cases for evaluation.

Acknowledgements

The authors wish to thank the reviewers for their valuable comments on an earlier draft of this paper.

References

Aegyptus.89.240 = HGV P.Flor. 3 324 = Trismegistos 25457 = p.flor.3.324. (2011). Duke Databank of Documentary Papyri. http://papyri.info/ddbdp/aegyptus;89;240

Assael, Y., Sommerschield, T., & Prag, J. (2019). Restoring ancient text using deep learning: A case study on Greek epigraphy. *Proceedings of the 2019 Conference on Empirical Methods in Natural Language Processing and the 9th International Joint Conference on Natural Language Processing (EMNLP-IJCNLP)*, 6367–6374. https://doi.org/10.18653/v1/D19-1668

Assael, Y., Sommerschield, T., Shillingford, B., Bordbar, M., Pavlopoulos, J., Chatzipanagiotou, M., Androutsopoulos, I., Prag, J., & De Freitas, N. (2022). Restoring and attributing ancient texts using deep neural networks. *Nature*, *603*(7900), 280–283. https://doi.org/10.1038/s41586-022-04448-z

Bamman, D., & Burns, P. J. (2020). *Latin BERT: A Contextual Language Model for Classical Philology*. https://doi.org/10.48550/ARXIV.2009.10053

Bray, T. (2014). *The JavaScript object notation (JSON) data interchange format* (7159). RFC Editor. https://doi.org/10.17487/RFC7159

Del Grosso, A. M., Zenzaro, S., Boschetti, F., & Ranocchia, G. (2023). GreekSchools: Making Traditional Papyrology Machine Actionable through Domain-Driven Design. *2023 7th IEEE Congress on Information Science and Technology (CiSt)*, 621–626. https://doi.org/10.1109/CiSt56084.2023.10409929

EDH HD056774. (2014, February 18). Epigraphic Database Heidelberg. https://edh.ub.uni-heidelberg.de/edh/inschrift/HD056774

Elliott, T., Bodard, G., & Cayless, H. (2006, 2024). *EpiDoc: Epigraphic Documents in TEI XML*. https://epidoc.stoa.org/

Epigraphic Database Heidelberg. (1993, 2021). https://edh.ub.uni-heidelberg.de/

Fitzgerald, W., & Barney, J. (2024). *The Machine-Actionable Ancient Text (MAAT) Corpus, Beta 1 (1.0.0)* . (MAAT Corpus) [dataset]. https://doi.org/10.5281/zenodo.12518435

Kleve, K., & Fonnes, I. (1981). Lacunology: On the use of computer methods in Papyrology. *Symbolae Osloenses*, *56*(1), 157–170. https://doi.org/10.1080/00397678108590755

Myerston, J. (2022, January 27). *aristoBERTo*. https://huggingface.co/Jacobo/aristoBERTo/blob/main/README.md

Packard Humanities Institute. (2023, July 12). *PHI Greek Inscriptions*. https://inscriptions.packhum.org/

Papavassileiou, K., Kosmopoulos, D. I., & Owens, G. (2023). A Generative Model for the Mycenaean Linear B Script and Its Application in Infilling Text from Ancient Tablets. *Journal on Computing and Cultural Heritage*, *16*(3), 1–25. https://doi.org/10.1145/3593431

Papyri.info. (2007, 2024). https://papyri.info/docs/about

Riemenschneider, F., & Frank, A. (2023). Exploring Large Language Models for Classical Philology. *Proceedings of the 61st Annual Meeting of the Association for Computational Linguistics (Volume 1: Long Papers)*, 15181–15199. https://doi.org/10.18653/v1/2023.acl-long.846

TEI: Text Encoding Initiative. (1994, 2024). https://tei-c.org/

Wilcken, U. (1932). *Das Leydener Klammersystem*. B.G. Teubner Verlagsgesellschaft.

Williams, A. C., Santarsiero, A., Meccariello, C., Verhasselt, G., Carroll, H. D., Wallin, J. F., Obbink, D., & Brusuelas, J. H. (2015). Proteus: A platform for born digital critical editions of literary and subliterary papyri. *2015 Digital Heritage*, 453–456. https://doi.org/10.1109/DigitalHeritage.2015.7419546

Lacuna Language Learning: Leveraging RNNs for Ranked Text Completion in Digitized Coptic Manuscripts

Lauren Levine[1], **Cindy Tung Li**[1],
Lydia Bremer-McCollum[2], **Nicholas Wagner**[3], **Amir Zeldes**[1]
[1]Georgetown University, [2]University of Oklahoma, [3]Duke University
{lel76, cl1579, amir.zeldes}@georgetown.edu
lcbm@ou.edu, nicholas.wagner@duke.edu

Abstract

Ancient manuscripts are frequently damaged, containing gaps in the text known as lacunae. In this paper, we present a bidirectional RNN model for character prediction of Coptic characters in manuscript lacunae. Our best model performs with 72% accuracy on single character reconstruction, but falls to 37% when reconstructing lacunae of various lengths. While not suitable for definitive manuscript reconstruction, we argue that our RNN model can help scholars rank the likelihood of textual reconstructions. As evidence, we use our RNN model to rank reconstructions in two early Coptic manuscripts. Our investigation shows that neural models can augment traditional methods of textual restoration, providing scholars with an additional tool to assess lacunae in Coptic manuscripts.

1 Introduction

Ancient manuscripts are an invaluable resource for linguists and historians, offering insights into the cultures and languages of the ancient world. Unfortunately, these manuscripts are often damaged, with sections of text missing, known as lacunae. In recent years, neural models have made significant advances in various areas of linguistic research. Nevertheless, attempts to apply neural methods to manuscript reconstruction have been limited, and none have specifically targeted Coptic (see Section 2.2).

In this paper, we explore the potential for neural language models to be utilized in the reconstruction of Coptic manuscripts. Leveraging a bidirectional RNN language model trained for Coptic character prediction, we explore how the model can be integrated into the workflow of scholars attempting textual reconstruction. We consider the ability of the model to predict the missing characters of lacunae directly, as well as to provide rankings for the likelihood of reconstruction candidates already under consideration. We show that scholars can use judgments from neural models as additional quantitative evidence, in conjunction with more traditional qualitative methods, to work towards manuscript reconstruction.

2 Background and Related Work

2.1 Coptic

Coptic belongs to the Afro-Asiatic language family and is the latest stage of the Egyptian language, the longest continuously attested language on Earth. Coptic utilizes the 24 glyphs of the Greek alphabet and adds additional Demotic (Egyptian) glyphs (a minimum of 6 depending on dialect) to represent sounds not found in Greek. In late antiquity, more than a dozen regional dialects were spoken and written (Layton, 2011). Owing to these dialect variations, the use of superlinear strokes and other diacritical marks, and irregular orthography of Greek loan words, Coptic provides a highly complex dataset.

Coptic manuscripts preserve the diverse textual tradition of late-antique and medieval Egypt. Inscribed on papyrus and other perishable media, many Coptic manuscripts contain small gaps or holes (lacunae), which often cannot be restored on the basis of other extant manuscripts. Scholars use qualitative methods to restore lacunae, chiefly through study of the manuscript's context and (con)textual parallels. Occasionally, appeal is made to traditional canons of textual criticism, but here too the scholar's own judgment guides the restoration (Wasserman, 2013). Initial testing has shown that human methods of textual restoration have a high error rate at both the word level and the character level (Sommerschield et al., 2023, 711–712).

2.2 Manuscript Reconstruction

Following early attempts using n-gram models to approach the Indus Valley script (Rao et al., 2009),

Proceedings of the 1st Workshop on Machine Learning for Ancient Languages (ML4AL 2024), pages 61–70

most previous work on reconstructing lacunae in manuscripts, as well as in epigraphic data, has focused on Greek and Latin (Novokhatko and Maier, 2022; Matsumoto, 2022). Early projects included eAQUA (Schubert, 2011), which pioneered proposing automatic reconstructions of lacunae based on statistical methods from larger datasets (in the context of ancient languages). More recently, studies using neural methods for the reconstruction of Greek (Assael et al., 2019) and Latin (Brunello et al., 2023) have appeared, with papers in the last three years specifically proposing to leverage transformer based language model architectures for both born-digital and (OCRed) handwritten inputs in a range of languages (Vogler et al., 2022).

We are not aware of previous papers applying language models to the reconstruction of Coptic texts, though a recent Web page prepared by the CoptOT project[1] provides a 'Manuscript Speculation Tool' which helps in laying out missing letters on predefined digitized manuscript spaces. However, in the tool's operating scenario, a base text to be laid out is known (e.g. a chapter of the Bible), and the question is how many letters of each verse might fit into each missing line or part of a line. To our knowledge, this paper is the first attempt to leverage language modeling for lacuna reconstruction in Coptic.

2.3 Masked Language Models

In 2019, Devlin et al. introduced BERT, a foundational masked language model (MLM), where random tokens in the input were masked, and the model was trained to predict the masked token based on the context. For 15% of the tokens in training, each one is replaced with either [MASK], a random token, or the original token, without change. Masking mimics gaps and teaches the model to fill in missing segments of strings, which makes the MLM approach highly applicable to our lacuna reconstruction task.

In the same paper, Devlin et al. found that a model with only left to right context performed worse than a bidirectional masked language model, which is able to use context from before and after the masked token. They advocate for a bidirectional model that can use left and right context at every layer over concatenating a left to right model and a right to left model, as proposed earlier in ELMo (Peters et al., 2018). As we are framing our lacuna reconstruction task as a prediction of masked characters, parallel to the masked token prediction done by models such as BERT, this finding regarding bidirectionality leads us to adopt a bidirectional strategy for our model as well.

As the masked language model strategy was popularized with transformer based models such as BERT, there is not much existing work regarding the implementation of masked language models with an RNN-based architecture. However, in scenarios with relatively small quantities of data and limited long distance dependencies, it can still be preferable to use an RNN-based architecture over a transformer-based architecture (Mishra, 2021). Considering that we have almost 1.22 million tokens of Coptic data, and we are looking to fill in character gaps at the sentence level, we consider our Coptic lacuna prediction task to be one such scenario, and we opt to use an RNN based architecture in our model.

While we have done some preliminary prototyping with transformer based architectures, such as ELECTRA (Clark et al., 2020), so far our experiments with RNN-based architectures have made the most progress. As such, we present those finding here. However, we still believe it would be worthwhile to return to the exploration of various transformer architectures in future work.

3 Data

For training and testing the model, we leverage the data from the Coptic SCRIPTORIUM Corpora (Schroeder and Zeldes, 2016). This project compiles text from a variety of manuscript sources and totals almost 1.22 million tokens of Sahidic Coptic. The Coptic SCRIPTORIUM project is an ongoing effort to create an open online database and tool set for digital research in Coptic. This effort includes creating normalized, machine readable versions of Coptic manuscripts with a variety of linguistic annotations created using the online, version controlled GitDox annotation tools (Zhang and Zeldes, 2017). The full data set is publicly available on GitHub[2] in various machine readable formats, and the corpora are searchable via an online query interface.[3]

The digitized manuscripts have a normalized version (with regard to spelling, etc.) of the text

[1] https://coptot.manuscriptroom.com/manuscript-speculation-tool

[2] https://github.com/CopticScriptorium/corpora

[3] https://annis.copticscriptorium.org/annis/scriptorium

as well as a version representing the original text. We leverage the original text version, annotated as `orig_group`, as we are creating a system to aid scholars who want a reconstruction of the original text of the manuscripts. Within the digitized original text, damaged and missing sections of the manuscripts are represented with brackets and dots, which can be used to convey different levels of damage and manual reconstruction in the manuscript. This information is represented in the Leiden+[4] documentation format: missing sections are denoted with brackets with dots inside, where the number of dots is equal to the estimated number of characters missing in the line of text (so [...] would indicate 3 missing characters); brackets with letters inside indicate a damaged section which was reconstructed by a scholar; and characters with some damage that have been manually reconstructed by a scholar can appear outside of brackets with a dot beneath them. Immediately below are example sentences from the data showing these formatting styles:

Blank Lacunae:
ⲁϥⲃⲉⲉⲃⲉ[...]ⲁϥϫⲓⲥⲉ[...]
Reconstructed Lacunae:
ⲁⲩⲱⲁϥϣⲗⲏⲗ[ⲁϥ]ⲧⲛⲛⲟⲟⲩϥ
ⲁⲩⲱⲙⲛⲡ̣ⲉⲧⲥϩⲟⲩⲟⲣⲧⲉⲡ̣ⲉⲧⲥⲟⲛⲥⲙⲛⲛⲩⲧⲉ

The completely blank sections are the target use case for our system, and we use the manually reconstructed lacunae as the gold standard test data for our model. As this gold standard test data is a limited proportion of the corpora, we also mask characters from the sentences of the corpora without lacunae to create training data and additional test data for our model. The Coptic SCRIPTORIUM Corpora have a total of 36,252 complete sentences (no lacunae) with over 2.8 million characters. The lengths of these sentences range from 5 characters to 1067 characters, with an average sentence length of 80 characters. We created a train/dev/test data partition from these complete sentences, with the proportions 90:5:5, giving us a training data set of 32,676 sentences, a dev data set of 1,815 sentences, and a test set of 1,816 sentences.

In addition to the complete sentences, there is a portion of sentences in the Coptic SCRIPTORIUM Corpora which contain lacunae. There are a total of 792 sentences, with approximately 60,000 characters, which contain only those lacunae that have

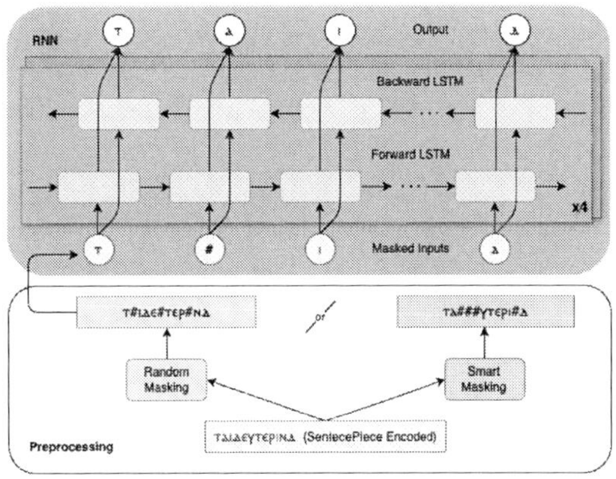

Figure 1: Model architecture and preprocessing

been manually reconstructed by Coptic language scholars. This set of sentences is our gold standard test data. The average sentence length in this set is 75 characters. The total number of missing characters in this test set is 3,594, with an average gap length of ~2 characters. There are also 780 sentences, with approximately 52,000 characters, that contain at least one empty lacuna which has not been reconstructed by a scholar. This set of sentences is the target data that we are building our system to fill in, so there is no gold standard to evaluate against directly. The average sentence length in this set is 68 characters, and the total number of missing characters is 3,658, with an average gap length of ~3 characters. The similarities in average sentence length and average lacuna gap length between these two data sets suggest that the model should be able to perform well on the target data set if it performs well on the test data set.

4 Model Architecture

For our lacuna prediction model, we implement a character based bidirectional RNN model, trained with a character-level masked language modeling task. We start with a character-level vocabulary and embedding layer, generated with SentencePiece (Kudo and Richardson, 2018). The vocabulary is 134 characters, including some control symbols, the mask token, the lower-cased Coptic alphabet, and some punctuation. Our final model has an embedding size of 200, hidden size of 300, and projection size of 150. For the body of the model, we then create a four layer bidirectional LSTM, an AdamW optimizer, and learning rate of 0.0003 (selected as the optimal parameters after conducting an extensive hyperparameter search). The LSTM

[4] https://papyri.info/docs/leiden_plus

architecture was chosen over other architectures, such as GRU, for its ability to capture long distance dependencies, which provide relevant context for lacuna reconstruction. We use categorical cross entropy for our loss criterion, evaluating only on predictions for masked characters. A diagram of our model architecture and preprocessing is shown in Figure 1.

The resulting model is fairly small model, and training on the full training data set can be accomplished in a few hours, with or without GPU hardware. As such, with our model code and the publicly available data from the Coptic SCRIPTORIUM project, models at the performance level presented in this paper will be accessible to interested parties. The code for our model is available on GitHub[5], and instructions for recreating the data partition, training the model, and running/interacting with the model are included in the README.

We explore several different masking strategies in the training of our model. For the first masking strategy, which we refer to as "random masking", we used the BERT masking strategy of randomly masking 15% of the characters. When creating the index vector for the sentence, each character has a 15% chance of being masked. If the character is masked, there are three possible masking options. 80% of the time, the character is replaced with a special mask token, while 10% of the time it is replaced with a random character, and finally, 10% of the time, the character is not replaced.

We also implement a masking strategy called "smart masking", which mimics the distribution of lacunae in the gold standard test set (described in Section 3). In the reconstructed lacuna test set, the sentences range from having one gap to as many as twenty. Over 60% of the sentences have just one gap, 35% have two to nine gaps, and just 5% have more than nine gaps. To mimic the variable number of gaps, we randomly incorporate one to five gaps per sentence. Of the 1,470 gaps in the 782 sentences, almost half of them are just one character long. The length of each gap has 48% of being just one character long, 22% chance of being two characters long, 12% chance of being 3 characters long, and for the final 18% of the time, the gap length is randomly generated to be between four and thirty-four characters.

[5]https://github.com/lauren-lizzy-levine/coptic_char_generator.git

In addition to the two different masking strategies for distribution, we also had two strategies relating to the re-masking frequency of the data. The first strategy is to mask one time, when loading the data initially, which we call "once masking". The second option is to re-mask the training data at each epoch, which we call "dynamic masking". Between the two masking distribution strategies and these two re-masking frequency strategies, we ended up with four different model types: random-once, random-dynamic, smart-once, and smart-dynamic. For training, we auto-generated masked dev data that matched the distribution masking strategy (random or smart) of the model being trained.

5 Evaluation

For evaluation, we had three different test sets. From the test partition made from the complete sentences that had no lacunae, we created two test sets: one with random masking and one with smart masking. Our final test data set was the gold standard data of manually reconstructed lacunae described in Section 3. We had our models predict on the data in all three test sets and scored their performance with a simple accuracy metric (number of masked characters correctly predicted / total number of masked characters in data set).

5.1 Baselines

We applied three rudimentary heuristic baselines to our three test data sets, the results of which are shown in the bottom half of Table 1. The first baseline selected a random character from the SentencePiece character model vocabulary for each character prediction. The second baseline always predicted the most common letter in the data set (mode character), "ϵ". The third baseline is a simple tri-gram language model. Results for "Test Random" and "Test Smart" are the performance of the baselines on the auto-generated random masked test data and smart masked test data respectively, while "Test Reconstructed Lacunae" is the performance on the gold standard data of manually reconstructed lacunae.

5.2 RNN Evaluation

We started our model training by doing hyperparameter searches on four different model configurations, using combinations of the masking strategies for masking distribution and re-masking frequency (random-once model, random-dynamic model, smart-once model, smart-dynamic model).

	Test Random	Test Smart	Test Reconstructed Lacunae
Models			
Random-Once	0.703	0.323	0.336
Random-Dynamic	**0.722**	0.338	**0.369**
Smart-Once	0.610	**0.366**	0.334
Smart-Dynamic	0.603	0.359	0.319
Baselines			
Tri-gram	0.259	0.134	0.155
Mode Character	0.126	0.124	0.121
Random	0.008	0.007	0.007

Table 1: Model and baseline accuracy results on the three test sets

After we selected the best performing hyperparameters for each masking configuration with regard to accuracy scoring on the correspondingly masked dev data, we ran the four best performing models (one for each masking configuration) on the three test data sets outlined at the top of this section. The results from these runs are shown in the top section of Table 1.

The random test set has the highest scores on average, while the reconstructed lacuna test set has the lowest scores on average, indicating that the reconstructed lacuna test set is the more difficult scenario. However, it is also the most realistic scenario out of all three test sets, so performance on this test set should be considered the most significant. We observe that all of the tested model configurations outperform the baselines, showing a substantial increase in performance on all test sets. Out of the four different masking strategies we explored, we found that the model utilizing the random-dynamic masking strategy had the highest performance on the random test set and the reconstructed lacuna test set, while the smart-once masking strategy had the highest performance on the smart test set.

It is somewhat surprising that the model utilizing the random strategy outperforms the model using the smart strategy on the reconstructed lacuna set, considering that the smart masking strategy was developed to better reflect the conditions in which actual lacunae occur. This result is likely because the reconstructed lacuna data set is composed of only sentences with fully reconstructed lacunae, and thus is biased towards containing shorter lacunae than we might otherwise expect. As such, in Figure 2 we consider the accuracy of each of our models with respect to the length (in characters) of the lacuna being reconstructed, and we observe that overall performance decreases as lacuna length increases. We also see that while the random-dynamic model has the best performance for lacunae of length 1-2, the smart-once model actually has better performance for lacunae of length 6+. For this reason, we recommend the smart-once model configuration for cases where the lacuna is more than a few characters. For our use case studies in Section 6, we consider outputs from both the random-dynamic model and the smart-once model.

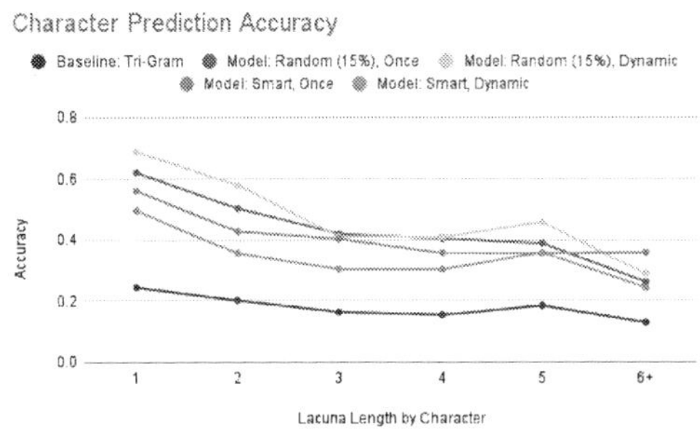

Figure 2: Accuracy of the various model configurations and tri-gram baseline relative to lacuna length in characters

5.3 Relative Ranking

As we saw in the previous section evaluating the quality of our RNN model outputs, performance on the more realistic reconstructed lacuna test set was relatively low, peaking at 37% accuracy. As such, we cannot consider the model by itself to be a definitive means of manuscript reconstruction. The model is better thought of as an additional tool in the toolbox of scholars attempting to reconstruct manuscript lacunae. To this end, we propose to use the RNN model as a means of ranking the likelihood of potential candidates for the lacuna reconstruction.

If a scholar has several candidates for a lacuna

from various qualitative methods of reconstruction, in addition to getting the model to predict what it considers to be the most likely reconstruction, we can also extract the probabilities associated with each of the scholar's potential reconstructions. Once we have these probabilities, we can sort them in descending order to get a ranking of which potential reconstructions the model considers to be more likely.[6] This will give a sense of which option is statistically the most likely considering the distribution of characters present in the training data of the model. While still not definitive, this ranking gives scholars another piece of evidence to consider when putting forward an argument for a particular reconstruction.

6 Case Studies

In this section, we demonstrate how our RNN model may be integrated into the workflow of a Coptic scholar working on manuscript reconstruction by looking at use cases in two early Coptic manuscripts. We use the model to predict reconstructions, or to produce relative rankings of potential reconstructions under consideration. We explore how this additional information may contribute to a scholar's considerations during the reconstruction process.

6.1 Isaiah 37:24

The manuscript P.Duk. inv. 282 comprises four contiguous fragments from a parchment codex and is currently held at Duke University, pictured in Figure 3 (Wagner, 2022). The manuscript contains portions of Isaiah chapters 36–38 in the Sahidic dialect. The manuscript's date is unknown. Some lacunae in the manuscript can be restored on the basis of the only other Sahidic manuscript containing these chapters, Morgan Library M 568. For example, at Isaiah 36:16 there are two small lacunae in the Duke manuscript: ⲁ[..]ⲛⲧ̣ⲉ[.]ⲛ̄ⲥⲉⲙⲟⲟⲩ. We can restore the original reading with confidence from the Morgan manuscript: ⲁ[ⲩⲱ] ⲛⲧ̣ⲉ[ⲧ]ⲛ̄ⲥⲉ ⲙⲟⲟⲩ ("and you will drink water").

Other lacunae in the Duke manuscript cannot be restored entirely on the basis of the Morgan manuscript. For example, at Isaiah 37:24 there are four lacunae: ⲁⲕⲛⲟ[.......]ⲉⲓⲥ-ⲁ[.....]ϫⲉϩⲙⲡ̣̄[.......]ⲁ̣ⲣⲙⲁϯ[.......]ⲣⲁⲓ̈ⲉⲛ

Figure 3: P.Duk. inv. 282 fr. B verso

[....]. The Morgan manuscript helps restore the passage excluding the penultimate lacuna: ⲁⲕⲛⲟ[ϭⲛⲉϭ ⲡϫⲟ]ⲉⲓⲥ ⲁ[ⲕϫⲟⲟⲥ] ϫⲉϩⲙⲡ̣̄[ⲁϣⲁⲓ̈ ⲛⲛϩ]ⲁ̣ⲣⲙⲁ ϯ[..... ⲉϩ]ⲣⲁⲓ̈ ⲉⲡ[ϫⲓⲥⲉ] ("You have reproached the Lord. You said, 'with the multitude of my chariots [...] to the height."). Where the Duke manuscript has ϯ[, the Morgan manuscript contains the past tense conjugation base verb: ⲁⲓ̈ⲁⲗⲉ ⲉϩⲣⲁⲓ̈ ⲉⲡϫⲓⲥⲉ ("I have gone up to the height."). Still, as in the Morgan manuscript, the Duke manuscript must contain a verb in the lacuna followed by ⲉϩⲣⲁⲓ "up". Thus the letter before the lacuna can only be the personal subject prefix ϯ - "I", which must be followed by a present or future tense verb. Restricting our search to verbs that are both contextually appropriate and appear in high frequency in the database of the Coptic SCRIPTORIUM project, we propose three reconstructions. The models rank each reconstruction as a sequence of consecutive characters, including uninterrupted context following and especially before the gap: ⲁⲕⲛⲟϭⲛⲉϭⲡ̄ϫⲟⲉⲓⲥⲁⲕϫⲟⲟ-ⲥϫⲉϩⲙⲡⲁϣⲁⲓⲛⲛϩⲁⲣⲙⲁϯ[.....]ⲉϩⲣⲁⲓ. The three reconstructions from the random-dynamic model are as follows, in order of probability (the log probability[7] of each sequence is included in parenthesis):

[6]One limitation of this is that in order for the probabilities to be compatible, the input context for the model must be the same. This means that all candidates being compared must be of the same character length.

[7]Log probabilities are used to avoid potential numerical underflow that can result from the multiplication of standard probabilities when calculating the likelihood of a sequence.

1. ⲙⲟⲟϣⲉ (-11.16) → ϯ[ⲙⲟⲟϣⲉ] ⲉϩⲣⲁⲓ
   "I am walking up"

2. ⲛⲁⲃⲱⲕ (-12.27) → ϯ[ⲛⲁⲃⲱⲕ] ⲉϩⲣⲁⲓ
   "I will go up"

3. ⲛⲁⲁⲗⲉ (-12.60) → ϯ[ⲛⲁⲁⲗⲉ] ⲉϩⲣⲁⲓ
   "I will rise up"

The first result, which is in the durative present tense, is less appealing than the other results when considering the other ancient language witnesses to this passage in Isaiah. To the best of our knowledge, all witnesses approximate the Morgan manuscript's past tense, except for two witnesses that give the future: the Syriac Peshitta (*'n' 'sq*, 'I will go up") and some manuscripts of Jerome's *Commentary on Isaiah* (11.7: *ego ascendam*, "I will go up"). These two witnesses increase the probability of the second and third result, both of which are in the future tense (signaled by the auxiliary ⲛⲁ). Although ranked lower by the model, some scholars would surely prefer the third result over the second, since, as we saw above, the same verb (ⲁⲗⲉ) appears in this passage in the Morgan manuscript. On the other hand, beyond its higher ranking, ⲃⲱⲕ appears far more often in Old Testament books and especially in Isaiah: in the Morgan manuscript ⲃⲱⲕ is used five times in ch. 37 alone, while ⲁⲗⲉ appears only here at the point of disagreement with the Duke manuscript. Thus the most plausible restoration of the passage: ⲁ[ⲕϫⲟⲟⲥ] ϫⲉϩⲙⲡ̄[ⲁϣⲁⲓ̈ ⲛⲛϩ]ⲁⲣⲙⲁ ϯ[ⲛⲁⲃⲱⲕ ⲉϩ]ⲣⲁⲓ̈ ⲉⲡϫⲓⲥⲉ "You have reproached the Lord. You said, 'with the multitude of my chariots I will go up to the height."

6.2 The Nag Hammadi Library – *Gospel of Philip*

The *Gospel of Philip* (*GPhilip*) is the third composition included in codex II of the Nag Hammadi (NH) library, a collection of thirteen papyrus codices containing a diverse range of ancient Christian texts. Unlike the example discussed in Section 6.1, there are no other surviving manuscript versions of (*GPhilip*). The codex sustained moderate damage to the top and bottom margins and most of its leaves contain peninsula-shaped lacunae[8].

The restoration of Saying 55 (63.30-64.5) has been a particular point of scholarly intrigue. While smaller gaps in the Saying can be restored with some confidence, scholars have proposed various readings for one lacuna of 5-6 letters, which contains the object of the verb ⲁⲥⲡⲁⲍⲉ or "kiss." The passage, which describes Jesus kissing Mary Magdalene, reads: ⲡⲉϥⲁⲥⲡⲁⲍⲉ ⲙⲙⲟⲥ ⲁ-ⲧⲉⲥ...ⲛϩⲁϩ ⲛⲥⲟⲡ, "He used to kiss her on the ..... many times" (63.35-36).

This case presents an especially challenging reconstruction due to the size of the lacuna. As discussed above (Section 5.2), the accuracy of the model degrades as the size of the lacuna increases. We consider outputs from both the smart-once model, which provides the highest accuracy rates for longer lacunae, and the random-dynamic model, which provides the highest accuracy rates for short lacunae.

Since the model is trained on Sahidic texts, the Saying needs to follow the orthographic conventions of the Sahidic dialect. Thus we changed the prenominal preposition ⲁ- 'towards, on' to ⲉ- (in the Sahidic dialect ⲁ is the past tense marker), resulting in the input text: ⲁⲥⲡⲁⲍⲉ ⲙ̄ⲙⲟⲥ ⲉ-ⲧⲉⲥ[.....] ⲛ̄ϩⲁϩ ⲛ̄ⲥⲟⲡ "kissed her on her ... on many occasions".

The four letters before the lacuna includes an indirect object construction headed with preposition ⲁ followed by a feminine possessive article ⲧⲉⲥ- "hers." Due to this syntactic environment, reconstructions are limited to feminine nouns, likely a body part in this case. To fill the lacuna, we have the models produce their predictions for either a 5 character gap or a 6 character gap:

Smart-Once:

- 5 spaces: ϩⲏⲧⲉⲛ
- 6 spaces: ϩⲏⲧⲉⲉⲉ

Random-Dynamic:

- 5 spaces: ϩⲟⲟⲉⲉ
- 6 spaces: ϩⲟⲟⲉⲉⲉ

Unfortunately, none of the reconstructions produce an attested Coptic lemma.

However, the models can still be leveraged to compare editorial suggestions and assign greater or lesser probability of editorial reconstructions. In this case, editors Bentley Layton and Hans-Martin Schenke propose several options for a 5 letter feminine body part: Schenke proposes "mouth" (ⲧⲁ-ⲡⲣⲟ). Layton offers multiple readings: "mouth" (ⲡⲁⲓϭⲉ or ⲧⲁⲡⲣⲟ), "cheek" (ⲟⲩⲟϭⲉ), "foot" (ϭⲁ-ⲗⲟϫ), and "forehead"(ⲧⲉϩⲡⲉ) as possible candidates (Schenke, 1997; Layton and Isenberg, 1989).

[8] Archival photo of the manuscript: https://ccdl.claremont.edu/digital/collection/nha/id/2962/rec/182

The editors present these candidates in an unordered manner, not singling out any one as being particularly more likely than the others.

Table 2 compares the output of smart-once model and the random-dynamic model, and contrasts the confidence of each model's top two predictions (again, not attested Coptic lemmas) with the list of attested feminine nouns supplied by the editors. As the table details, the lemma (ⲟⲩⲟϭⲉ), "cheek" is favored by the smart-once model and the lemma (ⲧⲉϩⲛⲉ), "forehead" is preferred by the random-dynamic model. Both of these results differ from Schenke's reconstruction of ⲧⲁⲡⲣⲟ, "mouth" (Schenke, 1997).

Table 2 also compares the effect of normalization on the model reconstructions. As discussed above in Section 3, the Coptic SCRIPTORIUM data utilized to train the model includes both normalized and original (un-normalized) data. We hypothesized that the normalization of dialect differences to conform to Sahidic orthography would greatly impact the results. However, in the end, the normalization had little impact and only slightly modified the ranking orders and confidence as Table 2 documents. Note the slightly different ranking of ⲛⲁⲓϭⲉ and ⲧⲁⲡⲣⲟ, two different words meaning "mouth," by the smart-once model.

These models provide quantitative data about reconstructions and offers a relative ranking of the alternatives proposed by text editors. In cases like the one discussed above in *GPhilip* where editors have provided multiple possible reconstructions to fill the lacuna and comparison to other manuscripts is not possible, this is an especially valuable tool in assisting readers in deciding which reading best fits within their comprehension of the passage.

7 Conclusion

In this paper, we presented a bidirectional RNN architecture to reconstruct lacunae in Coptic manuscripts. When training our masked language model for character prediction, we explored different masking strategies for masking distribution (random and smart) and re-masking frequency. We evaluated our models against both artificially masked data and scholar-reconstructed lacunae. We found that the performance of our models declined as the length of the lacunae being reconstructed increased, peaking at above 70% for single character reconstruction and below 40% for lacunae of length 6+ characters. And while the model trained with random masking performed with higher accuracy for single character reconstruction, the model trained with smart masking performed with higher accuracy on the reconstruction of longer lacunae, which is more similar to the real world use case, as it is more difficult for scholars to qualitatively reconstruct longer lacunae.

Using the judgments from these models, we explored two use cases of lacuna reconstruction from ancient Coptic manuscripts. We considered not only the direct predictions from the models, but also the likelihood ranking of reconstruction candidates already under consideration from the past proposals of various scholars of Coptic. Despite the low accuracy of the models on reconstructing lacunae of more than a few characters, we see that the rankings can still be leveraged to provide additional quantitative evidence alongside traditional qualitative methods. This initial application of neural methods to Coptic manuscript reconstruction shows the potential for integrating the judgments of models with the existing qualitative methods used by scholars working on manuscript reconstruction.

Limitations

As previously discussed in Section 5, the quality of our RNN models is relatively low, limiting the utility of its judgments. As we primarily consider a single model architecture in this investigation, in future work it would be beneficial to explore architectures beyond RNNs and training tasks beyond masked language modeling. In addition to different architectures, we believe there is much room for exploring different inputs for model training, including lexicographic information (what possible words might be, for example using a digital Coptic dictionary such as Feder et al. 2018), or linguistic annotations, such as morphosyntactic information provided by Coptic treebank data and corresponding parsers (Zeldes and Abrams, 2018; Zeldes and Schroeder, 2016).

Additionally, our current model does not account for the diacritics used in Coptic writing, and it is trained on a sentence-wise basis without incorporating document-level information, such as the surrounding sentences, or details about the page layout. Future work may benefit from incorporating diacritics and additional context into the training paradigm for the model. Future work should also include the ability to give a ranking of lacuna candidates of different lengths, which is not currently

Smart-Once Norm	Smart-Once Orig	Random-Dynamic Norm	Random-Dynamic Orig
ϩⲏⲧⲉⲛ *NA* (-6.89)	ϩⲏⲧⲉⲛ *NA* (-7.69)	ϩⲟⲟⲉⲉ *NA* (-7.88)	ϩⲟⲟⲉⲉ *NA* (-8.05)
ϩⲟⲟⲉⲉ *NA* (-8.08)	ϩⲟⲟⲉⲉ *NA* (-7.99)	ϩⲏⲧⲉⲛ *NA* (-11.51)	ϩⲏⲧⲉⲛ *NA* (-11.90)
ⲟⲩⲟϭⲉ *cheek* (-16.11)	ⲟⲩⲟϭⲉ *cheek* (-15.64)	ⲧⲉϩⲛⲉ *forehead* (-12.95)	ⲧⲉϩⲛⲉ *forehead* (-13.08)
ⲧⲉϩⲛⲉ *forehead* (-16.53)	ⲧⲉϩⲛⲉ *forehead* (-16.42)	ⲟⲩⲟϭⲉ *cheek* (-13.16)	ⲟⲩⲟϭⲉ *cheek* (-14.39)
ϭⲁⲗⲟϫ *foot* (-17.35)	ϭⲁⲗⲟϫ *foot* (-17.42)	ⲧⲁⲡⲣⲟ *mouth* (-14.66)	ⲧⲁⲡⲣⲟ *mouth* (-14.79)
ⲡⲁⲓϭⲉ *mouth* (-18.74)	ⲧⲁⲡⲣⲟ *mouth* (-18.64)	ⲡⲁⲓϭⲉ *mouth* (-16.12)	ⲡⲁⲓϭⲉ *mouth* (-15.36)
ⲧⲁⲡⲣⲟ *mouth* (-19.02)	ⲡⲁⲓϭⲉ *mouth* (-18.71)	ϭⲁⲗⲟϫ *foot* (-16.94)	ϭⲁⲗⲟϫ *foot* (-16.48)

Table 2: Rankings of lacuna candidates for the *GPhilip* use case (English translation in italics and log probabilities in parenthesis)

possible because model inputs must be of the same sequence length for their probabilities to be comparable.

Acknowledgements

This research was generously supported by a major grant from the National Endowment for the Humanities Humanities Collections and Reference Resources (PW-290519-23).

References

Yannis Assael, Thea Sommerschield, and Jonathan Prag. 2019. Restoring ancient text using deep learning: a case study on Greek epigraphy. In *Proceedings of the 2019 Conference on Empirical Methods in Natural Language Processing and the 9th International Joint Conference on Natural Language Processing (EMNLP-IJCNLP)*, pages 6368–6375, Hong Kong, China. Association for Computational Linguistics.

Andrea Brunello, Emanuela Colombi, Alessandro Locaputo, Stefano Magnani, Nicola Saccomanno, and Giuseppe Serra. 2023. Usage of language model for the filling of lacunae in ancient Latin inscriptions: A case study. In *Proceedings of the 2nd Workshop on Artificial Intelligence for Cultural Heritage (IAI4CH 2023) co-located with the 22nd International Conference of the Italian Association for Artificial Intelligence (AIxIA 2023), Roma, Italy, November 6, 2023*, volume 3536 of *CEUR Workshop Proceedings*, pages 113–125. CEUR-WS.org.

Kevin Clark, Minh-Thang Luong, Quoc V. Le, and Christopher D. Manning. 2020. ELECTRA: Pre-training text encoders as discriminators rather than generators. In *ICLR*.

Jacob Devlin, Ming-Wei Chang, Kenton Lee, and Kristina Toutanova. 2019. Bert: Pre-training of deep bidirectional transformers for language understanding. *Preprint*, arXiv:1810.04805.

Frank Feder, Maxim Kupreyev, Emma Manning, Caroline T. Schroeder, and Amir Zeldes. 2018. A linked Coptic dictionary online. In *Proceedings of the Second Joint SIGHUM Workshop on Computational Linguistics for Cultural Heritage, Social Sciences, Humanities and Literature*, pages 12–21, Santa Fe, New Mexico. Association for Computational Linguistics.

Taku Kudo and John Richardson. 2018. SentencePiece: A simple and language independent subword tokenizer and detokenizer for neural text processing. In *Proceedings of the 2018 Conference on Empirical Methods in Natural Language Processing: System Demonstrations*, pages 66–71, Brussels, Belgium. Association for Computational Linguistics.

Bentley Layton. 2011. *A Coptic Grammar*, third edition, revised and expanded edition. Porta linguarum orientalium 20. Harrassowitz, Wiesbaden.

Bentley Layton and Wesley W. Isenberg. 1989. *The Gospel of Philip, Nag Hammadi Codex II, 2-7*. NHS 20. Brill, Leiden.

Mallory E. Matsumoto. 2022. Archaeology and epigraphy in the digital era. *Journal of Archaeological Research*, 30(2):285–320.

Deepak Mishra. 2021. [Masked] Language Modeling with Recurrent Neural Networks. *Medium*.

Anna Novokhatko and Felix K. Maier. 2022. Digital methods of analysing and reconstructing Ancient Greek and Latin texts. *Classics@*, 20.

Matthew E. Peters, Mark Neumann, Mohit Iyyer, Matt Gardner, Christopher Clark, Kenton Lee, and Luke

Zettlemoyer. 2018. Deep contextualized word representations. In *Proceedings of the 2018 Conference of the North American Chapter of the Association for Computational Linguistics: Human Language Technologies, Volume 1 (Long Papers)*, pages 2227–2237, New Orleans, Louisiana. Association for Computational Linguistics.

Rajesh P. N. Rao, Nisha Yadav, Mayank N. Vahia, Hrishikesh Joglekar, R. Adhikari, and Iravatham Mahadevan. 2009. A markov model of the indus script. *Proceedings of the National Academy of Sciences*, 106(33):13685–13690.

Hans-Martin Schenke. 1997. *Das Philippus-Evangelium (Nag-Hammadi-Codex II,3). Neu herausgegeben, übersetzt und erklärt.* Texte und Untersuchungen 143. Akademie, Berlin.

Caroline T Schroeder and Amir Zeldes. 2016. Raiders of the Lost Corpus. *Digital humanities quarterly*, 10(2). Place: Providence.

Charlotte Schubert. 2011. Das portal eaqua: Neue methoden in der geisteswissenschaftlichen forschung ii. Technical report, Universität Leipzig.

Thea Sommerschield, Yannis Assael, John Pavlopoulos, Vanessa Stefanak, Andrew Senior, Chris Dyer, John Bodel, Jonathan Prag, Ion Androutsopoulos, and Nando de Freitas. 2023. Machine Learning for Ancient Languages: A Survey. *Computational Linguistics*, 49(3):703–747.

Nikolai Vogler, Jonathan Allen, Matthew Miller, and Taylor Berg-Kirkpatrick. 2022. Lacuna reconstruction: Self-supervised pre-training for low-resource historical document transcription. In *Findings of the Association for Computational Linguistics: NAACL 2022*, pages 206–216, Seattle, United States. Association for Computational Linguistics.

Nicholas E. Wagner. 2022. Fragments of Sahidic Isaiah at Duke University (P.Duk. inv. 282). *Journal of Coptic studies*, 24:319–330.

Tommy Wasserman. 2013. Criteria for evaluating readings in New Testament textual criticism. In Bart D. Ehrman and Michael W. Holmes, editors, *The Text of the New Testament in Contemporary Research: Essays on the Status Quaestionis*, pages 579–612. Brill, Leiden, The Netherlands.

Amir Zeldes and Mitchell Abrams. 2018. The Coptic Universal Dependency treebank. In *Proceedings of the Second Workshop on Universal Dependencies (UDW 2018)*, pages 192–201, Brussels, Belgium. Association for Computational Linguistics.

Amir Zeldes and Caroline T. Schroeder. 2016. An NLP pipeline for Coptic. In *Proceedings of the 10th SIGHUM Workshop on Language Technology for Cultural Heritage, Social Sciences, and Humanities*, pages 146–155, Berlin, Germany. Association for Computational Linguistics.

Shuo Zhang and Amir Zeldes. 2017. GitDOX: A linked version controlled online XML editor for manuscript transcription. In *Proceedings of FLAIRS-30*, pages 619–623, Marco Island, FL.

Deep Learning Meets Egyptology: a Hieroglyphic Transformer for Translating Ancient Egyptian

Mattia De Cao*[†], Nicola De Cao[‡], Angelo Colonna[†], Alessandro Lenci[†]
[†]Universitá di Pisa, [‡]Google DeepMind
mattia.dc96@gmail.com, ndecao@google.com
angelo.colonna@unipi.it, alessandro.lenci@unipi.it

Abstract

This work explores the potential of Transformer models focusing on the translation of ancient Egyptian hieroglyphs. We present a novel Hieroglyphic Transformer model, built upon the powerful M2M-100 multilingual translation framework and trained on a dataset we customised from the *Thesaurus Linguae Aegyptiae* database. Our experiments demonstrate promising results, with the model achieving significant accuracy in translating hieroglyphic into both German and English. This work holds significant implications for Egyptology, potentially accelerating the translation process and unlocking new research approaches. Source code at `https://github.com/mattia-decao/hiero-transformer`.

1 Introduction

Egyptology, with its rich trove of texts and inscriptions, has recently begun to embrace the potential of computational linguistics. However, a notable scarcity of publications on the topic is evident, with existing efforts primarily focused on optical recognition of hieroglyphs rather than their translation (Sommerschield et al., 2023). Notably, the development of these resources primarily originates from computer science disciplines and highlights the need for deeper integration with Egyptology field.

We bridge this gap by proposing an Egyptology-driven automatic translation approach, merging Egyptology with Natural Language Processing (NLP) tools. Our Hieroglyphic Transformer translates ancient Egyptian using an adaptation of M2M-100 multilingual model (Fan et al., 2021) to address hieroglyphic writing's challenges. We construct a meticulously curated dataset derived from the renowned database project *Thesaurus Linguae Aegyptiae* (TLA; Richter and Werning, 2023),[1] ensuring its compatibility with the model through rigorous data filtering, cleaning and structuring.

Experiments yield promising results, with the Hieroglyphic Transformer achieving reasonable accuracy in translating hieroglyphs into both German and English. Furthermore, we evaluate the model's performance on texts of varying grammatical complexity and literary styles, highlighting its capacity to handle diverse linguistic structures.

This work holds significant implications for Egyptology. NLP-powered approaches like ours can potentially accelerate and improve translation accuracy and depth. Furthermore, it paves the way for applying Deep Learning models to decipher and translate other ancient languages.

The main contributions of our work can be summarised as follows:

1. presenting a new dataset extracted from the TLA database;
2. adapting a pretrained model to translate Hieroglyphic;
3. showing an automatic and a human evaluation of the model's performance.

2 Background

2.1 Machine Translation for Ancient Languages

The linguistic diversity of the world encompasses over 7,000 distinct languages. Of these, English, Chinese, Spanish, Japanese, and other Eu-

*Mattia De Cao made the most significant contributions to this study, including developing the study conception and its elaboration, designing the experiments, mining/analyzing the data and writing the manuscript. Nicola De Cao supported the implementation of computational models, created the paper layout, and revised the manuscript. Angelo Colonna reviewed the human evaluation process and ancient Egyptian background material. Alessandro Lenci contributed to widening the automatic evaluation phase and provided technical review.

[1]`https://thesaurus-linguae-aegyptiae.de`

Proceedings of the 1st Workshop on Machine Learning for Ancient Languages (ML4AL 2024), pages 71–86
August 15, 2024

ropean languages represent the most extensive corpora (Summer Institute of Linguistics, 2024; UNESCO, 2024), while languages spoken primarily in Asia and Africa often lack comparable data resources (even thousands of times less). These "low-resource" languages attract research from both humanistic and engineering perspectives, with studies offering novel ideas (Aharoni et al., 2019) or exploring understudied niches (Ahia and Ogueji, 2020).

Ancient languages are also part of this wave, but most of their data remains non-machine-readable (i.e., images of objects with text on them or scans of parchment or papyri). Thus most of the recent attention from the machine learning community was directed to Optical Character Recognition (OCR). Major case of these studies include: (i) Kuzushiji, a Japanese cursive script of 8th-18th centuries (Lamb et al., 2020); (ii) Mayan hieroglyphs (Roman-Rangel et al., 2009); (iii) ancient Chinese character manuscripts (Sun et al., 2022); (iv) Sumerian cuneiform (Ahmed H. et al., 2020); and (v) Akkadian cuneiform (Gutherz et al., 2023).

While ancient Egyptian has a decent amount of data available, a substantial portion remains non-machine-readable, primarily in physical books and articles. Even though these sources are accessible online, they necessitate significant digitization efforts for effective utilization in language processing.[2]

Fortunately, the Egyptian language benefits from the numerous publications digitized and translated into German and English collected in the monumental project *Thesaurus Linguae Aegyptiae* (TLA; Richter and Werning, 2023) which we use as the source of data in this work.

2.2 Related Work

The majority of recent research in Egyptology using AI focuses primarily on OCR. Examples of such studies include those conducted by Franken and Van Gemert (2013); Hossam et al. (2018); Barucci et al. (2021); Moustafa et al. (2022); Barucci et al. (2023).

Apart from OCR, to the best of our knowledge, only a single publication addresses the task of translation. This work was undertaken by Wiesenbach and Riezler (2019), who sought to address the scarcity of resources by incorporating transliteration and POS tags into the training process. This scarcity of publications highlights the need for further research in the application of AI to Egyptology.

2.3 Ancient Egyptian Language

The ancient Egyptian language is a member of the so-called Afro-Asiatic language family and one of the longest continuously attested, having been used from approximately 3200 BCE to 1100 CE (Allen, 2014). Its historical development is usually articulated in six phases: Archaic Egyptian, Old Egyptian, Middle Egyptian, Late Egyptian, Demotic, and Coptic.

Notably, Middle Egyptian (2100-1600 BC) retained its status as a "classical" language for the production of historical and religious texts even after its decline as a spoken language, persisting until the end of ancient Egyptian history. For this reason, we opted for Middle Egyptian as the reference language to train the models in our study (to which we added Old Egyptian as later explained in Section 3.2).

Throughout its existence, ancient Egyptian employed four primary writing systems: hieroglyphic, hieratic, demotic, and coptic. **Hieroglyphic** consists of pictorial signs mostly carved in stone and used in monumental contexts. **Hieratic**, was a simplified and cursive form of hieroglyphic, used for writing on ostraca and papyri. **Demotic**, a late cursive script developed from hieratic, was exclusively employed during the language phase of the same name. **Coptic** writing was derived from the Greek alphabet, with seven additional letters from Demotic to express sounds absent in Greek , and was solely used to write Coptic.

In this work, we used hieroglyphic (or hieratic transcribed to hieroglyphic) because demotic and coptic scripts were used to write language phases other than the ones we chose to employ, i.e., Old and Middle Egyptian. Therefore we will not expand on the other writing systems. For more information about the ancient Egyptian language system, we redirect the reader to Loprieno (1995).

2.4 Hieroglyphs

A hieroglyph can be classified into three distinct categories: *ideogram*, *phonogram*, and *determinative* (Allen, 2014).

Ideograms indicate the word that they depict. In this way, for example, the hieroglyph 𓂋 repre-

[2]A significant portion of Egyptological articles and books available online have been digitized as images or in a format that hinders machine data extraction. Thus, the first step in making these data usable would be transcribing them into a machine-readable format.

Sign	Gardiner code	Transliteration	Description
𓄿	G1	ꜣ	Egyptian vulture
𓆑	I9	f	Horned viper
𓍑	V24	wd□	Cord wound on stick
𓋞	S12	nbw	Bead collar

Table 1: Example of hieroglyphs and their Gardiner code, Transliteration and Description.

senting a mouth writes the word "mouth", while the hieroglyph 𓉐 representing a house's top view is actually the word "house".

Phonograms represent the phonetic structure (sounds) of the individual word depicted according to the rebus principle. For example the sign 𓂋 is used to express the phoneme *r*.

Determinatives are used to indicate the semantic sphere of the preceding words, and so these signs are not meant to be pronounced. For example, the hieroglyph 𓉐 , used as determinative, refers to words belonging in the semantic sphere of enclosed spaces and is not read.

2.5 Gardiner Code

The Gardiner code, also called Gardiner's Sign List, represents the standard system used to identify hieroglyphic signs through alphanumeric codes. It was compiled by the English egyptologist and phololologist Alan H. Gardiner as an integral part of his Egyptian grammar (Gardiner, 1957), which remains a standard reference in the Egyptian language study.

The Gardiner code consists of main categories identified by a capital letter of the English alphabet and a descriptive label (e.g., "A. Human beings, male"). Within these sections, each hieroglyph is assigned a progressive number (e.g., 𓀀 = A1, 𓀁 = A2). For subsequent additions of sign variants, later than the original Gardiner's list itself, a lowercase letter was added after the number (e.g., in the section "N. Sky, earth, water", we find 𓈖 = N35, 𓈗 = N35a).

2.6 Transliteration

In Egyptology, transliteration is the process of converting hieroglyphs into alphabetical symbols to represent the consonants of ancient Egyptian. It is a convention that makes it possible to organize hieroglyphic signs into dictionaries. The transliteration can also be pronounced, but it should always be remembered that only consonants were written (not vowels), and in many cases, the phonetic value of the signs is unknown. We can only infer the pronunciation based on the Coptic forms as well as on the spelling of Egyptian words in other ancient languages, and vice versa (Allen, 2014). Phonograms and most ideograms can be transliterated into one, two, or three consonants, depending on the number of sounds they represent. For instance, the sign 𓅓 represents one consonant *m*, the sign 𓄟 represents *ms*, and the sign 𓋞 represents *nbw*. See Table 1 for examples of hieroglyphs with their Gardiner code, transliteration, and description.

3 Dataset Construction

This work is based on a snapshot collected from the database that also feeds the *Thesaurus Linguae Aegyptiae* (TLA; Richter and Werning, 2023)[3] and last updated in 2018.

3.1 Thesaurus Linguae Aegyptiae

The TLA project aims "to document and annotate the Ancient Egyptian language through its entire lifespan" (Richter and Werning, 2023). This objective manifests in two primary digital outcomes: the text corpus (*corpus dataset*) and the lemma list (*vocabulary dataset*).

The *corpus* encompasses a vast collection of hieroglyphic texts, transliterations, and translations. All entries come enriched with metadata such as production dates, script types and connections among data points. Notably, each corpus word is "lemmatized", i.e. linked to a specific entry in the lemma list. This allows researchers to access broader information spectrum per data point, including part-of-speech (POS) tags, for each element.

While most texts have German translations, some include English or both, promoting cross-language accessibility and the project's global reach.

[3]Project *Strukturen und Transformationen des Wortschatzes der ägyptischen Sprache: Text- und Wissenskultur im Alten Ägypten (Structure and Transformation in the Vocabulary of the Egyptian Language: Texts and Knowledge in the Culture of Ancient Egypt).*

3.2 Data Extraction

One of the major contributions of this study consists in the construction of a new dataset from the data collected by the TLA project. We chose Middle Egyptian as the reference language, as explained in section 2.3. However, limited data availability led us to include Old Egyptian (2700-2100 BC) due to its close linguistic relationship with Middle Egyptian, enriching the language representation. Our dataset includes specific elements for each data point. Unfortunately, not all elements were consistently present, preventing a complete construction. In Figure 1 we outline the structure of a data point in our dataset. Taking into account all the diverse elements, these include:

- **Gardiner code:** A unique identifier for each hieroglyph.
- **Transliteration:** The alphabetical representation of hieroglyphs.
- **Translation:** Either German or English.
- **Lemma IDs:** Numerical identifiers for lemmas (basic forms of words).
- **Token inflection codes:** Information about the inflectional forms of the lemmas morphologically marked in the script, such as gender and number of nouns.
- **Datapoint ID:** A unique identifier for the datapoint (each one is a text[4] containing several sentences).
- **Sentence ID:** A unique identifier for a single sentence in a text.
- **Part-of-speech tags:** Labels used to classify the lexical category of lemmas (e.g., noun, verb, adjective).
- **Metadata:** Unique IDs for data such as language phase, and historical period.

During the mining process, preliminary cleansing was performed to eliminate inconsistencies and irregularities, including: (i) tabs, (ii) carriage returns, (iii) line separators, (iv) excessive white space, and (v) multiple hyphens within hieroglyphs.

The total number of data points extracted was 103,906. We then focused on selecting Old and Middle Egyptian data points delving into language phase metadata. In cases where this information was absent but reliably inferable, we examined historical metadata to reconstruct it.[5] The total number of datapoints after filtering was 61,605.

```
{
 "source": <Source as Gardiner code>,
 "transliteration": <Transliteration>,
 "target": <Translation>,
 "lKey": <Lemma IDs>,
 "wordClass": <Part-of-speech tags>,
 "flexCode": <Inflection codes>,
 "metadata": {
  "target_lang": <Target language>,
  "id_datapoint": <Datapoint ID>,
  "id_sentence": <Sentence ID>,
  "language": <Language phase>,
  "date": <Historical period>,
  "script": <Script type>,
  "id_tree": <Assigned ID"
 }
}
```

Figure 1: Structure of a datapoint.

3.3 Data Cleaning

A crucial aspect of our work was the development of comprehensive cleansing operations. Initially, we meticulously hand-cleaned several texts, enabling the identification of recurring patterns and the formulation of generalizable cleansing procedures. This iterative process resulted in the creation of over 280 distinct cleaning operations (e.g., elimination of brackets '(', ')' and their contents in German translation, elimination of brackets '[' and ']' while maintaining the content in the transliteration, elimination of '!' from the hieroglyphs). In particular, *lacunae* were treated differently if they were reconstructed or not. If reconstruction was present, we used it; if not, we discarded the datapoint element (e.g. transliteration) as the training process could be altered. Reconstructions were always used.

An example of a datapoint cleansing process is presented in Table 2. A comprehensive compendium of the cleansing operations, including detailed descriptions, treatment methods, and underlying motivations, is provided in the GitHub repository for our project. [6]

3.4 Validation and Test sets

We randomly selected a validation and a test set comprising 100 distinct sources each. Some

[4]From Richter and Werning (2023): "A 'text' [...] in the TLA is an entity marked as an independent textual unit by clearly marked text delimiters (beginning and end). An individual text may either consist of writing only, or it may be a multimodal composition of writing and illustrations."

[5]In Appendix A we reported datapoint counts relating to both language and historical phases.

[6]`https://github.com/mattia-decao/hiero-transformer`

Gardiner code	Translation	Transliteration
	Raw	
Aa1-:D21 M17-S29 [?-*”□”-*I10-*”?”-*?]-:[?-*”□”-*D46-*”?”-*?] N25-:X1-*Z1 V30	and then every foreign land [says]:	ḫr js ꜥ⸢d□d⸣? ḫꜣs,t nb(.t)
	Cleaned	
Aa1 D21 M17 S29 I10 D46 N25 X1 Z1 V30	and then every foreign land says:	ḫr js d□d ḫꜣs,t nb.t

Table 2: Example of raw and cleaned datapoint (ID Sentence: `IBUBd91QAVzxpUWnqYiwnwLVrbI`. ID tree: `aaew_corpus_sawlit_687_107`).

sources had multiple translations (i.e., both in English and German) thus we included both versions in the set to (i) increase its size, and (ii) avoid contamination in the training set. Eventually, the validation set had 125 parallel data points, 25 of which possessed English translation, 75 German translation, and 25 containing only transliteration and hieroglyphic. Similarly, the test set had 150 data points, comprising 50 that possessed English translation, 50 German translation, and 50 containing only transliteration and hieroglyphic.

Source	Target	Datapoints
egy	de	16,075
egy	en	2,105
egy	τ	20,155
egy	lKey	21,036
egy	wordClass	20,045
τ	de	45,760
τ	en	2,174
τ	lKey	56,240
τ	wordClass	54,039

Table 3: Data pairs and their distribution among the datapoints.

4 Experimental Design

4.1 Data Pairing

Prior to feeding the data into the model, it was essential to organize the data points into source-target pairs. These represent the input-output pairings employed during training (e.g. Hieroglyphs to German). We used two sources as inputs: *egy*, i.e. Gardiner code of ancient Egyptian hieroglyphs; and τ, i.e., transliteration. Both of them were paired with five targets as outputs: (i) *de*, i.e. German; (ii) *en*, i.e. English; (iii) τ ; (iv) *lKey*, i.e. lemma IDs; and (v) *wordClass*, i.e. part-of-speech tags. We reported in Table 3 the list of all different data pairs employed, together with the count of data points in which each pair is present.

4.2 Training

We did not aim to develop novel machine learning techniques or models but rather to harness the capabilities of an existing one and apply it to the Ancient Egyptian language. We then chose to use the finetune M2M-100 model (Fan et al., 2021) for its versatility and effectiveness in multilingual machine translation. M2M-100, originally designed for translating between 100 modern languages, including English and German, was a compelling choice due to its open-source availability and relative novelty. By utilizing this pre-trained model, we effectively employed *transfer learning*, a powerful technique that leverages knowledge acquired from a related task to improve performance on a new task. For each experiment, we trained for between 6 and 20 epochs.[7]

We checked validation loss for model selection every 10% per epoch and employed early stopping if no improvement happened for the past 15-20 evaluations.[8] We used the Adam optimizer (Kingma and Ba, 2015) with batch size 16 and a fixed learning rate 3e-5.

We experimented with different mixtures of source and target (e.g., some included/ excluded the use of transliteration or POS tags). Overall, 11 models were trained,[9] and we reported a selection

[7]Initial experiments used 20 epochs, subsequently reduced due to: (i) no improvements after the third epoch, (ii) increased data pairs significantly extended execution time, and (iii) the 12-hour execution limit of the experimentation platform (Google Colab) rendered maintaining the same epochs impractical.

[8]This value was dynamically adjusted for each experiment due to variations in the amount of data-pairs.

[9]Due to cost constraints, we conducted most of our experiments with one NVIDIA T4 Tensor Core (16 GB), and the last model (ALL) that mixes all the data available, with one NVIDIA A100-SXM4 Tensor Core (40 GB). For ALL we

	SacreBLEU					RougeL				
Source	**egy**			$\mathcal{T}$		**egy**			$\mathcal{T}$	
Target	**de**	**en**	$\mathcal{T}$	**de**	**en**	**de**	**en**	$\mathcal{T}$	**de**	**en**
DE (raw)	4.0	-	-	-	-	18.4	-	-	-	-
DE	54.4	-	-	-	-	62.8	-	-	-	-
DE+EN	52.6	28.4	-	-	-	63.1	33.5	-	-	-
DE+EN^{B}	**61.5**	**36.4**	-	-	-	**67.7**	**38.1**	-	-	-
DE+$\mathcal{T}$	43.2	-	57.7	54.0	-	55.4	-	78.9	61.8	-
DE+$\mathcal{T}$+EN^{B}	47.6	20.1	58.4	47.1	30.3	58.8	27.9	80.2	**63.1**	37.5
ALL	54.4	31.6	**59.9**	**56.2**	**35.3**	64.5	35.5	**82.1**	62.7	**38.1**

Table 4: Results of automatic evaluation (SacreBLEU, RougeL). **Bold** results are best and underlined are second best.

in Table 4. The comprehensive table of all experiment metrics results can be found in Tables 8 and 9 in Appendix E.

In the training phase, we gave single data (e.g., transliteration or German translation) to the model by assigning them a special language id token (used as prefix in both the source and target text) already present within the model itself. These were *en* for English, *de* for German, *ar* (Arab) for ancient Egyptian, *th* (Thai) for POS tags, *lo* (Lao) for transliteration and *my* (Burmese) for lemma IDs. Except for German, English, and ancient Egyptian[10], the codes were arbitrarily selected from Fan et al. (2021) in order to avoid their duplication in the list where data quantities derived from other languages and language groups are presented (Figure 3 of the same article).

Backtranslation Due to the scarcity of data points containing English translations, we employed the M2M-100 model to translate our entire dataset from German to English and incorporated these translations into training.

4.3 Metrics

To assess the performance of the conducted experiments, we employed two automated evaluation metrics: SacreBLEU (Post, 2018) and RougeL (Lin, 2004).

Automatic metrics do not always correlate with human judgment, so we also employed a human evaluation. For that, we applied the model to a series of examples, 16 in total,[11] exhibiting a variety of grammatical constructions (listed in Appendix B), subsequently comparing the model's output against our own translations or those derived from established publications (Bresciani, 1969; Allen, 2015; Grapow, 1952; Gardiner, 1969; Vogelsang, 1913). During the comparison, we rigorously examined all the distinct data pairs generated by the model, evaluating both the quantity and quality of its correct and erroneous outputs.

5 Results

5.1 Data Cleaning

To assess the effectiveness of our cleaning operations, we conducted and compared two experiments: (i) DE (raw), with raw data; (ii) DE, after the cleaning. Cleaning the data increased the resulting SacreBLEU from 4.0 to 54.4 and RougeL from 18.4 to 62.8. As evident, results have demonstrated that our cleaning procedure significantly improves the model's training performance.

5.2 Main Results

As evident in Table 4, for translation and transliteration the ALL model (i.e., trained with all data) exhibits the best or second-best performance. This suggests that the model successfully incorporates signals from different forms (e.g., POS tags and transliteration).

Unsurprisingly, mixing back-translation data (DE+EN v.s. DE+EN^{B}) significantly increases performance in English (SacreBLEU 52 $\rightarrow$ 61 and RougeL 33 $\rightarrow$ 38). However, it surprisingly increases performance in German as well.

Notably, the DE+EN^{B} model shows the highest accuracy from hieroglyphic to German and English translation. Moreover, both DE+$\mathcal{T}$ and DE+$\mathcal{T}$+EN^{B}

increased the batch size to 180.

[10]We hypothesized that using Arab for ancient Egyptian could potentially enhance model performance due to its similarities in sentence construction, i.e. verb-subject-object. Further research is required to corroborate this hypothesis.

[11]Of these, 15 were composed of one to three sentences, 1 of eleven.

do not perform better than DE and DE+EN^{B} in German and English. These results suggest that adding transliteration during training may have some detrimental effects on accuracy. We reported a comprehensive list of results in Tables 8 and 9 in Appendix E.

5.3 N-fold cross validation analysis

We did a 10-fold cross-validation to DE and ALL experiments.[12] The M2M-100 model was subjected to the same conditions as the previous DE and ALL experiments, allowing for a direct comparison of their performance under different evaluation methods.

The results for the DE experiment exhibited a significant discrepancy, while the performance metrics for ALL were more consistent with the previous findings. This suggests that the validation and test datasets employed previously may have introduced a selection bias, which was mitigated by the larger and more diverse data submitted to training ALL. We reported the full results of n-fold cross validation analysis in Table 10 of Appendix E.

This finding highlights the importance of employing rigorous evaluation strategies to ensure reliable machine learning models, particularly in the context of low-resource languages like ancient Egyptian.

5.4 Human Evaluation

Following the training phase, the model ALL was identified as the most promising candidate due to its superior performance across all data pairs. In this phase, its effectiveness was assessed through a comprehensive trial procedure.

We divided the evaluation process into three distinct steps: (i) Grammatical Complexity, (ii) Literary Passages, and (iii) Stress Test. For every step our evaluation proceeded to analyze all the data pairs (detailed in Section 4.1).

For each Human Evaluation step, the model was submitted to two separate testing waves. In the first wave, the input was presented to the model as Gardiner code, while in the second wave, it was presented as transliteration.

We assessed the sentences based on specific criteria, including: (i) Morphological accuracy; (ii) Grammatical correctness; (iii) Verb-subject agreement in number and gender; (iv) Adequacy of terminology; (v) Semantic coherence.

This two-pronged approach aimed to assess the model's performance under both input representations, i.e. hieroglyphic and transliteration. Through this trial procedure, the effectiveness of the ALL model was thoroughly evaluated, demonstrating its potential for a quite accurate and versatile writing of hieroglyphic into transliteration, and both inputs into German, English, Lemma IDs and POS tags. We reported the list of grammatical forms submitted as input in Appendix B.

5.4.1 Grammatical Complexity

We presented exercises of increasing grammatical complexity to the model to assess its ability to handle diverse grammatical structures. All the exercises were extracted from Gardiner's grammar (Gardiner, 1957). An excerpt is reported in Table 5. The model exhibits no significant difficulties, but rather, it is more sensitive to variations in sentence construction due to low-resource training.

5.4.2 Literary Passages

Passages taken from literary works, encompassing a wide range of grammatical elements and one to three clauses in length, were fed into the model to examine its performance in natural language contexts. The works selected were the "Story of Sinuhe", the "Tale of the Shipwrecked Sailor", the "Admonitions of Ipuwer", and "The Eloquent Peasant". We observed that the model performs slightly better than the previous phase. Additionally, we noticed higher translation accuracy with transliteration input compared to the Gardiner code.

5.4.3 Stress Test

We submitted a lengthy passage extracted from the "Story of Sinuhe" to thoroughly evaluate the model's robustness, testing its ability to handle extended and complex linguistic structures. After that, we submitted the same passage divided into single units. Due to the length of the passage, it has been reported in the GitHub repository for our project. [13] We observed that the model fails with lengthy sentences that exceed three clauses but, when provided with a sentence of one or two clauses, it produces quite accurate results.

5.4.4 Human Evaluation Conclusion

The ALL model performed better with short and medium-length input texts comprising one to two sentences. The generated outputs were effective,

[12] This technique was not applied to every experiments due to resource limitations.

[13] `https://github.com/mattia-decao/hiero-transformer`

Source

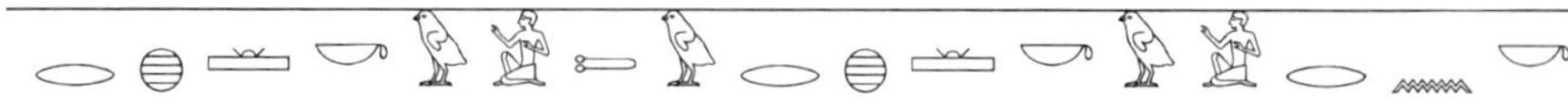

D21 Aa1 Y1 V31 G43 A1 V13 G43 D21 Aa1 Y1 V31 G43 A1 D21 N35 V31

Target	Prediction (from hieroglyphic)	Prediction (from transliteration)	Reference
DE	Ich kenne dich, ich kenne deinen Namen	Ich kenne dich und ich kenne deinen Namen	Ich kenne dich, ich kenne deinen Namen
EN	You know me, I know your name	I know you, I know your name	I know you, I know your name
$\mathcal{T}$	r.kwj ṯw r.kwj rn =k	–	rḫ.kw ṯw rḫ.kw rn =k
lkey	95620 44000 174900 95620 44000 94700 10110	95620 174900 95620 94700 10110	95620 174900 95620 94700 10110
pos	verb_2-lit personal_pronoun personal_pronoun verb_2-lit personal_pronoun personal_pronoun substanti	verb_2-lit personal_pronoun verb_2-lit substantive_masc personal_pronoun	verb_2-lit personal_pronoun verb_2-lit substantive_masc personal_pronoun

Table 5: Example of a grammar complexity exercise manually evaluated.

but there are occasional inconsistencies in completing the fields of transliteration, POS tags and occasionally lemma IDs. For input texts exceeding three sentences, the model struggles to produce exact predictions, particularly in terms of precision and completeness of writing.

Regarding the choice of input, despite transliteration is more accurate than Gardiner code, we recommend comparing both results to obtain a more comprehensive understanding.

We observed great accuracy in generating lemma IDs, indicating that they could be actively used to extract additional information from the TLA database.

Finally, the model exhibits no significant difficulties when submitted to an increasing grammatical complexity. Conversely, it struggles as the input length grows and the rare terms increase.

6 Conclusions

We publicly released our dataset and source code and designed them for easy utilization and assessment. The AI model produces suitable results for research applications and is user-friendly.

This work opens up avenues for future research, including expanding the dataset by incorporating other language phases (Late Egyptian, Demotic and Coptic), integrating additional modern languages , and conducting more comprehensive and diversified experiments.

These efforts could pave the way for enhanced model precision and contribute significantly to the advancement of research in Egyptology and the application of NLP to the translation and study of ancient languages.

References

Roee Aharoni, Melvin Johnson, and Orhan Firat. 2019. Massively multilingual neural machine translation. In *Proceedings of the 2019 Conference of the North American Chapter of the Association for Computational Linguistics: Human Language Technologies, Volume 1 (Long and Short Papers)*, pages 3874–3884, Minneapolis, Minnesota. Association for Computational Linguistics.

Orevaoghene Ahia and Kelechi Ogueji. 2020. Towards supervised and unsupervised neural machine translation baselines for nigerian pidgin. In *Eight International Conference on Learning Representations (ICLR2020) AfricaNLP Workshop.*

Al-Noori Ahmed H., Talib Moahaimen, and Saeed Mohammed Alhakimi Jamila. 2020. The classification of ancient sumerian characters using convolutional neural network. *Proceedings of the 1st International Conference on Computing and Emerging Sciences (ICCES)*, 1:31–35.

James P. Allen. 2014. *Middle Egyptian: An Introduction to the Language and Culture of Hieroglyphs*, 3 edition. Cambridge University Press.

James P. Allen. 2015. *Middle Egyptian Literature, Eight Literary Works of the Middle Kingdom*. Cambridge University Press, Cambridge.

Andrea Barucci, Michela Amendola, Fabrizio Argenti, Chiara Canfailla, Costanza Cucci, Tommaso Guidi,

Lorenzo Python, and Massimiliano Franci. 2023. *Discovering the ancient Egyptian hieroglyphs with Deep Learning*. Consiglio Nazionale delle Ricerche (CNR), Rome, Italy.

Andrea Barucci, Costanza Cucci, Massimiliano Franci, Marco Loschiavo, and Fabrizio Argenti. 2021. A deep learning approach to ancient egyptian hieroglyphs classification. *IEEE Access*, 09:123.438–123.447.

Edda Bresciani. 1969. *Letteratura e poesia dell'Antico Egitto*. Giulio Einaudi Editore, Turin.

Jan Buurman, Nicolas-Christophe Grimal, Michale Hainsworth, Jochen Hallof, and Dirk Van der Plas. 1988. *Inventaire des signes hieroglyphiques en vue de leur saisie informatique: Manuel de codage des textes hieroglyphiques en vue de leur saisie sur ordinateur*, volume 2 of *Informatique et egyptologie*. Imprimerie Lienharte et Cie.; Difussion Boccard, Paris.

Angela Fan, Shruti Bhosale, Holger Schwenk, Zhiyi Ma, Ahmed El-Kishky, Siddharth Goyal, Mandeep Baines, Onur Celebi, Guillaume Wenzek, Vishrav Chaudhary, Naman Goyal, Tom Birch, Vitaliy Liptchinsky, Sergey Edunov, Michael Auli, and Armand Joulin. 2021. Beyond english-centric multilingual machine translation. *J. Mach. Learn. Res.*, 22:107:1–107:48.

Morris Franken and Jan Van Gemert. 2013. Automatic egyptian hieroglyph recognition by retrieving images as texts. *MM 2013 - Proceedings of the 2013 ACM Multimedia Conference*, pages 765–768.

Alan H. Gardiner. 1957. *Egyptian Grammar, Being an Introduction to the Study of Hieroglyphs*, third edition. Griffith Institute, Oxford.

Alan H. Gardiner. 1969. *The Admonitions of an Egyptian Sage, from a Hieratic Papyrus in Leiden (pap. Leiden 344 recto)*. Georg Olms Verlag, Hildesheim.

Hermann Grapow. 1952. *Der stilistische Bau der Geschichte des Sinuhe*, volume 1 of *Untersuchungen zur ägyptischen Stilistik*. AkademieVerlag, Berlin.

Gai Gutherz, Shai Gordin, Luis Sáenz, Omer Levy, and Jonathan Berant. 2023. Translating Akkadian to English with neural machine translation. *PNAS Nexus*, 2(5):96–105.

Reham Hossam, Mohammed Abdel-Megeed Mohammed Salem, and Rimon Elias. 2018. Image based hieroglyphic character recognition. In *International Conference on Signal Image Technology & Internet-Based Systems (SITIS)*, pages 32–39, Las Palmas de Gran Canaria, Spain.

Diederik P. Kingma and Jimmy Ba. 2015. Adam: A method for stochastic optimization. In *3rd International Conference on Learning Representations, ICLR 2015, San Diego, CA, USA, May 7-9, 2015, Conference Track Proceedings*.

Alex Lamb, Tarin Clanuwat, and Asanobu Kitamoto. 2020. Kuronet: Regularized residual u-nets for end-to-end kuzushiji character recognition. *SN Computer Science*, 1.

Chin-Yew Lin. 2004. ROUGE: A package for automatic evaluation of summaries. In *Text Summarization Branches Out*, pages 74–81, Barcelona, Spain. Association for Computational Linguistics.

Antonio Loprieno. 1995. *Ancient Egyptian: A Linguistic Introduction*. Cambridge University Press.

Ragaa Moustafa, Farida Hesham, Samiha Hussein, Badr Amr, Samira Refaat, Nada Shorim, and Taraggy Ghanim. 2022. Hieroglyphs language translator using deep learning techniques (scriba). In *International Mobile, Intelligent, and Ubiquitous Computing Conference (MIUCC)*, pages 125–132, Cairo, Egypt.

Matt Post. 2018. A call for clarity in reporting BLEU scores. In *Proceedings of the Third Conference on Machine Translation: Research Papers*, pages 186–191, Brussels, Belgium. Association for Computational Linguistics.

Tonio Sebastian Richter and Daniel A. Werning. 2023. Thesaurus Linguae Aegyptiae v2.0.2.1. `https://thesaurus-linguae-aegyptiae.de`. [Online; accessed 17-September-2023].

Edgar Roman-Rangel, Carlos Pallan, Jean-Marc Odobez, and Daniel Gatica-Perez. 2009. Retrieving ancient maya glyphs with shape context. *2009 IEEE 12th International Conference on Computer Vision Workshops, ICCV Workshops 2009*, pages 988 – 995.

Thea Sommerschield, Yannis Assael, John Pavlopoulos, Vanessa Stefanak, Andrew Senior, Chris Dyer, John Bodel, Jonathan Prag, Ion Androutsopoulos, and Nando de Freitas. 2023. Machine Learning for Ancient Languages: A Survey. *Computational Linguistics*, 49(3):703–747.

Summer Institute of Linguistics. 2024. Ethnologue: Languages of the world. `https://www.ethnologue.com/`. Accessed: 2024-01-18.

Jinhu Sun, Peng Li, and Xiaojun Wu. 2022. Handwritten ancient chinese character recognition algorithm based on improved inception-resnet and attention mechanism. In *2022 IEEE 2nd International Conference on Software Engineering and Artificial Intelligence (SEAI)*, pages 31–35.

UNESCO. 2024. The world atlas of languages. `https://en.wal.unesco.org/world-atlas-languages`. Accessed: 2024-01-18.

Hans Van den Berg. 1997. "Manuel de Codage" A standard system for the computer-encoding of Egyptian transliteration and hieroglyphic texts. `http://www.catchpenny.org/codage/`. [Online; accessed 28-July-2023].

Friedrich Vogelsang. 1913. *Kommentar zu den Klagen des Bauern*, volume 6 of *Untersuchungen zur Geschichte und Altertumskunde Ägyptens*. Leipzig.

Philip Wiesenbach and Stefan Riezler. 2019. Multi-task modeling of phonographic languages: Translating middle egyptian hieroglyphs. In *International Workshop on Spoken Language Translation*.

A Taxonomy Analysis of Data Mining

Language	Datapoints
Absent	70,559
Egyptian	28
Middle Egyptian	23,997
Late Egyptian	8,615
Demotic	707

Table 6: Amount of datapoints for each language phase. Counts done on the datapoints mined from TLA (before filtering) and corresponding to 103.906.

Date	Datapoints
Absent	1,165
Old Kingdom	35,849
First Intermediate Period	571
XI Dynasty	466
Middle Kingdom	7,633
Second Intermediate Period	3,634
New Kingdom	38,078
Third Intermediate Period	3,590
Late Period	2,191
600 to 200 BC	2,977
Hellenistic Period	7,133
Roman Period	619

Table 7: Amount of datapoints for each historical period. Counts done on the datapoints mined from TLA (before filtering) and corresponding to 103.906.

B Grammatical Inputs of Human Evaluation

The examples submitted to the model during the human Evaluation comprised various type of sentences. The Grammatical Complexity included: adverbial, nominal (A B), verbal (sḏm =f), negative verbal (sḏm =f), pseudo-verbal and stative. The Literary passage included: verbal (sḏm =f and sḏm.n =f), verbal negative (sḏm.n =f), adverbial, nominal (A + pw), infinitive, participle, and two longer sentences. The Stress Test included: infinitive, verbal (causative (sḏm =f), stative, subject-stative, adverbial and containing dates or epithets.

C Data Entry Methods

The approach described below ensures that the model receives a clean and standardized representation of hieroglyphic and transliteration, minimizing potential misinterpretations that could arise from extraneous elements and enhancing its ability to produce accurate translations.

C.1 Hieroglyphic Input

To input hieroglyphs, it is essential to employ Gardiner code. Each hieroglyph must be meticulously cleansed of any brackets, letters, or graphic symbols that extraneously adhere to it, altering its visual representation (it can be checked using Jsesh[14]). To divide hieroglyphs, a single space should be inserted between them, while any other extraneous character should be eliminated.

The model has been trained on Ancient and Middle Egyptian hieroglyphs and may encounter challenges with inputs from later linguistic phases and grammatical structures postdating the Second Intermediate Period.

We recommend utilizing signs list of Gardiner's grammar (Gardiner, 1957), or preferably Allen's (Allen, 2014), for a more accurate use of Gardiner code.

C.2 Transliteration Input

For transliteration input, it is necessary to adhere to conventions similar to the one employed by the TLA.

- Proper nouns should have the first letter capitalized.
- It may be beneficial, but not compulsory, to incorporate hyphens between individual lemmas of proper nouns or concepts (e.g., *sḥtp-jb-rʿ* or *wꜣḏ-wr*)
- The equal sign (=) to indicate a suffixed pronoun must always be preceded by a space and followed directly by the pronoun, without any additional characters (e.g., *zꜣ =f m pr*)
- The *j* is utilized for the strong yod while *i̯* for the weak yod.
- A dot should be employed to distinguish the root of verbs from a suffix other than a pronoun (e.g., *n* in *sḏm.n =f* form) and occasionally for the plural/dual.
- A comma should be employed for the feminine ending and occasionally also for the plural/dual.

[14]https://jsesh.qenherkhopeshef.org

Transliterated characters can be submitted to the model both as a proper character (e.g., ꜣ) or according to the computer-encoding system of Manuel de Codage (e.g., A for the ꜣ; Buurman et al., 1988; Van den Berg, 1997).

To enable the insertion of both upper and lowercase letters, while preserving the encoding of MdC, we have implemented a simple mechanism that allows you to capitalize a letter by preceding it with an asterisk. In practice, a straightforward substitution operation has been created in the section where inputs are entered. For instance, since to obtain *ḏ* you must insert *D*, then to get *Ḏ* you have to type **D*; similarly, to attain *D*, you must enter **d*. To input the weak radical *i̯* simply enter an *i*.

D Experiments Graphs

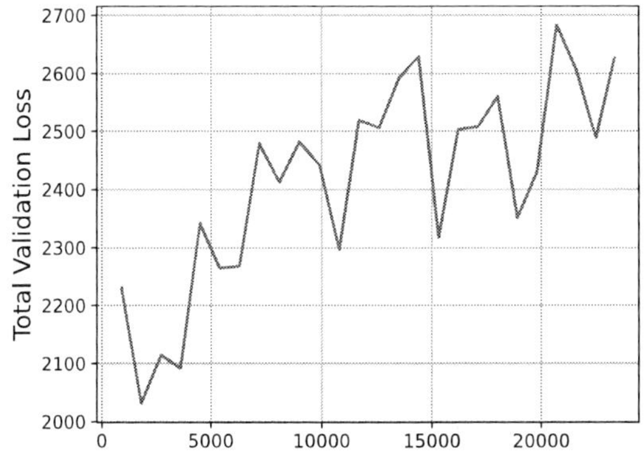

(a) Model DE (raw). Best loss: step 1,800.

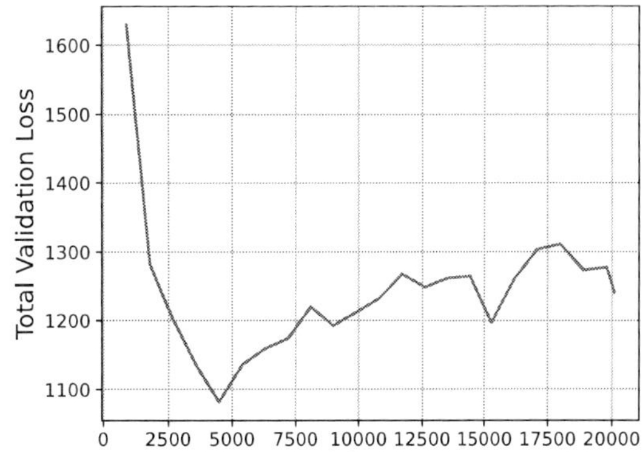

(b) Model DE. Best loss: step 4,500.

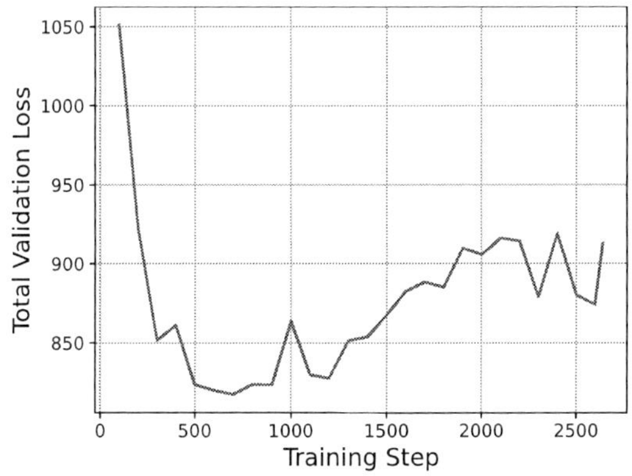

(c) Model EN. Best loss: step 700.

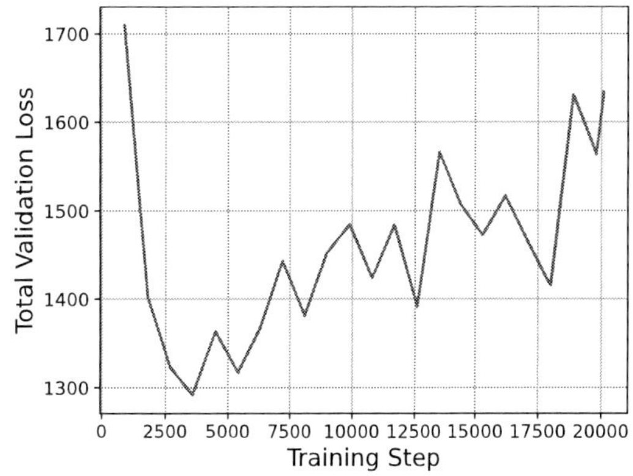

(d) Model DE (lem). Best loss: step 3,600.

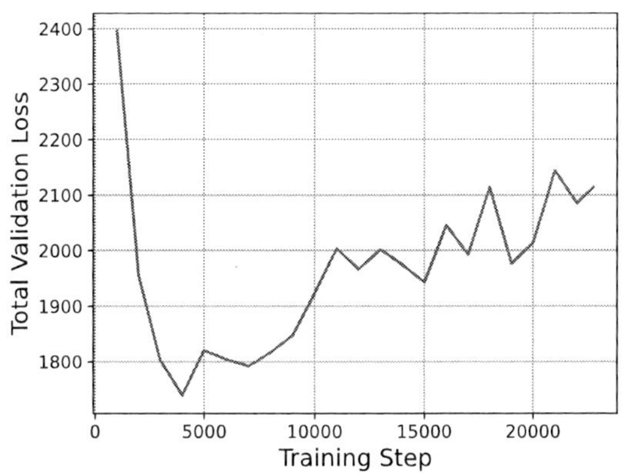

(e) Model DE+EN. Best loss: step 4,000.

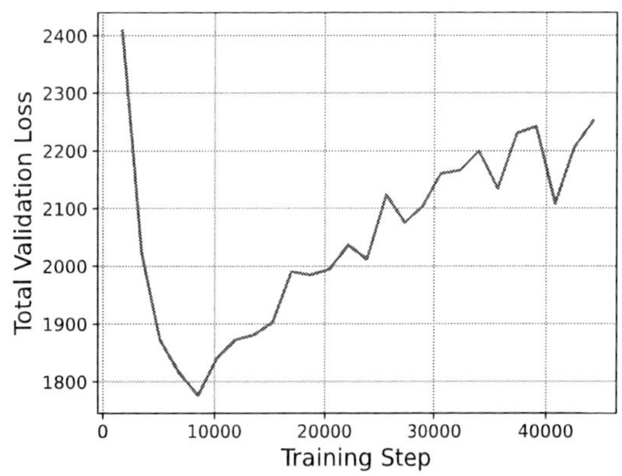

(f) Model DE+EN^{B}. Best loss: step 8,500.

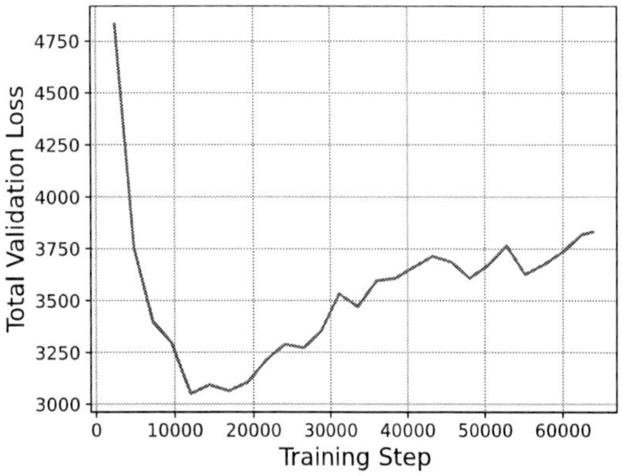

(g) Model DE+τ. Best loss: step 12,000.

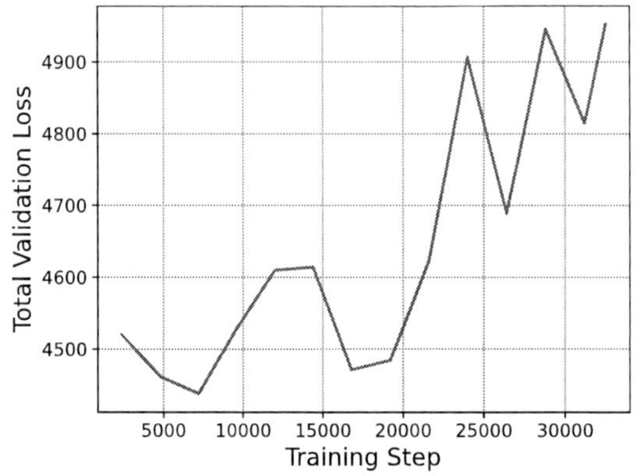

(h) Model DE+τ+EN^{B}. Best loss: step 7,200.

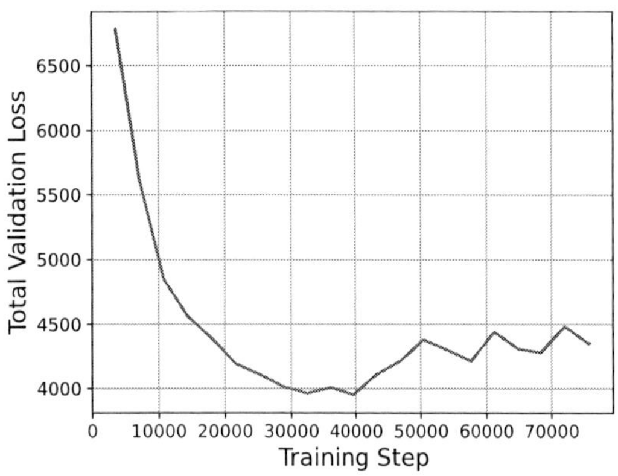

(i) Model DE+τ+POS. Best loss: step 39,600.

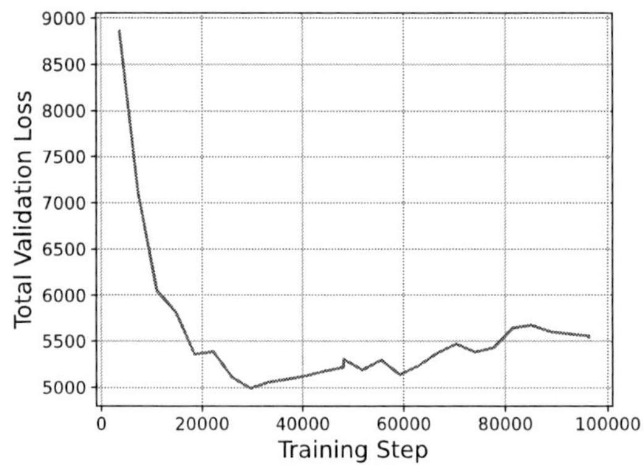

(j) Model DE+τ+LKEY. Best loss: step 29,600.

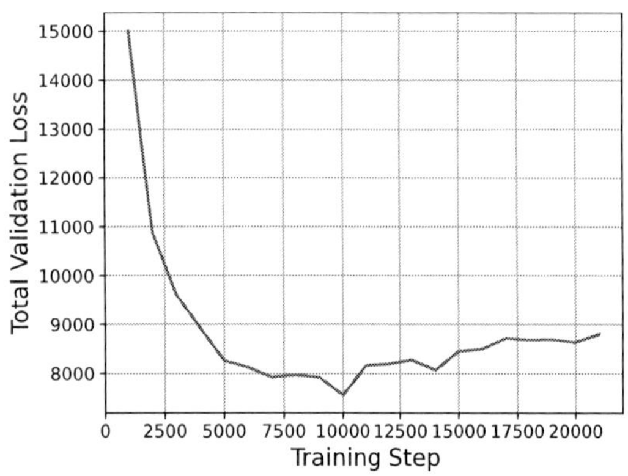

(k) Model ALL. Best loss: step 10,000.

Figure 2: Validation losses of different models and at which step the loss is at its minimum.

E Taxonomy Analysis of Generated Models: SacreBLEU, RougeL and 10-fold Cross Validation

	SacreBLEU								
Source	egy					τ			
Target	**de**	**en**	τ	**lkey**	**POS**	**de**	**en**	**lkey**	**POS**
DE (raw)	4.0	-	-	-	-	-	-	-	-
DE	54.4	-	-	-	-	-	-	-	-
EN	-	22.6	-	-	-	-	-	-	-
DE (lem)	25.9	-	-	-	-	-	-	-	-
DE+EN	52.6	28.4	-	-	-	-	-	-	-
DE+EN^B	**61.5**	**36.4**	-	-	-	-	-	-	-
DE+τ	43.2	-	57.7	-	-	54.0	-	-	-
DE+τ+EN^B	47.6	20.1	58.4	-	-	47.1	30.3	-	-
DE+τ+POS	53.2	-	**60.0**	-	**82.1**	49.6	-	-	**87.1**
DE+τ+LKEY	55.1	-	59.4	**64.4**	-	**58.9**	-	70.9	-
ALL	54.4	31.6	59.9	63.9	79.0	56.2	**35.3**	**74.0**	86.4

Table 8: Results of automatic evaluation, in particular SacreBLEU, of all models along with POS tags and lKey. **Bold** results are best and underlined are second best.

	RougeL								
Source	egy					τ			
Target	**de**	**en**	τ	**lkey**	**POS**	**de**	**en**	**lkey**	**POS**
DE (raw)	18.4	-	-	-	-	-	-	-	-
DE	62.8	-	-	-	-	-	-	-	-
EN	-	25.1	-	-	-	-	-	-	-
DE (lem)	42.0	-	-	-	-	-	-	-	-
DE+EN	63.1	33.5	-	-	-	-	-	-	-
DE+EN^B	**67.7**	**38.1**	-	-	-	-	-	-	-
DE+τ	55.4	-	78.9	-	-	61.8	-	-	-
DE+τ+EN^B	58.8	27.9	80.2	-	-	63.1	37.5	-	-
DE+τ+POS	62.9	-	**83.1**	-	**83.8**	**67.3**	-	-	87.6
DE+τ+LKEY	59.6	-	82.6	71.5	-	63.8	-	75.4	-
ALL	64.5	35.5	82.1	**71.7**	82.6	62.7	**38.1**	**77.7**	**88.4**

Table 9: Results of automatic evaluation, in particular RougeL, of all models along with POS tags and lKey. **Bold** results are best and underlined are second best.

SacreBLEU									
Source			**egy**				τ		
Target	**de**	**en**	τ	**lkey**	**POS**	**de**	**en**	**lkey**	**POS**
DE	32.0±2.0	10.2±1.2	-	-	-	5.4±2.0	0.2±0.3	-	-
ALL	45.5±1.4	35.9±3.7	52.7±1.3	57.9±5.1	71.9±1.3	59.6±1.4	42.6±2.9	74.3±2.4	79.2±0.7
RougeL									
Source			**egy**				τ		
Target	**de**	**en**	τ	**lkey**	**POS**	**de**	**en**	**lkey**	**POS**
DE	41.1±0.9	14.7±1.1	-	-	-	3.9±1.3	0.3±0.4	-	-
ALL	53.4±1.1	40.9±2.4	78.9±0.6	65.2±4.3	81.6±0.6	68.0±1.0	47.9±1.5	79.1±2.1	88.0±0.8

Table 10: Results of 10-fold cross validation.

Neural Lemmatization and POS-tagging models for Coptic, Demotic and Earlier Egyptian

Aleksi Sahala
University of Helsinki
Helsinki, Finland
aleksi.sahala@helsinki.fi

Eliese-Sophia Lincke
Freie Universität Berlin & Berlin-Brandenburg
Academy of Sciences and Humanities
Berlin, Germany
e.lincke@fu-berlin.de

Abstract

We present BabyLemmatizer models for lemmatizing and POS-tagging Earlier Egyptian, Coptic and Demotic to test the performance of our pipeline for the ancient languages of Egypt.[1] Of these languages, Demotic and Earlier Egyptian are known to be difficult to annotate due to their high extent of ambiguity. We report lemmatization accuracy of 86%, 91% and 99%, and XPOS-tagging accuracy of 89%, 95% and 98% for Earlier Egyptian, Demotic and Coptic, respectively.

1 Introduction

Lemmatization is an annotation task that aims to label word forms with their dictionary forms, known as lemmata. This is necessary for languages with complex writing systems or morphology that would otherwise preclude effective word searches using simple keywords. By enabling the location of all inflected forms and spelling variants of any searched word, lemmatization opens several interesting avenues for quantitatively studying historical texts and their language.

POS tagging is another annotation task that aims to label word forms with their part-of-speech tags. This can be useful for simple named entity recognition, syntactic parsing, and disambiguation of lemmatization results. The more fine-grained the POS tagging is, the more information it can provide about the words in the corpus.

In this paper, we present lemmatizer and POS-tagger models for Earlier Egyptian, Coptic, and Demotic. Earlier Egyptian and Demotic pose particular challenges for lemmatization due to their ambiguous word forms, which are often only one or two characters long. To our knowledge, neural lemmatization of these languages has not been attempted before. Our models are based on BabyLemmatizer, an OpenNMT-based neural lemmatizing and POS-tagging pipeline designed primarily for historical languages. Previously, BabyLemmatizer has been evaluated on Sumerian, Babylonian, Neo-Assyrian, Urartian, Latin, and Ancient Greek with promising results (Sahala and Lindén, 2023).

2 Languages and Datasets

Egyptian-Coptic existed as a spoken language long before its first written records (Pre-Old Egyptian, (Kammerzell, 2005)). It is attested in writing from approximately 3000 BCE until around 1400 CE. For several millennia, it was the majority language of the lower Nile valley until it was gradually displaced by Arabic, leading to its eventual extinction. Today, only the Bohairic dialect of Coptic remains, serving as the liturgical language of the Coptic Orthodox Church. Egyptian-Coptic is classified as the only member of a now extinct branch of Afroasiatic, with its closest relatives being the Semitic and Berber languages (Schenkel, 1990; Grossman and Richter, 2015). Its placement within the Afroasiatic language family has recently become a topic of renewed debate (Almansa-Villatoro and Štubňová Nigrelli, 2023). The language history is generally divided into two major phases: Earlier Egyptian, which includes Old Egyptian (2700–2000 BCE) and Middle Egyptian (2000–1400 BCE), and Later Egyptian, which encompasses Late Egyptian (1350–600 BCE), Demotic (800 BCE-450 CE), and Coptic (300–1400 CE). Numerous comprehensive linguistic overviews discuss the phonology, morphology, and syntax of the language and its long-term developments (Allen, 2013; Haspelmath, 2015; Loprieno, 1995, 2004; Loprieno and Müller, 2012; McLaughlin, 2022; Müller, 2020; Schenkel, 1990; Stauder, 2020).

According to Egyptological conventions, Egyptian texts (including Demotic) are presented in several layers: (1) in the original script (e.g., as a facsimile, as a handcopy, or printed in a hieroglyphic

[1] The models are available at https://huggingface.co/asahala

Proceedings of the 1st Workshop on Machine Learning for Ancient Languages (ML4AL 2024), pages 87–97
August 15, 2024 ©2024 Association for Computational Linguistics

font) or, in the case of hieratic, transliterated into hieroglyphs, (2) in Egyptological transcription (commonly referred to as transliteration in English), and (3) in translation. In linguistic studies, morphological analyses are often presented as interlinear glosses following the Leipzig Glossing Rules (Di Biase-Dyson et al., 2009). Coptic, using a Greek-based alphabetic script, is usually not transliterated unless it is presented to an audience not familiar with ancient languages (Grossman and Haspelmath, 2015).

Like the native writing systems that do not represent vowels—except for the Coptic script—Egyptological transcription focuses exclusively on consonants. It does not attempt to encode the spellings on a character level, but rather aims to represent the consonantal skeleton (roots). Consequently, distinctions made in the indigenous Egyptian scripts are not captured, leading to a high number of homographs in the scholarly representation of Egyptian, including Demotic (see Figure 1). In response to this, lexicographical projects have adopted lemma IDs in addition to lemma forms, and have established chronolect-specific lemma lists (Egyptian and Demotic: TLA = Thesaurus Linguae Aegyptiae, (Grallert et al., 2024); Coptic: CCL = Comprehensive Coptic Lexicon, (Burns et al., 2020)). As a result, a lemmatizer designed for scholarly purposes must be trained to map tokens to lemma IDs, not just to lemma forms, to effectively integrate with existing digital corpora.

For Coptic, which is typically not transliterated, the issue of homonymy is less pronounced but nonetheless present, often resulting from phonetic changes or only obvious when considering material from several different dialects (see Figure 2).

2.1 Earlier Egyptian

Earlier Egyptian encompasses the chronolects Old Egyptian (Allen, 2015) and Middle Egyptian (Schenkel, 2001). It is classified as a fusional language, characterized by root-and-pattern morphology (roots inflection). The word order is relatively fixed; in sentences with a verbal predicate, the structure follows a V-S-O schema (Loprieno, 1988). Additionally, there are three other sentence types with non-verbal predicates: nominal, adjectival, and adverbial (Loprieno et al., 2017).

Texts from these periods are written either in monumental hieroglyphic or in hieratic, a cursive script. Both scripts are mixed systems that utilize various sign function classes (Polis and Rosmorduc, 2015; Polis, 2023): logograms, mono- or multiconsonantal phonograms, classifiers (traditionally termed determinatives), and interpretants (also known as phonetic complements). Some researchers propose more nuanced categorizations of these sign functions, e.g. by including radicograms (Schenkel, 2003; Polis and Rosmorduc, 2015: pp. 166-167).

Although the Thesaurus Linguae Aegyptiae currently includes almost 1.16 million tokens, a significant number of corpora and texts, while published in print, remain unavailable in digital format. This includes important works such as the Coffin Texts, the Netherworld Books, and the Heqanakhte papyri (letters). Other materials still not digitized include most temple inscriptions or recently discovered texts like the letters from Balat and the Wadi al-Jarf papyri. Additionally, many inscriptions on objects located on-site, in collections and storerooms have yet to be cataloged and are neither available in print nor electronically.

The Earlier Egyptian dataset (TLA-Egy 2024) is derived from the Thesaurus Linguae Aegyptiae, corpus v18, 2023 (Richter et al., 2023). The TLA is the largest digital corpus of Egyptian texts, currently comprising approximately 1.16 million tokens (Grallert et al., 2023). This dataset includes texts from the 3rd to the early 2nd millennium BCE (Old Kingdom to the so-called Second Intermediate Period) across various genres: archival, historical-biographical (royal and non-royal), tomb inscriptions (non-royal), Letters to the Dead, religious texts (Pyramid Texts), literary works (narratives, dialogues, wisdom literature, hymns), magical and medical texts, votive labels and inscriptions, rock inscriptions, and stelae inscriptions (offering formulas). From this corpus, only sentences from the pre-New Kingdom era without emendations, lacunae, questionable readings or questionable translations were selected, ensuring the dataset consists solely of complete sentences from Old and Middle Egyptian. Sentences were further filtered to include only those with fully encoded hieroglyphic spellings and lemmatization. The final dataset comprises 12,773 sentences, totaling 70,267 tokens.

The data is organized in a spreadsheet format, with each sentence displayed on a separate row (tokens are separated by spaces) and various columns providing detailed annotations: hieroglyphic spelling (hieratic script is transliterated

Egyptian (Old–Late Egyptian)			Demotic			Coptic (B = Bohairic, else: Sahidic)		Translation
	mn	69560		mn	d2418	ⲙⲛ-	C1890	there is no (non-existence)
			—	mn	dm733	ⲙⲙⲟⲛ	C1897	really
	mn	69590		mn	d2422	ⲙⲟⲩⲛ	C1913	remain, continue
	mn	69610		mn	d2419	ⲙⲁⲛ (B)	C1900	so and so (a certain person)
	mn	69630		mn	d2424	ⲁⲙⲓⲛ (B)	C89	jug, pot
	mn	70110		mn	d2429			establish, examine
	mn	69660	—	mn	d9203			be ill, suffer
	mn	69670						sick person
	mn	69640						[a kind of fabric]
				mn	dm5140	ⲙⲟⲟⲛⲉ	C1925	pasture, feed
			—	mn	dm7835	ⲙⲛ-	C1903	prefix of neg. imperative
				mn	d2420	ⲙⲁⲉⲓⲛ	C1904	dvine statue; sign, mark
			—	mn	d9297	ⲁⲙⲟⲛⲓ (B)	C91	seize, possess

Figure 1: Homonymy (homography) in Egyptological transcription illustrated by the lemma 'mn'. (Lemma forms and IDs from the Thesaurus Linguae Aegyptiae (TLA) for Earlier Egyptian and Demotic, and from the Comprehensive Coptic Lexicon (CCL) for Coptic. Demotic spellings—written right-to-left— are sourced from the variant list of the Demotic Palaeographical Database Project (Quack et al., 2024).

into hieroglyphs) presented in Unicode[2], Egyptological transcription (following the Leiden Unified Transliteration),[3] lemmatization (including both lemma-ID numbers from the TLA and lemma forms), Part-of-speech tags (UPOS),[4] morphological glossing of the word form (in the following treated as XPOS), and contextual translation into German (translating the entire sentence rather than word-by-word). The dataset also includes the dates (*post quem* and *ante quem*) of the manuscripts and credits to the editors/translators. All annotations have been made by trained Egyptologists. This dataset is published under the CC-BY-SA 4.0 International license.

[2]Currently, not all hieroglyphs are available as Unicode code points. Those not included in the Unicode standard are represented by alphanumeric codes (e.g., Gardiner numbers, JSesh numbers) and enclosed within a tag, e.g., <g>M134</g>.

[3]https://www.iae-egyptology.org/the-leiden-unified-transliteration/

[4]https://universaldependencies.org/u/pos/

2.2 Demotic

The term 'Demotic' refers to the chronolect predominantly used in the second half of the 1st millennium BCE and the early part of the current era, as well as to the cursive script used to write it. Following Alexander the Great's conquest (332 BCE), Greek emerged as the prestige and administrative language, significantly influencing the linguistic environment. Demotic, however, remained dominant in the literary and religious genres as well as for personal communication and in documentary texts. Demotic represents the stage of the language where the evolutionary trends initiated in (late) Middle Egyptian or Late Egyptian fully manifest, such as the shift from a V-S-O to an (AUX-)S-V-O word order (McLaughlin, 2022, pp. 274-275), the analyticization of constructions that were still synthetic in Middle and Late Egyptian, and the (re-)syntheticization of Late Egyptian analytic constructions (McLaughlin, 2022). Thus, Demotic exhibits par-

Dialect	Coptic			Egyptian (Old–Late Egyptian)		
Sahidic	ⲙⲉ	'to love'	C1785	*mrj*	'to love'	72470
Sahidic	ⲙⲉ	'love'	C1786			
Sahidic	ⲙⲉ	'truth, justice'	C1789	*mꜣꜥ.t*	'truth, right order'	66620
Fayyumic	ⲙⲉ	'with, and'	C1901 C1902	*jrm*	'together with'	29840
Fayyumic	ⲙⲉ	'there is no'	C1890	*mn*	'there is no'	69560
Fayyumic, Mesokemic	ⲙⲉ	'place'	C1771	*mjꜣ.t*	'loom'(?)	68200
Fayyumic, Mesokemic	ⲙⲉ	'there'	C2155	*(m/n-)jm*	'there'	24640

Figure 2: Homonymy in the Coptic dialects Sahidic, Fayyumic and Mesokemic illustrated by a selection of lemmata with the form ⲙⲉ. (Lemma forms and IDs for Earlier Egyptian from the Thesaurus Linguae Aegyptiae (TLA); lemma IDs for Coptic from the Comprehensive Coptic Lexicon (CCL); lemma forms for Sahidic also from the Comprehensive Coptic Lexicon, for Fayyumic and Mesokemic from (Westendorf, 1977)).

tial alignment with both Late Egyptian and Coptic. This dual alignment is reflected in linguistic overviews, where Demotic is often characterized by its similarities to or contrasts with Late Egyptian (Quack, 2006; Winand, 2018) and Coptic (Richter, 2023), respectively.

Despite its significance for understanding the Egyptian Late and Greco-Roman periods, and the substantial amount of material preserved, Demotic remains largely underrepresented in digital corpora. This underrepresentation is attributed to the challenging nature of the material—marked by fragmentation and extremely cursive script—and the limited number of experts capable of editing it. In 1998, Kim Ryholt estimated that since the 1930s, 'less than one per cent of the known material' in the literary corpus had been published (Ryholt, 1998, p. 151). Although many texts have been edited and are available in print since that time, the number of texts available in electronic form remains limited, both for literary and documentary texts.

The Demotic dataset (tla-demotic-v18-premium, TLA-Dem 2024) represents a well-balanced selection of genres, encompassing literary works (narratives, mythological texts, wisdom texts, etc.), religious texts, documentary/administrative records (priestly decrees, temple inventories, letters, receipts, ration lists, among others), legal documents (codes, marriage and divorce settlements, sales deeds, wills, guarantees), graffiti/dipinti, oracular, omen, dream, medical and magical texts, as well as school exercises. Similar to the Earlier Egyptian dataset, this dataset is derived from corpus v18 of the TLA from 2023. It comprises 13,383 sentences totaling 117,314 tokens. The selection, presentation, and licensing criteria mirror those of the Earlier Egyptian dataset, with the exceptions that (1) the tokens are represented exclusively in scholarly transcription ('transliteration'), not in any indigenous script, and (2) XPOS pertains to the lemma, not to the word form. The corpus has been annotated by trained Demotists.

2.3 Coptic

Coptic was the vernacular language during the Christian period in Egypt, while Greek continued to serve as the prestige and administrative language. Following the Arab conquest of Egypt, Arabic began to spread. By the 8th century CE, Greek had been replaced by Coptic in all domains, only to be gradually overtaken by Arabic. During the emergence of Coptic, indigenous writing systems were abandoned in favor of an alphabetic script that included vowels, primarily based on Greek with an addition of 6 or 7 characters borrowed from Demotic, varying by dialect. Coptic does not exhibit root inflection and displays polysynthetic features, including noun incorporation (Grossman, 2019; Miyagawa, 2023). Grammatical morphemes are typically affixed, which categorizes Coptic as an agglutinative language. Particularly in the early centuries CE, the linguistic landscape was marked by significant dialectal variation (Funk, 1988; Richter,

2023). The commonly preferred Coptic word order is (AUX-)S-V-O, and the adjectival sentence pattern has disappeared.

The Coptic data utilized in this study is sourced from the Coptic Scriptorium project (Schroeder and Zeldes, 2016). The corpus, spanning versions 4.2.0 to 4.5.0, primarily comprises Christian literary and biblical texts, along with some letters from a monastic setting in the Sahidic dialect. Available for download in various formats, including CoNLL-U, from the Coptic Scriptorium's GitHub repository, the CoNLL-U formatted data includes 515,142 tokens. The annotation layers in the CoNLL-U files, used for this paper, adhere to the standard CoNLL-U format specifications: ID, form, lemma, Universal POS (UPOS), project-specific POS (XPOS), morphological features, and, to some extent, syntactic head, Universal Dependencies Relation, along with other annotations not pertinent to our study. Unlike the Earlier Egyptian and Demotic corpora, the lemmatization in this corpus maps tokens to surface forms (strings) rather than to IDs, and does not disambiguate homonyms. The numerous Greek loanwords in Coptic are annotated in the same manner like the Egyptian-based vocabulary. The annotation quality varies across three levels: automatic (machine-only annotations), checked (verified for accuracy by a Coptic expert), and gold (extensively reviewed for accuracy). The data is licensed under CC-BY-SA 3.0 and 4.0, except for the 'Sahidica' New Testament sub-corpus, which is copyrighted (c) 2000-2006 by J Warren Wells.

3 Previous Work

Schroeder and Zeldes trained the TreeTagger for POS-tagging and lemmatization, achieving an average accuracy of 95.12% for POS-Tagging and of 96.78% for lemmatization (Zeldes and Schroeder, 2016, 2015), both in ten-fold cross-validation. The same authors implemented a look-up based lemmatizer for the Coptic Scriptorium in Python, which first POS tags the word forms and then assigns the wordform + POS combination to its most common lemma (Schroeder and Zeldes, 2016). As of now, this system does not do disambiguation in case multiple lemmatization options are possible. Smith and Hulden built the first finite-state grammar for Sahidic Coptic (Smith and Hulden, 2016). The lexicon of this implementation comprised 95 verbs, 50 nouns, 65 productive prefixes, 36 closed-class words such as demonstratives and conjuctions, and numerous proper names, all represented in Latin transliteration. The authors reported their system to achieve a recall of 94.6% (precision is not reported), every input word form having 2.9 analyses on average. This implementation does not feature lemma disambiguation either.

SIGTYP 2024 Shared Task on Word Embedding Evaluation for Ancient and Historical Languages had Coptic as one of its languages. The tasks included POS-tagging, lemmatization, prediction of morphological labels and gap filling. In the constrained track that disallowed the use of additional data the best POS-tagger model was reported to have an accuracy of 96.92% (predicting top-1 label) and the lemmatizer an weighted average accuracy of 95.07% over predicting top-1 and top-3 labels (Dereza et al., 2024, Table 5).

4 Preprocessing

For Earlier Egyptian and Demotic we converted the JSON into CoNLL□U. For Coptic, the data was already in the CoNLL□U format, and could be used for BabyLemmatizer as it was.

The Demotic and Earlier Egyptian lemmatization use identifiers to disambiguate between homophonic lemmata. This is necessary, because Demotic and Earlier Egyptian word forms are often ambiguous and short, as already demonstrated earlier in this paper. The identifiers are encoded as integer sequences up to six digits in length, separated from the lemma with a pipe, as in $550034|nfr$. In our initial tests, these sequences seemed to cause slight performance issues for the lemmatizer in terms of accuracy, as accidental incorrect prediction of a single identifier digit resulted into a wrong lemma even if the phonetic part of the lemma was predicted correctly. In addition, it turned out that prediction of long arbitrary integer sequences with no relation to the phonetic form for out-of-vocabulary (OOV) lemmata was very unreliable, rendering predictions for word forms with OOV forms nearly impossible.

To overcome this issue, we compressed the identifiers by replacing them with shorter number sequences tied to the phonological representations of the lemmata. For instance, in the case of a lemma *wr* having four different senses, we enumerated them as *0|wr*, *1|wr*, *2|wr* and *3|wr* instead of using arbitrarily long integer sequences. We based the compressed identifiers on the lemma frequency, 0 having the highest frequency. We hoped that this decision would make leading zero the most likely prediction for OOV word forms, and therefore, the model would suggest the statistically most probable lemmata for word forms the model has not seen in the training data.[5]

Based on our experiments, identifier compression effectively doubles the accuracy of OOV lemmatization and increases the overall accuracy on average by 3%. After the lemmatization, the original identifiers can be restored by a simple dictionary mapping for all in-vocabulary words with known lemmata. For OOV word forms with previously unseen lemmata, the identifiers have to be defined manually. As Babylemmatizer marks the predictions for OOV word forms automatically in the output CoNLL-U, finding these instances is relatively easy.

Due to character encoding issues with the Egyptian hieroglyphs, we represented them as their Unicode code points in 8-character long sequences separated from each other with a dash symbol.[6] The input encoding will be discussed in a closer detail in the following section.

5 BabyLemmatizer

BabyLemmatizer is a lemmatization and POS-tagging pipeline designed especially for historical languages.[7] It has been optimized for the cuneiform writing system used in Mesopotamia from 3200 BCE to 100 CE, but its tokenizer has been recently extended to also support alphabetic scripts (Sahala and Lindén, 2023).

BabyLemmatizer uses a deep attentional encoder-decoder network, with a two layer BiLSTM encoder that reads the input as a character sequence. The output sequence is generated by a two layer unidirectional LSTM decoder with input feeding attention. In our models we use the default batch size of 64 and start the learning rate decay halfway through the training process.

The system is based on the Open Neural Machine Translation Toolkit (Klein et al., 2017) and it handles POS-tagging and lemmatization as machine translation tasks by mapping two sequences of symbols with each other and trying to learn their relation to each other. Examples are given in the following section.

BabyLemmatizer combines the strengths of neural and look-up based lemmatizers by first lemmatizing the input text using the neural network and then using a look-up to verify the labels predicted for all in-vocabulary words. The system also scores the lemmatizations by their confidence, which allows human annotators to first focus on the most likely incorrect lemmata instead of going through the whole dataset. This scoring system is designed for cuneiform languages and has a slightly less relevance for non-logosyllabic scripts, but it still labels the words with scores as shown in Table 1. These scores are included in the output CoNLL-U file.

5.1 Input Encoding

For all models except the Egyptian Hieroglyphic model, we use BabyLemmatizer's alphabetic tokenization, which splits the inputs into character sequences. We use the default context window sizes for POS and lemma prediction: two preceding and two following word forms for POS tagging, and the preceding and following POS tags for lemmatization. Examples of the source and target sequences are shown for the POS tagger in Table 2 and for the lemmatizer in Table 3, using Demotic transliteration.

We use transliteration as input for Demotic because the Demotic script is not supported by Unicode. For Coptic, we use the Unicode representation of the Coptic script. For Earlier Egyptian, which appeared to be the most difficult dataset to annotate, we use two different input formats: transliteration and a concatenation of hieroglyphs and transliteration. In our initial tests, using the hieroglyphic script alone yielded poor results, so we have not reported these results.

We represent hieroglyphs as their Unicode code points in hexadecimal format merged in pairs, the pairs separated from each other with dashes, as in D80CDEA2-D80CDC9D from \ud80c\udea2\ud80c\udc9d. We concatenated these representations in the beginning of the transliterations and used BabyLemmatizer's cuneiform tokenizer to treat the hieroglyphs as monolithic indivisible tokens, but preserving the transliterations as divisible character sequences to retain substring information.

Our motivation for concatenating hieroglyphs and transliteration came from the transliteration of the cuneiform script, where homophonic transliter-

[5] Alternative option would have been to handle the ID sequences as monolithic tokens, but this would have required modifications to the BabyLemmatizer source code.

[6] We had issues reading UTF-16 characters when converting the JSON data into ConLL-U on Windows and had to read them in binary to get the code points.

[7] The tool is available at https://github.com/asahala/BabyLemmatizer

Score	Description of the word form
0 & 1	Reserved for cuneiform languages only (out-of-vocabulary logograms)
2	Out-of-vocabulary (does not occur in training data)
3	Ambiguous (distribution of lemmata assigned for this word form in training data is close to uniform)
4	Slightly ambiguous (of all lemmata given to this word form in training data one occurs 70% of the time.)
5	Likely unambiguous (as in score 4, and occurs in a known XPOS context)

Table 1: Confidence scoring.

Source	= y | (r) | « d y . t » | w y | = f
Target	V

Table 2: POS-tagger input and output label. The center word is enclosed in double angle brackets and the words are separated from each other with pipes.

Source	d y . t P0=PTCL P1=V P2=V
Target	0 | d y

Table 3: Lemmatizer input and output label. The input word form is given first, followed by its POS tag and the POS tags immediately before and after it.

ations are distinguished from each other by adding an index number to indicate which sign was used in the original text (for example, u_2 and u_3 are written using different cuneiform signs despite having the same phonetic value in Akkadian). Since Egyptological transliteration does not use indexing, we hypothesized that adding information about the hieroglyphs would alleviate some of the ambiguity in the transliterations. As reported in the evaluation section, this did not significantly impact the results, but it did improve the out-of-vocabulary (OOV) lemmatization accuracy.

We made various unsuccessful attempts to deal with the ambiguity, especially in the Earlier Egyptian texts, by altering the input and output strings. First, we attempted to use the UPOS tags instead of XPOS tags as context information for the lemmatizer, due to UPOS tags being easier to predict correctly and being simpler. Second, we predicted lemmata without the numeric identifiers alongside the XPOS tags and used these simplified lemmata as context information for predicting the final lemma. Third, we attempted to produce the lemmata with identifiers by using a concatenation of word forms as the input format, taking one or more preceding and following word forms into account.

Finally, we also modified the BabyLemmatizer source code to use a larger context window when predicting POS tags and lemmata for Earlier Egyptian, but this did not improve the results either. In fact, increasing the context window for lemmatization was generally detrimental to accuracy, possibly due to the small dataset, which rendered the model unable to make generalizations based on very long input sequences.

As none of these experiments consistently improved accuracy, we will report only the results for the default BabyLemmatizer settings in the evaluation section.

6 Evaluation

We make a 80/10/10 train/dev/test split of our datasets and evaluate our models using 10-fold cross-validation. We use accuracy as our evaluation metric, that is, the percentage word forms that were assigned the correct label (LEMMA, XPOS, UPOS) by the system. As out baseline, we use a dictionary-based lookup that assigns the word forms with their most common UPOS, XPOS and LEMMA labels (see Table 5). Our final results are summarized in Table 6, confidence intervals of the cross-validation shown in parentheses.

Category	Coptic	Demotic	E. Egy.
XPOS	61	46	234
UPOS	15	11	10
LEMMA	8 557	5 683	6 270
FORM	8 977	7 807	8 109
Tokens	515,142	117,314	70,267

Table 4: Number of unique labels and word forms in our datasets. Earlier Egyptian word form count is based on the number of unique Latin transliterations.

The performance for Coptic is high, but this is partly explainable due to the low number of out-of-vocabulary words, and as for lemmatization, due to the lack of lemma identifiers. Yet, even when the

	Coptic	Demotic	E. Egyptian T	E. Egyptian H+T
XPOS	83.74	87.06	71.52	68.09
UPOS	87.41	88.22	84.99	78.54
LEMMA	90.20	81.19	75.73	71.21

Table 5: Baseline results. Average labeling accuracy (%) over the test sets.

Whole dataset				
	Coptic	**Demotic**	**E. Egyptian T**	**E. Egyptian H+T**
XPOS	97.98 (±0.05)	95.14 (±0.13)	88.43 (±0.18)	88.65 (±0.10)
UPOS	97.96 (±0.07)	96.83 (±0.31)	94.32 (±0.22)	94.70 (±0.21)
LEMMA	98.60 (±0.03)	91.40 (±0.20)	85.52 (±0.33)	85.42 (±0.33)
OOV-rate	0.91	3.90	5.90	14.59

OOV word forms only				
	Coptic	**Demotic**	**E. Egyptian T**	**E. Egyptian H+T**
XPOS	77.60 (±1.15)	71.11 (±1.53)	59.14 (±1.99)	66.70 (±0.89)
UPOS	75.33 (±2.13)	82.51 (±2.05)	76.88 (±2.15)	82.92 (±1.11)
LEMMA	87.44 (±0.76)	48.16 (±1.57)	50.47 (±1.36)	61.38 (±2.16)

Table 6: Results of the 10-fold cross-validation. OOV-rate shows the average percentage of OOV word forms in the test set in respect to training corpus. E. Egyptian T stands for transliteration and H+T for concatenated hieroglyphs and transliteration. The upper table shows overall results and the lower table the results for OOV word forms only.

number of OOVs are taken into account, the labels seem to be easy to predict compared to our other two datasets. Coptic dataset is also likely easier due to it being almost five times larger than that of Demotic, for instance. The word form to corpus size ratio is thus significantly lower, allowing the system to better learn their relations to the labels in context (cf. Table 4). For bench marking purposes, we also evaluated our system on the SIGTYP 2024 Shared Task dataset for Coptic. Our POS-tagger achieved an accuracy of 94.76% and our lemmatizer an accuracy of 96.20%. Although our POS-tagger underperformed the winner by 2.16%, the performance of our lemmatizer was at least on par with the best implementation, taking into account our system predicted only one label, whereas the best SIGTYP 2024 model's accuracy of 95.07% was based on the average two scores: predicting the correct lemma among the top-3 predictions and predicting only the top-1 lemma (Dereza et al., 2024).

The results for Demotic are on par with those earlier reported for Akkadian, Greek and Latin (Sahala and Lindén, 2023), except for lemmatization that performs slightly worse than expected due to high degree of ambiguity.

Low performance on Earlier Egyptian XPOS tagging is partly explainable by the size of its XPOS label set that also encodes the morphological analysis of the word. This makes the set four times larger than that of Coptic and five times the size of that of Demotic (Table 4). Another factor is the ambiguity of Egyptian word forms, which makes predicting the morphological labels difficult. The ambiguity also affects lemmatization performance, which is untypically low compared to other languages lemmatized with BabyLemmatizer. For UPOS tagging the results are better, but still slightly lower than for our other two datasets.

It seems that using the concatenation of hieroglyphs and transliteration yields slightly better results, but as it increases the portion of OOV word forms, the overall accuracy remains same. Noticeable improvement takes place in OOV lemmatization and POS-tagging, where including information about the hieroglyphs increases the accuracy up to ca. 10% (compare the E. Egyptian T and E. Egyptian H+T results in the lower section of Table 6).

7 Conclusions

We presented models for predicting lemma, UPOS and XPOS labels for Earlier Egyptian, Demotic and Coptic. Our models achieved an accuracy of 88% to 98% for XPOS tagging and 85% to 99% for lemmatization, depending on the input format and the language in question. We attempted various techniques to improve the accuracy of Earlier Egyptian lemmatization and POS tagging but were unable to achieve significantly better results. We hypothesized that the poor results are likely due to the small corpus size and the proportionally higher number of word form types compared to our other datasets.

Acknowledgments

We wish to thank the Academy of Finland for funding the project Origins of Emesal (PI Krister Lindén) and the Centre of Excellence in Ancient Near Eastern Empires (PI Saana Svärd). We are grateful to Daniel A. Werning (Berlin-Brandenburg Academy of Sciences and Humanities) for extracting the training data from the TLA corpus, discussing it with us, and providing comments on the manuscript of this paper. We also value the feedback from our reviewers which added valuable insights to the paper.

Sources

Coptic Scriptorium 2024: Coptic Scriptorium Corpora v4.2.0–v4.5.0 (downloaded 2023-11-20). Caroline T. Schroeder, Amir Zeldes, et al., Coptic SCRIPTORIUM, 2013-2024, urlhttp://copticscriptorium.org, https://github.com/CopticScriptorium/corpora

TLA-Dem 2024: Thesaurus Linguae Aegyptiae, Demotic sentences, corpus v18, premium, https://huggingface.co/datasets/thesaurus-linguae-aegyptiae/tla-demotic-v18-premium, v1.1, 2/16/2024 ed. by Tonio Sebastian Richter & Daniel A. Werning on behalf of the Berlin-Brandenburgische Akademie der Wissenschaften and Hans-Werner Fischer-Elfert & Peter Dils on behalf of the Sächsische Akademie der Wissenschaften zu Leipzig.

TLA-Egy 2024: Thesaurus Linguae Aegyptiae, Original Earlier Egyptian sentences, corpus v18, premium, https://huggingface.co/datasets/thesaurus-linguae-aegyptiae/tla-Earlier_Egyptian_original-v18-premium, v1.1, 2/16/2024 ed. by Tonio Sebastian Richter & Daniel A. Werning on behalf of the Berlin-Brandenburgische Akademie der Wissenschaften and Hans-Werner Fischer-Elfert & Peter Dils on behalf of the Sächsische Akademie der Wissenschaften zu Leipzig.

References

James P. Allen. 2013. *The Ancient Egyptian Language: An Historical Study*. Cambridge University Press, Cambridge.

James P. Allen. 2015. Old Egyptian. In Julie Stauder-Porchet, Andréas Stauder, and Willeke Wendrich, editors, *UCLA Encyclopedia of Egyptology*. Los Angeles.

María Victoria Almansa-Villatoro and Silvia Štubňová Nigrelli, editors. 2023. *Ancient Egyptian and Afroasiatic: Rethinking the Origins*, volume 11 of *Languages of the Ancient Near East*. Eisenbrauns, University Park, PA.

Dylan Michael Burns, Frank Feder, Katrin John, and Maxim Kupreyev. 2020. Comprehensive Coptic Lexicon: Including loanwords from Ancient greek v 1.2.

Oksana Dereza, Adrian Doyle, Priya Rani, Atul Kr. Ojha, Pádraic Moran, and John McCrae. 2024. Findings of the SIGTYP 2024 shared task on word embedding evaluation for ancient and historical languages. In *Proceedings of the 6th Workshop on Research in Computational Linguistic Typology and Multilingual NLP*, pages 160–172, St. Julian's, Malta. Association for Computational Linguistics.

Camilla Di Biase-Dyson, Frank Kammerzell, and Daniel A. Werning. 2009. Glossing Ancient Egyptian: Suggestions for adapting the Leipzig Glossing Rules. *Lingua Aegyptia*, 17:343–366.

Wolf-Peter Funk. 1988. Dialects wanting homes: A numerical approach to the early varieties of Coptic. In Jacek Fisiak, editor, *Historical Dialectology, Part 1: Regional and Social*, volume 37 of *Trends in Linguistics. Studies and Monographs*, pages 149–192. Mouton de Gruyter, Berlin/New York/Amsterdam.

Silke Grallert, Tonio Sebastian Richter, Simon D. Schweitzer, and Daniel A. Werning. 2023. TLA Text Corpus, corpus issue 18. In Tonio Sebastian Richter, Daniel A. Werning, Hans-Werner Fischer-Elfert, and Peter Dils, editors, *Thesaurus Linguae Aegyptiae*. Berlin-Brandenburgische Akademie der Wissenschaften and Sächsische Akademie der Wissenschaften zu Leipzig. Web-App-Version 2.1.3, Accessed: 5/15/2024.

Silke Grallert, Tonio Sebastian Richter, and Daniel A. Werning. 2024. TLA-Lemmalisten, corpus issue 18. In Tonio Sebastian Richter, Daniel A. Werning, Hans-Werner Fischer-Elfert, and Peter Dils, editors, *Thesaurus Linguae Aegyptiae*. Berlin-Brandenburgische Akademie der Wissenschaften and Sächsische Akademie der Wissenschaften zu Leipzig. Web-App-Version 2.1.3, Accessed: 5/16/2024.

Eitan Grossman. 2019. Language-specific transitivities in contact: The case of Coptic. *Journal of Language Contact*, 12(1):89–115.

Eitan Grossman and Martin Haspelmath. 2015. The Leipzig-Jerusalem transliteration of Coptic. In (Grossman et al., 2015), pages 145–153.

Eitan Grossman, Martin Haspelmath, and Tonio Sebastian Richter, editors. 2015. *Egyptian-Coptic Linguistics in Typological Perspective*, volume 55 of *Empirical Approaches to Language Typology*. De Gruyter Mouton, Berlin/Munich/Boston.

Eitan Grossman and Tonio Sebastian Richter. 2015. The Egyptian-Coptic language: its setting in space, time and culture. In (Grossman et al., 2015), pages 69–101.

Martin Haspelmath. 2015. A grammatical overview of Egyptian and Coptic. In (Grossman et al., 2015), pages 104–143.

Frank Kammerzell. 2005. Old Egyptian and Pre-Old Egyptian: Tracing linguistic diversity in archaic Egypt and the creation of the Egyptian language. In Stephan J. Seidlmayer, editor, *Texte und Denkmäler des ägyptischen Alten Reiches*, number 3 in Thesaurus Linguae Aegyptiae, pages 165–246. Achet, Berlin.

Guillaume Klein, Yoon Kim, Yuntian Deng, Jean Senellart, and Alexander M Rush. 2017. OpenNMT: Open-source toolkit for neural machine translation. *arXiv preprint arXiv:1701.02810*.

Antonio Loprieno. 1988. On the typological order of constituents in Egyptian. *Journal of Afroasiatic Languages*, 1:26–57.

Antonio Loprieno. 1995. *Ancient Egyptian: A Linguistic Introduction*. Cambridge University Press, Cambridge.

Antonio Loprieno. 2004. Ancient Egyptian and Coptic. In Roger D. Woodard, editor, *The Cambridge Encyclopedia of the World's Ancient Languages*, pages 160–217. Cambridge University Press, Cambridge.

Antonio Loprieno and Matthias Müller. 2012. Ancient Egyptian and Coptic. In Zygmunt Frajzyngier and Erin Shai, editors, *The Afroasiatic Languages*, pages 102–144. Cambridge University Press, Cambridge.

Antonio Loprieno, Matthias Müller, and Sami Uljas. 2017. *Non-Verbal Predication in Ancient Egyptian*, volume 2 of *The Mouton Companions to Ancient Egyptian*. De Gruyter Mouton, Berlin/Boston.

Rachael Hannah McLaughlin. 2022. *The Linguistic Cycle in Ancient Egyptian Verbal Constructions*. Phd thesis, University of Liverpool.

So Miyagawa. 2023. Noun incorporation in Coptic. In Diliana Atanassova, Frank Feder, and Heike Sternberg el Hotabi, editors, *Pharaonen, Mönche und Gelehrte: Auf dem Pilgerweg durch 5000 Jahre ägyptische Geschichte über drei Kontinente: Heike Behlmer zum 65. Geburtstag*, volume 4 of *Texte und Studien zur Koptischen Bibel*, pages 565–574. Harrassowitz, Wiesbaden. Festschrift for Heike Behlmer's 65th Birthday.

Matthias Müller. 2020. Egyptian. In Rebecca Hasselbach-Andee, editor, *A Companion to Ancient Near Eastern Languages*, pages 107–128. Wiley Blackwell, Hoboken, NJ.

Stéphane Polis, editor. 2023. *Guide to the Writing Systems of Ancient Egypt*, volume 4 of *Guides de l'Institut Français d'Archéologie Orientale*. IFAO, Cairo.

Stéphane Polis and Serge Rosmorduc. 2015. The hieroglyphic sign functions: Suggestions for a revised taxonomy. In Hans Amstutz, Andreas Dorn, Matthias Müller, et al., editors, *Fuzzy Boundaries: Festschrift Antonio Loprieno I*, pages 149–174. Kai Widmaier, Hamburg.

Joachim F. Quack, Claudia Maderna-Sieben, Jannik Korte, and Fabian Wespi. 2024. The Demotic Palaeographical Database Project. Accessed: 15 May 2024.

Joachim Friedrich Quack. 2006. En route vers le copte. notes sur l'évolution du démotique tardif. *Faits de langues, Les langues chamito-sémitiques (afro-asiatiques), Vol. 2*, 27:191–216.

Tonio Sebastian Richter. 2023. Coptic. In Andréas Stauder and Willeke Wendrich, editors, *UCLA Encyclopedia of Egyptology*. Los Angeles.

Tonio Sebastian Richter, Daniel A. Werning, Hans-Werner Fischer-Elfert, and Peter Dils, editors. 2023. *Thesaurus Linguae Aegyptiae, Corpus issue 18*. Berlin-Brandenburgische Akademie der Wissenschaften and Sächsische Akademie der Wissenschaften zu Leipzig. Web-App-Version 2.1.3, Accessed: 5/13/2024.

Kim Ryholt. 1998. A parallel to the Inaros Story of P. Krall (P. Carlsberg 456+P CtYBR 4513): Demotic narratives from the Tebtunis temple library (I). *Journal of Egyptian Archaeology*, 84:151–169.

A. J. Aleksi Sahala and Krister Lindén. 2023. A neural pipeline for lemmatizing and POS-tagging cuneiform languages. In *Proceedings of the Ancient Language Processing Workshop at the 14th International Conference on Recent Advances in Natural Language Processing RANLP 2023*, pages 203–212.

Wolfgang Schenkel. 1990. *Einführung in die altägyptische Sprachwissenschaft*. Wissenschaftliche Buchgesellschaft, Darmstadt.

Wolfgang Schenkel. 2001. Middle Egyptian. In Donald B. Redford, editor, *The Oxford Encyclopedia of Ancient Egypt*, volume 2, pages 52–56. Oxford University Press, Oxford.

Wolfgang Schenkel. 2003. *Die hieroglyphische Schriftlehre und die Realität der hieroglyphischen Graphien*, volume 138 of *Sitzungsberichte der Sächsischen Akademie der Wissenschaften zu Leipzig. Philologisch-historische Klasse*. Hirzel, Stuttgart.

Caroline T. Schroeder and Amir Zeldes. 2016. Raiders of the lost corpus. *Digital Humanities Quarterly*, 10(2).

Daniel Smith and Mans Hulden. 2016. Morphological analysis of Sahidic Coptic for automatic glossing. In *Proceedings of the Tenth International Conference on Language Resources and Evaluation (LREC'16)*, pages 2584–2588.

Andréas Stauder. 2020. History of the Egyptian Language. In Ian Shaw and Elizabeth Bloxam, editors, *Oxford Handbook of Egyptology*, pages 930–956. Oxford University Press, Oxford.

Wolfhart Westendorf. 1977. *Koptisches Handwörterbuch*, 2nd edition. Universitätsverlag Winter, Heidelberg.

Jean Winand. 2018. Late Egyptian. In Julie Stauder-Porchet, Andréas Stauder, and Willeke Wendrich, editors, *UCLA Encyclopedia of Egyptology*. Los Angeles.

Amir Zeldes and Caroline T. Schroeder. 2015. Computational Methods for Coptic: Developing and Using Part-of-Speech Tagging for Digital Scholarship in the Humanities. *Digital Scholarship in the Humanities*, 30(suppl1):i164–i176.

Amir Zeldes and Caroline T. Schroeder. 2016. An NLP pipeline for Coptic. In *Proceedings of the 10th SIGHUM Workshop on Language Technology for Cultural Heritage, Social Sciences, and Humanities*, pages 146–155, Berlin, Germany. Association for Computational Linguistics.

UFCNet: Unsupervised Network based on Fourier transform and Convolutional attention for Oracle Character Recognition

Guoqi Liu[1,2,3], Yanan Zhou *[1,3], Yiping Yang[1,3], Linyuan Ru[1,2], Dong Liu[1,2,3], and Xueshan Li[2]

[1]College of Computer and Information Engineering, Henan Normal University, Henan, China
[2]Oracle Bone Intelligent Computing Laboratory, Henan Normal University, Henan, China
[3]Big Data Engineering Laboratory for Teaching Resource & Assessment of Education Quality, Henan, China

Abstract

Oracle bone script (OBS) is the earliest writing system in China, which is of great value in the improvement of archaeology and Chinese cultural history. However, there are some problems such as the lack of labels and the difficulty to distinguish the glyphs from the background of OBS, which makes the automatic recognition of OBS in the real world not achieve the satisfactory effect. In this paper, we propose a character recognition method based on an unsupervised domain adaptive network (UFCNet). Firstly, a convolutional attention fusion module (CAFM) is designed in the encoder to obtain more global features through multi-layer feature fusion. Second, we construct a Fourier transform (FT) module that focuses on the differences between glyphs and backgrounds. Finally, to further improve the network's ability to recognize character edges, we introduce a kernel norm-constrained loss function. Extensive experiments perform on the Oracle-241 dataset show that the proposed method is superior to other adaptive methods. The code will be available at https://github.com/zhouynan/UFCNet.

1 Introduction

The oracle bone inscriptions (OBIs) mainly refer to the OBIs of Yinxu, which are carved on tortoises in the Shang Dynasty. It is the earliest self-contained writing system in China,which is of great significance to the improvement of Chinese cultural history and the study of the formation and evolution of Chinese characters (Xie et al., 2020). The oracle bone character (OBC) image of rubbings is mainly the original image obtained by experts on the unearthed tortoise shell, animal bone, and other text carriers. As the oracle bones have been buried underground for a long time, they are badly damaged or contaminated, and there is serious noise (Huang et al., 2019), which makes it very challenging to recognize OBCs.

Early research methods mainly combine graph theory and topological properties. (Li and Zhou, 1996) proposed an OBIs recognition method based on graph theory. They abstracted oracle into an undirected graph composed of only points and lines, and extracted its topological features. (Li and Zhou, 1996) introduced the information of the adjacent points of the endpoint, and improved the recognition accuracy through the continuous recognition of multi-level feature coding. However, these methods cannot meet the real-world oracle recognition, which requires a lot of manpower and time.

To help with the excavation of new oracle bones and the identification of unseen characters, the advent of deep neural networks has a great impact on the recognition of oracle bone character (OBC) images. (Zhang et al., 2019) used CNNs to map character images into Euclidean space for classification by nearest neighbor rules. (Guo et al., 2015) utilized a low-level representation associated with Gabor and an intermediate representation associated with a sparse encoder and combines it with a CNN-based model. However, training a depth model requires a large number of labeled samples. (Wang et al., 2022) proposed an unsupervised structured Texture separation network (STSN) for Oracle identification and a dataset of 241 classes of Oracle-241 (Wang et al., 2022) for unsupervised identification. They took handprint characters transcribed by experts with high resolution and clean backgrounds as source domains. Accordingly, the original oracle character (scanned image) is taken as the target domains. They have achieved good results by finding a domain invariant feature space to align the distribution between two domains.

In this paper, we propose a network (UFCNet) combining Fourier transform and convolutional attention for oracle character recognition. The convolution attention fusion module (CAFM) combines deep and shallow features to obtain more global information and a better position location of char-

*Corresponding author: 2208283102@stu.htu.edu.cn

Proceedings of the 1st Workshop on Machine Learning for Ancient Languages (ML4AL 2024), pages 98–106
August 15, 2024

acters. Additionally, we further design the Fourier transform (FT) module that converts the image from the spatial domain to the frequency domain, aiming to capture the edge details of the glyphs more efficiently and provide rich functionality for the CAFM. We utilize the FT module to capture the high-frequency information of character images and extract rich edge information. We also introduce a kernel norm-constrained loss function to improve the network's discriminative performance on edges. We conduct extensive experiments on the Oracle-241 dataset, and the results demonstrate that our network exhibits better recognition performance in the realm of unsupervised adaptation.

Our main contributions are summarized as follows:

- We deploy CAFM can better extract and fuse features at different levels, and establish a global relationship between multi-layer features.
- We design the FT module, the OBIs are converted to the frequency domain, which can extract the edge features, and provide more effective detail features for the CAFM.
- To validate the effectiveness of our method, we conduct extensive experiments on the Oracle-241 dataset and results demonstrate that UFCNet has better classification accuracy than the existing state-of-the-art (SOTA) unsupervised OBIs recognition method STSN.

2 Related work

2.1 Oracle character recognition

The recognition and deciphering of oracle characters is one of the major topics in the study of oracle bones. With the development of technology, many researchers have tried to recognize oracle characters by image processing. For example, by using non-directed graphs, DNA methods, and template matching (Lin et al., 2016). The earliest studies were (Zhou et al., 1995), (Li and Woo, 2000), (Gu, 2016) which considered oracle features as an undirected graph and used its topological properties as features for classification. (Li et al., 2011) proposed an algorithm based on graph isomorphism. They transformed inscriptions into labeled graphs and used an adjacency matrix of the labeled graphs to encode the inscriptions. (Lv et al., 2010) proposed a Fourier descriptor based on curvature histogram to identify OBIs. (Guo et al., 2015) regarded the oracle bone recognition problem as a sketch recognition task and constructed a hierarchical representation for it.

In addition, (Liu and Liu, 2017) extracted block histogram-based features and applied support vector machines (SVM) to recognize characters. (Gu et al., 2008) believed that the topological structure of OBIs was relatively stable, and calculated the fractal dimension of OBIs according to their fractal characteristics. However, most of these methods are complex large-scale systems composed of multi-layer features, so these methods mainly rely on artificial feature design, which is highly subjective. In particular, they are mostly suitable for small-scale datasets, not for large-scale dataset design and evaluation.

In recent years, convolutional neural networks (CNNs) have made great progress in some computer vision tasks and have been introduced into the recognition of oracle characters. (Huang et al., 2019) published a dataset of scanned oracle characters called OBC306 and proposed a CNN-based evaluation of this dataset as a benchmark, (Guo et al., 2015) aimed to use a CNN-based learning (Wang and Deng, 2018) model to represent oracle characters. They generated a dataset named Oracle-20K and trained and tested it with the proposed CNN. However, they did not discuss the real images of the OBIs and their features such as noise, fracture, and non-uniformity. (Zhang et al., 2019) proposed a deep metric learning-based nearest neighbor classification for oracle recognition and trained a DenseNet (Huang et al., 2017) with triplet state loss to classify manually printed and scanned dataset in a supervised manner. However, the difference in distribution between handprint and scanned characters is not taken into account.

2.2 Unsupervised domain adaptation

Cross-domain tasks are often encountered in computer vision and pattern recognition, there are two types of data, one with labeled information and the other without or little labeled information. To discard the target labeled data, unsupervised domain adaptation (UDA) was proposed in the literature (Wang and Deng, 2018) to solve the problem of domain drift between the labeled source domain and unlabeled target domain.

Popular UDA methods (Long et al., 2015), (Peng et al., 2019) align distributions by moment matching. For example, maximum mean difference

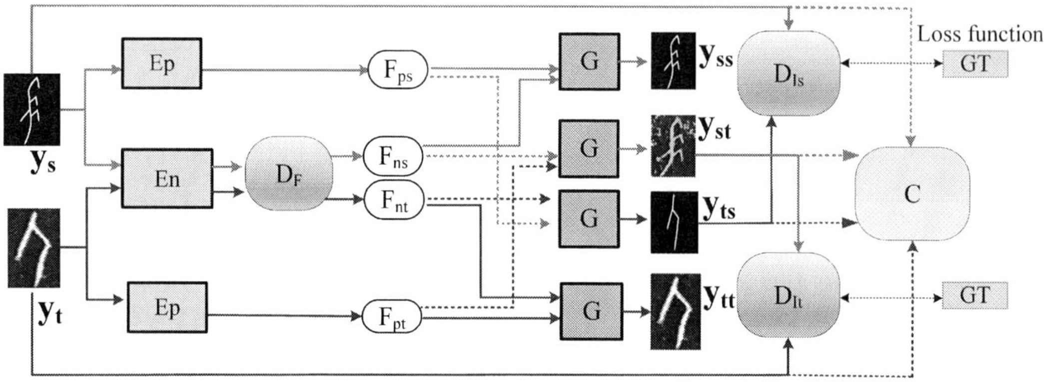

Figure 1: The overall structure of the proposed UFCNet includes a shared encoder E_n for extracting font, which uses RseNet-18 as the backbone network, and an independent encoder E_p. A generator G, a classifier and discriminators D_F and D_I for distinguishing features.

(MMD) (Long et al., 2015), (Chen et al., 2019) were used to reduce distribution mismatch. With a labeled source dataset and an unlabeled target dataset, their main goal is to train the recognition model on the source domain dataset so that it can be generalized to the target domain.

Another common approach to address unsupervised domain adaptation is through adversarial learning strategies (Yaroslav and Victor, 2015),(Eric et al., 2017) where the differences between domains are minimized by jointly training a network of recognizers and a network of domain discriminators. Adversarial learning (Yaroslav and Victor, 2015), (Long et al., 2018) were widely used for alignment of source and target domains. Domain adversarial neural networks (DANN)(Yaroslav et al., 2016) made it impossible for domain classifiers to predict the domain labels of features by the gradient inversion layer (GRL), making the distribution of features on two domains similar. Conditional adversarial domain adaptation (CDAN)(Long et al., 2018) built an adversarial adaptation model based on the discriminative information passed in the classifier prediction. In both methods, a subnetwork called a domain discriminator is used, trained to distinguish between source and target dataset and to learn depth features to confuse the discriminator in domain adversarial training.

If a model is trained directly in the source domain and applied to the target domain, the results are often poor because the feature distributions of the two may be somewhat different. (Wang et al., 2022) proposed the use of UDA to transfer knowledge from easily accessible handprint dataset to the scanned domain. They used a secure distributed alignment in the feature space associated with the structure (glyphs), which can mitigate the negative effects of severe noise and wear and tear. Second, with the idea of Generative Adversarial Networks (GANs), they designed a generator and duplex discriminator to realize the exchange of learned texture (background) information between any pair of images to transform the image. This approach successfully transfers the knowledge of handprint oracle character recognition to the scanned dataset and improves the recognition performance.

3 Methods

The UFCNet network proposed in this paper is shown in Figure 1. It adopts the unsupervised idea of STSN to transfer the knowledge of handprint oracle character recognition to scanned dataset. It consists of three encoders, one of which is a glyph-sharing encoder E_n for extracting both handprint and scanned characters. It is a ResNet-18 pre-trained on the ImageNet dataset as a structural encoder. The other two are independent encoders E_p used to extract the background features of handprint and scanned characters. Specifically, E_p consists of one convolution unit with a kernel size of 7x7 (convolution, BatchNormalization, and ReLU) and four convolution units with a kernel size of 3, CAFM and FT. The CAFM can cascade the high-level and low-level features of handprint and scanned images to obtain rich global features. The FT module can capture more edge features of characters by using the advantage of converting the image to the frequency domain. Alternatively, it includes a generator G, a feature-level discriminator

Generator(G)
Input: f_n, f_p
Deconv(k4n256s2), IN, Relu, ConvBlock(k3n128s1)
Deconv(k4n128s2), IN, Relu, ConvBlock(k3n64s1)
Deconv(k4n64s2), IN, Relu, ConvBlock(k3n32s1)
Deconv(k4n32s2), IN, Relu, ConvBlock(k3n32s1)1x2
Conv(k3n3s1)Tanh
Output: $y^{ss}/y^{st}/y^{ts}/y^{tt}$

Table 1: Network architecture of the generator is used for oracle characters recognition.

Discriminator(D_I)	Discriminator(D_F)
Conv(k6n64s2), IN, Relu(0.2)	Linear(1024), Relu
Conv(k6n128s2), IN, Relu(0.2)	Dropout(0.5)
Conv(k6n256s2), IN, Relu(0.2)	Linear(1024), Relu
Conv(k6n256s2), IN, Relu(0.2)	Dropout(0.5)
Linear(1)	Linear(1), Sigmoid
Output: Real/Fake	Output: Source/Target

Table 2: The discriminator is used for the network architecture Identify.

D_F, two image-level discriminators $\{D_{Is}, D_{It}\}$ and a classifier that is finally used to classify the recognized scanned characters. For the discriminators of images and features, the discriminative network structure uses in this paper is detailed in Table 1 and Table 2.

3.1 Convolutional attention fusion module

To get rich features, we try to fully mine the global and local information of the glyph to improve the dependency extraction of the glyph in the image. We pass the starting image $\chi \in R^{H\times W\times 3}$ through three multi-scale feature maps (i.e., S_1', S_2' and S_3') generated by serialized convolution blocks at different stages. Among these feature maps, S_1' and S_2' provide detailed information about the appearance of oracle characters, while S_3' provides high-level features. Specifically, we consider F as a convolutional unit containing 3×3 convolution, batch normalization (Sergey and Christian, 2015), and ReLU (Xavier et al., 2015). As shown in Figure 2. CAFM is divided into three parts.

Firstly, for the high-level feature S_3', we use an upsampling operation to make the highest-level feature maps S_3' and S_2' have the same size. In this paper, we use the convolutional operation units F1 and F2 with kernel size 3×3 to provide the required information for the network and filter out the unnecessary background texture noise, get the results S_{31} and S_{32}, multiply S_{31} with S_2', this can establish a global relationship between multi-layer features. And input the results obtained from the multiplication into the channel and spatial attention model (CSAM) to get C1. CSAM utilizes channel and spatial weighting on these basic features to better focus on interdependence between some features on channels and space to improve the sensitivity of the model to channels as well as spatial features. Denote the current process as Eq.1.

$$\begin{cases} S_{31} = F1\left[U\left(S_3'\right)\right] \\ S_{32} = F2\left[U\left(S_3'\right)\right] \\ S_{22} = F4\left[U\left(S_2'\right)\right] \\ C1 = CSM\left(S_{31} \times S_2'\right) \end{cases} \tag{1}$$

Secondly, for the features S_2' and S_1' in the lower two layers, we also use the same way of processing the higher-level features by performing convolutional upsampling operations on S_2' and S_3' respectively to reach the same size as S_1'. By multiplying the three features, we can build global features between multiple layers of features. The details of the low-level features are added to the high level after using convolutional attention to CSM to obtain C2. This process is denoted as Eq.2.

$$C2 = CSM\left\{F3\left[U\left(S_3'\right)\right] \times S_1'\right\} \tag{2}$$

Finally, we pass the feature through CSM and smoothly concatenate the resulting C1 with S_{32}, and the feature is mapped to two convolutional units (F5 and F6). Due to the potential loss of crucial detail information during the convolution process, and considering that C2 has already acquired rich local features following the CSM, we opt to integrate the output of the convolution unit with C2. This fusion strategy effectively harnesses some of the original structural information, enhancing the overall feature representation. Finally, we input the connected feature maps into F for dimensionality reduction to get the result T1, which is also the output of CAFM.

3.2 Fourier transform module

The discrete Fourier transform plays an important role in image processing and pattern recognition as an effective computational tool. Several studies (Justin et al., 2016) , (Leon A et al., 2015) have shown that higher feature layers are beneficial in maintaining structural information, while lower feature layers help to maintain what is associated with

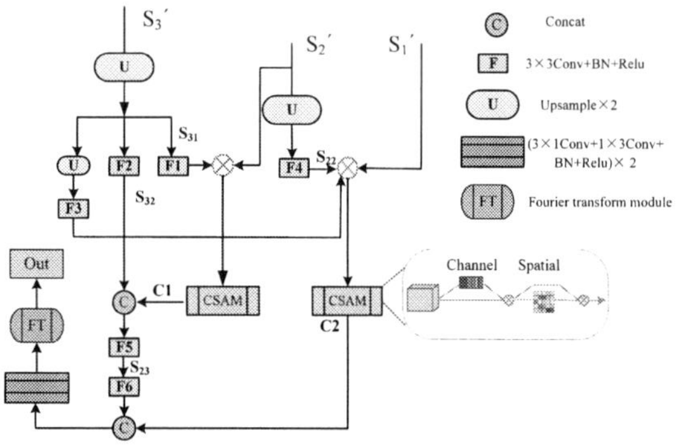

Figure 2: An architecture that passes shallow features into deep features and merges them.

texture. However, in the scanned dataset, it is difficult to distinguish the edge outline of the font because of the similarity between the characters and the background, which makes it difficult to identify the oracle characters accurately. Studies have shown that Fourier transform method can obtain high-frequency information of the object (the edge of the object). At the same time, compared with the spatial domain filtering with large number of cores, frequency domain filtering has obvious advantages. Therefore, we further consider to transfer the image recognition of text to the frequency domain for more detailed feature extraction.

In particular, high-pass filtering can make high-frequency components unimpeded, allowing only high-frequency features to be transmitted, and suppressing low frequencies. The high frequencies in the frequency domain correspond to the Outlines (edges) of the objects in the image. Therefore, FT combines with Gaussian filter is used to extract rich edge information of the oracle bone text image in the frequency domain, so that background pixels and text pixels can be effectively distinguished. The FT module is structured as shown in Figure 3.

It is worth noting that the global feature is obtained by aggregation at the bottom of the encoder. We transform global feature to a single-line greyscale image, performed a two-dimensional discrete FT, and obtained a frequency domain map.

After the discrete FT, it is transmitted to the center of the spectrum graph to obtain the low-frequency information. The number of frequencies of an image in the frequency domain corresponds to the number of pixels of that image in the time domain, indicating that the image has the same number of dimensions in the time and frequency domains. For an input grey-scale image of size

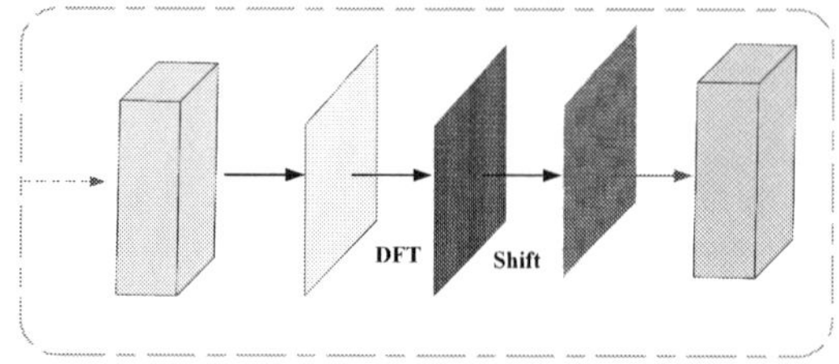

Figure 3: The structure of fourier transform module.

$H_1 \times W_1$, the two-dimensional DFT is expressed as Eq.3.

$$F(k,l) = \frac{1}{H_1 W_1} \sum_{c=0}^{H_1-1} \sum_{d=0}^{W_1-1} f(c,d)\, e^{-j\frac{2\pi}{H_1}kc} e^{-j\frac{2\pi}{W_1}ld} \tag{3}$$

The discrete function is for the spatial domain image. We use a combination of Gaussian filter and Fourier transform to extract rich edge information in the frequency domain. Notably, we set the radius of the circular filter to 0.5, which can prevent the loss of details after image reconstruction. Where $F(0,0)$ shows the lowest frequency and $F(H_1-1, W_1-1)$ is the highest frequency. Then, the high-frequency portion is processed using the Fourier inverse transform to obtain high-frequency images to explicitly model the dependencies between channels. It can be written as Eq.4.

$$f(c,d) = \frac{1}{H_1 W_1} \sum_{k=0}^{H_1-1} \sum_{l=0}^{W_1-1} F(k,l)\, e^{j\frac{2\pi}{H_1}kc} e^{j\frac{2\pi}{W_1}ld} \tag{4}$$

3.3 Loss function

To generate more realistic OBCs, the following perceptual loss (l_{pre}) (Wang et al., 2022) and reconstruction loss (l_{rec}) (Wang et al., 2022) are introduced in this paper to impose constraints on the structural similarity and texture similarity during image reconstruction. The first part, perceptual loss, constraints y_{st} to be similar to y_t in texture; it also requires y_{st} to be similar to y_s in structure. A similar constraint is imposed on the transformed image y_{ts}. The second part of the reconstruction loss ensures that the reconstructed images y_{ss} and y_{tt} should be the same as the original input images y_s and y_t. In addition, we apply the mean square loss (MSE) and the cross entropy loss function CrossEntorpyLoss.

In particular, we also propose a key loss function l_{bcem}, which is a loss function based on BCELoss.

Specifically, we introduce the nuclear norm constraint BNM (Leon A et al., 2015) to improve the edge discrimination ability of the network. In the case of insufficient labels, the performance of the network on the decision boundary will be degraded. To improve discriminability, we introduce nuclear norm maximization to improve target prediction ability. Experiments show that when the weighting factor is 0.5, BNM enables the network to obtain the optimal result for the discrimination of the target domain edge that lacks labels. So the total loss of our l_{bcem} is Eq.5.

$$l_{bcem} = l_{bce} - l_{BNM} \tag{5}$$

Thus, the overall loss in this paper is Eq.6.

$$l_{loss} = l_{mse} + l_{ce} + l_{pre} + l_{rec} + l_{bcem} \tag{6}$$

4 Experiment

4.1 Datasets

In this section, we use the Oracle dataset of Oracle-241 for character recognition, using our network to transfer knowledge from the handprint data to the scanned data. Oracle-241 contains 78,565 handprint and scanned characters in 241 categories. The handprint samples used for training and the unlabeled scan samples are 10861 and 50168, respectively. The dataset use for testing contains 3730 handprint data and 13806 scan data. As shown in Table 3.

4.2 Implementation details

The proposed method uses Pytorch as a framework and runs on a single NVIDIA GeForce GTX 3090Ti 24G GPU. We perform 150,000 iterations on data with a batch size of 16. For preprocessing, we randomly crop and flip the training samples, setting the weight decay and initial learning rate to 5e-4 and 2.5e-4, respectively. This paper follows standard protocols for unsupervised domain adaptation, e.g. (Yaroslav et al., 2016), (Long et al., 2018). Train with all marked source characters and all unmarked target characters. To quantitatively evaluate the recognition performance of UFCNet on handprint and scan datasets, classification accuracy is used as the evaluation metric in this paper, and the calculation method is as follows Eq.7.

$$ACC = \frac{TP + FN}{TP + TN + FP + FN} \tag{7}$$

Where TP and TN represent the number of pixels and background texture pixels of correctly identified oracle font structure, respectively. Similarly,

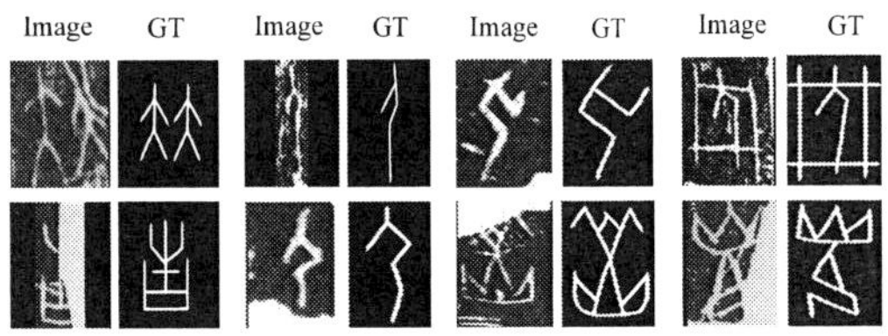

Figure 4: Eight images are misclassified with the "single-source" model, but our model classified them correctly.

	Train	Test
handprint	10861	3730
Scan	50168	13806

Table 3: Statistics from the ORACLE-241 dataset.

FP represents a background pixel incorrectly identified as an oracle glyph structure, while FN represents an oracle glyph structure pixel incorrectly predicted as a background pixel.

4.3 Comparative experiment

To demonstrate the effectiveness of our network, we compare the UFCNet with some of the methods used to identify (Huang et al., 2019). Since they only use handprint samples to train the network model, the model trained on the source domain has no adaptation, they are referred to as " single-source " models in this paper. In addition, we compare with other SOTA adaptive methods for image classification, such as CDAN, DANN, BSP (Chen et al., 2019), and GVB (Cui et al., 2020). All of these data are used with ResNet-18 as the backbone and experimented in the same environment to make a fair comparison.

Method	Accuracy (%)	
	Handprint	Scan
ResNet	94.9	2.9
CDAN	86.5	37.8
DANN	88.7	31.4
BSP	91.7	33.7
GVB	87.8	36.8
STSN	92.2	44.9
Ours	**94.7**	**56.5**

Table 4: Source and target Accuracy (MEAN %) on ORACLE-241 dataset is statistically compared with various state-of-the-art (SOTA) methods. The best numbers are represented in bold.

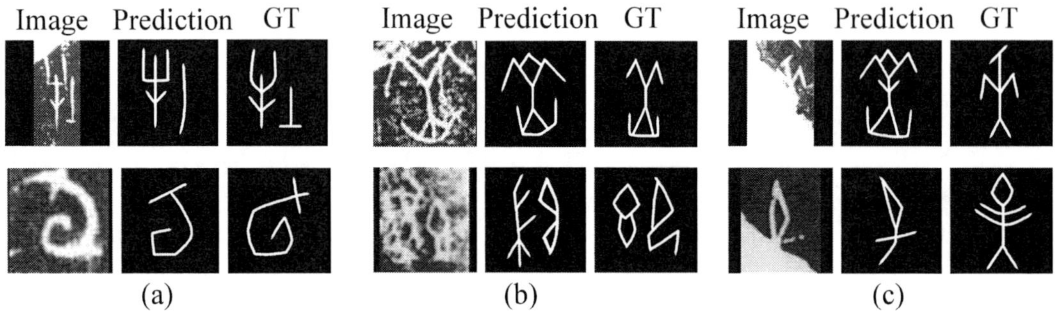

Figure 5: The example samples which are misclassified by UFCNet. For each set of characters, the left, middle, and right images represent the scan sample, model prediction, and ground-truth (GT), respectively. (a) represents characters that look similar, (b) denotes characters that contain heavy noise, and (c) is heavily polluted or occlusion characters.

We can see from the results in Table 4. Firstly, training on handprint dataset and testing on the same domain, the model trained and tested only on the source domain model can obtain higher accuracy. When directly apply to scanned dataset, the model's performance undergoes a marked degradation. Figure 4 shows some example images that are misclassified by the "single-source" model but correctly classified by our model. From these results, we can find that the "single-source" model has difficulty in identifying scanned images with severe noise and contaminated wear, while our model can successfully identify them. Our method in this paper transfers the knowledge from handprint dataset to scanned dataset by unsupervised domain transfer, and better results can be obtained on scanned dataset.

Secondly, we note that although the existing unsupervised domain adaptation methods can use domain invariant features to improve the performance of the target domain, this phenomenon illustrates the importance of mitigating domain transfer. However, if this method does not consider the texture feature information contained in the source domain and the target domain, it is still difficult to align the entire source domain and the target domain. In addition, the characteristics of having two domains meanwhile will also have a certain degree of negative impact on alignment, thus affecting the performance of the two domains. GVB uses a fully connected bridge to model domain-specific parts. Compared with the single domain method, the success rate of GVB for scanning sample recognition is 36.8%. However, the simple structure of the bridge makes it difficult to capture the characteristics of different fields very well.

Finally, DANN does not consider the relationship between samples and labels, but only directly connects samples and labels to form a higher-dimensional vector. This approach will hurt distinguishing the source domain and the target domain. Compared with DANN, CDAN has improved the scanned dataset by 6.4%. CDAN introduces sample weighting in the discriminator for both the source and target domains. As the classifier converges, the weight assigned to source domain samples will gradually approach unity, leading to equal weighting for source samples. Although BSP applies the singular value decomposition method to obtain the maximum k singular values of the source and target eigenmatrices, respectively. The BSP is utilized as the regularization term in these maximum k singular values. Nevertheless, due to the discrepancies between domains, the eigenvectors might not receive equal contributions from the source and target domains, potentially leading to distortions.

In particular, for the classical adaptive models CDAN and DANN, benefiting from the joint adaptation of STSN, pick-up entanglement and transformation and freedom from contamination by background textures during the adaptive process, our network model's improvements on top of them are more advantageous for the recognition and classification of scanned dataset. Inspired by the Fourier transform, detailed features of the character structure are extracted from a frequency domain perspective, especially the edge part of high frequency. In addition, a convolutional attention module is introduced to extract more comprehensive features at the encoder

However, due to the existence of some similar characters, the model classification fails. For ex-

Method	Accuracy (%)	
	Handprint	Scan
Baseline	92.2	44.9
Baseline+CAFM	93.2	50.7
Baseline+CAFM+FT	94.6	54.6
Baseline+CAFM+FT+bcem	94.7	56.5

Table 5: Statistical comparison of ablation experiments of two key components in UFCNet. CAFM stands for convolution attention fusion module. FT stands for Fourier transform module.

ample, the characteristics of prediction and groundtruth (GT) categories differ only in a few details. Secondly, as shown in Figure 5, severe noise, severe image degradation, even for humans, there are certain challenges.

4.4 Ablation experiments

To verify the experimental effectiveness of each block in our network, we conduct ablation experiments on UFCNet. The baseline network is a U-shaped codec structure where the private encoder consists of one convolution unit with a kernel size of 7x7 (convolution, BatchNormalization, and ReLU) and four convolution units with a kernel size of 3. After each convolution, the input feature is downsampled twice, the size of the feature map is reduced, and then it is re-amplified through the upsampling operation, which is used to transfer information between the encoder and the decoder, so as to retain more detailed information. Then the average pooling operation is performed to reduce the noise effect of irrelevant features. We add a convolutional attention module and a Fourier transform module to this and tested the baseline+CAFM and baseline+FT and loss function on dataset Oracle-241, respectively. All the ablation experiments are performed in the same computational environment. The test results are shown in Table 5.

Effectiveness of CAFM: Compared to the base network, the performance optimization of adding CAFM, especially in the classification accuracy of the scanned dataset, increased by 5.8%. This further indicates that adding the CAFM module to the base network can capture more global feature information, helping to locate the location of the object.

Effectiveness of FT: The addition of the FT module to the base network shows the superiority of our FT module by Table 5, especially the recognition accuracy for scanned dataset increases by 6.8%. In particular, the FT module can obtain more edge information when extracting high frequencies from images

Effectiveness of the loss function: We use the improved l_{bcem} function, and the results in Table 5 shows that our loss function can improve the discriminative property of the network for edges and can better extract the detailed features of oracle characters.

5 Conclusion

In this paper, we propose a new network UFCNet for the recognition of oracle character images. Different from the recognition method of OBCs based on CNNs, we use the Fourier transform to transfer the recognition of oracle character images from the image domain to the frequency domain and extract rich edge information. At the same time, we use the convolutional attention fusion module to fuse shallow features with deep features in multiple layers, which makes up for the important detailed features lost in the sampling process of the CNN. A large number of experiments show that our UFCNet has better recognition accuracy compared with SOTA methods. However, due to the serious incompleteness and blurring of OBCs, our network still needs to be further improved in recognition.

Acknowledgments

The work was supported by the National Natural Science Foundation of China (No.U1904123, No.61901160).

References

F Li and XL Zhou. 1996. The graph theory method of oracle bone inscriptions automatic recognition. *J. Electron*, 18(1):41–47.

F Li and X.L Zhou. 1996. Study on computer identification method of oracle. *J. Fudan Univ*, 481–486.

Jun Guo et al. 2015. Building hierarchical representations for oracle character and sketch recognition. *IEEE Transactions on Image Processing*, 25(1):104–118.

Yi-Kang Zhang et al. 2019. Oracle character recognition by nearest neighbor classification with deep metric learning. *2019 International Conference on Document Analysis and Recognition (ICDAR)*, 309–314.

Mei Wang et al. 2022. Unsupervised Structure-Texture Separation Network for Oracle Character Recognition. *IEEE Transactions on Image Processing*, 31:3137–3150.

Meng Lin et al. 2016. Recognition of oracular bone inscriptions using template matching. *International Journal of Computer Theory and Engineering*, 8(1):53.

Xin-Lun Zhou et al. 1995. A method of Jia Gu Wen recognition based on a two-level classification. *Proceedings of 3rd International Conference on Document Analysis and Recognition*, 2:833–836.

Feng Li and Peng-yung Woo. 2000. The coding principle and method for automatic recognition of Jia Gu Wen characters. *International Journal of Human-Computer Studies*, 53(2):289–299.

Qingsheng Li et al. 2011. Recognition of inscriptions on bones or tortoise shells based on graph isomorphism. *Jisuanji Gongcheng yu Yingyong(Computer Engineering and Applications)*, 47(8):112–114.

Shaotong Gu. 2016. Identification of oracle-bone script fonts based on topological registration. *Computer & Digital Engineering*, 10:029.

Xiaoqing Lv et al. 2010. A graphic-based method for Chinese Oracle-bone classification. *Journal of Beijing Information Science and Technology University*, 25(Z2): 92-96.

Yongge Liu and Guoying Liu. 2017. Oracle bone inscription recognition based on SVM. *Journal of Anyang Normal University*. 2:54–56.

Shuangping Huang et al. 2019. OBC306: A large-scale oracle bone character recognition dataset. *2019 International Conference on Document Analysis and Recognition (ICDAR)*, 681–688.

Gao Huang et al.(2017). Densely connected convolutional networks. *Proceedings of the IEEE conference on computer vision and pattern recognition*, 4700–4708.

Mei Wang and Weihong Deng. 2018. Deep visual domain adaptation: A survey. *Neurocomputing*, 312:135–153.

Mingsheng Long et al.(2015). Learning transferable features with deep adaptation networks. *International conference on machine learning*, 97–105.

Xingchao Peng et al. 2019. Moment matching for multi-source domain adaptation. *Proceedings of the IEEE/CVF international conference on computer vision*, 1406–1415.

Yiming Chen et al. 2019. A graph embedding framework for maximum mean discrepancy-based domain adaptation algorithms. *IEEE Transactions on Image Processing*, 29:199–213.

Ganin Yaroslav and Lempitsky VVictor. 2015. Unsupervised domain adaptation by backpropagation. *International conference on machine learning*, 1180–1189.

Ganin Yaroslav et al. 2016. Domain-Adversarial Training of Neural Networks. *Journal of Machine Learning Research*, 17(1):2096-2030.

Tzeng Eric et al. 2017. Adversarial discriminative domain adaptation. *Proceedings of the IEEE conference on computer vision and pattern recognition*, 7167–7176.

Mingsheng Long et al. 2018. Conditional adversarial domain adaptation. *Advances in neural information processing systems*, 31.

Ioffe Sergey and Szegedy Christian. 2015. Batch normalization: Accelerating deep network training by reducing internal covariate shift. *International conference on machine learning*, 448–456.

Glorot Xavier et al. 2015. Deep sparse rectifier neural networks. *Proceedings of the fourteenth international conference on artificial intelligence and statistics*, 315–323.

Johnson Justin et al. 2016. Perceptual losses for real-time style transfer and super-resolution. *Computer Vision–ECCV 2016: 14th European Conference, Amsterdam, The Netherlands, October 11-14, 2016, Proceedings*, 694–711, Part II 14.

Gatys Leon A et al. 2015. A neural algorithm of artistic style. arXiv preprint arXiv:1508.06576.

Shuhao Cui et al. 2020. Gradually vanishing bridge for adversarial domain adaptation. *Proceedings of the IEEE/CVF conference on computer vision and pattern recognition*, 12455–12464.

Shaotong Gu al. 2008. A study of oracle input encoding based on glyph topology. *Chinese Journal of Informatics*, 22(4):123–128.

Xinyang Chen et al. 2019. Transferability vs. discriminability: Batch spectral penalization for adversarial domain adaptation. *Proceedings of International conference on machine learning*, pp. 1081–1090.

Naihe Xie et al. 2020. Flourishing from Yin Ruins to the world—a review of "Busan, south Korea international symposium commemorating the 120th anniversary of oracle bone inscription discovery". *[J]. Guan zi journal*, pp. 125–128.

Coarse-to-Fine Generative Model for Oracle Bone Inscriptions Inpainting

Shibin Wang *[1,2], Wenjie Guo[1], Yubo Xu[1,2], Dong Liu[1,2], and Xueshan Li[1,2]

[1]School of Computer and Information Engineering, Henan Normal University (Henan), China.
[2]Oracle Bone Intelligent Computing Laboratory, Henan Normal University (Henan), China.

Abstract

Due to ancient origin, there are many incomplete characters in the unearthed Oracle Bone Inscriptions(OBI), which brings the great challenges to recognition and research. In recent years, image inpainting techniques have made remarkable progress. However, these models are unable to adapt to the unique font shape and complex text background of OBI. To meet these aforementioned challenges, we propose a two-stage method for restoring damaged OBI using Generative Adversarial Networks (GAN), which incorporates a dual discriminator structure to capture both global and local image information. In order to accurately restore the image structure and details, the spatial attention mechanism and a novel loss function are proposed. By feeding clear copies of existing OBI and various types of masks into the network, it learns to generate content for the missing regions. Experimental results demonstrate the effectiveness of our proposed method in completing OBI compared to several state-of-the-art techniques.

1 Introduction

Since the earliest discovery of Oracle Bone Inscriptions(OBI), over 5,000 distinct character forms have been identified, which have significantly advanced our comprehension of many characters' meanings. These deciphered OBIs provide invaluable historical information crucial for understanding various aspects of ancient Chinese politics, society, religion, and more.

Recognizing and interpreting are important topics in the field of OBI research. Due to the lack of physical objects, the images of rubbings in the recorded books are the main carriers of research. However, some OBIs have suffered varying degrees of residual erosion and damage on their surface, resulting in a large number of incomplete fonts in the inscriptions and rubbings seen today. With the rapid development of image generation technology, many image restoration problems difficult to solve in traditional methods have found new research avenues. The comprehensive application of artificial intelligence and other technologies has become a new research direction in the restoration of OBIs.

Zeng et al. (2019) proposed the Pyramid Context Encoder Network (PEN). It is based on the U-Net structure and encodes and decodes contextual semantics to ensure visual and semantic consistency. Li et al. (2020) developed the Recurrent Feature Reasoning (RFR) network, featuring a plug-and-play RFR module and a Knowledge Consistent Attention (KCA) module. They infer the hole boundaries and capture the distant feature information. Wu et al. (2021) introduced a two-stage (coarse-to-fine) model. It combines a Local Binary Pattern (LBP) Waller et al. (2013) network and incorporates a new spatial attention mechanism. These methods have enhanced image processing. However, they only grasp limited connections between textures and edges. They fail to fully comprehend image semantics and complex structures. Additionally, they overlook the interplay between global and local features. Given the complexities behind incomplete fonts and unique font features, existing image restoration models struggle to effectively complete OBI image inpainting tasks.

To meet these challenges, we propose a two-stage (coarse-to-fine) font inpainting network. Our network incorporates a dual discriminator structure to capture both global and local image information. Specifically, we employ a global discriminator to focus on the spatial correlation between damaged and undamaged regions. The local discriminator concentrates on the local patch information. To effectively understand the intrinsic features of the image, we introduce a novel loss function to accurately restore the structure and details. Through extensive comparisons, our framework demonstrates

*Corresponding author: wangshibin@htu.edu.cn

Proceedings of the 1st Workshop on Machine Learning for Ancient Languages (ML4AL 2024), pages 107–114
August 15, 2024 ©2024 Association for Computational Linguistics

state-of-the-art performance in OBI image inpainting tasks.

2 Method

2.1 Network Architecture

The network is a two-stage deep generative model. Both stages consist of encoder-decoder pipeline and follow an adversarial model Goodfellow et al. (2014). The network architecture is shown as Figure. 1. The damaged image consists of the missing regions filled with white pixels, represented as I_{in}. L_{in} denotes the LBP Waller et al. (2013) structural information extracted from the damaged oracle I_{in} in the grayscale channel. M represents a binary mask, where 1 indicates the missing regions and 0 indicates the known regions.

In the first stage, the generator G_1 includes seven feature extraction blocks and feature restoration modules. Each feature extraction block consists of LeakyReLU Xu et al. (2015), a convolutional layer, and InstanceNorm2d Ulyanov et al. (2016). The decoder generates the content of the missing region through seven feature restoration modules, which consist of ReLU Nair and Hinton (2010), transposed convolution, and InstanceNorm2d Ulyanov et al. (2016). Finally, G_1 and D_1 generate the completed LBP structural information L_{out} and L_o.

In the second stage, an additional spatial attention layer is added to the fifth layer of the encoder. This layer builds the correlations not only within the known region but also among the missing regions.

Due to a single discriminator judging the image authenticity solely from a global perspective and being unable to handle the details, artifacts and structural inconsistencies may arise in the restoration results. The dual discriminator, on the other hand, judges the image from both global and local perspectives. They compete with each other to learn more effective weights.

2.2 Dual Discriminator

The structure of Dual PatchGAN Isola et al. (2017) Discriminator (DP) is as shown in Figure. 2. The left branch is a global discriminator that focuses on the spatial correlation between damaged and undamaged regions. Its input consists of an image and a mask, and output is a 3D feature. Each CSL block consists of a 5×5 convolution, SpectralNorm Miyato et al. (2018) and LeakyReLU with α= 0.2. In the first two CSL blocks, the number of convolutional output channels is 64 and 128, while in the others it is 256. The right branch is a local discriminator with five 4×4 convolutions, which focuses on the local patch. The first four layers use the LeakyReLU with α= 0.2, the Sigmoid for the last layer and the BatchNorm2d for normalization in the middle three layers. The local discriminator can be formulated as:

$$\begin{aligned}\tau_{\text{adv2}} = \min_{G_2}\max_{D_2}\mathbb{E}_{I_g}\left[\log D_2(I_{\text{g}})\right] \\ +\mathbb{E}_{I_{in}}\left[\log\left(1-D_2\left(G_2\left(I_{\text{in}}, M\right)\right)\right)\right]\end{aligned} \quad (1)$$

Our objective function for the global discriminator can be formulated as:

$$\tau_{\text{adv3}} = -\mathbb{E}_{I_{in}\sim\mathbb{P}_{I_{in}}(I_{in})}\left[D_3\left(G_2\left(I_{\text{in}}\right)\right)\right] \quad (2)$$

$$\begin{aligned}\tau_{\text{D}_3} = \mathbb{E}_{I_g\sim\mathbb{P}_{data}(I_g)}\left[\text{ReLU}\left(1-D_3\left(I_g\right)\right)\right] \\ +\mathbb{E}_{I_{in}\sim\mathbb{P}_{I_{in}}(I_{in})}\left[\text{ReLU}\left(1+D_3\left(G_2\left(I_{\text{in}}\right)\right)\right)\right]\end{aligned} \quad (3)$$

where G_2 represents the second stage generator, D_2 and D_3 represent the right and left branches of the dual discriminator, respectively.

2.3 Multi-level Fusion Loss Function

We reduce the difference between the original image and the inpainting image by using a multi-level fusion loss function(MLFLF) to enhance the stability of training.

The reconstruction loss is defined as:

$$L_{\text{r}} = \left\|L_{\text{o}} - L_{\text{g}}\right\|_2 \quad (4)$$

$$L_{\text{o}} = L_{\text{in}} \odot (1-M) + L_{\text{out}} \odot M \quad (5)$$

The adversarial loss Yan et al. (2018) is defined as:

$$\begin{aligned}\tau_{\text{adv1}} = \min_{G_1}\max_{D_1}\mathbb{E}_{L_g}\left[\log D_1(L_{\text{g}})\right] \\ +\mathbb{E}_{L_{in}}\left[\log\left(1-D_1\left(G_1\left(L_{\text{in}}, M\right)\right)\right)\right]\end{aligned} \quad (6)$$

The pixel-level reconstruction loss is responsible for directly comparing each pixel of the generated image with the target image:

$$\begin{aligned}&\text{L}_{\text{valid}} \\ &= \frac{1}{\text{Sum}(1-M)}\left\|\left(L_{\text{out}} - L_g\right)\odot(1-M)\right\|_1\end{aligned} \quad (7)$$

$$\text{L}_{\text{hole}} = \frac{1}{\text{Sum}(M)}\left\|\left(L_{\text{out}} - L_g\right)\odot M\right\|_1 \quad (8)$$

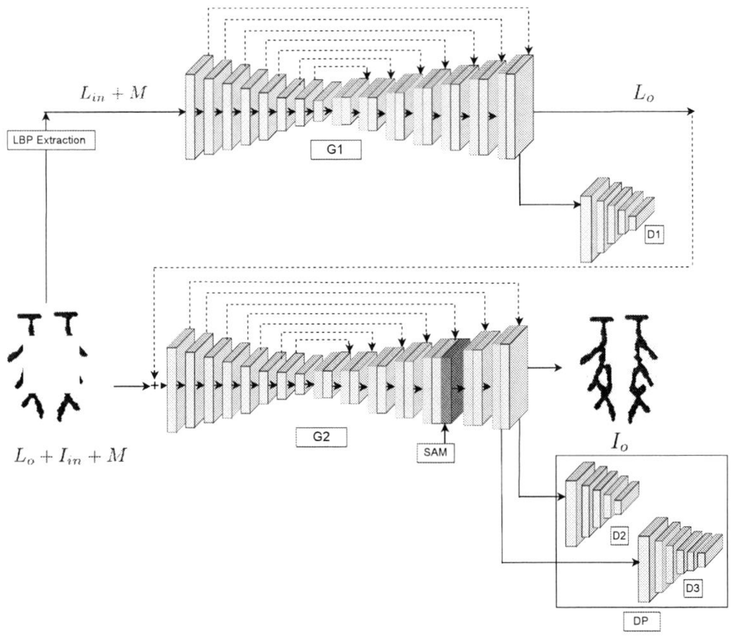

Figure 1: The network architecture of our proposed method.

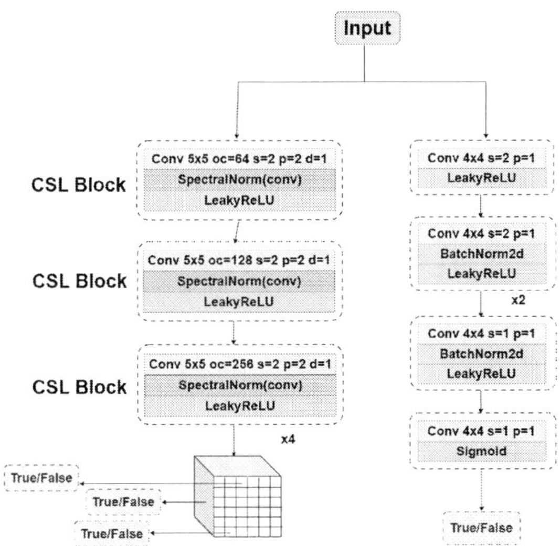

Figure 2: Proposed DP to introduce efficient local and global consistencies.

The Total Variation (TV) Liu et al. (2018) loss reduces noise and discontinuities, resulting in a smoother and more continuous appearance:

$$L_{\text{tv}} = \|L_o(i, j+1) - L_o(i, j)\|_1 + \|L_o(i+1, j) - L_o(i, j)\|_1 \tag{9}$$

The multi-scale loss compares the differences between ground truth images and mapping results of different scales:

$$\tau_m = \sum_{h \in d} \|\Phi_h(I_o) - \Phi_h(I_g)\|_2 \tag{10}$$

$$I_{\text{o}} = I_{\text{in}} \odot (1 - M) + I_{\text{out}} \odot M \tag{11}$$

We apply the perceptual loss Johnson et al. (2016) and style loss Gatys et al. (2016) defined on the VGG-16 Simonyan and Zisserman (2014) (pre-trained on ImageNet Deng et al. (2009)) to enhance the recovery of structural and textual information.

$$I_{\text{per}} = \sum_i \|\Psi_i(I_o) - \Psi_i(I_g)\|_1 \tag{12}$$

$$I_{\text{style}} = \sum_i \|\delta_i(I_o) - \delta_i(I_g)\|_1 \tag{13}$$

where Ψ_i is the feature map of $i - th$ layer in ImageNet-pretrained VGG-16 network, $\delta_i(\cdot) = \Psi_i(\cdot)\Psi_i(\cdot)^T$ is from (Buades et al., 2005).

3 Experiments

3.1 Dateset

We select 2000 OBI images for training and 100 for testing from the oracle bone images produced by the Key Laboratory of Oracle Information Processing of the Ministry of Education in Henan Province. To better validate the results of the experiment, we use the masks to simulate the broken regions of

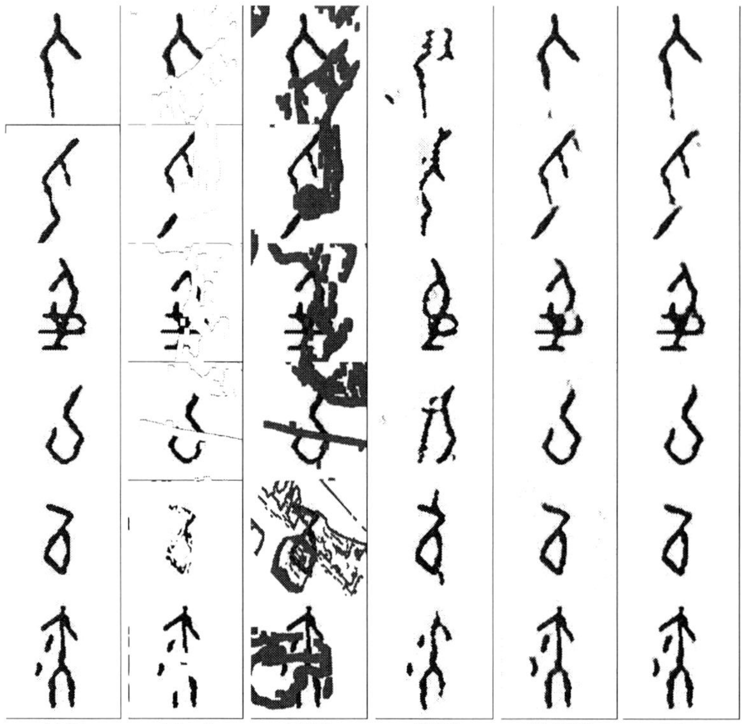

Figure 3: Comparison of qualitative results between the proposed method and other approaches on the irregular mask. Our proposed method generates more effective structural and texture information.

OBIs. These masks are divided into irregular and regular types. The irregular masks are obtained from the NVIDIA dataset Liu et al. (2018), while the regular masks are square masks of fixed size (25% of the total image pixels) placed in the center of the image.

3.2 Qualitative Comparisons

In this section, we conduct the experimental comparisons with other image restoration models.

For the restoration of OBI with irregular masks, the visualization results are shown in Figure. 3. The input image (b) shows the damaged OBI images. (c) demonstrates the results of using the PEN network Zeng et al. (2019) with a mode collapse. (d) using the RFR network Li et al. (2020) fails to accomplish the complementation task effectively. Note in particular the comparison between (e) the LBPLSA network Quan et al. (2022) and (f) our network. Our network evidently produces more realistic completion results from the smoother strokes in the first row of Figure. 3. And fewer or no artifacts appear at the end of the strokes in the rest of the lines. In contrast, the LBPLSA network exhibits severe artifacting and discontinuities in strokes. It fails to adequately complete the objectives. The presence of artifacts indicates that the network did not accurately understand the missing content in the image. As a result, it fills in unrealistic textures and structures.

We also explore the classic center mask completion scenario in image inpainting. Given that most of the OBI content lies in the center, it is challenging for the network to infer the main content of the characters from just one stroke at the boundary. The generated results are depicted in Figure. 4. We can see that the generated results of the PEN network (c) collapse again and the RFR network (d) fails to meet the target requirement. Focus on the comparison between LBPLSA (e) and our method (f) again, LBPLSA generates the images with more artifacts and doesn't effectively learn the semantic information of the OBIs. For instance, in the second row of Figure. 4, the strokes generated by the LBPLSA are opposite to the ground truth. More artifacts are present in rows 5 and 6. Under the same experimental configuration, our network achieves results that are closer to the ground truth.

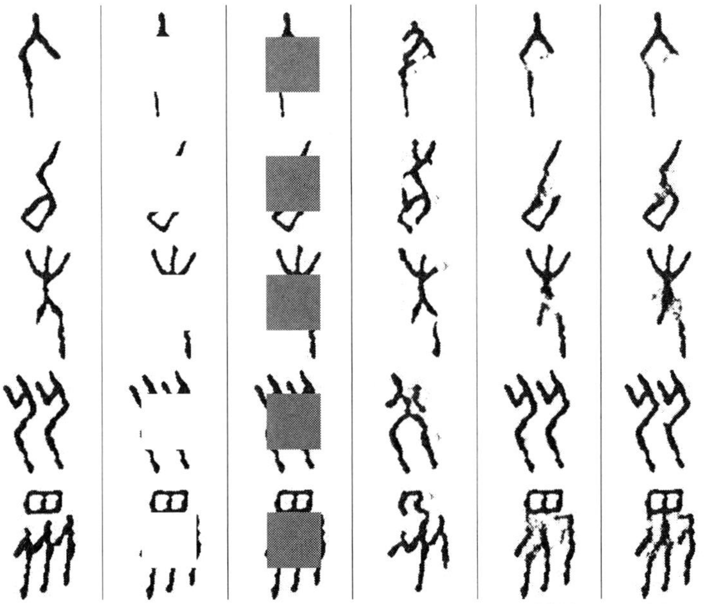

Figure 4: Comparison of qualitative results between the proposed method and other approaches on the rectangle mask. Our proposed method generates more effective structural and texture information.

	method	PEN	RFR	LBPLSA	LG	Ours
PSNR+	Irregular	8.67	14.67	25.67	27.01	**29.61**
	rectangle	9.08	14.30	26.73	22.46	**33.27**
SSIM+	Irregular	0.6337	0.8507	0.9719	0.9781	**0.9826**
	rectangle	0.7800	0.8397	0.9497	0.9449	**0.9623**
L1-	Irregular	0.1628	0.0567	0.0091	0.0066	**0.0058**
	rectangle	0.1425	0.0598	0.0162	0.0197	**0.0143**

Table 1: Comparison between the proposed method and state-of-the-art methods on the oracle dataset (+ indicates higher is better, - indicates lower is better).

3.3 Quantitative Comparisons

In terms of evaluation metrics, we follow the structural similarity index (SSIM) Wang et al. (2004) and peak signal-to-noise ratio (PSNR) as outlined in references Ren et al. (2019). The evaluation results are presented in Table 1.

Compared with other methods, the scores of each indicator in our model have been improved. The DP structure can effectively capture both the global and local image information. Additionally, the loss function component introduced MLFLF optimizes semantic plausibility and structural consistency. The integration of DP structure and MLFLF component produces the images with reduced pixel-level differences and leads to significant improvements across SSIM, PSNR, and L1 distance metrics, which indicates the high accuracy and effectiveness in image inpainting tasks.

3.4 Ablation Studies

The ablation studies are conducted under mask rates ranging from 20% to 30%. We evaluate the effectiveness of our proposed method by contrasting three different experimental settings, including the LBPLSA method, the SN method only with DP component and the complete method. The generated results are depicted in Figure. 5. Part (a) represents the ground truth OBIs. The input images with various degrees of damage are generated by masks, shown in (b). The completion results of LBPLSA (c), SN (d), and ours (e) are sequentially displayed.

Compared with the LBPLSA method, the SN method shows some improvement with the introduction of the DP structure. The incorporation

Figure 5: Qualitative results comparison of ablation study.

	method	NO	DP	DP+MLFLF
PSNR+	Irregular	25.67	28.66	**29.61**
	rectangle	26.73	26.88	**33.27**
SSIM+	Irregular	0.9719	0.9798	**0.9826**
	rectangle	0.9497	0.9566	**0.9623**
L1-	Irregular	0.0091	0.0068	**0.0058**
	rectangle	0.0162	0.0159	**0.0143**

Table 2: Quantitative results of ablation study on oracle dataset. (+ indicates higher is better, - indicates lower is better).

of the DP structure enables the model to better capture both global and local image information, which improves the restoration results to a certain extent. However, the SN method lacks the further optimization from the MLFLF component. It still has certain limitations and fails to fully exploit the intrinsic features of the images.

Furthermore, our complete method achieves further improvements across all metrics within the experimental scope. By leveraging the dual advantages of DP and MLFLF, our method can more accurately restore the structure and details of the images. This makes the restoration results closer to the original images. Compared to the methods only with DP, the addition of the MLFLF component further enhances the clarity and quality of the restored images. This leads to better performance across metrics, such as SSIM, PSNR, and L1 distance, as demonstrated in the ablation study metrics presented in Table 2.

Through the ablation studies, we validate the crucial roles of DP and MLFLF in image restoration tasks. The DP structure enhances the model's understanding of images, while the MLFLF module further optimizes detail and texture restoration. This showcases significant advantages across all metrics. These experimental results validate our method's effectiveness. They emphasize the importance of leveraging the dual advantages of DP and MLFLF in image inpainting tasks.

4 Conclusion

We propose the two-stage (coarse-to-fine) network for efficient OBI image inpainting. This new framework consists of an enhanced LBP network and integrated DP and MLFLF components. Specifically, we design a novel dual discriminator network. The first stage LBP learning network adopts a U-Net architecture, aimed at accurately predicting structural information in missing regions. This guides the second image inpainting network in better filling missing pixels. In the second stage image generation network, we employ dual discriminators to complete the masked regions. Compared to several state-of-the-art methods, experimental results demonstrate the effectiveness of DP and MLFLF components in the proposed method in completing OBI image inpainting tasks.

In the future, we plan to further develop our network to achieve more powerful functions, such as increasing the speed, realizing editing functions, and improving the efficiency of paleographers. Our goal is to solve the problem of more complex noise or higher mask coverage. We believe that our two-stage (coarse-to-fine) generation model can be extended to very high-resolution coloring applications by improving the first-stage generation results.

Acknowledgments This study was funded by the scientific and technological project in Henan Province in 2022 (Grant No. 222102210187), the Key Research Project for Higher Education Institutions in Henan Province (Grant No. 24A520018).

References

Antoni Buades, Bartomeu Coll, and J-M Morel. 2005. A non-local algorithm for image denoising. In *2005 IEEE computer society conference on computer vision and pattern recognition (CVPR'05)*, volume 2, pages 60–65. Ieee.

Jia Deng, Wei Dong, Richard Socher, Li-Jia Li, Kai Li, and Li Fei-Fei. 2009. Imagenet: A large-scale hierarchical image database. In *2009 IEEE conference on computer vision and pattern recognition*, pages 248–255. Ieee.

Leon A Gatys, Alexander S Ecker, and Matthias Bethge. 2016. Image style transfer using convolutional neural networks. In *Proceedings of the IEEE conference on computer vision and pattern recognition*, pages 2414–2423.

Ian Goodfellow, Jean Pouget-Abadie, Mehdi Mirza, Bing Xu, David Warde-Farley, Sherjil Ozair, Aaron Courville, and Yoshua Bengio. 2014. Generative adversarial nets. *Advances in neural information processing systems*, 27.

Phillip Isola, Jun-Yan Zhu, Tinghui Zhou, and Alexei A Efros. 2017. Image-to-image translation with conditional adversarial networks. In *Proceedings of the IEEE conference on computer vision and pattern recognition*, pages 1125–1134.

Justin Johnson, Alexandre Alahi, and Li Fei-Fei. 2016. Perceptual losses for real-time style transfer and super-resolution. In *Computer Vision–ECCV 2016: 14th European Conference, Amsterdam, The Netherlands, October 11-14, 2016, Proceedings, Part II 14*, pages 694–711. Springer.

Jingyuan Li, Ning Wang, Lefei Zhang, Bo Du, and Dacheng Tao. 2020. Recurrent feature reasoning for image inpainting. In *Proceedings of the IEEE/CVF conference on computer vision and pattern recognition*, pages 7760–7768.

Guilin Liu, Fitsum A Reda, Kevin J Shih, Ting-Chun Wang, Andrew Tao, and Bryan Catanzaro. 2018. Image inpainting for irregular holes using partial convolutions. In *Proceedings of the European conference on computer vision (ECCV)*, pages 85–100.

Takeru Miyato, Toshiki Kataoka, Masanori Koyama, and Yuichi Yoshida. 2018. Spectral normalization for generative adversarial networks. *arXiv preprint arXiv:1802.05957.*

Vinod Nair and Geoffrey E Hinton. 2010. Rectified linear units improve restricted boltzmann machines. In *Proceedings of the 27th international conference on machine learning (ICML-10)*, pages 807–814.

Weize Quan, Ruisong Zhang, Yong Zhang, Zhifeng Li, Jue Wang, and Dong-Ming Yan. 2022. Image inpainting with local and global refinement. *IEEE Transactions on Image Processing*, 31:2405–2420.

Yurui Ren, Xiaoming Yu, Ruonan Zhang, Thomas H Li, Shan Liu, and Ge Li. 2019. Structureflow: Image inpainting via structure-aware appearance flow. In *Proceedings of the IEEE/CVF international conference on computer vision*, pages 181–190.

Karen Simonyan and Andrew Zisserman. 2014. Very deep convolutional networks for large-scale image recognition. *arXiv preprint arXiv:1409.1556.*

Dmitry Ulyanov, Andrea Vedaldi, and Victor Lempitsky. 2016. Instance normalization: The missing ingredient for fast stylization. *arXiv preprint arXiv:1607.08022.*

Ben M Waller, Mark S Nixon, and John N Carter. 2013. Image reconstruction from local binary patterns. In *2013 International Conference on Signal-Image Technology & Internet-Based Systems*, pages 118–123. IEEE.

Zhou Wang, Alan C Bovik, Hamid R Sheikh, and Eero P Simoncelli. 2004. Image quality assessment: from error visibility to structural similarity. *IEEE transactions on image processing*, 13(4):600–612.

Haiwei Wu, Jiantao Zhou, and Yuanman Li. 2021. Deep generative model for image inpainting with local binary pattern learning and spatial attention. *IEEE Transactions on Multimedia*, 24:4016–4027.

Bing Xu, Naiyan Wang, Tianqi Chen, and Mu Li. 2015. Empirical evaluation of rectified activations in convolutional network. *arXiv preprint arXiv:1505.00853*.

Zhaoyi Yan, Xiaoming Li, Mu Li, Wangmeng Zuo, and Shiguang Shan. 2018. Shift-net: Image inpainting via deep feature rearrangement. In *Proceedings of the European conference on computer vision (ECCV)*, pages 1–17.

Yanhong Zeng, Jianlong Fu, Hongyang Chao, and Baining Guo. 2019. Learning pyramid-context encoder network for high-quality image inpainting. In *Proceedings of the IEEE/CVF conference on computer vision and pattern recognition*, pages 1486–1494.

Restoring Mycenaean Linear B 'A&B' series tablets using supervised and transfer learning

Katerina Papavassileiou and **Dimitrios I. Kosmopoulos**
Postdoc researcher and Associate Professor
Department of History and Archaeology, Computer Engineering and Informatics Department
University of Patras
Patra, Greece
cpapavas@upatras.gr, dkosmo@upatras.gr

Abstract

We investigate the problem of restoring Mycenaean linear B clay tablets, dating from about 1400 B.C. to roughly 1200 B.C., by using text infilling methods based on machine learning models. Our goals here are: first to try to improve the results of the methods used in the related literature by focusing on the characteristics of the Mycenaean Linear B writing system (series D), second to examine the same problem for the first time on series A&B and finally to investigate transfer learning using series D as source and the smaller series A&B as target. Our results show promising results in the supervised learning tasks, while further investigation is needed to better exploit the merits of transfer learning.

1 Introduction

For many years the language attributed by the Linear B script (c. 1400-1200 B.C.) was a point of contention among scientists, who argued over the origin of the Mycenaean syllabary. The answer was given in 1952 by Michael Ventris (Chadwick, 1990; Fox, 2013) who, together with the philologist John Chadwick, proved that the syllables of the Linear B script form words of the Greek language and that the Mycenaean world was both linguistically and culturally linked to ancient Greece.

Mycenaean Linear B is a syllabic script. It includes syllables as well as logograms or ideograms. In summary, Linear B is structured by groups of phonetic symbols, which are accompanied by ideograms. The surviving tablets typically refer to human names, place names, agricultural production, land ownership, religious offerings, or military equipment. The Mycenaean inscriptions have been classified based on their place of origin, but also based on the category to which they belong. The place of origin is indicated by the following abbreviations: KN (Knossos), PY (Pylos), MY (Mycenae), TH (Thebes), TI (Tiryns), KH (Khania), MI (Midea), etc. The classification into categories was based on the ideograms of the tablets: Series A&B, (lists of personnel), series C (animal records), series D (sheep records), series E (grain records), series F&G (records of oil, agricultural products and their offerings), series L (textile records), etc. (Kober, 1945), (Kober, 1946), (Kober, 1948), (Ruijgh, 1977).

The main challenge faced by those dealing with the study and restoration of the Mycenaean Linear B texts, either manually (Ventris and Chadwick, 1953, 1956; Killen, 1964; Doria, 1965; Ventris et al., 1988; Meissner, 2001; Robinson and Eisenman, 2002; Pope, 2008; Duhoux and Davies, 2008; Fox, 2013; Ventris and Chadwick, 2015; Freo and Perna, 2019; Bernabé and Luján, 2020) or computationally (Papavassiliou et al., 2020; Papavassileiou et al., 2023), is the scarcity of data. Furthermore, we have to take into account the particularities presented by the Mycenaean inscriptions: a) Their eminently administrative content, b) their subject as they deal extensively with people and places and c) their state of preservation since most of them are broken, worn out or burnt. These make the infilling task very challenging.

This article contributes by investigating Transfer Learning (TL) techniques to alleviate the above mentioned data scarcity. TL is the process of taking a model that has been trained to do one task (pre-trained model) and fine-tuning it to work on a related (different or similar) task. In Natural Language Processing (NLP), pre-trained models are often used as the starting point for a wide range of NLP tasks, such as language translation, sentiment analysis, and text summarization. By using a pre-trained model, we can save time and resources, as they don't have to train a model from scratch on a large dataset (Devlin et al., 2019; Radford et al., 2019; Peters et al., 2018; Liu et al., 2019).

In this work we deal with series A&B and series D to find out the effect of TL from a series to

Proceedings of the 1st Workshop on Machine Learning for Ancient Languages (ML4AL 2024), pages 115–129
August 15, 2024

another one. To this end we have chosen to investigate the effect of TL from the series D, since it is the largest with the most tablets and resulting sequences, to the series A&B, as opposed to training the series as a whole.

We also contribute by investigating whether there is an improvement in the predictions of models learned from series D (Papavassileiou et al., 2023; Papavassiliou et al., 2020) if we remove the ideograms from the sequences. This choice is based on the observation that in Linear B, typically there is consistent separation of phonographic (syllabograms) and non-phonographic (ideograms as well as signs for measurement units and numbers) graphemes (Petrakis, 2017).

Finally we apply generative methods for the infilling problem of series A&B. Following the same tactic with series D, we create a dataset of sequences derived from the Mycenaean tablets of series A&B, excluding ideograms, and use it to learn a generative model in order to predict damaged parts of this series' tablets.

The rest of the paper is organized as follows: In Section 2 we provide an overview of previous research and studies on various methods of restoring ancient inscriptions. In Section 3 we present the dataset for our experiments. Section 4 demonstrates supervised learning for language modelling and for missing symbol recovery. Section 5 presents transfer learning techniques for infilling series A&B. Finally, in Section 6 we present our conclusions and the future work.

2 Related work

The problem of text restoration through infilling is attracting more and more attention from researchers community; however most recent results from the Natural Language Processing (NLP) community have been only partially applied, obviously due to the lack of sufficient data.

Some of the simplest models are the n-grams. These are probabilistic models for predicting the next item in a sequence of n elements and can be used to model almost any type of sequential data. They have been used for machine translation (Wolk and Marasek, 2014), but also for textual restoration. (Rao et al., 2009) and (Yadav et al., 2010) use n-gram Markov chains for texts in the Indus script. The benefits of n-gram models are their simplicity and scalability. With larger n, a model can store more context, enabling small experiments to scale up. However, when n increases, the number of possible n-grams increases exponentially and therefore the out-of-vocabulary n-grams increase as well and actually undermine the performance of the model. Obviously, the n-grams are not appropriate for long sequences.

(Roued-Cunliffe, 2010) uses a decision support system called DUGA for reading ancient documents in the Latin language found in Vindolanda (Britain). She uses the so-called cruciverbalistic approach: it begins by establishing the letters that are legible and uses them as a foundation for a subsequent hypotheses. A knowledge-base of previously interpreted documents from the same period is used to extract word lists and frequencies. These are then used to suggest different interpretations of words and letters, as well as missing parts, using a hierarchical approach from individual symbols to whole sentences. The system is therefore largely based on the experts' decisions. (Kang et al., 2021) present a multi-task learning approach based on the Transformer networks to effectively restore and translate ancient historical documents based on a self-attention mechanism, specifically utilizing two Korean historical records, one of the most voluminous historical records in the world. This work combines 3 different studies: the restoration of damaged documents (recovering), neural machine translation (translating), and the analysis of historical records (mining). The proposed model consists of embedding and output layers for Hanja and Korean, and three Transformer modules: the shared encoder (for both the restoration and translation tasks), the restoration encoder (for the restoration task), and the translation decoder (for translating Hanja sentences into modern Korean sentences). However, a large-scale training corpus is required.

Similar to our work is the PYTHIA system (Assael et al., 2019) and its follow-up system Ithaca (Assael et al., 2022). It aims to fill the missing symbols (characters) in ancient Greek inscriptions. The authors use a sequence-to-sequence framework (Sutskever et al., 2014) with Long Short-Term Memory (LSTM) networks in the encoder and the decoder. The encoder involves the input character embeddings sequence with missing characters, and a separate stream is also modelled using the word sequence as embeddings as well; an attention layer is also used. The decoder is trained to output the missing characters. They use a dataset that results from processing the epigraphical corpora of the Packard Humanities Institute (Packard Humanities Institute, 2005), the PHI-ML. As (Shen et al., 2020) argue in their ancient text restoration experiment, (Assael et al., 2019) perform restoration at the character-level where the number of characters to recover is assumed to be known and indicated by a corresponding number of '?' symbols. In reality, when epigraphists restore a deteriorated document, the length of the lost fragment is unknown and needs to be guessed as a first step. BLM, in essence a variant of BLM, the L-BLM, can bypass this limitation and flexibly generate completions without this additional knowledge. A single token, sized equal to the number of '?' symbols, is defined and the L-BLM is trained to predict a character to fill in and the length of the new blank to its left. Compared to our work, the problem presented by the authors of these articles (Assael et al., 2019; Shen et al., 2020) is similar in the sense that it concerns a known script and known language and uses a machine learning architecture. However, our task is more challenging, due to the fact that the corpus is of much smaller size (over 40000 inscriptions available in the aforementioned articles versus 1100 inscriptions in ours); that impedes training.

(Fetaya et al., 2020) use recurrent neural networks (LSTM) to restore fragmentary Babylonian texts. These involve ancient texts in the Akkadian language, which belong to the Semitic language family. Comparisons to simple 2-gram baseline approach (considering the previous and the next word) are made, resulting in better performance. The experiments use a dataset of 3000 transliterated archival documents belonging to economic, juridical and administrative genres. Similarly to this work, (Lazar et al., 2021) also introduce BERT-based models aiming to solve the task of predicting missing signs in Akkadian texts. The difference with the previous article (Fetaya et al., 2020) is that the completion of missing signs is done by combining large-scale multilingual pretraining with Akkadian language finetuning. Although (Fetaya et al., 2020) have small-scale data at their disposal to train the learning algorithm (c. 3000 Babylonian transliterated texts, 539-331 B.C.E.), what is emphasized by the authors is that the late Babylonian texts are structured official bureaucratic documents, e.g., legal proceedings, receipts, promissory notes, contracts and so on. This is in stark contrast to Linear B tablets, which are significantly impeded by syntactic inconsistencies. This is proved by the fact that the pre-processing of each Mycenaean tablet requires special handling, so as to extract valid sequences of Mycenaean words in accordance with the principles of Mycenaean language. Another BERT-based model, Latin BERT, is proposed by (Bamman and Burns, 2020). They pre-trained BERT model on Latin texts from Perseus, PROIEL and Index Thomisticus Treebank, targeting restoration and several other downstream tasks. (Sommerschield et al., 2023) offer a review on published research using machine learning for the study of ancient texts. They also classify the studies of ancient texts into tasks: digitisation, restoration, attribution, linguistic analysis, textual criticism, translation and decipherment. Finally, a similar review task takes place in the article (Braović et al., 2024), but focusing on the computational techniques related to the Bronze Age Aegean and Cypriot scripts, namely the Archanes script and the Archanes formula, Cretan hieroglyphic (including the Malia Altar Stone and Arkalochori Axe), Phaistos Disk, Linear A, Linear B, Cypro-Minoan and Cypriot scripts.

The work in (Papavassileiou et al., 2023) is similar to ours and is the only one that we are aware of that does infilling for the Linear B tablets. However, that work is limited to series D tablets and considers both phonogrpahic and non-phonographic symbols. Furthermore, like all aforementioned methods, it does not investigate transfer learning.

3 The Mycenaean dataset

Here we present the modifications we made to the Mycenaean dataset of series D, that was initially created as described in (Papavassiliou et al., 2020) and (Papavassileiou et al., 2023). We also present the way to create the new dataset of series A&B.

The Linear B script uses two basic symbol systems, one phonetic (phonographic component) and one logographic (non-phonographic component). The symbols of the phonetic system are called syllabograms-syllables. The phonetic system is usually represented transcribed, i.e., the syllable is rendered in letters, and in most cases by a combination of consonant and vowel. The system of the phonetic symbols, includes at least 87 different syllables. For the symbols of the logographic system, the term 'ideograms' or 'logograms' is used, sometimes modified by ligatured signs or 'adjuncts' (mostly acrophonic abbreviations) (Petrakis, 2017). The ideograms are 143. For their representation a transcription is used, based on the abbreviation of the Latin name of the represented object or being, e.g., VIR 'man', MUL(ier) 'woman'. Additionally

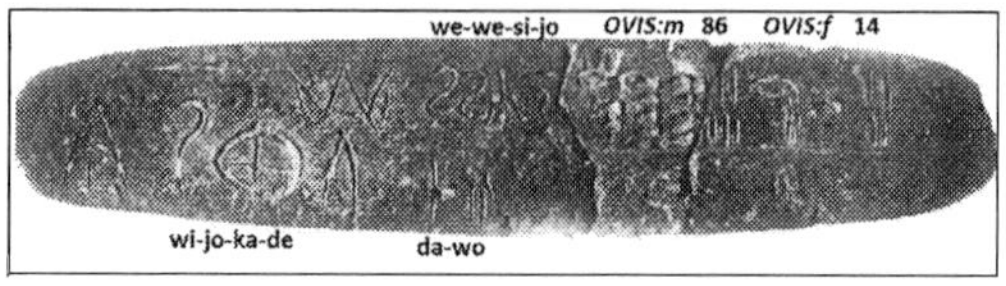

Figure 1: The image of the Mycenaean Linear B tablet KN Dd 1155 + 5378 + 5688 (the copyright of the images belongs to the Hellenic Ministry of Culture and Sports - "Hellenic Organization of Cultural Resources Development"). Translation of the Mycenaean tablet "Wiokados (shepherd's name): at Dawos (place name) belonging to Werwesios (collector's name), rams 86, ewes 14"

there are numbers that follow the decimal system and measurements units of weight and capacity (Ruiperez and Melena, 1996; Duhoux, 2014).

The assumption for the creation of both datasets was based on the clear separation of the signs of the Linear B writing system into phonograms and non-phonograms. The phonographic part is made up of the syllables, while the non-phonographic component includes the ideograms sometimes modified by ligatured signs or 'adjuncts' (mostly acrophonic abbreviations), as well as signs for measurement units, numbers, and other marks, such as signgroup dividers or 'check-marks' (Petrakis, 2017). Therefore, we decided to exclude the ideograms.

3.1 The dataset of series D

The series D of Knossos, which is the largest classification, comprises the accounts of sheep herds in around 1100 tablets. Most of them were probably written by the same scribe and have a similar structure. From those tablets 513 complete sequences were extracted, without missing syllables. From the augmentation rules (similar to (Papavassileiou et al., 2023)) were obtained 2052 sequences (725 augmented samples and 1327 duplicated samples). So, 2565 constitute the training set of the model. The remaining sequences were more or less damaged, making about 145 sentences. The new Vocabulary was defined by [77 syllables, space].

In essence, the modification we made in the dataset of series D, (Papavassileiou et al., 2023), concerns the removal of ideograms from the sequences, along with the numeric signs and the measurement units of weight and capacity. Thus, only the signs which occur in groups, i.e., the words, make up the new corpus. An example of such a sequence is shown in Table 1 derived from Figure 1.

Mycenaean sequence with ideograms
wi-jo-ka-de da-wo we-we-si-jo $OVIS^m$ $OVIS^f$
Mycenaean sequence without ideograms
wi-jo-ka-de da-wo we-we-si-jo

Table 1: Mycenaean sequence extracted from the Mycenaean Linear B tablet KN Db 1155 + 5378 + 5688 (Fig. 1) including ideograms (up), excluding ideograms (down).

3.2 The dataset of series A&B

We chose to include in the dataset the documents of series A&B found in Knossos (site of origin), to facilitate transfer learning from series D tablets, which originate from Knossos.

The tablets of series A&B write on staff lists/ staff statuses/ personnel situations; more specifically they include work groups. The introductory words, describing these groups, can be either a Cretan place-name, or a man's name (sometimes in genitive), or a feminine ethnic adjective from a place-name (ethnic-name), or an occupational name (trade-name) or some combination of these.

Some specific rules applied in this series are:

1. The tablets that contain complex (compound) sentences, are converted into simple ones. E.g., tablet KN Ai 63, Figure 2, writes "pe-se-re-jo e-e-si MUL 1 ko-wo 1 ko-wa 1" translated as "To Psellos belong one woman, one girl and one boy" (family or chattel slavery record). This tablet provides 3 sequences for our dataset: "pe-se-ro e-e-si", "pe-se-ro e-e-si ko-wa" and "pe-se-ro e-e-si ko-wo".

2. The second rule has to do with abbreviations. Most of the time the syllables are placed one after the other to form recognizable words. But, there are also cases where the syllables are used individually. When this happens, the syllable functions either as a ligature with an ideogram, or as an ideogram adjunct, or as an abbreviation of a word. There are numerous such annotations in series A&B that refer to the third case, abbreviations. In cases where we know the full form of abbreviated words, then the abbreviations are replaced by the full words. E.g., the tablet KN Ak 627, Figure 3, writes "da-*22-to a-no-zo-jo TA 1 DA 1 MUL 9 pe di 2 ko-wa me-zo-e 7 ko-wa me-wi-jo-e 10 ko-wo me-zo-e 2 ko-wo me-wi-jo-e 10". Here, the abbreviations 'pe' and 'di' appear.

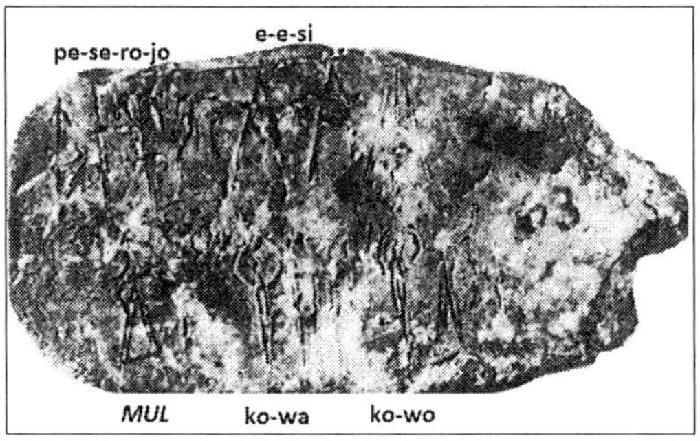

Figure 2: The image of the Mycenaean Linear B tablet KN Ai 63(image copyright belongs to the Hellenic Ministry of Culture and Sports - "Hellenic Organization of Cultural Resources Development"). Translation of the Mycenaean tablet *To Psellos (name of a person) belong one woman, one girl and one boy.*

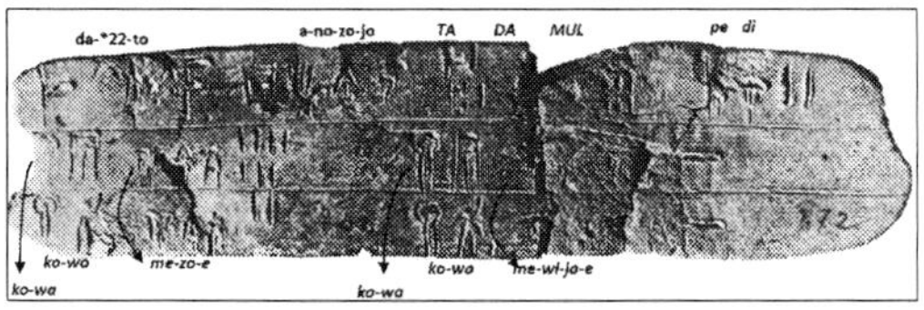

Figure 3: The image of the Mycenaean Linear B tablet KN Ak 627 + 7025 + fr (image copyright belongs to the Hellenic Ministry of Culture and Sports - "Hellenic Organization of Cultural Resources Development"). Translation of the Mycenaean tablet *In area da-*22-to the work group belonging to a-no-zo consists of one leader, one damar, nine women, of which two come from the censuses of the previous year in a period of apprenticeship, 7 older girls, 10 younger girls, 2 older boys and 10 younger boys.*

> These are the shortened forms of the words 'pe-ru-si-nu-wo' (last year's) and 'di-da-ka-re' (during apprenticeship/under instruction) (Ventris and Chadwick, 2015), which will appear in their full form in the dataset.

We gathered all the sequences that emerged from the tablets of series A&B, without missing symbols, 426 in number. The sequences resulting from the damaged tablets of this category were around 159. We defined a Vocabulary of [75 syllables, space].

The augmentation used in series D cannot be applied to series A&B tablets due to the fact that in A&B we mostly encounter lists of human names.

4 Supervised learning for infilling Mycenaean tablets

In the first place, we employ a symbol-level Bidirectional Recurrent Neural Network (BRNN), (as has been employed in (Papavassileiou et al., 2023)) to fill in the gaps in the Mycenaean tablets of series D and A&B. The goal in this case is to check if the predictions of the model improve by removing the ideograms from the Mycenaean sequences.

4.1 Modeling series D

A variation of Leave One Out Cross Validation (LOOCV) procedure was followed, the *Leave-"one and its derivatives"-Out Cross Validation*, in order to evaluate the BRNN model on unseen data, considering the scarcity of data. The derivatives are the samples/sequences resulting from applying an augmentation step to the real sample/sequence that is currently left out for testing. So, the samples resulting from augmentation of the current test sample sequences were excluded from the respective training set to avoid contamination of the test set by including sample sequences of the same origin (through augmentation). Furthermore, only the original sequences were used for testing (not the augmented or the duplicated ones), to make results comparable to those where no augmented data were used. Thus, the model is trained 513 times and the final performance is based on all these runs.

We implemented a function that performs one step of stochastic gradient descent with gradient clipping, $ClippingValue = 0.5$. We applied the greedy heuristic approach to search for the best hyperparameters, ending up with: 110.000 iterations ($epochs = 43$), number of neurons in hidden layer $N_{hl} = 57$, and learning rate $l_r = 0.01$. As an output activation function was set the softmax function and for the hidden layer the hyperbolic tangent (Tanh) function was chosen. For the initialization of weight matrices and bias vectors, we ended up in *"Glorot/Xavier"* as the most suitable for use. Given those choices we came to the results for the BRNN shown in Table 2, which demonstrate an improvement when compared to the baseline.

We used the trained model to infill gaps for which experts made educated guesses on the missing parts (Chadwick et al., 1987), mainly based on the visual cues, since some small parts of the syllables remain visible. The experts didn't use the sequences' structure unlike our method. Eight (8) of our TOP-5 predictions agree with the literature recommendations. This number shows an improvement of 2 units compared to the corresponding training of the BRNN model on the dataset including ideograms (Papavassileiou et al., 2023). See the Appendix A for more details.

SERIES D - with ideograms				
TOP-1	**TOP-5**	**TOP-10**	**TOP-15**	**TOP-20**
48.34	65.30	71.93	74.85	78.17
SERIES D - without ideograms				
TOP-1	**TOP-5**	**TOP-10**	**TOP-15**	**TOP-20**
48.56	65.50	72.12	76.02	80.12

Table 2: Estimated scores (percentages) of finding the correct missing symbol among the top-k most likely symbols (k=1,5,10,15,20) according to the probabilities estimated by the BRNN model. Up, the training dataset includes the ideograms. Down, the training dataset does not include the ideograms.

4.2 Modeling series A&B

At this point we evaluate the performance of the model learnt from A&B series. In a similar fashion to D series, we conducted two experiments, one with synthetic gaps and one with real ones.

4.2.1 Infilling synthetic sequences

To estimate the performance of the model on unseen data, the Leave-One-Out Cross-Validation (LOOCV) is used, since the data are scarce.

We randomly removed syllables from the 426 sequences in order to test the prediction capability of the BRNN model. The creation of the synthetic gaps follows the distribution of the real gaps appearing in the damaged tablets of this category. 67% of the real gaps occur at the beginning of the sequence, 17% somewhere in the middle of the sequence and 26% in the end of the sequence. We created a similar distribution for synthetic gaps.

The model is trained 426 times and the final performance estimate is based on all these runs. We used the Cross-Entropy loss along with the stochastic gradient descent optimizer with gradient clipping value of 0.5. The network is trained for 55.000 iterations ($epochs$ = 129) - $batch-size = 1$, with 58 neurons in the single hidden layer and learning rate, $lr = 0.01$. For the hidden layer of the neural network was used the hyperbolic tangent (Tanh) activation function and as an output activation function was chosen the softmax function since it is a d-way classification problem. Finally, *"Glorot/Xavier"* was chosen for the initialization of weight matrices and bias vectors.

Given those choices we came up with the results in Table 3. The model's prediction rates on series A&B are lower than those of its counterpart (Table 2 (down)) on series D. This is mainly due to the fact that the tablets of series A&B offer fewer sequences and we could not formulate augmentation rules.

SERIES A&B				
TOP-1	**TOP-5**	**TOP-10**	**TOP-15**	**TOP-20**
30.28%	50.23%	57.75%	61.97%	66.20%

Table 3: Estimated scores (percentages) of finding the correct missing symbol among the top-k most likely symbols (k=1,5,10,15,20) according to the probabilities estimated by the BRNN model. The training dataset does not include the ideograms.

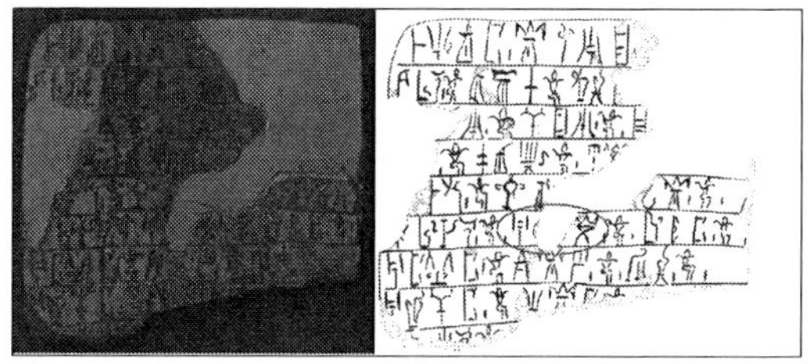

Figure 4: The image of the damaged Mycenaean tablet KN Bk 799 + 8306. (© Hellenic Ministry of Culture) (left) and its drawing (right). It lists men's names. Thirteen of them are complete. Around 6 names remain unknown.

4.2.2 Infilling real sequences

In this experiment, the model is applied in some real cases. In order to predict the missing syllables from the 159 sequences obtained from the damaged tablets of series A&B, we used the BRNN model from the previous experiment (A) which was trained on the 426 complete sequences.

In this category, experts have offered their opinion on a number of cases, 29 in all, as to what the missing syllable might be, based on the visual similarity that the remnant might have with the Mycenaean syllables. For example, experts suggest that the residue on the tablet in Figure 4 is equally likely to match the syllables 'ka' and 'qe', thus completing the man's name 'a-ka-de' or 'a-qe-de'. More such results are presented in the Appendix A.

Of the model's TOP-10 predictions, slightly more than half (15) match the experts' estimates. Of these correct predictions, always in agreement with the visual assessments of the experts, 9 are in the top 5 predictions (TOP-5), Table 5. This gives an indication that the model can learn effectively from the data. More details are given in the Tables of the Appendix A.

One way to increase the data of series A&B is to include the tablets of this series from other sites, namely Pylos, Thebes, Mycenae etc. However, that process has to be done with great caution so as not to contaminate the content of the dataset.

5 Transfer learning for infilling series A&B

In the following we investigate different transfer learning approaches for enhancing the model for series A&B (target) using the model learnt from series D (source). Series D data involves more tablets and is syntactically richer while the data in series A&B is scarce. However, for the NLP standards both series are considered very scarce.

We have essentially experimented with 2 simple TL techniques:

(A) Use the parameters of the model trained on D, see Section 4.1, as initialization for the training of the A&B series model (CASE A).

(B) Freeze the D model while training a second hidden layer using Tanh activation, finally fed to a softmax output layer (CASE B).

5.1 Case A: Weights initialization from D

We use the pre-trained D model only to initialize the A&B model.

By replacing, in the weight initialization procedure, the *"Glorot/Xavier"* method with the optimal parameters extracted from the training of another neural network model, we seek to examine whether there will be an improvement in the results.

The first goal is to use the optimal parameters extracted from the pre-trained model in series D corpus, as weight initialization for the training of series/corpus A&B.

In each LOOCV evaluation/iteration, the optimal parameters from the training of corpus D are used as weight initialization. The best results from the training of series D were collected with hyperparameters; learning rate = 0.01, mini batch size = 1, epochs = 43 (110.000 iterations), one hidden layer with 57 neurons/units.

We experimented with the number of iterations as hyperparameter and the results of Table 4 (CASE A) were achieved with 12.000 iterations ($epochs \approx 28$).

5.2 Case B: Add and train a second hidden layer

In this case we connected the D model with an additional neural network layer of 55 neurons (emerged after many tests), in order to train the A&B corpus, and to experiment with the following technique: Freeze the trained model in D and train the attached layer (CASE B).

CASE A				
TOP-1	**TOP-5**	**TOP-10**	**TOP-15**	**TOP-20**
25.65%	43.66%	54.23%	62.91%	67.37%
CASE B				
TOP-1	**TOP-5**	**TOP-10**	**TOP-15**	**TOP-20**
24.71	42.96	50.70	57.28	63.15

Table 4: Estimated scores (percentages) of finding the correct missing symbol among the top-k most likely symbols (k=1,5,10,15,20) according to the probabilities estimated by the TL models, CASE A and CASE B

Here we kept the weights of the pre-trained layer frozen while we trained only the attached neural network layer. The initial layer has 57 neurons, $N_{hl_1} = 57$, since it corresponds to the pre-trained model in series D, and the second layer has 55 neurons, $N_{hl_2} = 55$. In each iteration, $iters = 6.000$ ($epochs \approx 14$), the weights of the initial layer remain frozen, while the weights of the higher/second layer were readjusted/updated. Thus, we ended up with a bidirectional recurrent neural network with two hidden layers, which on the second layer performs one step of stochastic gradient descent with gradient clipping, $ClippingValue = 0.8$, and learning rate, $lr = 0.01$. Table 4 (CASE B) illustrates the results of this architecture.

5.3 Assessment

Comparing the experiments of TL with that of training on series A&B from scratch, we observe the following:

- There is no overall improvement in synthetic gap infilling in comparison to learning from scratch as displayed in Table 3 and Table 4.
- The results of the trained model of cases A and B on the 29 real cases of the series A&B are presented in Table 5. The TL again does not seem to outperform the model trained from scratch in A&B series. However, the model behaves better and actually gives solutions in some complex cases, in cases where only one syllable has survived from the incomplete word (e.g., Mycenaean tablets KN Ak 7022 [+] 7024 and KN Ai 7745), while the model from supervised learning does not. These are described in detail in Appendix A.

Surely further investigation is needed on TL methods. The relative success for the real gap infilling task let us assume that if the data of series D (pre-trained model) increases then we will probably get better prediction rates.

Series A&B	BRNN		TL CASE A		TL CASE B	
29 sugges-tions	TOP5: 9	TOP10: 15	TOP5: 9	TOP10: 12	TOP5: 8	TOP10: 14

Table 5: Number of predictions (TOP-5 and TOP-10) in agreement with the visual assessments of the experts in the 29 instances for the three cases concerning the training of category A&B.

6 Conclusions and future work

Our model exploits a character-level Bidirectional Recurrent Neural Network and two Transfer Learning approaches in order to capture the statistical structure of the Mycenaean documents. Our methodology is expected to assist the experts recover the missing parts by offering alternatives along with their probability, which are complementary to the visual channel. The key takeaways are described in the following.

Training the BRNN model on the different series D datasets, by excluding the ideograms, we experienced a small improvement over the with-ideograms dataset.

The training of a similar BRNN model in series A&B from Knossos gives reasonable results. The prediction rates are reasonably lower, since the dataset includes significantly fewer tablets and consequently offers fewer sequences; these sequences are much shorter, most of them a single word, compared to those of series D.

We explored the potential of transfer learning techniques in a small dataset, with mixed results. Although the overall performance is not better than training from scratch, the TL should not be rejected because it exhibits some complementarity with supervised learning. Further investigation is needed, potentially with more data series.

The research can be extended to incorporate more series (apart from series D and A&B there are about 12 more series to investigate), including newly discovered or previously unexplored Mycenaean tablets. Increasing the size and diversity of the dataset can contribute to the robustness and generalization of the models, enabling them to handle a broader range of linguistic variations and complexities. Furthermore, we can incorporate Mycenaean tablets from other sites, not only from Knossos, for example from Pylos, Thebes, etc. Such an attempt will not only increase the dataset but will also contribute to enhancing the diversity of the data.

The incorporation of the visual modality is another aspect that we have not investigated so far, but should do in our next steps.

References

Yannis Assael, Thea Sommerschield, and Jonathan Prag. 2019. Restoring ancient text using deep learning: a case study on Greek epigraphy. In *Empirical Methods in Natural Language Processing*, pages 6369–6376.

Yannis Assael, Thea Sommerschield, Brendan Shillingford, Mahyar Bordbar, John Pavlopoulos, Maria Chatzipanagiotou, Ion Androutsopoulos, Jonathan Prag, and Nando Freitas. 2022. Restoring and attributing ancient texts using deep neural networks. *Nature*, 603:280–283.

David Bamman and Patrick J. Burns. 2020. Latin BERT: A contextual language model for classical philology. *CoRR*, abs/2009.10053.

A. Bernabé and E.R. Luján. 2020. *Introducción al griego micénico. Gramática, selección de textps y glosario*. Monografías de Filología Griega. Prensas de la Universidad de Zaragoza.

Maja Braović, Damir Krstinić, Maja Štula, and Antonia Ivanda. 2024. A systematic review of computational approaches to deciphering bronze age aegean and cypriot scripts. *Computational Linguistics*, pages 1–54.

J. Chadwick. 1990. *The Decipherment of Linear B*. Canto. Cambridge University Press.

J. Chadwick, L. Godart, J. T. Killen, J. P. Olivier, A. Sacconi, and I. A. Sakellarakis. 1987. *Corpus of Mycenaean Inscriptions from Knossos: Volumes 1-4*. Cambridge University Press.

Jacob Devlin, Ming-Wei Chang, Kenton Lee, and Kristina Toutanova. 2019. BERT: Pre-training of deep bidirectional transformers for language understanding. In *Proceedings of the 2019 Conference of the North American Chapter of the Association for Computational Linguistics: Human Language Technologies, Volume 1 (Long and Short Papers)*, pages 4171–4186, Minneapolis, Minnesota. Association for Computational Linguistics.

Mario. Doria. 1965. *Avviamento allo studio del Miceneo : struttura, problemi e testi / Mario Doria*. Incunabula Graeca ; v.8. Edizioni dell'Ateneo, Roma.

Y. Duhoux. 2014. *A companion to linear B : Mycenaean Greek texts and their world*. Number v. 3 in Series: Bibliothèque des Cahiers de l'Institut de Linguistique de Louvain (BCILL), 133. Peeters.

Y. Duhoux and A.M. Davies. 2008. *A Companion to Linear B: Mycenaean Greek Texts and Their World*. Bibliothèque des Cahiers de l'Institut de Linguistique de Louvain. Peeters.

Ethan Fetaya, Yonatan Lifshitz, Elad Aaron, and Shai Gordin. 2020. Restoration of fragmentary babylonian texts using recurrent neural networks. *Proceedings of the National Academy of Sciences*, 117(37):22743–22751.

Margalit Fox. 2013. *Riddle of the labyrinth: the quest to crack an ancient code and the uncovering of a lost civilisation*. Profile Books.

M.D. Freo and M. Perna. 2019. *Manuale di epigrafia micenea: introduzione allo studio dei testi in lineare B*. Libreriauniversitaria.it edizioni.

Kyeongpil Kang, Kyohoon Jin, Soyoung Yang, Soojin Jang, Jaegul Choo, and Youngbin Kim. 2021. Restoring and mining the records of the Joseon dynasty via neural language modeling and machine translation. In *Proceedings of the 2021 Conference of the North American Chapter of the Association for Computational Linguistics: Human Language Technologies*, pages 4031–4042, Online. Association for Computational Linguistics.

J. T. Killen. 1964. The interpretation of mycenaean greek texts by l. r. palmer. oxford: the clarendon press, 1963. 501 pp., frontispiece, 4 figs. 70s. *Antiquity*, 38(150):148–150.

Alice Elizabeth Kober. 1945. Evidence of inflection in the "chariot" tablets from knossos. *American Journal of Archaeology*, 49:143 – 151.

Alice Elizabeth Kober. 1946. Inflection in linear class b: 1-declension. *American Journal of Archaeology*, 50:268 – 276.

Alice Elizabeth Kober. 1948. The minoan scripts: Fact and theory. *American Journal of Archaeology*, 52:82 – 103.

Koren Lazar, Benny Saret, Asaf Yehudai, Wayne Horowitz, Nathan Wasserman, and Gabriel Stanovsky. 2021. Filling the gaps in Ancient Akkadian texts: A masked language modelling approach. In *Proceedings of the 2021 Conference on Empirical Methods in Natural Language Processing*, pages 4682–4691, Online and Punta Cana, Dominican Republic. Association for Computational Linguistics.

Yinhan Liu, Myle Ott, Naman Goyal, Jingfei Du, Mandar Joshi, Danqi Chen, Omer Levy, Mike Lewis, Luke Zettlemoyer, and Veselin Stoyanov. 2019. Roberta: A robustly optimized bert pretraining approach.

Torsten Meissner. 2001. F. m. j. waanders: Studies in local case relations in mycenaean greek. pp. vii 134. amsterdam: J. c. gieben, 1997. paper, hfl. 65. isbn: 90-5063-107-x. *The Classical Review*, 51(1):179–180.

The Packard Humanities Institute. 2005. PHI Greek inscriptions. https://inscriptions.packhum.org/. Online accessed 2021.

Katerina Papavassileiou, Dimitrios I. Kosmopoulos, and Gareth Owens. 2023. A generative model for the mycenaean linear b script and its application in infilling text from ancient tablets. *J. Comput. Cult. Herit.*, 16(3).

Katerina Papavassiliou, Gareth Owens, and Dimitrios Kosmopoulos. 2020. A dataset of Mycenaean Linear B sequences. In *Proceedings of the Twelfth Language Resources and Evaluation Conference*, pages 2552–2561, Marseille, France. European Language Resources Association.

Matthew E. Peters, Mark Neumann, Mohit Iyyer, Matt Gardner, Christopher Clark, Kenton Lee, and Luke Zettlemoyer. 2018. Deep contextualized word representations. In *Proceedings of the 2018 Conference of the North American Chapter of the Association for Computational Linguistics: Human Language Technologies, Volume 1 (Long Papers)*, pages 2227–2237, New Orleans, Louisiana. Association for Computational Linguistics.

Vassilis Petrakis. 2017. Figures of speech? observations on the non-phonographic component in the linear b writing system. In *Aegean Scripts: Proceedings of the 14th International Colloquium on Mycenaean Studies*, v. 105, pt. 1, pages 127–167. Edizioni Consiglio nazionale delle ricerche, Istituto di studi sul Mediterraneo antico.

Maurice Pope. 2008. The decipherment of linear b. In Anna Morpurgo Duhoux, Yves; Davies, editor, *A Companion to Linear B: Mycenaean Texts and their World*, volume 1, pages 3–11. Louvain-la-Neuve, Belgium: Peeters.

Alec Radford, Jeff Wu, Rewon Child, David Luan, Dario Amodei, and Ilya Sutskever. 2019. Language models are unsupervised multitask learners.

Rajesh P. N. Rao, Nisha Yadav, Mayank N. Vahia, Hrishikesh Joglekar, R. Adhikari, and Iravatham Mahadevan. 2009. A markov model of the indus script. *Proceedings of the National Academy of Sciences*, 106(33):13685–13690.

A. Robinson and S. Eisenman. 2002. *The Man who Deciphered Linear B: The Story of Michael Ventris*. World of Art Series. Thames & Hudson.

Henriette Roued-Cunliffe. 2010. Towards a decision support system for reading ancient documents. *Literary and Linguistic Computing*, 25(4):365–379.

C.J. Ruijgh. 1977. E. L. Bennett J.P. Olivier, the Pylos tablets transcribed, i : Texts and notes, ii : Hands, concordances, indices (incunabula graeca, 51 et 59). Rome, edizioni dell'Ateneo, 1973 et 1976. 287 et 146 p. pr. l. 10.600 et 14.000. *Mnemosyne*, 30(3):296 – 298.

M. S. Ruiperez and J. L. Melena. 1996. *The Mycenaean Greeks*. Athens: Kardamitsa.

Tianxiao Shen, Victor Quach, Regina Barzilay, and Tommi Jaakkola. 2020. Blank language models. In *Proceedings of the 2020 Conference on Empirical Methods in Natural Language Processing (EMNLP)*, pages 5186–5198, Online. Association for Computational Linguistics.

Thea Sommerschield, Yannis Assael, John Pavlopoulos, Vanessa Stefanak, Andrew Senior, Chris Dyer, John Bodel, Jonathan Prag, Ion Androutsopoulos, and Nando de Freitas. 2023. Machine Learning for Ancient Languages: A Survey. *Computational Linguistics*, pages 1–44.

Ilya Sutskever, Oriol Vinyals, and Quoc V Le. 2014. Sequence to sequence learning with neural networks. In *Advances in Neural Information Processing Systems*, volume 27, pages 3104–3112. Curran Associates, Inc.

M. Ventris and J. Chadwick. 1953. *Evidence for Greek Dialect in the Mycenaean Archives*. Journal of Hellenic Studies. Journal of Hellenic Studies.

M. Ventris and J. Chadwick. 1956. *Evidence for a Greek Dialect in the Mycenaean Archives*. Council of the Society for the Promotion of Hellenic Studies.

M. Ventris and J. Chadwick. 2015. *Documents in Mycenaean Greek*. Cambridge University Press.

M. Ventris, A. Sacconi, and J. Chadwick. 1988. *Work Notes on Minoan Language Research and Other Unedited Papers*. Incunabula Graeca. Edizioni dell'Ateneo.

Krzysztof Wolk and Krzysztof Marasek. 2014. Polish-English speech statistical machine translation systems for the IWSLT 2014. In *Proceedings of the 11th International Workshop on Spoken Language Translation: Evaluation Campaign*, pages 143–149, Lake Tahoe, California.

Nisha Yadav, Hrishikesh Joglekar, Rajesh P. N. Rao, Mayank N. Vahia, Ronojoy Adhikari, and Iravatham Mahadevan. 2010. Statistical analysis of the indus script using n-grams. *PLoS ONE*, 5(3):e9506.

A Appendix

Here we present the damaged Mycenaean tablets, along with the experts' guesses based on the visual cues of some small parts of the missing syllables (Chadwick et al., 1987). We compare our models (Bidirectional Recurrent Neural Network and Transfer Learning) with those estimations.

The bibliographic comments on the missing symbol, are shown in the third column, and the results of the model in the fourth one. The symbol *'bl'* corresponds to the 'space' symbol.

In Table 1 are presented the D series BRNN predictions for the 15 cases for which we have the opinions of the experts. Eight of our TOP-5 predictions agree with the literature recommendations. In the following we try to give some possible explanations for the remaining 7 model's predictions, since there is no hard evidence available:

- On the tablet Dl 933 we find a syllable, '*83' (its phonetic value has not been determined with certainty), which is quite rare and is observed only twice in the training dataset. As a result, the model is probably not sufficiently trained in such a context.

- The TOP-5 BRNN predictions are not consistent with the remnant in the KN Dv 1213 and KN Dv 5236 + 532. The model prioritizes other syllables, probably due to the short sequence length, which conveys rather poor context information. Inclusion of visual evidence in our model in the future could handle such issues.

- The tablet Da 1341 is a difficult case, since the visual evidence is very weak and even the experts note that their degree of certainty is low.

- For the tablet KN Db 5310 + 6062 + 837 we notice that the predictions of our model, and in fact the 'ka' and 'ra', are not completely irrelevant/unrelated to the remnant.

- The tablet Db 5359 + 5565 +7214 is another difficult case as acknowledged by experts and their degree of certainty is also low.

- The remnant in tablet KN Do 7740 largely matches the syllable 'ke', suggested by the bibliography. The model in this case probably failed to predict part of a human name; human names are typically unique.

As regards Tables 2, 3 and 4 related to the experts' suggestions in the 29 real cases of series A&B, we observe the following:

- There is a convergence of the models after Transfer Learning with the estimations of the experts for real gaps. If we observe the predictions of the BRNN model on the damaged tablets of series A&B, Table 2, in relation to those after applying the Transfer Learning technique, Tables 3 and 4, we will see that when the predictions of all three models agree with the bibliographic annotation, tablets KN Bk 806 + 6053 + frr (eighth row) and KN As 1516 (thirteenth row), then the predictions of the TL models rank higher (among the TOP-5 predictions).

- Another important observation, concerning the TL method, results from the tablet KN Ak 7022 [+] 7024. This tablet offers 6 sequences (twenty-first - twenty-sixth row), Tables 2, 3 and 4. The bibliography for the incomplete word, "*-ki", suggests the syllable "do". This syllable begins to appear in the BRNN predictions of the Table 4, which concerns TL method (CASE B). It is quite difficult to predict the rest of a word when there is only one syllable left. These cases are more likely to be approached with TL techniques rather than training from scratch.

- It is no coincidence that results for tablet KN Ai 7745 (twenty-ninth row), in agreement with the experts' opinion, we only have with TL method and indeed in CASE B (Table 4) it is the first choice.

- Something similar happens with tablets KN Bk 5134 (fifteenth row) and KN As 5932 [+] 8342 (twentieth row). Only the TL method manages to display the desired syllable in the TOP-10 predictions, Table 4 for the KN Bk 5134 and Table 3 for the KN As 5932 [+] 8342, with the difference that they are not in the TOP-5.

Due to these reasons we believe that TL methods need further investigation.

Damaged Tablets	Sequences	Bibliographic annotation	BRNN TOP-5
KN Dq 447	*-ta-wo da-mi-ni-jo	*possibly 'ka' or 'qe'*	***'ka'***, *'si', 'ku', 'qo', 'ti'*
KN Dl 933 + 968 + 975	*-*83-re-to si-ja-du-we po-ti-ni-ja-we-jo	*perhaps 'ko'*	*'no', 'a3', 'ra', 'wi', 'do'*
KN Dp 1061	*-sa pa-i-ti-ja	*probably 'to'*	***'to'***, *'sa', 'te', 'po', 'qa'*
KN Dv 1213	*-so u-ta-no	*'to', 'jo' possible*	*'pu', 'ko', 'nwa', 'i', 'wi'*
KN Da 1341 [+] 1454 + 8777	*-no-qa-ta pa-i-to da-mi-ni-jo	*'po' possible, but difficult*	*'a', 'wi', 'jo', 'ka', 'ti'*
KN Db 1344 + 6017 + 7268 + 7950 + 8235	*-tu-to pa-i-to we-we-si-jo-jo	*perhaps 'ti'*	*'bl', 'ku', 'ra',* ***'ti'***, *'pa'*
KN Da 1401 + 7998 + fr.	*-wi da-*22-to	*perhaps 'na'*	*'ro', 'ri',* ***'na'***, *'nu', 'ra'*
KN Df 5198 + 5238 + 5269	wi-na-jo ra-* ki-ri-jo-te	*traces favour 'ja'*	*'to',* ***'ja'***, *'su', 'nwa', 'pe'*
KN Dv 5236 + 5329	*-jo ra-to	*perhaps 'qa' or 'wo'*	*'te', 'ku', 'ri', 'wa', 'ro'*
KN Dv 5278 + 5338 + 8557	*-ma-we qa-mo	*'ko' not impossible*	*'ja', 'i',* ***'ko'***, *'sa', 'no'*
KN Db 5310 + 6062 + 8375	e-*-jo ku-ta-to	*perhaps 'qa' or 'ri'*	*ka', 'ra', 'wa', 'te', 'se'*
KN Db 5359 + 5565 + 7214	*-ma-na-so ra-su-to u-ta-jo	*'pi' not impossible*	*'bl', 'ta', 'wa', 'ru', 'di'*
KN Dv 5690	du-ni-*	*'jo' possible*	***'ja'***, *'to', 'po', 'ki', 'mi'*
KN Dc 7161 + 7179 + 8365 + fr.	*-to ku-ta-to u-ta-jo-jo	*possibly 'ke'*	*'ra', 'ta',* ***'ke'***, *'ro', 'ko'*
KN Do 7740	*-ta ka-to-ro se-to-i-ja	*'ke' or 'de'*	*'u', 'ku', 'wa', 'si', 'qo'*

Table 1: Bibliographic annotations (Chadwick et al., 1987) comparing to BRNN predictions in the 15 sequences appear in the real cases of series D.

Damaged Tablets	**Sequences**	**Bibliographic annotation**	**BRNN TOP-10**
KN B 164 + 5666 + 7136 + 7544 + 8120 + frr.	o-da-*	*'ke' or 'je'*	*'wa', 'wi', 'ra', '*22', 'mo', 'ro', 'wo', 'mi', 'ma', 'zo'*
KN As 605 + 5869 + 5911 + 5931 + frr.	*-no pe-ro-qe	*'me' or 'ro'*	*'wo', 'tu', 'jo', 'ne', 'wi', 'ta',* ***'ro'****, 're', 'no', 'qa'*
KN Bk 799 + 8306 (Fig. 4)	a-*-de	*'ka' or 'qe'*	*'to', 'me', 'ke', 'pe', 'ta', 'mi', 'di', 'pi', 'ko', 'pa'*
KN Bk 802	ra-ti-*	*'jo'*	*'ja',* ***'jo'****, 'ri', 'pu', 'zo', 're', 'wa', 'nu', 'no', 'to'*
KN Bk 804	a-pa-re-*	*'u'*	*'jo', 'we',* ***'u'****, 'da', 'ta', 'ne', 'ti', 'te', 'wa', 'pa'*
KN Bk 806 + 6053 + frr.	ko-*-no	*'pi' or 'wi'*	*'wa', 'wo', 'no', 'to', 'so', 'ko', 'ma', 'qa', 'a', 'ta2'*
KN Bk 806 + 6053 + frr.	*-wo-ta	*'pi' or 'e'*	*'ne', 're', 'a', 'qi', 'wo', 'po', 'mo', 'ko', 'u', 'ri'*
KN Bk 806 + 6053 + frr.	ko-*-ka-ra-te-ne	*'wo'*	*'tu', 'we', 'bl', 'so', 'no', 'wa', 'da',* ***'wo'****, 'ma', 'u'*
KN B 809	*-sa-do-ro-jo	*'ke'*	***'ke'****, 'bl', 'to', 'pi', 'te', 'a', 'we', 'u', 'po', 'mi'*
KN As 1516	ko-no-si-ja ra-wa-ke-si-ja *-ki-wa-ta	*'a' or 'a3'*	***'a'****, 'e', 'pa', 'pi', 'mi', 'ni', 'du', 'wa',* ***'a3'****, 'do'*
KN As 1516	ko-no-si-ja ra-wa-ke-si-ja wa-du-*-to	*'ni' or 'sa'*	*'na', '*22', 'we', 'du', 'se',* ***'ni'****, 'de', 'ra2', 'za', 'nu'*
KN As 1516	*-ti-jo qa-si-re-wi-ja a-nu-to	*'ta' or 'ra'*	*'a', 'bl', 'do', 'i', 'po',* ***'ta'****, 'so', 'du', 'wa', 'o'*
KN As 1516	ku-*-ti-jo qa-si-re-wi-ja a-nu-to	*'ta' or 'ra'*	*'a', 'du', 'do', 'tu', 'i',* ***'ta'****, 'to', 'ku', 'ro2', 'au'*
KN As 1516	se-to-i-ja qa-si-re-wi-ja pi-*-jo	*'ri'*	*'si',* ***''ri'****, 'wi', 'ni', 'ra', 'u', 'mi', 'ro', 'mo', 'qi'*
KN Bk 5134	to-ke-*	*'u'*	*'qa', 're', 'zo', 'pu', 'ti', 'su', 'da', 'ka', 'no', 'ta'*
KN Bk 5172	*-wa-ta	*'ku'*	*'a', 'ki', 'ko', 're', 'i', 'po', 'wo', 'ne', 'ta', 'qi'*
KN Bk 5172	wi-do-*-wi	*'wo'*	*'e', 'ro', 'da',* ***'wo'****, 'ra', 'qe', 'ta', 'tu', 'to', 're'*
KN As 5609 + 6067	*-ke-u	*'i' or 'pa'*	*'e', 'ta', 'nu', 'ne', 'mi', 'wa', 'pi',* ***'pa'****, 'we', 'do'*
KN Am 5882 + 5902	*-so ka-ma-jo	*'to'*	***'to'****, 'no', 'tu', 'u', 'ni', 'ne', 'wo', 'wi', 'ko', 'ta2'*
KN As 5932 [+] 8342	a-*-we	*'ro'*	*'ke', 're', 'te', 'mi', 'pe', 'nu', 'pa', 'pi', 'ku', 'to'*
KN Ak 7022 [+] 7024	*-ki	*'do'*	*'to', 'jo', 'wo', 'bl', 'ni', 'ne', 'te', 'we', 'e', 'po'*
KN Ak 7022 [+] 7024	*-ki ko-wa me-zo-e	*'do'*	*'re', 'jo', 'e', 'wo', 'ni', 'ne', 'mi', 'to', 'qa', 'ri'*
KN Ak 7022 [+] 7024	*-ki ko-wa me-wi-jo-e	*'do'*	*'re', 'jo', 'e', 'wo', 'to', 'wi', 'ka', 'pu', 'mi', 'ni'*
KN Ak 7022 [+] 7024	*-ki ko-wo me-zo-e	*'do'*	*'re', 'to', 'wo', 'ni', 'tu', 'jo', 'mi', 'e', 'su', 'ri'*
KN Ak 7022 [+] 7024	*-ki ko-wo me-wi-jo-e	*'do'*	*'to', 're', 'jo', 'wo', 'ni', 'e', 'a', 'su', 'o', 'ri'*
KN Ak 7022 [+] 7024	*-ki do-e-ra	*'do'*	*'to', 're', 'qa', 'te', 'ke', 'ka', 'e', 'i', 'pi', 'qe'*
KN Bo 7043 + 7925	*-ra-so	*'ka' or 'qe' or 'we'*	***'ka'****, 'bl', 'ta',* ***'qe'****, 'si', 'pa', 'sa', 'a', 'wo', 're'*
KN Bg 7682	ri-si-*	*'jo'*	***'jo'****, 'ja', 'ra', 'nu', 'pu', 'mi', 'wi', 'no', 'ro', 'zo'*
KN Ai 7745	*-ja-to si-qa	*'ri'*	*ti', 'i', 're', 'qe', 'si', 'ta', 'wi', 'ni', 'bl', 'me'*

Table 2: Bibliographic annotations (Chadwick et al., 1987) comparing to BRNN predictions in the 29 sequences appear in the real cases of series A&B.

Damaged Tablets	Sequences	Bibliographic annotation	BRNN TOP-10
KN B 164 + 5666 + 7136 + 7544 + 8120 + frr.	o-da-*	*'ke' or 'je'*	*'te', 'su', 'ka', 'ra', 'no', 'wi', 'wo', 'se', 'bl', 'so'*
KN As 605 + 5869 + 5911 + 5931 + frr.	*-no pe-ro-qe	*'me' or 'ro'*	*'a', 'bl', 'no',* ***'ro'****, 'i', 'ko', 'ka', 'ta2', 'qi', 'na'*
KN Bk 799 + 8306 (Fig. 4)	a-*-de	*'ka' or 'qe'*	*'ta', 'ra', 'to', 'pi', 'no', 're', 'ja', 'nu', 'wo', 'jo'*
KN Bk 802	ra-ti-*	*'jo'*	***'ja'****, 'bl', 'ke', 'ka', 'wa', 'ti', 'a',* ***'jo'****, 'qa', 'to'*
KN Bk 804	a-pa-re-*	*'u'*	*'so', 'ta', 'ka', 'te', 'se', 'si', 'wa', 'ti', 'we', 'po'*
KN Bk 806 + 6053 + frr.	ko-*-no	*'pi' or 'wi'*	*'a', '*56', 'ko', 'ta', 'bl', 'wo', 'mo', 'wa', 'no', 'ka'*
KN Bk 806 + 6053 + frr.	*-wo-ta	*'pi' or 'e'*	*'ro', 'to', 'da', 'jo', 'no', 'qo', 'nu', 'ko', 'du', 'di'*
KN Bk 806 + 6053 + frr.	ko-*-ka-ra-te-ne	*'wo'*	*'bl', 'no', 'a',* ***'wo'****, 'ja', 'wa', 'ta', 'si', 'i', 'e'*
KN B 809	*-sa-do-ro-jo	*'ke'*	*'bl', 'ta', 'ro', 'no', 'jo', 'ka', 'ja', 'ne', 'e', 'so'*
KN As 1516	ko-no-si-ja ra-wa-ke-si-ja *-ki-wa-ta	*'a' or 'a3'*	*'no', 'mi', 'ru', 'so', 'pe', 'da', 'si', '*56', 'to', 'do'*
KN As 1516	ko-no-si-ja ra-wa-ke-si-ja wa-du-*-to	*'ni' or 'sa'*	*'ri', 'se', '*22', 'qa',* ***'ni'****, 'su', 'ru', 'no', '*56', 'ka'*
KN As 1516	*-ti-jo qa-si-re-wi-ja a-nu-to	*'ta' or 'ra'*	*'i', 'do', 'se', 'ku', 'wi', 'po', 'na', 'tu', 'wa', 'a'*
KN As 1516	ku-*-ti-jo qa-si-re-wi-ja a-nu-to	*'ta' or 'ra'*	*'i',* ***'ta'****, 'se', 'do', 'qe', 'o', 'su', 'ra2', 'ko', 'nwa*
KN As 1516	se-to-i-ja qa-si-re-wi-ja pi-*-jo	*'ri'*	***'ri'****, 'ro', 'si', 're', 'sa', 'da', 'mi', 'ra', 'tu', 'ru'*
KN Bk 5134	to-ke-*	*'u'*	*'a', 'bl', 'ka', 'to', 'o', 'ja', 'e', 'ti', 'ru', 'ta'*
KN Bk 5172	*-wa-ta	*'ku'*	*'ro', 'bl', 'ki', 'di', 're', 'ko', 'so', 'u', 'a3', 'qo'*
KN Bk 5172	wi-do-*-wi	*'wo'*	*'ti', 'bl', 'so',* ***'wo'****, 'ro', 'si', 'su', 'sa', 'ne', 'o'*
KN As 5609 + 6067	*-ke-u	*'i' or 'pa'*	*'to', 'ro', 'te', 'nu', 'sa', 'e', 'ne', 'ke', 'de', 'zo'*
KN Am 5882 + 5902	*-so ka-ma-jo	*'to'*	***'to'****, 'po', 'na', 'ko', 'no', 'nu', 'du', 'pu', 'ro', 'e'*
KN As 5932 [+] 8342	a-*-we	*'ro'*	*ta', 'ko', 're', 'te', 'ma',* ***'ro'****, 'ra', 'pi', 'nu', 'du'*
KN Ak 7022 [+] 7024	*-ki	*'do'*	*'si', 'jo', 'ro', 'to', 'no', 'bl', 'ta', 'ja', 'ne', 'so'*
KN Ak 7022 [+] 7024	*-ki ko-wa me-zo-e	*'do'*	*'to', 'te', 'jo', 'po', 'qo', 'e', 'na', 'si', 'no', 'me'*
KN Ak 7022 [+] 7024	*-ki ko-wa me-wi-jo-e	*'do'*	*te', 'to', 'po', 'jo', 'qo', 'si', 'e', 'ro', 'we', 'no'*
KN Ak 7022 [+] 7024	*-ki ko-wo me-zo-e	*'do'*	*'to', 'te', 'po', 'jo', 'si', 'e', 'na', 'qo', 'no', 'ro'*
KN Ak 7022 [+] 7024	*-ki ko-wo me-wi-jo-e	*'do'*	*te', 'po', 'jo', 'to', 'e', 'we', 'si', 'qo', 'na', 'no'*
KN Ak 7022 [+] 7024	*-ki do-e-ra	*'do'*	*'si', 'ta', 'no', 'ro', 'qa', 'di', 'wi', 'we', 'sa', 'i'*
KN Bo 7043 + 7925	*-ra-so	*'ka' or 'qe' or 'we'*	*'bl', 'ti', 'e', 'ta', 'ku', 'pa', 'zo', 'si',* ***'ka'****, 'wo'*
KN Bg 7682	ri-si-*	*'jo'*	***'ja'****,* ***'jo'****, 'no', 'ta', 'se', 'ni', 'mi', 're', 'ke', 'de'*
KN Ai 7745	*-ja-to si-qa	*'ri'*	*'ra',* ***'ri'****, 'ni', 'ti', 'na', 'i', 'mi', 'bl', 'ku', 're'*

Table 3: Bibliographic annotations (Chadwick et al., 1987) comparing to TL predictions in the 29 sequences appear in the real cases of series A&B (CASE A).

Damaged Tablets	**Sequences**	**Bibliographic annotation**	**BRNN TOP-10**
KN B 164 + 5666 + 7136 + 7544 + 8120 + frr.	o-da-*	*'ke' or 'je'*	*'ra', 'ko', 'wo', 'zo', 'su', '*22', 'to', '*56', 'sa', 'wa'*
KN As 605 + 5869 + 5911 + 5931 + frr.	*-no pe-ro-qe	*'me' or 'ro'*	*'a', 're', 'qa', 'to', 'da', 'wi', 'ki', 'su', 'ne', 'ti'*
KN Bk 799 + 8306 (Fig. 4)	a-*-de	*'ka' or 'qe'*	*'to', 'ta', 'no', 'po', 'te', 'nu', 'mi', 'tu', 'pe', 'a'*
KN Bk 802	ra-ti-*	*'jo'*	*'ri', 'to', 'e', 'so', 'we', 'i', 'ti', 'qa', 'ni', 'di'*
KN Bk 804	a-pa-re-*	*'u'*	*'ta', 'so', 'i', 'wa', 'po', 'jo', 'si', 'we',* ***'u'***, *'ka'*
KN Bk 806 + 6053 + frr.	ko-*-no	*'pi' or 'wi'*	*'a', 'wo', 'ko', 'to', 'ta', 'no', 'ma', 'ro', 'du', 'po'*
KN Bk 806 + 6053 + frr.	*-wo-ta	*'pi' or 'e'*	*'a', 'we', 'ko', 'po', 'ra', 'u', 'da', 'qi', 'bl', 'o'*
KN Bk 806 + 6053 + frr.	ko-*-ka-ra-te-ne	*'wo'*	*'a',* ***'wo'***, *'to', 'ta', 'e', 'tu', 'o', 'bl', 'ku', 'da'*
KN B 809	*-sa-do-ro-jo	*'ke'*	*'u', 'bl', 'to', 'a', 'qa', 'pi', 'te', 'di', 'we', 'ka'*
KN As 1516	ko-no-si-ja ra-wa-ke-si-ja *-ki-wa-ta	*'a' or 'a3'*	*'pu',* ***'a'***, *'ro', 'pe', 'si', 'wi', 'pi', 'se', 'di', 'su'*
KN As 1516	ko-no-si-ja ra-wa-ke-si-ja wa-du-*-to	*'ni' or 'sa'*	*'se', 'si', 'ri', 'ke', '*22', 'we', 'to', 'po', 'o', 'pe', 'mi'*
KN As 1516	*-ti-jo qa-si-re-wi-ja a-nu-to	*'ta' or 'ra'*	*'pe', 'pa', 'wa', 'i', 'do', 'ni', 'du',* ***'ta'***, *'ma', 'su'*
KN As 1516	ku-*-ti-jo qa-si-re-wi-ja a-nu-to	*'ta' or 'ra'*	***'ta'***, *'su', 'po', 'to', 'pa', 'du', 'pe', 'i', 'ko', 'ro2'*
KN As 1516	se-to-i-ja qa-si-re-wi-ja pi-*-jo	*'ri'*	***'ri'***, *'ra', 'ni', 'da', 'ti', 'si', 'ki', 'wa', 'mi', 'pi'*
KN Bk 5134	to-ke-*	*'u'*	*'ko', 'ja', 'so', 'qa', 'ku', 'da', 'to',* ***'u'***, *'a', 'ru'*
KN Bk 5172	*-wa-ta	*'ku'*	*'we', 'a', 'po', 'bl', 'si', 'o', 'ki', 'te', 'ti', 're'*
KN Bk 5172	wi-do-*-wi	*'wo'*	*'pe', 'e', 'sa', 'po', 'ra', 'do', 'te', 'zo', 'ti', 'pa'*
KN As 5609 + 6067	*-ke-u	*'i' or 'pa'*	*'pe', 'te', 'ri', 'ke', 'no', 'ro', 'se', 'zo', 'wo', 'do'*
KN Am 5882 + 5902	*-so ka-ma-jo	*'to'*	***'to'***, *'ta', 'ke', 'do', 'sa', 'ni', 'qa', 'te', 'ne', 'e'*
KN As 5932 [+] 8342	a-*-we	*'ro'*	*'ko', 'pe', 'te', 'po', 'nu', 'ke', 'a', 'da', 'me', 'no'*
KN Ak 7022 [+] 7024	*-ki	*'do'*	*'jo', 'pe', 'ni', 'wo', 'tu', 'te', 'no', 'to', 'ja', 'ta'*
KN Ak 7022 [+] 7024	*-ki ko-wa me-zo-e	*'do'*	*'ni', 'ka', 'wi', 'tu', 'mi', 'te', 'na', 'pe', 'to', 'ki'*
KN Ak 7022 [+] 7024	*-ki ko-wa me-wi-jo-e	*'do'*	*'ni', 'mi', 'te', 'tu', 'na', 'wi', 'ki', 're', 'e', 'ti'*
KN Ak 7022 [+] 7024	*-ki ko-wo me-zo-e	*'do'*	*'to', 'ka', 'ni', 'na', 'wi', 'tu', 'pe', 'te',* ***'do'***, *'ja'*
KN Ak 7022 [+] 7024	*-ki ko-wo me-wi-jo-e	*'do'*	*'ni', 'ka', 'to', 'na', 'wi', 'tu', 'pe', 'ki', 'se',* ***'do'***
KN Ak 7022 [+] 7024	*-ki do-e-ra	*'do'*	*'ka', 'ki', 'to',* ***'do'***, *'wi', 'su', 'mi', 'ti', 'tu', 'ni'*
KN Bo 7043 + 7925	*-ra-so	*'ka' or 'qe' or 'we'*	***'ka'***, *'si', 'zo', 'se', 'wo',* ***'qe'***, *'ta', 'a', 'nu', 'mo'*
KN Bg 7682	ri-si-*	*'jo'*	*'ja', 'wo',* ***'jo'***, *'ra', 'ni', 'to', 'ta', 'ti', 'de', 'ri'*
KN Ai 7745	*-ja-to si-qa	*'ri'*	***'ri'***, *'ro', 'ni', 'di', 'ti', 'mi', 'ke', 'pe', 'te', 're'*

Table 4: Bibliographic annotations (Chadwick et al., 1987) comparing to TL predictions in the 29 sequences appear in the real cases of series A&B (CASE B).

CuReD: Deep Learning Optical Character Recognition for Cuneiform Text Editions and Legacy Materials

Shai Gordin
Ariel University
Open University of Israel
shaigo@ariel.ac.il

Morris Alper
Tel Aviv University
morrisalper@mail.tau.ac.il

Avital Romach
Yale University
avital.romach@yale.edu

Luis Sáenz
Heidelberg University
luissaenzs@gmail.com

Naama Yochai
Tel Aviv University
naamayochai@mail.tau.ac.il

Roey Lalazar
roey@gerev.ai

Abstract

Cuneiform documents, the earliest known form of writing, are prolific textual sources of the ancient past. Experts publish editions of these texts in transliteration using specialized typesetting, but most remain inaccessible for computational analysis in traditional printed books or legacy materials. Off-the-shelf OCR systems are insufficient for digitization without adaptation. We present CuReD (Cuneiform Recognition-Documents), a deep learning-based human-in-the-loop OCR pipeline for digitizing scanned transliterations of cuneiform texts. CuReD has a character error rate of 9% on clean data and 11% on representative scans. We digitized a challenging sample of transliterated cuneiform documents, as well as lexical index cards from the University of Pennsylvania Museum, demonstrating the feasibility of our platform for enabling computational analysis and bolstering machine-readable cuneiform text datasets. Our result provide the first human-in-the-loop pipeline and interface for digitizing transliterated cuneiform sources and legacy materials, enabling the enrichment of digital sources of these low-resource languages.

1 Introduction

The cuneiform writing system was used to write around a dozen different ancient languages over a period of more than three millennia. Many of these complex writing systems were logo-syllabic and of different language families, from the agglutinative Sumerian in southern Mesopotamia, to the family of Hurrian and Urartian in northern Mesopotamia and Armenia, to Indo-European Hittite and Luwian in Anatolia. While the records of many of these languages are in the hundreds or thousands, it is Semitic Akkadian with its main Babylonian and Assyrian dialects that is attested on hundreds of thousands of ancient texts (Vita, 2021). What all of them share is a similar critical apparatus: a standard Latin transcription and notation system, developed by experts in scholarly publications, from the mid-19th century to the early 20th century (see Appendix A), and is still used to this day. Legacy materials such as personal notebooks of curators or researchers, or card catalogues in universities and museums use this notation system extensively (Fig. 1).

Many publications and legacy materials have been scanned or photographed, but are largely unavailable as machine-readable text. The ability to automatically digitize them using optical character recognition (OCR) would make their contents readily available to experts and the general public. They can be further used in computational research into the languages, cultures, and history of these societies, as well as a wider use of natural language processing (NLP) techniques, such as part-of-speech tagging, named entity recognition, sentiment analysis, machine translation, and more. This in turn can further enhance cross-lingual research and the creation of linked open data entities as well as knowledge graphs (Gutherz et al., 2023; Homburg et al., 2023; Sahala and Lindén, 2023; Ong and Gordin, 2024; Smidt et al., 2024).

Existing OCR models trained on texts in other languages such as English are not suitable for this task. They do not recognize the diacritics, typographical oddities like mixed upper- and lower-case or sub- and super-script, as well as special symbols required for digitizing cuneiform transliterations. Furthermore, many off-the-shelf models are biased by their prior training on character sequences in the

Proceedings of the 1st Workshop on Machine Learning for Ancient Languages (ML4AL 2024), pages 130–140

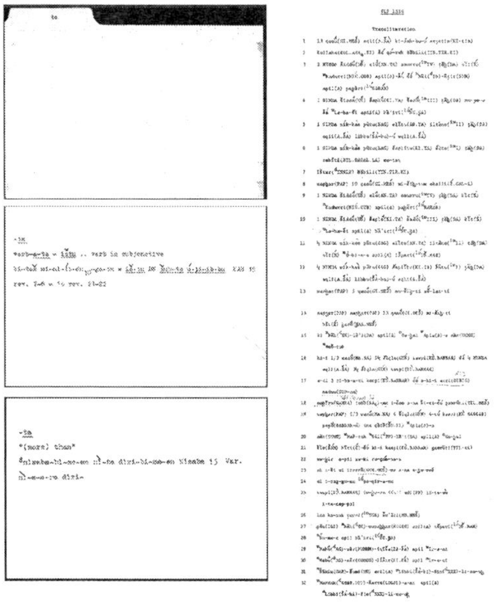

Figure 1: On the left examples of scanned lexical cards from the University of Pennsylvania Sumerian lexicography collection digitized by Anna Glenn for the University of Munich (Sjöberg, 2023). On the right an example of cuneiform transliteration from the Neo-Babylonian text corpus published in the dissertation of R. B. Dillard (Dillard, 1975).

source language. They are also typically trained on large datasets of scans with manually-labelled text, which is not available for more niche use cases such as those of cuneiform scholars.

In order to overcome these challenges, we trained a custom deep-learning based OCR model on transliterations of Akkadian, bootstrapping with artificially-generated data, and then fine-tuned with a small set of manually-labelled examples. The data for training and testing the model were taken from Open Richly Annotated Cuneiform Corpus (ORACC) and their equivalent print publications in PDF format.

However, those texts were from one period (Neo-Assyrian) and followed the same editorial conventions. To estimate the real-world usability of the model, we performed two additional digitization experiments on transliterated text produced with a typewriter during the 1970s and 80s: (1) 81 previously undigitized Neo-Babylonian administrative and archival daily documents published in the 1975 dissertation of Raymond B. Dillard (Dillard, 1975); (2) 30 index cards produced by Å. W. Sjöberg in the late 1970s and early 1980s as part of the Sumerian Lexicography collection housed in the Babylonian Section of the University of Pennsylvania Museum, now scanned in their entirety by Anna Glenn for LMU Munich, and published on the LMU library online catalogue (Sjöberg, 2023).

Both were particularly difficult to OCR, and were not a part of the model's training. In the case of the Dillard texts, we show that with fine-tuning on only 10 texts, the models' results rose from 53% to 85% accuracy. Similarly, in the case of the Sumerian lexical cards, after only 60 text lines, the model improved from 87% to 94% accuracy.

Thus, the model requires a minimal number of examples in order to be a significant assistant in the digitization process of ancient documents. The model is published on the Digital Pasts Lab GitHub repository and is freely available as an online tool in the Babylonian Engine website, which is undergoing a transformation into a standalone browser-based application. The tool and model will facilitate the digitization of hundreds of thousands of published cuneiform text lines in transliteration, which were previously unavailable for further computational or quantitative study.

2 Methods

2.1 Data preparation for training the OCR model

We used texts from the State Archives of Assyria (SAA), which are available in both print and digital forms. The transliterated Akkadian texts are hosted on the Open Richly Annotated Cuneiform Corpus (ORACC) as the State Archives of Assyria online (SAAo), which are part of the Munich Open-access Cuneiform Corpus Initiative (MOCCI) (Radner et al., 2015). Also available are scans of the books containing the texts in print; however, these cannot directly be used to train an OCR model because there is no alignment between the digitized Akkadian text and the location of its print equivalent on the scanned pages.

In order to collect usable pairs of images and corresponding digital Akkadian transliterations, we ran a heuristic algorithm which segmented and localized the transliterations within these scans, as well as extracting the digitized Akkadian transcribed text hosted on the Open Richly Annotated Cuneiform Corpus (ORACC) and aligning them. The algorithm uses computer vision (CV) methods such as thresholding and dilation to determine where there are paragraphs, and then runs a regular OCR on each paragraph to check whether this is an English

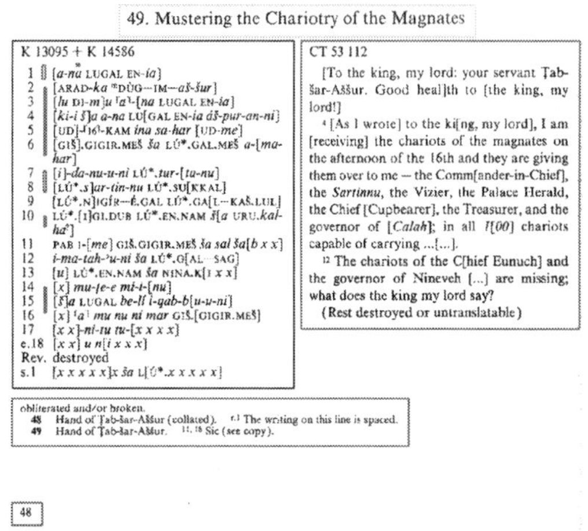

Figure 2: Segmentation Example from the State Archives of Assyria volume 1 (Parpola, 2015). Akkadian paragraph marked in blue, title marked in green.

paragraph or an Akkadian one. It also tries to locate titles (Fig. 2).

This method generated pairs of images and Akkadian text. The results were highly approximate and not clean enough to be used directly for training an OCR system, but allowed us to find examples for use in fine-tuning and evaluating our final model. In total, we manually labelled 30 of these images.

Because of this scarcity of labelled data, in order to train our OCR model from scratch we decided to bootstrap it with artificially-generated image data. We took all the digital text editions of the SAAo and generated images by rendering each line of text in the dataset as an image file. Our core OCR model was based on the open-source Kraken OCR framework developed by Benjamin Kiessling as described in Romanov et al. (2017).

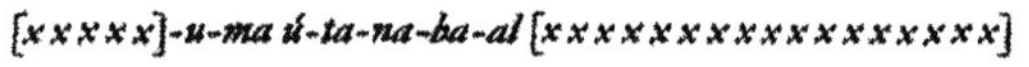

Figure 3: Artificial data example generated from the SAAo corpus.

In order to increase the robustness of the model to noise and typeface variation, we added noise to the images by using Kraken's data augmentation API, with parameters alpha=0.3 (mean of folded normal distribution of foreground pixel flip probabilities) and distortion=3 (mean of folded normal distribution from which distortion values are sampled). We found that results were significantly improved by using multiple fonts to render the images. In order to match the typefaces most commonly found in the source materials, we rendered the texts in three fonts: (1) DejaVu Serif, (2) Garamond, (3) IM Fell Double Pica.

We also found that it was important to consider italic text since in Akkadian transliterations lowercase letters are normally printed in italics. Therefore, for each font we rendered all lines of the dataset in both normal and italic letters. Although this did not exactly match the scanned texts in which normal-styled uppercase letters and italic-styled lowercase letters were mixed, we found that it gave acceptable results upon bootstrapping our model.

After generating all lines of the SAAo textual dataset in all three fonts and in both normal and italic styles (416,000 images in total), we took a random subset of 194,000 of these images to use as our artificially-generated bootstrapping dataset.

In summary the data that we collected and used in our final model consisted of:

1. 30 manually-labelled pairs of scanned Akkadian transliterations and their corresponding digital texts.
2. 194,000 automatically generated images of lines of Akkadian transliterations, using various fonts and both normal and italic font styles

Since the SAAo data was used for training, we used scanned data from The Royal Inscriptions of the Neo-Assyrian Period (RINAP) as test data. We manually labeled 10 pages of these books, which gave us about 350 lines of test data.

2.2 OCR workflow and architecture

The typical OCR workflow consists of steps similar to the following:

- Preprocess images (deskewing, image binarization)
- Segmentation (localizing text on page, line segmentation)
- Core OCR (converting line to text)
- Post-processing (language model-based correction)

We found that Kraken's default preprocessing and segmentation methods were sufficient for our purposes, and focused on adapting the core OCR model to Akkadian transliterations. We assume input of the form similar to the data we collected, with paragraphs already localized.

After binarization and line segmentation, each line of input was first dewarped and resized to be of appropriate dimensions for the OCR model. After dewarping, the height of each line was resized to be 48 units, with the width scaled by the same factor and with 16 units of (white) padding added to the left and right sides of the line. Therefore, each sample input into the OCR model is a tensor of shape (48, ?, 1), with ? representing the variable width of a single line of input and 1 the single (grayscale) channel of input.

The core OCR model that we trained was a hybrid CNN-RNN neural network (CRNN) selected from Kraken with the following sequential architecture:

- 2D convolutional layer (32 filters, kernel size 4×2, 4×2 stride, 1×0 padding)
- 2D convolutional layer (64 filters, kernel size 4×2, 1×1 stride, 1×0 padding)
- Max-pooling (kernel size 4×2, stride 4×2, no padding, dilation 1)
- 2D convolutional layer (128 filters, kernel size 3×3, 1×1 stride, 1×1 padding)
- Max-pooling (kernel size 1×2, stride 1×2, no padding, dilation 1)
- Reshape (converting input of shape (2, ?, 128) to output of shape (?, 256))
- BiLSTM (hidden size 256)
- BiLSTM (hidden size 512)
- BiLSTM (hidden size 256)
- Fully-connected (output size 103, linear activation)

The output of the final layer was chosen to match the size of the character-level vocabulary: 102 characters found in the training set data, plus the 0 index to indicate the "blank symbol" meaning no character.

Additionally, each convolutional and recurrent layer was followed by a regularization layer, and the BiLSTM layers by dropout layers:

- Each convolutional layer was followed by a group normalization layer with group size 32. Group normalization is a variant of batch normalization adapted to computer vision tasks where small batch sizes are required due to memory constraints. Instead of normalizing across multiple samples in a batch, group normalization normalizes across channels within a single sample. In our case, this grouped channels into groups of 32 and normalized activations within each group. For more details, see Wu and He (2018)
- Each BiLSTM layer was followed by a dropout layer with dropout probability 0.5.

The outputs of the model for each step are interpreted as logits corresponding to the probability that each character in the vocabulary is present at that horizontal location in the line of text. We then used greedy decoding to identify the most likely character at each step.

Interpreting the output of such a model requires an additional merger step. For example, consider the following output of a similar OCR system (Fig. 4):

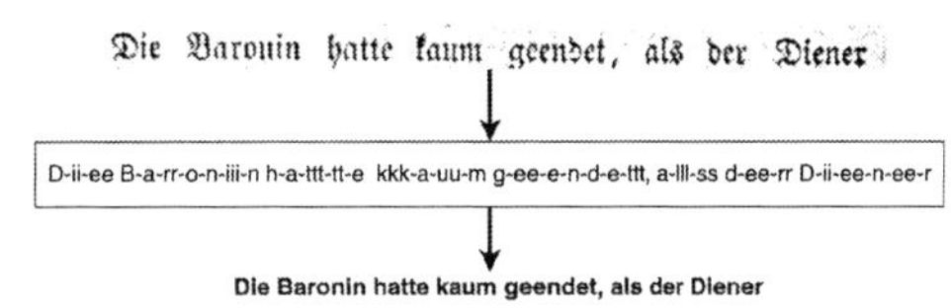

Figure 4: Old German OCR, reproduced from Fig. 10 in Martínek et al. (2020).

Since the model's output represents small displacements in the horizontal direction, the same character will be identified multiple times in a row. Therefore we merge the same label when it appears multiple times in a row, without another label or the blank symbol appearing in between. This is the *connectionist temporal classification (CTC) alignment* introduced by Graves et al. (2006).

2.3 Training

The model was trained in two stages: First, it was trained from scratch on the 194,000 artificially generated textual images from SAAo. Then, it was fine-tuned on the 30 manually labelled paragraph images from SAA books (about 900 lines of text). Although our manually labelled dataset was quite small, we found that the fine-tuning stage was critical for achieving acceptable results.

The objective used was the so-called *connectionist temporal classification (CTC) loss*. Similar to the CTC alignment described above, CTC loss is used to compare the output of a continuous recognition system like OCR or speech recognition to a desired string of tokens. The motivation for CTC loss is twofold:

- The training data available to us is pairs of images and desired text, without spatial alignments.
- The network's outputs are character scores for each horizontal position, so the same token may be identified in multiple adjacent positions.

As first described in Graves et al. (2006), the CTC loss function solves these issues as follows. First, it takes as input the ground truth text and the network's outputs (probabilities per character for each horizontal position). It then calculates the likelihood of the ground truth text for each possible *path* (possible alignment) and sums them together over all possible paths. This is the objective function we used to train the network.

For both stages of training, we used the recommended settings from Kraken: batch size 1, Adam optimizer (learning rate $1e-3$ and momentum 0.9). In both stages, minimum validation loss was achieved after a single epoch of training, after which the model began to overfit, so we used the results of training on a single epoch.

3 OCR Results on Training and Testing Data

Results in Table 1 were calculated as follows: The **accuracy** we present was measured by computing the edit distance between the output of the OCR and the ground truth text in the test data images, divided by text length (averaged between the ground truth and OCR output texts). Before calculating edit distance, we normalized newlines and whitespace and combined together period (.) and dash (-) characters, since these can always be distinguished in context.

The new CuReD model has a character error rate (CER) of 9% on clean data and 11% on representative scans. We observe that manually fine-tuning the model with real dataset images greatly improves our accuracy, even though the fine-tuning dataset was extremely small. The baseline model, only trained on artificial data, overfit to this type of data and did not generalize well to real scans. Visually observing the baseline model output showed that it regularly had trouble distinguishing certain characters (e.g. "a" vs. "u"), and we hypothesize that this is because of the different appearance of these characters in the artificial training data fonts and the fonts used in the test data. Fine-tuning likely helps the model to quickly adapt to these differences.

Model	Validation Accuracy	Test Accuracy
Baseline	99.8%	77%
Fine-tuned 10 Images	91%	89%
Fine-tuned 30 Images	91%	89%

Table 1: OCR performance when training on artificially generated SAAo data, and finetuned on manually labelled SAA scanned transliterations. Accuracy tested on manually labelled transliterations from RINAP.

The columns "Validation Accuracy" is the accuracy of OCR prediction on a validation set selected from the training data. For the baseline model this is calculated on artificially generated SAAo transliteration images, while for fine-tuning it is calculated on a validation set of manually-labelled scanned images of SAA books from the fine-tuning set. The column "Test Accuracy" is the final accuracy of OCR predictions on the test dataset of real scanned transliterations from RINAP books (Fig. 5).

We also observe that even after fine-tuning on 10 images, we already reach a plateau in performance, and adding another 20 manually-labelled images to the fine-tuning does not noticeably improve performance. Thus, minimal data is needed to fine-tune the model on previously unseen published transliterations.

4 Real-world Experiments with the CuReD Tool

4.1 A human-in-the-loop pipeline

The OCR model released with this paper on GitHub can continuously improve on new datasets through fine-tuning. Yet, there remains a gap between cuneiform specialists and their ability to fine-tune and improve machine learning (ML) models. A set of *Cuneiform Recognition* tools, abbreviated CuRe, was therefore created. These tools are currently an online interactive platform for cuneiform experts as part of the Babylonian Engine project, but are in the process of becoming a standalone browser application for the sake of long-term upkeep; such as server maintenance costs. The *Cuneiform Recognition Documents* or CuReD tool provides a platform

na-ki-ri áš-tak-ka-nu
ù mim-ma ep-šet e-tep-pu-šu qé-reb-šu
ú-šaṭ-ṭir-ma i-na tem-me-en-ni É.GAL *be-lu-ti-ia*
e-zib aḫ-ra-taš
a-na ar-kàt u_4*-me i-na* LUGAL.MEŠ*-ni*
DUMU.MEŠ*-ia ša* [d]*aš-šur a-na* RE.É.UM*-ut* KUR *ù*
UN.MEŠ *i-nam-bu-u zi-kir-šu e-nu-ma* É.GAL
šá-a-tu i-lab-bi-ru-ma en-na-ḫu
an-ḫu-sa lu-ud-diš MU.SAR*-a ši-ṭir šu-mi-ia*
li-mur-ma Ì.GIŠ *lip-šu-uš* UDU.SISKUR *liq-qí a-na*
áš-ri-šú li-ter [d]*aš-šur ik-ri-bi-šu i-šem-me*

(a) Sample scan from RINAP test data

```
na-ki-ri áš-tak-ka-m
ut mim-ma ep-šat e-tap-pu-šu qé-reb-šu
i-šag-rir-ma i-na tem-me-en-ni É ṣa be-lu-ri-i
e-zib aḫ-ra-taš
a-na ar-kdt u-me i-na LUGAL-MEŠ-n
UMU-MEŠ-ia ša dšaš-šur a-na 15.É.UM-ur gk ù
UN-MEŠ i-nam-bu-u zi-kir-šu e-nu-ma É SAL
šá-a-tu i-lab-bi-ru-ma en-na-ḫu
an-ḫu-sa lu-ud-diš MU.SAR-a ši-ṭir šu-m-ie
li-mur-ma Ì.GIŠ lip-šu-uš UDU.SISKUR kq-qí a-n
áš-ri-šú li-rer škaš-šur ik-ri-bi-šu i-šem-mq
```

(b) Final (fine-tuned) CuReD model output

Figure 5: Comparison of source image with CuReD OCR output.

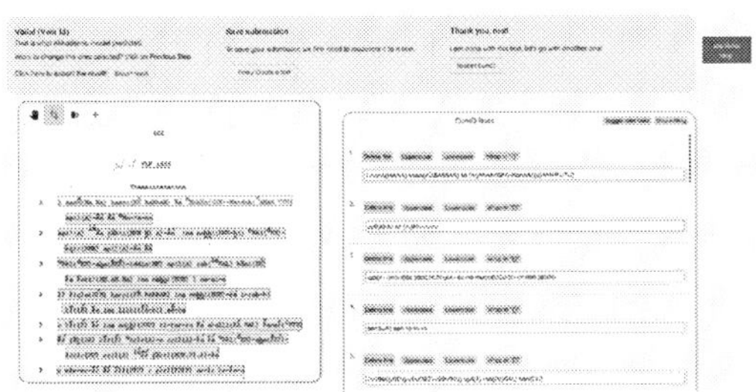

Figure 6: The CuReD tool interface.

for correcting the initial results of the OCR model presented above, and fine-tuning the model on new, unfamiliar types of transliterations.

There, users can upload currently one-by-one a PDF or image, place a bounding box around a text. Then lines of transliteration are automatically identified, and a corresponding line by line digital text is generated that can be manually edited for corrections (Fig. 6). Corrected text is saved for fine-tuning the model at a later stage, and the machine-readable output can be downloaded immediately as plain text. All OCR'ed transliterations are also searchable in the Babylonian Engine gallery.

The ML models are envisioned as "co-workers" which provide likely suggestions to the user, aiding the process of cuneiform scholarly edition publication, and improving as the user corrects them. This way, it is not only the ML models that benefit from the corrections and labeled data created by experts, but also the experts can enjoy a designated work environment for cuneiform studies, and download the results of their work–already advancing cuneiform scholarship.

In what follows we present two real-world scenarios of cuneiform scholarship: text editions published in book form, and legacy materials in the form of lexical cards. Both were created with typewriter in the late 1970's and early 80's of the 20th century.

4.2 Experiment 1: Text editions

We chose to digitize the texts edited in the dissertation of Raymond B. Dillard (1975). Namely, 81 Neo-Babylonian archival and administrative documents from the Free Library of Philadelphia (FLP), purchased on the antiquities market in the early 20th century by John Frederik Lewis.

Why Dillard? First, these texts are not digitized on any of the large online databases, such as CDLI, Achemenet, ORACC, or eBL. Second, it is a diverse corpus chronologically, geographically, and stems from a variety of archives (see metadata file on GitHub).

We initially had quite poor results of 53% accuracy, but after correcting only 10 texts, the OCR model reached 85% accuracy. Additional training on 47 texts increased the model's performance only incrementally to 89%. Thus, similarly to our initial fine-tune phase, the model requires a minimal number of ca. 10 documents in order to be a significant assistant in the digitization process of ancient texts (Fig. 7).

4.3 Experiment 2: Legacy collections

The Sumerian Lexicography collection is housed in the Babylonian Section of the University of Pennsylvania Museum of Archaeology and Anthropology. This collection consists of approximately 200,000 index cards (see Fig. 1) compiled by Å. W. Sjöberg in the late 1970's and early 1980's. These cards serve as the foundation for the intended Pennsylvania Sumerian Dictionary (PSD). No other collection of lexicographic cards in the field of Sumerian Lexicography matches its scale.

The PSD was never completed. From 1984 to 1992, only the letters A-B were published. In May 2004, the project transitioned to a digital format, evolving into the electronic Pennsylvania Sumerian

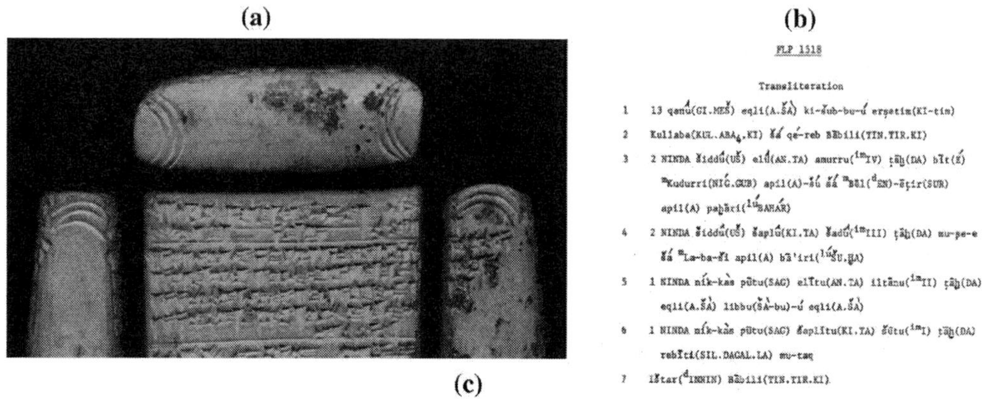

(c)

```
13 qanû(GI.MEŠ) eqli(A.ŠÀ) ki-šub-bu-ú erṣetim(KI-tim)
Kullaba(KUL.ABA4.KI) šá qé-reb Bābili(TIN.TIR{KI})
2 NINDA šiddû(UŠ) elû(AN.TA) amurru(IM.4limmu) ṭāḫ(DA) bīt(É) {m}Kudurri(NÍG.GUB) apil(A)-šú šá {m}
Bēl({d}EN)-ēṭir(SUR) apil(A) paḫāri({lú}BAHÁR)
2 NINDA šiddû(UŠ) šaplû(KI.TA) šadû(IM.3) ṭāḫ(DA) mu-ṣe-e šá {m}La-ba-ši apil(A) bā'iri({lú}ŠU.HA)
1 NINDA ník-kàs pūtu(SAG) elītu(AN.TA) iltānu(IM.2) ṭāḫ(DA) eqli(A.ŠÀ) libbu(ŠÀ-bu)-ú eqli(A.ŠÀ)
1 NINDA ník-kàs pūtu(SAG) šaplītu(KI.TA) šūtu(IM.1) ṭāḫ(DA) rebīti(SIL.DAGAL.LA) mu-taq
Ištar({d}INNIN) Bābili(TIN.TIR{KI})
```

Figure 7: (a) Neo-Babylonian cuneiform tablet from the Free Library of Philadelphia collection; (b) Its transliteration in Dillard (1975); (c) Its plain text output from CuReD.

Dictionary (ePSD). It has undergone significant changes in editorial principles, replacing the manually compiled catalog with a much larger digital corpus.

The index card collection was digitized in May 2023 by Dr. Anna Glenn on behalf of the Institute for Assyriology und Hittitology of the LMU Munich. Hosted by the university library, this digitized collection forms the dataset for the study case presented here (Sjöberg, 2023).

The project plans to convert these scans into machine-readable text, and to link the results with other lexical collections, as part of the eBL platform. For test purposes, we uploaded to CuReD in the first step 30 cards, a little bit more than 60 lines, and corrected the results for fine-tuning. Prior to the training, the accuracy level stood at 87%. Note that the model at this time was already fine-tuned on the texts published by Dillard (see above). Following the first training session on this corpus, the accuracy improved to 94%.

Although the results improved significantly, a new issue emerged: the OCR fails to recognize a line when it consists of only a single word (compare to other lexical index cards digitized by Idziak et al. (2021)). This is particularly critical because many lemmas, i.e., lexemes in the Sumerian language, are made up of a single phoneme, that is, one letter.

5 Related Literature

To the best of our knowledge, this is the first custom-trained OCR model for transliterated cuneiform documents, trained initially on transliterations. See, however, the Tesseract-based model used for OCR'ing secondary literature in assyriology, which includes text editions (Anderson, 2023).

Human-in-the-loop pipelines for transcribing historical and epigraphical documents from other periods, however, are revolutionizing how those are being recorded and studied in the humanities and the galleries, libraries, archives, and museums (GLAM) sector. Some of the most impactful tools in this regard are Transkribus and eScriptorium, each of which has produced hundreds of studies based on their OCR/HTR engine, and several more are on the rise (Idziak et al., 2021; Nockels et al., 2022, 2024; Calvelli et al., 2023).

It is important to separate, however, the OCR/HTR efforts from Latin transliterations and OCR/HTR of cuneiform signs themselves on clay tablets, stone inscriptions, etc. Identifying cuneiform signs requires other designated models, and the several advances in recent years are summarized in Bogacz and Mara (2022); see also the newly published contribution by Yugay et al. (2024).

The high-performance of our model on minimal ground-truth data was possible due to the relative simplicity of generating representative artificial training data. Improvements in recent years in the generation of data that is similar enough to ground truth is proving more and more vital in aiding the digitization of low-resource languages, such as cuneiform (Rusakov et al., 2019) and Aramaic inscriptions (Aioanei et al., 2024), to name a few. These methods are probably to be vital in the upcoming years to push forward the digitization of ancient languages (Sommerschield et al., 2023).

Although our work only covers OCR digitization of transliterations as printed in published sources, there has also been work on automatic conversion of such transliterations to phonological transcriptions representing how texts were pronounced in the Akkadian language. See Sahala et al. (2020) for an example of a such deep-learning based model.

6 Conclusion

To aid the community of cuneiform experts in digitizing published records of cuneiform texts, we developed an OCR system for recognizing Akkadian Latin transliterations written using standard scholarly conventions. Because of a lack of natural labelled training data, we bootstrapped an OCR model using the Kraken open-source framework by generating artificial training data, rendering text from the SAA corpus using various fonts and text styles. After fine-tuning the resulting model on a small set of manually-labelled scans, we achieved 89% accuracy on a representative set of scans.

We integrated this model in a human-in-the-loop tool called CuReD (Cuneiform Recognition Documents), to allow scholars and students to OCR various scanned or photographed materials, and help continuously improve their model. We further showed this tool in practice, by performing two real-world experiments OCR'ing text editions and legacy lexical materials in machine typeface, both of which included handwritten notation. The fine-tuning of the two experiments was integrated into our model, which is also on the CuReD online tool, making it already highly effective for OCR'ing machine typed transliterations. Minimal fine-tuning is needed to improve its results on unseen texts, and the same should hold true for transliterations of other languages using the cuneiform script.

We provide this model as an open-source contribution to researchers of the ancient Near East and the general public, in hopes that it will make cuneiform inscriptions more accessible in machine-readable form.

Limitations

Our current OCR system has been tested only on Latin transliterations of Akkadian and Sumerian cuneiform texts, but not on the other languages of the ancient Near East using the cuneiform script. While we assume this transfer learning would be easy for the model given the similarities in the transliteration practices (see Appendix A), that remains to be seen.

Additionally, both experiments show how the model can be effectively fine-tuned with few examples to drastically improve performance. However, the results are never perfect. A common challenge in both experiments is the presence of many handwritten notes, such as accents, subscripts, diacritics, special characters, square brackets, or simply marginalia scribbled around the text. These factors lead to inaccuracies in the OCR results, particularly creating errors in the line segmentation.

The CuReD model, with its human-friendly interface, permits users to quickly correct the remaining errors. The fine-tuning process makes the correction phase extremely efficient. It may not completely make typing of editions a thing of the past, but it reduces the time by at least 90%. In addition, further manual improvements can be considered, such as validating the OCR'ed results against known cuneiform sign readings, or combining CuReD with Handwritten Text Recognition (HTR) (Nockels et al., 2022) to identify marginalia etc.

Furthermore, the continual fine-tuning of the model makes it familiar with additional typefaces and editorial conventions. The significant uptick in accuracies before fine-tuning between the experiments (from 53% on the Dillard texts to 87% on the PSD card catalogue) shows this quality, as both experiments share a similar typeface. Initial results on unseen texts will thus continue to improve as more corpora are added for training, and fewer and fewer examples will be required for fine-tuning.

Ethics Statement

The training data used in this work consists of publicly available scholarly publications and does not contain any sensitive personal information. The resulting OCR system is intended as a tool to aid scholarly research and all code and data is made freely available under a CC-BY 4.0 license. We do not anticipate any major ethical concerns stemming from this work.

Acknowledgements

We would like to thank the Babylonian Section of the University of Pennsylvania Museum of Archaeology and Anthropology for providing access to their Sumerian Lexicography card collection, to Enrique Jiménez for suggesting this case study for CuReD, and to Anna Glenn for digitizing the cards.

References

Andrei C. Aioanei, Regine R. Hunziker-Rodewald, Konstantin M. Klein, and Dominik L. Michels. 2024. Deep Aramaic: Towards a synthetic data paradigm enabling machine learning in epigraphy. *PLOS ONE*, 19(4):1–29. Publisher: Public Library of Science.

Adam Anderson. 2023. FactGrid Cuneiform Discovery Project: Building Linked Open Data Repositories.

Bartosz Bogacz and Hubert Mara. 2022. Digital Assyriology—Advances in Visual Cuneiform Analysis. *Journal on Computing and Cultural Heritage*, 15(2):1–22.

Lorenzo Calvelli, Federico Boschetti, and Tatiana Tommasi. 2023. EpiSearch. Identifying Ancient Inscriptions in Epigraphic Manuscripts. *Journal of Data Mining & Digital Humanities*, Historical Documents and...(Sciences of Antiquity and...):10417.

Raymond B. Dillard. 1975. *Neo-babylonian texts from the john frederick lewis collection of the free library of philadelphia*. Doctoral Dissertation, The Dropsie University, Philadelphia, PA.

Ignace J. Gelb. 1970. Comments on the akkadian syllabary. *Orientalia*, 39:516–546.

Alex Graves, Santiago Fernández, Faustino Gomez, and Jürgen Schmidhuber. 2006. Connectionist temporal classification: Labelling unsegmented sequence data with recurrent neural networks.

Gai Gutherz, Shai Gordin, Luis Sáenz, Omer Levy, and Jonathan Berant. 2023. Translating Akkadian to English with neural machine translation. *PNAS Nexus*, 2(5):pgad096.

Timo Homburg, Tim Brandes, Eva-Maria Huber, and Michael A. Hedderich. 2023. From an Analog to a Digital Workflow: An Introductory Approach to Digital Editions in Assyriology. *Cuneiform Digital Library Bulletin*, 2023(4). Publisher: Cuneiform Digital Library Initiative.

Jan Idziak, Artjoms Šeļa, Michał Woźniak, Albert Leśniak, Joanna Byszuk, and Maciej Eder. 2021. Scalable Handwritten Text Recognition System for Lexicographic Sources of Under-Resourced Languages and Alphabets. In *Computational Science – ICCS 2021*, pages 137–150, Cham. Springer International Publishing.

Jiří Martínek, Ladislav Lenc, and Pavel Král. 2020. Building an efficient OCR system for historical documents with little training data. *Neural Computing and Applications*, 32(23):17209–17227.

Joe Nockels, Paul Gooding, Sarah Ames, and Melissa Terras. 2022. Understanding the application of handwritten text recognition technology in heritage contexts: a systematic review of Transkribus in published research. *Archival Science*, 22(3):367–392.

Joseph Nockels, Paul Gooding, and Melissa Terras. 2024. The implications of handwritten text recognition for accessing the past at scale. *Journal of Documentation*, 80(7):148–167. Publisher: Emerald Publishing Limited.

Matthew Ong and Shai Gordin. 2024. Linguistic annotation of cuneiform texts using treebanks and deep learning. *Digital Scholarship in the Humanities*, 39(1):296–307.

Simo Parpola. 2015. *The correspondence of Sargon II, Part I: Letters from Assyria and the West*, reprinted edition. Number 1 in State Archives of Assyria. Eisenbrauns, Winona Lake, Indiana.

Karen Radner, Jamie Novotny, and et al. 2015. State Archives of Assyria Online (SAAo). Publisher: The SAAo Project.

Maxim Romanov, Matthew Thomas Miller, Sarah Bowen Savant, and Benjamin Kiessling. 2017. Important new developments in arabographic optical character recognition.

Eugen Rusakov, Kai Brandenbusch, Denis Fisseler, Turna Somel, Gernot A Fink, Frank Weichert, and Gerfrid GW Müller. 2019. Generating cuneiform signs with cycle-consistent adversarial networks. In *Proceedings of the 5th international workshop on historical document imaging and processing*, pages 19–24.

Aleksi Sahala and Krister Lindén. 2023. A neural pipeline for POS-tagging and lemmatizing cuneiform languages. In *Proceedings of the ancient language processing workshop*, pages 203–212, Varna, Bulgaria. INCOMA Ltd., Shoumen, Bulgaria.

Aleksi Sahala, Miikka Silfverberg, Antti Arppe, and Krister Linden. 2020. Automated phonological transcription of akkadian cuneiform text.

Åke W. Sjöberg. 2023. The university of pennsylvania collection of sumerian lexicography.

Gustav Ryberg Smidt, Katrien De Graef, and Els Lefever. 2024. At the Crossroad of Cuneiform and NLP: Challenges for Fine-grained Part-of-Speech Tagging. European Language Resources Association.

Thea Sommerschield, Yannis Assael, John Pavlopoulos, Vanessa Stefanak, Andrew Senior, Chris Dyer, John Bodel, Jonathan Prag, Ion Androutsopoulos, and Nando De Freitas. 2023. Machine Learning for Ancient Languages: A Survey. *Computational Linguistics*, 49(3):703–747.

Juan-Pablo Vita. 2021. *History of the Akkadian language*. Number 152 in Handbook of Oriental studies. Brill, Leiden.

Wolfram von Soden. 1995. *Grundriss der akkadischen grammatik*, 3 edition. Editrice Pontificio Instituto Biblico, Rome.

Yuxin Wu and Kaiming He. 2018. Group normalization.

Vasiliy Yugay, Kartik Paliwal, Yunus Cobanoglu, Fabian Simonjetz, Luis Sáenz, Ekaterine Gogokhia, Shai Gordin, and Enrique Jiménez. 2024. Stylistic Classification of Cuneiform Signs Using Convolutional Neural Networks. *it - Information Technology*. Publisher: De Gruyter Oldenbourg.

A Appendix: Akkadian Latin Transliteration

We include here a short description of the main features of the conventions used for Akkadian Latin transliteration. This standard system was described in Gelb (1970) and von Soden (1995), each with some modifications. It is in large part also used for other languages written in the cuneiform writing system, most notably Sumerian, but also with necessary modifications for Eblaite, Elamite, Hurrian, Urartian, Hittite, Luwian and several minor Anatolian languages written in cuneiform (like Hattian).

Besides the usual characters of the Latin alphabet, cuneiform transliterations can contain the following special characters used to represent particular sounds:

- Š š, equivalent to the English *sh*-sound
- □ □, equivalent to the *ts*-sound
- □ □, an emphatic *t*-sound (e.g. **th**eatre)
- □ □, the voiceless uvular fricative (e.g. German a**ch**t)
- □ and □, aleph (glottal stop) and ayin (pharyngeal fricative), respectively
- G̃ g̃, nasal g (*ng*-sound)
- Ř ř, alveolar trills (see řeka)

Cuneiform symbols may be used phonetically to represent syllables with structure V, VC, CV, or CVC. When used in this way, the transliteration of these signs is written in italic lowercase letters with dashes separating syllables of the same word. For example, the word *iddin* 'he gave' may be written phonetically as *id-din*, *id-di-in*, or using other variants.

Uppercase, normal-style (i.e. non-italic) letters are used to represent logograms; cuneiform symbols representing words or morphemes rather than phonetic values. Some editions represent the logographic values in small caps instead. The text in uppercase represents the reading of the logogram in Sumerian, from which it was borrowed, although the Akkadian speaker would have probably read it in their native language. For example, the transliteration DINGIR represents a cuneiform sign that would have been read in context as Akkadian *ilu* ("god"). Logogram compounds are separated with periods in transliterations; for example, DUMU.MUNUS-*ia* "my daughter".

The Sumerian language for which cuneiform was originally developed had a large number of homonymic symbols (symbols with the same phonetic value). In order to distinguish these in transliteration, scholars use accents and subscript digits. For example, *gu, gú, gù* represent three different cuneiform symbols with the same pronunciation *gu*; the fourth such symbol and onwards would be notated as gu_4, the fifth as gu_5, and so on. Newer resources may only use superscript numbers instead of accents (gu_2, gu_3). Many homonymic readings are used simultaneously in cuneiform languages.

Superscript symbols are used to represent determinatives, also known as classifiers, which are cuneiform signs that do not have an independent reading but rather clarify the meaning of following or preceding sign(s). For example, superscript *d* represents the determinative indicating a divine name, and superscript *m* indicates a male name.

Since cuneiform inscriptions are often broken or not fully legible, a number of special symbols are used to indicate textual anomalies. The most common of these are:

- Square brackets [ ] - used to indicate missing signs, such as when there is a hole in the text. May contain editorial guesses as to the missing contents, or X to indicate a missing sign.
- Half brackets ⸢ ⸣ - indicate fragmentary but legible signs

- Superscript ! - indicates a scribal error
- Superscript ? - indicates an uncertain sign
- angle brackets < > - used to add signs that the modern editor thinks the ancient scribe has omitted.
- double angle brackets « » - indicate signs which the modern editor thinks the ancient scribe has erroneously added, and believes should be ignored for phonetic and linguistic reconstruction.

The notation system for homonymic signs and editorial marks for textual anomalies are shared across the transliteration conventions of texts written in the cuneiform script, as well as combinations of lowercase, uppercase, and italics. Furthermore, the Sumerian readings of logograms are shared across the many languages written in the cuneiform script. Thus, CuRed is likely to be an efficient baseline model of transliterations from other cuneiform languages.

Towards Context-aware Normalization of Variant Characters in Classical Chinese Using Parallel Editions and BERT

Florian Kessler
Friedrich-Alexander-University Erlangen-Nuremberg
florian.kessler@fau.de

Abstract

For the automatic processing of Classical Chinese texts it is highly desirable to normalize *variant characters*, i.e. characters with different visual forms that are being used to represent the same morpheme, into a single form. However, there are some variant characters that are used interchangeably by some writers but deliberately employed to distinguish between different meanings by others. Hence, in order to avoid losing information in the normalization processes by conflating meaningful distinctions between variants, an intelligent normalization system that takes context into account is needed. Towards the goal of developing such a system, in this study, we describe how a dataset with usage samples of variant characters can be extracted from a corpus of paired editions of multiple texts. Using the dataset, we conduct two experiments, testing whether models can be trained with contextual word embeddings to predict variant characters. The results of the experiments show that while this is often possible for single texts, most conventions learned do not transfer well between documents.

1 Introduction

A lack of orthographic norms is a common feature of ancient writing systems. In the case of Classical Chinese, the written language of ancient China, this manifests prominently in a high number of *variant characters* (*yitizi* 異體字), that is in a broad sense, characters that are graphically distinct from each other but are used to write the same morpheme. For many downstream tasks such as full-text search, identification of parallel passages or the analysis of vocabulary, normalization of variant characters is desirable, as often, they are completely interchangeable and merely reflect arbitrary choices of copyists or woodblock carvers. However, there is also a class of *quasi-variant* characters that are only interchangeable in some

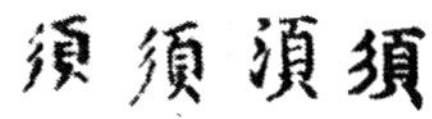

Figure 1: Images of four characters taken from the *Sibu congkan* editions of the *Zhaimin yaoshu* (first and second from the left) and the *Baishi changqing ji* (third and fourth from the left), all representing the same word "*xu* to need", transcribed as 「*xu* 湏」 (first and third from the left) and 「*xu* 須」 (second and fourth from the left) in the digital editions.

contexts, with one variant often being preferred for one of multiple words[1] that can be written with the characters, more strongly associated with a particular word sense, or only found in certain compounds. For example, the two homophonous and etymologically related words "*li* to experience, to undergo" and "*li* calender" should, according to most dictionaries, be written with the two characters 「*li* 歷」[2] and 「*li* 曆」 respectively. While the usage of these two characters in some editions of Classical Chinese texts agrees with this distinction, in others, we find either character used to write both words, or other variant forms such as 「*li* 歴」 replacing them. Hence, a simplistic approach to normalization based on lists of variant characters must either risk conflating variants that were intentionally kept apart such as 「*li* 歷」 and 「*li* 曆」, potentially impacting the understanding of the text, or ignore such cases, which could e.g. mean missing a parallel passage in two texts just because one scribe decided to use 「*li* 歴」 for both "to experience" and "calender".

[1] Since Classical Chinese is a largely monosyllabic language, most morphemes are also words, so in the following, we will be mostly concerned with words rather than morphemes, although this is of course a simplification.

[2] In order to distinguish between characters and the words they represent, we use English quotation marks "" for our glosses for the latter, and Chinese quotation marks 「」 for the former. To improve readability for readers unfamiliar with Chinese, Pinyin transliterations for both are supplied, although it should be noted that characters can represent multiple words with different pronunciations.

Proceedings of the 1st Workshop on Machine Learning for Ancient Languages (ML4AL 2024), pages 141–151
August 15, 2024

The complex history of many characters further complicates matters, with specialised variants appearing and disappearing and characters being borrowed to write additional words over time (for a detailed overview, see Qiu et al., 2000, Chapters 10-12). Also, in China there traditionally was a taboo on using characters from the ruler's name, which was sometimes avoided by using existing variant forms or even coining new ones (Wang, 1997, 4)[3]. Furthermore, the physical quality of texts might vary, and OCR systems as well as preferences of human transcribers can have an impact on which variant characters are presented to us in digital versions of the texts. For example, in Figure 1 four characters are shown that represent the same word but are transcribed into two different, but very similar variant forms, which the *Dictionary of Chinese Character Variants* (DCCV) (Ministry of Education, R.O.C) lists as having overlapping but not identical usage. One case matches fine variations in the writing style of the original text while the other appears to be a transcription error. Thus, we anticipate a considerable amount of variability and noise in the data, and it is to be expected that there is no single normal form that "normalization" will result in.

In order to cope with these difficulties, an intelligent system for character normalization should ideally satisfy the following conditions:

1. It should be able to detect in which cases variants are completely interchangeable, and when there is a meaningful difference in their usage.
2. Using that information, when substituting characters to a more regular form, it should do so in the direction of higher differentiation, e.g. replacing「*li* 歷」with「*li* 歷」or「*li* 曆」depending on which word it represents in its specific context.

Towards the development of such a system, in this study, we have extracted a dataset of variant characters in context from a corpus of texts in two editions. In two experiments, we have tested whether contextual word embeddings can be used to train models to predict variant characters.

[3]We would like to thank one of the anonymous reviewers for pointing out the importance of considering this taboo when studying the usage of variant characters.

2 Related work

Given the fact that many quasi-variant characters are distinguished from each other by being preferred for specific words or word senses, we expect the problem to be highly similar to word sense disambiguation. For Classical Chinese, Shu et al. (2021) and Pan et al. (2022) have recently used BERT for this task, with some success, although results for some characters were mixed. Our approach of using a parallel corpus has already been successfully applied for learning word sense disambiguation, using alignments of translated sentences (Ng et al., 2003).

Wang et al. (2023) have developed a dataset of loangraphs, i.e. characters used to write a word that is commonly written with another character, and used BERT embeddings to detect them and predict the more usual character for writing the word in question. Many variant characters originate from loangraphs (Qiu et al., 2000, 371-372), and the tasks share the problem of having to decide whether a character should be replaced by another character, so the study is very similar to the subject of this study. However, the authors use a hand-annotated dataset, which compared to ours, has the advantage of higher accuracy, and greater coverage of rare loangraph usage. On the other hand, the number of samples for each type of character is quite limited in comparison to our automatically derived dataset, and since there is no systematic annotation of an entire corpus, it is impossible to quantify how widespread the phenomenon is, and how the usage of loangraphs differs between texts.

A somewhat comparable task for modern Chinese is conversion from simplified to traditional characters, as one simplified character often replaces several traditional ones, such as「*li* 历」replacing both「*li* 歷」and「*li* 曆」. Hence, machine learning techniques that take context into account have been investigated for this task (Pang and Yao, 2015). The problem of substituting one character with another, more common character is shared with spelling correction, for which BERT has also been used (Wu et al., 2023). An important difference to modern languages is of course that for Classical Chinese, there is no uniformly accepted normative authority, so it is not *a-priori* clear which character is "correct" in a given context.

For Western languages, normalization of historic spelling variations has been intensively studied. Bollmann (2019) gives an overview over different techniques, including machine learning approaches. Jurish (2010) and among others more recently Makarov and Clematide (2020) introduce techniques to take context into account to differentiate words, similar to what is attempted here. However, a key difference between alphabetical languages and Chinese is that techniques for the former often rely on edit distances between words, which is not directly transferable to Chinese characters.

3 Building a dataset

To the best of our knowledge, no comprehensive annotated corpus to train and test a system for variant normalization exists. However, there is a readily available data source which has high potential: works for which different prints or handwritten editions are digitally available. Since the usage of variant characters can vary considerably between several editions of the same text, aligning them allows for the mining of variant characters. Crucially, using an algorithm that will be described in detail below, we were able to automatically extract instances of variant characters that are used concurrently in one edition but correspond to only a single variant in another, giving potential cases of quasi-variant characters differentiated by one writer but not the other.

3.1 A corpus of parallel editions

All texts used in this study were obtained from two collections of pre-modern Chinese works, the *Wenyuange* copy of the *Siku quanshu* (SKQS), compiled in the late 18th century, and the 1919 edition of the *Sibu congkan* (SBCK), digital versions of which were sourced from the Kanseki repository (Wittern, 2016). In the repository, there are 286 works with editions from both collections.[4] For our purposes, an important distinction between the two collections is that the editions in the SKQS were produced as the result of an organised editing process over some 15 years in the 18th century (Guy, 1987, 67-120), whereas the SBCK consists of photographic reproductions of older editions from different periods of time, prioritizing early prints where available (Cui and Wang, 2011). Nevertheless, a comparison of different historical copies of the SKQS has revealed considerable freedom in the choice of variant characters, which might be attributed to preferences of scribes (Lan, 2015, 49). Hence, the combination of both should give a good overview of variant character usage by different editors or scribes from different times.

Period	**Num. of works**	**Num. of chars.**
Zhou (1046 BC-256 BC)	8	467 505
Qin (221 BC-206 BC)	2	353 858
Han (202 BC-220 AD)	32	2 644 549
Three Kingdoms (220-280)	6	537 497
Jin (265-420)	4	411 061
Northern and Southern Dynasties (420-589)	11	1 665 058
Sui (581-618)	2	84 228
Tang (618-907)	62	7 694 484
Song (960-1279)	87	17 754 465
Yuan (1271-1368)	29	5 938 237
Ming (1368-1644)	10	3 008 885
Qing (1636-1912)	7	1 622 437
Other	8	859 096

Table 1: Composition of the corpus by period assigned in the Kanseki repository, with dates from Wilkinson (2018, 4-5) and length in characters in the SKQS version after truncation.

Table 1 shows the composition of the corpus by time of origin of the works as recorded in the Kanseki repository. Of course, the editions of the works contained in the repository will often be later.[5] As can be seen, although both collections contain many ancient works, they are in no way exclusively composed of works in Classical Chinese in the strict sense, i.e. the written language of China before ca. 0 AD. Instead, they also contain numerous works from medieval and late imperial China. We expect that the choice of variant characters is often more strongly influenced by the copyists than the original authors of documents, and since the earliest extant editions of ancient texts are often not that ancient, understanding writing conventions of later times is highly relevant to our

[4] According to the catalogue of the repository, there should be another 30 parallel editions, but our script failed to retrieve them.

[5] Given the high degree of intertextuality present in the corpus, for any given work, significant parts of the textual content might not actually originate from the period assigned in the repository. However, it should at least give a rough approximation.

understanding of ancient texts. Hence, we did not exclude any material based on the time of origin of the work, and have tested as part of the second experiment below whether learning conventions for variant character usage transfers between documents from different time periods.

From the raw text files obtained from the Kanseki repository, all metadata was removed, and all characters that are not Chinese characters deleted. In order to limit the influence of extraordinarily long documents, the length of each text was truncated to 500 000 characters. Afterwards, an optimal global alignment for each pair of editions of the same work was computed using Hirschberg's algorithm, using the implementation from the Python package `sequence-align` (Kensho Technologies LLC), with gap and mismatch penalty both at -1, and match score at 1.

3.2 Searching for quasi-variant characters

Subsequently, each pair of aligned sequences was searched for potential instances of quasi-variant characters using an algorithm that looks for instances of a single character in one edition corresponding to more than one character in the other edition, applying some frequency thresholds to avoid noise. We exclude cases where more than one of the differentiated characters occurs in both editions (with a small margin of error of a single occurrence), because this indicates either noise or intentional but divergent differentiation by both writers. While including these cases would be interesting for a future study, it was decided to err on the side of caution here and not consider them, reducing the amount of noise in the dataset.

For an aligned pair of sequences $x = x_1, x_2, \ldots, x_n$ and $y = y_1, y_2, \ldots, y_n$, the algorithm proceeds by the following steps:[6]

1. Let $C \leftarrow \{c \mid c \neq \sqcup \wedge |\{i \mid x_i = c\}| \geq 100\}$, the set of all characters that are not the gap character $\sqcup$ and that occur at least 100 times in x.

2. For each $c \in C$ and each $d \neq \sqcup$, let $S_{c,d} \leftarrow \{i \mid 11 \leq i \leq n - 10 \wedge x_i = c \wedge y_i = d \wedge \sum_{j=i-10}^{i+10} \delta_{x_j,y_j} > 10\}$, the set of all indices where c is aligned to d (which might or might not be equal to c) in y, and where at least half the characters in a 21 character span are equal between the two editions to avoid passages with alignment errors (δ_{x_j,y_j} denotes the Kronecker delta taking the value 1 if $x_j = y_j$ and 0 otherwise).

3. For each c and d such that $|S_{c,d}| < 20$, let $S_{c,d} \leftarrow \emptyset$, deleting substitutions without sufficient support.

4. Return as candidates for quasi-variant characters all $c, d_1, d_2, \ldots, d_k$ with $k \geq 2$ and the respective indices S_{c,d_i} such that the $d_1, \ldots, d_k$ are exactly those characters d for which $S_{c,d}$ is not empty, and such that at most one of the $d_1, \ldots, d_2$ occurs more than once in x.

For example, when running the algorithm on the *Xunzi*, an ancient philosophical text, with the SKQS edition as sequence x and the SBCK edition as sequence y, we start by collecting in C a list of characters that occur at least 100 times in the SQKS edition, giving in this case 283 different characters.

Next, in step two, for all the locations where one of these 283 characters occurs in the SQKS edition and where in the surrounding context, a reasonably good alignment was computed by Hirschberg's algorithm, the two characters in the two editions are recorded in S. For example, in the *Xunzi*, after this step, $S_{\text{彊},\text{彊}}$ contains 241 indices, indicating that for that number of occurrences of 「*qiang/jiang* 彊」 in the SKQS edition, the parallel passages in the SBCK edition have the same character. In $S_{\text{彊},\text{強}}$, there are another 66 indices of passages where the SBCK has 「*qiang/jiang* 強」 instead. This pattern of non-substitution and substitution is potentially relevant for our purposes, as the DCCV lists 「*qiang/jiang* 彊」 as a variant form of 「*qiang/jiang* 強」, but also has a separate entry for it. On the other hand, $S_{\text{彊},\text{能}}$ also contains one entry, which in this case corresponds to a specific difference in a single passage between the two editions, which is not relevant for our study.

Hence, in the third step, entries like those in $S_{\text{彊},\text{能}}$ with less than 20 indices are deleted from S.

Finally, in the fourth step, it is checked for which characters from edition x alignments to more than one character in edition y are recorded in S, and whether these characters also occur in x itself. For the *Xunzi*, at this stage, there are only eleven characters left for which S contains alignments to more than one character. Out of these, seven are cases where a character in the SKQS edition is aligned to

[6]The implementation of the algorithm as well as all other code used in this paper can be accessed at `https://github.com/notiho/variants`.

two characters in the SBCK, both of which are also used in the SQKS edition. For example, the two visually highly similar variant forms「*de* 德」and「*de* 徳」are both used in both editions. Hence, the indices contained in $S_{德,徳}$ and $S_{徳,德}$ are not returned by the algorithm. On the other hand,「*qiang/jiang* 強」does not occur in the SKQS edition of the *Xunzi*. Thus,「*qiang/jiang* 彊」and its alignments to either itself or「*qiang/jiang* 強」are reported as one of the candidates from this invocation of the algorithm.

In general, candidates returned by the algorithm consist of one character that is differentiated into multiple characters in the other edition. In the following, a candidate $c, d_1, d_2, \ldots, d_k$ reported by the algorithm will be referred to as a *substitution profile* $c \leftrightarrow d_1, d_2, \ldots, d_k$, and the occurrences corresponding to it as samples of that substitution profile from the respective document. Note that a substitution profile may be attested in multiple pairs of editions, but that the samples are specific to each pair.

The algorithm is run on all aligned pairs in both directions, giving 563 substitution profiles. These were filtered to remove all instances where the DCCV lists one of the characters on the right hand side only as a variant of the other character, suggesting that no meaningful difference can be found.[7] For these, an unconditional normalization approach is sufficient. The remaining 108 profiles originate from 103 of the aligned documents, showing as a first result that using more than one variant form of a character is a widespread phenomenon in the corpus.

Table 2 shows four examples from the dataset. The upper two examples display a meaningful distinction between「*li* 歷」and「*li* 曆」, while the lower two are pulled from an edition that arbitrarily uses either「*mu* 母」or「*mu/wu* 毋」to write "*mu* mother".

The number of samples per substitution profile ranges from 41 to 5139 (mean 562.6, sd 830.3). On average, each substitution profile is found in 2.2 different documents (sd 2.5), with the highest number of documents for a single profile reaching 14.[8] For some of the profiles, one variant form is highly dominant, accounting for 96.9% of all samples in the most extreme case (mean 71.1%, sd 14.7).

Note that some of the substitution profiles do not consists of variant characters according to the dictionary. For example, we found a profile 留 ↔ 畱留, where「*wan* 畱」is listed as a variant of「*wan* 畹」and not「*liu* 留」. Since they are visually highly similar, this could be an artefact introduced by the digitalization process, for which normalisation is also desirable. The DCCV also has some variant characters with separate entries without noting any difference in usage. For example, in the profile 爾 ↔ 尓爾,「*er* 尓」is listed as a variant form of「*er* 爾」, but also has its own entry, which however only states that it is the same as「*er* 爾」. Since the first experiment described below is specifically designed to test which profiles represent or do not represent meaningful differentiations in usage, there is no need to remove these cases *a-priori*.

3.3 Contextual embeddings

For the 109 profiles found to be potential cases of quasi-variant characters differentiated in one edition but not in the other, contextualised BERT (Devlin et al., 2019) embeddings were collected, which have shown to be useful for a wide variety of tasks (Liu et al., 2019). Specifically, the model from Wang and Ren (2022) was used.[9] Compared to other BERT-family models for Classical Chinese, it has a relatively large vocabulary size of 38 208, making it especially useful for studying variant characters, some of which are quite rare.[10]

For the purposes of the study, we are interested in whether for the substitution profiles, the differentiation on the right hand side is meaningful. We

[7]Variants not found in the dictionary, which usually correspond to minor graphical alterations, were also removed. Another two profiles were removed as noise resulting from a difference in how the chapter (*juan*) number is stated in the beginning of each text file. The full unfiltered list can be found in the supplementary material. The filtered version is shown in Appendix A. After inspection of the results, it was further decided to normalize the minor graphical alterations「*li* 歴」to「*li* 歷」and「*li* 暦」to「*li* 曆」. This allows us to focus on the interesting semantic difference between「*li* 歷」and「*li* 曆」in the following.

[8]The profiles with the highest document frequencies highlight the importance of taboo characters, as two of the top-five profiles, 歴 ↔ 暦歴 and 歷 ↔ 曆歷, both involve the character「*li* 曆」, which was part of the personal name of the Qianlong emperor, under whose reign the SKQS was compiled, and whose name thus had to be avoided by the writers at the time (Wang, 1997, 276).

[9]Obtained from `https://huggingface.co/Jihuai/bert-ancient-chinese`.

[10]In fact, out of the left hand sides of the substitution profiles investigated, which are input into the model, only three characters,「*chuang* 窗」,「*chi* 勑」,「*mao* 皃」, were absent from the vocabulary. Even for these cases, the model still has the context available, so it is in principle capable of computing useful embeddings.

Profile	Edition	Text
歴 ↔ 曆歷	SKQS	非明 歴 理不足與共事
歴 ↔ 曆歷	SBCK	非明 曆 理不足與共事
Translation		If someone doesn't understand the principles of calenders it is not worth making common cause with them.
歴 ↔ 曆歷	SKQS	鄧山昌上人 歴 游諸方獨為此懼
歴 ↔ 曆歷	SBCK	鄧山昌上人 歷 游諸方獨爲此懼
Translation		Chang Shangren from Maoshan has experienced travelling in all the different directions, but was only ever worried over this.
母 ↔ 毋母	SKQS	母 年七十遠在絶域不知死生
母 ↔ 毋母	SBCK	毋 年七十遠在絶域不知死生
Translation		[My] 70 years old mother is far away in an inaccessible place, and [I] don't know whether she is alive or dead.
母 ↔ 毋母	SKQS	父 母 妻子徙日南
母 ↔ 毋母	SBCK	父 母 妻子徒日南
Translation		[Their] fathers, mothers, wives and children were banished to Rinan.

Table 2: Four examples from the dataset, showing passages with relevant context from editions of two works, belonging to two profiles. The relevant characters are highlighted in red in the original text and our translations.

take this to mean that it is in some way predetermined through the context it occurs in. Hence, when there is a meaningful difference, the model should be able to predict the variant used in the edition corresponding to the right hand side of the substitution profile having only seen the undifferentiated version from the left hand side edition. Accordingly, for each substitution profile $c \leftrightarrow d_1, d_2, \dots, d_k$ only the passages corresponding to the left hand side of the profiles were input into the BERT model. Specifically, for each occurrence of a c substituted by one of the $d_1, \dots, d_k$, the c, alongside with 200 characters each to the left and right, or less if the end of the document was reached before that, were extracted. The passages were then input the model. Since embeddings produced by different layers can have significantly different performance on various tasks (Liu et al., 2019), the output of all twelve hidden layers was collected to test which gives the best results.

4 Experiments

4.1 Can conventions in single documents be learned?

In the first experiment, it was tested which substitution profiles in which documents correspond to meaningful differentiations, and which are arbitrary. Since many substitution profiles are attested in more than one document, and it could be the case that for the same profile, substitutions are purely noise in one document, but meaningful in another, each pair of editions of documents was tested separately. For this purpose, we have fitted a logistic regression on the contextual embeddings computed from the non-differentiated editions, separately for each unique combination of substitution profile and document. If the resulting model is capable of predicting which of the differentiated variants should occur in a particular position, this indicates that the choice is in some way determined, and the differentiation meaningful for that particular set of variant characters in that particular edition.

For evaluation, ten-fold cross-validation was used, that is, for each substitution profile found in each document, the available samples were randomly partitioned into ten parts, and each part held out as test data for a model trained on the remaining nine parts. Following among others Shi et al. (2016), logistic regression was used to fit models on the contextual embeddings. In particular, we used the `sklearn` package (Pedregosa et al., 2011), with L2 regularization and softmax loss for those profiles with more than two alternative variants. After training, the R package **caret** (Kuhn, 2008) was used to test whether the model's predictions on the test set are significantly better than a naive predictor that always predicts the most fre-

	Above naive	Total
Combinations of profile and document	77 (32.4%)	283 (100%)
Profile (at least one document above naive)	45 (41.7%)	108 (100%)

Table 3: Counts of unique combinations of profile and document for which significantly better accuracy compared to a naive classifier was achieved (first row), and of profiles for which this was the case for at least one document (second row).

quent class, at a significance level of 0.05, adjusted for multiple testing with a Bonferroni correction.

The experiment is run twelve times, using the different hidden layers as input. The highest number of combinations of document and profile with prediction significantly better than a naive classifier was achieved when using the output of the final hidden layer, where 77 cases could be found, compared with 69 for the second best, the second-to-last hidden layer. This agrees with the intuition that the problem of predicting the precise variant used in a particular position is highly similar to the masking problem BERT is trained with, in contrast to most other tasks where embeddings taken from middle layers generalize better (Liu et al., 2019).

The results of the experiment, a summary of which is shown in Table 3, indicate that meaningful differentiation of variants is less common than free alteration of variants, even after having filtered out variants that are always interchangeable according to the DCCV as described in Section 3.2. Only for a minority of unique combinations of profile and document the model learns to predict samples significantly better than naively predicting the most frequent class.[11]

Interestingly, the model is able to predict some variants which we would expect to be completely interchangeable based on the DCCV, such as 「*er* 尔」 and 「*er* 爾」 described above, albeit only for a single document. A manual investigation of that document, the *Taiping yulan* reveals that indeed, one of the editions consistently writes the surname "Erzhu" as 「*erzhu* 尔朱」, but the name of a well-known gloss dictionary, the *Erya*, as 「*erya* 爾雅」, whereas the other edition uses 「*er* 爾」 for both. Thus, the method has successfully revealed a distinction not found in the dictionary.

[11]A complete list documenting for how many documents this was the case for each profile can be found in Appendix A.

Profile	Pairs above naive classifier / all pairs
歴 ↔ 曆歷	112/132
勑 ↔ 勅勑	0/20
明 ↔ 明明	0/20
歷 ↔ 曆歷	9/12
聲 ↔ 声聲	3/12
于 ↔ 于扵	0/2
巳 ↔ 己巳	0/2
歷 ↔ 歴歷	0/2
荅 ↔ 答荅	0/2
解 ↔ 解觧	0/2
須 ↔ 湏須	0/2
魯 ↔ 嚕魯	1/2

Table 4: Number of directed pairs for which a model trained on the first document was able to achieve performance significantly better than a naive classifier, by substitution profile.

The accuracy achieved by the model is difficult to compare between different profiles and documents. For those combinations of profile and document where the accuracy is significantly better than the naive predictor, it ranges from 51.2% to 100% (mean 89.2%, sd 8.7).

4.2 Do conventions transfer between documents?

The first experiment has shown that in principle, a simple logistic model is able to learn to predict differentiated variant characters from contextual embeddings taken from an edition that does not differentiate the variants. However, it was only tested whether this is possible for individual pairs of editions of documents. Hence, the logistic regression could have learned to overfit the conventions of an individual writer, which would not be useful for normalizing other texts. Thus, in a second experiment, we tested whether what was learned on one pair of editions of a document (u, v) can be applied to another pair of editions of a different document (x, y) that exhibits the same substitution profile.

For this purpose, all profiles were selected where in the first experiment, the model was able to learn to predict variants for more than one document. This was the case for only 12 profiles, which are listed in Table 4. Then, for each directed pair[12] of documents with above naive classifier performance, each consisting in turn of a pair of aligned editions, a model was fitted with the same basic setup as in the first experiment, using all samples from the first document as training data, and all samples from the second document for testing. That is, for documents a and b with aligned editions (u, v) and (x, y) respectively, the model is trained to predict the variants in v based on embeddings taken from u, and it is test on predicting variants in y based on embeddings from x. Finally, it was again tested whether the model has significantly higher accuracy than a naive classifier that always predicts the most frequent variant in the target document, at a significance level of 0.05 with Bonferroni correction. The counts of pairs where this was the case are also shown in Table 4.

As can be seen in the table, for most profiles, a convention learned on one document does not generalize to other documents in most cases. In fact, the only profiles where for a majority of directed pairs, a model trained on one document was successful in predicting variants in the target document were the two profiles having 「*li* 曆」and 「*li* 歷」on the right hand side. Other than that, only the profiles 聲 ↔ 声聲 and 魯 ↔ 嚕魯 had successful cross-training cases.

This result suggests that for the other profiles, idiosyncrasies rather than universal norms are more frequently found in the corpus. Of course, training on single documents means the model is exposed to only one type of content. To stay with an example from above, although we have only a single document for it, having learned to write the surname Erzhu with 「*er* 尔」 can't be successfully applied to a document that does not mention a person of that name. And even if it does contain that name, it would not necessarily agree in that choice of variant, as historically, there was no general consensus to write that name with 「*er* 尔」. Furthermore, there is also the possibility that for some documents, the model has simply learned to predict patterns in artefacts that are introduced by the digitalization process, which also should not transfer to other documents.

In a similar vein, a manual investigation of the two documents with successful transfer for the profile 聲 ↔ 声聲 shows that they share a strong preference for writing the name of tones, e.g. "*qusheng* departing tone", with the simplified form 「*sheng* 声」, another convention we do not expect to be widely adopted.

For the only group where a high degree of transferability could be observed, i.e. the two profiles 歴 ↔ 曆歷 and 歷 ↔ 曆歷, time of origin of the works doesn't appear to have an effect on transferability. Using the dating information in the form of dynasties provided by the Kanseki repository, a chi-squared test shows no dependency between documents originating from the same time period and above naive predictor performance of the model ($\chi^2 = 0.5232, df = 1, p = .4695$). Out of 94 pairs from different dynasties, 81 (86.2%) transferred successfully, whereas for pairs from the same dynasty, it was 40 (80%) out of 50. We take the result to indicate that conventions regarding the use of 「*li* 曆」and 「*li* 歷」were quite stable over time. Further research is needed to determine how this relates to the time of origin of editions instead of works.

Accuracy for the models of the same group calculated for each directed pair ranges from 71.8% to 97.8% (mean 88.4%, sd 6.3). A preliminary experiment suggests that accuracy can be much improved by training on more than one document, with mean per-document accuracy for the same set of documents reaching 99.5% (sd 0.9) when dividing the documents randomly into ten parts, using one part for testing and the others for training. We leave it to further studies to investigate how this might be further improved upon.

5 Conclusions

In this article, we have demonstrated the general viability of using parallel editions and contextual embeddings for context-aware variant character normalization for Classical Chinese, by showing that a simple logistic model can be trained to predict which of more than one differentiated variants could replace a character in a given context. At the same time, our analysis has also revealed that meaningful variation of variant characters is quite a rare phenomenon, while in the digital editions surveyed, alteration between variant characters without meaningful difference is ubiquitous. This confirms the need for some form of variant normalization. In this regard, the failure of the model to learn to distinguish variants can actually be highly useful, because it can increase confi-

[12]For two documents a and b, both (a, b) and (b, a) are considered distinct directed pairs.

dence that for those cases, a simple list based normalization approach does not run the risk of losing information.

For those cases where the model was able to learn a differentiation, the results of the second experiment indicate that idiosyncratic usage of variant characters is quite common in the corpus. Training a model on the conventions used by one writer of one edition of a document does often not generalize to other documents. Taken together with the high overall number of variant characters, this confirms that copyists had considerable freedom in choosing variant characters, and highlights the importance of considering the transmission process when reading received versions of ancient texts.

In terms of the two design goals for an intelligent system for variant normalization stated in the introduction, we have achieved more progress towards the first goal. As we have seen with the example of「*er* 尓」and「*er* 爾」, the system has shown itself capable of discovering deliberate variation in a case where we would not expect it to occur based on consulting a dictionary. It could be a worthwhile endeavour to rerun the experiments with the full list of substitution profiles, i.e. without removing instances that are completely interchangeable according to the DCCV, to see how widespread such cases are.

Towards the second goal of normalizing variants towards specialised forms, we have made significant progress only for a single case,「*li* 曆」and「*li* 歷」. In differentiating these two characters, our simple approach that did not require any manually annotated data achieved high accuracy. Since the second experiment has shown an apparent lack of uniform conventions in the usage of many variant characters, further endeavours in this direction will first need to decide which conventions to adopt.

6 Limitations

Since we did not systematically compare the original manuscripts or prints with the digitalized editions, for some visually similar variants we do not know whether they are merely the result of inconsistencies in the digitalization process.

Due to the lack of a manually annotated dataset, we do not know how good the recall of our approach of extracting quasi-variant characters from an aligned corpus of parallel editions is. Since the algorithm that computes the list of candidates contains some filters to reduce noise, it might miss cases where a variant only occurs with very low frequency.

The approach we took towards determining whether the variation of variant forms is meaningful or not can only detect differentiations that the BERT model is aware of, and that are encoded in a simple enough way for a logistic model trained on a limited set of data to extract them.

For the cases where the model was able to learn to predict variant characters, we do not know what factors the decisions are based on, and whether a human would find them meaningful.

References

Marcel Bollmann. 2019. A large-scale comparison of historical text normalization systems. In *Proceedings of the 2019 Conference of the North American Chapter of the Association for Computational Linguistics: Human Language Technologies, Volume 1 (Long and Short Papers)*, pages 3885–3898, Minneapolis, Minnesota. Association for Computational Linguistics.

Jianli Cui and Yun Wang. 2011. 《四部丛刊》编纂考略 (Brief Account of an Investigation of the Compilation of the "Sibu congkan"). *Shandong tushuguan xuekan*, 6:102–103.

Jacob Devlin, Ming-Wei Chang, Kenton Lee, and Kristina Toutanova. 2019. BERT: Pre-training of deep bidirectional transformers for language understanding. In *Proceedings of the 2019 Conference of the North American Chapter of the Association for Computational Linguistics: Human Language Technologies, Volume 1 (Long and Short Papers)*, pages 4171–4186, Minneapolis, Minnesota. Association for Computational Linguistics.

R. Kent Guy. 1987. *The Emperor's Four Treasuries: Scholars and the State in the Late Ch'ien-Lung Era*. Number 129 in Harvard East Asian Monographs. Harvard University Asia Center.

Bryan Jurish. 2010. More than words: Using token context to improve canonicalization of historical German. *Journal for Language Technology and Computational Linguistics*, 25(1):23–39.

Kensho Technologies LLC. Sequence-align: Efficient implementations of Needleman-Wunsch and other sequence alignment algorithms in Rust with Python bindings. `https://github.com/kensho-technologies/sequence_align`.

Max Kuhn. 2008. Building predictive models in R using the caret package. *Journal of statistical software*, 28:1–26.

Wen-Chin Lan. 2015. The Collation of Three Versions of Front Annotations of the Siku Quanshu: Based on

365 Pieces of Front Annotations. *Journal of Library and Information Studies*, 13(1):33–68.

Nelson F. Liu, Matt Gardner, Yonatan Belinkov, Matthew E. Peters, and Noah A. Smith. 2019. Linguistic knowledge and transferability of contextual representations. In *Proceedings of the 2019 Conference of the North American Chapter of the Association for Computational Linguistics: Human Language Technologies, Volume 1 (Long and Short Papers)*, pages 1073–1094, Minneapolis, Minnesota. Association for Computational Linguistics.

Peter Makarov and Simon Clematide. 2020. Semi-supervised contextual historical text normalization. In *Proceedings of the 58th Annual Meeting of the Association for Computational Linguistics*, pages 7284–7295, Online. Association for Computational Linguistics.

Ministry of Education, R.O.C. Dictionary of Chinese Character Variants. `https://dict.variants.moe.edu.tw/`. Accesssed: 3.05.2024.

Hwee Tou Ng, Bin Wang, and Yee Seng Chan. 2003. Exploiting parallel texts for word sense disambiguation: An empirical study. In *Proceedings of the 41st Annual Meeting of the Association for Computational Linguistics*, pages 455–462, Sapporo, Japan. Association for Computational Linguistics.

Xiaomeng Pan, Hongfei Wang, Teruaki Oka, and Mamoru Komachi. 2022. Zuo Zhuan Ancient Chinese Dataset for Word Sense Disambiguation. In *Proceedings of the 2022 Conference of the North American Chapter of the Association for Computational Linguistics: Human Language Technologies: Student Research Workshop*, pages 129–135, Hybrid: Seattle, Washington + Online. Association for Computational Linguistics.

Zhenjun Pang and Tianfang Yao. 2015. Chinese Bilateral Translation between Simplified and Complex-Character Texts based on Conversion Table and Context. In *14th Chinese National Conference on Computational Linguistics*.

F. Pedregosa, G. Varoquaux, A. Gramfort, V. Michel, B. Thirion, O. Grisel, M. Blondel, P. Prettenhofer, R. Weiss, V. Dubourg, J. Vanderplas, A. Passos, D. Cournapeau, M. Brucher, M. Perrot, and E. Duchesnay. 2011. Scikit-learn: Machine learning in Python. *Journal of Machine Learning Research*, 12:2825–2830.

Xigui Qiu, Gilbert L. Mattos, and Jerry Norman. 2000. *Chinese Writing*. Number 4 in Early China Special Monograph Series. Society for the Study of Early China, Berkely.

Xing Shi, Inkit Padhi, and Kevin Knight. 2016. Does string-based neural MT learn source syntax? In *Proceedings of the 2016 Conference on Empirical Methods in Natural Language Processing*, pages 1526–1534, Austin, Texas. Association for Computational Linguistics.

Lei Shu, Yiluan Guo, Huiping Wang, Xuetao Zhang, and Renfen Hu. 2021. 古汉语词义标注语料库的构建及应用研究 (the construction and application of Ancient Chinese corpus with word sense annotation). In *Proceedings of the 20th Chinese National Conference on Computational Linguistics*, pages 549–563, Huhhot, China. Chinese Information Processing Society of China.

Pengyu Wang and Zhichen Ren. 2022. The uncertainty-based retrieval framework for Ancient Chinese CWS and POS. In *Proceedings of the Second Workshop on Language Technologies for Historical and Ancient Languages*, pages 164–168, Marseille, France. European Language Resources Association.

Yankun Wang, editor. 1997. 历代避讳字汇典 *(Collection of Taboo Characters of Past Dynasties)*. Zhongzhou guji chubanshe, Zhengzhou.

Zhaoji Wang, Shirui Zhang, Xuetao Zhang, and Renfen Hu. 2023. The Construction and Application of an Ancient Chinese Language Resource on Tongjiazi. In *Proceedings of the 22nd Chinese National Conference on Computational Linguistics*, pages 535–546.

Endymion Wilkinson. 2018. *Chinese History - A New Manual*, 5. edition edition. Harvard University Asia Center, Cambridge, Massachusetts.

Christian Wittern. 2016. Kanseki Repository. *CIEAS Research Report 2015*, Special issue:1–80.

Hongqiu Wu, Shaohua Zhang, Yuchen Zhang, and Hai Zhao. 2023. Rethinking masked language modeling for Chinese spelling correction. In *Proceedings of the 61st Annual Meeting of the Association for Computational Linguistics (Volume 1: Long Papers)*, pages 10743–10756, Toronto, Canada. Association for Computational Linguistics.

A List of substitution profiles and results of first experiment

Profile	Docs. above naive classifier / docs.	Profile	Docs. above naive classifier / docs.
明 ↔ 明眀	5/14	歴 ↔ 曆歴	12/13
得 ↔ 得淂	0/12	歷 ↔ 歴歷	2/9
聲 ↔ 声聲	4/9	萬 ↔ 万萬	1/7
解 ↔ 解觧	2/7	於 ↔ 于扵	1/6
歷 ↔ 曆歷	4/6	爾 ↔ 尔爾	1/6
勑 ↔ 勅勑	5/5	玉 ↔ 玉王	0/5
等 ↔ 䓁等	1/5	須 ↔ 湏須	2/5
丘 ↔ 丘邱	1/4	京 ↔ 京亰	0/4
于 ↔ 于扵	2/3	巳 ↔ 已巳	1/3
幸 ↔ 幸㚔	0/3	爾 ↔ 尔爾	0/3
盡 ↔ 尽盡	0/3	總 ↔ 摠總	0/3
遷 ↔ 迁遷	0/3	體 ↔ 体體	1/3

玆 ↔ 玆玆	0/2
歴 ↔ 歴暦	1/2
文 ↔ 攵文	0/2
母 ↔ 毋母	0/2
篇 ↔ 篇萹	1/2
荅 ↔ 答荅	2/2
魯 ↔ 噜魯	2/2
牕 ↔ 牕窓	0/1
亦 ↔ 亦尔	0/1
以 ↔ 叺以	0/1
元 ↔ 元玄	1/1
克 ↔ 克克	0/1
勑 ↔ 勅勑	1/1
十 ↔ 十卄卅	1/1
同 ↔ 仝同	0/1
名 ↔ 名玄	1/1
多 ↔ 多朵	1/1
弘 ↔ 宏弘	0/1
憐 ↔ 怜憐	0/1
支 ↔ 支攴	0/1
暦 ↔ 歴歴	0/1
某 ↔ ム某	1/1
機 ↔ 机機	0/1
歸 ↔ 帰歸皈	0/1
無 ↔ 无無	0/1
燕 ↔ 燕鷰	0/1
爾 ↔ 児尔	1/1
牕 ↔ 忩窻	0/1
痕 ↔ 痕痕	0/1
窓 ↔ 忩窓窻	0/1
答 ↔ 答荅	1/1
脱 ↔ 托脱	1/1
舊 ↔ 旧舊	0/1
茂 ↔ 茂茂	1/1
謂 ↔ 爲謂	0/1
貌 ↔ 皃皃貌	0/1
貌 ↔ 皃皃	1/1
醫 ↔ 毉醫	0/1
野 ↔ 埜野	0/1
閑 ↔ 閑閒	0/1
體 ↔ 体躰體	0/1
體 ↔ 躰體	0/1
猒 ↔ 猒猒	0/2
巳 ↔ 己巳	2/2
最 ↔ 冣最	0/2
筆 ↔ 筆筆	1/2
總 ↔ 緫總	0/2
閒 ↔ 閑閒	0/2
皃 ↔ 貌貌	1/1
于 ↔ 于於	0/1
仙 ↔ 仙僊	0/1
伏 ↔ 伏伏	0/1
充 ↔ 充克	0/1
全 ↔ 全訂	1/1
勢 ↔ 勢埶	0/1
合 ↔ 合瑪	1/1
名 ↔ 名構	1/1
在 ↔ 在扗	0/1
已 ↔ 己已	0/1
彊 ↔ 強彊	1/1
揔 ↔ 揔摠總	0/1
明 ↔ 明朙明	1/1
望 ↔ 望朢	0/1
校 ↔ 挍校	0/1
檢 ↔ 撿檢	1/1
注 ↔ 注註	0/1
然 ↔ 然肰	0/1
爲 ↔ 為謂	0/1
爾 ↔ 尓尔爾	0/1
留 ↔ 畱留	0/1
皃 ↔ 貌貌	1/1
窻 ↔ 窓牕	0/1
總 ↔ 惣惚揔	0/1
與 ↔ 歟與	1/1
苟 ↔ 苟苟	0/1
草 ↔ 艸草	0/1
貌 ↔ 皃皃	1/1
貌 ↔ 貌貌	0/1
遊 ↔ 游遊	0/1
釋 ↔ 釋釋	0/1
鍼 ↔ 針鍼	1/1
閑 ↔ 閒闲	1/1
體 ↔ 体軆體	0/1
勑 ↔ 勅勑	0/1

"Gotta catch 'em all!": Retrieving people in Ancient Greek texts combining transformer models and domain knowledge

Marijke Beersmans[1], Alek Keersmaekers[1], Evelien de Graaf[1], Tim Van de Cruys[1], Mark Depauw[1], Margherita Fantoli[1], [1]KU Leuven,

Correspondence: marijke.beersmans@kuleuven.be

Abstract

In this paper, we present a study of transformer-based Named Entity Recognition (NER) as applied to Ancient Greek texts, with an emphasis on retrieving personal names. Recent research shows that, while the task remains difficult, the use of transformer models results in significant improvements. We, therefore, compare the performance of four transformer models on the task of NER for the categories of people, locations and groups, and add an out-of-domain test set to the existing datasets. Results on this set highlight the shortcomings of the models when confronted with a random sample of sentences. To be able to more straightforwardly integrate domain and linguistic knowledge to improve performance, we narrow down our approach to the category of people. The task is simplified to a binary PERS/MISC classification on the token level, starting from capitalised words. Next, we test the use of domain and linguistic knowledge to improve the results. We find that including simple gazetteer information as a binary mask has a marginally positive effect on newly annotated data and that treebanks can be used to help identify multi-word individuals if they are scarcely or inconsistently annotated in the available training data. The qualitative error analysis identifies the potential for improvement in both manual annotation and the inclusion of domain and linguistic knowledge in the transformer models.

1 Introduction

Identifying the mentions of people in texts is one of the goals of the broader task of Named Entity Recognition (NER). For scholars working on historical texts, accurately finding and identifying people is particularly valuable for studying the representation of individuals, both in qualitative and data-driven studies. The present research, for instance, is embedded in a broader project aiming at performing large-scale analysis on the mentions of individuals in Ancient Greek and Latin texts (NIKAW, Networks of Ideas and Knowledge in the Ancient World).

For classical languages, and Ancient Greek in particular, the task remains challenging to automate. This study capitalises on recent advancements in transformer models, which have shown promising improvements over previous approaches. After introducing the available methods and data for NER on Ancient Greek (Sections 2 and 3), in Section 4, we compare four recent transformer models of Ancient Greek and their performance for NER, with a focus on identifying mentions of people. This comparison allows the selection of a model for further exploration. Since the Ancient World has a wealth of domain-specific resources on offer, in Sections 5, we focus on the specific task of predicting PERS entities by simplifying the NER task, and we explore how integrating gazetteers (Section 5.2) and syntactic annotations (Section 5.3) can impact the process of pinpointing individuals in texts. In the qualitative error analysis in Section 5.4, we identify several shortcomings of the reduced transformer method and discuss how domain knowledge and linguistic information impact the performance. With this, we contribute to advancing NER for Ancient Greek, identifying the strengths and limitations of currently available models and data and offering concrete suggestions for the way forward.

2 Related Work

The task of NER for historical languages presents several challenges, which can be traced back to four main factors (Ehrmann et al., 2023): diversity of sources, noisiness of data, language change, and lack of resources. These challenges are transferable to Ancient Greek and Latin corpora. However, the use of transformer models yields promising results: this is demonstrated for Latin by Torres Aguilar (2022); Beersmans et al. (2023), and for Ancient Greek by Yousef et al. (2023); Pal-

Proceedings of the 1st Workshop on Machine Learning for Ancient Languages (ML4AL 2024), pages 152–164
August 15, 2024 ©2024 Association for Computational Linguistics

ladino and Yousef (2024). Palladino and Yousef (2024) present two transformer models finetuned for the task of Ancient Greek NER. This model was created by training a XLM-RoBERTa-based multilingual model that was previously fine-tuned on the word alignment task for ancient languages, including Ancient Greek (Yousef et al., 2022a,b) and an Ancient-Greek-BERT model (Singh et al., 2021) respectively.

In this paper, we compare the NER performance of four transformer models for Ancient Greek, described in detail in Section 4 and 5. In addition, recent studies highlight the advantages of incorporating domain knowledge, in particular gazetteers, in the training of NER models, especially for low-resource languages (Zafarian and Asghari, 2019; Fetahu et al., 2022; Song et al., 2020). Gazetteers are external resources that often take the form of name dictionaries, grouped by a specific entity type (e.g. location or person). To leverage the advantage of domain knowledge, we incorporate the Trismegistos Gazetteers of names and name variants (TM NamVar) (Broux and Depauw, 2015)[1] and of places (TM GeoVar)[2] in two approaches described in Section 5.2. This rejoins the efforts of exploiting available knowledge bases for annotating Ancient Greek texts, as discussed in Berti et al. (2019). Finally, we address the problem of multi-token entities, which are particularly difficult to label automatically given their sparsity in the training data and the potential complexity added by factors such as overlap, nesting, and non-consecutiveness (Xia et al., 2019; Alshammari and Alanazi, 2021; Byrne, 2007; Crane, 2011). In Section 5.3, we explore the effectiveness of expanding single-token entities into multi-token entities using syntactical dependencies.

3 Data

3.1 Datasets for training and testing

There is currently no dedicated openly available benchmark dataset for Ancient Greek NER.[3] However, scholars have been annotating entities in Ancient Greek texts for a variety of goals, such as the mapping of places.[4] We combined four of such annotated Ancient Greek texts and harmonised their annotation through rule-based means. Our harmonised corpus contains data from the following projects (details summarised in Table 1): First: the *Odyssey* (henceforth OD) (Pelagios, 2021). Second, the EpiDoc XML of the *Deipnosophistae* of Athenaeus of Naucratis (DEIPN), retrieved from the Perseus digital library.[5]. Third, the Stepbible corpus (SB), available on GitHub (STE, 2023), which contains the full Ancient Greek New Testament (for further details, see Section 3.2). And finally: Pausanias' *Periegesis Hellados* (PH), courtesy of the Periegesis project (Foka et al., 2021). For information on originally annotated entity types per dataset, please refer to Table 12 in appendix C.

In addition, we manually annotated a random sample of 596 sentences from the GLAUx corpus (Keersmaekers, 2021) to test the generalisability of the results to all literary Greek material (GLAUx TEST). GLAUx contains most of the literature produced in Greek between the 8th century BC and the 4th century CE (about 27 million tokens). It is partly manually and partly automatically annotated for morphology, lemmas and syntax. While the predictions were made on the (tokenized) text, the morphological and syntactic annotation and the lemmas were used for further experiments (for details, see Section 5.3). The annotation process of GLAUx is described in Section 3.3.

3.2 Data Harmonisation

Since the datasets described in the previous section followed different guidelines, data harmonisation was necessary, following the steps detailed here.

- All entities were projected from their original files onto the GLAUx XML files to ensure similar Unicode character encoding, linguistic enrichment, tokenization, and capitalisation standards.
- Similarly to Palladino and Yousef (2024), we mapped the original annotated entities to a PERS, LOC, GRP scheme (Appendix C). PERS is used for identifiable individuals, LOC for geographical locations (both natural and human-built) and GRP for ethnonyms, nationalities and organisations. As the OD lacked a category suitable for conversion to GRP, this dataset was not used in the full NER

[1] https://www.trismegistos.org/ref/about_naw.php.

[2] https://www.trismegistos.org/geo/about.php.

[3] Palladino and Yousef (2024) compiled a dataset similar to this one, but it is not publicly available.

[4] See for instance the geographical visualisation available for the *Odyssey*.

[5] For Named Entity retrieval tools for this text in particular, see *The Digital Athenaeus project* (Berti, 2021).

text	# tokens	annotation method	period	genre
PH	242,433	manual	2nd century AD	travelogue
DEIPN	314,256	semi-automatic	3rd century AD	encyclopedic dialogue
OD	104,364	manual	8th century BC	epic poetry
SB	158,325	manual	1st -2nd century AD	religious

Table 1: Available datasets for Ancient Greek NER

but only in the reduced model described in Section 5.

- We used the morphological tags available in the GLAUx corpus to convert all plural words annotated as a person (often Muses, Cyclopes, etc.) to GRP.
- The TITLE-category of the SB corpus also caused issues, including references to Jesus, the biblical God, and cults. To disambiguate, all capitalised singular titles (e.g. Jesus Christ) were re-annotated as PERS, all capitalised plural titles were re-annotated as GRP (e.g. Pharisees) and all non-capitalised titles (e.g. the non-capitalised word 'god') were discarded.
- The PH dataset contains annotated pronouns or references to entities that do not include a name (e.g. 'the island'). We rely on capitalisation and discard all entities that do not include at least one capitalised word. For consistency, this rule was adopted in all datasets, even though non-capitalised entities were rare in the others.
- For all datasets, all entities that were not annotated with one of our final entity types (i.e. PERS, LOC, GRP), e.g. Συμποσίῳ, 'in the Symposium', referring to the title of a work, were dropped.

Finally, we split the data in a train, validation and test set using a 75%-12.5%-12.5% split. After harmonisation, multi-token entities were scarce (see Table 2, a total of 2,376 on 55,454 entities). In DEIPN, for example, no multi-token entities were annotated.

3.3 Annotation of GLAUx

As mentioned before, the overarching goal of our project is to conduct a large-scale analysis of the mentions of individuals in Ancient Greek (and Latin) texts. For this purpose, we start from the GLAUx corpus (Keersmaekers, 2021), introduced in Section 3.

In order to evaluate the performance of the model on GLAUx, we annotated a random sample of 596 sentences, each containing at least one capitalised word, for a total of 1,012 entities (excluding the ones annotated as O),[6] as shown in Table 2. We annotated the entity types PERS, LOC, and GRP, following the definitions described in Section 3.2. For multi-token entities such as e.g. Ἀρχαγόρας Ἀργεῖος, 'Archagoras the Argive', we allowed nested annotation: in this case B-PERS I-PERS for the entire string, with an additional B-GRP for Ἀργεῖος.

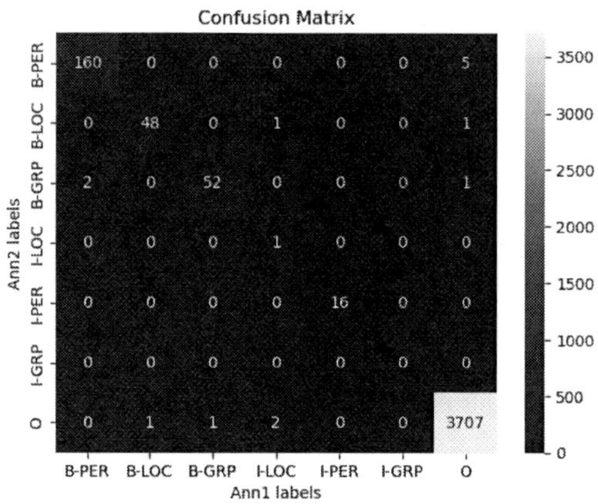

Figure 1: Confusion matrix for the IAA on GLAUx

172 sentences of the random GLAUx sample were annotated by two of the co-authors, resulting in an Inter Annotator Agreement (IAA) of 0.97 (Cohen's kappa coefficient), calculated on word level. When excluding the O's, the two annotators agreed on the label of 95% of the entities. The confusion matrix is shown in Figure 1. After IAA was calculated, both annotators discussed the differences to agree on a final annotation.[7] Surprisingly, the

[6]Entities annotated as O are those that do not fit the PERS, LOC, GRP scheme, such as, for example, book titles, titles of people without an actual named entity (e.g. Caesar or Pharaoh), and astronomical entities.

[7]Detailed information, both concerning the original annotations used to compute the IAA and the final annotation after discussion, can be found in the document *final_glaux_sample_iaa.csv* on our GitHub repository: https://github.com/NER-AncientLanguages/

	TRAIN	$TRAIN_{ody}$	VAL	VAL_{ody}	Held out TEST	$TEST_{ody}$	GLAUx TEST
B-PERS	21,307	2,033	4,054	381	3,090	400	578
I-PERS	290	25	122	1	83	0	51
B-LOC	8,261	699	1,345	85	1,105	76	233
I-LOC	1,061	18	278	0	196	0	11
B-GRP	8,884	41	1,291	2	1,384	4	201
I-GRP	182	0	9	0	49	0	0
O	494,668	75,248	81,968	12,547	83,182	12,519	13,454

Table 2: Entities annotated in the train, validation and tests sets. The *ody* datasets are exclusively used for the models predicting PERS/MISC. The GLAUx TEST dataset was annotated for this project to evaluate performance on data representative of all Ancient Greek literature.

main source of confusion was the attribution of the B-PER label, where one of the two annotators assigned O five times. This mostly concerned names mentioned as names or nicknames, that serve as additional specifications for a different, already mentioned entity. For instance, in the sentence "and they call his name 'the Emmanuel'", 'Emmanuel' was not considered an entity by one of the annotators. After discussion, these cases were considered entities in the final annotation. The annotators also disagreed twice on the annotation of a standalone ethnonym, here referring to a specific individual: the "Samaritan" was annotated by one annotator as B-PERS and by the other as B-GRP. The annotators agreed on B-GRP, to be consistent with the plural occurrences of ethnonyms. Concerning differences in boundaries, in the case of sequences such as Φᾶσιν ποταμὸν, 'river Phasis', only one of the two annotators included ποταμὸν, 'river', in the entity. The final annotation includes both words.

4 Models for normal NER

In this section, we compare the performance of four transformer-based models for NER. We have a twofold objective: determine the best-performing model for the general NER task,[8] and determine to what extent the inclusion of domain knowledge can improve the results of the best-performing transformer models.

4.1 Trained models

We trained a total of four models and tested them on both the Held out TEST and GLAUx TEST datasets. Two of these models are also included in Palladino and Yousef (2024): the first is Ancient Greek BERT (henceforth AG_BERT), a modern Greek BERT model fine-tuned on Ancient Greek text data from the Perseus Digital Library and the First1KGreek project (Singh et al., 2021). The second is a multilingual XLM-RoBERTa model fine-tuned on Perseus data, the First1KGreek project, and various treebank datasets for Ancient Greek translation alignment, developed in the context of the UGARIT project (henceforth UGARIT). Because our training data differ from theirs, we retrained the two models instead of comparing metrics for the fine-tuned models directly. In all cases, we used a random 10-fold hyperparameter search to optimise the weight decay, the learning rate, and the number of epochs to maximise the F1 score on the validation dataset. The search space and final hyperparameters are detailed in Tables 7 and 8 in Appendix A.

We added two other models for comparison. Firstly, Ancient Greek ELECTRA-small (henceforth ELECTRA) (Mercelis and Keersmaekers, 2022), trained on Ancient Greek texts from Homer up until the 4th century CE. It is smaller than the other models and significantly faster to train. Secondly, GrεBerta (Riemenschneider and Frank, 2023), an XLM-RoBERTa model trained on a corpus of 200 million Ancient Greek tokens. The texts are partially sourced from digitisation projects such as the Perseus Digital Library and First1KGreek and partially from OCRed text from the Internet Archive.

4.2 Results on test sets

Table 3 shows the results of the four models on the 'Held out TEST' and the 'GLAUx TEST' sets. Metrics are calculated on the entity level (e.g. for multi-word entities, all comprising words of said

NERAncientGreekML4AL.

[8]The best model will be published on HuggingFace upon acceptance, while the code for training the models is available on GitHub (ibid.)

entities must be correctly annotated by the model to be considered a true positive). Unless otherwise specified, we indicate the F1 score per category. The evaluation focuses on the assignment of entity type to every token and thus I-tags are not explicitly shown in the table because of the inconsistency of the annotation of these entities in the training data, as done by (Palladino and Yousef, 2024). However, it is important to note that Recall for I-tags of all types was low, as can be seen in Table 10 in Appendix B. This can be attributed to their relative scarcity in training and validation data, and a way to improve these results is discussed in Section 5.3.

First, it is notable that all the models perform better on the Held out TEST than on the GLAUx TEST. For PERS, the best-retrieved category, this translates into a minimum drop of 0.01 (GrεBerta) to a maximum of 0.05 (UGARIT). Secondly, while on the Held out TEST AG-BERT, ELECTRA and UGARIT have a very similar performance, on the GLAUx TEST, AG-BERT outperforms the other three.

5 Predicting PERS entities (Reduced models)

Because the overarching project in which this research is embedded is primarily interested in the mentions of people, and because, as demonstrated by Table 3, the prediction of LOC and GRP entities is more difficult than PERS, the next part of the paper focuses on adapting the NER task to predict individuals as comprehensively and consistently as possible. We propose the three following approaches:

- Simplify the task from standard NER to predicting whether a single token references a person (PERS) or not (MISC) (see 5.1).
- Incorporate information from the TM NamVar and GeoVar gazetteers as either a post-processing rule or a binary mask added to the model input (see 5.2).
- Utilise the GLAUx syntactic dependencies to (re)create multi-token entities after annotation by the models (see 5.3).

5.1 Training models to predict PERS-MISC

To create the data for the simplified NER task, which only predicts an entity label (PERS or MISC) for every capitalised token, and by default predicts O for all other tokens, we automatically re-annotated all capitalised words of the entity type PERS without B- or I- specifications: so, for example, the name 'Simon Petrus' was re-annotated as PERS PERS. This process causes a difference in entity count compared to the data used for the normal model, as visible in the 'support' columns of Tables 3 and 4. All other capitalised tokens were annotated as MISC. Non-capitalised tokens are always classified as non-entities. Critical editions of Ancient Greek text often lack a sentence-initial capital, so it is reasonable to assume that anything that is capitalised is an entity of some kind. In earlier work, capitalisation in critical editions of Ancient Greek (and Latin) texts has been similarly leveraged for NER e.g. in the Perseus Project (Crane, 2011) and Trismegistos (Broux and Depauw, 2015). We use the same base models and hyperparameter optimisation method as described above for the normal NER (details available in Table 9 in Appendix A). The results in Table 4 show that all models perform well on this task, with AG_BERT marginally outperforming the others. We thus only use this model (from now on AG_BERT_simple), for gazetteer and dependency incorporation.

5.2 Gazetteer approaches

As detailed in Section 2, including domain knowledge in the training of NER models may be advantageous. Here, in collaboration with the Trismegistos team, we explore the incorporation of the TM gazetteers NamVar and GeoVar (see Section 2), authoritative lists widely used in the field of ancient history.

TM NamVar aims at an exhaustive coverage of personal names attested in Ancient Greek (800 BCE - 800 CE), including all spelling and linguistic variants. For names outside Egypt, TM NamVar has integrated the Greek Lexicon of Personal Names (LGPN).[9] The coverage of the regional LGPN volumes varies over time, e.g. regarding the inclusion of non-Greek names. TM is in the process of adding whatever names are missing, both in epigraphic and in Greek literary texts. Currently there are 81,588 Greek name variants (out of a total of 239,201 for all languages and scripts). TM GeoVar for Ancient Greek currently focuses mainly on spelling and linguistic variants of place names found in texts from Egypt

5.2.1 Rule-based approach (AG_BERT_rule)

To create AG_BERT_rule, a post-processing rule was added to the prediction of AG_BERT_simple:

[9] https://www.lgpn.ox.ac.uk/.

	AG-BERT	**Electra**	**GrεBerta**	**UGARIT**	**support**
		Held out TEST			
PERS	**0.87**	0.86	0.76	0.86	3,090
LOC	**0.73**	0.71	0.57	0.73	1,105
GRP	0.81	0.80	0.68	**0.83**	1,384
Macro F1	0.80	0.79	0.67	**0.81**	5,579
		GLAUx TEST			
PERS	0.78	0.76	0.73	**0.79**	578
LOC	**0.75**	0.71	0.60	0.66	233
GRP	0.78	**0.78**	0.73	0.76	201
Macro F1	**0.77**	0.75	0.68	0.74	1,012

Table 3: Results (F1 score) for NER per label on in-domain (Held out TEST) and out-of-domain (GLAUx TEST) data

	AG_BERT	**Electra**	**GrεBerta**	**UGARIT**	**support**
		Held out TEST			
PERS	**0.90**	0.87	0.83	0.89	3,539
MISC	**0.90**	0.88	0.84	0.89	3,706
macro F1	**0.90**	0.88	0.83	0.89	7,245
		GLAUx TEST			
PERS	**0.88**	0.84	0.81	0.85	605
MISC	**0.88**	0.87	0.83	0.86	699
macro F1	**0.88**	0.86	0.82	0.86	1,304

Table 4: Results (F1 score) for the prediction of PERS and MISC labels on in-domain (Held out TEST) and out-of-domain (GLAUx TEST) data

if the lemma of a capitalised token appears in TM NamVar, but not in TM GeoVar, it is always classified as a person. Both on Held out TEST and on GLAUx TEST, this approach increases Recall (by ca. 0.03 points) but has a detrimental effect on Precision (drop of more than 0.06 points) (see Table 5).

5.2.2 Machine Learning approach (AG_BERT_mask)

For AG_BERT_mask, we incorporated the rule described in Section 5.2.1 as input for the model. A binary mask was added to the training data where 1 indicated the rule applied and 0 that it did not. This mask was provided as additional input information to the model. We retrained AG_BERT_simple with the same final hyperparameters as described in Section 5. The results in Table 5 show that while no effect is visible on Held out TEST, this approach improved Precision on GLAUx TEST from 0.84 to 0.90, with a slight drop in Recall (from 0.92 to 0.91). We thus conclude that the ML approach yields better results than the rule-based approach, and we integrate the syntax on the top of AG_BERT_mask.

5.3 Incorporating syntax for the retrieval of multi-token entities (AG_BERT_syntax)

In the training data, names with ethnonyms and patronyms are rarely annotated as multi-token entities. They are frequently annotated as two separate entities, as is the case DEIPN (e.g. Λεωνίδης ὁ Ἠλεῖος, 'Leonides of Elis', annotated as B-PERS O B-GRP) and PH (e.g. Δεκελεύς Σωφάνης, 'Sophanes of Decelea', annotated as B-GRP B-PERS), although there are exceptions (e.g. in PH Θεοδώρου τοῦ Σαμίου, 'Theodorus of Samos', annotated as a B-PERS I-PERS I-PERS). However, for the disambiguation and linking of people retrieving the full name is crucial.

	AG_BERT_simple			AG_BERT_rule			AG_BERT_mask			support
	Pr	Rc	F1	Pr	Rc	F1	Pr	Rc	F1	
					Held out TEST					
PERS	0.88	**0.93**	**0.90**	0.79	**0.96**	0.87	0.88	**0.93**	**0.90**	3,539
MISC	**0.93**	0.88	**0.90**	**0.96**	0.75	0.84	**0.93**	0.88	**0.90**	3,706
Macro	**0.90**	**0.90**	**0.90**	0.87	0.86	0.86	**0.90**	**0.90**	**0.90**	7,245
					GLAUx TEST					
PERS	0.84	0.92	0.88	0.78	**0.95**	0.86	**0.90**	0.91	**0.90**	605
MISC	0.92	0.84	0.88	**0.95**	0.76	0.85	0.92	**0.91**	**0.91**	699
Macro	0.88	0.88	0.88	0.86	0.86	0.85	**0.91**	**0.91**	**0.91**	1,304

Table 5: Results (Precision, Recall and F1 score) for the prediction of PERS and MISC labels on in-domain (Held out TEST) and newly annotated (GLAUx TEST) data, by not including the Gazetteer (AG_BERT_simple), including the Gazetteer with a rule-based approach (AG_BERT_rule) and with a mask (AG_BERT_mask).

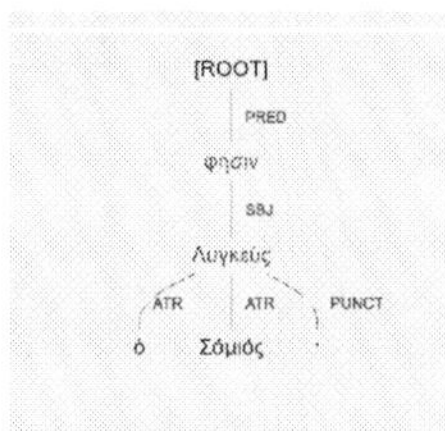

Figure 2: Dependency representation of sentence 1793 in DEIPN. `https://perseids-publications.github.io/glaux-trees/0008-001/2066`

In this approach, we rely on a dependency-based representation of Ancient Greek sentences as shown in Figure 2. If a capitalised word (in this case Λυγκεὺς) is annotated as a PERS by AG_BERT_mask, we check whether any of the direct children of said word is capitalised and re-annotate the entity as a multi-token. Thus, in this example, Λυγκεὺς ὁ Σάμίος, 'Lynceus of Samos', is re-annotated as B-PERS O I-PERS. Table 6 shows the results of dependency incorporation (AG_BERT_syntax) compared to the performances of the AG_BERT trained on the available data with respect to B-PERS, I-PERS. Only capitalised words are taken into account for calculating the metrics. For AG_BERT, the MISC category is created by grouping together all predictions of non-PERS tags. As shown in Table 6, dependency information greatly improves results for I-PERS tokens.

5.4 Qualitative error analysis

We performed a qualitative error analysis on the predictions of the models described in sections 5.2 and 5.3. We first describe the errors of AG_BERT_simple compared to AG_BERT_rule and AG_BERT_mask (as seen in ??), and second, evaluate the improvement on multi-token entities with AG_BERT_syntax (as seen in 6).

5.4.1 Difficult categories

Several entity categories can be identified where AG_BERT_simple failed to predict correctly and neither AG_BERT_rule nor AG_BERT_mask offered any improvement. First, all predict MISC for nicknames such as Κακεργέτης, 'the Evildoer', or for tokens that frequently appear as non-capitalised common nouns in the training data, e.g. the PERS entity Λύχνος, the name of a deity, identical to the non-entity λύχνος, with the meaning of 'candle'.

Second, PERS is predicted for many of the MISC entities that are capitalised tokens annotated by experts as O: for example, capitalised tokens such as mathematical notations to designate geometrical entities such as points, lines, circles, etc. in texts such as Euclid's *Elementa* (GLAUx ID: 1799-001). Other examples are capitalised tokens that are entities that do not fit the PERS, LOC, GRP scheme (see 3.3) such as titles of books (e.g. Γραφή, 'the Scripture', i.e. the Bible) and titles for people (e.g Φαραώ, 'Pharaoh', and Καίσαρα, 'Caesar'). Overall, these issues stem from mismatches between training and testing data: some, such as mathematical entities were not present in the training data, others, such as titles for people, were annotated differently.

	AG_BERT_syntax			AG_BERT			support
	Pr	Rc	F1	Pr	Rc	F1	
B-PERS	0.88	0.89	0.89	0.90	0.81	0.85	581
I-PERS	0.70	0.60	0.65	0.50	0.02	0.04	50
MISC	0.91	0.91	0.91	0.82	0.95	0.88	673
macro avg	0.83	0.80	0.81	0.74	0.59	0.59	1,304

Table 6: Results for retrieving multi-word PERS entities using the syntax approach compared to training on available data, on the newly annotated GLAUx_test

5.4.2 Difference between AG_BERT_rule and AG_BERT_mask

The predictions of the two gazetteer models show significant differences. AG_BERT_mask improves upon AG_BERT_rule in cases where an entity appears in TM NamVar but is a MISC entity, such as GRP entities that in singular could be a person, e.g. Νύμφαι, 'Nymphs'. Second, AG_BERT_mask is the only model that correctly predicts MISC for the majority of the mathematical entities described above. In the few cases where AG_BERT_rule was an improvement on AG_BERT_simple and AG_BERT_mask not, issues stem again from the inconsistencies in the training data. Sometimes forms of the same word appear annotated as different entity categories, e.g. Ἅιδου, 'Hades', annotated as O, PERS or LOC. The annotation with PERS and LOC stems from the inherent ambiguity of the word Hades, which can indeed refer both to the god Hades and the underworld. In other cases there are differences in annotation choices between the harmonised training data and our annotation, e.g. epithets annotated as PERS in GLAUx TEST, but as MISC in TRAIN. Lastly, for nested entities, AG_BERT_mask predicts the overarching level where the other two predict the second level, e.g. for Κωνσταντίνου [B-LOC nested B-PERS] ἀγορὰν [I-LOC], 'the Forum of Constantine', AG_BERT_mask predicts MISC for Κωνσταντίνου, 'Constantine'.

Under-representation of certain types of entities is also an issue for AG_BERT_mask. One example is personal names ending in an alpha. A specific case is personal names ending in -ίᾳ (feminine noun, dative ending): tokens with this ending are primarily annotated MISC (total: 441, total PERS: 83) in the training data (e.g. Ἀδρίᾳ, 'the Adriatic', MISC with mask = 1), resulting in the prediction of MISC instead of PERS for tokens ending in -ίᾳ such as for Ἀμεινίᾳ, 'Ameinias', with mask = 1. Only when the exact same form appears in the training data, is the prediction correct. For those tokens with mask = 1, naturally AG_BERT_rule's prediction is always correct. Training on the gazetteer mask had a detrimental effect for AG_BERT_mask in this case as several MISC entities in this category, like the examples given above, did receive a mask = 1, allowing the model the possibility that forms like this can be MISC even though they have mask = 1.

5.4.3 Syntax models

Last, AG_BERT_syntax shows significant improvement in predicting I-labels as compared to the AG_BERT model, as described in Section 5.3. This approach improved multi-token entity recognition for entities consisting of up to three separate tokens or with up to three non-entity tokens present between the B- and I- tokens. However, for multi-token entities that have both more than two tokens and gaps between the B- and I- tokens, performance is not increased. The majority of these errors are not caused by any error in the method but either by incorrect syntactic information encoded in GLAUx as the result of automatic analysis or because our rule-based method of using the syntactic trees could not retrieve all I-entities, e.g. we did not add special rules for coordination, which is complicatedly annotated in the syntactic annotation of GLAUx (see Section 3.3).

6 Conclusion

The goal of our study is to consistently and fully automatically annotate attestations of people using transformer-based NER. We trained several transformer models on available data for Ancient Greek NER and evaluated performance both on a Held out TEST set and on randomly annotated data representative for Greek literary data. While all models performed adequately, we conclude that inconsistency in annotation remains an obstacle in achieving high performance —which is in line with the findings by Palladino and Yousef (2024) and Beersmans et al. (2023), especially concerning multi-token entities. The approaches introduced in Sections 5.1-5.3 increase the performance for detecting persons specifically, but we recognise that there is still room for improvement (see Section 7). In future work, we will consider the integration of other available gazetteers,[10] and incorporate attestation counts as weights. The syntactically informed annotation of multi-token entities could equally benefit from an improvement of the rule-based extraction through a more careful analysis of the structure of I-entities in the dependency tree.

7 Limitations

One of the main limitations is our dependency on the capitalisation choices of the compilers of the (digital) editions we rely on. This also makes this approach difficult for truly transferring to even more low-resource languages. Secondly, gazetteers cannot ensure complete coverage of the attestations. In addition, we aimed at finding an exact match between the lemma in the text and the form resulting in the gazetteer. For this reason, small language variations resulted in a mismatch between the text and the gazetteer form. This could be addressed by allowing a certain degree of variation. For the use of syntactic relations, we largely relied on automatic parsing, a notably hard task, which resulted in some missed retrievals due to erroneous syntactic annotation. This aspect is hard to address because large-scale manual syntactical annotation is not achievable.

8 Acknowledgements

We thank the creators of data, and in particular Brady Kiesling, Elton Barker and Rainer Simon (Periegesis project and Recogito) and Chiara Palladino and Josh Kemp (Annotated Odyssey) for providing us with theirs as per our request.

References

2023. Stepbible data repository cc by 4.0.

Nasser Alshammari and Saad Alanazi. 2021. The impact of using different annotation schemes on named entity recognition. *Egyptian Informatics Journal*, 22(3):295–302.

Marijke Beersmans, Evelien de Graaf, Tim Van de Cruys, and Margherita Fantoli. 2023. Training and evaluation of named entity recognition models for classical Latin. In *Proceedings of the Ancient Language Processing Workshop*, pages 1–12, Varna, Bulgaria. INCOMA Ltd., Shoumen, Bulgaria.

Monica Berti. 2021. *Digital Editions of Historical Fragmentary Texts*. Propylaeum.

Monica Berti, K. Simov, and M. Eskevich. 2019. Named Entity Annotation for Ancient Greek with INCEpTION. In *Proceedings of CLARIN Annual Conference 201*, pages 1–4, Leipzig. CLARIN 2019.

Yanne Broux and Mark Depauw. 2015. Developing onomastic gazetteers and prosopographies for the ancient world through named entity recognition and graph visualization: Some examples from trismegistos people. In *Social Informatics*, Lecture Notes in Computer Science, page 304–313, Cham. Springer International Publishing.

Kate Byrne. 2007. Nested Named Entity Recognition in Historical Archive Text. In *International Conference on Semantic Computing (ICSC 2007)*, pages 589–596, Irvine, CA, USA. IEEE.

Gregory R. Crane. 2011. Scalable named entity identification in classical studies.

Maud Ehrmann, Ahmed Hamdi, Elvys Linhares Pontes, Matteo Romanello, and Antoine Doucet. 2023. Named entity recognition and classification in historical documents: A survey. *ACM Comput. Surv.*, 56(2).

Besnik Fetahu, Anjie Fang, Oleg Rokhlenko, and Shervin Malmasi. 2022. Dynamic Gazetteer Integration in Multilingual Models for Cross-Lingual and Cross-Domain Named Entity Recognition. In *Proceedings of the 2022 Conference of the North American Chapter of the Association for Computational Linguistics: Human Language Technologies*, pages 2777–2790, Seattle, United States. Association for Computational Linguistics.

Anna Foka, David A. McMeekin, Kyriaki Konstantinidou, Nasrin Mostofian, Elton Barker, O. Cenk Demiroglu, Ethan Chiew, Brady Kiesling, and Linda Talatas. 2021. *Mapping Ancient Heritage Narratives with Digital Tools*, page 55–65. Ubiquity Press.

Alek Keersmaekers. 2021. The glaux corpus: methodological issues in designing a long-term, diverse, multi-layered corpus of ancient greek. In *Proceedings of the 2nd International Workshop on Computational Approaches to Historical Language Change 2021*, page 39–50, Online. Association for Computational Linguistics.

Wouter Mercelis and Alek Keersmaekers. 2022. electra-grc.

[10]Another example of an Ancient Greek and Latin gazetteer is Pleiades,`https://pleiades.stoa.org/`

Chiara Palladino and Tariq Yousef. 2024. Development of robust ner models and named entity tagsets for ancient greek.

Pelagios. 2021. Beyond translation: Building better greek scholars.

Frederick Riemenschneider and Anette Frank. 2023. Exploring large language models for classical philology. In *Proceedings of the 61st Annual Meeting of the Association for Computational Linguistics (Volume 1: Long Papers)*, page 15181–15199, Toronto, Canada. Association for Computational Linguistics.

Pranaydeep Singh, Gorik Rutten, and Els Lefever. 2021. A pilot study for BERT language modelling and morphological analysis for ancient and medieval Greek. In *Proceedings of the 5th Joint SIGHUM Workshop on Computational Linguistics for Cultural Heritage, Social Sciences, Humanities and Literature (LaTeCH-CLfL 2021)*, pages 128–137. Association for Computational Linguistics.

Chan Hee Song, Dawn Lawrie, Tim Finin, and James Mayfield. 2020. Improving Neural Named Entity Recognition with Gazetteers. *arXiv preprint*. ArXiv:2003.03072 [cs].

Sergio Torres Aguilar. 2022. Multilingual named entity recognition for medieval charters using stacked embeddings and bert-based models. In *Proceedings of the Second Workshop on Language Technologies for Historical and Ancient Languages*, page 119–128, Marseille, France. European Language Resources Association.

Congying Xia, Chenwei Zhang, Tao Yang, Yaliang Li, Nan Du, Xian Wu, Wei Fan, Fenglong Ma, and Philip Yu. 2019. Multi-grained Named Entity Recognition. In *Proceedings of the 57th Annual Meeting of the Association for Computational Linguistics*, pages 1430–1440, Florence, Italy. Association for Computational Linguistics.

Tariq Yousef, Chiara Palladino, and Stefan Jänicke. 2023. Transformer-based Named Entity Recognition for Ancient Greek. In *Digital Humanities 2023. Book of Abstracts*, pages 420–422, Graz. Centre for Information Modelling - Austrian Centre for Digital Humanities.

Tariq Yousef, Chiara Palladino, Farnoosh Shamsian, Anise d'Orange Ferreira, and Michel Ferreira dos Reis. 2022a. An automatic model and gold standard for translation alignment of Ancient Greek. In *Proceedings of the Thirteenth Language Resources and Evaluation Conference*, pages 5894–5905, Marseille, France. European Language Resources Association.

Tariq Yousef, Chiara Palladino, David J. Wright, and Monica Berti. 2022b. Automatic translation alignment for Ancient Greek and Latin. In *Proceedings of the Second Workshop on Language Technologies for Historical and Ancient Languages*, pages 101–107, Marseille, France. European Language Resources Association.

Atefeh Zafarian and Habibollah Asghari. 2019. Improving NER Models by exploiting Named Entity Gazetteer as External Knowledge. In *Proceedings of the First International Workshop on NLP Solutions for Under Resourced Languages (NSURL 2019) co-located with ICNLSP 2019 - Short Papers*, pages 107–111, Trento, Italy. Association for Computational Linguistics.

A Hyperparameters

parameter	values
learning rate	uniform distribution: $[1 \times 10^{-6}, 1 \times 10^{-4}]$
weight decay	$\{0.1, 0.01, 0.001\}$
number of training epochs	$\{3, 4, 5, 6\}$

Table 7: Hyperparameter search space

	AG_BERT	ELECTRA	GrεBerta	UGARIT
learning rate	6.041e-05	9.889e-05	2.715e-05	5.784e-05
weight decay	0.01	0.1	0.01	0.01
epochs	3	5	4	5

Table 8: overview final hyperparameters on the regular NER task

	AG_BERT/AG_BERT_mask	ELECTRA	GrεBerta	UGARIT
learning rate	1.263e-05	8.703e-05	2.961e-05	2.490e-05
weight decay	0.01	0.1	0.1	0.001
epochs	6	5	4	6

Table 9: overview final hyperparameters on the PERS/MISC task

B Detailed results

	AG_BERT	Electra	GrεBerta	UGARIT	support
B-PERS	0.87	0.87	0.77	0.87	3,090
I-PERS	0.58	0.50	0.05	0.56	83
B-LOC	0.75	0.73	0.58	0.75	1,105
I-LOC	0.17	0.08	0.00	0.13	196
B-GRP	0.82	0.81	0.68	0.84	1,384
I-GRP	0.00	0.00	0.00	0.00	49
macro_f1	0.53	0.50	0.35	0.53	

Table 10: overview detailed results test set

	AG_BERT	Electra	GrεBerta	UGARIT	support
B-PERS	0.84	0.82	0.78	0.85	578
I-PERS	0.04	0.00	0.08	0.07	51
B-LOC	0.77	0.73	0.62	0.68	233
I-LOC	0.22	0.14	0.00	0.31	11
B-GRP	0.78	0.78	0.73	0.76	201
macro_f1	0.53	0.50	0.44	0.53	

Table 11: overview detailed results GLAUx_test

C Entity conversion

PH		DEIPN		OD		SB	
original	converted	original	converted	original	converted	original	converted
person	PERS/GRP	person	PERS/GRP	person	PERS/GRP	PERSON	PERS/GRP
place	LOC	ethnic	GRP	place	LOC	LOC	LOC
place.proxy	GRP	place	LOC			PERS-G	GRP
artwork	O	group	GRP			LOC-G	GRP
event	O	title	O			TITLE	O/PERS/GRP
work	O	festival	O				
epithet	O	month	O				
tx	O	language	O				
material	O	constellation	O				
attribute	O						
movement	O						
measure	O						
animal	O						
object	O						
focalisation	O						
intervention	O						
transformation	O						

Table 12: entity conversion table

Adapting transformer models to morphological tagging of two highly inflectional languages: a case study on Ancient Greek and Latin

Alek Keersmaekers
KU Leuven
Blijde-Inkomststraat 21, 3000 Leuven (BE)

alek.keersmaekers@kuleuven.be

Wouter Mercelis
KU Leuven*, Brepols Publishers†
*Blijde-Inkomststraat 21, 3000 Leuven (BE)
†Begijnhof 39, 2300 Turnhout (BE)
wouter.mercelis@kuleuven.be

Abstract

Natural language processing for Greek and Latin, inflectional languages with small corpora, requires special techniques. For morphological tagging, transformer models show promising potential, but the best approach to use these models is unclear. For both languages, this paper examines the impact of using morphological lexica, training different model types (a single model with a combined feature tag, multiple models for separate features, and a multi-task model for all features), and adding linguistic constraints. We find that, although simply fine-tuning transformers to predict a monolithic tag may already yield decent results, each of these adaptations can further improve tagging accuracy.

1 Introduction

Morphological information is an essential enrichment for corpora of highly inflectional languages such as Ancient Greek and Latin. Yet given that the field of natural language processing has traditionally been heavily oriented to Modern English, a relatively analytic language, the automated processing of morphologically rich languages has been a challenge for some time already (see e.g. Tsarfaty et al., 2010).

For Ancient Greek (henceforth simply 'Greek') and Latin, Sommerschield et al. (2023) have noted that, as for many other languages, the transformer-based approach has recently become popular for morphological tagging, showing promising results. However, it is still an open question what the most appropriate way is to employ transformer models for this task, i.e. whether specific adaptations are necessary for inflectional languages.

The aim of this paper is therefore to systematically compare a number of adaptations that were previously found to be beneficial for morphological tagging of Greek and Latin using older methods and assess the importance of these adaptations in a transformer context. We will first discuss previous work related to this topic (Section 2). Next, we will present the experimental set-up of this project (3), including the data and models we used, and assess which parameter combinations contribute to optimal performance for the two languages (4.1). We will also give a general evaluation of the errors of the best-performing models (4.2). Finally, we will summarize the main results of this study and discuss ways for further improvement (5), and address its limitations (6).

2 Previous work

Given the vast body of literature on morphological tagging, this section will focus on related work to the central topic of this paper, viz. transformer-based approaches to Greek and Latin morphological tagging, as well as earlier approaches that have explicitly aimed to adapt tagging techniques to the typological characteristics of these languages. We will therefore not discuss studies that focus on comparing a number of readily available tagging tools (e.g. Celano et al., 2016; Poudat and Longrée, 2009), since these tools typically differ on various parameters, so that it is difficult to tell why exactly certain tools are better to handle Greek and Latin than others.

The morphological richness of Greek and Latin has various consequences: data sparsity arises due to a high number of tokens compared to types,[1] the tag set (i.e. the number of possible combinations of

[1] For example, for each type (unique word form) in the GUM English Universal Dependencies Treebank (see https://universaldependencies.org/) there are 10.7 tokens. For the Latin PROIEL treebank there are only 6.5, and for the Greek Perseus treebank even less, viz. 4.8 (note that they are all roughly similar in size: 212K, 205K and 202K tokens respectively).

Proceedings of the 1st Workshop on Machine Learning for Ancient Languages (ML4AL 2024), pages 165–176
August 15, 2024

morphological features) is very large and morphology and syntax are often interrelated (e.g. with case marking). As for data sparsity, Hajic (2000) advocates for the use of morphological dictionaries for inflectional languages in general, viz. knowledge bases containing lists of morphologically inflected forms and their analysis. In this way the correct analysis for unattested or lowly attested forms can be retrieved from this dictionary instead of solely relying on the training data of the tagger (additionally, even if multiple analyses are present in the lexicon for a given form, the number of possible tags will be heavily constrained by it). Various researchers have observed a positive effect of employing such lexica for Greek (e.g. Dik and Whaling, 2008; Keersmaekers, 2020) and Latin (e.g. Eger et al., 2015).

As for the size of the tag set, it is important to remark that it is only large if we treat the combination of part-of-speech and all the morphological features as one singular label (as is customary for English), i.e. the tag would be 'noun, singular, feminine, dative'. Some researchers on inflectional languages have recommended 'splitting' the tags, i.e. making separate predictions for all the individual morphological features, instead (e.g. Schmid and Laws, 2008; Tkachenko and Sirts, 2018). Such an approach has been advocated by e.g. Keersmaekers (2020), Riemenschneider and Frank (2023) for Greek and Eger et al. (2015) for Latin, but so far it has not been compared to a 'singular label'-approach yet.

Finally, as for the interrelatedness of morphology and syntax, some scholars (e.g. Lee et al., 2011) have shown that performing morphological tagging and syntactic parsing jointly can help both tasks, but since this requires a high performing syntactic parsing model as well, such an approach falls outside the scope of this paper.

As noted in the introduction of this paper, recently (encoder-only) transformer models have become popular for Greek and Latin morphological tagging. They have been employed in various ways, including directly finetuning a pretrained large language model (LLM) for this task (Mercelis and Keersmaekers, 2022a; Wróbel and Nowak, 2022; Riemenschneider and Frank, 2023), by extracting the embeddings of a pretrained LLM and processing them combined with other information through a simpler architecture (Straka and Straková, 2020; Singh et al., 2021; Swaelens et al., 2023), or, occasionally, utilizing prompts on generative transformer architectures (Stüssi and Ströbel, 2024).

The effect of the various parameters described above, including the use of a morphological lexicon and the 'splitting' of morphological tags, has so far not been systematically investigated in a transformer context. In fact, there are reasons to suspect that their effect may be diminished, given that transformer architectures have specific adaptations to handle data sparsity and morphological richness. Firstly, transformer models are typically pre-trained on millions (or billions in the case of modern languages) of unannotated tokens, allowing them to recognize forms beyond the specific training set for morphological tagging. Nevertheless, the problem remains that morphological richness inherently implies a proportionally larger number of word form types, and due to the closed nature of historical language corpora these pre-trained models are also typically trained on lower amounts of data as compared to modern languages. [2] Secondly, in most modern transformer architectures subword tokenization is typically employed (see e.g. Kudo and Richardson, 2018), which splits morphologically complex words in several parts, based on statistical pattern recognition. For example, the tokenizer of the transformer model we will employ for Latin (see 3.1) splits the morphologically complex verb *honorificentur* into *honorific+entur*, so that even if the full form *honorificentur* might be scarcely attested, the individual parts *honorific-* and *-entur* would be more frequent. In this paper we will therefore systematically investigate whether modern transformer architectures have completely superseded the need for any special adaptations for inflectional languages, or if morphological lexica and splitting tags may still offer improvements.

3 Methodology

3.1 Data and models

In this paper, we compare morphological tagging for Greek and Latin. While these languages are typologically rather similar (both highly

[2] Although sometimes a modern language model is finetuned for ancient languages, as e.g. in Singh et al., 2021.

inflectional Indo-European languages), the external resources we used for each of them respectively results in two very different experimental conditions.

For Greek we have a relative large and diverse body of manually tagged data (1.46M tokens, of which we reserved 1.24M as training data and 219K as test data), which is a result of a data homogenization effort of various treebanks by the GLAUx project (Keersmaekers, 2021). This dataset consists of various text genres (29 in total according to the GLAUx classification) from all three major Ancient Greek time periods (archaic, classical and post-classical). We could also make use of a morphological lexicon from GLAUx which was specifically developed to be compatible with the treebank data (see 3.3).

In contrast, while for Latin various treebank project exists and some effort has recently been undertaken to homogenize them (Gamba and Zeman, 2023), these efforts have only been published very recently and we were not aware of them when we wrote this paper. We therefore instead made use of the largest dataset present in the Universal Dependencies (UD) project (Nivre et al., 2020) that was relatively diverse, viz. the PROIEL treebank (Haug and Jøhndal, 2008), consisting of 205K tokens, including the Vulgate New Testament, a late classical work by Palladius as well as more classical texts (by Caesar and Cicero). This dataset was therefore substantially smaller (we used the 'train' subset, consisting of 178K tokens, and the 'test' subset, 14K tokens). The lexicon we used was also not specifically developed to be compatible with this treebank (see 3.3). On the other hand, this allowed us to compare results for a situation that is rather typical for low-resource languages, where large datasets and standardized resources are typically absent.

As for our morphological tagging approach, our basic method was relatively simple: we fine-tuned pre-trained transformer models to predict either one or multiple labels (see 3.2) consisting of part-of-speech and morphological information. For Greek, we used *electra-grc* (Mercelis and Keersmaekers, 2022b), a small ELECTRA model trained on the GLAUx corpus, allowing us to use a model that was trained on a corpus with a data standard that was consistent with our tagging dataset. For Latin, we used LaBERTa, a base-size RoBERTa model offering state of the art performance for Latin morphological tagging (Riemenschneider and Frank, 2023). Since our data was tokenized into subwords, the training and predictions were always based on the final subwords of the token. We fine-tuned all models for a fixed number of 10 epochs, using a batch size of 16 and a learning rate of 5e-5.

3.2 Splitting tags

We evaluate the impact of predicting a single tag containing the part-of-speech proper and all morphological information (we call this approach *MonoTag* in what follows), vs. predicting each morphological feature separately. We compared two methods to perform the latter task: the simplest way is to train a tagging model for each feature (*MultiTag*). We then calculate the probability of a morphological tag as the product of the probabilities of each individual feature, and select the tag with the highest probability – this is the *Multiclass Multilabel model* described in Tkachenko and Sirts (2018). While this approach is statistically rather naïve, given that the probabilities of the various features are not independent,[3] it yielded decent results on the Greek and Latin datasets evaluated by them.

Another approach is to employ multi-task learning, as was done by Riemenschneider and Frank (2023) for Greek. In this approach (*MultiTag-MultiTask*), we do not train separate models for each feature, but rather train them all together. To achieve this, we use a shared encoder with for each feature a classification head on top. In this way, the model should generalize better and capture how the various morphological features interrelate during the training phase due to the shared loss function. Additionally, this method is computationally more efficient and less prone to overfitting.

Figure 1-3 visualize the three approaches.

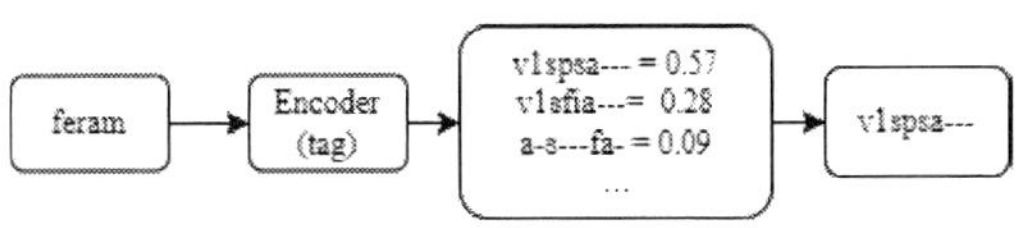

Figure 1: MonoTag approach.

[3] To give just one example, Greek possesses several feminine words that have an identical ending in the genitive singular and the accusative plural, viz. -ας. Obviously in such a case the probabilities of the features 'case' and 'number' are highly dependent on each other.

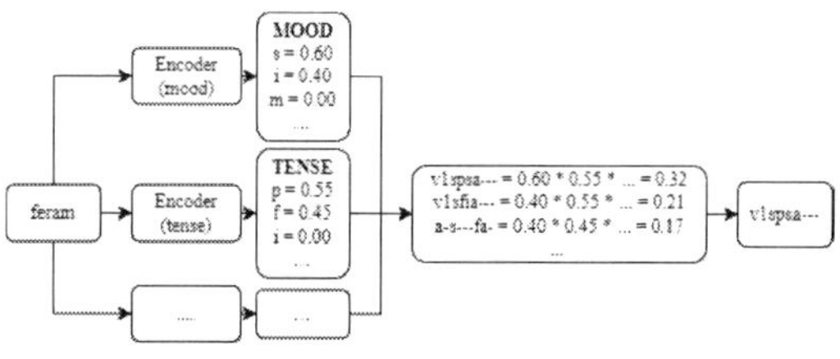

Figure 3: MultiTag approach.

3.3 Morphological lexica

We test the impact of employing an external lexicon consisting of inflected forms and their possible morphological analyses. For Greek, we used a lexicon from the GLAUx project, which was based on the morphological analysis tool Morpheus (Crane, 1991) and of which its output was converted and homogenized in order to be compatible with the morphological tagging of GLAUx. For Latin, we analyzed all forms in the test data with LEMLAT (3.0) (Passarotti et al., 2017). Since the output of this analyzer was not compatible with the UD annotation of PROIEL, we created a script in order to convert it to the latter format using a number of rules.

Concretely, we employed these lexica as follows: if an inflected form occurred in the lexicon, the possible tags that could be predicted were constrained to the ones corresponding to this form. To avoid the problem that some words may have analyses that are not present in this lexicon, we also added all forms from the training data and their tags to it. Our lexica covered the test data very well: for both languages only 0.4% of the forms in the test data were not present in the lexicon.

Figure 4 illustrates the integration of a lexicon in the *MultiTag-MultiTask* approach (in *MonoTag* and *MultiTag*, the integration happens analogically).

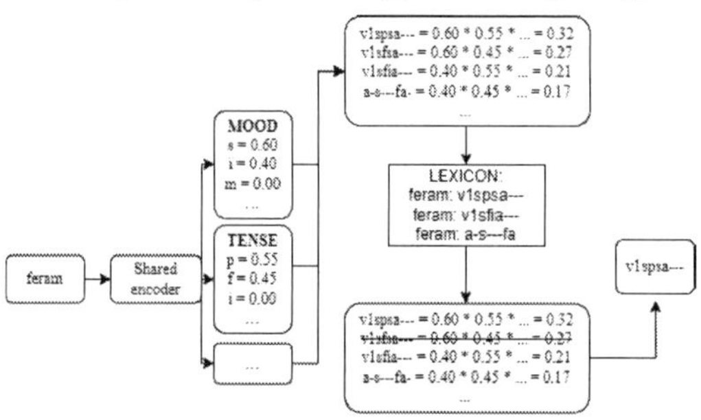

Figure 4: Integrating a lexicon in the tagging process.

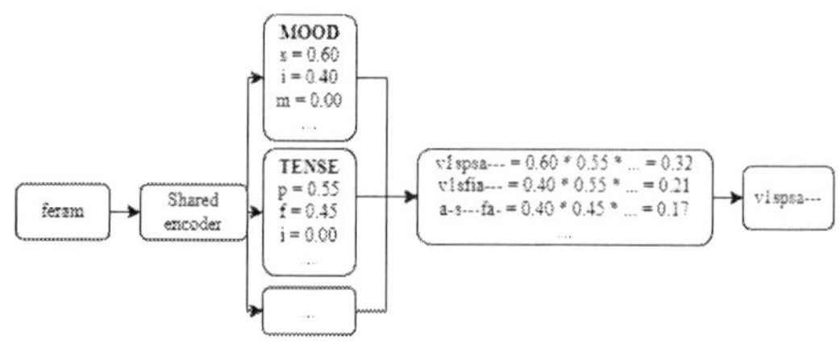

Figure 2: MultiTag-MultiTask approach.

3.4 Constraining the outcome space

When predicting the various features individually, one risk is that linguistically nonsensical feature combinations could be predicted (e.g. a passive noun). While the use of a lexicon may already reduce this problem to a great extent (since the possible combinations are limited to the ones occurring in the lexicon for a specific form), the problem potentially remains for forms that are not present in it. We therefore experiment with two approaches adding additional constraints on the tag outcomes: firstly, we restrict the possible tags that could be predicted to the ones occurring in the training data. A disadvantage of this approach is that if a feature combination does occur in the test data but not in the training data, it can never be predicted. [4] We therefore also tried a second approach, which consists of adding an external list of linguistically valid feature combinations for Greek and Latin to the list of tags occurring in the training data, based on a number of constraints that we defined for both languages (e.g. nouns cannot receive the feature voice, the future tense cannot occur in the subjunctive mood). In this way, all feature combinations that could logically occur in Greek and Latin could in theory be predicted.

Figure 5 illustrates the addition of constraints to the outcome space in the *MultiTag-MultiTask* (in *MonoTag* and *MultiTag* this again happens analogically), which can either come from the training data or an external list (e.g. in Figure 5, an external list has determined that the *s*[ubjunctive] mood and *f*[uture] tense are not compatible).

[4] Although this does not occur very often, for Latin there were 12 tokens and for Greek 18 where this was the case.

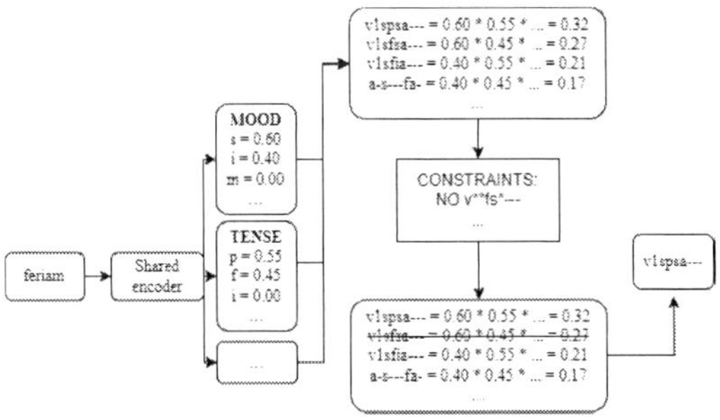

Figure 5: Constraining the outcome tag space.

4 Results

4.1 Parameter comparison

4.1.1 Greek

Tables 1-3 show the results for the three training approaches described in section 3.2 (*MonoTag*, *MultiTag*, *MultiTag-MultiTask*) for Greek. Firstly, it is clear that the use of a lexicon has a positive effect across all three approaches, allowing for a 15-20% error reduction. These differences are also statistically significant: with McNemar's test, $p<0.01$ in all cases when comparing the models with and without lexicon. Taking the *MonoTag* approach as an example, the lexicon corrected 1569 tagging mistakes, although it also introduced 240 new mistakes. An example of the former case is (1), in which φθιμένῃ (*phthiménēi*) was originally tagged as a present participle, but corrected by the lexicon to an aorist participle (the correct analysis). Given that the present of the same verb would be superficially similar (φθι(ν)ομένῃ *phthi(n)oménēi*), intricate knowledge of Greek verbal morphology is necessary to predict that it is an aorist, which the transformer model was not able to pick up. In particular, the lexicon was a valuable asset to handle Greek verbal morphology in a better way than the transformer model was able to do: verbs consisted of 26.5% of the mistakes when no lexicon was employed, but 22.0% when a lexicon was employed, the largest difference among all parts of speech.

(1) καίτοι **φθιμένῃ** μέγα κἀκοῦσαι τοῖς ἰσοθέοις σύγκληρα λαχεῖν. (Soph. Ant. 836-7)
kaítoi ***phthiménēi*** *mega kakoûsai toîs isothéois súgklēra lakheîn.*
"Yet it is great **for someone who died** to earn a fate equal to that of the gods."

Nevertheless, there were some new mistakes that the lexicon introduced. These were typically cases in which the lexicon was not strictly incorrect, but simply inconsistent with the data. For example, in (2), ὠμόφρονος *ōmóphronos* was tagged without the lexicon as an adjective (as it appears in the data) but with a lexicon as a noun. Since it has an adjectival meaning but morphologically it shares characteristics with nouns (having no gender inflection), both analyses could be argued to be correct, especially since there were no strict annotation guidelines in the data we used (see 3.1) to handle such cases.

(2) σίγα, τέκνον, μὴ κινήσῃς ἀγρίαν ὀδύνην πατρὸς **ὠμόφρονος**. (Soph. Trach. 975-6)
síga, téknon, mḗ kinḗsēis agrían odúnēn patrós ***ōmóphronos***.
"Be quiet, child, so that you will not stir the savage pain of your **savage-minded** father."

Comparing the three training approaches, the *MultiTag* approach performs slightly better than the *MonoTag* approach. In the best case (when also combined with constraints on the tag outcomes, see below), this allows for a 10% error reduction both with (96.9% to 97.2% accuracy) and without

Lexicon	Accuracy
No	0.963 (210635)
Yes	0.969 (211964)

Table 1: Greek tagger results (*MonoTag*), with accuracy and N correct predictions.

Lexicon	Tag constraints	Accuracy
No	None	0.964 (210891)
	Training data	0.967 (211569)
	Tag list	0.967 (211529)
Yes	None	0.972 (212567)
	Training data	0.972 (212596)
	Tag list	0.972 (212592)

Table 2: Greek tagger results (*MultiTag*), with accuracy and N correct predictions.

Lexicon	Tag constraints	Accuracy
No	None	0.964 (210805)
	Training data	0.964 (210950)
	Tag list	0.964 (210929)
Yes	None	0.970 (212169)
	Training data	0.970 (212177)
	Tag list	0.970 (212176)

Table 3: Greek tagger results (*MultiTag-MultiTask*), with accuracy and N correct predictions.

(96.3% to 96.7%) lexicon. These differences are also statistically significant ($p<0.01$ with McNemar's test in both cases). Taking the lexicon-based approach, without any constraints on the outcome tags, as an example, the *MultiTag* method was able to correct 1898 mistakes but unfortunately also introduced 1295 new mistakes. One obvious advantage of this approach is with scarcely attested tag combinations: for example, tag combinations that occur 50 times or less in the training data constitute 6.5% of mistakes with the *MonoTag* approach (448 in total) but 4.3% with the *MultiTag* approach (268). It introduced quite a large number of new mistakes, however. An example is (3), in which βέλτιστ' *béltist'* (literally 'best') was tagged correctly as a masculine singular vocative by the *MonoTag* approach but as a neuter (plural) vocative by the *MultiTag* approach. Obviously in this case the morphological features are highly dependent on each other: if βέλτιστ' *béltist'* is analyzed as a vocative (used in appellative contexts), it is much more likely that it refers to a masculine than a neuter entity. Cases such as this one might explain why the statistically 'naïve' approach of predicting each feature individually, assuming independence between these features, may return worse results than predicting one tag containing all morphological information.

(3) μὴ δὴ πράγματ', ὦ **βέλτιστ'**, ἔχε· (Men. Dysc. 338)
*mḗ dḗ prágmat', ô **béltist'**, ékhe.*
"Don't worry, **my dear friend**."

It would be expected that the multi-task model would improve in such cases (see Section 3.4), however, as can be judged from Tables 2-3, the multi-task models consistently performed slightly worse than the separately trained models. Taking again the lexicon-based approach without any constraints on the tag outcomes as an example, while the multi-class model corrected 1163 of the mistakes of the separately trained model, it also introduced 1561 new mistakes. It is difficult to explain why this is the case: the general qualitative characteristics of the errors of the multi-class models were similar to those of the separately trained models (see 4.2), but simply quantitatively more numerous.

Finally, the effect of adding constraints to the possible tag outcomes is rather mixed. If the possible tags are restricted to those occurring in the training data, this has a somewhat visible positive effect for the *MultiTag* model when no lexicon is employed (about an 8% error reduction) and a tiny positive effect with a lexicon as well (about a 0.5% error reduction) – note that these constraints only apply for forms that do not occur in the lexicon (since the lexicon already acts as a constraint for the other forms), which are only 3% of all errors of this model (215/6220), so a large error reduction is not expected. For the multi-task model, the differences are barely visible. Focusing on the *MultiTag* approach with a lexicon, constraining the tag outcomes to the ones occurring in the training data corrected 29 mistakes while not introducing a single new mistake. Most of these 29 mistakes were impossible feature combinations: for example, in (4) ἐξόπιστο *eksópisto* 'from behind' was predicted as an adverb with the aorist tense, presumably because the tagger was conflicted between an adverbial and a verbal analysis (since -το *-to* is a common verbal ending).

(4) εἰ σπόδρ' ἐπιτυμεῖς τὴ γέροντο πυγίσο, τὴ σανίδο τρήσας **ἐξόπιστο** πρώκτισον. (Aristoph. Thesm. 1123-4)
*ei spódr' epitumeîs tḗ géronto pugíso, tḗ sanído trḗsas **eksópisto** prṓktison.*
"If you desperately want, have anal sex with the old man, make a hole in the board and penetrate him **from behind**."

Restricting the possible tag combinations to the ones occurring in the training data has an obvious disadvantage: if the feature combination does not occur in the training data, it cannot be predicted. For Greek this occurs very rarely due to the size of the training data, but there are still 18 tokens in the test where this is the case (typically containing very rare features: 13/18 cases have dual number, which died out in an early stage in Greek). As argued in Section 3.4, adding an external list of possible tag combinations might help in these cases. Unfortunately, as can be judged from the numbers in Tables 2-3, in all cases this has a very small net negative effect instead. Again focusing on the *MultiTag* approach with a lexicon as an example, in all the 18 cases mentioned above a wrong tag was still predicted, while there were 4 new mistakes. Apparently the possible tags list was a little too permissive, introducing feature combinations that we would not expect to occur in the corpus and which were then erroneously applied in some cases. For example, one form (ἆπις *âpis*) was analyzed as a nominative masculine singular personal pronoun, which was present in the possible tags list but we would not expect to actually occur in Greek texts.[5]

4.1.2 Latin

Tables 4-6 show the results for the three training approaches (*MonoTag*, *MultiTag*, *MultiTag-MultiTask*) for Latin.

In contrast to Greek, adding a morphological lexicon does not seem to have a positive effect – in some cases even a slightly negative one, although the difference in absolute numbers is minimal. Taking the *MultiTag* model with the possible tags constrained by the training data as an example, even though the lexicon corrected 84 mistakes, it unfortunately also introduced 102 new ones. Many of these new mistakes involved proper nouns (36 out of 102), where the vocabulary of LEMLAT seemed to be incomplete. For example, the proper noun *Furio* (here in the dative case) is included in the lexicon as an adjective, or a verb form. Note that these are valid options, but the proper noun analysis should have been included as well.

In comparison with the Ancient Greek tagger, the multi-task model again falls just short of the simpler *MultiTag* approach. For Latin, the model corrects 202 mistakes, while it introduces 212 new mistakes. Again, it is difficult to explain why, since as for Greek, no general categories can be found in the newly introduced errors.

For the addition of constraints, we observe that constraining the output to combinations that occur in the training data has a positive effect on the *MultiTag* model, while the effect is much smaller for the *MultiTag-MultiTask* model. When we take the lexicon into account as well, the constraint options yield no differences at all.

As for Greek, the use of an external list of possible tags had a net negative effect on the result. More precisely, of the 12 tokens in the test data that had a tag that did not occur in the training data, only 1 received the correct tag (*primis*, an ablative masculine plural adjective without the degree feature). Meanwhile, the list introduced 13 new errors. Again, these were mainly cases where the list of possible tags was too permissive: for example, for the form *mi* (a dative of *ego*, *I*) the tagger predicted that it was in the vocative case, which would not be possible for a first person personal pronoun.

Lexicon	Accuracy
No	0.936 (13191)
Yes	0.933 (13151)

Table 4: Latin tagger results (*MonoTag*), with accuracy and N correct predictions.

Lexicon	Tag constraints	Accuracy
No	None	0.932 (13131)
	Training data	0.937 (13210)
	Tag list	0.937 (13198)
Yes	None	0.936 (13192)
	Training data	0.936 (13192)
	Tag list	0.936 (13192)

Table 5: Latin tagger results (*MultiTag*), with accuracy and N correct predictions.

Lexicon	Tag constraints	Accuracy
No	None	0.936 (13193)
	Training data	0.937 (13203)
	Tag list	0.937 (13200)
Yes	None	0.934 (13168)
	Training data	0.934 (13168)
	Tag list	0.934 (13168)

Table 6: Latin tagger results (*MultiTag-MultiTask*), with accuracy and N correct predictions.

4.2 Error analysis

In this section, we will analyze the remaining errors of two high-performing models, viz. the model with split tags, lexicon and morphological tags for both languages. We will do this by analyzing a random sample of 100 errors for both languages. In appendix, we also provide plots analyzing more general qualitative characteristics of the tagging errors, viz. the accuracy by morphological feature (appendix A) and by text type (appendix B).

Error	Proportion
Mistake gold data	41%
Data consistency	15%
Syntactic structure	11%
Mistake lexicon	10%
Various	24%

Table 7: Error analysis for Greek.

[5] Note that first and second person personal pronouns were never gendered in our corpus, since Greek makes no morphological gender distinctions. The only personal pronouns that can be gendered are reflexive third person personal pronouns, but these never occur in the nominative case.

4.2.1 Greek

A quantitative description of the mistakes we found is presented in Table 7. Strikingly, a very large part (41%) of them were actually cases where the gold data was incorrectly annotated and the tagger was correct, suggesting that the actual accuracy of the tagger is even higher than 97% (although it could also be the case that some analyses labeled as 'correct' were in fact wrongly annotated in the gold data as well). An additional 15% of errors were issues of data consistency, typically related to part-of-speech, where the boundaries between part-of-speech can be fluid and there are no consistent choices in the training/test data, as was already discussed above.

Moving to the actual errors, 11% of cases can be explained because the transformer model understood the syntactic structure of the sentence incorrectly. For example, in (5), βασιλήιον *basilēion* was analyzed as a noun by the tagger. The noun βασιλήιον *basilēion*, meaning 'palace', certainly exists, but in this case it is clearly an adjective 'royal' modifying the noun τεῖχός *teîkhós* 'fortress' (if it was a noun, it would not fit in the sentence context, given that the subject slot of ἐδέδμητο *edédmēto* 'it was built' is already taken up by τεῖχός *teîkhós*).

(5) ἐν τῷ τεῖχός τε ἐδέδμητο **βασιλήιον** τοῦτο τὸ δὴ Δορίσκος κέκληται... (Hdt. 7.59.1)
en tôi teîkhós te edédmēto ***basilēion*** *toûto tó dḗ Dorískos kéklētai...*
"at which that **royal** fortress was built which was called Doriscus..."

10% of errors were simply related to mistakes in the tagger lexicon: even though it had a net positive effect, fixing these mistakes could therefore further improve the results. The remaining 24% of errors were rather diverse. Interestingly, in 6% of cases the correct morphological analysis could only be made by logical inferences. For example, in (6) δακρύων *dakrúōn* was analyzed as a noun instead of the participle of δακρύω *dakrúō* 'to cry', which it could theoretically be: in that case θάλασσαν δακρύων *thálassan dakrúōn* would mean 'sea of tears'. While we could plausibly expect such an expression in e.g. a poetic context, it is much more logical that δακρύων *dakrúōn* means 'crying' in this context rather than that the farmer would curse his own massive torrent of tears. Obviously such logical inferences are easy to make for humans, but pose a challenge for a tagger.

(6) γεωργός τις ἰδὼν ναῦν ἐν θαλάσσηι κυμαινομένην καὶ βυθῶι πεμπομένην, κατηρᾶτο τὴν θάλασσαν **δακρύων**. (Aes. Fab.)
geōrgós tis idṓn naûn en thalássēi kumainoménēn kaí buthôi pempoménēn, katērato tḗn thálassan ***dakrúōn.***
"A farmer, seeing a ship being tossed on the waves and being sent into the deep sea, cursed the sea **while crying**."

Some other errors include cases related to the coreference chain (5, e.g. the gender of a pronoun was incorrectly determined, because the entity that the pronoun refers to occurs in another sentence), to the diversity of the Greek corpus (3, e.g. dialectal forms that were difficult to determine correctly) and general problems related to data sparsity (2), to damage/corruption to the actual text (2), 1 case clearly related to the issue that the morphological features were independently predicted (see 4.1), 1 case of true ambiguity (i.e. both the gold and the predicted tag can be argued to be correct, depending how the sentence is interpreted) and finally 3 cases where we did not find any explanation for.

Error	Proportion
Data consistency	45%
Mistake gold data	24%
Syntactic structure	16%
Various	15%

Table 8: Error analysis for Latin.

4.2.2 Latin

Our results (see Table 8) largely reflect similar problems to the ones for Greek. While the data contained less wrongly annotated forms than the Greek data (24%), an even larger proportion of the mistakes related to annotation conventions (45%). In this latter category, a very large proportion of problems (28/45) involved double- (23) and triple- (5, meaning no gender at all in the PROIEL annotation) gendered forms. In the error analysis, we considered a form to be triple-gendered if it does have a case and a number, but no gender. An example is (7), in which *multis* (which theoretically can be all three genders) agrees with *regionibus.* Since the PROIEL treebank is not very consistent in which cases forms are considered double/triple-gendered, it is not surprising that the tagger analyzed it as feminine (as *regionibus* is), even though it was triple-gendered in the gold data.

(7) et **multis** regionibus Samaritanorum evangelizabant (Acts 8:25) "and they preached the gospel to **many** villages of the Samaritans"

As for Greek, some errors were related to the transformer model misinterpreting the syntactic structure of the sentence (16%), while mistakes caused by errors in the lexicon are more rare (only 2% – specifically cases where the lexicon was incomplete, such as *Furio* as described in 4.1.2). As for the other problems (13%), they are rather analogous to the problems found for Greek, so we will not discuss them here.

5 Conclusions

The aim of this paper was to investigate whether transformer models need special adaptations to morphologically tag highly inflectional languages with data sparsity, using Ancient Greek and Latin as a test case. We show that, although the most simple approach – i.e. finetuning a transformer model on tags containing all morphological information – already performs decently, special adaptations tailored to the typological nature of these languages can still further improve tagging accuracy.

Firstly, the use of a morphological lexicon had a clear positive effect on Greek tagging accuracy. On Latin, conversely, the effect was negative in most cases. This can largely be explained by the quality of the respective lexica: the Latin lexicon contained a relatively large number of cases (primarily proper nouns) where not all possible analyses for a given token were recorded in the lexicon, and therefore introduced new tagging errors. Nevertheless, the proportion of errors that the Latin lexicon corrected (84/881, or about 10%) was still relatively modest. There are multiple explanations why a morphological lexicon might be less necessary than for Greek: this might be because Greek could be morphologically more complex, or because the pretrained transformer for Latin was trained on much more data than for Greek, or because the Latin data was simply more homogeneous.

Training separate models for each individual morphological feature had a positive, although very modest effect for both languages. Surprisingly, however, multi-task learning did not further improve the results, but had a (slight) detrimental effect instead. We were not able to explain why this was the case. In the future, however, we plan to experiment with other methods to combine the outputs of the individual feature models, as described in Tkachenko and Sirts (2018).

As for constraining the tag outcomes to the ones occurring in the training data, this had a very slight positive effect for Greek and no effect for Latin. Further adding a linguistically-based list of possible tags did have a slight negative effect for both languages, however. This was caused by a too permissive list of combinatory possibilities, so that feature combinations were predicted that could not co-occur. This is therefore a consequence of the quality of the concrete external list we used, and since it is only through such a list that feature combinations can be predicted that do not occur in the training data, we still generally recommend using this technique.

An error analysis revealed where there was room for further improvement. For both languages, data errors and consistency issues made up a very large proportion of errors. Most improvement can therefore not be made through more sophisticated machine learning algorithms, but by simply improving the quality of the data. Some other errors (e.g. related to logical inferencing or co-references across sentences) would also be hard to solve by the current generation of NLP techniques. A more promising category of errors were related to co-dependence of morphological and syntactic analysis. In this case, joint syntactic parsing and tagging may offer a possible solution.

Finally, we should note that, while this paper focused on Greek and Latin, the techniques we explore are not solely tied to these historical languages, given that there are many other inflectional languages with sparse datasets. We therefore hope that the solutions offered here could also inspire researchers working on similar languages.

For the sake of reproducibility and to allow other researchers to make use of the resources this study produced, all the code and datasets we used can be found on GitHub (see 'Supplementary Material').

6 Limitations

There are some limitations inherent to the experiments carried out in this paper. Firstly, to avoid having to compare too many models, we chose one specific method to employ transformer models for tagging, viz. finetuning the transformer network. As mentioned in Section 2, various alternative methods exist, and it would be interesting to compare which of them works best for our data. Similarly, for each language model we chose one pretrained transformer model, instead of comparing several of them. This, again, was in order to avoid having to run too many experiments, as well as the fact that the available transformer models for Greek and Latin differ on too many parameters (transformer architecture, data that it was trained on, tokenizer, training method etc.) so that a fair comparison could not be made.

Finally, this study was only limited to transformer-based approaches. While they are highly popular currently, there is no hard evidence that they are the best performing method for Greek and Latin morphological tagging. It would therefore be interesting to systematically investigate in the future whether they are actually the way to move forward or whether better performing approaches can be found.

Acknowledgments

Our work has been funded by grant no. G052021N of FWO/Research Council – Flanders and HBC.2021.0210 of Flanders Innovation and Entrepreneurship. We wish to thank all the annotators of the material we used in this study, as well as the three anonymous reviewers for their constructive comments which have helped to improve the quality of this paper.

References

Giuseppe G. A. Celano, Gregory Crane, and Saeed Majidi. 2016. Part of Speech Tagging for Ancient Greek. *Open Linguistics*, 2(1).

Gregory Crane. 1991. Generating and Parsing Classical Greek. *Literary and Linguistic Computing*, 6(4):243–245.

Helma Dik and Richard Whaling. 2008. Bootstrapping Classical Greek Morphology. In *Digital Humanities 2008*, pages 105–106, Oulu.

Steffen Eger, Tim vor der Brück, and Alexander Mehler. 2015. Lexicon-assisted tagging and lemmatization in Latin: A comparison of six taggers and two lemmatization models. In *Proceedings of the 9th SIGHUM Workshop on Language Technology for Cultural Heritage, Social Sciences, and Humanities*, pages 105-113, Beijing.

Federica Gamba and Daniel Zeman. 2023. Universalising Latin Universal Dependencies: a harmonisation of Latin treebanks in UD. In Loïc Grobol and Francis Tyers, editors, *Proceedings of the Sixth Workshop on Universal Dependencies (UDW, GURT/SyntaxFest 2023)*, pages 7–16, Washington, D.C. Association for Computational Linguistics.

Jan Hajic. 2000. Morphological Tagging: Data vs. Dictionaries. In *1st Meeting of the North American Chapter of the Association for Computational Linguistics*, pages 94-101, Seattle.

Dag Haug and Marius Jøhndal. 2008. Creating a Parallel Treebank of the Old Indo-European Bible Translations. In *Proceedings of the Second Workshop on Language Technology for Cultural Heritage Data (LaTeCH 2008)*, pages 27–34, Marrakech.

Alek Keersmaekers. 2020. Creating a richly annotated corpus of papyrological Greek: The possibilities of natural language processing approaches to a highly inflected historical language. *Digital Scholarship in the Humanities*, 35(1):67–82.

Alek Keersmaekers. 2021. The GLAUx corpus: methodological issues in designing a long-term, diverse, multi-layered corpus of Ancient Greek. In *Proceedings of the 2nd International Workshop on Computational Approaches to Historical Language Change 2021*, pages 39–50, Online. Association for Computational Linguistics.

Taku Kudo and John Richardson. 2018. SentencePiece: A simple and language independent subword tokenizer and detokenizer for Neural Text Processing. In Eduardo Blanco and Wei Lu, editors, *Proceedings of the 2018 Conference on Empirical Methods in Natural Language Processing: System Demonstrations*, pages 66–71, Brussels. Association for Computational Linguistics.

John Lee, Jason Naradowsky, and David A. Smith. 2011. A Discriminative Model for Joint Morphological Disambiguation and Dependency Parsing. In Dekang Lin, Yuji Matsumoto, and Rada Mihalcea, editors, *Proceedings of the 49th Annual Meeting of the Association for Computational Linguistics: Human Language Technologies*, pages 885–894, Portland. Association for Computational Linguistics.

Wouter Mercelis and Alek Keersmaekers. 2022a. An ELECTRA Model for Latin Token Tagging Tasks. In Rachele Sprugnoli and Marco Passarotti, editors, *Proceedings of the Second Workshop on Language Technologies for Historical and Ancient Languages*, pages 189–192, Marseille. European Language Resources Association.

Wouter Mercelis and Alek Keersmaekers. 2022b. electra-grc. https://huggingface.co/mercelisw/electra-grc

Joakim Nivre, Marie-Catherine de Marneffe, Filip Ginter, Jan Hajič, Christopher D. Manning, Sampo Pyysalo, Sebastian Schuster, Francis Tyers, and Daniel Zeman. 2020. Universal Dependencies v2: An Evergrowing Multilingual Treebank Collection. In Nicoletta Calzolari, Frédéric Béchet, Philippe Blache, Khalid Choukri, Christopher Cieri, Thierry Declerck, Sara Goggi, Hitoshi Isahara, Bente Maegaard, Joseph Mariani, Hélène Mazo, Asuncion Moreno, Jan Odijk, and Stelios Piperidis, editors, *Proceedings of the Twelfth Language Resources and Evaluation Conference*, pages 4034–4043, Marseille. European Language Resources Association.

Marco Passarotti, Marco Budassi, Eleonora Litta, and Paolo Ruffolo. 2017. The Lemlat 3.0 Package for Morphological Analysis of Latin. In *Proceedings of the NoDaLiDa 2017 Workshop on Processing Historical Language*, pages 24–31, Gothenburg. Linköping University Electronic Press.

Céline Poudat and Dominique Longrée. 2009. Variations langagières et annotation morphosyntaxique du latin classique [Linguistic variations and morphosyntactic annotation of Latin classical texts]. In Joseph Denooz and Serge Rosmorduc, editors, *Traitement Automatique des Langues, Volume 50, Numéro 2 : Langues anciennes [Ancient Languages]*, pages 129–148, France. ATALA (Association pour le Traitement Automatique des Langues).

Frederick Riemenschneider and Anette Frank. 2023. Exploring Large Language Models for Classical Philology. In Anna Rogers, Jordan Boyd-Graber, and Naoaki Okazaki, editors, *Proceedings of the 61st Annual Meeting of the Association for Computational Linguistics (Volume 1: Long Papers)*, pages 15181–15199, Toronto. Association for Computational Linguistics.

Helmut Schmid and Florian Laws. 2008. Estimation of Conditional Probabilities With Decision Trees and an Application to Fine-Grained POS Tagging. In Donia Scott and Hans Uszkoreit, editors, *Proceedings of the 22nd International Conference on Computational Linguistics (Coling 2008)*, pages 777–784, Manchester. Coling 2008 Organizing Committee.

Pranaydeep Singh, Gorik Rutten, and Els Lefever. 2021. A Pilot Study for BERT Language Modelling and Morphological Analysis for Ancient and Medieval Greek. In *The 5th Joint SIGHUM Workshop on Computational Linguistics for Cultural Heritage, Social Sciences, Humanities and Literature, co-located with EMNLP 2021*, pages 128–137, Online. Association for Computational Linguistics.

Thea Sommerschield, Yannis Assael, John Pavlopoulos, Vanessa Stefanak, Andrew Senior, Chris Dyer, John Bodel, Jonathan Prag, Ion Androutsopoulos, and Nando de Freitas. 2023. Machine Learning for Ancient Languages: A Survey. *Computational Linguistics*, 49(3):703–747.

Milan Straka and Jana Straková. 2020. UDPipe at EvaLatin 2020: Contextualized Embeddings and Treebank Embeddings. In Rachele Sprugnoli and Marco Passarotti, editors, *Proceedings of LT4HALA 2020 - 1st Workshop on Language Technologies for Historical and Ancient Languages*, pages 124–129, Marseille. European Language Resources Association.

Elina Stüssi and Phillip Ströbel. 2024. Part-of-Speech Tagging of 16th-Century Latin with GPT. In Yuri Bizzoni, Stefania Degaetano-Ortlieb, Anna Kazantseva, and Stan Szpakowicz, editors, *Proceedings of the 8th Joint SIGHUM Workshop on Computational Linguistics for Cultural Heritage, Social Sciences, Humanities and Literature (LaTeCH-CLfL 2024)*, pages 196–206, St. Julians, Malta. Association for Computational Linguistics.

Colin Swaelens, Ilse De Vos, and Els Lefever. 2023. Evaluating Existing Lemmatisers on Unedited Byzantine Greek Poetry. In Adam Anderson, Shai Gordin, Bin Li, Yudong Liu, and Marco C. Passarotti, editors, *Proceedings of the Ancient Language Processing Workshop*, pages 111–116, Varna. INCOMA Ltd., Shoumen, Bulgaria.

Alexander Tkachenko and Kairit Sirts. 2018. Modeling Composite Labels for Neural Morphological Tagging. In Anna Korhonen and Ivan Titov, editors, *Proceedings of the 22nd Conference on Computational Natural Language Learning*, pages 368–379, Brussels. Association for Computational Linguistics.

Reut Tsarfaty, Djamé Seddah, Yoav Goldberg, Sandra Kübler, Marie Candito, Jennifer Foster, Yannick Versley, Ines Rehbein, and Lamia Tounsi. 2010. Statistical parsing of morphologically rich languages (SPMRL): what, how and whither. In *Proceedings of the First Workshop on Statistical Parsing of Morphologically Rich Languages*, pages 1–12, Los Angeles. Association for Computational Linguistics.

Krzysztof Wróbel and Krzysztof Nowak. 2022. Transformer-based Part-of-Speech Tagging and Lemmatization for Latin. In Rachele Sprugnoli and Marco Passarotti, editors, *Proceedings of the Second Workshop on Language Technologies for Historical and Ancient Languages*, pages 193–197, Marseille. European Language Resources Association.

A Tagging accuracy by morphological feature

Feature	Accuracy
Person	0.999 (218532)
Voice	0.999 (218499)
Mood	0.998 (218443)
Tense	0.997 (218113)
Number	0.996 (217953)
Degree	0.995 (217745)
XPOS	0.993 (217279)
Case	0.991 (216736)
Gender	0.989 (216292)

Table 7: Tagging accuracy by morphological feature (Greek) (N=218,787)

Feature	Accuracy
Reflex	1.000 (14091)
Polarity	1.000 (14088)
Poss	1.000 (14085)
Mood	0.998 (14064)
Person	0.997 (14055)
Aspect	0.997 (14053)
VerbForm	0.997 (14049)
Voice	0.997 (14046)
Tense	0.995 (14023)
PronType	0.995 (14015)
Degree	0.993 (13991)
Number	0.992 (13980)
Case	0.989 (13934)
UPOS	0.983 (13854)
Gender	0.972 (13699)

Table 8: Tagging accuracy by morphological feature (Latin) (N=14,091)

B Tagging accuracy by text type

Text type	Accuracy
Mythography	0.994 (167/168)
Religious History	0.986 (17172/17419)
Religious Epistle	0.985 (7224/7333)
Religious Prophecy	0.983 (1686/1715)
Paradoxography	0.982 (639/651)
Religious Narrative	0.981 (254/259)
Dialogue	0.979 (1050/1072)
Biology	0.979 (94/96)
Alchemy	0.978 (391/400)
Biography	0.976 (8958/9181)
Oratory	0.975 (14905/15289)
Epistolography	0.975 (1234/1266)
Narrative	0.974 (12255/12584)
Philosophic Dialogue	0.973 (3833/3938)
Medicine	0.973 (803/825)
Epic poetry	0.973 (36641/37657)
History	0.973 (60353/62027)
Rhetoric	0.970 (2835/2924)
Geography	0.968 (1341/1385)
Polyhistory	0.966 (6460/6686)
Philosophy	0.965 (8847/9166)
Military	0.963 (2327/2417)
Tragedy	0.957 (15679/16384)
Engineering	0.951 (1402/1474)
Scientific Poetry	0.945 (52/55)
Mathematics	0.945 (240/254)
Comedy	0.944 (4085/4327)
Language	0.913 (506/554)
Lyric poetry	0.905 (1159/1281)

Table 9: Tagging accuracy by text type (Greek)

Text	Accuracy
Jerome's Vulgate	0.952 (6588/6922)
Commentarii belli Gallici	0.941 (1989/2114)
Epistulae ad Atticum	0.921 (2871/3116)
De officiis	0.921 (820/890)
Opus agriculturae	0.898 (942/1049)

Table 10: Tagging accuracy by text type (Latin)

C Supplementary Material

All the datasets used in this study can be found on https://github.com/alekkeersmaekers/transformer-tagging. The code (including the tagger settings for the experiments described here) can be found on https://github.com/alekkeersmaekers/glaux-nlp.

A deep learning pipeline for the palaeographical dating of ancient Greek papyrus fragments

Graham West[3], Matthew I. Swindall[1], James H. Brusuelas[2], Francesca Maltomini[5], Marius Gerhardt[4], Marzia D'Angelo[6], John F. Wallin[1]

[1]Middle Tennessee State University, [2]University of Kentucky, [3]Meharry Medical College,
[4]Ägyptisches Museum und Papyrussammlung, Staatliche Museen zu Berlin,
[5]Università Degli Studi Firenze, [6]Università Degli Studi Di Napoli Federico II,

Correspondence: graham.west@mmc.edu

Abstract

In this paper we present a deep learning pipeline for automatically dating ancient Greek papyrus fragments based solely on fragment images. The overall pipeline consists of several stages, including handwritten text recognition (HTR) to detect and classify characters, filtering and grouping of detected characters, 24 character-level date prediction models, and a fragment-level date prediction model that utilizes the per-character predictions. A new dataset (containing approximately 7,000 fragment images and 778,000 character images) was created by scraping papyrus databases, extracting fragment images with known dates, and running them through our HTR models to obtain labeled character images. Transfer learning was then used to fine-tune separate ResNets to predict dates for individual characters which are then used, in aggregate, to train the fragment-level date prediction model. Experiments show that even though the average accuracies of character-level dating models is low, between 35%-45%, the fragment-level model can achieve up to 79% accuracy in predicting a broad, two-century date range for fragments with many characters. We then discuss the limitations of this approach and outline future work to improve temporal resolution and further testing on additional papyri. This image-based deep learning approach has great potential to assist scholars in the palaeographical analysis and dating of ancient Greek manuscripts.

1 Introduction

With the meteoric rise in deep learning technologies, many fields are rapidly adopting these tools and incorporating them into their workflow. Palaeography, the study of the handwriting in ancient and medieval manuscripts, is one such discipline that has benefited from these methods. Projects such as READ (https://eadh.org/projects/read) and DigiPal (https://eadh.org/projects/digipal), for example, have focused on applying these methods to issues of writer identification, layout analysis, and frameworks for digital palaeographical content, especially via handwritten text recognition (HTR). One important project of note is Ithaca (Assael et al., 2022) which, among other uses, can attribute a date range to an inscription. Our approach differs in that while Ithaca takes digital transcriptions as input, our pipeline relies solely on images. In this paper, we present our latest contribution to this research effort, consisting of a dataset and deep learning pipeline for dating ancient Greek papyrus fragments. This pipeline takes as input an image of an ancient Greek papyrus fragment and outputs a predicted date range. We describe the training methodologies used to create the various models constituting the pipeline as well as a number of performance metrics.

1.1 Palaeography and the Dating of Greek Papyri

The method for dating Greek papyri begins with manuscripts that can be accurately dated. This mostly pertains to documentary texts (letters, petitions, taxes, leases, etc.) that preserve their date of composition. Documentary papyri lacking a date can, of course, still be dated accurately, if they mention historical events or figures that generally locate them within a given century. Palaeographic analysis of these papyri, i.e. the study of the handwriting and the features of the characters preserved, is important for those papyri that are not dated, especially the immense number of literary and sub-literary papyri that never contain the date of their production. Those papyri must be assigned a date based on a meticulous comparison between the Greek characters they preserve and those in reliably dated papyrus manuscripts. Palaeographical handbooks containing human observations, discernible patterns, and even conjectured styles have thus been published and they con-

Proceedings of the 1st Workshop on Machine Learning for Ancient Languages (ML4AL 2024), pages 177–185
August 15, 2024 ©2024 Association for Computational Linguistics

stitute the sources by which papyrologists assign dates to papyri (Roberts, 1955; Turner, 1987; Cavallo and Maehler, 2008).

In respect to the actual number of papyri preserved, however, these handbooks only contain a small number of manuscripts for comparison. It is not uncommon that an assigned date is later reevaluated and changed as more papyri are viewed and compared. The ability of deep learning methods to assist papyrologists in dating papyri by analyzing thousands of manuscript images holds great potential. To do so, this requires not only training models for the task at hand, but also creating a palaeography dataset to facilitate accurate dating. Previous work on the Ancient Lives Project provides a foundation for reaching these goals.

1.2 Ancient Lives & AL-ALL

Between 2011 and 2018, the Ancient Lives Project, a Zooniverse.org collaboration, enlisted the aid of citizen scientists in annotating the images of thousands of highly degraded, ancient Greek manuscripts (Williams et al., 2014). The project resulted in millions of annotations which were key to the creation of the first large-scale machine learning dataset for digital papyrology, AL-ALL (Swindall et al., 2021). This dataset consists of over 400,000 images of handwritten Greek characters on papyrus and has been successfully used to create various deep learning models. This dataset also includes images from fragments that are currently under papyrological study and have not been published. For a releasable dataset, a smaller, updated version of the published material, AL-PUBv2, has been made available at `https://www.kaggle.com/datasets/miswindall/al-pub-v2`.

1.3 HTR Models

The development of our dataset and pipeline for palaeographical dating rests on our two core HTR models, each of which perform a key HTR task: character detection and character classification.

1.3.1 Character Detection with YOLO

The character detection model is essentially an object detection model trained to locate Greek characters in images of papyri. Similar existing work refers to this process as *'character spotting'* (Majid and Smith, 2022; Mondal et al., 2022). To train this model, YOLOv5s (Ultralytics, 2023) was fine-tuned using 212 images of papyrus fragments from the Oxyhrynchus papyri (Bowman et al., 2007)

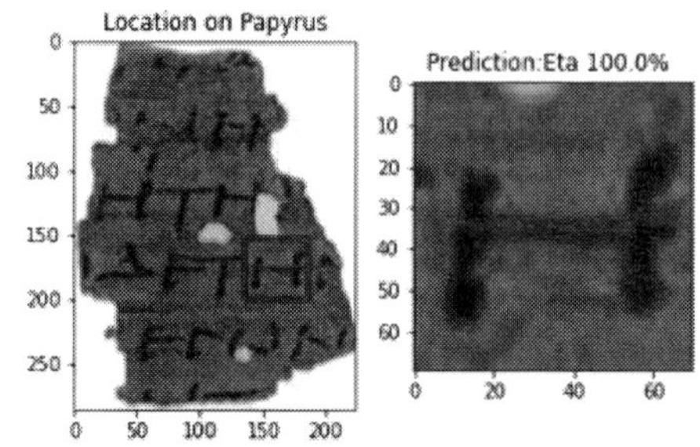

Figure 1: Example of character detection and classification using the HTR models. The YOLO model produces bounding boxes for each detected character. The bounded region is then cropped, resized, and given to the ResNet for classification.

containing 4097 character locations annotated during the Ancient Lives Project. YOLO is typically trained for multiple classes, but this model was fine-tuned to search for a single class: *Greek characters*. The model achieved precision and recall of 0.88 and 0.84, respectively, on the validation data, as well as validation box loss below 0.04. Further metrics are detailed in Figure 2.

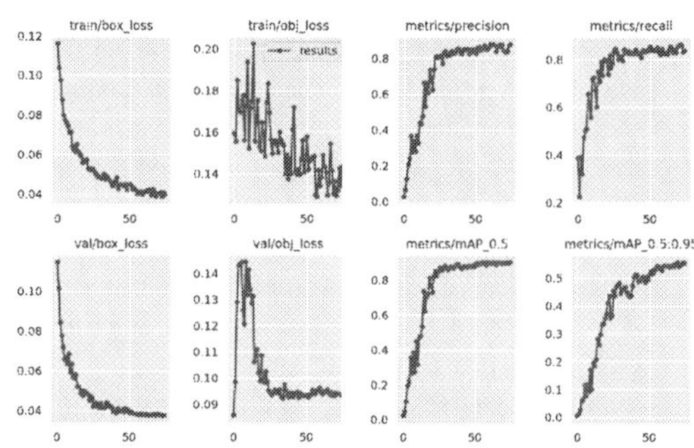

Figure 2: Training and validation metrics for the YOLO-based character detection model show that this model performs well on the task of locating Greek characters in images of damaged papryi.

1.3.2 Character Classification with ResNet

Our character classification model is a ResNet trained on the recently updated AL-ALLv2 dataset. The latest version of the dataset consists of 419,445 character images of all 24 characters in the ancient Greek alphabet, including the Lunate Sigma (C, ς) which typically replaces the more familiar Sigma (Σ, σ) in ancient papyri. This model achieved a training accuracy of 96.69% and a validation accuracy of 94.11%. Previous versions of this model

	4th-3rd BCE	2nd-1st BCE	1st-2nd CE	3rd-4th CE	5th-6th CE	Total
Fragments	299	729	3418	2002	570	7018

Table 1: The number of fragments from each century in the palaeography dataset.

	4th-3rd BCE	2nd-1st BCE	1st-2nd CE	3rd-4th CE	5th-6th CE	Total
α	6736	7582	36233	16548	4036	71135
β	302	219	1270	955	254	3000
γ	2914	2216	7765	3910	716	17521
ϵ	6508	5977	14132	7025	1795	35437
δ	903	1261	6679	2221	343	11407
ζ	354	288	2431	1158	284	4515
η	1741	3766	12873	7769	2105	28254
θ	299	729	3418	2002	570	7018
ι	4825	6951	24308	11785	4482	52351
κ	2886	2747	7343	5024	1828	19828
λ	971	2099	9766	3394	998	17228
μ	1362	2826	17883	7520	2573	32164
ν	4851	12339	28077	11578	3500	60345
ξ	62	93	653	410	106	1324
o	7011	13017	53709	24570	10146	108453
π	2293	3010	14785	7122	2043	29253
ρ	3389	4039	16570	9895	3414	37307
σ	4856	7732	28246	11490	4397	56721
τ	11823	14300	44502	23982	4910	99517
υ	2224	4727	12985	7165	1698	28799
ϕ	505	530	2652	1536	568	5791
χ	997	1944	6151	3557	1239	13888
ψ	135	108	499	265	53	1060
ω	1046	3176	20221	8912	2932	36287
Total	68993	101676	373151	179793	54990	778603

Table 2: The number of characters from each century in the palaeography dataset.

were released as a supplement to (Swindall et al., 2022), including models trained on a synthetically augmented version of AL-ALL in an effort to reduce sampling bias.

2 A Dataset for Palaeographical Dating

The development of the palaeographical dating pipeline necessitated the construction of a dataset containing images of papyrus fragments, their constituent characters, and their dates of composition. Three large papyrus databases were scraped for their fragment images and metadata (including dates of composition). The databases chosen were the Berlin Papyrus Database, Papiri della Società Italiana (PSI), and the Duke Papyrus Archive. For the first iteration of this dataset, we focused only on documentary papyri that preserve an exact date or are reliably dated within a range of a century or two. Since the format of the dates varied, the dates were processed and converted to a common format containing only the century or range of two centuries of composition. To reduce the difficulty of the dating task, we decreased the temporal resolution of the date classes from the one-century level to the two-century level: 4th-3rd BCE, 2nd-1st BCE, 1st-2nd CE, 3rd-4th CE, and 5th-6th CE (future work will consist of increasing the temporal resolution). The fragment images were then passed through our HTR models, thus obtaining cropped and classified images of each fragment's constituent characters. These character images are assigned the same date classes as the fragment on which they were written.

The character and fragment counts for each time-period in the dataset are detailed in Tables 1 and 2. As can be seen, we have examples of all 24 Greek characters from the 4th BCE to the 6th CE. There is also significant imbalance in both the characters and the dates. Concerning the characters, there are only 1,060 psis (Ψ, ψ) but 108,453 omicrons (O, o). Fortunately, transfer learning permits one to use a smaller dataset while still getting useful results since the majority of the layers have already been trained. Concerning the dates, 1st-2nd CE contains the largest number of characters and fragments (373,151 and 3,418, respectively) while 4th-3rd BCE contains the least (68,993 and 299, respectively).

It should be noted that this dataset is actually a subset of all that was scraped from the papyrus archives and run through the HTR pipeline. Many of the characters in the full dataset are of poor quality and were filtered out to create the final dataset. Filtering was done based on two factors: 1) image saturation entropy and 2) ResNet prediction entropy. The first is done in order to eliminate YOLO false positives which often consist of images with few ink pixels. Consequently, false positives of this type tend to have a low entropy in the distribution of their pixel saturation and can be reliably (though, not completely) eliminated by applying a simple threshold. The second filter removes images which

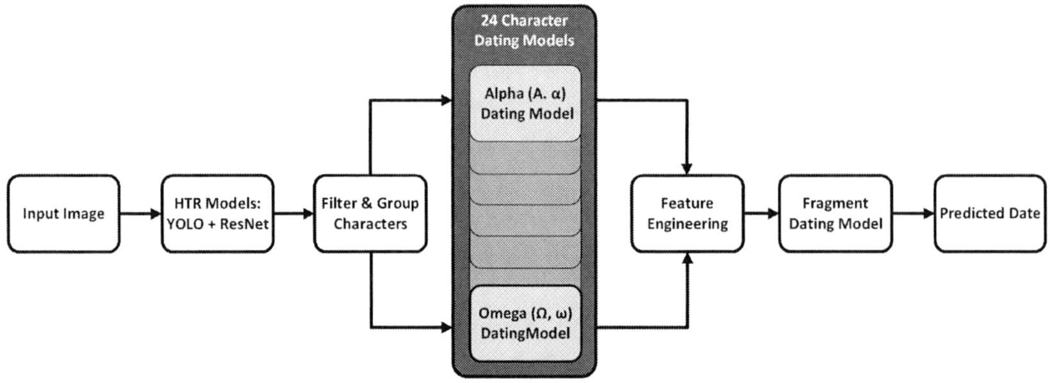

Figure 3: The palaeography pipeline performs HTR on the fragment image, obtaining images of individual characters. Poor character images (YOLO false positives, uncertain classifications, etc.) are filtered out. Remaining characters are grouped according to their character and sent to individual ResNet character dating models. These predicted character dates are then used as input to a final Gaussian Process fragment dating model.

were unreliably classified by the ResNet. Again, these can be fairly reliably eliminated by applying a threshold to the entropy of the ResNet's predicted class probabilities.

3 A Pipeline for Palaeographical Dating

Given the goal of producing a deep learning pipeline which can take an image of an ancient Greek papyrus fragment as input and output a predicted date of composition, the primary task is to determine the proper architecture for such a pipeline. Figure 3 depicts the chosen architecture, which consists of five core stages: HTR, filtering/grouping of characters, character dating, feature engineering, and fragment dating.

3.1 HTR, filtering, and grouping

The first step of the dating pipeline takes the input image and passes it through the HTR models, thus obtaining cropped and classified images of the fragment's constituent characters. The filtering steps described above are then applied to these character images to remove any unreliable samples. The characters are then grouped based on their character class (alpha, beta, etc.) before being sent to the next step of the pipeline.

3.2 Character dating models

Next, each group of characters is sent to another round of ResNet models which predict individual characters' date of composition. These models were developed via performing transfer learning on the ResNet discussed earlier. Naturally, the last two dense layers were retrained and the output layer was altered to have five output neurons (one per date class) instead of 24 (one per character).

While the transfer learning aspect was trivial, the data wrangling required to properly train these models was more complicated. Splitting the dataset into training and validation sets was done at the fragment level so that no fragment had constituent characters present in both sets of each individual ResNet model. As discussed above, there is a significant class imbalance with respect to the time periods (with 1st - 2nd CE having the overwhelming majority of samples). Thus, a great deal of balancing was performed. This was done by sampling the less frequent classes with replacement such that all classes had the same number of samples as the most frequent class. This was done separately for the training and validation sets. Additionally, data augmentation was performed using Keras's ImageDataGenerator so that there would not be identical copies of the images. The ranges for zoom, width shift, and height shift were all set to 0.1. No rotation was applied since the slant of characters is useful for determining their date of composition. This augmentation helps to increase the variability for less frequently occurring centuries which have many duplicated images due to sampling with replacement.

A custom loss function inspired by the Kolmogorov-Smirnov test was utilized since it is better suited for the ordinal nature of date labels than categorical cross entropy. Equation 1 illus-

	4th-3rd BCE	2nd-1st BCE	1st-2nd CE	3rd-4th CE	5th-6th CE
α	0	1	10	4	0
β	0	3	2	0	1

Table 3: An example of (one-hot encoded) raw features created from the output of the character dating models.

trates this loss function.

$$\text{loss} = \sum_{i=0}^{N-5} (t_i^c - p_i^c)^2 \quad (1)$$

Here, $N = 5$ is the number of classes and t_i^c, p_i^c are the true and predicted cumulative class probabilities, respectively. By comparing the cumulative probabilities, we can essentially form a metric which allows the ResNet's optimizer to take advantage of the fact that (given a true date of 5th-6th CE) a predicted date of 4th-3rd BCE is worse than 1st-2nd CE.

3.3 Feature engineering and fragment dating model

Once each character has received a predicted date, we then utilize these outputs to predict the date of the fragment as a whole. This is done via a simple dense neural network which outputs identical date classes as the ResNet in the previous step of the pipeline. Although the ordinal loss function described above worked well for the character models, it did not work well for the fragment model. Thus, categorical cross entropy was used.

For the fragment dating model's input, some clever feature engineering was done on the character dating model predictions. In what follows, all indices are assumed to start at zero. Let $C_k \in \{0, 1, 2, \cdots, 23\}$ (where k ranges over all the characters in a particular fragment) be the predicted character class. Also, let, p_{kj} (where $j = 0, \cdots, 4$ ranges over the number of date classes) be the predicted probability that character k belongs in date class j. Now, we construct the raw features X':

$$X'_{ij} = \sum_{k \ni (C_k = i)} p_{kj} \quad (2)$$

This sum adds the total probability for all α's, β's, etc. into separate columns. Table 3 shows a simplified example where, for the sake of simplicity, it is assumed that all of the probabilities are effectively one-hot encoded. These raw features are then processed with two more steps, obtaining the final features X:

$$X_{ij} = \frac{1 + X'_{ij}}{5 + \sum_j X'_{ij}} \quad (3)$$

First, Laplace's rule of succession is applied, adding a 1 to all entries of X' (we will explain the reason for this step below). Next, we normalize all of the rows (date-wise) by dividing by their sum. The normalization step ensures that all of the different fragments' feature values will be within the same range of values (between 0 and 1). The rule of succession is applied to preserve a kind of confidence that would otherwise be lost in the normalization step. Consider two fragments whose α rows are [0,0,1,0,0] and [0,0,5,0,0], respectively. Without application of the rule of succession, both columns would be normalized to [0,0,1,0,0]. Yet this is misleading since the second fragment has more α's predicted to be from 1st-2nd CE. We should want this increased confidence to be reflected in the features. Thus, by applying the rule of succession, we obtain [1,1,2,1,1] and [1,1,6,1,1] for the pre-normalization step and [0.166,0.166,0.333,0.166,0.166] and [0.1,0.1,0.6,0.1,0.1] for post-normalization. Notice how 0.6 is larger than 0.333, thus preserving the confidence due to having a larger number of characters.

Finally, as with the character-level data, there is also significant class imbalance at the fragment-level, though less severe. To combat this, we manually balance the training set of the fragment model by sampling with replacement.

4 Model Evaluation

In this section, we will discuss the performance of the models which comprise the palaeographical dating pipeline.

4.1 Character dating performance

Figure 4 shows the loss curves for each of the character dating models. Each model was trained for 200 epochs with a batch size of 256. A Keras callback was written which would store the model with the lowest validation loss in case of overfitting. The

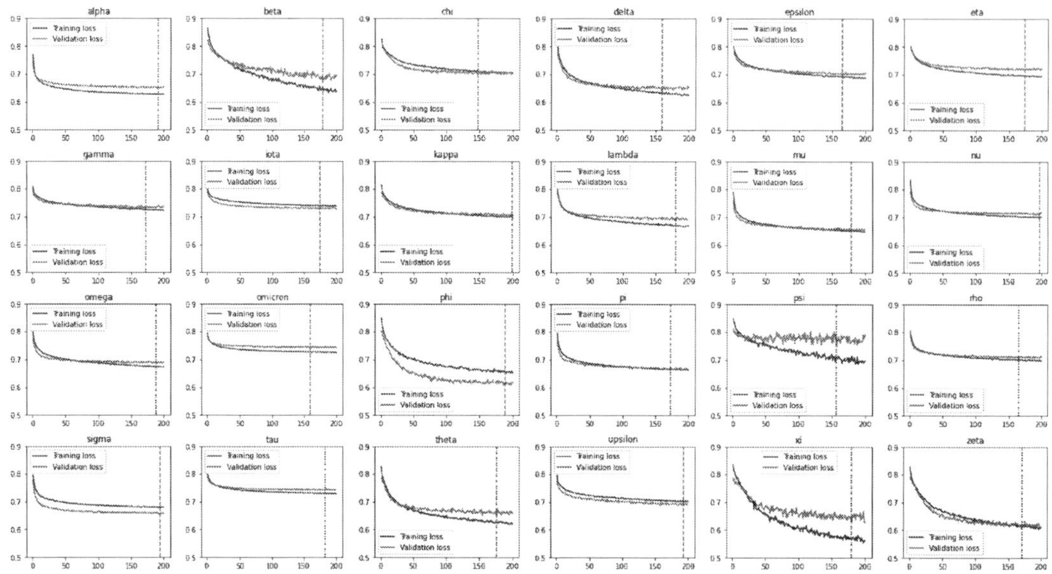

Figure 4: Loss curves for the character dating models. The vertical green line shows the epoch of lowest validation loss.

vertical green lines in the plots show when these best models were found. A range of behaviors can be seen across each of the model histories. Perhaps the most obvious is the range of optimal losses achieved. Note the difference in the values for omega and omicron. Also, some models converge in a fairly low number of epochs (such as alpha and omicron) while others have yet to converge after 200 epochs (beta and xi). This is likely due to the vast difference in sample size between the different characters. Characters with more samples are effectively trained more than those with fewer samples.

Figure 5 contains plots of the confusion matrices for each character dating model. To construct these statistics, we used Keras's ImageDataGenerator to create 1,000 augmented images per character/date combination and compare the character models' predictions on these images to the true date label (which is equivalent to that of the fragment from which the augmented character image was taken). The rows of the confusion matrices were then normalized for simplicity. All 24 models achieve overall accuracies between 35%-45%. These values are quite low, but we will see a significant increase once we see the fragment model's results.

There are several points to note about these confusion matrices. First, we can see that 3rd-4th CE is consistently the least accurately predicted date class across all characters. Second, the lower triangular portions of the matrices have a consistently higher value than the upper triangular portions. This is likely due to the fact that older handstyles can persist into the future but newer handstyles cannot retroject into the past. As such, we see a diffusion of the class probability as we move from earlier to later date classes (reading from top to bottom), causing confidence to decrease. Thirdly, we see a consistent trend in the final column which suggests that predictions of 5th-6th CE tend to have many false positives. This is likely due to the presence of a great variety of handstyles in this period, with papyri exhibiting character shapes present in older manuscripts.

4.2 Fragment dating performance

For our fragment dating model, we manually balanced the training set and performed 5-fold cross validation (five was chosen in order to keep the validation set from being too small). We present here the results obtained from a model trained on one of the folds. The accuracy of the fragment dating model depends heavily on the number of characters present in the fragment. As such, Figure 7 shows a boxplot of model accuracy (across the five folds). Note that the validation fragments have been grouped based on quartiles of the number of extant characters (which passed through the filter step). Additionally, we show in Figure 6 a set of confusion matrices for each of these groups.

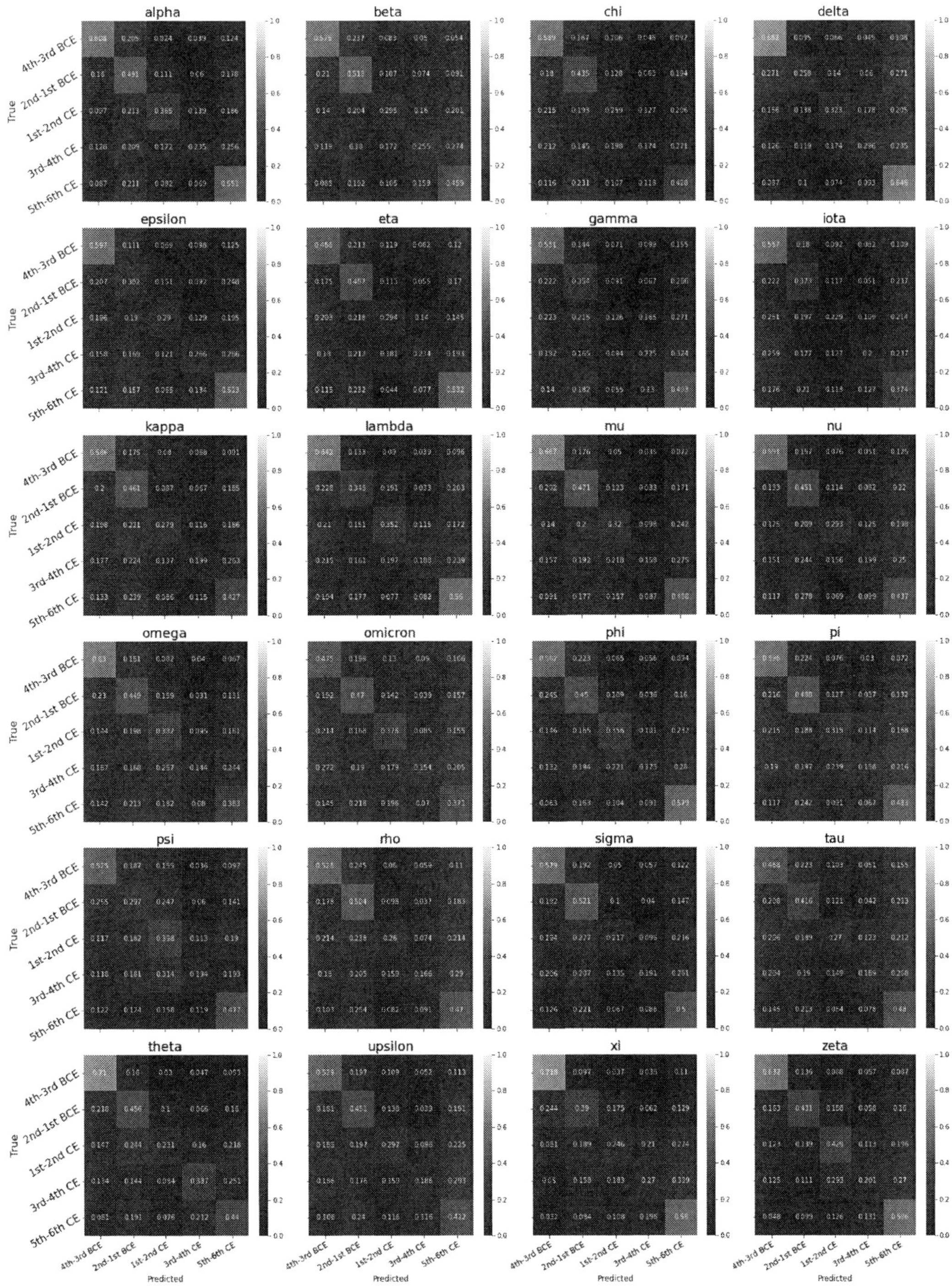

Figure 5. Confusion matrices for the character dating models.

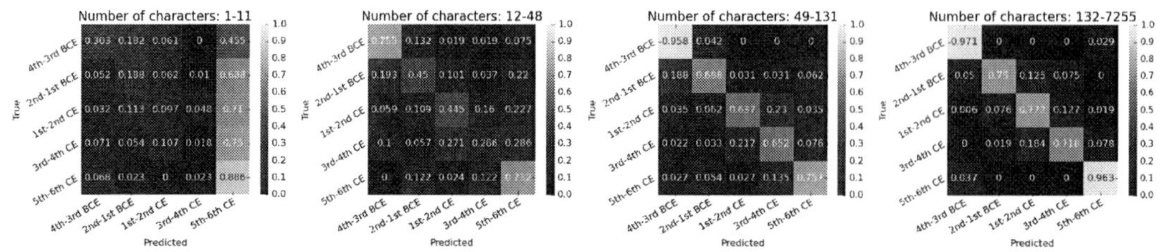

Figure 6: Confusion matrices for the fragment dating model. Each matrix contains only fragments within the specified range of number of characters.

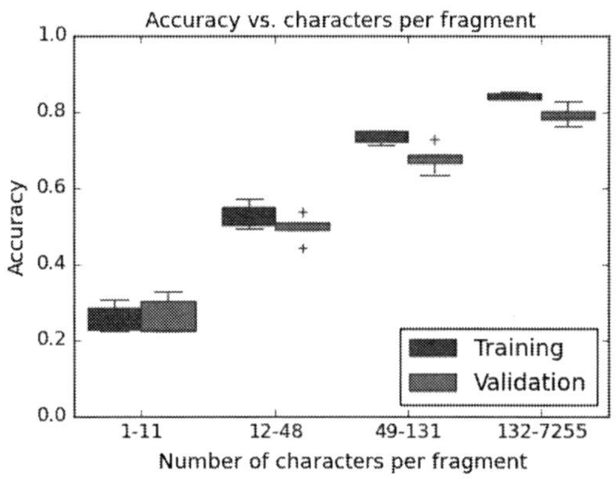

Figure 7: A box plot of the fragment dating model's accuracy of the five folds grouped based on quartiles of the number of characters in the fragments.

For the group of fragments with 1-11 characters, the average accuracy across the folds was 26% (only 6% above random chance). The confusion matrix corresponding to this group varied significantly across the folds, showing that dating fragments with a small number of characters is highly unreliable (as it is for humans). However, moving from left to right (increasing the number of characters in the fragment), we see increasing accuracy and a progressively more pronounced diagonal trend. A maximum accuracy of 79% (averaged over the folds) was achieved for fragments with between 132-7,255 characters. Thus, we can see the effect of something like the law of large numbers present in the fragment model. Although the character dating models are not very accurate, they are accurate enough that the most frequently predicted class will be correct (i.e., the probability of a correct prediction is significantly above chance). Therefore, the more characters contained within a fragment, the greater the probability of a correct date prediction.

5 Conclusions

While this research is still in its early stages, our results suggest that deep learning can perform the task of palaeographically dating ancient Greek papyri based solely on image input. This initial dataset and pipeline thus has the potential to further enhance the field of digital palaeography. Future work will pertain to increasing that temporal resolution and to leveraging the large number of individual characters in the dataset for analyzing handwriting features across time. Additionally, we plan to investigate the use of similar techniques for the location attribution of Greek papyri. More importantly, as noted above, this pipeline focuses on documentary papyri. Although these kinds of manuscripts constitute the ground truth for assigning dates to other papyri, literary and sub-literary papyri, which never preserve their date of production, have unique features of their own. How these models perform on and/or adapt to these manuscripts will also be a critical next step.

References

Y. Assael, B. Shillingford, M. Bordbar, N. de Freitas, T. Sommerschield, J. Pavlopoulos, M. Chatzipanagiotou, I. Androutsopoulos, and J. Prag. 2022. Restoring and attributing ancient texts using deep neural networks. *Nature*, 603(7900):280–283 – 283.

Alan K. Bowman, R.A. Coles, N. Gonis, Dirk Obbink, and P. J. Parsons. 2007. *Oxyrhynchus: a city and its texts*. Graeco-Roman Memoirs, v. 93. London: Published for the Arts and Humanities Research Council by the Egypt Exploration Society.

Guglielmo Cavallo and Herwig Maehler. 2008. *Hellenistic Bookhands*. Walter De Gruyter.

Nishatul Majid and Elisa H. Barney Smith. 2022. Character spotting and autonomous tagging: offline handwriting recognition for bangla, korean and other alphabetic scripts. *International Journal on Document Analysis and Recognition*, 25(4):245 – 263.

R. Mondal, R. Sarkar, S. Malakar, and E.H. Barney Smith. 2022. Handwritten english word recognition using a deep learning based object detection architecture. *Multimedia Tools and Applications*, 81(1):975–1000 – 1000.

Colin H. (Colin Henderson) Roberts. 1955. *Greek literary hands, 350 B.C.-A.D. 400*. Oxford palaeographical handbooks. At the Clarendon Press.

Matthew I. Swindall, Gregory Croisdale, Chase C. Hunter, Ben Keener, Alex C. Williams, James H. Brusuelas, Nita Krevans, Melissa Sellew, Lucy Fortson, and John F. Wallin. 2021. Exploring learning approaches for ancient greek character recognition with citizen science data. In *2021 17th International Conference on eScience (eScience)*, pages 128–137. IEEE.

Matthew I. Swindall, Timothy Player, Ben Keener, Alex C. Williams, James H. Brusuelas, Federica Nicolardi, Marzia D'Angelo, Claudio Vergara, Michael McOsker, and John F. Wallin. 2022. Dataset augmentation in papyrology with generative models: A study of synthetic ancient greek character images. In *The 31st International Joint Conference on Artificial Intelligence*. IJCAI-ECAI.

E. G. Turner. 1987. Greek manuscripts of the ancient world, second edition, revised and enlarged by p. j. parsons. bics supplement 46, london. *The Classical Review*.

Ultralytics. 2023. Comprehensive guide to ultralytics yolov5. `https://docs.ultralytics.com/yolov5/`. February 14, 2023.

Alex C. Williams, John F. Wallin, Haoyu Yu, Marco Perale, Hyrum D. Carroll, Anne-Francoise Lamblin, Lucy Fortson, Dirk Obbink, Chris J. Lintott, and James H. Brusuelas. 2014. A computational pipeline for crowdsourced transcriptions of ancient greek papyrus fragments. In *2014 IEEE International Conference on Big Data (Big Data)*, pages 100–105. IEEE.

UD-ETCSUX: Toward a Better Understanding of Sumerian Syntax

Kenan Jiang
Independent Researcher
kenanj11@berkeley.edu

Adam Anderson
University of California, Berkeley
adam.anderson@factgrid.eu

Abstract

Beginning with the discovery of the cuneiform writing system in 1835, there have been numerous grammars published illustrating the complexities of the Sumerian language. However, the one thing the published grammars have in common is their omission of dependency rules for syntax in Sumerian linguistics. For this reason we are working *toward a better understanding of Sumerian syntax*, by means of dependency-grammar in the Universal Dependencies (UD) framework. Therefore, in this study we articulate the methods and engineering techniques that can address the hardships in annotating dependency relationships in the Sumerian texts in transliteration from the *Electronic Text Corpora of Sumerian* (ETCSUX). Our code can be found at https://github.com/ancient-world-citation-analysis/UD-ETCSUX.

1 Introduction

The Sumerian language has been studied academically by philologists since Henry Rawlinson's discovery of the cuneiform writing system in 1835 (Cathcart, 2011). Since then, there have been numerous grammars published illustrating the complexities of the Sumerian language, including: epigraphy, orthography, phonology, morphology, and semantics. While not all of these grammars are in agreement, the one thing they have in common is their general lack of rules for dependency-grammar. This is because Sumerian is a highly inflected language with post-position particles for cases, numbers, and persons, and an agglutinative verbal system that reflects these same features for a given clause or sentence in the verbal chain, thereby reducing the need for complex syntax rules. For this reason, we are working *toward a better understanding of Sumerian syntax*, by means of dependency-grammar in the Universal Dependencies (UD) framework (Nivre et al., 2017), in order to model the many different dependencies of a polysemous sentence and illustrate the results using UD treebanks. This paper is meant to serve as the first step in motivating the much-needed collaboration of computational linguists and Sumerologists in the development of open-source tools for the Sumerian language, and the cuneiform writing system. Our contribution is summarized as follows:

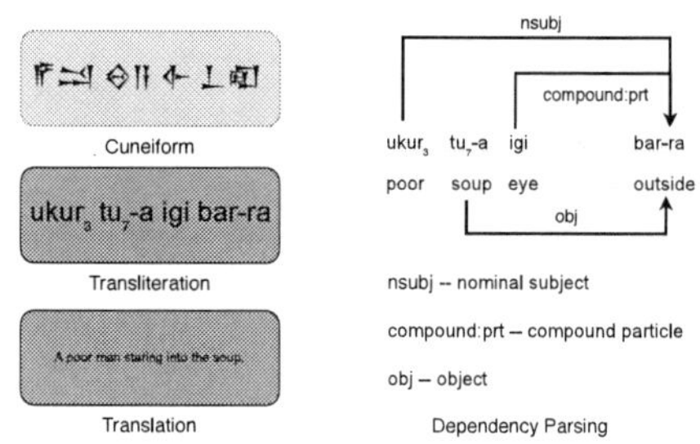

Figure 1: A dependency parsing example of Sumerian transliteration.

- We release the first dependency dataset for Sumerian UD-ETCSUX.
- We present a dependency parser for Sumerian texts in transliteration.
- We identify the two major challenges in Sumerian syntax studies.

2 Related Work

2.1 Sumerian Language

Sumerian has a problematic past from the moment of its decipherment, in that a few modern philologists were motivated to situate Sumerian as the progenitor of their own linguistic family trees (Cooper, 1991). Further compounding the historical linguistic study of Sumerian is the fact that the natural language died out near the end of the third millennium B.C. (Michalowski, 2000). From that point onward (i.e. from 2000 B.C. to

Proceedings of the 1st Workshop on Machine Learning for Ancient Languages (ML4AL 2024), pages 186–191
August 15, 2024

539 B.C.), the Sumerian language was studied and taught in scribal schools throughout Mesopotamia and was preserved much like Latin in Medieval Europe (Kraus, 2020). Our modern understanding of Sumerian relies on the Sumerian-Akkadian reference works (e.g. lexicons, syllabaries, commentaries, and translations) made by many generations of Mesopotamian scribes who continued to elaborate on Sumerian's complex morpho-graphemic orthography, and who integrated the frozen-form Sumerian logograms into the vocabulary of a considerable number of contemporary languages, like Akkadian, Elamite, and Hittite (Seri, 2010).

2.2 Computational Linguistics Tools

Due to the complex nature of Sumerian syntax, current computational tools for Sumerian transliteration have primarily focused on lemmatization and part-of-speech (POS) tagging. Of note are the recent contributions from specialists in Helsinki (Sahala and Lindén, 2023), who introduced BabyLemmatizer, a neural framework that applies machine translation methodologies to train annotators for POS and lemmatization. This approach conceptualizes tagging challenges as translation tasks, utilizing a sequence-based transformer model to generate tags. However, there remains a gap in the research as no existing studies have explored effective computational techniques for dependency labeling in Sumerian.

2.3 Cuneiform Corpora

Developing high-quality corpora is pivotal for advancing Sumerian language tools. Fortunately, the online (aka 'electronic') publications of Sumerian texts got an early start in ETCSL, the electronic text corpus of Sumerian literature (Black et al., 1998–2006), and ETCSRI, the Sumerian royal inscriptions (Zólyomi, Gábor - Tanos, Bálint - Sövegjártó, Szilvia, 2008). The first study to develop UD labels for Sumerian was the MTAAC project (Pagé-Perron et al., 2017), with a goal to translate 100,000 Sumerian texts from the Ur III period (2100-2000 B.C.). In preparation for this goal, they designed dependency sets tailored for Sumerian in transliteration, of which there are currently 370 published examples in the CDLI (CDLI contributors, 2024). The culmination of these efforts underscores a collaboration between NLP experts and Assyriologists to build a Sumerian text retrieval system, enhancing accessibility through a specialized NLP pipeline and linguistically linked open data. Although the

Sumerian	Lemma	Dependency	Head
ur-gir$_{15}$-gin$_7$	urgir	amod	5
ki	ki	compound:prt	3
za-za	zaza	aux	5
hul	hulu	compound:prt	5
a-ab-gig	gig	root+nsubj	5

Table 1: Examples from UD-ETCSUX dataset: "Like a dog, he hates to grovel."

focus has been on morphological annotation in the MTAAC workflow, comprehensive steps for dependency parsing remain less detailed, with only a handful of examples in CONLLU format documented by (Chiarcos et al., 2018).

2.4 Syntax Parsing

Dependency parsing is a syntactic parsing technique that represents the structure of a sentence in terms of binary relations between words, capturing the head-dependent relationship (Jurafsky and Martin, 2009). This parsing method facilitates the understanding of syntactic and semantic structures, aiding various applications such as machine translation and information extraction. Among contemporary models, spaCy's dependency parser (Honnibal et al., 2020) stands out due to its efficiency and accuracy. spaCy utilizes state-of-the-art neural network architectures and pre-trained word embeddings to capture complex linguistic patterns, making it highly effective for parsing diverse and morphologically rich languages. Its robust performance and ease of integration have made spaCy a popular choice for researchers and developers working on a wide range of NLP tasks.

3 UD-ETCSUX Dataset

In this section, we delineate the methodology of our dependency dataset, UD-ETCSUX. Initially, we extracted Sumerian transliterations along with their English equivalents from the ETCSRI (Zólyomi, Gábor - Tanos, Bálint - Sövegjártó, Szilvia, 2008) and ETCSL (Black et al., 1998–2006) datasets. Subsequently, we utilized the spaCy framework (Honnibal et al., 2020) to perform dependency tagging on the English translations. Using the dependency tags derived from the Universal Dependencies (UD) and the English translations, we manually transferred the UD labels from the English texts to the corresponding Sumerian transliterations, guided by the lemmatization and English gloss words provided in ETCSRI and ETCSL. This methodology enables annotators with limited expertise in Sumerian to initiate the annotation of basic structures in the language. With UD labels directly attached to Sumerian transliterations, this process facilitates the later migration of the labeled data into a UD-compatible format. We present an example from UD-ETCSUX in Table 1. Currently, we have curated dependency trees for 133 Sumerian transliterations, containing a total of 573 labeled data. We also plan to incorporate feedback from the scholarly community and will modify our labels based on their input in future versions. To address the challenge of a limited number of training examples, we employed data augmentation techniques. We selected 60 labeled Sumerian transliterations and used a trained embedding model to find the most semantically similar words in the corpus, replacing the original transliterations with new words of similar meaning. This process generated 60 new transliterations, with an example presented in Table 2.

Sumerian	Lemma	Dependency	Head
nita	nita	nsubj	4
zig	zig	acl	1
mumun	mumun	obj	4
al	al	root	4

Table 2: Example of augmented data: "A male aroused eats salt."

4 Sumerian Dependency Parser

In this section, we present the complete workflow that forms our dependency parser.

4.1 Compound Verbs

Compound verbs represent a distinctive but challenging aspect of Sumerian transliteration. Due to their extensive variety and frequent occurrences, coupled with morphological variations, accurately identifying compound verbs can be time-consuming for annotators (see Table 1). To streamline the annotation process and improve the accuracy of dependency labeling, we have developed a compound verb detector. This tool contains 674 general compound verbs, and a total of 1055 variations derived from the general compound verbs in its dictionary and is designed to automatically detect potential compound verbs and provide their corresponding English meanings given a Sumerian transliteration. We present some examples of our compound verb detector in the Appendix.

4.2 Word Embeddings

To enhance the performance of our dependency parser, we trained two types of word embedding models using the entire ETCSRI and ETCSL corpora, which contain 277,247 lines of Sumerian text in transliteration. We utilized FastText (Bojanowski et al., 2016) and Pointwise Mutual Information (PMI) (Church and Hanks, 1990) embedding techniques for this purpose. For exploration, we calculated one set of embeddings on transliterations and another on lemmas, setting the embedding dimension to 512. Four embedding models were incorporated into our dependency parsing training regimen. The comparative effectiveness of these models is thoroughly evaluated in the Experiments section.

4.3 Implementation Details

We built our dependency parser using the training framework of spaCy (Honnibal et al., 2020), tokenizing Sumerian transliterations by spaces. Given our dataset of 125 sentences, we performed a 10-fold cross-validation to evaluate the parser's effectiveness. Utilizing a custom embedding layer, the parser was trained for 20 epochs per fold with a minibatch size of 12. To prevent overfitting and enhance robustness against minor labeling errors, we applied a dropout rate of 0.8.

5 Experiments

We evaluated both PMI and FastText embedding methods trained on lemmas and transliterations, respectively. For each 10-fold cross-validation, we report the average Unlabeled Attachment Score (UAS) (Ratnaparkhi, 1996) and Labeled Attachment Score (LAS) (Buchholz and Marsi, 2006) across the folds.

The UAS measures the parser's ability to identify the sentence structure, focusing on the correctness of the head assignments. In contrast, the LAS evaluates the parser's performance on both dependency tags and sentence structure, assessing both head assignments and the correct labeling of dependency relations. Both scores are reported as percentage accuracy, ranging from 0 to 100, with 100 being complete correctness. The detailed scores are presented in Table 3.

From Table 3, we observe that our parser performs slightly better with FastText embed-

	Lemma		Transliteration	
	PMI	FastText	PMI	FastText
UAS	50.69	51.54	50.47	51.27
LAS	13.19	13.23	12.84	13.29

Table 3: Results for 10-fold validation.

dings compared to PMI embeddings, regardless of whether the embeddings were trained on lemmas or transliterations. Specifically, FastText embeddings trained on lemmas yield the highest UAS at 51.54, indicating a more effective approach in capturing syntactic structure. The LAS, which evaluates both dependency tags and sentence structure, shows a similar trend, with FastText generally outperforming PMI, though the differences are less pronounced. However, both UAS and LAS scores are relatively low across all methods, with the highest UAS at 51.54 and the highest LAS at 13.29, indicating significant room for improvement. These low scores reflect the challenges of parsing Sumerian text, likely due to the limited dataset size and the language's complexity. To improve accuracy with limited resources, we trained our parser with 60 additional augmented data. The same evaluation is presented in Table 4.

	Lemma		Transliteration	
	PMI	FastText	PMI	FastText
UAS	51.96	51.86	50.62	51.20
LAS	13.47	13.75	14.19	13.82

Table 4: Results for 10-fold validation with 60 augmented data.

Compared to Table 3, we observe consistent improvements in both UAS and LAS across all embedding settings. This highlights the promising potential of using data augmentation techniques to temporarily mitigate the negative impacts of low-resource data in enhancing parsing performance for Sumerian.

6 Qualitative Evaluation

We present two examples to illustrate the performance of our dependency parser.

Table 5 showcases a correct inference where the parser accurately identified the nominal subject (nsubj), object (obj), compound particle (comp.prt), and root. This demonstrates the parser's ability to handle straightforward Sumerian sentences effectively. Notably, it also highlights the effectiveness of our compound verb detector. During inference, the detector successfully identified "igi" and "bar" as a compound verb, assigning "igi" the compound particle label directly and thereby preventing potential confusion for the parser. The dependency relations and head assignments align with the expected structure, reflecting the parser's proficiency in parsing simple syntactic constructions.

	Truth		Predicted	
Sumerian	Dep.	Head	Dep.	Head
$ukur_3$	nsubj	4	nsubj	4
tu_7-a	obj	4	obj	4
igi	comp.prt	4	comp.prt	4
bar-ra	root	4	root	4

Table 5: Example of a correct inference: "A dog climbed up onto the roof."

	Truth		Predicted	
Sumerian	Dep.	Head	Dep.	Head
ur	nsubj	4	nsubj	4
si-im-si-im	amod	1	nsubj	4
e_2-e_2-a	obj	4	obj	4
ku_4-ku_4	root	4	root	4

Table 6: Example of an incorrect inference: "A sniffing dog entering all the houses."

Table 6 presents a failed case. The parser misclassified "si-im-si-im" as a nominal subject (nsubj) instead of an adjectival modifier (amod), which affected the overall dependency structure. We believe this misclassification is due to the parser's limited exposure to diverse sentence structures and the imbalance in the training data, making it challenging to accurately recognize and differentiate adjectival modifiers, which are less common, from nominal subjects. Such failures underscore the need to incorporate more diverse and complex sentences into UD-ETCSUX to broaden the parser's capabilities.

7 Future Directions

We plan to incorporate additional feedback from language experts and continuously expand and enhance the quality of UD-ETCSUX, with the ultimate goal of publishing it in the Universal Dependency Treebank. Additionally, we will conduct inter-annotator agreement studies in future work to ensure the reliability and consistency of our annotations. Furthermore, we have identified two issues that require targeted solutions in future research.

7.1 Morphology Inclusion

Sumerian has a highly-inflected morphology, which in many instances encapsulates multiple parts of speech and phrasal elements into a single word, as seen in Table 1, which contains both the subject and root in three signs or one token. In order to properly identify each of the phrasal elements of a sentence, it will be necessary to annotate these sub-word particles, especially for the verbs. Fortunately, this format has been clearly articulated in recent Sumerian grammars, but it has only been applied to the ETCSRI corpus, and has not yet been extended to the rest of the electronic text corpora of Sumerian. We see this as a critical step in order to allow for an automated process of dependency parsing. As such, we plan to provide the full repertoire of Sumerian texts with annotations for sub-word particles in subsequent versions of the UD-ETCSUX dataset.

7.2 Multiple Translations

Also mentioned above is the fact that much of the vocabulary and many of the literary texts in Sumerian exhibit forms of word-play, parallelism, polysemy, and double-entendre. (Alster, 1975) A good example of this may be seen in the sentence in Table 1, which ETCSL translates: "Like a dog, he hates to grovel," but which could also be read, "he hates to grovel like a dog." The former implies the dog's hatred of groveling and the latter only likens the subject's act of groveling to a dog's. Both readings are possible because there is no separate subject in the sentence outside of the verbal chain. While including such polysemy in our model might over-complicate the process from the start, we hope to include the plurality of dependency parsings in the future to reflect the rich layers of meaning embedded in the Sumerian text.

8 Conclusion

In this work, we presented UD-ETCSUX, a concise dataset for Sumerian dependency parsing. Additionally, we introduced tools to enhance parsing accuracy, such as compound verb detection and data augmentation techniques. Our dependency parsing analysis compared various embedding methods and identified areas for future improvement. We hope our contributions will prove valuable and inspire language experts to further advance the understanding of Sumerian syntax.

9 Acknowledgements

We would like to express our gratitude to Émilie Pagé-Perron for sharing the latest work from the MTAAC project, as well as Jason Moser, Matthew Ong, Andrew Pottorf, and Manuel Molina for their extensive feedback on our initial results.

10 Limitations

While our dataset effectively supports the initial objectives of this study, its current scope is limited, restricting our ability to fully explore the diverse linguistic scenarios in Sumerian languages. Furthermore, more extensive expert validations are required to enhance our dataset's robustness. We are still in the process of receiving and incorporating feedback from Sumerian language specialists, and we are committed to expanding the dataset and deepening expert collaborations to refine the quality and applicability of our findings.

References

Bendt Alster. 1975. Paradoxical proverbs and satire in sumerian literature. *Journal of Cuneiform Studies*, 27(4):201–230.

J.A. Black, G. Cunningham, J. Ebeling, E. Flückiger-Hawker, E. Robson, J. Taylor, and G. Zólyomi. 1998–2006. The electronic text corpus of sumerian literature. http://etcsl.orinst.ox.ac.uk/. Accessed: 2024-05-24.

Piotr Bojanowski, Edouard Grave, Armand Joulin, and Tomas Mikolov. 2016. Enriching word vectors with subword information. *Transactions of the Association for Computational Linguistics*, 5:135–146.

Sabine Buchholz and Erwin Marsi. 2006. CoNLL-X shared task on multilingual dependency parsing. In *Proceedings of the Tenth Conference on Computational Natural Language Learning (CoNLL-X)*, pages 149–164, New York City. Association for Computational Linguistics.

K. J. Cathcart. 2011. The Earliest Contributions to the Decipherment of Sumerian and Akkadian. *Cuneiform Digital Library Journal*, 2011(1). [Online; accessed 2024-05-15].

CDLI contributors. 2024. Cuneiform digital library initiative. https://cdli.mpiwg-berlin.mpg.de/. [Online; accessed 2024-05-24].

Christian Chiarcos, Ilya Khait, Émilie Pagé-Perron, Niko Schenk, Jayanth, Christian Fäth, Julius Steuer, William Mcgrath, and Jinyan Wang. 2018. Annotating a low-resource language with llod technology: Sumerian morphology and syntax. *Information*, 9(11).

Kenneth Ward Church and Patrick Hanks. 1990. Word association norms, mutual information, and lexicography. *Computational Linguistics*, 16(1):22–29.

Jerry S. Cooper. 1991. Posing the Sumerian question: Race and scholarship in the early history of assyriology. *Aula Orientalis*, 9:47–66.

Matthew Honnibal, Ines Montani, Sofie Van Landeghem, and Adriane Boyd. 2020. spaCy: Industrial-strength Natural Language Processing in Python.

Dan Jurafsky and James H. Martin. 2009. *Speech and language processing : an introduction to natural language processing, computational linguistics, and speech recognition*. Pearson Prentice Hall, Upper Saddle River, N.J.

Nicholas L. Kraus. 2020. *Scribal Education in the Sargonic Period*. Brill.

Piotr Michalowski. 2000. The life and death of the sumerian language in comparative perspective. *Acta Sumerologica*, 22:177–202.

Joakim Nivre, Daniel Zeman, Filip Ginter, and Francis Tyers. 2017. Universal Dependencies. In *Proceedings of the 15th Conference of the European Chapter of the Association for Computational Linguistics: Tutorial Abstracts*, Valencia, Spain. Association for Computational Linguistics.

Émilie Pagé-Perron, Maria Sukhareva, Ilya Khait, and Christian Chiarcos. 2017. Machine translation and automated analysis of the Sumerian language. In *Proceedings of the Joint SIGHUM Workshop on Computational Linguistics for Cultural Heritage, Social Sciences, Humanities and Literature*, pages 10–16, Vancouver, Canada. Association for Computational Linguistics.

A. Ratnaparkhi. 1996. A maximum entropy model for part-of-speech tagging. In *Conference on Empirical Methods in Natural Language Processing*.

Aleksi Sahala and Krister Lindén. 2023. A neural pipeline for POS-tagging and lemmatizing cuneiform languages. In *Proceedings of the Ancient Language Processing Workshop*, pages 203–212, Varna, Bulgaria. INCOMA Ltd., Shoumen, Bulgaria.

Andrea Seri. 2010. 3. adaptation of cuneiform to write Akkadian. In *Visible Language: Inventions of Writing in the Ancient Middle East and Beyond*, pages 85–98, Chicago, USA. Oriental Institute Museum Publications.

Zólyomi, Gábor - Tanos, Bálint - Sövegjártó, Szilvia. 2008. The electronic text corpus of sumerian royal inscriptions.

A Appendix

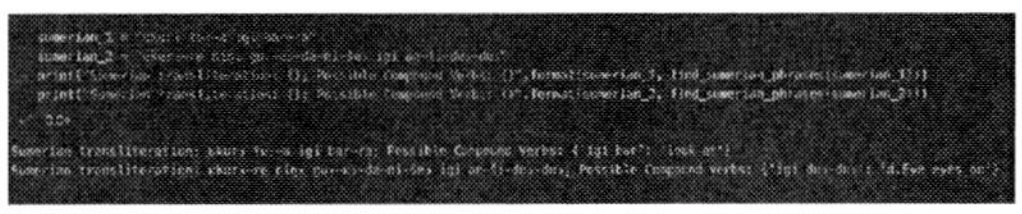

Figure 2: Use case for compound verb detector.

SumTablets:
A Transliteration Dataset of Sumerian Tablets

Cole Simmons
Stanford University
coles@stanford.edu

Richard Diehl Martinez
University of Cambridge
rd654@cam.ac.uk

Dan Jurafsky
Stanford University
jurafsky@stanford.edu

Abstract

Sumerian transliteration is a conventional system for representing a scholar's interpretation of a tablet in the Latin script. Thanks to visionary digital Assyriology projects such as ETCSL, CDLI, and Oracc, a large number of Sumerian transliterations have been published online, and these data are well-structured for a variety of search and analysis tasks. However, the absence of a comprehensive, accessible dataset pairing transliterations with a digital representation of the tablet's cuneiform glyphs has prevented the application of modern Natural Language Processing (NLP) methods to the task of Sumerian transliteration.

To address this gap, we present *SumTablets*, a dataset pairing Unicode representations of **91,606 Sumerian cuneiform tablets** (totaling **6,970,407 glyphs**) with the associated transliterations published by Oracc. We construct *SumTablets* by first preprocessing and standardizing the Oracc transliterations before mapping each reading back to the Unicode representation of the source glyph. Further, we retain parallel structural information (e.g., surfaces, newlines, broken segments) through the use of special tokens. We release *SumTablets* as a Hugging Face Dataset (CC BY 4.0) and open source data preparation code via GitHub.

Additionally, we leverage *SumTablets* to implement and evaluate two transliteration baselines: (1) weighted sampling from a glyph's possible readings, and (2) fine-tuning an autoregressive language model. Our fine-tuned language model achieves an average transliteration character-level F-score (chrF) of 97.55, demonstrating the immediate potential of transformer-based transliteration models in allowing experts to rapidly verify generated transliterations rather than manually transliterating tablets one-by-one.

colesimmons/SumTablets (CC BY 4.0)
colesimmons/SumTablets

Figure 1: An administrative Sumerian cuneiform tablet from Shuruppak, dated to the Early Dynastic IIIa period (ca. 2500 BCE). (British Museum, 1896)

1 Introduction

Sumerian is the world's earliest attested written language, marking the transition from prehistory into history as well as reflecting a rich written tradition spanning three thousand years. These texts are an invaluable resource in the study of ancient Near Eastern culture, politics, economics, and more.

During the latter half of the fourth millennium BCE, a sophisticated record-keeping system emerged in southern Mesopotamia, now known as proto-cuneiform (Selz, 2020). Over time this system evolved[1] to handle natural language. By about 2900 BCE this writing system, known as *cuneiform*, is concretely recognizable as encoding Sumerian.

Mesopotamian scribes originally devised the cuneiform script to write Sumerian. This script was later adapted to encode other languages throughout the Near East, such as Akkadian. To form glyphs, scribes would typically compose stylus impressions on a wet clay tablet[2]. Because

[1]There continues to be considerable ambiguity and disagreement about the extent to which evolution occurred gradually or was the result of a single inventor. For a more comprehensive treatment of the topic, see (Sproat, 2023).

[2]Although not all texts are clay or in the form of a tablet,

Proceedings of the 1st Workshop on Machine Learning for Ancient Languages (ML4AL 2024), pages 192–202
August 15, 2024 ©2024 Association for Computational Linguistics

ID	Period	Genre	Glyphs (Inputs)	Transliteration (Targets)
Q001103	Early Dynastic IIIb	Royal Inscription	<SURFACE> 𒀭𒂗𒆤 𒈗𒆳𒆳𒊏 𒀊𒁀𒀭𒀭𒊑𒉈𒆤 𒅗𒄀𒈾𒉌𒋫 ...	<SURFACE> {d}en-lil$_2$ lugal kur-kur-ra ab-ba dingir-dingir-re$_2$-ne-ke$_4$ inim gi-na-ni-ta ...

Table 1: A sample paired glyph–transliteration example from *SumTablets*, dating ca. 2600–2300 BCE.

cuneiform writing was impressed or inscribed on durable materials, texts have survived to the present in tremendous quantity (Finkel and Taylor, 2015). Uncovered during archaeological excavations of ancient cities beginning in the nineteenth century CE, these tablets had to be subsequently deciphered. Deciphering Sumerian, a language isolate, proved particularly challenging, and some periods and genres are still not completely understood.

Sumerian cuneiform glyphs are frequently polyvalent; that is, they have many possible readings (of no necessary semantic or phonetic relation) depending on the context. For instance, 𒅗 can be read as *ka* "mouth," *dug*$_4$ "to speak," *kiri*$_3$ "nose," *zuh* "to steal," the syllable *ka*, and more. When reading a tablet, an Assyriologist must often consider various possibilities for each glyph to achieve a set of consistent readings. They represent their interpretation through the process of transliteration.

Transliteration is a modern, conventional system for representing Sumerian in the Latin alphabet. Conventions were established at various points in the modern, 150-year history of Sumerian decipherment and do not necessarily reflect the current understanding of Sumerian phonology or morphology. In transliterations, homophones are distinguished via subscripts; for instance, *e* and e_2 are homophonic—but semantically unrelated—readings of different glyphs. Additionally, hyphens are used to join nominal/verbal roots with affixes (Michalowski, 2004).

In 1996, the Electronic Text Corpus of Sumerian Literature (ETCSL) (Black et al., 2016) project began publishing transliterations online. This project became archival in 2006, soon followed by other projects such as the Cuneiform Digital Library Initiative (CDLI) (CDLI contributors, 2024) and the Open Richly Annotated Cuneiform Corpus (Oracc) (ORACC contributors, 2024). Thanks to these and other projects, a large number of transliterations have been published online and their data made available for use with open licenses. Our work would not be possible without the decades of dedicated efforts by contributors to these projects.

Because Assyriologists are reading from either the physical text or an image, no digital representation of the original text's glyphs is typically recorded. Today, most cuneiform glyphs have been added to Unicode[3]. However, easily accessible[4], standardized datasets of paired Sumerian Unicode glyphs and transliterations remain limited, barring the development of transliteration models.

In this paper, we present the first large-scale, easily accessible dataset of **91,606 Sumerian tablets** as glyph–transliteration pairs, containing a total of **6,970,407 glyphs**. We additionally include IDs[5], period, and genre metadata for each tablet to be used for results analysis.

Our dataset, *SumTablets*, is derived from a collection of publicly available Sumerian language resources, primarily the Electronic Pennsylvania Sumerian Dictionary (ePSD2) (Tinney et al., 2024) and the Oracc Sign List (OSL) (Veldhuis et al., 2024). These projects aggregate and index transliteration data from across Oracc, which shares data with CDLI and includes data from other current and former projects[6].

Because of how they are formatted and because they do not include parallel Unicode glyph tablet representations, however, the data on Oracc are not immediately suited for glyph-to-transliteration tasks. We preprocess these data to clean and standardize them, converting structure-related anno-

we follow Assyriological convention by referring to texts generically as tablets.

[3]All online Sumerian data aggregation and collaboration was limited to ASCII for more than a decade: The first cuneiform was added to Unicode in 2006.

[4]We define *easily accessible* as being easily utilized programmatically and requiring no or minimal Assyriological expertise to contribute to development of models based on these datasets.

[5]IDs are consistent with those in Oracc and CDLI.

[6]ePSD2 credits

tations into special tokens. Then, since a given reading maps back to only one glyph, we utilize Unicode–reading dictionaries provided by ePSD2 and OSL to convert each reading back into its source glyph.

We upload our dataset to Hugging Face (HuggingFace Inc., 2024), the largest and most widely utilized library for sharing datasets for machine learning tasks. We intend to use Hugging Face's git-based version control to provide experiment reproducibility over time, with versions containing snapshots of the continuously updated Oracc data.

Our dataset, *SumTablets*, builds on previous open-source projects by:

1. **being the largest dataset of parallel glyph–transliteration examples.**
2. **standardizing the data available in Oracc**, optimizing formatting for the transliteration task while maintaining the morphosyntactic fidelity of the texts.
3. **vastly facilitating the use of this data in machine learning projects**, simplifying access via the common Hugging Face Datasets library.

Using our dataset, we develop and compare two baseline transliteration approaches. The first is a weighted dictionary mapping; for each glyph we sample one of the glyph's possible readings according to its frequency. The second is a language model that we fine-tune for the glyph-to-transliteration task. As far as we are aware, we are the first to develop an automatic Sumerian transliteration model. Evaluated on a held-out test set, the dictionary-lookup approach obtains a character-level F-score (chrF) (Popović, 2015) of 61.22, while the fine-tuned model achieves a chrF score of 97.54.

Our goals in releasing this dataset are to facilitate the development of transliteration models and to demonstrate the potential of adapting large pretrained multilingual models for the task. We envision web-based tooling built on top of neural transliteration models helping Assyriologists to generate transliterations more quickly—allowing them to rapidly validate model outputs rather transliterating each tablet from scratch—and target review of potential errors in existing transliterations. Additionally, transliteration models serve as an essential step in eventually developing a complete Sumerian translation pipeline. Finally, as a language isolate, Sumerian poses a unique syntactic challenge for cross-lingual models, and opens new avenues of research into the transfer of language understanding.

2 Related Work

To the best of our knowledge, our work represents the first to formulate Sumerian transliteration as an NLP task and to develop a transliteration model. However, prior works have utilized NLP techniques for other tasks in parsing and analyzing Sumerian cuneiform. The Machine Translation and Automated Analysis of Cuneiform Languages (MTAAC) project (Pagé-Perron et al., 2017) sought to develop a pipeline for Sumerian annotation, translation, and information extraction, working primarily with Ur III transliterations. Chiarcos et al. expanded this data to include the Electronic Text Corpus of Sumerian Royal Inscriptions (ETCSRI) (Zólyomi et al., 2019). Bansal et al. then used MTAAC data in conjunction with CDLI and ETCSL data to train models for part-of-speech (POS) tagging, named entity recognition (NER), and translation, aiming primarily to build generalizable cross-lingual methods for performing these tasks on low-resource languages. The COMPASS (Veldhuis, 2024) also explores using cuneiform data for research tasks, such as reconstructing social graphs. Perhaps most similar to our work, Gordin et al. develop a neural network to automatically transliterate Akkadian from Unicode cuneiform glyphs.

Others have built datasets also representing tablets' glyphs in Unicode. Jauhiainen et al. utilized Oracc dataset to build a dataset of 13,662 tablets for the task of language and dialect identification. More recently, Chen et al. used CDLI data to create CuneiML, a dataset of 38,947 tablets with photos, Unicode glyphs, transliterations, and metadata, also designed primarily for classification tasks. Both of these datasets include both Sumerian and Akkadian texts, whereas our dataset only includes monolingual Sumerian texts. Furthermore, our dataset is larger, designed specifically for the transliteration task, and is easily accessible through Hugging Face.

Outside of NLP, an exciting area of research is using computer vision methods to identify cuneiform signs from images (Dencker et al., 2020). Efforts in visual classification and transcription of cuneiform are enabled by projects that have open-sourced high-quality 2D and 3D images of tablets (Dahl et al., 2019; Mara and Homburg, 2023). And beyond cuneiform, Assael et al. used deep learning methods to restore fragmented ancient texts in ancient Greek.

As Sumerian is a low-resource language, it is infeasible to train a transformer-based language model on Sumerian from scratch rather than adapting cross-lingual representations in existing models. Fortunately, the recent success of large cross-lingual NLP models such as mBERT (Devlin et al., 2019), XLM-R (Conneau et al., 2020), m-T5 (Liu et al., 2020), and BLOOM (BigScience Workshop et al., 2023) have steadily raised the bar for zero- and few-shot cross-lingual performance on benchmarks such as XTREME (Hu et al., 2020) and MEGA (Ahuja et al., 2023). Recently, benchmarks to measure a model's ability to perform NLP tasks in extremely low-resource and orthographically-diverse languages have emerged, such as IndicXNLI (Aggarwal et al., 2022) for low-resource Indian languages, and Sukhareva et al. who develop a POS tagging benchmark for Hittite, another cuneiform language. *SumTablets* marks the first benchmark for Sumerian neural machine transliteration.

3 Creating *SumTablets*

SumTablets is built upon the metadata and transliterations provided by ePSD2 via JSON files[7]. These transliterations were created or manually typed by scholars working in different projects around the world over decades of evolving knowledge of Sumerian vocabulary and grammar; they also contain extensive (but not useful for our purposes) embedded ASCII annotation. We begin by preprocessing the transliterations to normalize conventions, remove annotations, and convert formatting information into special tokens. Then, we use dictionaries built from ePSD2 and OSL resources to map each reading back to a Unicode representation of its source glyph. The result is a set of Unicode glyph–transliteration pairs with parallel formatting, allowing language models to most effectively learn the relationships between the two representations.

[7]https://oracc.museum.upenn.edu/epsd2/json

3.1 Initial Data Cleaning

We first parse and type-check the ePSD2 JSON data using custom Pydantic[8] classes. The transliterations are structured in a recursive format called cdl (for the three node types: chunk, delimiter, and lemma) at the document level, which we navigate in order to reconstruct the transliteration as a single string with embedded formatting information.

We then remove annotations embedded in the transliterations. Many of these represent the editor's interpretation beyond what is visible on the tablet; for instance, text enclosed in square brackets represents the editor's belief of what was originally in a now-missing segment. While this information is academically useful, it can inject an undesirable bias when training transliteration models. Our goal is to best represent only what is on the tablet. We remove text enclosed in square brackets (broken) and single angle brackets (graphemes must be supplied for the sense but are not present), replacing the former with a **...** special token to indicate breakage. For text enclosed in upper square brackets (partially visible) and double angle brackets (graphemes are present but most be excised for the sense), we remove the notation but retain the text. These examples are a few of many conventions are used in the provided transliterations. For each type, we either remove the notation but retain the text, remove the notation and the text, or replace the notation and text with a special token (described in subsection 3.3).

The Oracc data are supplied with metadata that varies depending on the project in which a tablet was digitized. After performing an inner join on all of the data, we found the period and genre to be the most salient, universally-supplied metadata; because we provide the original Oracc IDs, removed fields can easily be reintegrated.

3.2 Mapping transliterations to glpyhs

For each of the transliterations, we generate the associated glyphs in three steps:

1. First, we split each transliteration by spaces to get a list of words, which we then split further into individual glyph readings (i.e., morphemes).

2. Next, for each reading, we look up the corresponding glyph name. Each glyph in Sumerian has a conventional name that is an up-

[8]https://docs.pydantic.dev/latest/

percase version of one of its readings; for instance, the glyph 𒅗 is referred to as KA. Like most glyphs, it can be read a number of different ways (e.g., *ka*, *dug_4*, *inim*). Importantly, these readings are readings only of KA and can be mapped back to it. If we cannot ascertain the glyph name, we replace the reading with <UNK>. Sign names are often used in place of a reading (to say that the reading is uncertain), in which case we replace the reading with <UNK> but will still use the corresponding Unicode. The first row of Table 2 shows the proportion of readings that we are able to map to glyph names.

3. Finally, we convert each glyph name to the Unicode representation of that glyph name; for instance, we convert BU to 𒁍. For the rare glyphs that are not represented in Unicode, we replace both the glyph and associated reading with <UNK> tokens. The bottom row of Table 2 shows the proportion of glyphs names that we able to map to Unicode.

To map from transliteration to glyph name and from glyph name to Unicode, we leverage ePSD2 and OSL.

Preprocessing Step	Success Rate
Readings → Glyph Name	6,724,498 (99.93%)
Glyph Name → Unicode	6,638,081 (99.96%)

Table 2: Preprocessing steps with associated amount of maintained glyphs in constructing *SumTablets*.

3.3 Extra-semantic tokens

In addition to the aforementioned preprocessing steps, we add the following special tokens to maintain structural information about each tablet in corresponding locations in the glyph and transliteration examples:

- **<SURFACE>** – The start of a surface. For a tablet, this may be the start of the obverse or reverse side. For other types of artifacts (like statues), the number of surfaces and their relationship to each other depends on the form.
- **\n** – A line break. These are important to retain because it is extremely rare that a word-form runs over to a subsequent line.
- **...** – Breakage. Ellipses on their own line indicate an indeterminate number of missing lines, while ellipses on a line with text indicate an indeterminate number of missing glyphs.
- **<RULING>** – A horizontal line drawn by the scribe to separate sections of the tablet.
- **<COLUMN>** – The start of a new column of text. Not all tablets are formatted in columns.
- **<BLANK_SPACE>** – The scribe left some amount of blank space before continuing on.

3.4 Metadata

As part of the dataset, we include additional metadata associated with each tablet: the time period each tablet dates from and the semantic genre of each tablet (e.g. administrative, legal). In total, we define 10 unique time periods and 14 genres (see Table 3).

Period	Train	Val	Test
Ur III	71,116	3,951	3,951
Old Akkadian	4,766	265	265
Early Dynastic IIIb	3,467	192	192
Old Babylonian	1,374	73	73
Lagash II	788	44	44
Early Dynastic IIIa	755	42	42
Early Dynastic I-II	77	4	4
Unknown	68	4	4
Neo-Assyrian	20	1	1
Neo-Babylonian	14	1	1
Middle Babylonian	7	0	0
Total	82,452	4,577	4,577
Genre	Train	Val	Test
Administrative	77,193	4,259	4,291
Royal Inscription	2,611	151	146
Literary	1,000	63	62
Letter	718	48	33
Legal	544	35	36
Unknown	269	14	7
Lexical	69	0	0
Liturgy	40	4	1
Math/Science	8	3	1
Total	82,452	4,577	4,577

Table 3: Composition of tablets by period and genre in *SumTablets*.

3.5 Data Partitions

For the purposes of developing automatic transliteration approaches, we split our corpus into train, validation, and test partitions using a 90%/5%/5% split. As an artifact both of what was produced as well as what sites have been excavated, there is a considerable imbalance in the number of examples between historical periods and genres. To ensure that we are training, validating, and testing evenly on how the language was used over time, we stratify the splits by period—Table 3 shows the number of examples in each by split. Because the genres of texts produced correlates strongly with period, stratifying by period results in a nearly equal split of genres, also shown in Table 3. Importantly, we removed the lexical texts before splitting, and then added them back to the train set after.[9]

4 Evaluating Transliteration Performance

The scale and standardization of *SumTablets* enables new methods to be applied to the task of Sumerian transliteration. In this section, we leverage our dataset to develop and compare two transliteration approaches: a straight-forward 'dictionary baseline' and a 'neural baseline'. First, we define the transliteration task.

4.1 The Transliteration Task

We model transliteration as a sequence-to-sequence conversion task, where the input sequence is defined as glyphs and the output as a sequence of alpha-numeric characters, hyphens and white spaces. Table 1 illustrates example pairs of input (glyphs) and output (transliterations). As we model it, the transliteration task is more akin to a translation task, where each input sequence can be mapped to a large space of output sequences, rather than a token classification task. Given our framing of the transliteration task, we use character-level chrF score as the evaluation metric, defined as:

$$\texttt{chrF} = (1+\beta)^2 \frac{\texttt{chrP} \cdot \texttt{chrR}}{\beta^2 \cdot \texttt{chrP} + \texttt{chrR}} \quad (1)$$

where chrP and chrR stand in for character-level precision and recall scores. Throughout our analysis, we set $\beta = 2$, and use a character n-gram order of 6, as proposed by Popović. We compute the chrF score over the transliterated tokens for each tablet individually and then average these scores together over the dataset.

4.2 Dictionary Baseline

As part of previous transliteration efforts, Sumerian language experts have hand-crafted dictionaries that map a glyph to all possible readings of that glyph. We cross-analyze our dataset with the ePSD2 and OSL Sumerian dictionaries and find that the average number of different readings for a glyph, weighted by glyph frequency, is 22.17.

The availability of these dictionaries yields a simple automatic Sumerian transliteration approach: for each glyph in the test set, sample over its possible readings in proportion to their frequency[10]. This baseline results in an average chrF score of 61.22.

4.3 Neural Baseline

We explore whether the cross-lingual abilities of existing multilingual language models can be leveraged to solve the Sumerian transliteration task. Although Sumerian is a language isolate, it shares grammatical features with other modern languages: like Basque, it has ergative–absolutive alignment; like Turkish and Japanese, it is agglutinative; and like Korean, it is SOV (Michalowski, 2004). Therefore, the key to our approach is to leverage XLM-R (Conneau et al., 2020), a transformer language model pre-trained on over 100 languages.

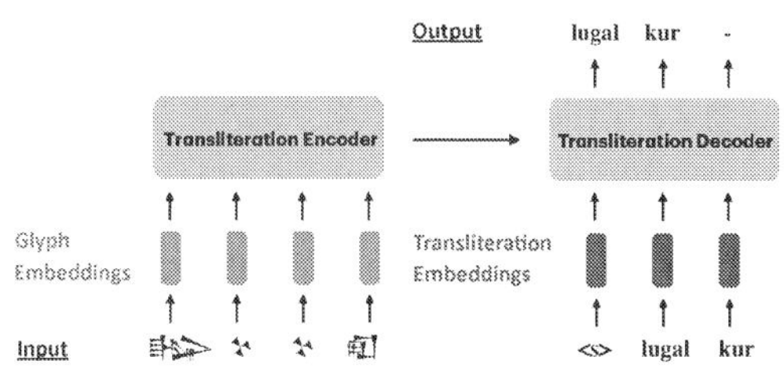

Figure 2: Illustration of the neural baseline model architecture. Inputs are read in as glyph tokens, while outputs are transliteration tokens.

The lack of tokenization support for Sumerian presents a first challenge in applying the XLM-R model to transliterating Sumerian. To deal with

[9]Lexical texts are lists of words that were used in scribal training. We believe that it does not make sense to evaluate against them, but leave it up to the user to decide whether they provide productive noise during training.

[10]We recorded occurrence counts in the process of constructing the dataset.

Period			Genre		
Category	Dictionary	Neural	Category	Dictionary	Neural
Ur III	62.89	**98.46**	Administrative	63.15	**98.14**
Old Akkadian	64.52	**94.03**	Royal Inscription	54.58	**95.15**
Early Dynastic IIIb	62.51	**97.08**	Literary	37.73	**90.67**
Old Babylonian	37.70	**90.38**	Letter	47.43	**90.99**
Lagash II	58.55	**93.97**	Legal	56.19	**96.14**
Early Dynastic IIIa	67.85	**95.02**	Unknown	69.84	**97.58**
Early Dynastic I-II	73.72	**96.82**	Liturgy	55.92	**77.68**
Unknown	64.98	**89.87**	Math/Science	62.00	**95.12**
Neo-Assyrian	40.83	**89.79**			
Neo-Babylonian	42.47	**97.81**			
Overall	61.22	**97.54**		61.22	**97.54**

Table 4: Results by period and genre. Average chrF scores of transliterations generated in the dictionary baseline compared against those generated in the neural baseline.

this, we retrain the default SentencePiece tokenizer (Kudo and Richardson, 2018) used by the XLM-R model twice: once to build a 'glyph tokenizer' that is trained only on the Sumerian glyphs in *SumTablets*, and once to build a 'transliteration tokenizer' that is trained only on the corresponding Sumerian transliterations in *SumTablets*. The 'glyph tokenizer' has a vocab size of 632 glyph tokens and is used by the encoder model to generate 'glyph embeddings' from a string of Unicode-encoded glyphs. The 'transliteration tokenizer' has a vocab size of 1024 transliteration tokens and is used by the decoder model to output transliterations. The vocabularies of both the glyph and transliteration tokenizers include eleven special tokens, including the extra-semantic special tokens discussed in section 3.3.

We structure our transliteration model as a sequence-to-sequence (encoder-decoder) model. We initialize both the encoder and decoder separately with the pre-trained weights of an XLM-R model.

We train the model in three stages: First, we independently fine-tune the pretrained encoder model on the Unicode cuneiform glyphs using a masked language modeling task (MLM). This step yields a model with effective internal representations for the glyphs. Then, we integrate the decoder, training the full encoder-decoder model to take glyph sequences as input and auto-regressively predict target transliterations token-by-token. To stabilize the auto-regressive training of the joint encoder-decoder model, we decompose this process two stages. We first freeze the encoder weights (only training the decoder) for one-third of the time that we train the joint encoder-decoder model. For the rest of training, we unfreeze the encoder weights and allow both the encoder and decoder to receive gradient updates. Figure 2 showcases the encoder–decoder model architecture. An added benefit of using both an encoder and a decoder is that the encoder can function independently from the decoder to predict missing or unknown glyphs, as illustrated in Figure 3.

Both the encoder and decoder are initialized with the pre-trained weights of a 279 million parameter XLM-R model [11]. We initially fine-tune the encoder on the MLM task for 50 epochs, with sequences lengths of 64 tokens, a learning rate of 5e-05, batch size of 2,048, and 200 warmup steps. We set the MLM masking probability to 0.10 and use the same 80-10-10 masking procedure as in Devlin et al.. Next, the encoder-decoder with frozen encoder weights is trained with a learning rate of 1e-04 for 2 epochs. Finally, we unfreeze the encoder weights and train the full encoder–decoder model with a learning rate of 5e-05 for a further 4 epochs. For both encoder–decoder learning procedures, we set the train batch size to 128 and the number of warmup steps to 100. All training used the AdamW optimizer (Loshchilov and Hutter, 2019) and was run on a single A100 SXM 80GB. For transliteration generation, we use beam search decoding with a beam size of 5.

[11]For a full description of the XLM-R model, refer to: https://huggingface.co/FacebookAI/xlm-roberta-base

Throughout our experiments, we set the maximum sequence length to 128. For tablets with more than 128 glyphs, we divide both the pre-tokenized glyphs and transliterations by newlines—these divisions align due to how we design *SumTablets* to preserve tablet structures. We then tokenize chunks of N lines, with N decreasing in size progressively from 16 down to 1, until the resulting chunk contains slightly less than 128 tokens. This segmentation ensures that all resultant chunks contain a maximum amount of tokens within the valid sequence length.

After processing the data into chunks of sequence length 128, we find that the dataset comprises 178,208 administrative examples and 23,282 non-administrative examples. To address the imbalance, we up-sample non-administrative examples by a factor of 5 for the initial two epochs of training and then reduce the up-sampling factor to 3 for the remaining epochs.

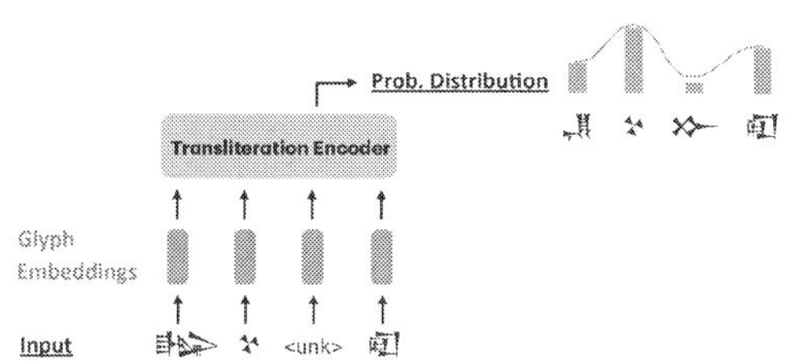

Figure 3: The encoder model can produce a probability distribution over possible glyphs that can replace an <UNK> token. This is because the encoder is trained using an MLM objective.

Our encoder-decoder model achieves an average character-level chrF score of 97.54 on unseen test data, setting, to the best of our knowledge, a new state-of-the-art benchmark performance on the transliteration task. We report results for both baselines and across all time periods and genres in Table 4. Our work demonstrates the capability of large multilingual models to model and transliterate Sumerian, despite the highly fragmented nature of these extant texts and the language being both low-resource and an isolate.

4.4 Analysis

We derive several key takeaways from our results.

The genre of the texts impacts transliteration performance. The difference in transliteration performance across genres that we observe in Table 4 is intuitive given the nature of the underlying data. Because the training data is dominated by administrative examples, it is natural that that would be the best performing category. These texts also tend to be relatively formulaic. Liturgical, letter, and literary texts, on the other hand, have a different style, form, and vocabulary from the rest of the corpus. These genres (liturgical in particular) are also some of the most challenging for experts. Genre also affects performance insofar as for most genres there are so few examples on which to train or evaluate.

Inconsistent transliteration conventions muddle performance. Some of the different readings for a glyph stem not from a tangible semantic difference but from phonetic or aesthetic disagreement. For instance, "saŋ" and "sag" represent the same thing, but Assyriologists have a preference in how they represent the nasal 'g.' A lack of standardization on matters like this fragments the patterns in which models observe a reading occurring.

It is difficult to predict phonemes in names. Manual error analysis showed that some errors occurred when selecting a reading that serves as part of a name (playing a phonetic role). Our neural baseline model would often predict a valid reading for a glyph, but a different one than in the true transliteration. Future work will incorporate expert evaluation to determine whether these predictions are any more or less plausible than those in the original transliteration.

5 Limitations

We note that our work has some limitations, both in terms of the *SumTablets* dataset and the transliteration model.

5.1 Dataset Limitations

Administrative documents have an outsized representation in the train, validation, and test data. This dataset imbalance is a natural by-product of the category of documents produced by Mesopotamian peoples and is an unavoidable consequence of working with Sumerian texts. Although we chose to oversample non-administrative tablets in the train set by a factor of 5 during training of our model, we leave the choice of how to best handle this imbalance to the consumer.

While the set of Unicode cuneiform glyphs is largely complete, there are still glyphs that are not represented in this set, particularly some complex compound glyphs. We currently convert these glyphs and their corresponding readings into <UNK> tokens, but future work could incorporate unique identifiers for these glyphs as a placeholder until they are added to the Unicode standard.

Finally, there is considerable orthographic variation in glyphs over time, and representing these in Unicode flattens these (potentially meaningful) variations into a single, universal representation.

5.2 Model Limitations

In this paper, we train an XLM-R model on *SumTablets* as a fully supervised neural baseline for Sumerian glyph transliteration. We give our model access to the entire training set to explore the limit of a pre-trained cross-lingual model to perform this novel task. Our work, however, does not study the zero- and few-shot abilities of cross-lingual models, which is typically of more interest when evaluating a model's cross-lingual abilities. Nor do we study the performance of a model trained from scratch on our dataset. We encourage future work to use *SumTablets* as a few- and zero-shot cross-lingual benchmark task to evaluate how a multilingual model's language understanding transfers to the Sumerian language.

Moreover, we recognize that the dictionary baseline that we implement is very simple, and that a better point of comparison would be an N-gram model.

6 Conclusion

We introduce *SumTablets*, the first collection of paired glyph-transliterations extracted from 91,606 Sumerian tablets. Our dataset provides a resource for experts and non-experts alike to contribute to the development of transliteration models. We define the transliteration task, evaluation method, and establish a baseline performance so that future results may be compared. We also demonstrate that—despite Sumerian's status as a low-resource language and language isolate—large pretrained multilingual language models can be adapted to perform the sequence-to-sequence task of transliterating a sequence of Unicode cuneiform glyphs with remarkable accuracy.

With such an abundance of extant texts and so few specialists capable of reading them, we believe transliteration models will enable Assyriologists to spent less time on tedious, from-scratch transliteration and more time on research and translation.

Acknowledgments

We would like to thank Niek Veldhuis for his assistance as we explored past digital and computational Assyriological work.

First and foremost we thank the relentless dedication of contributors to the countless open-source cuneiform and Sumerian language resources. We would also like to thank Niek Veldh, Sabri Eyuboglu and Geoff Angus for their many suggestions and guidance in creating SumTablets. Richard Diehl Martinez is supported by the Gates Cambridge Trust (grant OPP1144 from the Bill & Melinda Gates Foundation).

References

Divyanshu Aggarwal, Vivek Gupta, and Anoop Kunchukuttan. 2022. IndicXNLI: Evaluating Multilingual Inference for Indian Languages. In *Proceedings of the 2022 Conference on Empirical Methods in Natural Language Processing*, pages 10994–11006, Abu Dhabi, United Arab Emirates. Association for Computational Linguistics.

Kabir Ahuja, Harshita Diddee, Rishav Hada, Millicent Ochieng, Krithika Ramesh, Prachi Jain, Akshay Nambi, Tanuja Ganu, Sameer Segal, Mohamed Ahmed, Kalika Bali, and Sunayana Sitaram. 2023. MEGA: Multilingual Evaluation of Generative AI. In *Proceedings of the 2023 Conference on Empirical Methods in Natural Language Processing*, pages 4232–4267, Singapore. Association for Computational Linguistics.

Yannis Assael, Thea Sommerschield, Brendan Shillingford, Mahyar Bordbar, John Pavlopoulos, Marita Chatzipanagiotou, Ion Androutsopoulos, Jonathan Prag, and Nando de Freitas. 2022. Restoring and attributing ancient texts using deep neural networks. *Nature*, 603(7900):280–283.

Rachit Bansal, Himanshu Choudhary, Ravneet Punia, Niko Schenk, Émilie Pagé-Perron, and Jacob Dahl. 2021. How Low is Too Low? A Computational Perspective on Extremely Low-Resource Languages. In *Proceedings of the 59th Annual Meeting of the Association for Computational Linguistics and the 11th International Joint Conference on Natural Language Processing: Student Research Workshop*, pages 44–59, Online. Association for Computational Linguistics.

BigScience Workshop, Teven Le Scao, Angela Yu, Victor Sanh, Albert Webson, Mariama Barbu, Xingxing Yap, Cécile Gessler, Sonja Lovrić, Niklas Muennighoff, Stella Biderman, et al. 2023. BLOOM: A 176B-Parameter Open-Access Multilingual Language Model. *Preprint*, arXiv:2211.05100.

J.A. Black, G. Cunningham, J. Ebeling, E. Flückiger-Hawker, E. Robson, J. Taylor, and G. Zólyomi.

2016. Electronic Text Corpus of Sumerian Literature. https://etcsl.orinst.ox.ac.uk/.

British Museum. 1896. Tablet BM 15826. Clay tablet; Pre-Sargonic. Sumerian account of silver and other commodities; square tablet, 8 col.

CDLI contributors. 2024. Cuneiform Digital Library Initiative. https://cdli.mpiwg-berlin.mpg.de/.

Danlu Chen, Aditi Agarwal, Taylor Berg-Kirkpatrick, and Jacobo Myerston. 2023. CuneiML: A Cuneiform Dataset for Machine Learning. *Journal of Open Humanities Data*, 9(1).

Christian Chiarcos, Émilie Pagé-Perron, Ilya Khait, Niko Schenk, and Lucas Reckling. 2018. Towards a Linked Open Data Edition of Sumerian Corpora. In *Proceedings of the Eleventh International Conference on Language Resources and Evaluation (LREC 2018)*, Miyazaki, Japan. European Language Resources Association (ELRA).

Alexis Conneau, Kartikay Khandelwal, Naman Goyal, Vishrav Chaudhary, Guillaume Wenzek, Francisco Guzmán, Edouard Grave, Myle Ott, Luke Zettlemoyer, and Veselin Stoyanov. 2020. Unsupervised cross-lingual representation learning at scale. In *Proceedings of the 58th Annual Meeting of the Association for Computational Linguistics*, pages 8440–8451, Online. Association for Computational Linguistics.

Jacob L. Dahl, Hendrik Hameeuw, and Klaus Wagensonner. 2019. Looking both forward and back: imaging cuneiform. *Cuneiform Digital Library Preprints*, 2019(14.0). [Online; accessed 2024-07-04].

Tobias Dencker, Pablo Klinkisch, Stefan M. Maul, and Björn Ommer. 2020. Deep learning of cuneiform sign detection with weak supervision using transliteration alignment. *PLOS ONE*, 15(12):e0243039.

Jacob Devlin, Ming-Wei Chang, Kenton Lee, and Kristina Toutanova. 2019. BERT: Pre-training of deep bidirectional transformers for language understanding. In *Proceedings of the 2019 Conference of the North American Chapter of the Association for Computational Linguistics: Human Language Technologies, Volume 1 (Long and Short Papers)*, pages 4171–4186, Minneapolis, Minnesota. Association for Computational Linguistics.

Irving L. Finkel and Jonathan Taylor. 2015. *Cuneiform*. British Museum.

Shai Gordin, Gai Gutherz, Ariel Elazary, Avital Romach, Enrique Jiménez, Jonathan Berant, and Yoram Cohen. 2020. Reading Akkadian cuneiform using natural language processing. *PLOS ONE*, 15(10):e0240511.

Junjie Hu, Sebastian Ruder, Aditya Siddhant, Graham Neubig, Orhan Firat, and Melvin Johnson. 2020. XTREME: A massively multilingual multitask benchmark for evaluating cross-lingual generalisation. In *Proceedings of the 37th International Conference on Machine Learning*, volume 119 of *Proceedings of Machine Learning Research*, pages 4411–4421. PMLR.

HuggingFace Inc. 2024. Huggingface datasets. https://huggingface.co/docs/datasets/index.

Tommi Jauhiainen, Heidi Jauhiainen, Tero Alstola, and Krister Lindén. 2019. Language and Dialect Identification of Cuneiform Texts. In *Proceedings of the Sixth Workshop on NLP for Similar Languages, Varieties and Dialects*, pages 89–98, Ann Arbor, Michigan. Association for Computational Linguistics.

Taku Kudo and John Richardson. 2018. SentencePiece: A simple and language independent subword tokenizer and detokenizer for neural text processing. In *Proceedings of the 2018 Conference on Empirical Methods in Natural Language Processing: System Demonstrations*, pages 66–71, Brussels, Belgium. Association for Computational Linguistics.

Yinhan Liu, Jiatao Gu, Naman Goyal, Xian Li, Sergey Edunov, Marjan Ghazvininejad, Mike Lewis, and Luke Zettlemoyer. 2020. Multilingual denoising pretraining for neural machine translation. *Transactions of the Association for Computational Linguistics*, 8:726–742.

Ilya Loshchilov and Frank Hutter. 2019. Decoupled weight decay regularization. In *International Conference on Learning Representations*.

Hubert Mara and Timo Homburg. 2023. MaiCuBeDa Hilprecht - Mainz Cuneiform Benchmark Dataset for the Hilprecht Collection.

Piotr Michalowski. 2004. Sumerian. In Roger D. Woodard, editor, *The Cambridge Encyclopedia of the World's Ancient Languages*. Cambridge University Press, Cambridge ; New York.

ORACC contributors. 2024. Openly Richly Annotated Cuneiform Corpus. https://oracc.museum.upenn.edu/.

Émilie Pagé-Perron, Maria Sukhareva, Ilya Khait, and Christian Chiarcos. 2017. Machine Translation and Automated Analysis of the Sumerian Language. In *Proceedings of the Joint SIGHUM Workshop on Computational Linguistics for Cultural Heritage, Social Sciences, Humanities and Literature*, pages 10–16, Vancouver, Canada. Association for Computational Linguistics.

Maja Popović. 2015. chrF: Character n-gram F-score for automatic MT evaluation. In *Proceedings of the Tenth Workshop on Statistical Machine Translation*, pages 392–395, Lisbon, Portugal. Association for Computational Linguistics.

Gebhard J. Selz. 2020. The Uruk Phenomenon. In Karen Radner, Nadine Moeller, and D. T. Potts, editors, *The Oxford History of the Ancient Near East: Volume I: From the Beginnings to Old Kingdom Egypt and the Dynasty of Akkad*, pages 163–244. Oxford University Press.

Richard Sproat. 2023. *Symbols: An Evolutionary History from the Stone Age to the Future*. Springer Nature Switzerland, Cham.

Maria Sukhareva, Francesco Fuscagni, Johannes Daxenberger, Susanne Görke, Doris Prechel, and Iryna Gurevych. 2017. Distantly Supervised POS Tagging of Low-Resource Languages under Extreme Data Sparsity: The Case of Hittite. In *Proceedings of the Joint SIGHUM Workshop on Computational Linguistics for Cultural Heritage, Social Sciences, Humanities and Literature*, pages 95–104, Vancouver, Canada. Association for Computational Linguistics.

Steve Tinney, The Pennsylvania Sumerian Dictionary Project, and ePSD2 contributors. 2024. Electronic Pennsylvania Sumerian Dictionary. https://oracc.museum.upenn.edu/epsd2/index.html.

Niek Veldhuis. 2024. niekveldhuis/compass. https://github.com/niekveldhuis/compass.

Niek Veldhuis, Steve Tinney, and Robin Leroy. 2024. Oracc Sign List. https://oracc.museum.upenn.edu/osl.

Gábor Zólyomi, Bálint Tanos, and Szilvia Sövegjártó. 2019. The Electronic Text Corpus of Sumerian Royal Inscriptions. https://oracc.museum.upenn.edu/etcsri/index.html.

Latin Treebanks in Review: An Evaluation of Morphological Tagging Across Time

Marisa Hudspeth, Brendan O'Connor, Laure Thompson
University of Massachusetts, Amherst
{mhudspeth, brenocon, laurejt }@cs.umass.edu

Abstract

Existing Latin treebanks draw from Latin's long written tradition, spanning 17 centuries and a variety of cultures. Recent efforts have begun to harmonize these treebanks' annotations to better train and evaluate morphological taggers. However, the heterogeneity of these treebanks must be carefully considered to build effective and reliable data. In this work, we review existing Latin treebanks to identify the texts they draw from, identify their overlap, and document their coverage across time and genre. We additionally design automated conversions of their morphological feature annotations into the conventions of standard Latin grammar. From this, we build new time-period data splits that draw from the existing treebanks which we use to perform a broad cross-time analysis for POS and morphological feature tagging. We find that BERT-based taggers outperform existing taggers while also being more robust to cross-domain shifts.

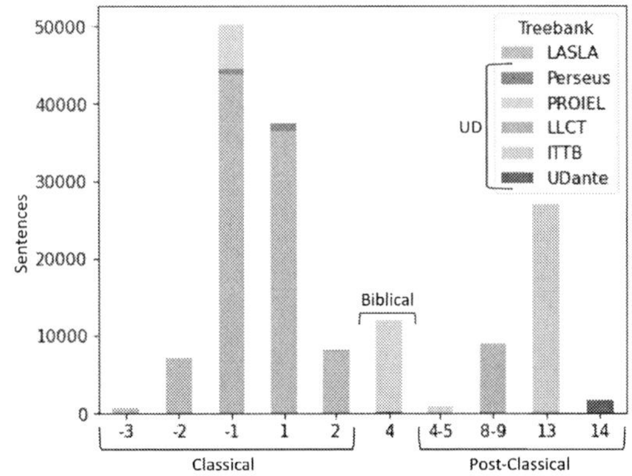

Figure 1: From our curated metadata (§2), the number of sentences per century (3rd BCE—14th CE) across the 5 UD treebanks and LASLA, shown with three broad time periods.

1 Introduction

Large-scale digitized Latin archives now document cultures across many centuries in wide a variety of genres from literature to legal documents. With increasingly powerful Latin natural language processing tools (e.g. Bamman and Burns, 2020; Burns, 2023), morphological feature tagging is a promising method for Latin-based computational humanities. The goal of morphological tagging is to identify a set of morphological feature-value pairs for each token of a given sentence. These features can help researchers analyze agency, power, and other morphosyntactically-signalled phenomena which have been fruitfully investigated in English (Sap et al., 2017; Greene and Resnik, 2009) and other languages (Rashkin et al., 2017). For example, Voice (active, passive verbs) and Case (e.g., nominative, accusative ablative nouns) are useful for studying power and agency.

Although Latin taggers have relatively good performance, in our experience they often perform poorly on rarer feature values—such as passive voice–that may prove crucial for downstream analyses. Toward this end, we hope to develop a Latin morphological tagger whose accuracy is robust across time and genre by leveraging the recent development of five separate Latin Universal Dependencies (UD; de Marneffe et al., 2021) treebanks and recent efforts to harmonize their morphological tags (Gamba and Zeman, 2023a). In this work we review these harmonized treebanks[1] plus the non-UD treebank LASLA (Denooz, 2004), and conclude that more data curation is required to fully evaluate and improve morphological tagging's cross-domain accuracy.

Our contributions include: **1)** precisely documenting genre and historical context for the 544 texts within the UD treebanks as a machine-readable, cross-treebank resource that will enable

[1]Perseus (Bamman and Crane, 2011), PROIEL (Haug and Jøhndal, 2008), LLCT (Cecchini et al., 2020b), ITTB (Passarotti, 2019), and UDante (Cecchini et al., 2020a)

Proceedings of the 1st Workshop on Machine Learning for Ancient Languages (ML4AL 2024), pages 203–218
August 15, 2024 ©2024 Association for Computational Linguistics

future work to examine morphosyntactic association against these variables; **2)** harmonizing the UD and LASLA treebanks to reduce annotation differences that can affect training; **3)** proposing edits to the UD tagset that better align with standard analyses of Latin grammar to facilitate work by researchers with standard Latin training; and **4)** conducting a cross-time analysis with experimental results broken down by historical period that show the promise of our harmonization efforts and BERT-based morphological taggers.[2]

2 Latin Treebanks Revisited

2.1 Time and Genre Metadata

Detailed metadata on the texts included in the Latin UD treebanks is difficult to aggregate or lacking altogether. Information on the included works' time period, genre, author, and relative size has not been compiled in one place. Our work takes major steps to fill this gap. For all 544 texts across the five UD treebanks, we manually collected the following metadata: the source treebank, time period, century, internal treebank identifiers, cumulative and split-level sentence counts, author, and exhaustive genre labels.

Genre. Figure 2 shows the genre coverage of the UD treebanks. Previous EvaLatin campaigns (Sprugnoli et al., 2020, 2022) have implicitly defined several genres (prose, poetry, epics, and histories), which were then used to analyze cross-genre tagging accuracy on Classical era, non-UD data. We expand upon these genres by including more fine-grained labels and by covering non-Classical texts.

We annotate nine exclusive genres: short poems, epics, letters, histories, satires, speeches, legal texts, treatises, and the Bible.[6]

Time. We define the (approximate) century of each text (Figure 1 and 2). For cross-time analysis, we define three very broad time periods:

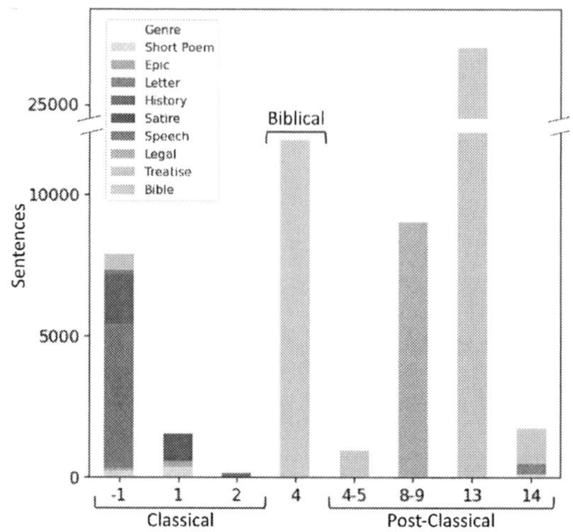

Figure 2: Number of sentences in the UD treebanks per century, colored by genre.

- **Classical** is defined as 3rd century BCE through the 2nd century CE, in line with conventional definitions of the Classical Latin language and periods (Sala and Posner, 2024) and previous Latin NLP literature (Sprugnoli et al., 2020, 2022).
- **Biblical** is defined as its own genre and time period, consisting solely of Jerome's *Vulgata* from the 4th century CE. It is significantly different from other texts given it is a translation (from much earlier material), and has relatively simpler grammar (Nunn, 1922).
- **Post-Classical** is defined as 4th century CE and later, excluding the Bible, thus including Late and Medieval Latin texts. For simplicity, we do not split it further.

Prior work in cross-time tagging either used a smaller set of time periods (Sprugnoli et al., 2022) or considered each UD treebank its own time period (Gamba and Zeman, 2023a), which we argue is too approximate given our metadata findings (§2.2).

2.2 UD Treebanks

Currently, there are five UD treebanks for Latin.[7] Four of these—Perseus, PROIEL, LLCT, and ITTB—were automatically converted to UD format, while the fifth, UDante, was annotated directly in UD. Collectively, this corresponds to about 58,000 annotated sentences and 979,280 annotated tokens. As Figure 1 shows, these treebanks cover a wide range of time but far from evenly.

[2]We have publicly released our new text-level metadata, standardized morphologically tagged text from described treebanks, and conversion software on Github.

[3]Although unreleased, we determined the feature-value set by examining LatinCy's outputs.

[4]EvaLatin 2020 also has annotated data that is not directly sourced from LASLA but consists of a subset of LASLA's texts. This data is not annotated with morphological features.

[5]EvaLatin 2022 is a near-subset of LASLA because it has one non-Classical text that is not in LASLA.

[6]We also annotate additional non-exclusive genres (§A.1).

[7]In May 2024, a sixth, CIRCSE, was added; it is a subset of LASLA.

	Name	Text Data	Standard Grammar?	Data Source	Paper/Version
1	Pre-UD	4 non-UD	Mixed	Perseus, PROIEL LLCT1,ITTB	Bamman and Crane 2011; Haug and Jøhndal 2008 Korkiakangas and Passarotti 2011; Passarotti 2019
2	UD v2.8+	5 UD	Mixed	UD Site	UD v2.8-11
3	LatinCy Edits	5 UD	Yes[3]	Unreleased	Burns 2023
4	Harmonized UD	5 UD	No	Github *(acc. 1/24)*	UD v2.13; Gamba and Zeman 2023a
5	LASLA	1 non-UD	Mixed	Github *(acc. 2/24)*	Denooz 2004
6	EvaLatin 2022[4]	near-subset of 5[5]	Mixed	Github	Sprugnoli et al. 2022
7	CIRCSE	1 UD; subset of 5	Mixed	Github	UD v2.14
8	Harmonized + Standardized	5 UD + LASLA, New Splits	Yes	Github	This work

Table 1: Summary of data sources and history of Latin treebanks (for morphological tagging only).

We find that the three Post-Classical treebanks (LLCT, ITTB, and UDante) are quite distinct from each other in terms of genre and time period. LLCT consists entirely of medieval legal charters from the 8th and 9th centuries. ITTB consists of three philosophical and religious works by Thomas Aquinas from the 13th century. Finally, UDante is comprised of Dante Alighieri's 14th century Latin works, including treatises, letters, and poems.

The two remaining treebanks, Perseus and PROIEL, are more diverse. Most texts in Perseus are Classical, although 154 sentences are from Jerome's *Vulgata* (the Book of Revelation). While PROIEL also includes Classical texts, the majority (11785) of its 18411 sentences are also taken from Jerome's *Vulgata*. There is overlap between Perseus and PROIEL, as both share at least 145 sentences from the Book of Revelation.[8] Aside from Classical and Biblical texts, PROIEL also includes one 4th-5th century work, *Opus Agriculturae* by Palladius.

2.3 LASLA: Additional Classical-era treebank

LASLA is a large, non-UD treebank for Latin (Denooz, 2004). By our own count, LASLA has 134 unique texts with 95,974 sentences and about 1.8M tokens.[9] All texts are Classical. All genres included in UD are covered, in addition to plays. Unlike the UD treebanks, LASLA does not have dependency relations.

[8]See Table 8 for a breakdown of annotation agreement between these duplicate sentences.

[9]A full list of authors, works, and tokens per text is available here.

3 Harmonizing UD and LASLA Annotations

In this section, we describe steps taken to reduce the annotation differences between the Harmonized UD treebanks (Table 1 row 4) and LASLA (1 row 5). Throughout this section, we sometimes use "UD" as a shorthand for Gamba and Zeman (2023a)'s Harmonized UD treebanks.

In §3.1, we outline the annotation agreement between Harmonized UD and LASLA before any intervention on our part. Then, we describe two types of changes: harmonization (§3.2) and standardization (§3.3). During harmonization, we enforce consistency of arbitrary values to have fair training and evaluation. Standardization is more involved, where we change the grammatical system to be more Latin-specific. Both of these steps are done automatically and simultaneously through conversion scripts.

3.1 Annotation Agreement Between UD and LASLA

Author	Work	# Dups
Caesar	Gallic War	1127
Cicero	De Officiis	447
Cicero	In Catilinam	118
Ovid	Metamorphoses	0[10]
Petronius	Satyricon	407
Propertius	Elegies	183
Sallust	Bellum Catilinae	228
Tacitus	Historiae	50
Vergil	Aeneid	47

Table 2: For the nine texts shared between LASLA and UD (collectively; specifically, Perseus and PROIEL), number of duplicate sentences.

[10]Ovid's *Metamorphoses* appears in both treebanks, but they cover different books of the text.

UD and LASLA happen to have re-annotated many of the same sentences, which gives a way to analyze annotation agreement between the projects. We detect sentences that appear in both datasets (§A.2), finding 2607 such duplicates across eight Classical texts (Table 2), which may be an underestimate since our duplicate detector will miss cases where sentence segmentation or tokenization differ.

We calculate annotation agreement before and after harmonization and standardization on our reduced set of features (Table 3). Some features, such as `Degree`, `Tense`, and `VerbForm`, have low agreement due to mismatches between their possible value sets in UD and in LASLA. Other features, such as `Gender`, `Person`, and UPOS have low agreement due to remaining annotation differences.[11]

3.2 Our Harmonization Efforts

Gamba and Zeman (2023a) have already performed the bulk of the harmonization necessary for the UD treebanks. However, we are additionally attempting to harmonize LASLA with the UD treebanks.

Remaining inconsistencies we've harmonized. We have found some remaining inconsistencies, both within the UD treebanks and between UD and LASLA. Usually, neither is incorrect in their annotation, but without normalization this will cause unfair evaluation. Thus, we enforce consistent, arbitrary values in these cases. See §A.4 for specifics.

Collapsing feature values. Another issue we encountered is that some UD treebanks lack certain feature values that are present in the others. Gamba and Zeman (2023a) were aware of this issue, and chose not to harmonize these values in order to preserve as much information as possible. This is understandable, as these features may be of interest to researchers. However, for our purposes, we have collapsed certain feature values together in order to have fairer evaluation of models trained on different treebanks.

For UPOS (universal part of speech), we have collapsed INTJ into PART across all treebanks, since two UD treebanks (ITTB and LLCT) do not use INTJ, instead using the value PART. Additionally, for `Degree`, we have collapsed `Degree=Pos` into `Degree=None`, since LASLA is the only treebank to use `Pos`. The distinction between `Degree=Pos` and `Degree=None` is debated.[12] We note that Gamba and Zeman (2023a) also collapsed `Degree=Pos` and `Degree=Dim` into `Degree=None`, so this decision has precedent.

3.3 Conversion to Standard Latin Grammar

	Before			After		
Feature	% same	# same	# total	% same	# same	# total
Case	97.8	20372	20821	97.8	20372	20821
Degree	8.5	598	6998	**69.5**	598	860
Gender	74.7	14965	20034	**75.2**	14964	19911
(loose)	97.2	19481	20034	**97.8**	19477	19911
Mood	99.4	5279	5312	**97.3**	8621	8864
VerbForm	93.2	8264	8867	–	–	–
Number	97.9	25672	26211	97.9	25543	26088
Person	91.0	6089	6692	91.0	6089	6692
Tense	77.3	5228	6766	**96.7**	8184	8465
Voice	96.0	7493	7809	**96.5**	8554	8864
UPOS	93.0	34814	37425	93.0	34821	37425

Table 3: Percent and number of tokens in the duplicate LASLA and Harmonized UD sentences that have the exact same value for each feature, before and after our harmonization and standardization. Percent is out of tokens that had a non-None value in either UD or LASLA. After our changes, Mood and VerbForm are collapsed into Mood only, but we list them separately before. Percentages after our changes are **boldfaced** when there is improved agreement.

UD was developed with cross-linguistic goals in mind, offering a set of universal tags applicable to all languages. However, prior to the harmonization efforts by Gamba and Zeman (2023a), many Latin UD treebanks employed standard Latin values for certain features, reflecting a long-standing desire for a more Latin-specific tagset. Harmonization and conversion to UD has relegated these Latin-specific values to a secondary status. This poses a key challenge for evaluation, as these two annotation styles are not comparable.

Although UD provides a valuable cross-linguistic framework, we believe Latin is also useful to study on its own, within long-standing approaches to Latin linguistics (e.g. Greenough and Allen 1903). The UD treebanks remain the most complete, high-quality source of morphological annotations for Latin. To bridge the gap between UD and standard Latin linguistics, we offer an alternative version that uses more standard Latin grammar. In particular, we standardize the treebanks to follow Pre-UD Perseus's (Table 1 row 1) features: UPOS, person, number, tense, mood, voice, gender, case, and degree. This set is nearly identical to Burns

[11] See appendix for agreement rates across all features (Table 9) and a comprehensive overview of the feature inventories (Table 12).

[12] See the UD documentation for Degree in Latin here.

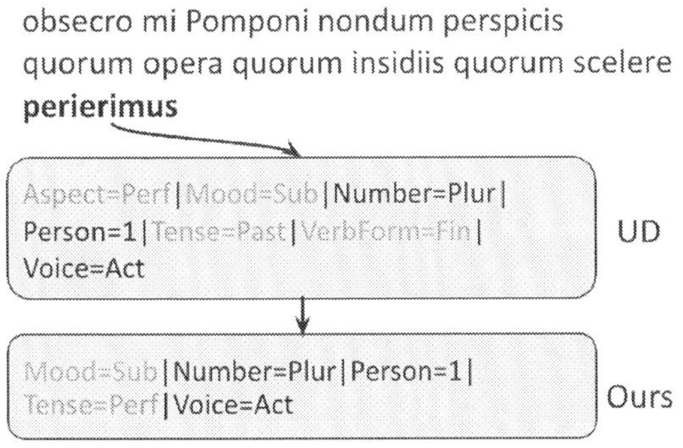

Figure 3: Example of how a token's set of morphological features changes after standardization, from Cicero's *Letters to Atticus* Book 3 Letter 9.

(2023)'s, except that LatinCy separately predicts Mood and VerbForm (which we combine). For most of these features, UD has a corresponding feature that we can easily extract. The exceptions are Tense and Mood, where we developed a more elaborate method of standardization (§A.5). For example, Latin tense traditionally has six possible values (present, imperfect, perfect, future, pluperfect, future perfect) which are standardized across pedagogical materials (Greenough and Allen, 1903; Wheelock and LeFleur, 2010). However, UD's `Tense` feature only includes four of these values (present, past, future, pluperfect), which is why we must perform a conversion.

We choose to convert to Standard Latin Grammar *before* training, rather than perform postprocessing on the predictions of a model trained on the UD tagset, for two reasons: 1) preprocessing allows for more precise conversions based on known treebank sources, addressing inconsistencies between treebanks, and 2) model predictions may combine features from various annotation schemes and be grammatically inconsistent, making postprocessing complex and potentially unreliable.

3.4 Remaining Inconsistencies

After our harmonization and standardization, most features have high annotation agreement between LASLA and UD (Table 3). Degree and UPOS, two features that already had low agreement within UD (Table 8), saw improved but not high agreement after UD-LASLA harmonization. These are likely due to fundamental differences in the annotation process which may require reannotation to fix.

We modify how our models are trained to account for the two following differences (§5.1):

- In LASLA, the `Gender` feature can take multiple values to represent possible genders based only on the word form (disregarding the context of the sentence). In the UD treebanks, `Gender` is assigned one value that depends on the sentence. This causes the low annotation agreement for `Gender` in Table 3. If we use a looser criterion—counting the annotations as the same when the UD gender value matches one of LASLA's gender values—we do see higher agreement (*(loose)* in Table 3).

- In LASLA, personal pronouns are annotated with `Person=None`, but in the UD treebanks personal pronouns have non-`None` values.[13]

We list additional differences in §A.6.

3.5 Our Custom Data Splits

Time	Train	Dev	Test
Classical (UD)	6524	201	1041
Classical (UD+LASLA)	102498	201	1041
Bible	10451	322	1021
Postclass	32661	1010	5003

Table 4: Number of sentences in our proposed train, dev, and test splits

We create new data splits to emulate EvaLatin's cross-time sub-task which evaluates models on texts of a different time period than what they are trained on. When creating train/test splits for each time period, we keep the following constraints in mind: **1)** Individual works should be within a single split. For example, Ovid's *Metamorphoses* should only appear in either the train or test set, rather than having a random sample of sentences in the train set with the rest in the test set. **2)** Make sure the test set is large enough for reasonable statistical power. We specifically choose to have a minimum of 1000 sentences in each test set. **3)** Only evaluate on UD data and not LASLA. Due to some annotation differences (see §3.4), UD treebanks have more complete information than LASLA. This is in contrast to EvaLatin campaigns which evaluate on subsets of LASLA.

To make our dev sets, we randomly sample 3% of sentences from each work in the train sets, making sure that we never sample from LASLA or any UD sentences that also appear in LASLA.

[13]This will be simple to fix in future work, since there are limited personal pronoun lemmas in Latin.

Due to these constraints, we are unable to keep the original UD test sets. Since we want test sets for each time period, we must construct Classical-specific splits. Perseus, despite being largely Classical, is too small for effective training. PROIEL contains some Classical texts but is mostly comprised of Biblical texts. We separate the Biblical content and combine the Classical texts from both treebanks to ensure a sufficiently large Classical train set. Due to the first constraint, we cannot use ITTB's original train/test splits since *Summa Contra Gentiles* appears in both the train and test set. To help meet our second constraint, we do not use UDante's and LLCT's original splits.

To achieve our third constraint, our Classical train set must include all works that appear in both LASLA and UD, shown in Table 2. We want to test two scenarios: training with and without LASLA data. In order to have enough training sentences in the UD-only scenario, we treat the letters of Cicero's *Letters to Atticus* as separate texts (i.e. that can be distributed across the Classical train and test set), even though this conflicts with our first constraint.

We include a detailed description of which works appear in our custom train and test sets in the Appendix (Table 13).

4 Related Work: Morphological Tagging

There is a long history of work analyzing POS and morphological tagging of Latin (Eger et al., 2015, 2016; Straka and Straková, 2020). Our work follows recent trends of using transformer-based contextual representations.

Several recent papers have explored morphological tagging for Latin. As part of the 2022 EvaLatin feature identification task (Sprugnoli et al., 2022), participants trained and tested on a subset of data from the LASLA corpus that had been automatically converted to UD format (Wróbel and Nowak, 2022; Mercelis and Keersmaekers, 2022). Only a subset of UD morphological features were retained, partly to limit the task to morphological features identifiable by the word form, and partly to avoid features affected by annotation differences. Participants were then able to train on combined UD and LASLA data if they wished, but models were only evaluated on EvaLatin test sets, not UD test sets.

Nehrdich and Hellwig (2022) used LatinBERT (Bamman and Burns, 2020) to train a morphological tagger predicting the case, gender, number, tense and verbform features. Its outputs were then fed into the authors' dependency parser, outperforming prior work using UDPipe and static word embeddings (Straka et al., 2019). Their training and test data came from three UD treebanks (ITTB, PROIEL, and Perseus).

Burns (2023) developed LatinCy, a full NLP pipeline for Latin which includes morphological feature classification.[14] Notably, this pipeline was trained on all five UD treebanks with early attempts made at harmonization, using a smaller tagset than UD that is closer to standard analyses of Latin grammar (Table 1 row 3). Recently, Gamba and Zeman (2023a) performed more rigorous harmonization of morphological features across the five UD Latin treebanks (Table 1 row 4). They reported accuracy before and after harmonization, training and testing on each pair of treebanks using fasttext embeddings (Grave et al., 2018) with UDPipe (Straka et al., 2016) or Stanza (Qi et al., 2020). Harmonization was shown to improve accuracy when training and testing on two different treebanks.

Part-of-speech (POS) tagging is closely related to morphological tagging. In the 2020 EvaLatin campaign, participants trained and tested POS taggers on a subset of the LASLA corpus (Sprugnoli et al., 2020). More recently, Riemenschneider and Frank pretrained a trilingual RoBERTa (Liu et al., 2019) model on English, Ancient Greek, and Latin which surpassed the 2022 EvaLatin competitors (Table 1 row 6). Thus, the current SOTA models for Latin POS tagging are all transformer-based. Additionally, Riemenschneider and Frank's trilingual model underperformed their monolingual Ancient Greek model, suggesting a monolingual Latin model could prove even stronger, given sufficient pretraining data.

Researchers have also experimented with using GPT3.5-Turbo and GPT4 for POS tagging of 16th century Latin texts (Stüssi and Ströbel, 2024). No POS-annotated data exists for 16th century Latin, so the authors experimented with zero-shot prompting and finetuning using data from the five UD treebanks. Although the UD testsets are not entirely comparable with EvaLatin's, the accuracy of these GPT-based approaches seems low when compared to the results of EvaLatin's POS tagging shared task.

Although substantial progress has been made in Latin morphological tagging, gaps still exist. Aside

[14] Using SpaCy (Honnibal and Montani, 2017)

from Gamba and Zeman (2023a) and Burns (2023), prior work has not leveraged all five UD treebanks for training *and* evaluation. While Gamba and Zeman (2023a) measure overall tagging accuracy, more detailed analysis of specific morphological features and diachronic trends has been left to future work. Moreover, to our knowledge no recent paper has evaluated the currently available taggers on UD test data.

5 Experiments

We use three metrics in our evaluations: whole string morphological accuracy, macro F1 for individual features, and F1 for particular feature-values. See A.8 for more detailed explanations.

5.1 Our LatinBERT-based Tagger

Following other recent working finding SOTA performance with transformer-based taggers (Sprugnoli et al., 2022; Riemenschneider and Frank, 2023), we finetune a tagger on top of LatinBERT (Bamman and Burns, 2020). Similar to Riemenschneider and Frank (2023), our tagger uses a separate classification head for every morphological feature, all trained simultaneously—a simple choice which could be improved upon in future work.

When training on LASLA, we sometimes do not train a particular feature head based on a token's feature values. First, if `Gender` has multiple values we do not train the Gender prediction head. We want to keep our set of possible `Gender` values limited to the standard three (`Masc`, `Fem`, and `Neut`). Second, if the token is a personal pronoun and `Person=None`, we do not train the Person prediction head. Having a null value here is inconsistent with the rest of our data. Since we do not know the true value, we choose not to train in this instance. If either of these two cases apply to a particular token, then that token will not contribute to the loss for either the Gender or Person classifier head. Other heads are unaffected.

5.2 Comparison to Previous Taggers

In this section, we use the official UD train/test splits for comparison to previous work but converted to our harmonized and standardized tagset. We compare our BERT taggers to two sets of taggers previously evaluated on UD data: LatinCy (Table 1 row 3) and five Stanza models trained on the five Harmonized UD treebanks (Table 1 row 4). LatinCy uses a non-transformer neural architecture as part of the SpaCy pipeline, along with

Model	Train Set(s)	perseus	proiel	llct	ittb	udante
LatinCy	All UD	.726	.740	.792	.809	.736
BERT	All UD	**.929**	.962	.969	.982	**.910**
Stanza	In-Domain UD	.787	.929	.969	.965	.819
BERT	In-Domain UD	.915	**.962**	**.977**	**.984**	.903

Table 5: Whole string accuracy of **morphological features**. Train set is either All 5 UD treebanks, or a single In-Domain UD Treebank (i.e., same as the Test column).

Model	Metric	perseus	proiel	llct	ittb	udante
Stanza	POS Macro F1	.072	.253	.284	.227	.122
BERT	POS Macro F1	**.066**	**.191**	**.185**	**.144**	**.101**
Stanza	Morph Acc	.058	.179	.275	.177	.077
BERT	Morph Acc	**.016**	**.069**	**.186**	**.074**	**.030**

Table 6: Average difference between in and out of domain performance, for each of the 5 UD treebank test sets (columns); this work (BERT rows) always attains a smaller difference.

static floret vectors (Boyd and Warmerdam, 2022). Stanza has a Bi-LSTM architecture for its POS and morphological taggers and uses either word2vec (Zeman et al., 2018) or fasttext (Bojanowski et al., 2017) embeddings, depending on the language. For a fair comparison, we must convert between the different tagsets used by each tagger. For LatinCy, rather than retraining the SpaCy pipeline ourselves, we convert its predictions on each official UD test set to our tagset. This required little modification as LatinCy predicts a near-identical set of features and values.[15] For the Stanza models, we retrain them on our harmonized and standardized versions of each UD training set (Table 1 row 8), since Gamba and Zeman (2023b)'s models and their predictions are unreleased. Replicating Gamba and Zeman (2023b), we only train the Stanza models on each individual treebank, rather than all UD data. We also use the same Latin fasttext embeddings (Grave et al., 2018) and default training parameters.

We report whole string morphological accuracy for each UD test set in Table 5. Our BERT taggers consistently have the highest accuracy. The smallest treebanks, Perseus and UDante, see the most benefit from the BERT architecture and the out-of-domain training data.[16]

[15] LatinCy lacks two possible `Tense` values, `Perf` and `FutP`, which our tagset includes. In a more generous evaluation, where `Fut` and `Imp` are considered correct predictions for gold `FutP` and `Perf`, respectively, all morphological accuracy scores in Table 5 increase by $\leq 5\%$, with maximum accuracy on the LLCT test set at 0.826.

[16] We see similar trends for UPOS; see Table 10.

Model	classical	bible	postclass
	UPOS Macro-F1		
classical-ud	**0.964**	0.937	0.864
classical-all	0.949	0.799	0.839
bible	0.868	**0.976**	0.834
postclass	0.866	0.920	**0.980**
all-ud-custom	0.961	0.975	0.976
all-both-custom	0.948	0.964	0.980
	Morph Accuracy		
classical-ud	0.946	0.936	0.905
classical-all	0.945	0.941	0.908
bible	0.914	0.956	0.885
postclass	0.916	0.931	0.973
all-ud-custom	**0.946**	0.956	0.973
all-both-custom	0.939	**0.960**	**0.974**

Table 7: Performance of our BERT-based taggers when evaluated on custom time-period test sets.

When comparing two models' performance, we calculate statistical significance via randomized permutation testing (Wasserman 2004).[17] When comparing our All-UD model to LatinCy and our in-domain models to Stanza, all comparisons were significant (p=0) for both UPOS Macro-F1 and morphological accuracy, except for LLCT UPOS Macro-F1 (p=0.13). So, in nearly all cases our BERT taggers performed significantly better at both UPOS and morphological tagging than previously released taggers, when trained on all or in-domain data.

We also find that our BERT taggers are more robust to out-of-domain data than the Stanza taggers. In Table 6, for each UD test set, we report the average difference between the in-domain test performance (training and testing on the same treebank) and out-of-domain test performance (training on a different treebank). This difference is always lower for our BERT models than for the Stanza models, suggesting that BERT has better cross-domain performance than Stanza.

5.3 Performance on Our Custom Splits

In total, we train six models including four trained on the sets described in Table 4. The other two models are `all-ud-custom`, trained on the Classical (UD Only), Bible, and Postclass train sets; and `all-both-custom`, trained on the Classical (UD+LASLA), Bible, and Postclass train sets. Since our LatinBERT taggers outperform the other taggers, we limit our focus to these BERT-based taggers. We find that it is generally unnecessary to train a period-specific model. As Table 7 shows, models trained on all time periods have only slightly reduced UPOS Macro F1 and have slightly increased morphological accuracy compared to the models trained on a single domain.

Addition of LASLA data boosts performance for some rare feature values, but decreases it for other features. Although there is only a slight difference in *overall* morphological accuracy with the addition of LASLA data, F1 of particular feature-values improves. When evaluating the `classical-ud` and `classical-all` models on the Classical test set, F1 increases from 0.907 to 0.941 for `Case=Dat` (p=0.0028), and 0.800 to 0.909 for `Mood=Ger` (p=0.0). We also found that some features' Macro F1 scores decreased with the inclusion of LASLA. This behavior is most prominent for Degree (0.96 to 0.91, p=0.0001) and UPOS (0.96 to 0.95, p=0.0). Since the duplicate sentences in LASLA and UD have low annotation agreement for Degree and UPOS (Table 3), the addition of LASLA data likely led to noisier training labels for these two features.

Most errors involve acontextual ambiguity. We randomly sample 100 tokens whose morphology was predicted incorrectly by our `all-ud-custom` model,[18] and annotated them according to six error types: illegal, lexical, genuine acontextual ambiguity, annotation differences, gold wrong, other.

Illegal. We found four illegal errors in which the model combined morphology and/or UPOS in a way that breaks rules of grammar. Three of these involved the token *quod*. For example, when the gold annotation labeled *quod* as SCONJ, the model correctly predicted SCONJ but incorrectly predicted `Gender=Neut` and `Number=Sing`, when a SCONJ should have no value for those features. In the fourth case, when the gold was PRON, the model again correctly predicted PRON but incorrectly predicted `Case=None` and `Number=None`, even though a PRON should have values for those features.

Lexical. We found eight *lexical errors* where the predicted combination of UPOS and morphological features is legal in general, but is impossible given the particular token based on lexical information. For example, let's consider the token *ista* whose gold annotation is a DET with `Case=Nom`, `Gender=Fem`, and `Num=Sing`. This word is a

[17]As detailed in §A.9, we simply report p-values based on 10,000 null simulations; thus p=0 is possible and could be more conservatively interpreted as $p < .0003$ ("rule of three": Eypasch et al. 1995).

[18]33 tokens from Classical texts, 33 from the bible, 12 from Aquinas' works, 11 from LLCT, 11 from Dante's works.

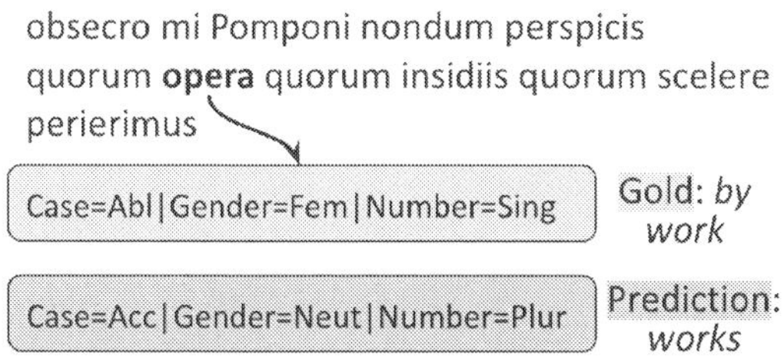

Figure 4: Example of an error in the model's prediction due to acontextual ambiguity, from Cicero's *Letters to Atticus* Book 3 Letter 9.

demonstrative adjective with 1st and 2nd declension endings, so out of context there are only a few combinations of morphological features possible: either `Case=Nom,Abl|Gender=Fem|Num=Sing` or `Case=Nom,Acc|Gender=Neut|Num=Plur`. Our tagger incorrectly predicted `Case=Acc` but correctly predicted `Gender=Fem` and `Num=Sing`. Even though its predictions for Gender and Number are correct, they do not form a valid combination of feature values for this token.

Genuine acontextual ambiguity. Most errors (67) were due to *genuine acontextual ambiguity*. This means that, out of context, the model's prediction is legal and valid given the particular token's lexical information, but in context it is incorrect. We would hope that BERT, as a contextual model, could still predict these cases correctly but it seems to struggle. Figure 4 shows an example of this error type. In other contexts, the token *opera* can be accusative plural, as the model predicted, but within this sentence it must be ablative singular. The verb *perierimus* (we have been ruined) does not take an object, so *opera* cannot be accusative. Additionally, the structure of *quorum opera* is repeated with *quorum insidiis* and *quorum scelere*. The nouns *insidiis* and *scelere* are clearly ablative, suggesting that *opera* should be the same case. This makes more sense contextually: *perierimus* (we have been ruined) *quorum opera* (by whose work).

Annotation differences. Nine errors were due to remaining annotation differences, discussed more thoroughly in §A.6.

Gold wrong. Nine errors were caused by incorrect gold annotations. These include missing `Case` value for nouns, and incorrect UPOS and morphological features.

Words segmented by the tokenizer have a higher error rate. Because of the presence of lexical errors in our model's predictions, we investigated whether the LatinBERT tokenizer segments words in a morphologically-aware manner. We find that the majority (81%) of words in our three custom test sets correspond to a single subtoken for the tokenizer. For these word tokens, our `all-ud-custom` model achieves 98.3% accuracy on UPOS and 97.2% accuracy on all morphological features. In the case that word tokens are split into *multiple* subtokens, performance degrades; Accuracy drops slightly for UPOS to 97.5% and more dramatically for morphological features to 93.6%. Since most words are not segmented and those that are have worse performance, we hypothesize that the model is not able to learn Latin's inflections, which could hypothetically aid in the tagging of rarer words. The relationship between token frequency, word segmentation, and downstream performance is a promising direction for analysis in future work. This aligns with previous findings for English that transformer models with WordPiece tokenizers have lower generalization ability than those with morphologically-aware tokenization (Hofmann et al., 2021).

6 Conclusion and Future Work

In this work, we consider the diverse time periods represented in the Latin treebanks when training and evaluating morphological taggers. We hope the genre metadata we provide can be used for future cross-genre analysis of Latin, similar to the cross-time analysis we present in this paper.

We also believe further improvements can be made through the harmonization of remaining annotation differences (§3.4) and more informed modeling choices. Specifically, we hypothesize that (1) conditioning morphological feature prediction on UPOS, or vice versa; (2) enforcing grammatical constraints through modeling, rather than only through training data; and (3) constructing a morphologically-aware tokenizer may all lead to improved performance.

Acknowledgments

We thank Gregory Crane, David Smith, Geoff Bakewell, the UMass NLP group, and anonymous reviewers for feedback. This work was supported by NSF CAREER 1845576. Any opinions, findings, and conclusions or recommendations expressed in this material are those of the authors and do not necessarily reflect the views of the National Science Foundation.

References

David Bamman and Patrick J. Burns. 2020. Latin BERT: A Contextual Language Model for Classical Philology. *ArXiv*, abs/2009.10053.

David Bamman and Gregory Crane. 2011. The Ancient Greek and Latin Dependency Treebanks. In *Language Technology for Cultural Heritage*, pages 79–98, Berlin, Heidelberg. Springer Berlin Heidelberg.

Piotr Bojanowski, Edouard Grave, Armand Joulin, and Tomas Mikolov. 2017. Enriching Word Vectors with Subword Information. *Transactions of the Association for Computational Linguistics*, 5:135–146.

Adriane Boyd and Vincent D. Warmerdam. 2022. floret: lightweight, robust word vectors.

Patrick J. Burns. 2023. LatinCy: Synthetic Trained Pipelines for Latin NLP. *Preprint*, arXiv:2305.04365.

Flavio Cecchini, Rachele Sprugnoli, Giovanni Moretti, and Marco Passarotti. 2020a. UDante: First Steps Towards the Universal Dependencies Treebank of Dante's Latin works.

Flavio Massimiliano Cecchini, Timo Korkiakangas, and Marco Passarotti. 2020b. A New Latin Treebank for Universal Dependencies: Charters between Ancient Latin and Romance Languages. In *Proceedings of the Twelfth Language Resources and Evaluation Conference*, pages 933–942, Marseille, France. European Language Resources Association.

Marie-Catherine de Marneffe, Christopher D. Manning, Joakim Nivre, and Daniel Zeman. 2021. Universal Dependencies. *Computational Linguistics*, 47(2):255–308.

Joseph Denooz. 2004. Opera Latina: une base de données sur internet. *Euphrosyne*, 32:79–88.

Steffen Eger, Rüdiger Gleim, and Alexander Mehler. 2016. Lemmatization and Morphological Tagging in German and Latin: A Comparison and a Survey of the State-of-the-art. In *Proceedings of the Tenth International Conference on Language Resources and Evaluation (LREC'16)*, pages 1507–1513, Portorož, Slovenia. European Language Resources Association (ELRA).

Steffen Eger, Tim vor der Brück, and Alexander Mehler. 2015. Lexicon-assisted tagging and lemmatization in Latin: A comparison of six taggers and two lemmatization methods. In *Proceedings of the 9th SIGHUM Workshop on Language Technology for Cultural Heritage, Social Sciences, and Humanities (LaTeCH)*, pages 105–113, Beijing, China. Association for Computational Linguistics.

Ernst Eypasch, Rolf Lefering, CK Kum, and Hans Troidl. 1995. Probability of adverse events that have not yet occurred: a statistical reminder. *BMJ*, 311(7005):619–620.

Federica Gamba and Daniel Zeman. 2023a. Latin Morphology through the Centuries: Ensuring Consistency for Better Language Processing. In *Proceedings of the Ancient Language Processing Workshop*, pages 59–67, Varna, Bulgaria. INCOMA Ltd., Shoumen, Bulgaria.

Federica Gamba and Daniel Zeman. 2023b. Universalising Latin Universal Dependencies: a harmonisation of Latin treebanks in UD. In *Proceedings of the Sixth Workshop on Universal Dependencies (UDW, GURT/SyntaxFest 2023)*, pages 7–16, Washington, D.C. Association for Computational Linguistics.

Edouard Grave, Piotr Bojanowski, Prakhar Gupta, Armand Joulin, and Tomas Mikolov. 2018. Learning Word Vectors for 157 Languages. In *Proceedings of the Eleventh International Conference on Language Resources and Evaluation (LREC 2018)*, Miyazaki, Japan. European Language Resources Association (ELRA).

Stephan Greene and Philip Resnik. 2009. More than Words: Syntactic Packaging and Implicit Sentiment. In *Proceedings of Human Language Technologies: The 2009 Annual Conference of the North American Chapter of the Association for Computational Linguistics*, pages 503–511, Boulder, Colorado. Association for Computational Linguistics.

James B. Greenough and Joseph Henry Allen. 1903. *Allen and Greenough's New Latin Grammar for Schools and Colleges*. Ginn Company.

Dag Trygve Truslew Haug and Marius L. Jøhndal. 2008. Creating a Parallel Treebank of the Old Indo-European BibleTranslations.

Valentin Hofmann, Janet Pierrehumbert, and Hinrich Schütze. 2021. Superbizarre Is Not Superb: Derivational Morphology Improves BERT's Interpretation of Complex Words. In *Proceedings of the 59th Annual Meeting of the Association for Computational Linguistics and the 11th International Joint Conference on Natural Language Processing (Volume 1: Long Papers)*, pages 3594–3608, Online. Association for Computational Linguistics.

Matthew Honnibal and Ines Montani. 2017. spaCy 2: Natural language understanding with Bloom embeddings, convolutional neural networks and incremental parsing. To appear.

Kyle P. Johnson, Patrick J. Burns, John Stewart, Todd Cook, Clément Besnier, and William J. B. Mattingly. 2021. The Classical Language Toolkit: An NLP Framework for Pre-Modern Languages. In *Proceedings of the 59th Annual Meeting of the Association for Computational Linguistics and the 11th International Joint Conference on Natural Language Processing: System Demonstrations*, pages 20–29, Online. Association for Computational Linguistics.

Timo Korkiakangas and Marco Carlo Passarotti. 2011. Challenges in Annotating Medieval Latin Charters. *J. Lang. Technol. Comput. Linguistics*, 26:103–114.

Yinhan Liu, Myle Ott, Naman Goyal, Jingfei Du, Mandar Joshi, Danqi Chen, Omer Levy, Mike Lewis, Luke Zettlemoyer, and Veselin Stoyanov. 2019. RoBERTa: A Robustly Optimized BERT Pretraining Approach. *Preprint*, arXiv:1907.11692.

Wouter Mercelis and Alek Keersmaekers. 2022. An ELECTRA Model for Latin Token Tagging Tasks. In *Proceedings of the Second Workshop on Language Technologies for Historical and Ancient Languages*, pages 189–192, Marseille, France. European Language Resources Association.

Sebastian Nehrdich and Oliver Hellwig. 2022. Accurate Dependency Parsing and Tagging of Latin. In *Proceedings of the Second Workshop on Language Technologies for Historical and Ancient Languages*, pages 20–25, Marseille, France. European Language Resources Association.

H. P. V. Nunn. 1922. *An introduction to ecclesiastical Latin*, page x–xi. Cambridge University Press.

Marco Passarotti. 2019. *The Project of the Index Thomisticus Treebank*, pages 299–320. De Gruyter Saur, Berlin, Boston.

Peng Qi, Yuhao Zhang, Yuhui Zhang, Jason Bolton, and Christopher D. Manning. 2020. Stanza: A Python Natural Language Processing Toolkit for Many Human Languages. In *Proceedings of the 58th Annual Meeting of the Association for Computational Linguistics: System Demonstrations*, pages 101–108, Online. Association for Computational Linguistics.

Hannah Rashkin, Eric Bell, Yejin Choi, and Svitlana Volkova. 2017. Multilingual Connotation Frames: A Case Study on Social Media for Targeted Sentiment Analysis and Forecast. In *Proceedings of the 55th Annual Meeting of the Association for Computational Linguistics (Volume 2: Short Papers)*, pages 459–464, Vancouver, Canada. Association for Computational Linguistics.

Frederick Riemenschneider and Anette Frank. 2023. Exploring Large Language Models for Classical Philology. In *Proceedings of the 61st Annual Meeting of the Association for Computational Linguistics (Volume 1: Long Papers)*, pages 15181–15199, Toronto, Canada. Association for Computational Linguistics.

Marius Sala and Rebecca Posner. 2024. Latin language. In *Encyclopedia Britannica*.

Maarten Sap, Marcella Cindy Prasettio, Ari Holtzman, Hannah Rashkin, and Yejin Choi. 2017. Connotation Frames of Power and Agency in Modern Films. In *Proceedings of the 2017 Conference on Empirical Methods in Natural Language Processing*, pages 2329–2334, Copenhagen, Denmark. Association for Computational Linguistics.

Rachele Sprugnoli, Marco Passarotti, Flavio Massimiliano Cecchini, Margherita Fantoli, and Giovanni Moretti. 2022. Overview of the EvaLatin 2022 Evaluation Campaign. In *Proceedings of the Second Workshop on Language Technologies for Historical and Ancient Languages*, pages 183–188, Marseille, France. European Language Resources Association.

Rachele Sprugnoli, Marco Passarotti, Flavio Massimiliano Cecchini, and Matteo Pellegrini. 2020. Overview of the EvaLatin 2020 Evaluation Campaign. In *Proceedings of LT4HALA 2020 - 1st Workshop on Language Technologies for Historical and Ancient Languages*, pages 105–110, Marseille, France. European Language Resources Association (ELRA).

Milan Straka, Jan Hajič, and Jana Straková. 2016. UDPipe: Trainable Pipeline for Processing CoNLL-U Files Performing Tokenization, Morphological Analysis, POS Tagging and Parsing. In *Proceedings of the Tenth International Conference on Language Resources and Evaluation (LREC'16)*, pages 4290–4297, Portorož, Slovenia. European Language Resources Association (ELRA).

Milan Straka and Jana Straková. 2020. UDPipe at EvaLatin 2020: Contextualized Embeddings and Treebank Embeddings. In *Proceedings of LT4HALA 2020 - 1st Workshop on Language Technologies for Historical and Ancient Languages*, pages 124–129, Marseille, France. European Language Resources Association (ELRA).

Milan Straka, Jana Straková, and Jan Hajič. 2019. Evaluating Contextualized Embeddings on 54 Languages in POS Tagging, Lemmatization and Dependency Parsing. *Preprint*, arXiv:1908.07448.

Elina Stüssi and Phillip Ströbel. 2024. Part-of-Speech Tagging of 16th-Century Latin with GPT. In *Proceedings of the 8th Joint SIGHUM Workshop on Computational Linguistics for Cultural Heritage, Social Sciences, Humanities and Literature (LaTeCH-CLfL 2024)*, pages 196–206, St. Julians, Malta. Association for Computational Linguistics.

Larry Wasserman. 2004. *All of Statistics*. Springer Science & Business Media.

F.M. Wheelock and R.A. LeFleur. 2010. *Wheelock's Latin: The Classic Introductory Latin Course, Based on Ancient Authors*. Elsie Giddings Helman Memorial. HarperCollins.

Krzysztof Wróbel and Krzysztof Nowak. 2022. Transformer-based Part-of-Speech Tagging and Lemmatization for Latin. In *Proceedings of the Second Workshop on Language Technologies for Historical and Ancient Languages*, pages 193–197, Marseille, France. European Language Resources Association.

Daniel Zeman, Jan Hajič, Martin Popel, Martin Potthast, Milan Straka, Filip Ginter, Joakim Nivre, and Slav Petrov. 2018. CoNLL 2018 Shared Task: Multilingual Parsing from Raw Text to Universal Dependencies. In *Proceedings of the CoNLL 2018 Shared Task: Multilingual Parsing from Raw Text to Universal Dependencies*, pages 1–21, Brussels, Belgium. Association for Computational Linguistics.

A Appendix

A.1 UD Genres

We mark the following 12 genres: narrative, poem, short poem, letter, epic, history, satire, speech, treatise, Christian, Bible, legal.

These genres are not exclusive, so each text will have at least one, but possibly more genres marked.

In Figure 2, for simplicity we showed a subset of genres which are mutually exclusive. This also ensures the number of sentences shown in the figure exactly matches the number of sentences that exist in the UD treebanks. The additional genres that we left out of the figure are broader, covering multiple sub-genres. Specifically, *narratives* includes some (not all) texts from every genre except for legal texts and speeches. *Poems* includes epics and short poems, the two of which are mutually exclusive. *Christian* includes the Bible itself, as well as the religious treatises of Thomas Aquinas.

A.2 Finding Duplicate Sentences in LASLA and UD Treebanks

In order to detect *duplicate sentences* between the treebanks, we first normalize the orthographic variation across the UD treebanks and LASLA. We used CLTK's (Johnson et al., 2021) JV replacer on the harmonized UD treebanks, since LASLA's texts do not use the letters 'j' or 'v'. We also remove any punctuation present in the UD treebanks, as LASLA does not have punctuation.

We search for duplicate sentences by finding sentence pairs with exact character or token overlap at the beginning or end of each sentence.

Within the duplicate sentences, we identify *duplicate tokens* by searching for the longest overlapping, contiguous subsequence of tokens of each sentence. We search for exact token matches. Our reported number of duplicate tokens is an underestimate, since there are sometimes token mismatches within sentences that are genuine duplicates. For example, one sentence may have a numeral where the other has the word form of the number.

A.3 Annotation Agreement

In Table 8, we show the annotation agreement between duplicate sentences in Perseus and PROIEL after our standardization and harmonization. Notably, these are both (Harmonized) UD treebanks (Table 1 row 4), and some annotation differences still remain, although agreement is generally still higher than between UD and LASLA.

Feature	% same	# same	Total
Case	96.1	794	826
Degree	50.0	5	10
Gender	94.7	767	810
Mood	93.1	349	375
Number	97.7	1097	1123
Person	100.0	347	347
Tense	95.4	356	373
Voice	98.4	369	375
UPOS	97.6	1538	1576

Table 8: Percent and number of tokens in the duplicate Perseus and PROIEL sentences that have the **exact same value** for each feature, after our harmonization and conversion to Standard Latin grammar

Feature	% same	# same	Total
AdpType	76.8	2115	2753
AdvType	0.0	0	357
Aspect	97.1	8608	8864
Case	97.8	20372	20821
Compound	0.0	0	1
ConjType	0.0	0	5
Degree	8.5	598	6998
Foreign	0.0	0	2
Gender	74.7	14965	20034
Gender_loose	97.2	19481	20034
InflClass	0.0	0	27580
InflClass[nominal]	0.0	0	3394
Mood	99.4	5279	5312
Number	97.9	25672	26211
Number[psor]	100.0	281	281
NumForm	0.0	0	268
NumType	71.2	497	698
PartType	6.2	4	65
Person	91.0	6089	6692
Person[psor]	96.3	501	520
Polarity	35.1	267	760
Poss	96.3	501	520
PronType	78.2	4952	6333
Reflex	91.7	584	637
Tense	77.3	5228	6766
Variant	0.0	0	43
VerbForm	93.2	8264	8867
Voice	96.0	7493	7809
UPOS	93.0	34814	37425

Table 9: Percent and number of tokens in the duplicate LASLA and Harmonized UD sentences that have the **exact same value** for each feature, before any harmonization or standardization by us.

In Table 9, we show the annotation agreement between Harmonized UD and LASLA, before our harmonization and standardization. This table also shows the union of UD and LASLA's feature sets. There are many features we did not consider which could benefit from harmonization.

Finally, Table 12 is a venn diagram showing all possible features and values in UD and LASLA, before our harmonization and standardization.

A.4 Remaining Inconsistencies We've Harmonized

Here is a full list of arbitrary values we've enforced for certain grammatical constructions. For each of these items, there are arguably multiple correct ways to annotate—and the Latin treebanks were annotating these differently.

- Gerunds, Infinitives, and Supines should have `Number=None`
- Gerunds, Gerundives, and Supines should have `Tense=None`
- If UPOS is AUX, then `Voice=Act`. This almost entirely applies to forms of *sum*.
- Gerunds should have `Voice=Act`, and Gerundives should have `Voice=Pass`.
- Supines have `Voice=Act`, unless used in a construction with *iri*, in which case `Voice=Pass`.
- Gerunds, Infinitives, and Supines should have `Gender=None`.

A.5 Standardizing Tense and Mood

Tense We use the `TraditionalTense` field of the harmonized treebanks (Gamba and Zeman, 2023a), rather than the UD approach to tense. Altogether, the UD Latin treebanks include four tenses (present, past, future, pluperfect) and four aspects (imperfective, perfective, prospective, inchoative). When tense and aspect are considered together, they can represent the seven traditional Latin tenses. However, this is less intuitive for Classicists or those whose goal is to study only Latin. We chose to revert back to the traditional tenses. We were able to use the `TraditionalTense` field for most tags, but to differentiate between future and future perfect it is also necessary to look at `Aspect`. Additionally, we found that infinitives did not have a `TraditionalTense`, so we looked to the `Aspect` feature value to determine the tense of infinitives.

For LASLA, since it does not have a `TraditionalTense` field, we look at both `Tense` and `Aspect` feature values to determine tense.

Our final set of tenses is: present, imperfect, perfect, pluperfect, future, and future perfect.

Mood Similar to tense, the non-finite moods are represented by a combination of the `Mood` and `VerbForm` fields in Gamba and Zeman (2023a)'s harmonized treebanks, with references to Latin-specific constructions being moved to the `TraditionalMood` field. Strictly speaking, non-finite verbs do not have mood, but traditional Latin grammars still classify the different non-finite verbforms as "mood."[19] Again, we opt to use the traditional terminology and follow the same tagset as the Perseus treebank. For finite verbs, this includes indicative, subjunctive, imperative; and for non-finite verbs, infinitive, participle, gerund, gerundive, and supine.

For LASLA, we are able to take the mood directly from the `Mood` feature for finite verbs, and from `VerbForm` feature for non-finite verbs. This is because LASLA uses the Latin-specific `Ger,Gdv,Sup` values for `VerbForm`, unlike the harmonized UD treebanks.

A.6 Remaining Inconsistencies We're Unable to Harmonize

We are aware of the following differences, but leave their harmonization to future work:

- The pre-UD Perseus treebank (Table 1 row 1) has an additional `Voice` value for deponent verbs. After Gamba and Zeman (2023a)'s harmonization, deponent verbs in Perseus always have `Voice=Act`, but deponent verbs in every other UD treebank have `Voice=Pass`. We would like a system more similar to pre-UD Perseus with an additional `Voice=Dep` value.
- ITTB is the only treebank that sometimes marks *esse*, the infinitive of *sum*, as NOUN with `Mood=None`.

The following annotation differences were found to cause 9% of sampled errors in our BERT tagger's morphological predictions:

[19]This is explained in the EvaLatin 2022 guidelines: https://github.com/CIRCSE/LT4HALA/blob/master/2022/data_and_doc/EvaLatin_2022_guidelines_v1.pdf

Model	Train Set(s)	per-seus	pro-iel	llct	ittb	uda-nte
LatinCy	All UD	.729	.800	.800	.786	.737
BERT	All UD	**.872**	.974	.982	.980	**.855**
Stanza	In-Domain UD	.809	.967	.982	.977	.841
BERT	In-Domain UD	.867	**.977**	**.984**	**.986**	.880

Table 10: Macro F1 of **UPOS**. Train set is either All 5 UD treebanks, or a single In-Domain UD Treebank (i.e., same as the Test column).

- Whether to have `Case=None` for undeclined nouns.
- Whether deponent verbs should be labeled as `Voice=Act` or `Voice=Pass`.
- Whether infinitives should have a value for `Case`.
- Whether infinitives can have their UPOS be NOUN, `Mood=None`, and `Tense=None`.
- Whether the pronoun *sui* should always have `Number=None`.

A.7 Finetuning Details

We use the same hyperparameters that Bamman and Burns (2020) used to finetune a POS tagger: Adam optimizer with learning rate 5×10^{-5}, early stopping patience of 10 epochs, batch size 32, dropout rate 0.25. We keep the model with the lowest validation loss across all epochs.

A.8 Metrics

Whole-String Morphological Accuracy Following the convention of Gamba and Zeman (2023a) and Sprugnoli et al. (2022), we consider the model's prediction correct when every morphological feature is correctly predicted. We construct a morphological feature string from the predicted feature set, making sure to sort the features alphabetically. Then, we can test whether the predicted morphological string is an exact match to the gold string. Although this is a strict criteria, it indicates whether the model understands how all the morphological features fit together.

Macro F1 for Individual Features For UPOS and each individual morphological feature, we report Macro F1 in order to see how the model performs on rare feature values. If we define F as a particular feature and $\mathcal{V}_F = \{v_1, ..., v_n\}$ as the set of possible values that F can take, then macro F1 is defined as $\frac{1}{n}\sum_{i=1}^{n} \mathrm{F1}(v_i)$. Note that $v =$ `None`

Feature	classical	bible	postclass
Case	0.946	**0.953**	0.948
Degree	0.977	**0.987**	0.965
Gender	0.968	0.977	**0.982**
Mood	0.859	0.938	**0.982**
Number	0.987	0.988	0.992
Person	0.994	0.993	0.992
Tense	0.955	0.977	0.954
Voice	0.969	0.973	0.990

Table 11: Macro f1 of each individual feature for the `all-ud-custom` model. Note that macro f1 for `Mood` on the Classical test set seems low (0.859) because the model never predicts `Mood=Sup` (supine). Excluding that value, its macro f1 is 0.967.

is a possible value for every morphological feature, and is included in our calculation.

A.9 Randomized Permutation Testing

Within a null simulation, for each test set sentence we shuffle the two models' predictions, and store the absolute difference in the performance metric calculated from the entire shuffled test set. We finally report the p-value as the fraction of 10,000 simulated absolute differences that are larger than the observed absolute difference. p=0 simply means the observed difference is larger than in all simulations; it could be more conservatively interpreted as $p < .0003$ (Eypasch et al., 1995) due to Monte Carlo error.

Feature Union	UD Only Values	Value Intersection	LASLA Only Values
Abbr		Yes	
AdpType	Post	Prep	
AdvType	Loc, Tim		
Aspect	Inch	Imp, Perf, Prosp	
Case		Loc, Acc, Abl, Voc, Nom, Dat, Gen	
Compound	Yes		
ConjType			Cmpr
Degree	Dim	Abs, Cmp	Pos
Foreign		Yes	
Form	Emp		
Gender		Fem, Neut, Masc	Fem,Neut, Fem,Masc,Neut, Fem,Masc, Masc,Neut
InflClass		LatPron, LatI, LatAnom, IndEurU, IndEurO, LatI2, IndEurI, LatA, IndEurE, IndEurA, LatX, Ind, IndEurX, LatE	IndEurA,IndEurO, IndEurInd
InflClass[nominal]	IndEurX	IndEurI, IndEurO, Ind, IndEurA	IndEurA,IndEurO, IndEurU
Mood		Ind, Sub, Imp	
NameType	Lit, Ast, Oth, Met, Giv, Nat, Let, Rel, Cal, Com, Sur, Geo		
Number		Plur, Sing	Plural
Number[psor]		Plur, Sing	
NumForm	Reference, Word	Roman	
NumType		Card, Dist, Mult, Ord	
NumValue	2		
PartType		Int, Emp	
Person		2, 3, 1	
Person[psor]		2, 3, 1	
Polarity			Neg
Poss		Yes	
PronType	Ind, Rel, Art, Rcp	Tot, Neg, Con, Prs, Rel, Int, Dem, Ind	Emp
Proper	Yes		
Reflex		Yes	
Tense		Past, Pqp, Fut, Pres	
Typo	Yes		
UPOS	PUNCT	SCONJ, ADP, ADJ, AUX, VERB, X, NUM, _, PART, INTJ, ADV, NOUN, DET, CCONJ, PROPN, PRON	
Variant			Greek
VerbForm	Conv, Vnoun	Fin, Inf, Part	Ger, Gdv, Sup
VerbType	Mod		
Voice		Pass, Act	

Table 12: Feature and Values Comparison between UD and LASLA. Note that Perseus and PROIEL (the only UD treebanks that overlap with LASLA) lack some feature values that the other UD treebanks have, but this shows the union of all UD features.

Classical (UD Only)		Bible		Post Classical	
Work	# Sents	Work	# Sents	Work	# Sents
BellumGallicum	1445	jerome_vulgata-Mark	1257	aquinas_summa-contra-gentiles	23687
DeOfficiis	557	jerome_vulgata-1-John	12	dante_de-vulgari-eloquentia	419
InCatilinam	137	jerome_vulgata-2-John	3	dante_letters	376
Metamorphoseon	183	jerome_vulgata-3-John	4	dante_questio-de-aqua-et-terra	133
PetroniusSatiricon	547	jerome_vulgata-John	1765	dante_eclogues	111
PropertiusElegiae	224	jerome_vulgata-Luke	2044	llct_39	165
Catilina	336	jerome_vulgata-Galatians	189	llct_79	670
TacHistoriae	64	jerome_vulgata-Titus	39	palladius_opus-agriculturae	955
Aeneis	68	jerome_vulgata-1-Thessalonians	97	llct_36	276
cicero_letters-to-atticus-1	703	jerome_vulgata-James	7	llct_80	571
cicero_letters-to-atticus-2	800	jerome_vulgata-Acts	1490	llct_72	271
cicero_letters-to-atticus-4	703	jerome_vulgata-Hebrews	13	llct_83	812
cicero_letters-to-atticus-5	688	jerome_vulgata-Colossians	29	llct_73	518
cicero_letters-to-atticus-6	270	jerome_vulgata-revelation	763	llct_40	324
		jerome_vulgata-1-Corinthians	736	llct_84	771
		jerome_vulgata-2-Peter	2	llct_86	826
		jerome_vulgata-Matthew	1978	llct_75	462
		jerome_vulgata-2-Corinthians	345	llct_38	276
				llct_74	404
				llct_81	288
				llct_77	333
				llct_76	216
				llct_85	807
Total	6725	**Total**	10773	**Total**	33671
phaedrus_fabulae	389	jerome_vulgata-1-Peter	5	aquinas_forma	3290
augustus_res-gestae	38	jerome_vulgata-1-Timothy	4	dante_monarchia	682
suetonius_life-of-augustus	109	jerome_vulgata-2-Thessalonians	37	llct_37	170
cicero_letters-to-atticus-3	420	jerome_vulgata-2-Timothy	47	llct_78	389
cicero_letters-to-atticus-7	85	jerome_vulgata-Ephesians	100	llct_82	472
		jerome_vulgata-Jude	22		
		jerome_vulgata-Philemon	25		
		jerome_vulgata-Philippians	97		
		jerome_vulgata-Romans	684		
Total	1041	**Total**	1021	**Total**	5003

Table 13: Number of UD sentences in our custom train (top) and test (bottom) splits. Works that appear only in LASLA are not listed, as there are too many. See LASLA's website for a full list.

The Metronome Approach to Sanskrit Meter: Analysis for the Rigveda

Yuzuki Tsukagoshi
Univeristy of Tokyo / Tokyo, Japan
yuzuki@l.u-tokyo.ac.jp

Ikki Ohmukai
Univeristy of Tokyo / Tokyo, Japan
i2k@l.u-tokyo.ac.jp

Abstract

This study analyzes the verses of the Rigveda, the oldest Sanskrit text, from a metrical perspective. Based on metrical structures, the verses are represented by four elements: light syllables, heavy syllables, word boundaries, and line boundaries. As a result, it became evident that among verses traditionally categorized under the same metrical name, there are those forming distinct clusters. Furthermore, the study reveals commonalities in metrical structures, such as similar metrical patterns grouping together despite differences in the number of lines. Going forward, it is anticipated that this methodology will enable comparisons across multiple languages within the Indo-European language family.

1 Introduction

The oldest of the Vedic literature, the Rigveda, possesses a metrical structure. Metrical analysis involves examining the patterns of syllables, word boundaries, and poetic line boundaries, which are foundational elements in the study of ancient Indo-European poetry. Metronome analysis that is solely based on the metrical structure was demonstrated in Latin and some languages (Section 3). Similar to Latin, Vedic Sanskrit also considers the elements of syllable weight, word boundaries, and poetic line boundaries as components of its metrical structure (Section 2). By focusing on the metrical structure, the same analysis as Latin can be applied to Sanskrit, especially Vedicpoetry, as discussed in Section 4. Consequently, analyzing the Rigveda based on its metrical elements revealed that even when assigned the same metrical name, they clearly belong to different clusters (Section 5). This research enables us to uncover patterns and structures that are not immediately apparent through traditional philological or linguistic methods (Section 6).

2 Vedic Meter

Sanskrit, belonging to the Indo-Aryan branch of the Indo-Iranian subfamily within the Indo-European language family, has literature with a metrical structure. In particular, the Vedic literatures, in which Vedic Sanskrit is used, an ancient stage of the Sanskrit language, are known for their metrical composition. The calculation of meter in Sanskrit is syllabic; that is, Sanskrit poetry shapes its rhythm based on the number of syllables and their weight.

In this context, an overview of the meter in the Rigveda, which is used for analysis, is provided. The Rigveda is the oldest among the Vedic literature and consists of metrical verses. In the tradition of Rigveda studies, "meter" refers to the rhythmic pattern of entire verses composed of lines with a consistent rhythm. The meters of the Rigvedic verses are mentioned in traditional literature written in Sanskrit (Macdonell, 1886), Anukramaṇī.

Table 1 lists some primary meters. Taking the Triṣṭubh meter as an example, verses with this meter consist of four lines, each having eleven syllables. Additionally, in each line, the last four syllables repeat the pattern –heavy + light– twice. Generally, heavy syllables are represented as —, light syllables as ◡, and when not specified as heavy or light, it is denoted as ⏓. Vedic metrical texts, including the Rigveda, are recited, and in the context of meter calculation, the last syllable of each line is pronounced long, whether it is heavy or light.

Although metrical patterns refer to the rhythmic patterns of entire verses in the Rigveda, the fundamental unit in actual structural patterns is the individual line. As shown in Table 1, when the number of syllables per line is determined, the cadence, which is the latter part of the line, tends to follow a certain syllabic pattern. Specifically, for an eight-syllable line, there is a repetition of the *light and heavy* pattern ◡ — ◡ ⏓, for an eleven-sylalble line, a repetition of the *heavy and light*

Proceedings of the 1st Workshop on Machine Learning for Ancient Languages (ML4AL 2024), pages 219–223
August 15, 2024 ©2024 Association for Computational Linguistics

Table 1: Poplular meters

Meter	Syllables per line	Lines in a verse	Syllabic pattern in the cadence
Triṣṭubh	11	4	— ◡ — ⏑̱
Gāyatrī	8	3	◡ — ◡ ⏑̱
Jagatī	12	4	— ◡ — ◡ ⏑̱
Anuṣṭubh	8	4	◡ — ◡ ⏑̱

pattern — ◡ — ⏑̱, and for a twelve-syllable line, a repetition of the *heavy and light* pattern twice, followed by one syllable — ◡ — ◡ ⏑̱. However, despite the relatively strict regularity of cadence patterns, there are irregular lines that deviate from the presented patterns (Oldenberg, 1888). Additionally, for eight-syllable lines, such as Gāyatrī and Anuṣṭubh, there are cases where the pattern is reversed, resulting in a repetition of the *heavy and light* pattern — ◡ — ⏑̱. [1]

In addition to these, there exists a less strict regularity in lines with eleven and twelve syllables. The forepart of lines of these syllable counts are further divided into two parts: opening and caesura. This division often aligns with word boundaries. Moreover, the rhythm patterns in the initial part of caesura also exhibit some regularity (Oldenberg, 1888; Arnold, 1905).

The representative studies of meters in the Rigveda (Oldenberg, 1888; Kuryłowicz, 1927; Arnold, 1905; Gippert, 1997, 1999) have frequently focused on aspects such as syllable counts and syllable weight patterns in the cadence. This emphasis arises from the strong tendency in the Rigveda to strictly determine the rhythm based on syllable counts and syllabic weight patterns in the cadence.

3 Related Research

Nagy et al. (2023) analyzed Latin poetry using four elements known as the *metronome*: *light syllable*, *heavy syllable*, *word boundary*, and *poetic line boundary*. Following the metronome analysis code, we represent light syllables as 'w', heavy syllables as 'S', word boundaries as '.', and poetic line boundaries as '|'. By substituting these elements in Latin poetry, the verse is considered as a sequence of these four elements. Texts composed of these four metrical elements are similar to genes consisting of four types of base pairs, akin to genetic sequences.

The study of Vedic meter made significant advancements following the research of Oldenberg (Oldenberg, 1888). About a century later, Gippert pioneered the computer-based analysis of meters (Gippert, 1999). Recent research on Vedic meter (Ittzés, 2012; Beguš, 2015), including the studies mentioned above (Oldenberg, 1888; Gippert, 1997, 1999), focuses on the phonology of Vedic Sanskrit and the historical changes of sounds from Proto-Indo-European to Sanskrit. While these studies focus on phonological aspects and the development of phonological theories based on metrical patterns, there has been limited exploration of Vedic meters from a stylometric perspective. Our research aims to bridge this gap by applying a stylometric approach to the analysis of Vedic poetry, inspired by the metronome analysis of Latin poetry.

4 Method

This study follows the metronome analysis proposed by Nagy (2023); Nagy et al. (2023). Similar to their approach, it converts all verses in the Rigveda into four elements of the metronome, 'w' for a light syllable, 'S' for a heavy syllable, '.' for a word boundary, and '|' for a verse boundary, to perform metrical analysis. An example of the transformation of Rigveda text into the metronome is provided in Table 2[2]. The skeleton structure represents short vowels by V, long vowels by W, and consonants by C.

Table 2: Examples of transformation into metronome

Text	*agním īḷe puróhitaṃ*
Skeleton	VCCVC WCW CVCWCVCVC
metronome	`Sw.SS.wSwS|`

Specifically, the steps for the analysis are as follows. The electronic text of the Rigveda (Martínez García and Gippert, 1995) is utilized, and it undergoes a transformation into the metronome. The metronome sequences are then subjected to a score calculation using the Python module

[1] Known as Trochaic Gāyatrī.

[2] The detailed steps for transformation are outlined in Section A.

metronome[3]. Subsequently, a hierarchical clustering analysis is performed on the metronome sequences of Rigvedic verses[4]. For distance calculations, Euclidean distance, normalized Euclidean distance, Chebyshev distance, and Minkowski distance are employed. As for linkage methods, average, centroid, complete, median, single, and ward are used. All possible combinations of these distances and methods, resulting in twenty-four variants, are employed for clustering. By employing all possible combinations of these distances and linkage methods (resulting in twenty-four variants), the study aims to ensure robustness in the clustering results.

For clarity in the analysis results, the scope of the text is limited. Since the Rigveda comprises ten books with a total of over 10,000 verses, the analysis is conducted book by book. Notably, Books 2 to 7 of the Rigveda are known as *family books*, consisting of verses attributed to a single poetic family. Family books are considered to contain relatively more ancient verses of the Rigveda, making them particularly significant (Oldenberg, 1888; Arnold, 1905).

5 Result

First, we shall focus on books 2 to 7 of the Rigveda, known as family books, and also include the first and second halves of book 8. [5]

Figure 1 shows the result of clustering on Book 7, whose author is Vasiṣṭha[6]. The color threshold is set to 15. While the upper three groups (brown, purple, and red) are mainly Triṣṭubh verses, the green group contains Triṣṭubh and Jagatī verses. Distant from these, the bottom yellow group contains eight-syllable verses. The other family books also have the tendency that some of Triṣṭubh verses are more similar to Jagatī than other Triṣṭubh and eight-syllable verses are close despite their difference in the number of syllable.

Upon closer examination of eight-syllable verses, it can be seen that Gāyatrī, Anuṣṭubh, Paṅkti (= 8 syllables × 5 lines), and Bṛhatī (= 8 syllables × 2 lines followed by two-syllable line and ending with eight-syllable line) form a cohesive group (Figure 2). However, it is not possible to discern the difference between Gāyatrī in ⏑ — tone and Gāyatrī in — ⏑ tone here.

6 Conclusion

The analysis in this study revealed that some verses with the Triṣṭubh meter, traditionally considered to have rhythmical pattern similar to that of the Jagatī meter (Arnold, 1905; Van Nooten and Holland, 1994)., are distinctly different from standard Triṣṭubh verses. Even though Triṣṭubh verses were traditionally labeled as such, it was empirically known that some lines within these verses exhibited the rhythmic pattern of Jagatī meter lines in the cadence. In practice, scholars have sometimes categorized Triṣṭubh and Jagatī as *trimeter* (= opening + caesura + cadence) and Gāyatrī, Anuṣṭubh, and so on as *dimeter* (= opening + cadence), respectively, while at other times making clear distinctions based on syllable counts.

Regarding eight-syllable verses, Gāyatrī, Anuṣṭubh, Paṅkti all share the commonality of having eight syllables per line, with the only difference being the number of lines. Generally, it is believed that the rhythmic pattern is determined by the number of syllables per line, regardless of the number of lines. This study reveals that various eight-syllable verses do form cohesive clusters, indicating that the rhythmic pattern is indeed primarily influenced by the number of syllables per line. Additionally, a closer look at this cluster reveals that Gāyatrī and Bṛhatī meters each form distinct subclusters, showcasing rhythmic similarities based on differences in the number of lines. Unlike previous studies mentioned in the section 3 that focus solely on cadence, our research examines the entire verse, leading to these significant findings of the similarity of different syllable counts. This comprehensive approach highlights the importance of considering the whole verse.

This study contributes to Vedic philology by providing a nuanced understanding of the rhythmic structures within Rigvedic verses. By identifying distinct clusters and subclusters based on metrical patterns, our research contributes to a better understanding of the development of Vedic meters over time and can offer insights into the chronological aspects of Rigvedic verses.

While this study primarily focuses on the

[3]https://github.com/bnagy/metronome

[4]Scripts for converting the Rigveda into metronome and for a clustering analysis are accesible in https://github.com/Yuzki/metronome_veda

[5]Book 8 consists of the first half by the Kaṇva family and the second half by the Aṅgirasa family. Therefore both are often treated as ones of family books.

[6]Due to space constraints, it is not possible to present all patterns in the figure. Representative examples are shown.

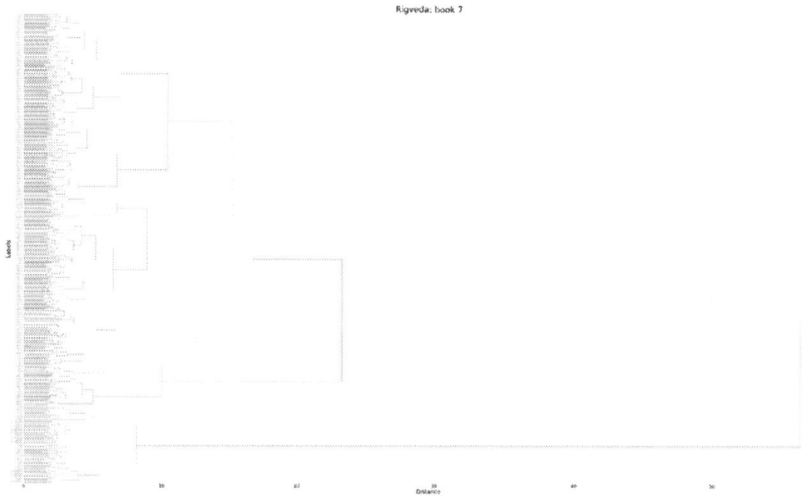

Figure 1: Rigveda Book 7, Euclidean distance, Ward's method

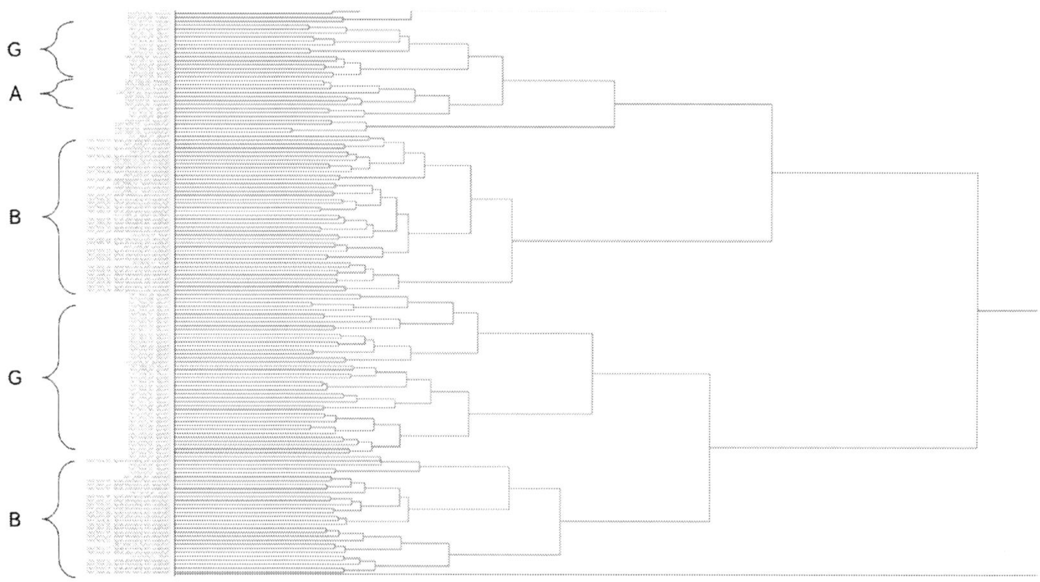

Figure 2: Enlarged view of the Gāyatrī section from Figure 1 (G: Gāyatrī, A: Anuṣṭubh, B: Bṛhatī)

Rigveda, the methodology and findings have broader implications for other Vedic texts and even extend to other Indo-European poetries. The rhythmic patterns and clustering identified in this study could serve as a model for analyzing similar meter structures in other Vedic texts, as well as later Sanskrit literatures.

Acknowledgments

This work was supported by JSPS KAKENHI Grant Number 23K18646.

References

Edward Vernon Arnold. 1905. Vedic metre in its historical development.

Gašper Beguš. 2015. A new rule in Vedic metrics. *Journal of the American Oriental Society*, 135(3):541–550.

Jost Gippert. 1997. Laryngeals and Vedic metre. In *Sound law and analogy. Papers in honor of Robert S.P. Beekes on the occasion of his 60th birthday*, pages 63–79. Amsterdam: Rodopi.

Jost Gippert. 1999. Neue Wege zur sprachwissenschaftlichen Analyse der vedischen Metrik. In *Compositiones Indogermanicae in memoriam Jochem Schindler*, pages 97–125. Praha: Enigma.

Máté Ittzés. 2012. Initial y in the Rigveda. In Roman Sukač and Ondřej Šefčik, editors, *The Sound of Indo-European 2. Papers on Indo-European Phonetics, Phonemics and Morphophonemics*, volume 41 of *LINCOM Studies in Indo-European Linguistics*, pages 86–115. LINCOM, München.

Jerzy Kuryłowicz. 1927. Les effets du ə en indoiranien. *Prace Filologiczne*, 11:201–243.

Arthur Anthony Macdonell. 1886. *Kâtyâyana's Sarvânukramanî of the Rigveda: with extracts from Shadgurusishya's commentary entitled Vedârthadîpikâ*. Anecdota oxoniensia: Aryan series. Clarendon Press, Oxford.

Francisco Javier Martínez García and Jost Gippert. Thesaurus indogermanischer text- und sprachmaterialien [online]. 1995.

Benjamin Nagy. 2023. Metre matters. In *DH2023 Workshop – SIG-DLS Seven Years on*.

Benjamin Nagy, Artjoms Šeļa, Mirella De Sisto, Wouter Haverals, and Petr Plecháč. 2023. Metronome: tracing variation in poetic meters via local sequence alignment. Poster presented at the CHR2023.

Hermann Oldenberg. 1888. *Metrische und textgeschichtliche Prolegomena*. Berlin: Verlag von Wilhelm Hertz.

Barend A. Van Nooten and Gary B. Holland. 1994. *Rig Veda: a metrically restored text with an introduction and notes*. Cambridge, Massachusetts: Department of Sanskrit and Indian Studies, Harvard University.

A Transformation Method to Metronome

This section demonstrates the method of transforming verses of the Rigveda into metronome format.

A.1 Metrical Calculation

First, we verify the metrical calculation method for Sanskrit, specifically clarifying the syllable structure and the definitions of light and heavy syllables.

Syllable formation spans word boundaries. For example, when a word ends with a consonant and the following word begins with a vowel, the final consonant of the first word and the initial vowel of the second word together form one syllable. In the case of *agním ī́ḷe* as seen in Table 2, the final consonant *-m* of *agním* forms a syllable with the initial vowel *ī́-* of the following word *ī́ḷ*. Thus, dividing *agním ī́ḷe puróhitaṃ* into syllables, we get the following:

ag ní mī́ ḷe pu ró hi taṃ ǀ
VC CV CW CW CV CW CV CVC.

The structure in the second line is called the skeleton structure, consisting of consonants (C) and vowels (short vowel V, long vowel W).

The lightness or heaviness of a syllable is determined by the length of the syllable nucleus vowel and the presence or absence of a final consonant. A light syllable has a short vowel as its nucleus and no final consonant. A heavy syllable has a long vowel as its nucleus or a final consonant. Based on this, the skeleton structure text shown above has the following light ◡ and heavy — syllable patterns:

ag ní mī́ ḷe pu ró hi taṃ ǀ
VC CV CW CW CV CW CV CVC.

A.2 From Skeleton Structure to Metronome

Using the skeleton structure seen in the previous section, we perform the conversion to metronome. In the original text, when there is a word boundary between the nuclei of two adjacent syllables, this word boundary is noted between the corresponding skeleton structures. These word boundaries within the defined skeleton structure are provisional. This is because word boundaries in the original text and those in the skeleton structure do not necessarily match, as syllable formation spans word boundaries. Additionally, due to a phonological phenomenon called sandhi, sounds at the boundary of adjacent words may merge. In such cases, the merged entity is not separated back into the original individual words.

Using the method shown so far, the original text can be transformed into metronome format as follows. For readability, light and heavy syllables are indicated by ◡ —, word boundaries by #, and verse boundaries by /.

ag ní mī́ ḷe pu ró hi taṃ,
VC CV CW CW CV CW CV CVC,
— ◡ # — — # ◡ — ◡ — /.

Ancient Wisdom, Modern Tools: Exploring Retrieval-Augmented LLMs for Ancient Indian Philosophy

Priyanka Mandikal
Department of Computer Science, UT Austin
mandikal@utexas.edu

Abstract

LLMs have revolutionized the landscape of information retrieval and knowledge dissemination. However, their application in specialized areas is often hindered by limitations such as factual inaccuracies and hallucinations, especially in long-tail knowledge distributions. In this work, we explore the potential of retrieval-augmented generation (RAG) models in performing long-form question answering (LFQA) on a specially curated niche and custom knowledge domain. We present VedantaNY-10M, a dataset curated from extensive public discourses on the ancient Indian philosophy of Advaita Vedanta. We develop and benchmark a RAG model against a standard, non-RAG LLM, focusing on transcription, retrieval, and generation performance. A human evaluation involving computational linguists and domain experts, shows that the RAG model significantly outperforms the standard model in producing factual, comprehensive responses having fewer hallucinations. In addition, we find that a keyword-based hybrid retriever that focuses on unique low-frequency words further improves results. Our study provides insights into meaningfully integrating modern large language models with ancient knowledge systems.

1 Introduction

Generic LLMs have proven to be highly effective for broad knowledge domains. However, they often encounter challenges in niche and less popular areas, suffering from issues such as factual inaccuracies and hallucinations for long-tail knowledge distributions (Kandpal et al., 2023; Mallen et al., 2023). Moreover, the inability to verify responses against authentic sources is particularly problematic in these long-tail domains, where LLMs can generate highly inaccurate answers with unwarranted confidence (Kandpal et al., 2023; Menick et al., 2022).

In response to these limitations, there has been a growing interest in retrieval-augmented generation (RAG) models (Guu et al., 2020; Karpukhin et al., 2020; Lewis et al., 2020b; Izacard et al., 2022; Ram et al., 2023). These models, which integrate external datastores to retrieve relevant knowledge and incorporate it into LLMs, have demonstrated higher factual accuracy and reduced hallucinations compared to conventional LLMs (Shuster et al., 2021; Borgeaud et al., 2022; Menick et al., 2022). Additionally, updating these external datastores with new information is more efficient and cost-effective than retraining LLMs.

Recent studies on the societal impact of LLMs (Malhotra, 2021; Yiu et al., 2023) have highlighted the increasing significance of LLMs as cultural technologies akin to libraries for search and retrieval. Analogous to earlier technologies like writing, print, libraries and internet search, the power of LLMs can be harnessed meaningfully to preserve and disseminate human knowledge (Sommerschield et al., 2023). In this vein, we argue that RAG models show immense potential for supplementing study in diverse knowledge domains. Hence, there is a growing need to examine the applications of RAG models for unconventional, custom knowledge domains that are often niche and scarcely represented in pre-training data. The capability of RAG models to provide verified, authentic sources when answering questions is particularly advantageous for end-users.

In this work, we develop and evaluate a RAG-based language model specialized in the ancient Indian philosophy of Advaita Vedanta (Upanishads, >3000 B.C.E.; Bhagavad Gita, 3000 B.C.E.; Shankaracharya, 450 B.C.E.). To ensure that the LLM has previously not been exposed to the source material, we construct VedantaNY-10M, a custom philosophy datastore comprising transcripts of over 750 hours of public discourses on YouTube from Vedanta Society of New York. We evaluate standard non-RAG and RAG models on this domain, and find that RAG models perform significantly

Proceedings of the 1st Workshop on Machine Learning for Ancient Languages (ML4AL 2024), pages 224–250
August 15, 2024

better. However, they suffer from a number of issues, including irrelevant retrievals, sub-optimal retrieval passage length, retrieval-induced hallucinations, and reliance on outside knowledge. In early attempts to mitigate some of these issues, we find that traditional sparse retrievers have a unique advantage over dense retrievers in niche domains having specific terminology—Sanskrit terms in our case. Hence, we propose a keyword-based hybrid retriever that effectively combines sparse and dense embeddings to upsample low-frequency or domain-specific terms. In addition, a simple keyword-based retrieval refinement serves to shorten or lengthen retrievals to further refine context.

We conduct an extensive evaluation comprising both automatic metrics and human evaluation with 5 computational linguists and 3 domain experts, assessing the models along three dimensions: transcription, retrieval, and generation. Our findings are twofold. First, the standard RAG model significantly outperforms the generic non-RAG model along all axes, offering more factual, comprehensive, and specific responses while minimizing hallucinations. User preference for the RAG model over the generic counterpart is evident, with a preference rate of 81%. Second, the keyword-based hybrid RAG model further outperforms the standard deep-embedding based RAG model in both automatic and human evaluation metrics. Our study also includes detailed long-form responses from the evaluators, with domain experts specifically indicating the likelihood of using such LLMs to supplement their day-to-day study. Our work offers a step toward building and evaluating real-world RAG models for niche and esoteric ancient knowledge domains, highlighting the opportunities and challenges arising thereof.

2 Related Work

Language models for ancient texts Sommerschield et al. (2023) recently conducted a thorough survey of machine learning techniques applied to the study and restoration of ancient texts. Spanning digitization (Narang et al., 2019; Moustafa et al., 2022), restoration, (Assael et al., 2022), attribution (Bogacz and Mara, 2020; Paparigopoulou et al., 2022) and representation learning (Bamman and Burns, 2020), a wide range of use cases have benefitted from the application of machine learning techniques to study ancient texts. Recently, Lugli et al. (2022) released a digital corpus of romanized Buddhist Sanskrit texts, training and evaluating embedding models such as BERT and GPT-2 on them. However, the use of LLMs as a question-answering tool to enhance understanding of ancient esoteric knowledge systems has not yet been systematically studied. To the best of our knowledge, ours is the first work that studies the effects of RAG-based models in the niche knowledge domain of ancient Indian philosophy.

Retrieval-Augmented LMs. In current LLM research, retrieval augmented generation models (RAGs) are gaining popularity (Izacard et al., 2022; Ram et al., 2023; Khandelwal et al., 2020; Borgeaud et al., 2022; Menick et al., 2022). A key area of development in RAGs has been their architecture. Early approaches involved finetuning the language model on open-domain question-answering before deployment. MLM approaches such as REALM (Guu et al., 2020) introduced a two-stage process combining retrieval and reading, while DPR (Karpukhin et al., 2020) focused on pipeline training for question answering. RAG (Lewis et al., 2020b) used a generative approach with no explicit language modeling. ATLAS (Izacard et al., 2022) combined RAG with retrieval-based pre-training, employing an encoder-decoder architecture. Very recently, in-context RALM (Ram et al., 2023) showed that retrieved passages can be used to augment the input to the LLM in-context without any fine-tuning like prior work. In this work, we adopt the in-context retrieval augmented methodology similar to (Ram et al., 2023), where neither the retriever nor the generator is fine-tuned. This also enables us to use any combination of retrieval and generation models that best suits our application.

Applications of RAGs. The applications of RAGs are diverse and evolving. ATLAS (Izacard et al., 2022) and GopherCite (Menick et al., 2022) have shown how fine-tuning and reinforcement learning from human feedback can enhance RAGs' ability to generate verifiable answers from reliable sources. GopherCite notably focused on producing answers with verifiable quotes without modifying the retrieval model. Prompting techniques have also seen innovation. kNNPrompt (Shi et al., 2022) extended kNN-LM for zero or few-shot classification tasks, and retrieval in-context approaches (Ram et al., 2023; Shi et al., 2023) have proven effective in utilizing retrieval at the input stage. Retrieval-LMs have been shown to be particularly valuable for handling long-tail or less frequent entities (Kandpal et al., 2023; Mallen et al., 2023), updating knowledge (Izacard et al., 2022), improving parameter efficiency (Izacard et al., 2022; Mallen et al., 2023), and enhancing verifiability (Bohnet et al., 2022), making them increasingly relevant in a wide range of applications. In our work, we examine the application of RAGs for long-tail knowledge, conducting an extensive study on a niche knowledge domain of ancient Indian philosophy.

Evaluation of LFQA The field of long-form question answering (LFQA) is an emerging area of active research (Krishna et al., 2021; Nakano et al., 2021; Xu et al., 2023). Recently, Xu et al. (2023) conducted a thorough examination of various LFQA metrics, encompassing both human and automatic evaluation methods, and found that existing automatic metrics don't always align with human preferences. Based on their suggestions, we place special emphasis on conducting an extensive human evaluation utilizing the expertise of experienced computational linguists and domain experts.

3 The VedantaNY-10M Dataset

We first describe our niche domain dataset creation process. The custom dataset for our study needs to satisfy the following requirements: (1) **Niche:** Must be a specialized niche knowledge domain within the LLM's long-tail distribution. (2) **Novel**: The LLM must not have previously encountered the source material. (3) **Authentic:** The dataset should be authentic and representative of the knowledge domain. (4) **Domain experts:** should be available to evaluate the model's effectiveness and utility.

Knowledge domain. To satisfy the first requirement, we choose our domain to be the niche knowledge system of Advaita Vedanta, a 2500-year-old Indian school of philosophy (Shankaracharya, 450 B.C.E.) based on the Upanishads (>3000 B.C.E.), Bhagavad Gita (3000 B.C.E.) and Brahmasutras (3000 B.C.E.)[1]. It is a contemplative knowledge tradition that employs a host of diverse tools and techniques including analytical reasoning, logic, linguistic paradoxes, metaphors and analogies to enable the seeker to enquire into their real nature. Although a niche domain, this knowledge system has been continuously studied and rigorously developed over millenia, offering a rich and structured niche for the purposes of our study. Being a living tradition, it offers the additional advantage of providing experienced domain experts to evaluate the language models in this work.

Composition of the dataset. Considering the outlined criteria, we introduce VedantaNY-10M, a curated philosophy dataset of public discourses. To maintain authenticity while ensuring that the LLM hasn't previously been exposed to the source material, we curate our dataset from a collection of YouTube videos on Advaita Vedanta, sourced from the Vedanta Society of New York. It contains 10M tokens and encompasses over 750 hours of philosophical discourses by Swami Sarvapriyananda, a learned monk of the Ramakrishna Order. These discourses provide a rich and comprehensive exposition of the principles of Advaita Vedanta, making them an invaluable resource for our research.

Languages and scripts. The dataset primarily features content in English, accounting for approximately 97% of the total material. Sanskrit, the classical language of Indian philosophical literature, constitutes around 3% of the dataset. The Sanskrit terms are transliterated into the Roman script. To accommodate the linguistic diversity and the specific needs of the study, the dataset includes words in both English and Sanskrit, without substituting the Sanskrit terms with any English translations. Translating ancient Sanskrit technical terms having considerably nuanced definitions into English is a non-trivial problem (Malhotra and Babaji, 2020). Hence, our dual-language approach ensures that the Sanskrit terms and concepts are accurately represented and accessible, thereby enhancing the authenticity of our research material. For a sample of the Sanskrit terms present in the corpus, please refer to Appendix Tab. 2.

4 In-context RAG for niche domains

We now discuss the methodology adopted to build an in-context retrieval augmented chatbot from the custom dataset described above.

We first define a generic chatbot C_g that does not use retrieval as follows: $C_g : q \to a_g$ where q

[1]Currently there exists no consensus on accurately dating these ancient scriptures. The Upanishads (which are a part of the Vedas) have been passed on orally for millennia and are traditionally not given a historic date. However, they seem to have been compiled and systematically organized sometime around 3000 B.C.E. by Vyasa. Likewise, the time period of Adi Shankaracharya also varies and he is usually placed between 450 B.C.E to 700 C.E.

Figure 1: **Sanskrit terms in VedantaNY-10M.** Frequently occurring Sanskrit terms in the corpus.

is the user query and a_g is the answer generated by the chatbot. Now, let D_t represent the textual data corpus from our knowledge domain and R be the retriever. Our goal is to build a retrieval-augmented generation chatbot $C_r : q \times R(D_t, q) \rightarrow a_r$ that will generate answer a_r for the query by retrieving relevant context from D_t using R. An overview of our approach is illustrated in Fig. 2. We first build D_t from 765 hours of public discourses on Advaita Vedanta introduced in Sec. 3. When deployed, the system processes q by first using retriever R to identify the top-k most relevant passages P from D_t using a similarity metric. Subsequently, a large language model (LLM) is prompted with both the query and the retrieved passages in-context, following Ram et al. (2023), to generate a contextually relevant response.

We now describe each of the components in detail. We follow a four-stage process as follows:

Transcription. We first need to create a dense textual corpus targeted at our niche domain. Since our dataset consists of YouTube videos, we first employ a transcription model to transcribe the audio into text. Our video corpus D_v consists of 612 videos totaling 765 hours of content, with an average length of 1.25 hours per video. We extract audio content from D_v and transcribe it using OpenAI's Whisper large-v2 model (Radford et al., 2023). This step converts the spoken discourses into a transcribed textual corpus D_t consisting of 10M tokens in total. Since Whisper is a multilingual model, it has the capacity to support the dual-language nature of our dataset. We evaluate the transcription quality of Whisper in Sec. C.1.

Datastore creation. The transcribed text in D_t is then segmented into shorter chunks called passages P, consisting of 1500 characters each. These chunks are then processed by a deep embedder to produce deep embedding vectors z_{dense}. These embedded chunks are stored in a vector database D_z. Ultimately, we store approximately 25,000 passage embeddings $z \in D_z$, each representing a discrete chunk of the philosophical discourse in D_t.

Retrieval. To perform retrieval-augmented generation, we first need to build a retrieval system $R : D_z \times q \rightarrow P$ that retrieves contextually relevant textual passages P from D_t given D_z and q. The retriever performs the following operation to retrieve relevant passages: $P = D_t[argTop\text{-}k_{z \in D_z} sim(q, z)]$, where we use cosine similarity as the similarity metric. Standard RAG models employ state-of-the-art deep embedders to encode documents and retrieve them during inference. However, these semantic embeddings can struggle to disambiguate between specific niche terminology in custom domains (Mandikal and Mooney, 2024). This can be particularly problematic in datasets having long-tail distributions such as ours. In addition, retrieved fixed-length passages are suboptimal. Short incomplete contexts can be particularly damaging for LFQA, while longer contexts can contain unnecessary information that can confuse the generation model. To mitigate these two issues, we experiment with two key changes: (1) a keyword-based hybrid retriever to focus on unique low-frequency words, and (2) a context-refiner to meaningfully shorten or expand retrieved context.

1. **Keyword-based retrieval.** To emphasize the importance of key terminology, we first employ keyword extraction and named-entity recognition techniques on the query q to extract important keywords κ. During retrieval, we advocate for a hybrid model combining both deep embeddings as well as sparse vector space embeddings. We encode the full query in the deep embedder and assign a higher importance to keyphrases in the sparse embedder. The idea is to have the sparse model retrieve domain-specific specialized terms that might otherwise be missed by the deep model. Our hybrid model uses a simple weighted combination of the query-document similarities in the sparse and dense embedding spaces. Specifically, we score a document D for query q and keywords κ using the ranking function:

$$S_{hybrid}(D, q) = \lambda \, Sim\big(z_d(D), z_d(q)\big) + (1 - \lambda) \, Sim\big(z_s(D), z_s(\kappa)\big) \quad (1)$$

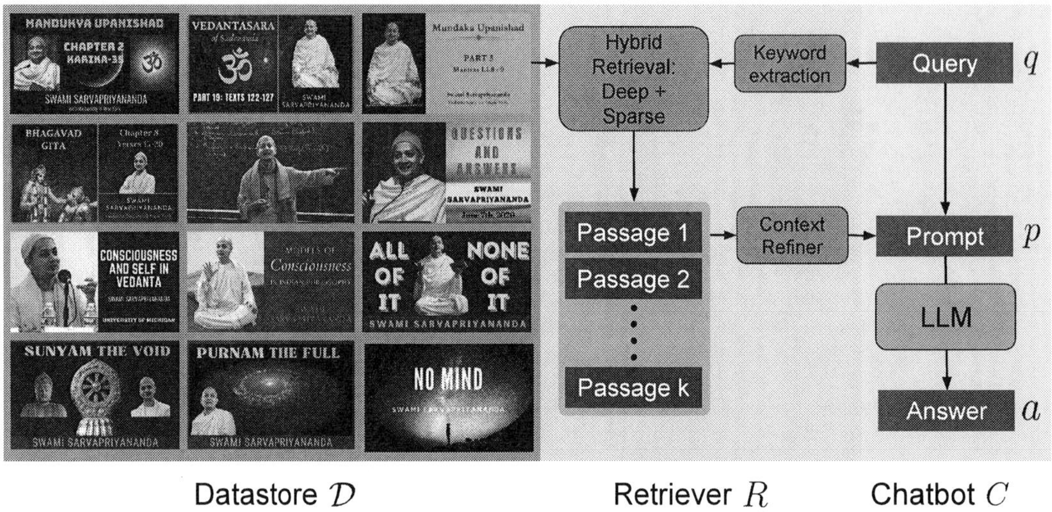

Figure 2: **Overview of the RAG model.** We build VedantaNY-10M, a datastore from 750+ hours of public discourses on the ancient Indian philosophy of Advaita Vedanta and build a Retrieval-Augmented Generation (RAG) chatbot on this knowledge domain. At deployment, given a query q, the retriever R first retrieves the top-k most relevant passages P from the datastore using a hybrid keyword-based retriever. It then refines this retrieved context using a keyword-based context reshaper to shorten or lengthen the passage. Finally, an LLM is invoked by prompting it with the query and the retrieved passages in-context. An extensive evaluation is conducted to evaluate this model with the help of computational linguists and domain experts to assess its real-world utility and identify challenges.

Where z_d and z_s denotes the dense and sparse embedding functions and Sim is cosine similarity measuring the angle between such vector embedddings. In our experiments, we set $\lambda = 0.2$. Amongst the top-n retrieved passages, we choose k passages containing the maximum number of unique keywords.

2. **Keyword-based context refinement.** Furthermore, we refine our retrieved passages by leveraging the extracted keywords using a heuristic-based refinement operation to produce $P' = Ref(P, \kappa)$. For extension, we expand the selected passage to include one preceding and one succeeding passage, and find the first and last occurrence of the extracted keywords. Next, we trim the expanded context from the first occurrence to the last. This can either expand or shorten the original passage depending on the placement of keywords. This ensures that retrieved context contains relevant information for the generation model.

Generation. For answer generation, we construct prompt p from the query q and the retrieved passages $(P'_1, P'_2, ..., P'_k) \in P$ in context. Finally, we invoke the chatbot C_r to synthesize an answer a_r from the constructed prompt. For an example of the constructed RAG bot prompt, please refer to Fig. 4. This four-stage process produces a retrieval-augmented chatbot that can generate contextually relevant responses for queries in our niche domain.

Implementation Details. For embedding and generation, we experiment with both closed and open source language models. For RAG vs non-RAG comparison, we use OpenAI's text-embedding-ada-002 model (Brown et al., 2020) as the embedder and GPT-4-turbo (OpenAI, 2023) as the LLM for both C_r and C_g. For comparing RAG model variants, we use the open source nomic-embed-text-v1 (Nussbaum et al., 2024) as our deep embedder and Mixtral-8x7B-Instruct-v0.1 (Jiang et al., 2024) as our generation model. For keyword extraction, we use an ensemble of different models including OpenKP (Xiong et al., 2019), KeyBERT (Grootendorst, 2020) and SpanMarker (Aarsen, 2020). We experimented with using language models such as ChatGPT for keyword extraction, but the results were very poor as also corroborated in Song et al. (2024). For further implementation details of the eval metrics, see Appendix Sec. A. The VedantaNY-10M dataset, code and evaluation is publicly available at `https://github.com/priyankamandikal/vedantany-10m`.

5 Evaluation

We now evaluate the model along two axes: automatic evaluation metrics and a human evaluation survey. To ensure a broad and comprehensive evaluation, we categorize the questions into five distinct types, each designed to test different aspects of the model's capabilities:

1. **Anecdotal:** Generate responses based on stories and anecdotes narrated by the speaker in the discourses.
2. **Comparative**: Analyze and compare different concepts, philosophies, or texts. This category tests the model's analytical skills and its ability to draw parallels and distinctions.
3. **Reasoning** Require logical reasoning, critical thinking, and the application of principles to new scenarios.
4. **Scriptural**: Test the model's ability to reference, interpret, and explain passages from religious or philosophical texts.
5. **Terminology**: Probe the model's understanding of specific technical terms and concepts.

For a sample set of questions across the above five categories, please refer to Appendix Tab. 4.

5.1 Automatic Evaluation

Inspired by Xu et al. (2023), we conduct an extensive automatic evaluation of the two RAG models on our evaluation set. We describe each metric type below and provide implementation details in Appendix Sec. A. Due to the lack of gold answers, we are unable to report reference-based metrics.

Answer-only metrics: We assess features like fluency and coherence by analyzing responses with specific metrics: (1) **Self-BLEU** (Zhu et al., 2018) for text diversity, where higher scores suggest less diversity, applied in open-ended text generation; (2) **GPT-2 perplexity** for textual fluency, used in prior studies on constrained generation. We also consider (3) **Word** and (4) **Sentence** counts as length-based metrics, owing to their significant influence on human preferences (Sun et al., 2019; Liu et al., 2022; Xu et al., 2023).

(Question, answer) metric: To ensure answers are *relevant* to the posed questions, we model $p(q|a)$ for ranking responses with **RankGen** (Krishna et al., 2022). This encoder, leveraging the T5-XXL architecture, is specially trained via contrastive learning to evaluate sequences generated by models based on their congruity with a given prefix, in this context, the question. A higher RankGen score indicates a stronger alignment between the question and the answer, serving as a measure of relevance.

(Answer, evidence) metric: A key challenge in LFQA is assessing answer correctness without dedicated factuality metrics, akin to summarization's faithfulness. We apply **QAFactEval** (Fabbri et al., 2022), originally for summarization, to LFQA by considering the answer as a summary and evidence documents as the source. Answers deviating from source content, through hallucinations or external knowledge, will score lower on this metric.

5.2 Human Evaluation

We have three experienced domain experts evaluate the models across the five categories. Each of these experts is closely associated with Vedanta Society of New York, and has extensively studied the philosophy in question for up to a decade on average, being well-versed with domain-specific terminology and conceptual analysis. We conduct the human survey along two dimensions: retrieval and generation. For retrieval, we evaluate relevance and completeness, and for generation we evaluate factual correctness and completeness. In addition, we ask the reviewers to provide free-form justification for their choices, which proves to be very useful in analyzing the two models.

Relevance: Defined as the relevance of the retrieved passages to the user query, this metric is scored on a scale from 1 to 5 (where 1 = Not at all relevant, 5 = Extremely relevant).

Correctness: Factual accuracy of the generated answer (1 = Factually inaccurate, 5 = No inaccuracies)

Completeness: This metric measures if the retrieved passage and generated answer comprehensively cover all parts of the query (1 = Not at all comprehensive - misses crucial points, 5 = Very comprehensive and specific).

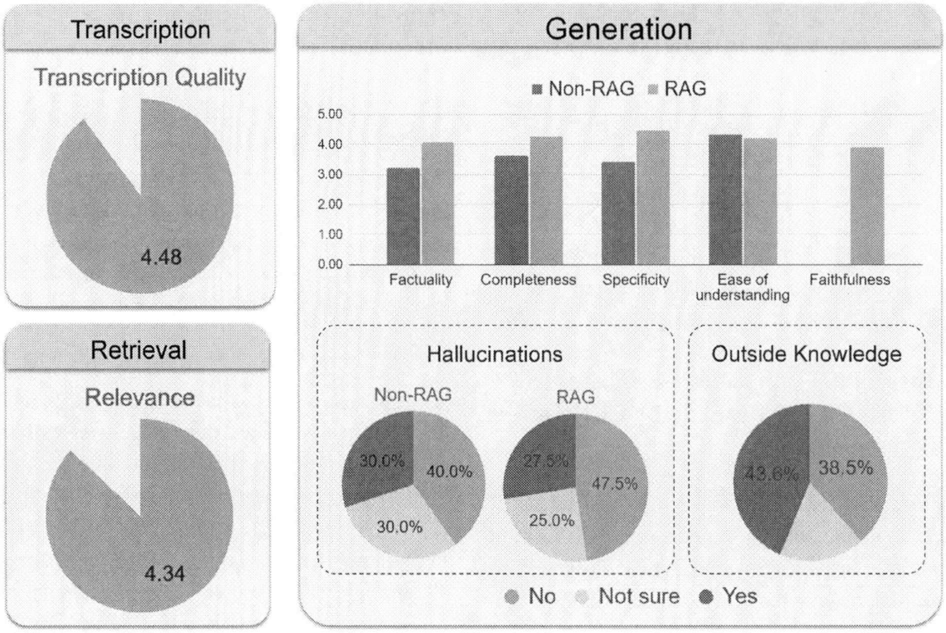

Figure 3: **Human evaluation: RAG vs non-RAG.** The RAG model outperforms the generic model across various metrics, particularly in factuality, completeness and specificity, while being marginally lower in ease of understanding.

5.3 Results: RAG vs Non-RAG

We first conduct a human evaluation survey with 5 computational linguists and 3 domain experts on RAG vs non-RAG models. In the evaluation of the generation capabilities of our models, we consider five metrics: factuality, completeness, specificity, ease of understanding, and faithfulness. The performance of the RAG model is compared against a baseline non-RAG model across these dimensions in Fig. 3. The RAG model substantially outperforms the non-RAG model across various metrics, particularly in factuality, completeness and specificity, while being marginally lower in ease of understanding. Sample responses in Figs. 6-10.

5.4 Results: Standard RAG vs Keyword-based RAG

We report results in Tab. 1. All human evaluation scores are normalized between 0 to 1. The keyword based RAG model shows strong improvement across all automatic metrics while significantly outperforming the standard model in the human evaluation. Amongst the answer-only metrics, the model tends to produce longer, more comprehensive answers (indicated by longer length), which are more coherent (lower self-bleu and perplexity). The question-answer RankGen (Krishna et al., 2022) metric evaluates the probability of the answer given the question. A higher score for the model suggests more relevant answers to the question. Most notably, the keyword model does very well on QAFactEval (Fabbri et al., 2022). It evaluates faithfulness by comparing answers from the summary (in our case, the answer) and the evidence document (retrievals). A higher score indicates greater faithfulness of the answer to retrieved passages, indicating fewer hallucinations and reliance on outside knowledge.

Coming to the human evaluation, from Tab. 1, a relevance rating of 0.87 for keyword-based RAG vs 0.58 for standard RAG indicates a strong alignment between the retrieved content and the users' queries for our model, demonstrating the efficacy of the retrieval process. On the other hand, the standard model sometimes fails to disambiguate unique terminology and retrieves incorrect passages (see Fig. 11). In assessing the accuracy of the generated answer, the keyword-based RAG model significantly outperforms the standard model, indicating better alignment with verifiable facts. Refer to Fig. 12 for an example of a factually inaccurate response from the generic model. The keyword model gets higher completeness scores for both the retrievals as well as generation. Sample responses

Category	Mean	Anecdotal	Comparative	Reasoning	Scriptural	Terminology
RAG Model	M1/M2	M1/M2	M1/M2	M1/M2	M1/M2	M1/M2
			Automatic metrics			
Answer-only						
Self-bleu ↓	0.16/**0.13**	0.11/**0.05**	0.10/**0.06**	**0.15**/0.27	**0.13**/0.16	**0.09**/0.14
GPT2-PPL ↓	16.6/**15.3**	**16.6/16.6**	16.9/**15.7**	13.9/**11.9**	**14.2**/14.7	21.5/**17.7**
# Words ↑	196/**227**	**189/189**	174/**206**	218/**282**	225/**243**	216/**261**
# Sentences ↑	9.0/**10.1**	**8.2**/7.6	7.8/**9.4**	9.6/11.8	10.0/**10.6**	9.4/**11.0**
(Question, answer)						
RankGen ↑	0.46/**0.48**	0.42/**0.52**	0.44/**0.47**	0.41/**0.43**	0.51/**0.52**	**0.52**/0.46
(Answer, retrievals)						
QAFactEval ↑	1.36/**1.60**	1.01/**1.14**	1.53/**1.94**	1.18/**1.61**	**1.52**/1.36	1.56/**1.95**
			Human evaluation			
Retrieval						
Relevance ↑	0.59/**0.82**	0.41/**0.88**	0.79/**0.85**	0.73/**0.83**	0.48/**0.73**	0.55/**0.81**
Completeness ↑	0.52/**0.79**	0.41/**0.86**	0.72/**0.79**	0.57/**0.83**	0.37/**0.68**	0.52/**0.79**
Answer						
Correctness ↑	0.61/**0.86**	0.40/**0.89**	0.81/**0.88**	0.71/**0.85**	0.52/**0.81**	0.63/**0.89**
Completeness ↑	0.58/**0.85**	0.42/**0.92**	0.80/**0.85**	0.72/**0.81**	0.49/**0.77**	0.63/**0.91**

Table 1: **Automatic and human evaluation: standard RAG (M1) vs keyword-based RAG (M2).** We report both automatic and human evaluation metrics calculated on 25 triplets of {question, answer, retrievals} across 5 different question categories. The key-word based RAG model shows strong improvement across all automatic metrics while significantly outperforming the standard model in the human evaluation.

are shown in Figs. 11-15.

6 Challenges

The evaluation in Sec. 5 shows that the RAG model provides responses that are not only more aligned with the source material but are also more comprehensive, specific, and user-friendly compared to the responses generated by the generic language model. In this section, we discuss the challenges we encountered while building the retrieval-augmented chatbot for the niche knowledge domain of ancient Indian philosophy introduced in this work.

Transcription. Our requirement of using a niche data domain having long-tail knowledge precludes the use of source material that the LLM has previously been exposed to. To ensure this, we construct a textual corpus that is derived from automated transcripts of YouTube discourses. These transcripts can sometimes contain errors such as missing punctuations, incorrect transcriptions, and transliterations of Sanskrit terms. A sample of such errors is shown in Appendix Tab. 3. A proofreading mechanism and/or improved transcription models can help alleviate these issues to a large extent.

Spoken vs written language. Unlike traditional textual corpora that are compiled from written sources, our dataset is derived from spoken discourses. Spoken language is often more verbose and less structured than written text, with the speaker frequently jumping between concepts mid-sentence. This unstructured nature of the text can be unfamiliar for a language model trained extensively on written text, which expects a more coherent and structured input. A peculiar failure case arising from this issue is shown in Appendix Fig. 5. This can be addressed by converting the spoken text into a more structured prose format with the help of well-crafted prompts to LLMs, followed by human proofreading.

Context length. The passages retrieved in the standard model are of a fixed length and can sometimes be too short for many queries, especially for long-form answering. As an example, the retrieved passage may include a snippet from the middle of the full context. As a result, the chatbot response may be incomplete or incoherent (Fig. 10). This motivated us to employ a keyword-based context-expansion mechanism to provide a more comprehensive context. While this results in much better answer generation, the retrieved passage may contain too much information, making it difficult for the generator to reason effectively. Moreover, the increase in the number of tokens increases processing time. Future work can explore more advanced retrieval models capable of processing longer contexts and summarizing them effectively before input to the LLM.

Retrieval-induced hallucinations. There are scenarios when the RAG models can latch onto a particular word or phrase in the retrieved passage and hallucinates a response that is not only irrelevant but also factually incorrect. A sample of such a hallucination is shown in Fig. 9. This is a more challenging problem to address, however retrieval models that can extract the full context, summarize it and remove irrelevant information should be capable of mitigating this issue to a reasonable extent.

7 Conclusion

In this work, we integrate modern retrieval-augmented large language models with the ancient Indian philosophy of Advaita Vedanta. Toward this end, we present VedantaNY-10M, a large dataset curated from automatic transcriptions of extensive philosophical discourses on YouTube. Validating these models along various axes using both automatic and human evaluation provides two key insights. First, RAG models significantly outperform non-RAG models, with domain experts expressing a strong preference for using such RAG models to supplement their day-to-day study. Second, the keyword-based hybrid RAG model underscores the merits of integrating classical and contemporary deep learning techniques for retrieval in niche and specialized domains. While there is much work to be done, our study underscores the potential of integrating modern machine learning techniques to unravel ancient knowledge systems.

Limitations and Future Work

While our study demonstrates the utility of integrating retrieval-augmented LLMs with ancient knowledge systems, there are limitations and scope for future work. First, this study is conducted for a single niche domain of Advaita Vedanta as taught by a single teacher. Extending this study to include other ancient systems of philosophy such as the Vedantic schools of Vishishtadvaita, Dwaita, as well as the various Buddhist and Jain schools will be an interesting extension of this work. Second, expanding the evaluation set and involving more subjects for evaluation and will considerably strengthen the scope of the study. Third, in addition to the spoken discourses, incorporating the primary scriptural sources that the philosophical school is based on will further enhance the authenticity of the RAG model generation. Fourth, while we only experiment with RAG models in this study, fine-tuning the language models themselves on the philosophy datasets is an interesting future direction. Finally, while the language models in this work are primarily in English and in the Latin script, building native LLMs having the capacity to function in the original Sanskrit language of the scriptures using Devanagari script is essential future work.

Acknowledgments

The author would like to thank Prof. Kyle Mahowald for an insightful course on form and functionality in LLMs. The material covered in the course served as a guide to evaluate the models presented in this paper. Fangyuan Xu helped with information on the automatic metrics for LFQA evaluation. The author would also like to thank all the human evaluators who participated in the RAG bot evaluation survey and provided valuable feedback—special thanks to Dr. Anandhi who coordinated the effort amongst domain experts. Finally, the author would like to extend their gratitude to the Vedanta Society of New York and Swami Sarvapriyananda for the 750+ hours of public lectures that served as the dataset for this project.

References

Tom Aarsen. 2020. SpanMarker for Named Entity Recognition.

Yannis Assael, Thea Sommerschield, Brendan Shillingford, Mahyar Bordbar, John Pavlopoulos, Marita Chatzipanagiotou, Ion Androutsopoulos, Jonathan Prag, and Nando de Freitas. 2022. Restoring and attributing ancient texts using deep neural networks. *Nature*, 603.

David Bamman and Patrick J Burns. 2020. Latin bert: A contextual language model for classical philology. *arXiv preprint arXiv:2009.10053*.

Bhagavad Gita. 3000 B.C.E. The Bhagavad Gita.

Bartosz Bogacz and Hubert Mara. 2020. Period classification of 3d cuneiform tablets with geometric neural networks. In *2020 17th International Conference on Frontiers in Handwriting Recognition (ICFHR)*. IEEE.

Bernd Bohnet, Vinh Q Tran, Pat Verga, Roee Aharoni, Daniel Andor, Livio Baldini Soares, Jacob Eisenstein, Kuzman Ganchev, Jonathan Herzig, Kai Hui, et al. 2022. Attributed question answering: Evaluation and modeling for attributed large language models. *arXiv preprint arXiv:2212.08037*.

Sebastian Borgeaud, Arthur Mensch, Jordan Hoffmann, Trevor Cai, Eliza Rutherford, Katie Millican, George Bm Van Den Driessche, Jean-Baptiste Lespiau, Bogdan Damoc, Aidan Clark, et al. 2022. Improving language models by retrieving from trillions of tokens. In *International conference on machine learning*. PMLR.

The Brahmasutras. 3000 B.C.E. The Brahmasutras.

Tom Brown, Benjamin Mann, Nick Ryder, Melanie Subbiah, Jared D Kaplan, Prafulla Dhariwal, Arvind Neelakantan, Pranav Shyam, Girish Sastry, Amanda Askell, et al. 2020. Language models are few-shot learners. *Advances in neural information processing systems*.

Anthony Chen, Gabriel Stanovsky, Sameer Singh, and Matt Gardner. 2020. MOCHA: A dataset for training and evaluating generative reading comprehension metrics. In *Proceedings of the 2020 Conference on Empirical Methods in Natural Language Processing (EMNLP)*, pages 6521–6532, Online. Association for Computational Linguistics.

Kevin Clark, Minh-Thang Luong, Quoc V. Le, and Christopher D. Manning. 2020. ELECTRA: Pre-training text encoders as discriminators rather than generators. In *ICLR*.

Alexander Fabbri, Chien-Sheng Wu, Wenhao Liu, and Caiming Xiong. 2022. QAFactEval: Improved QA-based factual consistency evaluation for summarization. In *Proceedings of the 2022 Conference of the North American Chapter of the Association for Computational Linguistics: Human Language Technologies*, pages 2587–2601, Seattle, United States. Association for Computational Linguistics.

Maarten Grootendorst. 2020. Keybert: Minimal keyword extraction with bert.

Kelvin Guu, Kenton Lee, Zora Tung, Panupong Pasupat, and Mingwei Chang. 2020. Realm: Retrieval augmented language model pre-training. In *International conference on machine learning*. PMLR.

Matthew Honnibal, Ines Montani, Sofie Van Landeghem, and Adriane Boyd. 2020. spaCy: Industrial-strength Natural Language Processing in Python.

Gautier Izacard, Patrick Lewis, Maria Lomeli, Lucas Hosseini, Fabio Petroni, Timo Schick, Jane Dwivedi-Yu, Armand Joulin, Sebastian Riedel, and Edouard Grave. 2022. Atlas: Few-shot learning with retrieval augmented language models. *Journal of Machine Learning*.

Albert Q. Jiang, Alexandre Sablayrolles, Antoine Roux, Arthur Mensch, Blanche Savary, Chris Bamford, Devendra Singh Chaplot, Diego de las Casas, Emma Bou Hanna, Florian Bressand, Gianna Lengyel, Guillaume Bour, Guillaume Lample, Lélio Renard Lavaud, Lucile Saulnier, Marie-Anne Lachaux, Pierre Stock, Sandeep Subramanian, Sophia Yang, Szymon Antoniak, Teven Le Scao, Théophile Gervet, Thibaut Lavril, Thomas Wang, Timothée Lacroix, and William El Sayed. 2024. Mixtral of experts. *Preprint*, arXiv:2401.04088.

Nikhil Kandpal, Haikang Deng, Adam Roberts, Eric Wallace, and Colin Raffel. 2023. Large language models struggle to learn long-tail knowledge. In *International Conference on Machine Learning*. PMLR.

Vladimir Karpukhin, Barlas Oğuz, Sewon Min, Patrick Lewis, Ledell Wu, Sergey Edunov, Danqi Chen, and Wen-tau Yih. 2020. Dense passage retrieval for open-domain question answering. *EMNLP*.

Urvashi Khandelwal, Omer Levy, Dan Jurafsky, Luke Zettlemoyer, and Mike Lewis. 2020. Generalization through memorization: Nearest neighbor language models. *ICLR*.

Kalpesh Krishna, Yapei Chang, John Wieting, and Mohit Iyyer. 2022. Rankgen: Improving text generation with large ranking models. *arXiv preprint arXiv:2205.09726*.

Kalpesh Krishna, Aurko Roy, and Mohit Iyyer. 2021. Hurdles to progress in long-form question answering. Association for Computational Linguistics.

Philippe Laban, Tobias Schnabel, Paul N. Bennett, and Marti A. Hearst. 2022. Summac: Re-visiting nli-based models for inconsistency detection in summarization. *Transactions of the Association for Computational Linguistics*, 10:163–177.

Mike Lewis, Yinhan Liu, Naman Goyal, Marjan Ghazvininejad, Abdelrahman Mohamed, Omer Levy, Veselin Stoyanov, and Luke Zettlemoyer. 2020a. BART: Denoising sequence-to-sequence pre-training for natural language generation, translation, and comprehension. In *Proceedings of the 58th Annual Meeting of the Association for Computational Linguistics*, pages 7871–7880, Online. Association for Computational Linguistics.

Patrick Lewis, Ethan Perez, Aleksandra Piktus, Fabio Petroni, Vladimir Karpukhin, Naman Goyal, Heinrich Küttler, Mike Lewis, Wen-tau Yih, Tim Rocktäschel, et al. 2020b. Retrieval-augmented generation for knowledge-intensive nlp tasks. *Advances in Neural Information Processing Systems*.

Yixin Liu, Alexander R. Fabbri, Pengfei Liu, Yilun Zhao, Linyong Nan, Ruilin Han, Simeng Han, Shafiq R. Joty, Chien-Sheng Wu, Caiming Xiong, and Dragomir R. Radev. 2022. Revisiting the gold standard: Grounding summarization evaluation with robust human evaluation. *ArXiv*, abs/2212.07981.

Ligeia Lugli, Matej Martinc, Andraž Pelicon, and Senja Pollak. 2022. Embeddings models for buddhist Sanskrit. In *Proceedings of the Thirteenth Language Resources and Evaluation Conference*.

Rajiv Malhotra. 2021. *Artificial Intelligence and the Future of Power: 5 Battlegrounds*. Rupa Publications.

Rajiv Malhotra and Satyanarayana Dasa Babaji. 2020. *Sanskrit Non-Translatables: The Importance of Sanskritizing English*. Amaryllis.

Alex Mallen, Akari Asai, Victor Zhong, Rajarshi Das, Hannaneh Hajishirzi, and Daniel Khashabi. 2023. When not to trust language models: Investigating effectiveness and limitations of parametric and non-parametric memories. *ACL*.

Priyanka Mandikal and Raymond Mooney. 2024. Sparse meets dense: A hybrid approach to enhance scientific document retrieval. In *The 4th CEUR Workshop on Scientific Document Understanding, AAAI.*

Joshua Maynez, Shashi Narayan, Bernd Bohnet, and Ryan McDonald. 2020. On faithfulness and factuality in abstractive summarization. In *Proceedings of the 58th Annual Meeting of the Association for Computational Linguistics*, pages 1906–1919, Online. Association for Computational Linguistics.

Jacob Menick, Maja Trebacz, Vladimir Mikulik, John Aslanides, Francis Song, Martin Chadwick, Mia Glaese, Susannah Young, Lucy Campbell-Gillingham, Geoffrey Irving, et al. 2022. Teaching language models to support answers with verified quotes. *arXiv preprint arXiv:2203.11147.*

Ragaa Moustafa, Farida Hesham, Samiha Hussein, Badr Amr, Samira Refaat, Nada Shorim, and Taraggy M Ghanim. 2022. Hieroglyphs language translator using deep learning techniques (scriba). In *2022 2nd International Mobile, Intelligent, and Ubiquitous Computing Conference (MIUCC)*. IEEE.

Reiichiro Nakano, Jacob Hilton, Suchir Balaji, Jeff Wu, Long Ouyang, Christina Kim, Christopher Hesse, Shantanu Jain, Vineet Kosaraju, William Saunders, et al. 2021. Webgpt: Browser-assisted question-answering with human feedback. *arXiv preprint arXiv:2112.09332.*

Sonika Narang, MK Jindal, and Munish Kumar. 2019. Devanagari ancient documents recognition using statistical feature extraction techniques. *Sādhanā*, 44.

Zach Nussbaum, John X. Morris, Brandon Duderstadt, and Andriy Mulyar. 2024. Nomic embed: Training a reproducible long context text embedder. *Preprint*, arXiv:2402.01613.

OpenAI. 2023. Gpt-4 technical report.

Asimina Paparigopoulou, John Pavlopoulos, and Maria Konstantinidou. 2022. Dating greek papyri images with machine learning. In *ICDAR Workshop on Computational Paleography, https://doi. org/10.21203/rs*, volume 3.

Alec Radford, Jong Wook Kim, Tao Xu, Greg Brockman, Christine McLeavey, and Ilya Sutskever. 2023. Robust speech recognition via large-scale weak supervision. In *International Conference on Machine Learning*, pages 28492–28518. PMLR.

Ori Ram, Yoav Levine, Itay Dalmedigos, Dor Muhlgay, Amnon Shashua, Kevin Leyton-Brown, and Yoav Shoham. 2023. In-context retrieval-augmented language models. *arXiv preprint arXiv:2302.00083.*

Ramakrishna Order. Belur math.

Adi Shankaracharya. 450 B.C.E. Commentary on the upanishads.

Weijia Shi, Julian Michael, Suchin Gururangan, and Luke Zettlemoyer. 2022. Nearest neighbor zero-shot inference. In *Proceedings of the 2022 Conference on Empirical Methods in Natural Language Processing.*

Weijia Shi, Sewon Min, Michihiro Yasunaga, Minjoon Seo, Rich James, Mike Lewis, Luke Zettlemoyer, and Wen-tau Yih. 2023. Replug: Retrieval-augmented black-box language models. *arXiv preprint arXiv:2301.12652.*

Kurt Shuster, Spencer Poff, Moya Chen, Douwe Kiela, and Jason Weston. 2021. Retrieval augmentation reduces hallucination in conversation. *ACL.*

Thea Sommerschield, Yannis Assael, John Pavlopoulos, Vanessa Stefanak, Andrew Senior, Chris Dyer, John Bodel, Jonathan Prag, Ion Androutsopoulos, and Nando de Freitas. 2023. Machine Learning for Ancient Languages: A Survey. *Computational Linguistics.*

Mingyang Song, Xuelian Geng, Songfang Yao, Shilong Lu, Yi Feng, and Liping Jing. 2024. Large language models as zero-shot keyphrase extractors: A preliminary empirical study. *Preprint*, arXiv:2312.15156.

Simeng Sun, Ori Shapira, Ido Dagan, and Ani Nenkova. 2019. How to compare summarizers without target length? pitfalls, solutions and re-examination of the neural summarization literature. *Proceedings of the Workshop on Methods for Optimizing and Evaluating Neural Language Generation.*

Upanishads. >3000 B.C.E. The Upanishads.

Vedanta Society of New York. Swami Sarvapriyananda's Vedanta discourses.

Lee Xiong, Chuan Hu, Chenyan Xiong, Daniel Campos, and Arnold Overwijk. 2019. Open domain web keyphrase extraction beyond language modeling. *arXiv preprint arXiv:1911.02671.*

Fangyuan Xu, Yixiao Song, Mohit Iyyer, and Eunsol Choi. 2023. A critical evaluation of evaluations for long-form question answering. In *Association of Computational Linguistics.*

Eunice Yiu, Eliza Kosoy, and Alison Gopnik. 2023. Imitation versus innovation: What children can do that large language and language-and-vision models cannot (yet)? *ArXiv*, abs/2305.07666.

Yaoming Zhu, Sidi Lu, Lei Zheng, Jiaxian Guo, Weinan Zhang, Jun Wang, and Yong Yu. 2018. Texygen: A benchmarking platform for text generation models. In *The 41st International ACM SIGIR Conference on Research & Development in Information Retrieval*, pages 1097–1100.

A Implementation Details

A.1 Automatic Metrics

Following Xu et al. (2023), we implement a number of automatic evaluation metrics for LFQA as described below.

Length We use the Spacy package (Honnibal et al., 2020) for word tokenization.

Self-BLEU We calculate Self-BLEU by regarding one sentence as hypothesis and all others in the same answer paragraph as reference. We report self-BLEU-5 as a measure of coherence.

RankGen For a given question q and a model-generated answer a, we first transform them into fixed-size vectors $(\boldsymbol{q}, \boldsymbol{a})$ using the RankGen encoder (Krishna et al., 2022). To assess their relevance, we compute the dot product $\boldsymbol{q} \cdot \boldsymbol{a}$. We utilize the T5-XXL (11B) encoder, which has been trained using both in-book negative instances and generative negatives.

QAFactEval QAFactEval is a QA-based metric recently introduced by Fabbri et al. (2022). It has demonstrated exceptional performance across multiple factuality benchmarks for summarization (Laban et al., 2022; Maynez et al., 2020). The pipeline includes four key components: (1) Noun Phrase (NP) extraction from sentence S represented as $Ans(S)$, (2) BART-large (Lewis et al., 2020a) for question generation denoted as Q_G, (3) Electra-large (Clark et al., 2020) for question answering labeled as Q_A, and (4) learned metrics LERC (Chen et al., 2020), to measure similarity as $Sim(p_i, s_i)$. An additional answerability classification module is incorporated to assess whether a question can be answered with the information provided in document D. Following Xu et al. (2023), we report LERC, which uses the learned metrics to compare Ans_S and Ans_D(a).

A.2 Chat Prompt

For an example of the constructed RAG bot prompt, please refer to Fig. 4. In this scenario, the RAG bot C_r is presented with the top-k retrieved passages alongside the query for generating a response, whereas a generic bot C_g would only receive the query without additional context.

RAG Bot

You are a helpful assistant that accurately answers queries using Swami Sarvapriyananda's YouTube talks. Use the following passages to provide a detailed answer to the query: **{query}**
Passages:
{Passage 1}
{Passage 2}
...
{Passage k}

Generic Bot

You are a helpful assistant that accurately answers queries using Swami Sarvapriyananda's YouTube talks. Provide a detailed answer to the query: **{query}**

Figure 4: **Prompts for the RAG and generic chatbots.** RAG Bot receives the top-k retrieved relevant passages in the prompt along with the query, while the generic bot only receives the query.

B Sample Sanskrit terms

Tab. 2 contains excerpts from passages containing Sanskrit terms. The Sanskrit terms are italicized and underlined. Notice that the passages contain detailed English explanations of these terms. To retain linguistic diversity, authenticity and comprehensiveness of the source material, we retain these Sanskrit terms as is in our passages as described in Sec. 3. Note that these are direct Whisper (Radford et al., 2023) transcriptions with no further post-processing or proofreading. Transcriptions may not always be accurate.

C Transcription

We asses the transcript quality and list out some common errors.

C.1 Transcript Evaluation

Transcription quality is scored on a scale from 1 to 5 (where 1 = Poor, 5 = Perfect). On 10 randomly sampled transcripts, evaluators assign a high average score of 4.48 suggesting that the transcription of YouTube audio into text is highly accurate and clear, indicating that our constructed custom dataset D_t is of high quality.

C.2 Transcript Errors

Tab. 3 contains a few sample transcription errors. The transcriptions are largely good for English words and sentences. However, errors often arise from incorrectly transcribing Sanskrit terms and verses. Other less common errors include missing or incorrect punctuation. Human proofreading will remove these errors to a large extent.

D Spoken vs written language

Unlike traditional textual corpora that are compiled from written sources, our dataset is derived from spoken discourses. Spoken language is often more verbose and less structured than written text, with the speaker frequently jumping between concepts mid-sentence. This unstructured nature of the text can be unfamiliar for a language model trained extensively on written text, which expects a more coherent and structured input. Fig. 6 shows a peculiar failure case arising from this issue. The speaker jumps between speaking about Aldous Huxley and Alan Watts. As a result, the RAG bot incorrectly attributes information about Huxley to Watts while answering the query. Due to the unstructured nature of the spoken text, such errors can occur. This can be addressed by converting the spoken text into a more structured prose format with the help of well-crafted prompts to LLMs, followed by human proofreading.

E Question Categories

To ensure a broad and comprehensive evaluation, we categorize the questions into five distinct types—anecdotal, teminology, scriptural, comparative and reasoning. Questions from each of these categories is provided in Tab. 4. Each category is designed to test different aspects of the model's capabilities. For details, refer to Sec. 5.

F Sample Responses: RAG vs Non-RAG

In Figs. 6-10, we present the sample queries and responses from the RAG and generic chatbots for five sample queries. The query is highlighted in yellow, RAG response is in the green box. Non-RAG response is in the red box. We use GPT-4-turbo (OpenAI, 2023) as the large language model for both of them.

G Sample Responses: Standard RAG vs Keyword-based Hybrid RAG

In Figs. 11-15, we present the sample queries and responses from the standard RAG and keyword-based hybrid RAG model for one query each from five categories. We additionally also show the human-annotated and model generated keywords. Keyword-RAG response is in the green box. Standard-RAG response is in the red box.

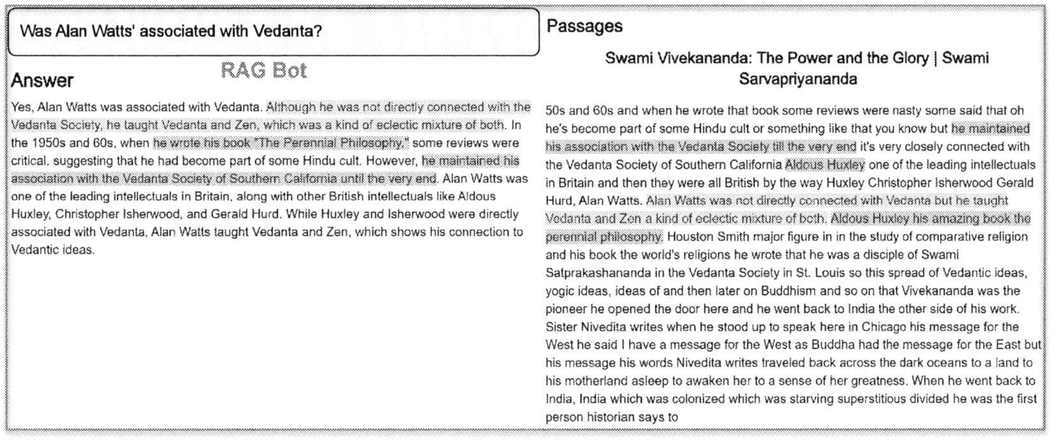

Figure 5: **Subject confusion: Aldous Huxley vs Alan Watts.** In the retrieved passage, the speaker jumps between speaking about Aldous Huxley and Alan Watts. Moreover, the transcription has poor punctuation. As a result, the RAG bot incorrectly attributes information about Huxley to Watts in the response. Due to the unstructured nature of the spoken text, such errors can occur. This can be addressed by converting the spoken text into a more structured prose format with the help of well-crafted prompts to LLMs, followed by human proofreading.

Sl. No.	Excerpts from passages	Notes
1.	*Om Bhadram Karne Bhishrinu Yamadevaha Bhadram Pashyam Akshabhirya Jatraaha Sthirai Rangai Stushta Vagam Sasthanubhi Vyase Madevahitaiyadayoh Swasthina Indro Vriddha Shravaha Swasthina Phusa Vishwa Vedaaha Swasthina Starksho Arishta Nemi Swasthino Brihas Patir Dadhatu Om Shanti Shanti Shanti*.	This is a Sanskrit chant which is directly Romanized and processed. The automatic transcriptions often contain errors in word segmentation for Sanskrit verses.
2.	*Samsara* is our present situation, the trouble that we are caught in, the mess that we are caught in. *Samsara* is this. In Sanskrit, normally when you use the word *samsara*, it really means this world of our life, you know, being born and struggling in life and afflicted by suffering and death and hopelessness and meaninglessness.	*Samsara* is a Sanskrit term. The excerpt contains an explanation of the concept in English.
3.	The problem being ignorance, solution is knowledge and the method is *Jnana Yoga*, the path of knowledge. So what is mentioned here, *Shravana Manana Nididhyasana*, hearing, reflection, meditation, that is *Jnana Yoga*. So that's at the highest level of practice, way of knowledge.	The excerpt contains an explanation of *Jnana Yoga*, the path of knowledge.
4.	In Sanskrit, *ajnana* and *adhyasa*, ignorance and superimposition. Now if you compare the four aspects of the self, the three appearances and the one reality, three appearances, waker, dreamer, deep sleeper, the one reality, *turiyam*, if you compare them with respect to ignorance and error, you will find the waker, that's us right now. We have both ignorance and error.	*Ajnana*, *adhyasa* and *turiyam* are Sanskrit terms. Notice that the passage implicitly contains rough English translations of these terms in the context of the overall discourse. For instance, *ajnana* is translated as ignorance and *adhyasa* is translated as superimposition.
5.	*Mandukya* investigates this and points out there is an underlying reality, the *Atman*, pure consciousness, which has certain characteristics. This is causality, it is beyond causality. It is neither a cause nor an effect. The *Atman* is not produced like this, nor is it a producer of this. It is beyond change. No change is there in the *Atman*, *nirvikara*. And third, it is not dual, it is non-dual, *advaitam*. This is *kadyakarana* in Sanskrit, this is *kadyakarana vilakshana Atma*. In Sanskrit this is *savikara*, this is *nirvikara Atma*. This is *dvaita*, this is *advaita Atma*. So this is *samsara* and this is *moksha*, freedom.	The excerpt contains an explanation of different Sanskrit technical terms.

Table 2: **Excerpts from passages containing Sanskrit terms.** These excerpts contain detailed English descriptions of technical terms in Sanskrit (italicized and underlined). To retain authenticity to the source material, we retain these Sanskrit terms as is in our passages. Note that these are direct Whisper (Radford et al., 2023) transcriptions with no further post-processing or proofreading, so transcriptions may not always be accurate. For more details, refer to Sec. B.

Sl. No.	Transcription errors	Notes
1.	That's what Sam Altman, Chachjipiti, somebody asked him.	Should be ChatGPT
2.	Last year, you studied extensively with Professor Garfield, I believe, studying *Vajamaka* and the teachings of the *Garjuna*.	Should be *Madhyamaka* and *Nagarjuna*, respectively
3.	From attachment comes desire, *raga*, I want it and if that desire is satisfied then there is no end to it, greed, *lobha*. But if it is somehow thwarted, then anger, *kama krodho vijayate*.	Should be *bhijayate*
4.	In fact, one of the terms which is used in Mandukya Upanishad, Brahman is *abhyavaharyam*.	Should be *avyavaharam*
5.	So, one of them was the *Brahmo Samad*, which was quite popular in Calcutta in those days.	Should be *Samaj*
6.	I am awareness I'm eternal consciousness Aldous Huxley Christopher Isherwood Gerald Hurd all of them were very close to Swami Prabhavananda in Southern California in Hollywood and look at the product of that Isherwood wrote that one of the most amazing biographies	The transcripts sometimes miss punctuation marks, making the passage difficult to comprehend for both humans and language models

Table 3: **Sample transcription errors.** For constructing our text corpus, we directly use the transcripts obtained from Whisper (Radford et al., 2023) with no further post-processing or proofreading. The transcriptions are largely good (with a score of 4.5/5 from human evaluators). However, errors arise from incorrectly transcribing Sanskrit terms, missing punctuations, etc. Human proofreading will remove these errors to a large extent.

Category	Description	Questions
Anecdotal	Stories and anecdotes narrated by the speaker in the discourses	• Does Swami speak about Wittgenstein's thesis defense? • Does Swami narrate any incident surrounding Shivaratri? • Does Swami speak about The Matrix movie? • Does Swami speak about Vachaspati Mishra? Does he narrate how Bhamati came to be written? • What was Christopher Isherwood's contribution to Vedanta?
Terminology	Probe the model's understanding of specific terms and concepts	• What is Adhyaropa Apavada? • What is Vikshepa Shakti? • What is the significance of the word 'Shraddha'? • What is Upadana Karana? • What constitutes Sadhana Chatushtaya?
Scriptural	Reference, interpret, and explain passages from religious or philosophical texts	• In Mandukya Upanishad, what is the significance of the word 'Om'? • In the Gospel, what parable does Sri Ramakrishna use to portray intense longing for God? • In the Mundaka Upanishad, how do we interpret the parable of the two birds? • How is Phala Vyapti and Vritti Vyapti defined in Vedantasara? • In the Gospel of Sri Ramakrishna, how do we understand the analogy of the salt doll that Thakur provides?
Comparative	Analyze and compare different concepts, philosophies, or texts	• As mentioned in the Yoga Sutras, is Samadhi necessary to attain enlightenment according to Advaita Vedanta? • Would Sri Ramakrishna's teachings be considered purely Advaitic? • In Kashmir Shaivism, Chit is both Prakasha and Vimarsha i.e. it is both self-lumious and self-reflective. Would Advaita Vedanta agree with this? • How does Sankhya differ from Advaita Vedanta? • What is the main difference between Buddhist Shunyavada and Advaita Vedanta?
Reasoning	Require logical reasoning, critical thinking, and the application of principles to new scenarios	• Can AI ever become conscious? • Is the waking state similar to a dream or absolutely indistinguishable from the dream state? • Do our senses report reality to us? • Dis-identifying myself from the body-mind seems to require a lot of effort. Did the reverse process of identification also involve as much effort? • If Brahman as Existence-Consciousness-Bliss is the eternal subject that cannot be objectified, yet eternally reveals itself to give rise to apparent objects through the principle of Maya, can we infer that Brahman is Existence-Consciousness-Bliss-Maya? That is, is Brahman inseparable from Maya?

Table 4: **Question categories.** To ensure a broad and comprehensive evaluation, we categorize the questions into five distinct types, each designed to test different aspects of the model's capabilities. For details, refer to Sec. 5.

Figure 6: **RAG vs Non-RAG: Sam Altman on Atman and Brahman.** The retrieved passages are very good at capturing the context of the query. The first passage references the monk speaking about Sam Altman and his views on Atman and Brahman. The second passage contains a brief explanation of Atman and Brahman that is helpful to answer the query. The generic bot also generates a reasonable answer. However, it has a sentence stating that, "Atman is a part of Brahman". This is incorrect in the context of Advaita Vedanta as it is not the same as equivalence—this point was highlighted by the domain experts in the survey.

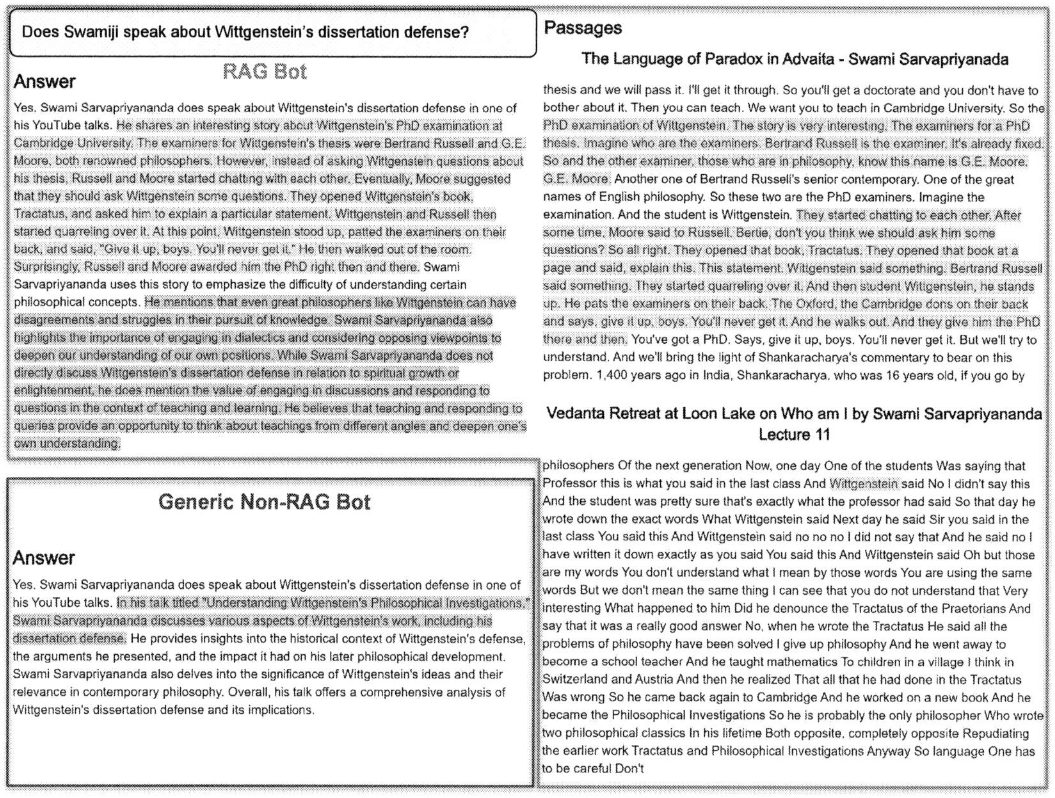

Figure 7: **RAG vs Non-RAG: Wittgenstein's thesis defense.** The retrieved passage is about the monk narrating a story about Wittgenstein's thesis defense, which is highly relevant to the query. The generated RAG bot response makes use of this passage to answer the query. However, the latter half of the response is not relevant to the query and is purely hallucinated. The generic bot response, on the other hand, is completely fabricated and references a non-existent YouTube talk.

Figure 8: **RAG vs Non-RAG: AI and Consciousness.** The retrieved passages are again highly relevant to the query and the generated answer is coherent. However, it does contain a statement about "a mirror reflecting a face" which is not present in the passages. This was pointed out by the experts as a relevant statement possibly drawn from outside knowledge. The generic bot's response is highly general and does not represent the monk's views on the topic.

Figure 9: **RAG vs Non-RAG: Senses and reality.** In this scenario, the retrieved passages provide only partial context needed to answer the query, with additional irrelevant information. For example, one passage mentions cognitive scientist Donald Hoffman, inadvertently influencing the LLM to generate a response linking the Swami's views to Hoffman's concept of the world as a virtual reality. This is an instance where the LLM diverges from the query, using incomplete information from the passage. To mitigate this, implementing retrieval models capable of processing longer contexts and summarizing them effectively before input to the LLM could be beneficial. Despite this, the rest of the response aligns reasonably well with Advaita Vedanta philosophy, similar to the generic bot's response, which is also congruent with the philosophical context.

Dreams feel absolutely real while dreaming. What is the guarantee that I am not fast asleep in my bed and dreaming right now?

Answer — RAG Bot

According to Swami Sarvapriyananda, the question of whether we are dreaming or awake at any given moment is a profound one. In his talks, he refers to the insights of Gaudapada, an ancient Advaita Vedanta philosopher, who explored the nature of reality and the relationship between the dream state and the waking state. Gaudapada's insight is that there is no definitive way to differentiate between the dream state and the waking state. He argues that the clear distinction we make between dreaming and waking in our understanding is actually fuzzy. He reduces the status of our waking state experience to that of our dream state experience. One objection that often arises is the feeling of reality in dreams. Dreams can feel absolutely real while we are experiencing them. We may interact with people, objects, and environments that seem just as solid and permanent as in the waking state. This raises the question: What is the guarantee that we are not currently dreaming and that our waking experience is not just another dream? Gaudapada's response to this objection is that the feeling of reality in dreams does not necessarily indicate the truth or permanence of the objects and experiences within the dream. In a dream, we may perceive objects and people as real, but upon waking up, we realize that they were mere appearances, not possessing any substantial reality. Similarly, Gaudapada argues that the objects and experiences we perceive in the waking state are also appearances, just like in a dream. Our beloved friends, family, and surroundings may seem real and permanent, but they are as real as the "I" or the self that perceives them. In other words, the reality of the waking state is dependent on the perceiving consciousness, just as the reality of the dream state is dependent on the dreaming mind. Gaudapada's perspective is balanced and nuanced. He acknowledges that our waking experience feels real to us, just as the dream experience feels real to the dreamer. However, he also emphasizes that the reality of both states is ultimately dependent on consciousness itself. It is important to note that Gaudapada's insights are not meant to dismiss the waking state as illusory or insignificant. Rather, they invite us to question the nature of reality and our assumptions about it. The ultimate aim of Advaita Vedanta is to realize the true nature of consciousness and the underlying unity of all existence. In conclusion, according to Gaudapada's teachings, there is no guarantee that we are not currently dreaming. The feeling of reality in dreams does not provide a definitive proof of the waking state's permanence or truth. Both the dream state and the waking state are appearances within consciousness, and their reality is dependent on the perceiving consciousness itself. The exploration of these insights can lead us to a deeper understanding of the nature of reality and our own existence.

Answer — Generic Non-RAG Bot

Dreams can indeed feel incredibly real while we are experiencing them. However, it can be difficult to determine with absolute certainty whether we are currently dreaming or awake. One way to approach this question is by considering the concept of reality testing. Reality testing involves examining the characteristics of our current experience to determine whether it aligns with what we typically perceive as reality. There are several techniques that people use to reality test, such as checking the time, looking for inconsistencies, or attempting to perform actions that are impossible in dreams, like flying or walking through walls. In the case of your query, if you are unsure whether you are dreaming or awake, you can try reality testing. For example, you could check the time on a clock or a digital device. In dreams, the time often appears distorted or inconsistent. Another approach could be to look for inconsistencies in your surroundings or try to perform actions that are impossible in reality. It is important to note that while reality testing can be helpful, it is not foolproof. In some cases, dreams can be incredibly vivid and realistic, making it challenging to distinguish them from waking reality. Additionally, some individuals may experience conditions like lucid dreaming, where they are aware that they are dreaming and can exert some control over the dream. Ultimately, the guarantee that you are not currently dreaming while asking this question is difficult to provide. However, by employing reality testing techniques and reflecting on the consistency of your experience, you can increase your confidence in determining whether you are awake or dreaming.

Passages

20. Mandukya Upanishad | Chapter 2 Karika 6 | Swami Sarvapriyananda

main... Well, I mean, how would that... Yes. But let's take it in a very simple way. The person in the dream and every other thing that you see in the dream are actually not there. You are with me? Are actually not there. They are all your own mind. You are actually sleeping on the bed. Just follow the facts as they... as you know them to be. You are actually on your bed and sleeping and your mind generates all of this. Now compare it with what you actually experience in a dream, that you are in some place and you have a body and you are meeting with other people. But when you wake up, all of that is falsified. Why is it falsified? Because it has no existence apart from the mind which was dreaming it. Right? So that's the example. Those things are false because they were dreamt up by a mind. They did not exist apart from you which you... it felt like. It felt like they were things apart from me. Similarly, now he wants to prove in this waking world, it seems to be a real world apart from me. It seems to be real. But just like that those things do not... dream entities do not exist apart from the dreamer's mind, these waking entities also do not exist apart from consciousness. Proof, they cannot be experienced without consciousness. They are clearly in consciousness. Yes, I'll come to you. Yes. I'll come to you. Okay, don't go there now. Don't go there. Just look at it from the point of view of the witness consciousness. From the point of view of witness consciousness, this waking

4. Mandukya Upanishad | Chapter 1 Mantra 5-6 | Swami Sarvapriyananda

from every dream to dream it's different. Answer in reply, the dream state is a waking state for the dreamer. As has already been pointed out. And one knows a state to be a waking state only when there is a feeling that the objects seen are real and as such remain the same in all waking states. The answer is, in the dream state, in a dream when you see objects, they are not felt to be temporary and about to disappear at the end of this dream. They feel felt to be absolutely real. My friend feels real. The table, chair I'm sitting with feels real. The food I eat feels as real as necessary. They don't feel temporary. Just as these ones seem pretty permanent, the dream objects also seem pretty permanent in the dream. Ninth, if the objects of the waking state are exactly like those of the dream state, then our beloved friends, kith and kin, would be no more than ideas, like those of our dream world relatives. Such an attitude is repugnant to our feelings. The reply is that our relatives seen in the waking or the dream state, again a very subtle and powerful answer, are as real as the I, as you yourself. What you consider yourself as real as the waker considers himself to be, so real does the waker's world seem to be. As real as the dreamer considers himself or herself to be, so real does the dream world seem to be. Advaita's answer here is balanced and nuanced. Why? Because you know actually what Advaita wants to say is that, yes, your relatives are appearances. They are dreams

Figure 10: **RAG vs Non-RAG: Waking and dreaming.** The passages retrieved for the query are relevant but only offer a segment from a broader context. As stated earlier, this can be mitigated by using more advanced retrieval models that summarize longer contexts before input to the LLM. The RAG bot's response, while relevant, is lengthy and complex, making it challenging to comprehend. The generic bot's response although more concise and coherent, is completely general and has no relation to the Advaita Vedanta philosophy.

Category: Anecdotal

Query: Does Swami narrate any incident surrounding Shivaratri?

Keywords

Human-annotated: Shivaratri

Model ensemble: Shivaratri

Keyword-based RAG

Yes, in the lecture "Raja Yoga: The Path of Meditation (Part 1)," Swami Sarvapriyananda does share an incident related to the Hindu festival of Shivaratri. He talks about his own experience of fasting on Shivaratri for the first time when he became a monk. He explains that on this day, devotees of Lord Shiva observe a strict fast, which means no food or water from sunrise to sunrise the next day.

Swami Sarvapriyananda also narrates an incident where a mathematics teacher approached a Swami and asked if he could fast on Shivaratri. The Swami responded sarcastically, pointing out that even young children are able to fast on this day, implying that the teacher should not find it difficult. This story highlights the significance of Shivaratri and the spiritual strength and dedication it is associated with.

Source:

Raja Yoga: The Path of Meditation (Part 1) | Swami Sarvapriyananda

back and meditate Then think about that So for asceticism also that Remember Common sense So Shivaratri I remember fasting I never fasted earlier The first time I fasted Was when I became a monk On Shivaratri And So You get some fruits in the afternoon But otherwise no food, no breakfast, no lunch, no dinner Whole night puja Next day in the morning you get food But in the afternoon you get some fruits So I never ate so many fruits Not because I was hungry In anticipation of being hungry Maybe I will be hungry You won't be Not really So that's what happens That's the mind I still remember this poor young man He was a teacher of mathematics And He went to a Swami very proudly And he said Tomorrow is Shivaratri I will also fast Can I also fast And the Swami I still remember He said What kind of question is that 10 year old little children are going to fast Aren't you ashamed of asking such a question Am I going to fast or not Of course you are going to fast And you should

Standard RAG

In the provided passage, Swami Sarvapriyananda shares an incident involving Swami Shivamayanji, but it does not explicitly mention Shivaratri. However, the narrative does offer insights into the experiences and teachings of the swamis.

According to the passage, Swami Shivamayanji once told a group of young monks, including Swami Sarvapriyananda, about an experience he had with his guru, Swami Gambhirananda. Swami Gambhirananda, at the time a vice president and later president of the Ramakrishna Math and Ramakrishna Mission, was describing the nature of God realization. He explained that the living form of the chosen deity appears in one's heart as a blazing or flaming form (Bengali: Amin jakhoni chok bhoji. Ishta murti. Jaljal kare bhaveshe othe). Swami Gambhirananda further emphasized the importance of realizing Brahman in all beings, indicating a deep understanding and connection with the divine in everything and everyone.

Swami Shivamayanji used this story to teach the young monks about the expectations of people who show respect and reverence to them. He wanted to remind them of the importance of their conduct and the impact they have on others.

While this narrative does not directly mention Shivaratri, it does provide a glimpse into the teachings and values of the swamis, which likely influenced their celebrations and observations of various Hindu festivals, including Shivaratri.

Source:

79 Bhagavad Gita I Chapter 6 Verse 15 I Swami Sarvapriyananda

just talking about. He says not even an effort. Anytime I close my eyes. The presence the living form of the chosen deity. Is vivid and it's a living form. It's not an. Not imagined. Not just visualized. That blazes forth. Of course he didn't explain all this. He just said in Bengali. Bhagavan lab bolte tumi ki bojo. What do you mean? What exactly do you mean by God realization? He said in Bengali. Amin jakhoni chok bhoji. Ishta murti. Jaljal kare bhaveshe othe. Bengali. It would just simply mean. It's like a flaming form or a blazing form. Of the. Ishta Devata. Appears in my heart. Next he said. But is this all? One has to realize Brahman in all beings. Bengali he said. So imagine. That was Swami Gambhiranji. Long time before he actually became the vice president. And the president. Anyway Swami Shivamayanji told us this incident. And then he looked at us. The young monks present there. And he said. Look this is what people expect. When they bow down to you. And touch your feet. And call you know like this. Or show you so much respect. This is what people expect. This is what they want. In a moment to see in a monk. So never forget that. So it's really ingrained in my memory. That incident. I can still see him looking at straight at us. And telling us. He is a wonderful monk. Swami Shivamayanji. You have so many wonderful incidents to share about. Humorous, straightforward, very simple. One little incident shows the heart of the man. He must have been in the 60s at that

Figure 11: **Keyword-RAG vs Standard-RAG: Anecdotal.** The keyword-based retriever accurately retrieves the correct snippet, while the dense retriever confuses "Shivaratri" with "Shivamayananda", possibly owing to similar embeddings and completely misses the context. As a result, the generated standard RAG answer is meaningless and lacks substance. The keyword-RAG model identifies the two key incidents relating to Shivaratri correctly and effectively summarizes them.

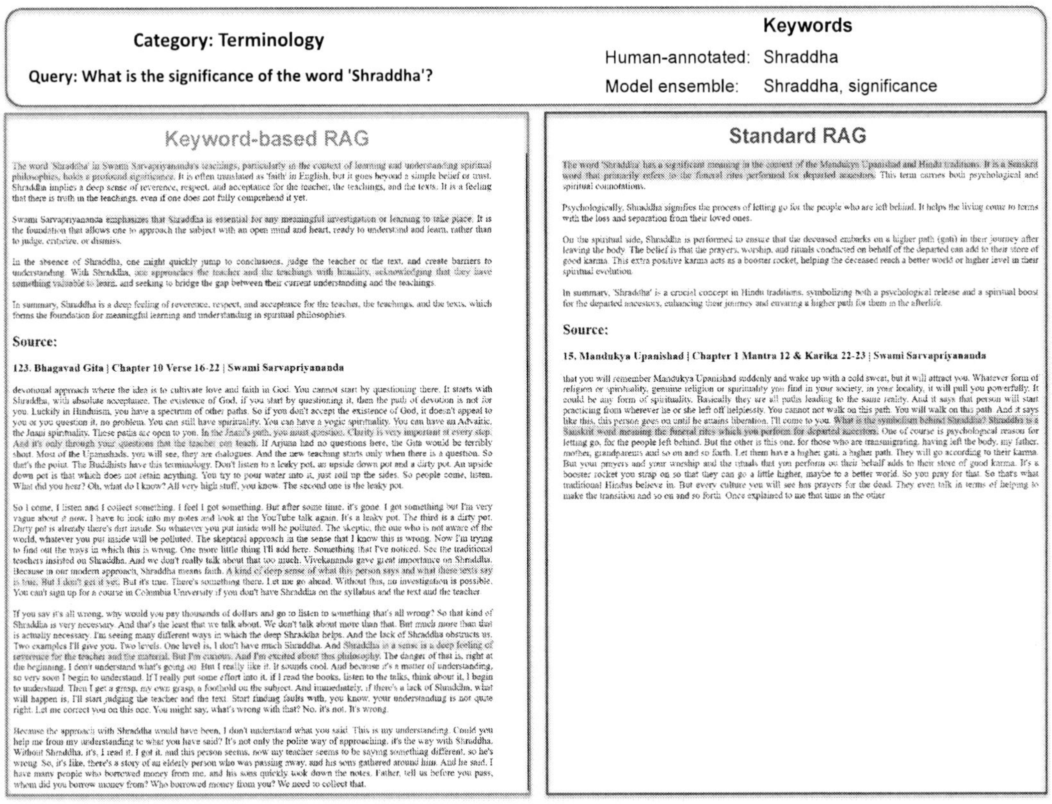

Figure 12: **Keyword-RAG vs Standard-RAG: Terminology.** The keyword-RAG model retrieves a comprehensive exposition on the concept of Shraddha, loosely translated as conviction, in the context of qualifications for the study of Advaita Vedanta. The standard RAG although retrieves a passage containing the word, it is however not directly related to what the questioner intends. This seems to be an unfortunate case of false positive for standard RAG due to inadequate or implied meaning in the query.

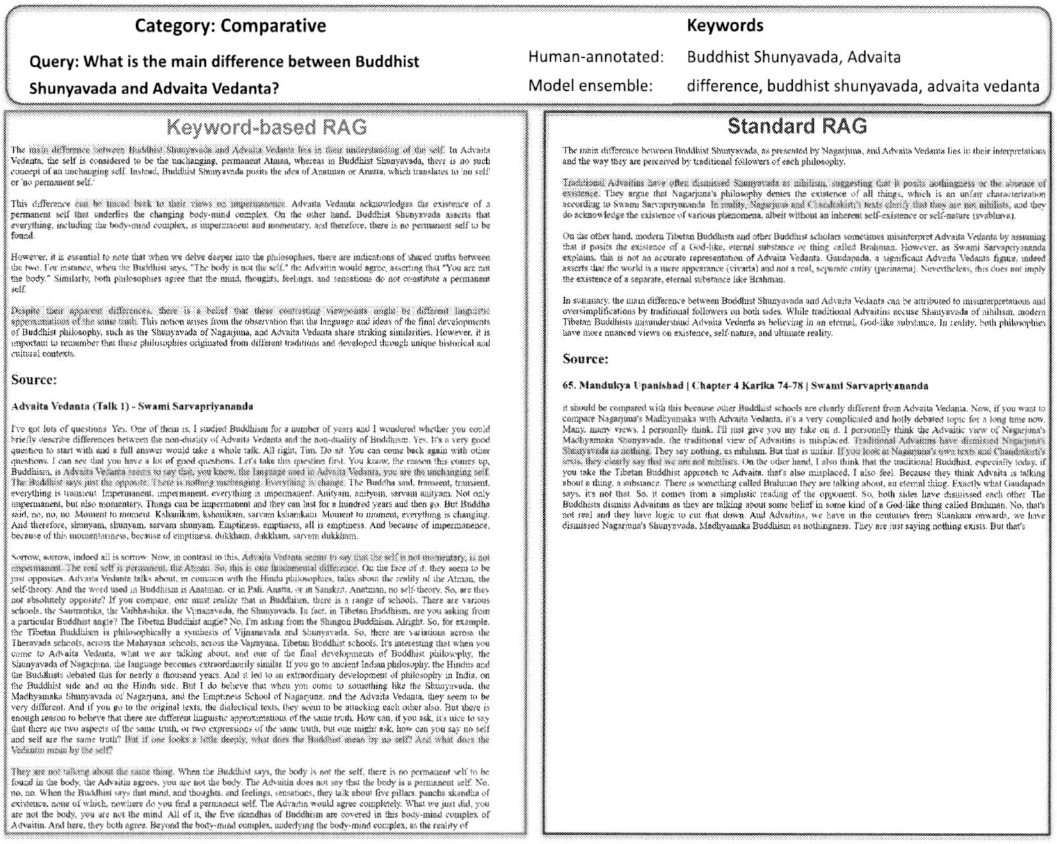

Figure 13: **Keyword-RAG vs Standard-RAG: Comparative.** This is a case where both models retrieve meaningful passages, with the keyword-based model providing greater context due to retrieval expansion. The standard model also seems to be using outside knowledge not mentioned in the passage.

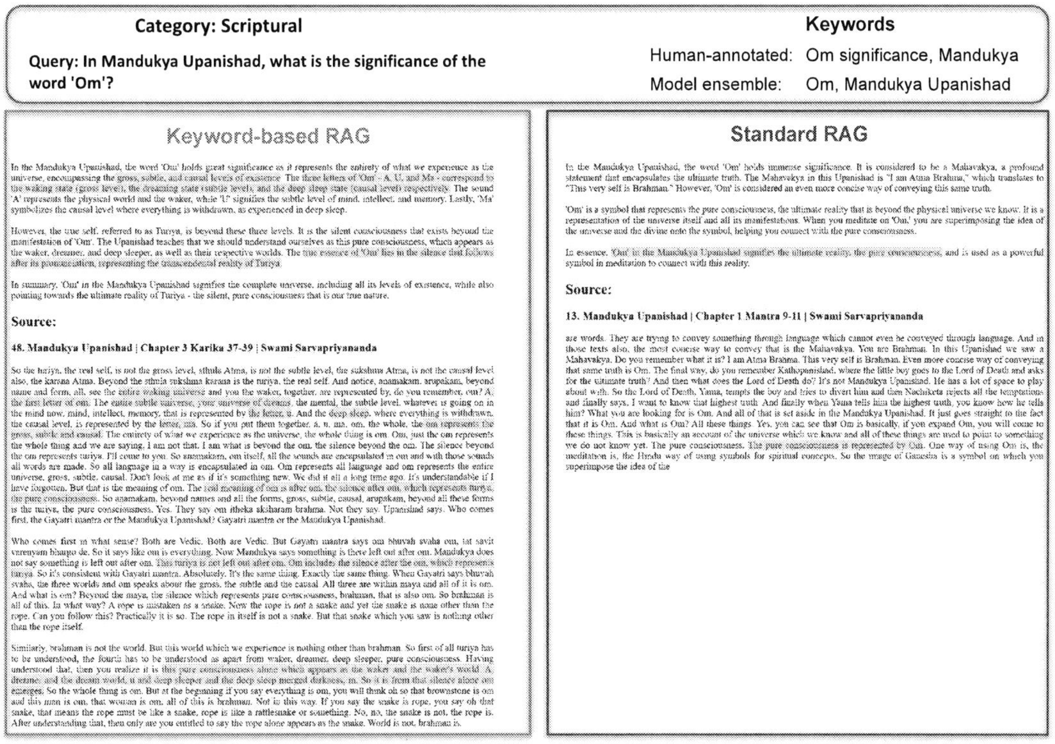

Figure 14: **Keyword-RAG vs Standard-RAG: Scriptural.** Both models retrieve from the correct scripture. However, while the retrieved passage in keyword-RAG is very comprehensive and accurately captures the context of the question, the standard RAG misses the point of the question and gives a generic answer.

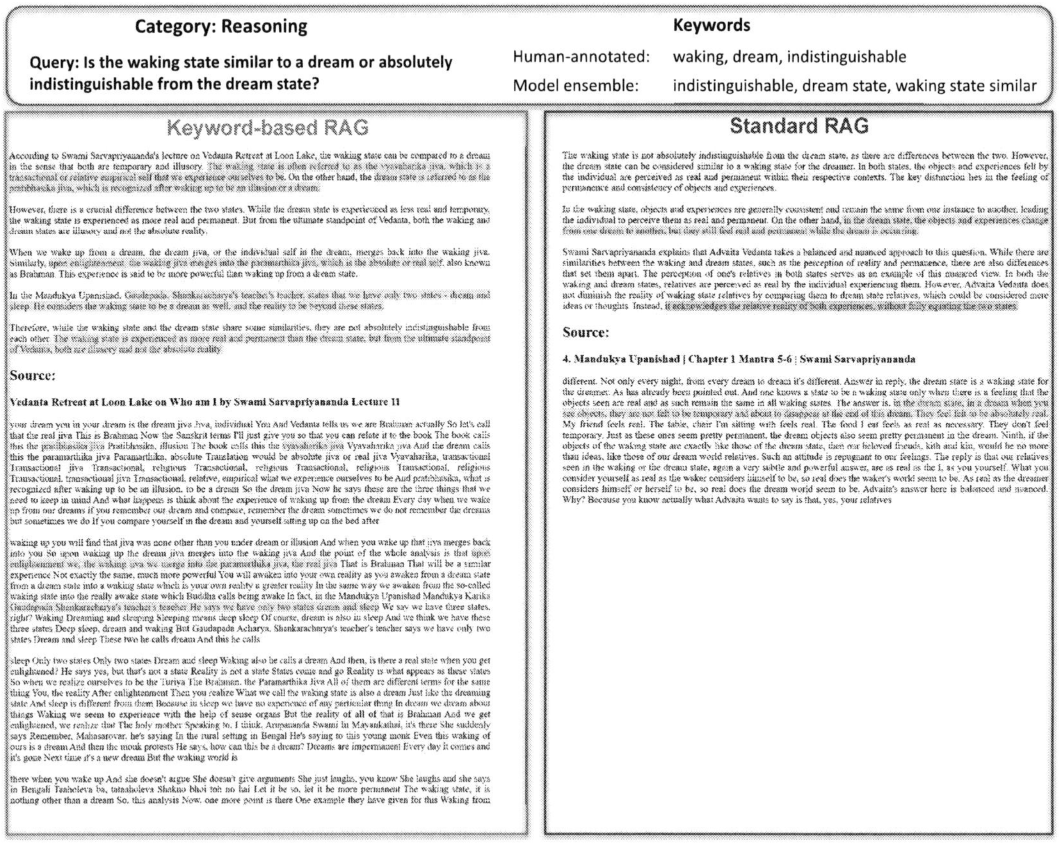

Figure 15: **Keyword-RAG vs Standard-RAG: Reasoning.** The retrieved passage in keyword-RAG is technical and comprehensive and the generated answer effectively summarizes the main points. The standard model is also good, although the explanation is not as effective owing to the quality of retrieval.

Leveraging Part-of-Speech Tagging for Enhanced Stylometry of Latin Literature

Sarah Li Chen,[1,2,3] **Patrick J. Burns,**[4] **Thomas J. Bolt,**[5] **Pramit Chaudhuri,**[6] **Joseph P. Dexter**[7,8†]

[1] Phillips Academy Andover
[2] Research Science Institute, Center for Excellence in Education
[3] Department of Computer Science, Stanford University
[4] Institute for the Study of the Ancient World, New York University
[5] Department of Languages & Literary Studies, Lafayette College
[6] Department of Classics, University of Texas at Austin
[7] Institute of Collaborative Innovation and Department of Computer and Information Science, University of Macau
[8] Data Science Initiative and Department of Human Evolutionary Biology, Harvard University
[†] Corresponding author: `jdexter@um.edu.mo`

Abstract

In literary critical applications, stylometry can benefit from hand-curated feature sets capturing various syntactic and rhetorical functions. For premodern languages, calculation of such features is hampered by a lack of computational resources for accurate part-of-speech tagging and semantic disambiguation. This paper reports an evaluation of POS taggers for Latin and their use in augmenting a hand-curated stylometric feature set. Our analyses show that POS-augmented features not only provide more accurate counts but also perform well on tasks such as genre classification. In the course of this work, we introduce POS n-grams as a feature for Latin stylometry.

1 Introduction

Although most associated with studies of authorship attribution and chronology (Stamatatos, 2009; Jockers and Witten, 2010; Stover and Kestemont, 2016), computational stylometric methods have increasingly been deployed to address broader literary questions and to augment more traditional approaches to criticism (Jockers, 2013; Moretti, 2013; Long and So, 2016; Piper, 2019; Underwood, 2019). For premodern literary traditions, such work has encompassed applications ranging from profiling the evolution of Latin prose style to computational restoration of Greek inscriptions and manuscripts (Dexter et al., 2017; Assael et al., 2022; Graziosi et al., 2023), as well as genre classification across multiple languages (Chaudhuri et al., 2019; Gianitsos et al., 2019; Storey and Mimno, 2020). For instance, for their genre classification work Chaudhuri et al. (2019) developed a set of 26 Latin stylometric features, including curated function word lists (e.g., prepositions, conjunctions, and pronouns), subordinate clauses, and sentence and clause length. Although calculated using only word or character n-gram counts and a small number of language-specific heuristics, these features proved highly effective for genre classification of classical texts, with the best-performing models achieving F1 > 97%.

It is the strength of a model, however, that it can withstand the frailties of individual features, at least up to a point. Hand-curated lists of words, such as those employed by Chaudhuri et al. (2019), may be insensitive to homonyms, semantic ambiguity, and other potentially challenging facets of natural language. While such issues may not impede success on certain tasks, increasing the accuracy of feature counts may be essential for others, especially those involving fine distinctions. Recent developments in NLP for Latin have led to the creation of tools that can plausibly improve on existing stylometric methods. Notably, the EvaLatin 2020 campaign (Sprugnoli et al., 2020) proposed shared tasks in lemmatization and part-of-speech (POS) tagging for classical Latin. Submissions introduced POS tagger models based on gradient boosters (Celano, 2020), ensemble methods (Stoeckel et al., 2020), and LSTMs (Straka and Straková, 2020) that achieved accuracies of up to 96%.

Here, we evaluate several POS taggers and assess how they improve and expand the feature set published by Chaudhuri et al. (2019). We perform error analysis on our POS-augmented features to quantify these improvements. We also train a classifier to distinguish Latin verse from

Proceedings of the 1st Workshop on Machine Learning for Ancient Languages (ML4AL 2024), pages 251–259
August 15, 2024 ©2024 Association for Computational Linguistics

prose using either a POS-augmented or the original feature set, and we compare the accuracy and feature importances for each set. In doing so, we demonstrate the stylometric and literary relevance of POS-augmented features and showcase a transition from general tool development to specific literary applications in a lower-resource language.

2 Methods

2.1 POS taggers and test corpora

We evaluate 4 POS taggers to identify an optimal model for feature augmentation. Two models are pre-trained: a gradient boosting model developed as the Leipzig team's submission (Celano, 2020) for the EvaLatin 2020 task using LightGBM (Ke et al., 2017), and a FLAIR model developed by Stoeckel et al. (2020) for the EvaLatin 2020 task. We also consider Lapos (Tsuruoka et al., 2011) and MarMoT (Mueller et al., 2013), 2 well-established POS taggers that are not specific to Latin and were not pre-trained.

We test the models on the Perseus (Bamman and Crane, 2011), PROIEL (Haug and Jøhndal, 2008), and ITTB (Cecchini et al., 2018) Universal Dependencies (UD) Treebanks in addition to EvaLatin's (Sprugnoli et al., 2020) test corpora: a classical dataset consisting of texts from the same genre and time period as the training data, a cross-genre dataset consisting of Latin poetry rather than prose, and a cross-time dataset consisting of medieval rather than classical Latin. These datasets are annotated using the UD POS tag set (Petrov et al., 2012), and training and test sets are pre-split by EvaLatin or the respective UD treebank. We directly evaluate the 2 pre-trained POS taggers on the test data, and we train Lapos and MarMoT on the corresponding training data before evaluating them on each test set.

2.2 Augmenting existing stylometric features

We leverage predicted POS tags in 3 primary ways: to reduce the need for hand-engineered heuristics, to disambiguate polysemous function words, and to calculate additional features based on POS n-grams. Table 1 summarizes our modifications and additions to the published feature set (Chaudhuri et al., 2019).

2.2.1 Minimization of hand-engineered heuristics

Chaudhuri et al. (2019) compute the frequency of conjunctions and frequency of prepositions by identifying the tokens in a text that are in a hand-curated list of words. POS tagging eliminates the need for such lists by enabling direct counts of the corresponding POS tags. POS tagging also allows for frequency calculations with parts of speech that are too numerous to list exhaustively (e.g., all nouns or verbs).

In addition, Chaudhuri et al. (2019) identify superlatives by searching for the infix *-issim-*. We take a first step in improving that feature by only considering words tagged as ADJ or ADV and omitting non-adjective and non-adverb matches. Although an improvement, this count still does not encompass irregular Latin superlatives. We also supplement the hand-engineered feature calculating the frequency of vocatives with a new feature counting the frequency of contiguous blocks of words tagged as INTJ, reflecting the frequency of interjection and exclamation within a text. We exclude lone instances of 'O' to avoid redundancy with the vocative feature and to capture a more specific interjective subset.

2.2.2 Disambiguation of function words

Chaudhuri et al. (2019) rely on n-gram matching to identify keywords and compute corresponding features such as pronoun frequencies. For features that count largely monosemous words (e.g., *ipse*), this approach presents no problems. Some feature computations, however, involve words that can take on multiple meanings in different contexts. In these cases, blunt token matching cannot distinguish between a polysemous word's various usages. This ambiguity limits the value of counting 3 words in particular, *ut* (which can be an adverb or conjunction), *cum* ("when" or "with"), and *quod* ("because" or "which").

As noted above, the frequency of *ut* feature fails to distinguish between adverbial and conjunctive usages. Using POS tagging, we can inspect *ut* at a higher resolution and tabulate separate frequency features for its adverbial (ADV) and conjunctive (SCONJ) meanings. In addition, the feature calculating the frequency of *cum* clauses attempts to isolate conjunctive *cum* from prepositional *cum* by requiring that the word immediately following *cum* not have a standard ablative ending. This rule-based requirement is leaky and prone to false negative calls, in which instances of *cum* are unintentionally excluded from the count. Compared to a gold standard annotation of Livy 22.1-15, Chaudhuri et al. (2019) identify *cum* clauses with a precision of 1 but a recall of only 0.52. POS tags can directly distinguish between *cum* as "when" (SCONJ) or "with" (ADP) and remove this source of error.

Finally, the features concerning relative clauses (fraction of sentences containing a relative clause and mean length of relative clauses) rely on searching for inflected instances of *qui* (*qui, cuius, cui, quem, quo, quae, quam, qua, quod, quorum, quibus, quos, quarum*, or *quas*). This token matching incorrectly includes *quod* when used as a subordinating conjunction. POS tagging can again distinguish *quod*'s 2 meanings (PRON vs. SCONJ), reducing the error in relative clause features and also enabling the tabulation of a new feature, the frequency of *quod* as a subordinating conjunction.

2.2.3 Frequency of POS tag n-grams

POS tagging enables additional features based on the frequency of POS tag n-grams. These frequency features have been proposed and implemented in English stylometric work (Iyer and Ostendorf, 1999) but, to our knowledge, have never been applied to Latin. The number of possible n-grams, and therefore the number of frequency features, grows exponentially as n increases. We consider up to 2-grams in the current analysis.

2.3 Application to prose vs. verse classification

POS augmentation yields 3 distinct feature sets:

- **Original**: The original set of 26 features published by Chaudhuri et al. (2019).
- **Modified**: Feature set with POS-augmented preposition, conjunction, *ut*, *cum* clause, relative clause, and superlative features replacing the corresponding original features (see the direct modifications in Table 1).
- **Expanded**: All possible features, including the union of the original and modified feature sets and additional features enabled by POS tagging (see the additions in in Table 1).

We extract these 3 feature sets for a selection of 154 prose texts and 180 verse texts drawn from the Tesserae Project (Coffee et al., 2012) and train a random forest model to classify the texts by genre using each individual feature set.

3 Results

3.1 POS tagger evaluation and selection

We first consider the overall accuracy and F1 scores for the 4 taggers' POS tag predictions (Table 2). Among these, the LightGBM and FLAIR models are pre-trained on EvaLatin data, while we train MarMoT and Lapos on EvaLatin training data for the EvaLatin test sets and UD treebank training data for each treebank test set. This retraining accounts for MarMoT and Lapos' higher performance on the UD treebank test sets, compared to to the LightGBM and FLAIR models.

Inconsistencies between dataset annotations provide further explanation for the LightGBM and FLAIR models' worse performance on the UD treebanks. POS annotation guidelines vary between the EvaLatin data and the treebank data (as well as between different UD treebanks). For example, the Perseus Treebank does not use the UD DET tag, whereas EvaLatin does; this difference in annotation accounts for 32% of the FLAIR model's incorrect predictions (6% of its overall error on the Perseus test set). Therefore, treebank datasets impose inherent limits on the performance of the EvaLatin models.

Given these inconsistencies in annotation, we narrow our focus to the 3 EvaLatin test sets and more closely evaluate the 4 taggers trained on the EvaLatin training set: FLAIR, LightGBM, Lapos, and MarMoT. Out of these taggers, FLAIR exhibits the highest accuracies and F1 scores in the classical and cross-genre tasks but the poorest performance in the cross-time task (83% accuracy) (Figure 1). However, the accuracies of all the taggers are generally comparable and have a range of only 2% in the classical test data. We break down these seemingly similar performances by considering subclasses particularly relevant to feature augmentation: the tokens *cum*, *ut*, and *quod*. When considering tokens that fall into these subclasses of interest, the margin between FLAIR and the other taggers on the classical and cross-genre classes widens considerably. For instance, the gap between the F1 scores of the highest and lowest performing classifiers in the classical subtask increases from 0.04 overall to 0.21 in the *ut* class (Figure 1).

Furthermore, performance on these subclasses of interest demonstrates trends that contrast with overall performance. Although FLAIR has the worst overall performance on the cross-time task, it has the highest performance on *quod* and *cum* tokens

Original Feature	**Modification or Addition**
Frequency of prepositions	Count ADP tags (eliminate need for hand-curated list)
Frequency of conjunctions	Count SCONJ and CCONJ tags (eliminate need for hand-curated list)
Frequency of *ut*	Frequency of *ut* tagged as ADV
	Frequency of *ut* tagged as SCONJ
Frequency of *cum* clauses	Only consider *cum* tagged as SCONJ
Fraction of sentences containing relative clause	Only consider forms of *qui* tagged as PRON (exclude instances of *quod* used as SCONJ)
Mean length of relative clauses	
Frequency of superlative adjectives and adverbs	Only consider words tagged as ADJ or ADV
N/A	Frequency of *quod* used as a SCONJ
N/A	Frequency of contiguous instances of INTJ tags
N/A	Frequency of POS tag n-grams and n-skip-grams

Table 1: Table of selected original features from Chaudhuri et al. (2019) (left) and modifications or additions enabled by POS tagging (right). POS augmentation of the feature set includes direct modifications of existing features (indicated by a completed left and right column) as well as additions to the feature set (indicated by "N/A" in the left column).

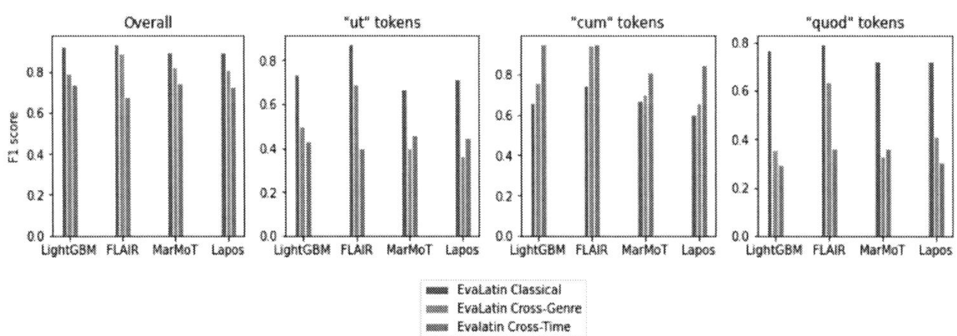

Figure 1: F1 score for LightGBM, FLAIR, MarMoT, and Lapos on EvaLatin test sets overall and on subsets most relevant to feature augmentation (*ut*, *cum*, *quod*).

	Accuracy				F1			
	LightGBM	FLAIR	MarMoT	Lapos	LightGBM	FLAIR	MarMoT	Lapos
EvaLatin Classical	0.96	0.97	0.95	0.95	0.92	0.93	0.89	0.89
EvaLatin Cross-Genre	0.89	0.91	0.87	0.87	0.79	0.89	0.82	0.81
EvaLatin Cross-Time	0.82	0.83	0.85	0.84	0.74	0.68	0.74	0.72
UD Perseus Treebank	0.77	0.80	0.84	0.84	0.50	0.53	0.72	0.73
UD PROIEL Treebank	0.79	0.82	0.95	0.95	0.69	0.73	0.95	0.94
UD ITTB Treebank	0.69	0.73	0.97	0.97	0.46	0.48	0.89	0.90

Table 2: POS tagger accuracy and F1 score across 3 EvaLatin test sets and 3 UD treebank test sets for 2 EvaLatin taggers (LightGBM and FLAIR) and 2 models that are not Latin-specific (MarMoT and Lapos) trained on EvaLatin or treebank data.

in that task. All taggers exhibit their highest performance on the classical subtask and poorer performance on the cross-time and cross-genre subtasks, but F1 scores for *cum* tokens for each tagger show the opposite trend, albeit with smaller margins. Given the pre-trained FLAIR model's strong performance overall as well as on *ut*, *cum*, and *quod* tokens, we use the model to augment the stylometric feature set. We apply the model to texts only within the classical and cross-genre domains, in which it demonstrates high performance.

3.2 Error analysis for POS-augmented features

Calculating stylometric features requires identifying tokens of interest and tabulating their frequency or some other summary metric. The method of token identification underlying a feature determines its accuracy. For example, it is necessary to identify identify conjunctive *cum* accurately to calculate the frequency of *cum* clauses. We perform an error analysis to compare the tokens identified by the original features and by POS-augmented features to the tokens marked by ground truth labels in the EvaLatin classical test dataset.

POS-augmented features overcome some limitations of the original methodology (see Table 3). When identifying conjunctions, counting words tagged as XCONJ (SCONJ or CCONJ) rather than using a hand-curated list increases F1 score from 0.69 to 0.97, an improvement of 0.28. When identifying prepositions, using the ADP tag decreases precision from 1 to 0.99 but increases recall by 0.67, from 0.33 to 1. The identification of *cum* clauses and relative clauses also improves when considering predicted POS tags. In this EvaLatin dataset, Chaudhuri et al. (2019)'s strict, rule-based method identifies *cum* with a precision of 0.92 but a recall of 0.55. Recall increases to 0.91 when counting instances of *cum* marked as SCONJ (Table 3). Chaudhuri et al. (2019)'s relatively loose criteria for identifying relative clauses (retrieve all instances of inflected *qui*) leads to a recall of 1 but a precision of only 0.59. Requiring instances of *qui* to be tagged as PRON increases the recall to 0.67 but still results in 353 false positives, suggesting that the method would benefit from further improvements (Table 3).

We also inspect token identification for features that lack definite ground truth labels in our dataset (Table 4). Requiring superlatives to be tagged as ADJ or ADV reduces the superlative count from 330 to 318. Manual inspection reveals that the 12 words omitted are forms of the verb *dissimulo* and are false positive hits. In addition, we count 6 vocatives and 13 INTJ blocks in the test data. There is no overlap between those sets. While the vocative feature identifies instances of direct address following 'O', the INTJ block feature identifies direct address without an 'O' marker and more general interjections such as *age* ("go"), *me hercule* ("by Hercules"), and *ecce* ("behold"). We thus improve the calculated frequency of superlatives feature and complement the calculated frequency of vocatives. Error analyses of remaining POS-augmented features, which include the frequency of conjunctive *quod*, conjunctive *ut*, adverbial *ut*, subordinating conjunctions, and pronouns, yield varying F1 scores with a minimum of 0.74 for conjunctive *quod* (Table 5).

3.3 POS-augmented features in prose vs. verse classification

We evaluate classifier performances with the original, modified, and expanded feature sets described above. There is no significant difference between the accuracy distributions for the different feature sets, although mean accuracy does increase to 98% for the expanded feature set (Table 6).

We also rank features in each set according to

	Cum Clauses		Relative Clauses		Conjunctions		Prepositions	
	SCONJ	Original	PRON	Original	XCONJ	Original	ADP	Original
TP	217	132	725	729	5549	3743	3726	1227
FP	7	11	353	501	151	1425	36	0
FN	21	106	4	0	135	1941	16	2515
Precision	0.97	0.92	0.67	0.59	0.97	0.72	0.99	1.00
Recall	0.91	0.55	0.99	1.00	0.98	0.66	1.00	0.33
F1	0.94	0.69	0.80	0.74	0.97	0.69	0.99	0.49

Table 3: Use of POS tag information improves the identification of *cum* clauses, relative clauses (marked by forms of *qui*), conjunctions, and prepositions. TP denotes true positives, FP denotes false positives, and FN denotes false negatives. Relative clause identification requires punctuation information omitted by EvaLatin, so we evaluate relative clauses on the UD ITTB test data instead.

	Superlatives	**Superlatives (ADJ and ADV)**	**Vocatives**	**INTJ Blocks**
Instance count (predicted POS)	330	318	6	13
Instance count (true POS)	N/A	318	N/A	13

Table 4: Number of tokens counted by the original superlative feature, POS-augmented superlative feature, original vocative feature, and INTJ block feature enabled by POS information. Predicted POS tags match POS ground truth labels with 100% accuracy for all words relevant to the features shown, so the instance counts using predicted POS tags and ground truth POS labels are identical.

Gini importance (Table 7). The original and modified feature sets share 5 out of their 10 most highly ranked features (and 7 out of 10 when considering the POS-augmented versions of the superlatives and prepositions features). Furthermore, 4 of the top 6 features in the modified feature set are POS-augmented (frequencies of prepositions, conjunctions, and conjunctive *ut*). In addition, in the fully expanded set, the top 10 features include frequency of relative clauses (notably not the POS-augmented version), prepositions, *quidam*, and gerunds, all of which are also highly ranked in the original or modified set. However, POS n-gram features have the 2 highest Gini importances and represent 6 of the 10 most important features in the set, demonstrating their relevance to the differentiation of Latin genre.

3.4 POS-augmented features in differentiating epic vs. didactic

Despite the improvements enabled by POS-tagged features, the interpretive payoff can seem modest because of the relative simplicity of the evaluation task: even the original approach of using hard-coded lists achieves F1 > 97% in distinguishing prose and verse. We therefore apply our suite of feature sets to the subtler question of distinguishing works of Latin narrative epic and didactic poetry, which are composed in the same hexameter verse form. These genres differ in topical content and rhetorical structure: epic typically recounts stories of war, while didactic describes technical and scientific matters; epic alternates between narrative and speech, while didactic consists of philosophical argument and explanation. These characteristic qualities are not directly captured in the feature sets, which focus on functional and syntactic elements rather than literary ones. Prior research has demonstrated, however, that these genres can be distinguished on the basis of such features (Chaudhuri et al., 2019), and we find reasonably discrete groupings in our selective hexameter corpus; in particular, certain didactic authors are more clearly separated from their epic peers.

Fig. 2 shows that this central result replicates for POS-augmented features. The inclusion of POS n-gram features, however, reduces generic separation, with the notable exception of Lucretius' *De Rerum Natura*, which remains emphatically distinct. The differences in results across the 3 feature sets therefore illustrate the complex relationship between the 2 genres as a whole and the individual works comprising each genre – on the one hand, broadly similar in their sequences of parts of speech; on the other hand, crucially different in sentence length and sentence subordination, and above all different from one author to another.

	quod (SCONJ)	*ut* (SCONJ)	*ut* (ADV)	SCONJ	PRON
TP	125	365	112	1553	4172
FP	45	26	27	137	105
FN	43	27	26	130	136
Precision	0.74	0.93	0.81	0.92	0.98
Recall	0.74	0.93	0.81	0.92	0.97
F1	0.74	0.93	0.81	0.92	0.97

Table 5: Performance metrics for POS-augmented features not discussed in the main text. These features identify conjunctive *quod*, conjunctive *ut*, adverbial *ut*, subordinating conjunctions, and pronouns with F1 scores ranging from 0.74 to 0.97. TP denotes true positives, FP denotes false positives, and FN denotes false negatives.

	Fold 1	Fold 2	Fold 3	Fold 4	Fold 5	Mean	SD
Original	0.96	0.99	0.96	0.99	0.97	0.97	0.015
Modified	0.99	0.97	1.00	0.97	0.95	0.98	0.017
Expanded	1.00	1.00	1.00	0.95	0.97	0.98	0.021

Table 6: 5-fold classifier accuracies for models using the original feature set, the directly modified feature set, and the fully expanded feature set in the prose vs. verse classification task.

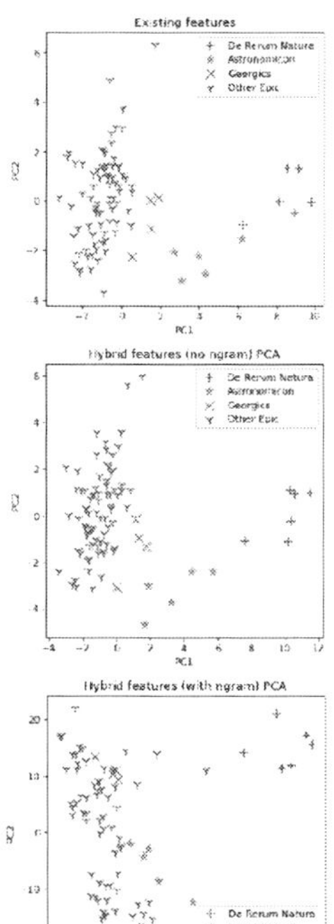

Figure 2: Principal component analyses of Latin narrative and didactic epic with the original (top), POS-augmented (middle), and hybrid stylometric and POS n-gram (bottom) feature sets.

4 Conclusion

We evaluate state-of-the-art POS taggers and select a FLAIR tagger to augment the stylometric feature set published by Chaudhuri et al. (2019). Using predicted POS tags, we first reduce dependency on hand-engineered heuristics in feature calculations to gain more complete POS counts, increasing recall by 0.32 for conjunctions and 0.67 for prepositions when comparing POS-augmented features to their original counterparts. Second, we disambiguate polysemous words such as *cum*, *ut*, and *quod*, increasing F1 score from 0.69 to 0.94 for *cum* clause identification and from 0.74 to 0.80 for relative clause identification. Finally, we calculate newly enabled features including POS n-gram frequencies.

We then train a random forest classifier to distinguish verse from prose, and through feature importance analysis we demonstrate that POS-augmented and POS n-gram features in particular quantify stylometric qualities highly relevant to genre classification. In these ways, we apply advances in Latin NLP to literary critical questions regarding generic style. More generally, we showcase a methodology for Latin that we hope will inform the quantitative criticism of other premodern languages as well.

5 Limitations

The current work uses established models for which performance on benchmark tasks has been well documented, such as the EvaLatin UDPipe

Rank	Original		Modified		Expanded	
1	superlatives	0.31	superlatives*	0.14	AUX*	0.13
2	*quidam*	0.14	*quidam*	0.13	SCONJ ADP 2-gram*	0.09
3	gerunds	0.13	prepositions*	0.10	relative clauses	0.07
4	relative clauses	0.09	conjunctions*	0.09	prepositions*	0.07
5	vocatives	0.08	gerunds	0.07	*quidam*	0.06
6	*idem*	0.07	*ut* (SCONJ)*	0.07	gerunds	0.05
7	personal pronouns	0.04	*antequam*	0.05	ADJ PROPN 2-gram*	0.04
8	*antequam*	0.03	alius	0.05	INTJ blocks*	0.04
9	prepositions	0.02	mean sentence length	0.05	PART ADP 2-gram*	0.04
10	*alius*	0.01	*idem*	0.05	ADP PRON 2-gram*	0.03

Table 7: For the original, modified, and expanded feature sets, the 10 features with highest Gini importance (feature name in left subcolumn, Gini importance in right subcolumn). Features improved or newly enabled by POS augmentation are denoted with *. Unless otherwise noted, each feature name in the table corresponds to the frequency of the indicated class.

model, which won all subtasks of the EvaLatin open division (Straka and Straková, 2020). The use of other models that reflect more recent advances is likely to have an effect on tagger accuracy and downstream performance for specific applications. Furthermore, models trained on a more diverse corpus may improve performance on cross-time tasks in particular. Finally, our use of POS n-grams as a stylometric feature is limited to 2-grams. Given their relatively high ranking among features contributing to successful classification, consideration of longer sequences, as well as of n-skip-grams, may be warranted.

6 Acknowledgments

This work was conducted under the auspices of the Quantitative Criticism Lab (www.qcrit.org), an interdisciplinary group co-directed by P.C. and J.P.D. and supported by an American Council of Learned Societies Digital Extension Grant and a National Endowment for the Humanities Digital Humanities Advancement Grant (grant number HAA-271822-20). T.J.B. was supported by an Engaged Scholar Initiative Fellowship from the Mellon Foundation., P.C. by a Mellon New Directions Fellowship, and J.P.D. by a Neukom Fellowship and a Harvard Data Science Fellowship. S.L.C. conducted part of this research as a 2020 Research Science Institute Scholar. We are grateful to TTLab for sharing the FLAIR model before public release.

References

Yannis Assael, Thea Sommerschield, Brendan Shillingford, Mahyar Bordbar, John Pavlopoulos, Marita Chatzipanagiotou, Ion Androutsopoulos, Jonathan Prag, and Nando de Freitas. 2022. Restoring and attributing ancient texts using deep neural networks. *Nature*, 603(7900):280–283.

David Bamman and Gregory Crane. 2011. The ancient Greek and Latin dependency treebanks. In *Language Technology for Cultural Heritage*, pages 79–98. Springer.

Flavio Massimiliano Cecchini, Marco Passarotti, Paola Marongiu, and Daniel Zeman. 2018. Challenges in converting the *Index Thomisticus* treebank into Universal Dependencies. In *Proceedings of the Second Workshop on Universal Dependencies (UDW 2018)*, pages 27–36, Brussels, Belgium. Association for Computational Linguistics.

Giuseppe G. A. Celano. 2020. A gradient boosting-Seq2Seq system for Latin POS tagging and lemmatization. In *Proceedings of LT4HALA 2020 - 1st Workshop on Language Technologies for Historical and Ancient Languages*, pages 119–123, Marseille, France. European Language Resources Association (ELRA).

Pramit Chaudhuri, Tathagata Dasgupta, Joseph P. Dexter, and Krithika Iyer. 2019. A small set of stylometric features differentiates Latin prose and verse. *Digital Scholarship in the Humanities*, 34(4):716–729.

Neil Coffee, Jean-Pierre Koenig, Shakthi Poornima, Christopher W. Forstall, Roelant Ossewaarde, and Sarah L. Jacobson. 2012. The Tesserae Project: intertextual analysis of Latin poetry. *Literary and Linguistic Computing*, 28(2):221–228.

Joseph P. Dexter, Theodore Katz, Nilesh Tripuraneni, Tathagata Dasgupta, Ajay Kannan, James A. Brofos, Jorge A. Bonilla Lopez, Lea A. Schroeder, Adriana Casarez, Maxim Rabinovich, Ayelet Haimson Lushkov, and Pramit Chaudhuri. 2017. Quantitative criticism of literary relationships. *Proceedings of the National Academy of Sciences*, 114(16):E3195–E3204.

Efthimios Gianitsos, Thomas Bolt, Pramit Chaudhuri, and Joseph P. Dexter. 2019. Stylometric classification of Ancient Greek literary texts by genre. In *Proceedings of the 3rd Joint SIGHUM Workshop on Computational Linguistics for Cultural Heritage, Social Sciences, Humanities and Literature*, pages 52–60, Minneapolis, USA. Association for Computational Linguistics.

Barbara Graziosi, Johannes Haubold, Charlie Cowen-Breen, and Creston Brooks. 2023. Machine learning and the future of philology: A case study. *TAPA*, 153(1):253–284.

Dag T.T. Haug and Marius L. Jøhndal. 2008. Creating a parallel treebank of the old Indo-European Bible translations. In *Proceedings of the Second Workshop on Language Technology for Cultural Heritage Data (LaTeCH 2008)*, pages 27–34.

Rukmini Iyer and Mari Ostendorf. 1999. Relevance weighting for combining multi-domain data for n-gram language modeling. *Computer Speech & Language*, 13(3):267–282.

Matthew L. Jockers. 2013. *Macroanalysis: Digital Methods and Literary History*. University of Illinois Press.

Matthew L. Jockers and Daniela M. Witten. 2010. A comparative study of machine learning methods for authorship attribution. *Literary and Linguistic Computing*, 25(2):215–223.

Guolin Ke, Qi Meng, Thomas Finley, Taifeng Wang, Wei Chen, Weidong Ma, Qiwei Ye, and Tie-Yan Liu. 2017. LightGBM: A highly efficient gradient boosting decision tree. In *Advances in Neural Information Processing Systems*, volume 30. Curran Associates, Inc.

Hoyt Long and Richard Jean So. 2016. Literary pattern recognition: Modernism between close reading and machine learning. *Critical Inquiry*, 42(2):235–267.

Franco Moretti. 2013. *Distant Reading*. Verso Books.

Thomas Mueller, Helmut Schmid, and Hinrich Schütze. 2013. Efficient higher-order CRFs for morphological tagging. In *Proceedings of the 2013 Conference on Empirical Methods in Natural Language Processing*, pages 322–332, Seattle, Washington, USA. Association for Computational Linguistics.

Slav Petrov, Dipanjan Das, and Ryan McDonald. 2012. A universal part-of-speech tagset. In *Proceedings of the Eighth International Conference on Language Resources and Evaluation (LREC'12)*, pages 2089–2096, Istanbul, Turkey. European Language Resources Association (ELRA).

Andrew Piper. 2019. *Enumerations: Data and Literary Study*. University of Chicago Press.

Rachele Sprugnoli, Marco Passarotti, Flavio Massimiliano Cecchini, and Matteo Pellegrini. 2020. Overview of the EvaLatin 2020 evaluation campaign. In *Proceedings of LT4HALA 2020 - 1st Workshop on Language Technologies for Historical and Ancient Languages*, pages 105–110, Marseille, France. European Language Resources Association (ELRA).

Efstathios Stamatatos. 2009. A survey of modern authorship attribution methods. *Journal of the American Society for Information Science and Technology*, 60(3):538–556.

Manuel Stoeckel, Alexander Henlein, Wahed Hemati, and Alexander Mehler. 2020. Voting for POS tagging of Latin texts: Using the flair of FLAIR to better ensemble classifiers by example of Latin. In *Proceedings of LT4HALA 2020 - 1st Workshop on Language Technologies for Historical and Ancient Languages*, pages 130–135, Marseille, France. European Language Resources Association (ELRA).

Grant Storey and David Mimno. 2020. Like two Pis in a pod: Author similarity across time in the Ancient Greek corpus. *Journal of Cultural Analytics*, 5(2).

Justin Stover and Mike Kestemont. 2016. Reassessing the Apulein corpus: A computational approach to authenticity. *The Classical Quarterly*, 66(2):645–672.

Milan Straka and Jana Straková. 2020. UDPipe at EvaLatin 2020: Contextualized embeddings and treebank embeddings. In *Proceedings of LT4HALA 2020 - 1st Workshop on Language Technologies for Historical and Ancient Languages*, pages 124–129, Marseille, France. European Language Resources Association (ELRA).

Yoshimasa Tsuruoka, Yusuke Miyao, and Jun'ichi Kazama. 2011. Learning with lookahead: Can history-based models rival globally optimized models? In *Proceedings of the Fifteenth Conference on Computational Natural Language Learning*, pages 238–246, Portland, Oregon, USA. Association for Computational Linguistics.

Ted Underwood. 2019. *Distant Horizons: Digital Evidence and Literary Change*. University of Chicago Press.

Exploring intertextuality across the Homeric poems through language models

Maria Konstantinidou[1]*, John Pavlopoulos[2], Elton Barker[3]

[1]Democritus University of Thrace, Greece
[2]Athens University of Economics and Business, Greece
[3]The Open University, U.K.

Abstract

Past research has modelled statistically the language of the Homeric poems, assessing the degree of surprisal for each verse through diverse metrics and resulting to the HoLM resource. In this study we utilise the HoLM resource to explore cross-poem affinity at the verse level, looking at Iliadic verses and passages that are less surprising to the Odyssean model than to the Iliadic one and vice-versa. Using the same tool, we investigate verses that evoke greater surprise when assessed by a local model trained solely on their source book, compared to a global model trained on the entire source poem. Investigating deeper on the distribution of such verses across the Homeric poems we employ supervised learning to further analyse quantitatively cross-poem affinity in selected books.

1 Background

The precise process by which the monumental ancient Greek epics, the Iliad and the Odyssey, came into being remains a point of speculation. That they have survived to the present day may be traced back to the Hellenistic period of ancient Greece (c. 330 BCE), when early scholars focused on issues of textualisation, primarily editing, in order to curate the canonical version of Homer. Less clear is how the poems arrived at this point. Though ever more detailed and in-depth references to them had been occurring over the previous two centuries, there is no documentation relating to the moment of their composition, primarily because they were the product of a vibrant oral society. Rather than being seen as the beginning of a Western tradition, it is more fruitful to think of the Homeric poems as coming at the end of a long tradition of in-performance improvisation, where poets recut the cloth of what they had inherited to weave new stories. The way into thinking about the oral traditionality (Foley, 1991) of these poems is through their language, and, in particular, the repeated phrases or epithets that have long been regarded as a characteristic feature of them. Phrases such as "swift-footed Achilles" — a line that recurs throughout the Iliad, for example – are not designed to capture a moment in a specific way but rather "trigger a chain of associations" (Graziosi and Haubold, 2005, p. 53) in the minds of audiences, who have grown up with these stories and poems of this kind. The more familiar with other (earlier) uses of such phrases, the more an audience can derive meaning from their present application (Barker and Christensen, 2019). Since "oral poetry works like a language, only more so" (Foley, 2002, p. 127), there is great potential in leveraging language modelling for better understanding how the Homeric poets have been put together. Such work might not be able to resolve the so-called Homeric Question: whether, that is, one person — let's call him Homer — composed both (or one of) the Iliad and Odyssey in the form that have come down to us. Yet, it is the contention of this paper that language modelling can lift the curtain on the mechanics of oral competitive poetics, either by drawing attention to the points of connection between the poems or to other epics (such as those of Hesiod), or, on the contrary, by revealing moments of rupture from the norm. In this way, we hope to set out some ground rules for identifying, and thinking about, the practice by which individual passages generate meaning by playing on audience expectations and their very familiarity with traditional story patterns, themes, and phraseology.

Our starting point is the HoLM resource, developed to assist scholars studying linguistic heterogeneity within the Homeric poems at the level of different structural elements (verses, passages and books) (Pavlopoulos et al., 2024), where related work is also discussed. In this study, we use the cross-score metric to calculate the number of verses per book exhibiting greater linguistic affinity (i.e.,

*Corresponding author: mkonst@helit.duth.gr.

Proceedings of the 1st Workshop on Machine Learning for Ancient Languages (ML4AL 2024), pages 260–268
August 15, 2024 ©2024 Association for Computational Linguistics

reduced surprise) with the opposite poem than to their original source poem. Such verses, either individual or in clusters, suggest complexities beyond simple interpolations. They hint at potential contamination between the poems or common origins for specific passages. As a means of generating supplementary data complementing existing material, we train three text classifiers to assess the verses of nine books selected from both poems, five from the Iliad and four from the Odyssey.

1.1 The HoLM resource

The HoLM resource uses character level statistical language models to score the Iliad and the Odyssey with a variety of metrics that assess each verse's linguistic unexpectedness to the trained models (Pavlopoulos et al., 2024). The dataset comprises a 'cross-score' computed for each verse, designed to compare the degree of unexpectedness across the two poems. In this work, we also consider relations between books of the same poem. To compare unexpectedness between the individual source book (local model) of a verse and its entire source poem (global model), we use the two Perplexity (PPL) scores provided in HoLM, 'local PPL' and 'global PPL'.

1.2 The formulaic character of Homeric poetry

Homeric poetry, much like other forms of oral literature, fundamentally relies on repetition, both linguistic and thematic. These repetitions serve several crucial purposes, acting as mnemonic devices that aid the poet in structuring the material, and as triggering devices that enable an audience to derive meaning from it — all the more critical for narratives as extensive and all-encompassing as the Iliad and the Odyssey. As has been long recognised, the use of formulas — repetitive epithets, phrases, half-verses, and even entire verses — constitutes a significant feature of Homeric poetry (Parry, 1971). These formulas function as the building blocks of the poetry, ensuring a smooth and continuous poetic flow. For instance, recurring phrases like "rosy-fingered dawn" or "swift-footed Achilles" serve not only to describe characters and scenes vividly but also to fit the metrical requirements of the epic's dactylic hexameter. This technique provides the poet with ready-made segments of verse that can be adapted to various narrative contexts, thus facilitating the composition of long, complex stories in real-time performance. At the same time, these repetitive elements also enhance an audience's understanding of the thematic coherence of the story-in-performance, as well as appreciation for the story it has to tell. They help create a sense of continuity and unity, by enabling an audience to anchor different parts of the narrative and grasp key ideas, particularly when heard in and against the stories that have been sung before. The extensive use of these formulas results in a high degree of repetition within the Homeric poems, both intra- and inter-poem. Identical or near-identical verses, often repeated multiple times, are scattered across the poems. Of the 15,683 verses in our version of the Iliad, 2,019 are duplicate (approximately 13%); that is, they are repeated one or more times. In the Odyssey 1,884 out of the 12,107 verses (approximately 15.5%) are duplicates.[1] There are many more near-duplicate verses, typically hemistichs (half-verses), and a lot of shorter formulas consisting of two or three words. So well-established is the idea of formularity in oral poetry, that scholars need to argue in favour of the uniqueness and the non-formulaic nature of Homeric diction, estimating that at least one third of it is *not* affected by formulas (Finkelberg, 2020). Dealing with formulas in a computational study presents several complex challenges that necessitate a comprehensive, separate investigation. Key issues include defining what constitutes a formula (e.g., whether two words should be considered as one) and understanding how these formulas interact with the metrical structure of the verses (Bozzone, 2022). Additionally, the overall language modelling of the text must be considered in connection with repeated expressions: recent studies have established that the density of formulas in Homeric texts is not exceptional and that contemporary speech exhibits a comparable degree of formularity (Erman and Warren, 2000). In our study, duplicate and near-duplicate verses are not excluded for training. Additionally, they score, as expected, a lower PPL both with the source poem model and the other poem model, since the same formulas can be found in both works. Table 1 presents examples of duplicate verses repeated within the Iliad. Table 2 shows recurrent verses in both poems.

[1] HoLM uses the (Allen, 1931) edition for the Iliad and for the Odyssey the (von der Mühll, 1962) one.

Verse no	Text
16,711	μῆνιν ἀλευάμενος ἑκατηβόλου ἀπόλλωνος
1,297	ἄλλο δέ τοι ἐρέω σὺ δ᾽ ἐνὶ φρεσὶ βάλλεο σῇσι
5,444	μῆνιν ἀλευάμενος ἑκατηβόλου ἀπόλλωνος
20,19	τὸν δ᾽ ἀπαμειβόμενος προσέφη νεφεληγερέτα ζεύς
22,182	τὴν δ᾽ ἀπαμειβόμενος προσέφη νεφεληγερέτα ζεύς
24,64	τὴν δ᾽ ἀπαμειβόμενος προσέφη νεφεληγερέτα ζεύς
8,477	τὴν δ᾽ ἀπαμειβόμενος προσέφη νεφεληγερέτα ζεύς
5,764	τὴν δ᾽ ἀπαμειβόμενος προσέφη νεφεληγερέτα ζεύς
23,93	τὸν δ᾽ ἀπαμειβόμενος προσέφη πόδας ὠκὺς ἀχιλλεύς
14,311	τὴν δ᾽ ἀπαμειβόμενος προσέφη νεφεληγερέτα ζεύς

Table 1: The verses with the ten lowest PPL scores in the Iliad are all duplicates

2 Motivation and method

Our objective is to broaden the scope of research on the phenomenon of unexpectedness by moving beyond the mere identification of surprising verses or passages within a model trained on the source text. Among the verses identified as unexpected in HoLM, we perform a quantitative analysis specifically on verses/passages that appear to be linguistically more surprising to their immediate surroundings than to other, more remote parts of the Homeric poems. In short, we focus on three levels of surroundings that provide increasingly broader contexts for assessing the linguistic surprise of verses or passages:

- **Immediate surroundings**: This refers to the immediate context of a verse or passage within its own book; specifically, the verses directly preceding and following the target verse. We investigate this level by seeking consecutive or near-consecutive outlier verses.
- **Individual book > Source poem**: This level expands the scope beyond the immediate surroundings to include the entirety of the book containing the verse or passage, compared to the source poem from which it originates. It assesses the verse's surprise factor within the context of its book in relation to the entirety of its source poem.
- **Source poem > Other poem**: This evaluates the level of surprise of a verse or passage within its source poem, juxtaposed with the surprise calculated using a model trained on the entirety of the other Homeric poem (e.g., the Iliad compared to the Odyssey, or vice versa). Specifically, it examines how the unexpectedness of the verse within its own context contrasts with its unexpectedness when assessed against the entirety of the alternative Homeric work.

This method lays the groundwork for investigating internal transposition of text within each poem, as well as Odyssean elements in the Iliad and vice versa. Further systematic study of such passages may help not only unveil patterns of interpolation itself, but also to shed light on what is consciously or instinctively perceived as 'Iliadic' or 'Odyssean', thereby ultimately unlocking insights into the agonistic, compositional basis of either poem.

3 Assessing proximity with the other poem

3.1 Positive cross-score

To identify verses and passages that may be linguistically more distant to their source poem than to the other one, we use the cross score. For a given verse, this is the difference between the PPL for that verse computed with the model trained on the source poem and the equivalent PPL computed with the model trained on the other poem. A positive cross value (PCV) for a verse means that the verse is more surprising to the source poem model than it is to the model trained on the other poem. We used PCVs to identify possible passages that may exhibit greater source poem surprise (clusters of more than two PCVs). Since a PCV is a rarity and to ensure that individual verses are not isolated from their surroundings, we also took into account the top 10% of verses with the highest negative scores (NCV). As mentioned above, few verses have a positive cross score: in the Iliad there are 511 PCVs in total and 375 if we remove the duplicate verses among them. In the Odyssey, we identified 272 PCVs (235 after duplicate verse elimination). Thus, the Iliad contains far more such verses, even after allowing for its greater length compared to the Odyssey (Fig. 1).

The greatest concentration is found in Books 24 (Fig. 3), 9 and 1 of the Iliad. The lowest concentration is found in Odyssey 7. Of the 783 PCVs, approximately one in five (173) are duplicates. Far less duplicate verses have a positive cross-score in the Odyssey (0.3%) than in the Iliad (0.87%). This could be due to the fact that in the Odyssey, unique common verses that appear across poems are fewer in number but are repeated more frequently compared to those in the Iliad(Fig. 2 and Table 2).

The low number of PCVs does not allow a reliable statistical analysis at the book level and a

Verse	Total count	Iliad count	Odyssey count
καί μιν φωνήσας ἔπεα πτερόεντα προσηύδα	30	15	15
τὸν δ᾽ ἀπαμειβόμενος προσέφη πολύμητις ὀδυσσεύς	30	5	25
ἦμος δ᾽ ἠριγένεια φάνη ῥοδοδάκτυλος ἠώς	22	2	20
αὐτὰρ ἐπεὶ πόσιος καὶ ἐδητύος ἐξ ἔρον ἕντο	21	7	14
ἀλλ᾽ ἄγε μοι τόδε εἰπὲ καὶ ἀτρεκέως κατάλεξον	17	4	13
διογενὲς λαερτιάδη πολυμήχαν᾽ ὀδυσσεῦ	17	7	10
ὀχθήσας δ᾽ ἄρα εἶπε πρὸς ὃν μεγαλήτορα θυμόν	11	7	4
τὸν δ᾽ ἠμείβετ᾽ ἔπειτα γερήνιος ἱππότα νέστωρ	11	8	3
ἀτρεΐδη κύδιστε ἄναξ ἀνδρῶν ἀγάμεμνον	10	8	2
τὴν δ᾽ ἀπαμειβόμενος προσέφη νεφεληγερέτα ζεύς	10	7	3

Table 2: The common verses in the two poems with the most occurances.

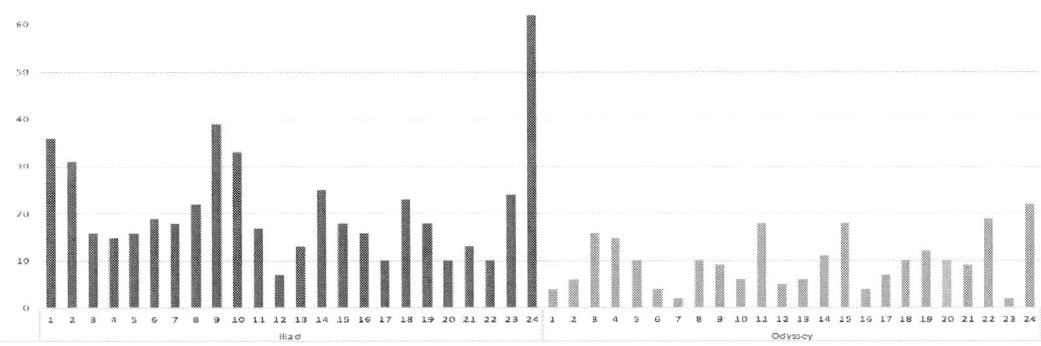

Figure 1: Number of verses with positive cross scores per book in the Iliad and the Odyssey

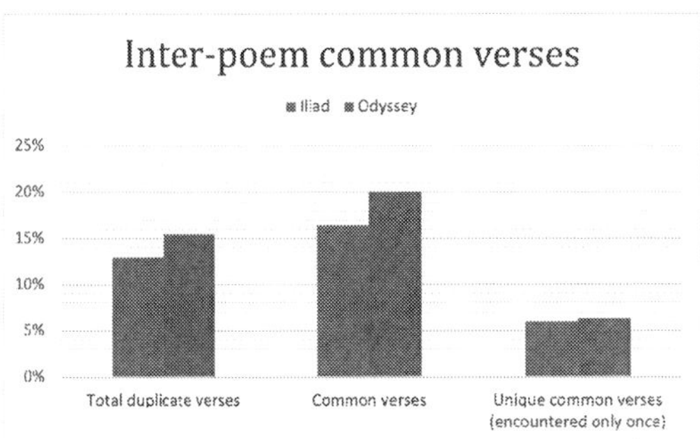

Figure 2: Verses in each poem also found in the other (percentage of total poem verses)

more decisive tool should be used for this purpose. Nevertheless, the cross-score metric can be useful to identify potential passages of interest.

4 Intra-poem unexpectedness: global versus local PPL

Local PPL is computed by training a statistical language model on the whole of the source book, excluding only the textual part that is being scored. As global PPL we consider the PPL score computed by a model trained on the source poem. In the Iliad, of the 1568 verses within the top 10 percentile of global PPL score, only 510 also rank among the top 10 percentile of Local PPL score. This means that 66% of the top surprising verses to the Global Iliad model are not surprising to their local Book model (and vice versa). If we examine the top 20 percentile, then 1536 out of the 3233 (48%) are equally surprising both globally and locally. In the Odyssey, it is a similar ratio, with 1123 verses universally surprising out of the 2421 globally surprising ones. The books with the greatest number of high local PPL verses are: Iliad 12, 22 and 24, and 1, 8 and 11 of the Odyssey (Fig. 4).

5 Zooming in

As is appropriate for works with such a lengthy and involved compositional history, the macroscopic book-level analysis ultimately aims at identifying distinctive narrative segments with higher concentration of PCVs, indicating a closer affinity with the other poem than their source poem. Using the books that stood out in the statistical analysis of PCVs, we focus on Iliad 1, 2, 9, 10 and 24. Book 10 is probably the most discussed book in terms of its authenticity; it is still commonly regarded as interpolated (or at least extended parts of it)

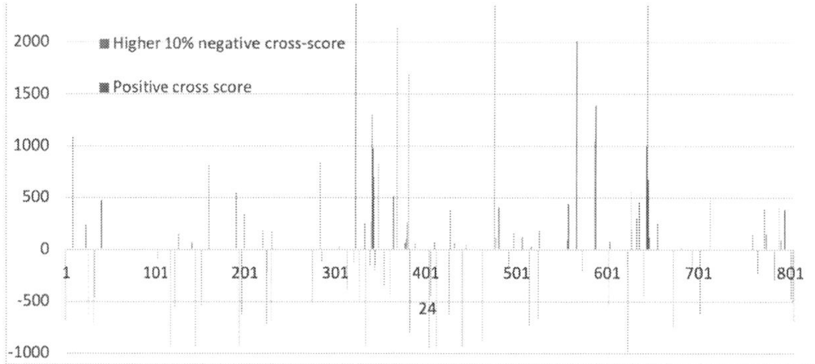

(a) HoLM SLM

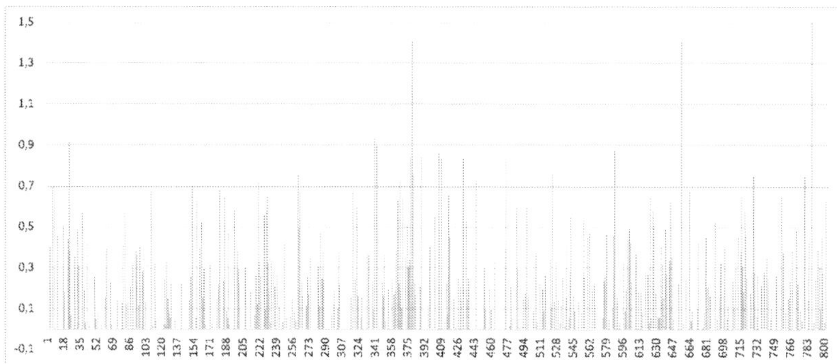

(b) RNNLM

Figure 3: Iliad book 24: (a) PCV and near positive cross-score verses computed with the HoLM SLM models and (b) PCV computed with the RNN model

(Danek, 2012). Book 2, which heralds 'the great gathering of armies', has also been discussed extensively in the literature (see for instance (Karanika, 2020)), again due to its atypical content, since it includes extensive lists, not least of which is the famous catalogue of ships. However, it is Book 24 that stands out from our book-level analysis of the HoLM resource: it exhibits the highest number of PCVs (Fig. 1) as well as the highest rate of locally surprising verses (Fig. 4). From the Odyssey, we selected books 11, 15, 22 and 24, the ones with the highest number of PCVs. Book 11 demonstrates in addition the highest number of high local PPL in the poem. Together with Book 24, they also present a more coherent picture of surprising passages with high concentration of PCVs (groups of verses clustered in close proximity).

5.1 Machine Learning for verse classification

To capture greater depth and range of language dependencies, we trained supervised learning algorithms to classify verses between the two poems (i.e., source v. other poem). This results in each unseen verse being marked as 'source-surprising' or not. We opted for three traditional machine learning algorithms for this experiment,[2] K-nearest neighbours (KNN), logistic regression (LR), and random forests (RF). All the algorithms operated on top of term-frequency inverse-document-frequency (TFIDF; documents are verses in our case) features, using character n-grams (i.e., sequences of two to five characters), maximum document frequency of 0.5 and minimum document frequency of 5 (i.e., we ignore n-grams in more than half and less than 5 verses).

The classifiers were trained on the whole of both poems, excluding books 1, 2, 9, 10 and 24 of the Iliad and books 11, 15, 22, and 24 of the Odyssey. We kept 20% of the verses, randomly selected across both poems, for evaluation purposes. This left us with 12,103 verses from Iliad and 9,861 verses from Odyssey for training. As is shown in Table 3, LR was the best in classifying the poem a verse belongs in, followed by RF and KNN. All

[2]We used the scikit-learn library for the implementations.

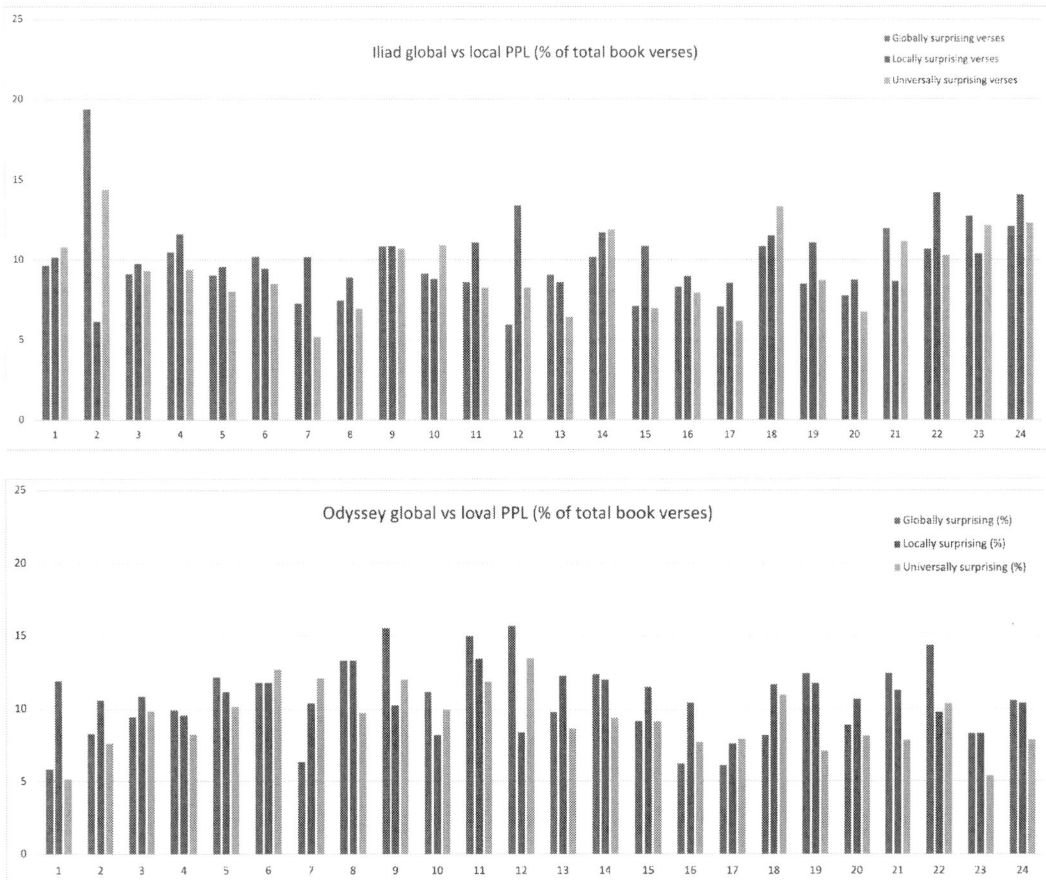

Figure 4: Global vs local PPL per book in the two poems

	ODYSSEY			ILIAD		
	P	R	F1	P	R	F1
LR	**0.75**	**0.68**	**0.72**	**0.76**	**0.82**	**0.79**
KNN	0.70	0.66	0.68	0.73	0.77	0.75
RF	0.73	0.65	0.69	0.74	0.81	0.77
RAND	0.45	0.50	0.47	0.55	0.50	0.52

Table 3: Precision, Recall and F1 per algorithm per poem. In bold the best per column.

three algorithms, however performed considerably better than a random baseline (RAND), classifying the verse randomly.

We also used these three classifiers to yield predictions per verse from the left out books. The distribution of source-surprising verses across the 9 books is shown in Fig. 6, but we observe that there is a positive correlation between the classifications of the three models (Fig. 5).

5.2 Classification vs PCV

Comparing the attribution of verses to the other poem in the four books, the classifiers largely support the SLM PCVs. In the Iliad, 79% of the PCVs are also flagged by the classifiers as Odyssean; in the Odyssey, 71% of PCVs are flagged as Iliadic. At the same time, the three classifiers substantially increase the quantity of source-surprising verses, revealing a clearer view. Among then, they mark as source-surprising another 1,622 verses in the Iliad and 1,192 in the Odyssey.

6 Discussion

Compared to the PCVs, a large number of groups of source-surprising verses (up to four excluding duplicates) can be readily observable in all of the individual books evaluated by the ML classifiers. Further merging groups located closely together requires closer examination and carefully selected criteria. It is, however, feasible to discern poten-

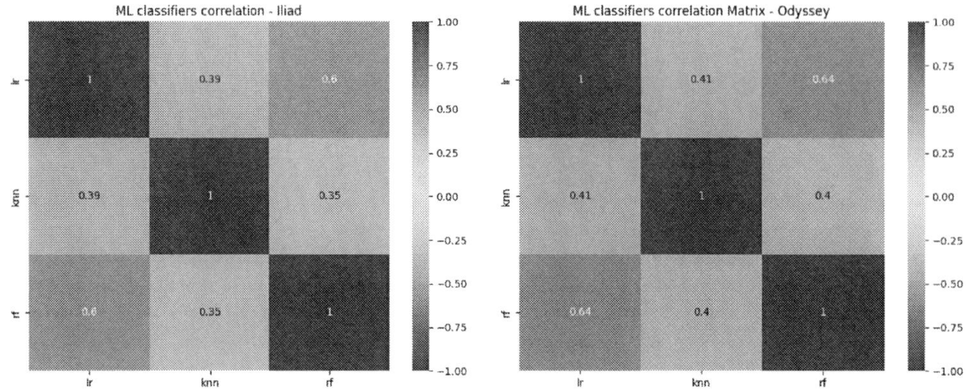

Figure 5: Pearson correlation between the machine learning classifiers on verses from held-out books of Iliad (the heatmap on the left) and Odyssey (on the right).

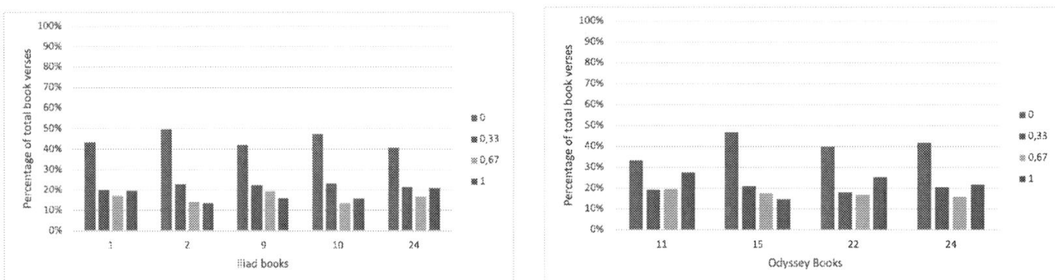

Figure 6: ML rate agreement in identifying source-surprising verses per book (0: no model classifies the verse as source-surprising; 1: all three models classify the verse as source-surprising). Number of verses shown as percentage of the book's total verses.

tial patterns among some of the passages picked out. These include lists (such as the catalogue of ships in Iliad 2 and the list of women in Odyssey 11), but also a number of similes, as well as narrations referring to the past. From a literary perspective, the books that emerge as related to the 'other' poem reveal close correspondences. These moments of contact could simply be down to the protagonist of either poem and their prominence in the other poem, namely Odysseus in Iliad 2, 9 and 10, and Achilles in Odyssey 11 (noting that the wrath of Achilles is the headline of the Iliad, and the return home of Odysseus the subject of the Odyssey). But, as well as being insufficient to explain all the cases (particularly in the Odyssey), the presence of the protagonist arguably better indicates heightened moments of thematic cross-over between the epics. As well as being prominent in these books of the Iliad, Odysseus also acts in an 'Odyssean' manner, most notably in Iliad 10, the book which some critics still doubt or consider as a late 'add on', precisely because of its seemingly unIliadic story of night adventure, ambush and deceit (led, of course, by Odysseus) (Barker, 2009). In Iliad 9 Odysseus is prominent as the leader of the embassy to Achilles, where his rhetorical skills are on display (and seen through by Achilles). In Iliad 2, Odysseus again takes control of the narrative, after Agamemnon's disastrous 'testing' of the troops: it is Odysseus to whom Athena goes (as she so often does in the Odyssey) and who notably holds back the Achaeans as they rush to the ships to go home, an event that, the Homeric narrator remarks, would have been 'beyond fate' (Barker, 2009).. The rivalry between these alternative epic traditions is taken up in Odyssey 11, where an ambushed Achilles is left behind in the Underworld bemoaning his early death and anxious for news of his son, even as Odysseus continues on his journey home to reunite with his l(Edwards, 1985). Odyssey 22 is the moment when Odysseus's banqueting halls become an Iliadic battleground, as Odysseus takes on and slaughters all the suitors who have been eating his son out of house and home. Odyssey 24 opens with another scene of (un)Iliadic heroes in the underworld — Achilles and Agamemnon praising each other no less — and culminates in another battle, when Odysseus, accompanied by both his father and son, takes on and kills the families of the suitors (Barker, 2009; Barker and Christensen, 2019). It is also striking that the beginning and ending of the Iliad is marked out as resonating strongly with the other tradition, as if self-consciously aware of its place in the tradition. Analysing individual passages is simultaneously more straightforward and open to speculation, especially in defining their boundaries. Nevertheless, a number clearly stand out when considering both PCVs and the ML models classifications. Such an example of source-surprising verses is in Iliad book 10 (263-279) where the arming of Odysseus is described in a distinct section of the book. In the Odyssey, the models mark as source-surprising the catalogue of women in book 11 (specifically verses 255-272 and 299-330). This is also a section mentioned in literature as a possible interpolation and further discussed in the same context in (Pavlopoulos and Konstantinidou, 2023).

7 Conclusions

Our two methods for assessing the level of inter-poem surprise largely converge in identifying specific books and passages as notably surprising within their respective poems. An initial expert analysis of the flagged passages reveals potential patterns recognized by the models; notably, Books 1, 9, 10, and 24 of the Iliad and Books 11, 15, 22, and 24 of the Odyssey contain the highest concentration of such verses. Within these books, shorter passages appear to contribute more significantly to these findings.

Further analysis of shorter verse clusters with positive or almost positive cross score seem promising in revealing both linguistic and thematic criteria associated with either poem. It may also reveal lexical features that weigh more in each poem's language modelling.

Future research may focus on these aspects, including catalogs, direct speech, gender-related topics and discourse, as well as proper names and content words. Additionally, it should aim to examine the Homeric poems within their closer historical context and model them alongside other ancient authors and genres, such as Hesiod and lyric poetry.

References

T.W. Allen. 1931. *Homeri Ilias*, volume 2 and 3. Clarendon Press, Oxford.

Elton T. E. Barker. 2009. *Entering the Agon: Dissent and Authority in Homer, Historiography, and Tragedy*. Oxford University Press.

Elton T. E. Barker and Joel P. Christensen. 2019. *Homer's Thebes: Epic Rivalries and the Appropriation of Mythical Pasts*. Center for Hellenic Studies.

Chiara Bozzone. 2022. Technologies of orality: Formularity, meter, and kunstsprache in homer. In *Rethinking Orality II: The Mechanisms of the Oral Communication System in the Case of the Archaic Epos*, pages 51–82, Berlin, Boston. De Gruyter.

Georg Danek. 2012. The Doloneia revisited. In Øvind Andersen and Dag T. T. Haug, editors, *Relative Chronology in Early Greek Epic Poetry*, pages 106–121. Cambridge University Press, Cambridge.

Anthony T. Edwards. 1985. *Achilles in the Odyssey : ideologies of heroism in the Homeric epic*. Verlag Anton Hain.

Britt Erman and Beatrice Warren. 2000. The idiom principle and the open choice principle. *Text & Talk*, 20(1):29–62.

Margalit Finkelberg. 2020. 6. oral theory and the limits of formulaic diction. In *Homer and Early Greek Epic, Collected Essays*, pages 53–65, Berlin, Boston. De Gruyter.

John Miles Foley. 1991. *Immanent art : from structure to meaning in traditional oral epic*. Bloomington (Ind.) : Indiana University Press.

John Miles Foley. 2002. *How to Read an Oral Poem*. University of Illinois Press.

Barbara Graziosi and Johannes Haubold. 2005. *Homer: The Resonance of Epic*. Duckworth. EPrint Processing Status: DRO Team to ask author to provide full text (pre-publication version).

Andromache Karanika. 2020. Catalogues. In *The Cambridge Guide to Homer*, page 108–109. Cambridge University Press.

Milman Parry. 1971. *The Making of Homeric Verse: The Collected Papers of Milman Parry; Edited by Adam Parry*. Oxford University Press, Oxford.

John Pavlopoulos and Maria Konstantinidou. 2023. Computational authorship analysis of the Homeric poems. *International Journal of Digital Humanities*, 5:45–64.

John Pavlopoulos, Ryan Sandell, Maria Konstantinidou, and Chiara Bozzone. 2024. HoLM: Analysing Linguistic Unexpectedness in Homeric Poetry. In *LREC-COLING*.

P. von der Mühll. 1962. *Homeri Odyssea*. Helbing & Lichtenhahn, Basel.

Author Index

Association for Computational Linguistics
209 N. Eighth Street
Stroudsburg, Pennsylvania 18360

ISBN 979-8-3313-0170-5

CURRAN ASSOCIATES INC.
proceedings.com